LONGMAN
ENGLISH DICTIONARY

ISIS Large Print Edition

LONGMAN ENGLISH DICTIONARY

ISIS Large Print Edition

ISIS Large Print
Oxford

Introduction

Here is a clear and handy guide to the most common and useful words and phrases in current English.

It explains the language we meet in everyday use, in conversation, in reading a newspaper, in watching a TV news broadcast – including terms from science, technology, politics, sport, and other specialized subjects. New words like *microprocessor* are included, as well as new senses of old words like *chip*, and the essential vocabulary of our rich and changing language.

The material has been carefully selected from Longman's huge dictionary data base, which was assembled by experts and is constantly updated. Definitions are written simply and concisely, and many shades of meaning and peculiarities of usage are illustrated by phrases or sentences showing a word in context.

1. **Main entries** Main entries are printed in bold type and arranged in alphabetical order, whether they are single words or compounds of two or more words. Words spelt alike but different in pronunciation, history, or grammar are listed separately, and distinguished by a small number preceding each.

2. **Alternatives** When a main entry can be spelt in two ways, both spellings are given, with the commonest one first. If the words are long, only the parts of the second spelling which differ from the first are shown.

    Sometimes another word with the same meaning as the main entry, although with a quite different spelling, is shown at this point.

3. **Parts of speech** A part of speech is shown, in italic type, after each main entry. When a word can be used in two ways in a sentence (eg as a noun and as a verb), the two parts of speech are combined; brackets are used to mark off the part of the definition of such a word that applies to only one of the parts of speech.

4. **Inflections** After the part of speech, information is given about any unusual changes in a word's form, such as nouns whose plural is not formed by adding *-s* or *-es*, and verbs whose past tense and present participle are not formed by adding *-ed* and *-ing*. Only the changed part of these forms is written out when only the end of a word alters, or a letter is doubled, or *-c* changes to *-ck-*.

5. **Usage** Labels in italic type mark words or meanings whose usage is specialized. They may be used particularly in one country (*'US'*), or mainly by specialists (*'law'*, *'medicine'*, *'technical'*), or they may be no longer in normal use although found in some books (*'old use'*, *'literature'*). Some words may be felt to belong particularly to serious writing (*'esp. written'*), to friendly conversation (*'esp. spoken'*), or to very informal speech (*'slang'*); others may suggest a particular tone or attitude (*'pompous'*, *'humour'*, *'offensive'*, etc). Items marked *not standard* may be in common use, but are thought by many people to be incorrect. Words or phrases borrowed from foreign languages and still felt to be not fully English are marked *French*, *Latin*, etc. Official names under which products are sold are labelled *trademark*.

6. **Meanings** When a word has two or more meanings, each sense is separately numbered, with the commonest or most important usually coming first. Special phrases and expressions including the word are shown after its ordinary meanings.

   In many cases, the explanation of a word or meaning is followed by an example of its use in a phrase or sentence; these examples are printed in italic type, and two or more examples of a single meaning are separated by a straight line.

7. **Undefined words** At the end of an entry, related words formed by adding an ending to the main form are shown in black type. Their meanings are not explained, since they can easily be guessed from their part of speech and the meaning of the main form. Such words are not usually written out in full, but are shown in either of two ways:
   a. **dark**[1] *adj* . . . ~**ness** *n*
   This means that the ending *ness* is added to the main form *dark*, so making the noun *darkness* (whose meaning may be deduced as 'the state of being dark').

   b. **brilliant** *adj* . . .-**liance** *n*
   Here the main form changes its spelling slightly before the ending is added, so more of the undefined form is shown in order to make clear its spelling *brilliance*.

Abbreviations used in this dictionary

abbrev.	abbreviation
adj	adjective
adv	adverb
conj	conjunction
E	East
esp.	especially
fem.	feminine
interj	interjection
masc.	masculine
n	noun
N	North
part.	participle
pl.	plural
prep	preposition
pres.	present
pron	pronoun
S	South
sing.	singular
sl	slang
US	America; American English
usu.	usually
v	verb
W	West

a –also (*before a vowel sound*) **an** – *indefinite article* **1** one: *I gave him a pound/an egg* **2** one member of a class or group: *a cat spits* **3** each; every: *6 times a day*

¹abandon v **1** to leave completely and for ever: *They abandoned the burning ship* **2** to give up, esp. without finishing: *The search was abandoned* **3** to give (oneself) up completely to a feeling, desire, etc. – **-donment** n

²abandon n the state when one's feelings and actions are uncontrolled: *They shouted in gay abandon*

abbey n **abbeys** (esp. formerly) a building in which Christian monks or nuns live apart from other people and work as a group for God; monastery or convent

abbreviation n **1** the act of making shorter **2** a shortened form of a word (such as *Mr*)

abdicate v **-cated, -cating** to give up (officially): *to abdicate (from) the throne / He abdicated all responsibility for the child* – **-cation** n

abdomen n *medical* a main part of the body in animals, being in man the part between the chest and legs and in insects the end part of the body joined to the thorax – **-dominal** adj

ability n **-ties** power and skill: *great musical ability*

able adj **1** having the power, skill, knowledge, time, etc., necessary to do something: *I was able to help her* **2** skilled: *an able rider*

aboard adv, prep on or into (a train, aircraft, bus, etc.): *They went aboard the ship*

abolish v to stop: *Bad laws ought to be abolished*

abolition n the act of putting an end to something: *the abolition of slavery* –~**ist** n

abortion n **1** the act or an example of giving birth or causing to give birth early, esp. within the first 20 weeks of the baby's existence inside a woman, so that the child cannot live **2** a badly-formed creature produced by such a birth **3** a plan or arrangement which breaks down before it can develop properly

¹about adv **1** also **around** – here and/or there: *I've left my purse somewhere about* **2** esp. spoken almost: *I'm about ready*

²about prep **1** also **around** – here and there in: *They walked about the streets* **2** also **around** – surrounding: *the wall about the the prison* **3** concerning: *What about father?* **4** concerned with: *Do the shopping and don't be long about it*

³about adj **1** moving; active: *He was up and about very early* **2** just ready: *We're about to start*

¹above adv **1** in or to a higher place: *the clouds above* **2** on an earlier page or higher on the same page: *See above for the address* **3** higher; more: *20 and above*

²above prep **1** higher than: *We flew above the clouds. / An admiral is above a captain. / He's above stealing* **2** **over and above** in addition (to) **3 above oneself a** self-satisfied **b** excited

abreast *adv* **1** side by side: *cycling 2 abreast* **2 keep/be abreast of** to have the latest information on

abroad *adv* **1** to or in another country: *living abroad* **2** over a wide area: *The news spread abroad that the results were out* **3** *old use* out of doors: *He was abroad early*

abrupt *adj* **1** sudden and unexpected: *an abrupt stop* **2** rough and impolite −~**ly** *adv* −~**ness** *n*

absence *n* **1** the state or a period of being away: *Behave yourself during my absence* **2** non-existence; lack: *absence of information*

¹**absent** *adj* **1** not present: *How many are absent today?* **2** showing lack of attention: *an absent look* −~**ly** *adv*

²**absent** *v esp. written* to keep away: *He absented himself from the meeting*

absolutely *adv* **1** completely: *You are absolutely wrong* **2** without conditions: *You must agree absolutely* **3** *esp. spoken* certainly: *'Do you think so?' 'Absolutely!'*

absorb *v* **1** to take or suck in (liquids) **2** to take in (knowledge, ideas, etc.) **3** to take up all the attention, time, etc., of: *absorbed in a book* **4** (of a big country, business, etc.) to make into a part of itself; take over

absurd *adj* **1** against reason or common sense: *Even sensible men do absurd things* **2** funny because clearly unsuitable, false, foolish, or impossible: *You look absurd in your wife's hat!* −~**ly** *adv* −~**ity** *n*

abundant *adj* more than enough: *abundant supplies of firewood* −~**ly** *adv*

¹**abuse** *v* **abused, abusing 1** to say unkind or rude things to or about **2** to put to wrong use: *to abuse one's power*

²**abuse** *n* **1** unkind or rude words: *He shouted a stream of abuse* **2** wrong use: *the use and abuse of figures to prove things* **3** an unjust or harmful custom

¹**academic** *adj* **1** concerning teaching or studying **2** concerning those subjects taught to provide skills for the mind **3** of a college or university: *academic dress* **4** *offensive* not concerned with practical examples: *The question of how many souls exist in heaven is academic*

²**academic** *n* a member of a college or university, esp. one who teaches

accelerate *v* **-rated, -rating 1** to move faster **2** *esp. written* to cause to happen earlier

¹**accent** *n* **1** importance given to a word, a vowel, or syllable by saying it with more force or on a different musical note: *The accent in the word 'important' is on the 2nd syllable* **2** the mark used, esp. above a word or part of a word, in writing or printing to show how to say it **3** a particular way of speaking, usu. connected with a country, area, or class: *a thick German accent*

²**accent** *v* **1** to pronounce with added force or on a different musical note **2** to mark with an accent

accept *v* 1 to take or receive, esp. willingly: *I cannot accept your gift* 2 to believe; admit; agree to: *I accept your reasons for being late* 3 to take responsibility for: *I'll accept the blame*

accident *n* 1 something, esp. something unpleasant or damaging, that happens unexpectedly or by chance: *I had an accident and broke all the glasses* 2 **by accident of** by the chance or fortune of: *By accident of birth he was rich*

accidental *adj* happening by chance —~**ly** *adv*

accommodation *n* 1 a place to live: *Accommodation is expensive in this city* 2 the act of changing something so that it suits new conditions 3 the act of settling a (business) disagreement 4 something that helps

accompany *v* **-nied, -nying** 1 to go with, as on a journey 2 to happen or exist at the same time as: *Lightning usually accompanies thunder* 3 to make supporting music for

accomplish *v* to succeed in doing; perform: *We accomplished nothing*

accordance *n* agreement: *in accordance with your orders*

according to *prep* 1 as stated or shown by: *According to my watch it is 4 o'clock* 2 in a way that agrees with: *Pay is according to ability*

¹account *n* 1 a written or spoken report; story: *Give us an account of what happened* 2 consideration: *Take into account the boy's illness* 3

advantage; profit: *He put his knowledge to good account* 4 a statement of money received and paid out, as by a bank or business: *The accounts show we have spent more than we received* 5 a statement of money owed: *Add the cost of this to my account* 6 a sum of money kept in a bank which may be added to and taken from: *My account is empty* 7 **bring/call (someone) to account (for) a** to cause or force (someone) to give an explanation (of) **b** to punish (someone) (for) 8 **on account of** because of 9 **on no account** also **not on any account**— not for any reason 10 **on one's own account a** so as to advance one's own interests **b** at one's own risk **c** by oneself

²account *v* to consider: *He was accounted a wise man*

accumulate *v* **-lated, -lating** to make or become greater in quantity or size: *He quickly accumulated a large fortune*

accurate *adj* careful and exact: *an accurate statement* – **-acy** *n* –~**ly** *adv*

accuse *v* **accused, accusing** to charge with doing wrong or breaking the law: *The police accused him of murder* –~**r, -sation** *n* –**accusingly** *adv*

accustom *v* to make used to: *He accustomed himself to the cold*

ace *n* 1 a playing card or other object, used in games, that has a single mark or spot and which usu. has the highest or the lowest value **2** *esp. spoken* a person of the highest skill in something: *an ace at cards* **3** (in tennis) a service that the opponent cannot hit back **4 within an ace of** *esp. spoken* very close to

¹ache *v* **ached, aching 1** to have or suffer a continuous dull pain: *I ache all over* **2** to have a strong desire: *He was aching to go*

²ache *n* a continuous pain

achieve *v* **achieved, achieving 1** to finish successfully: *He will never achieve anything* **2** to get as the result of action: *He hopes to achieve all his aims soon* **–achievable** *adj*

achievement *n* **1** the successful finishing or gaining of something **2** something successfully finished or gained esp. through skill and hard work

¹acid *adj* **1** having a bitter taste like that of vinegar **2** bad-tempered **3** of or concerning a chemical acid

²acid *n* a chemical substance containing hydrogen the place of which may be taken by a metal to form a salt

acknowledge *v* **-edged, -edging 1** to recognize the existence (of): *I acknowledge the truth of your statement* **2** to admit (as): *He was acknowledged to be the best player* **3** to show that one is grateful for: *His long service was acknowledged with a present* **4** to state that one has received: *We must acknowledge his letter*

acorn *n* the fruit or nut of the oak tree, which grows in a cuplike holder

acquaintance *n* **1** information or knowledge, as obtained through personal experience: *I have some acquaintance with the language* **2** a person whom one knows, esp. through work, but who may not be a friend

acquire *v* **acquired, acquiring 1** to get for oneself by one's own work, skill, action, etc.: *He acquired a knowledge of the language by careful study* **2** to come into possession of: *He acquired some property*

acquit *v* **-tt- 1** to give a decision that (someone) is not guilty, esp. in a court of law: *They acquitted him of murder* **2** *literature* to cause to act in the stated way: *He acquitted himself rather badly*

acre *n* a measure of land; 4,840 square yards or about 4,047 square metres: *The area of a football field is a little over 2 acres*

acrobat *n* a person skilled in walking on ropes or wires, balancing, walking on hands, etc., esp. at a circus **–~ic** *adj* **–~ically** *adv*

across *adv, prep* **1** from one side to the other (of): *a bridge across the river* **2** to or on the opposite side (of): *We swam across*

¹act *v* **1** to represent, esp. on the stage: *Olivier is acting ('Othello') tonight* **2** *offensive* to play the part of, as in a play: *He is always acting the experienced man* **3** *offensive* to behave as if performing on the

stage: *She always seems to be acting*
4 to take action: *Think before you
act!* **5** to behave as stated: *to act
bravely* **6** to produce an effect: *Does
the drug take long to act?*

²**act** *n* **1** *esp. written* a deed (of the
stated type): *an act of cruelty* **2** a
law: *Parliament has passed an Act
forbidding the killing of animals for
pleasure* **3** one of the main divisions
of a stage play: *Hamlet kills the king
in Act 5 Scene 2* **4** one of a number
of short events in a theatre or circus
performance **5** *offensive, esp. spoken*
an example of insincere behaviour
used for effect (often in the phrase
put on an act) **6 get in on the/
someone's act** *esp. spoken* to get a
share of an/someone's activity, and
esp. any advantages that may come
as a result

action *n* **1** movement using force or
power for some purpose: *Take
action before it is too late* **2** something done: *Actions are more
important than words* **3** the way in
which a body moves: *The horse has
a fine action* **4** the way in which a
part of the body or a machine
works: *the action of the heart* **5** the
moving parts of a machine or
instrument: *The action of this piano
is stiff* **6** effect: *the action of light on
photographic film* **7** a charge in a
court of law: *to bring an action
against someone* **8** a fight between
armies or navies: *The action lasted
5 hours* **9** the chain of events in a
play or book rather than the charac-

ters in it: *The action took place in a
village* **10** *sl* the most productive,
interesting, or exciting activity in
a particular field, area, or group:
London is where the action is! **11
out of action** out of operation; no
longer able to do a typical activity

¹**active** *adj* **1** doing things or always
ready to do things: *He is very active*
2 able to produce the typical effects
or act in the typical way: *Be careful!
That dangerous chemical is still
active!* **3** (of a verb or sentence)
having as the subject the person or
thing doing the action (as in *The
boy kicked the ball*) **–~ly** *adv*

²**active** *n* also **active voice–** the active
part or form of a verb

activity *n* **-ties 1** the condition of
being active **2** something that is
done or is being done, esp. for
interest or education **3** action

actor *n* a man who acts a part in a
play or film

actress *n* a female actor

actual *adj* existing as a real fact: *The
actual amount was not large*

actually *adv* **1** in actual fact; really **2**
strange as it may seem: *The vicar
actually offered me a drink!*

adapt *v* to change so as to be or make
suitable for new needs, different
conditions, etc.: *He adapted an old
car engine to drive his boat*

add *v* **1** to put together with something else so as to increase the
number, size, importance, etc.: *The
fire is going out; will you add some
wood?* **2** to join so as to find the

sum: *If you add 5 and/to 3 you get 8* **3** to say also: *I should add that we are very pleased* **4 add fuel to the fire** *esp. spoken* to make someone feel even more strongly about something

¹**addict** *v* to cause to need or be in the habit of having, taking, etc.: *He became addicted to the drug*

²**addict** *n* a person who is unable to free himself from a harmful habit, esp. of taking drugs – ~**ive** *adj*

addition *n* **1** the act of adding, esp. of adding two or more numbers together **2** something added: *A new baby is often called an addition to the family*

¹**address** *v* **1** to write (on an envelope, parcel, etc.) the name of the person meant to be the receiver, usu. with the place where that person lives or works **2** to direct speech or writing to **3** *esp. written* to cause (oneself) to begin to speak to a person or group **4** *esp. written* to put (oneself) to work at: *He addressed himself to the problem* **5** to speak or write to, using a particular title of rank: *Don't address me as 'officer'* **6** (in golf and other games) to bring one's club, cue, etc., into the correct position before hitting (the ball)

²**address** *n* **1 a** the number of the building, name of the street and town, etc. where a person lives or works **b** such information written down **2** a speech, esp. one that has been formally prepared, made to a group of people **3** *esp. written* manner of expression; behaviour **4** skill and readiness, esp. in conversation **5** also **form of address** – the correct title to be used to someone in speech or writing

adequate *adj* **1** enough for the purpose: *We took adequate food for the holiday* **2** having the necessary ability or qualities: *I hope you will prove adequate to the job* **3** only just good enough: *The performance was adequate* – ~**ly** *adv* – **-quacy** *n*

adjective *n* a word which describes the thing for which a noun stands (such as *black* in the sentence *She wore a black hat*) – **-tival** *adj* – **-tivally** *adv*

adjourn *v* **1** to bring (a meeting, trial, etc.) to a stop, esp. for a particular period or until a later time; to come to such a stop **2** to go to another place, esp. for a rest: *We adjourned to the garden* – ~**ment** *n*

adjust *v* **1** to change slightly, esp. in order to make suitable for a particular job or new conditions: *I must adjust my watch, it's slow* **2** to put into order: *Your collar needs adjusting* – ~**able** *adj* – ~**ment** *n*

administer *v* **1** to control (esp. the business or affairs of a person or group) **2** to put into operation: *The courts administer the law* – **-tration** *n*

admirable *adj* worthy of admiration: *an admirable meal* – **-bly** *adv*

admiration *n* **1** a feeling of pleasure and respect: *She was filled with* *admiration for his courage* **2** a person or thing that causes such feelings: *His skill made him the admiration of his friends*

admire *v* **admired, admiring 1** to regard with pleasure and respect; have a good opinion of: *I admire her for her bravery* **2** to look at with pleasure

admission *n* **1** allowing or being allowed to enter or join a school, club, building, etc. **2** an act of allowing someone to enter or join **3** the cost of entrance: *Admission £1* **4** a statement saying or agreeing that something is true (usu. something bad): *He made an admission of guilt*

admit *v* **-tt- 1** to permit to enter: *I cannot admit you yet* **2** to have space or room for: *The church admits only 200 people* **3** to confess: *The thief admitted his crime*

ado *n* anxious activity; trouble; excitement: *Without more ado he jumped into the water and swam off*

adolescent *adj, n* (of) a boy or girl in the period between being a child and being a grown person; young teenager of about 13–16 − **-cence** *n*

adopt *v* **1** to take (someone, esp. a child) into one's family to look after as one's own, taking on the full responsibilities in law of the parent **2** to take and use as one's own: *I adopted their methods* **3** to approve formally: *The committee adopted his*

suggestions **4** to choose, esp. as a representative

adore *v* **adored, adoring 1** to worship as God **2** to love deeply and respect highly: *an adoring look* **3** *esp. spoken* to like very much: *She adores the cinema*

adorn *v* **1** to add beauty or ornament to **2** to add importance or attractiveness to: *He adorned his story with improbable adventures*

adult *adj, n* (of) a fully grown person or animal, esp. a person over an age stated by law, usu. 18 or 21

¹advance *v* **advanced, advancing 1** to move or come forward: *The soldiers advanced* **2** to improve or move forward: *His employer advanced him (to a higher position)* **3** to bring forward to an earlier date or time **4** to move forward: *The work is not advancing*

²advance *n* **1** forward movement: *Our advance was slow* **2** a development: *advances in space travel* **3** money that is paid before the proper time or lent: *an advance of a month's pay* **4** in advance (of) **a** before in time **b** in front (of)

¹advantage *n* **1** something that may help one to be successful or to gain a desired result: *He had the advantage of wealth* **2** profit; gain **3** take advantage of **a** to make use of; profit from **b** to make use of somebody, as by deceiving them

²advantage *v* **-taged, -taging** *esp. written* to be of profit to; benefit

adventure *n* **1** a journey, activity, etc.,

that is exciting and often dangerous: *an adventure in the mountains* **2** excitement, as in a journey or activity; risk: *He lived for adventure*

adverb *n* a word which adds to the meaning of a verb, an adjective, another adverb, or a sentence, and which answers such questions as *how? when?* or *where?* (as in 'He ran *slowly.*') –~**ial** *n, adj* –~**ially** *adv*

advertise *v* **-tised, -tising 1** to make known to the public, as in a newspaper, or on film or television: *They advertised a used car for sale* **2** to ask by placing an advertisement in a newspaper, shop window, etc.: *We should advertise for a gardener* –~**r** *n*

advertisement *n* **1** also **ad** – a notice of something for sale, services offered, etc., as in a newspaper, painted on a wall, or made as a film **2** the action of advertising

advice *n* **1** opinion given by one person to another on how that other should act: *I asked the doctor for his advice* **2** a letter or report, esp. from a distant place giving information about delivery of goods

advise *v* **advised, advising 1** to tell (somebody) what one thinks should be done **2** *esp. written* to inform: *I have advised her that we are coming*

¹**aerial** *adj* **1** of, in, from, or concerning the air **2** moving or happening in the air –~**ly** *adv*

²**aerial** *n* a wire, rod, or framework put up, often on top of a house, to receive radio or television broadcasts

aeroplane *n* a flying vehicle that is heavier than air, that has wings, and has usu. at least one engine

aerosol *n* a small container from which liquid can be sprayed in a fine mist

affair *n* **1** something that has been done or is to be done ; business: *affairs of state* **2** a happening: *The meeting was a noisy affair* **3** a sexual relationship between 2 people not married to each other, esp. one that lasts for some time

affect *v* **1** to cause some result or change in: *Smoking affects health* **2** to cause feelings in: *She was deeply affected by his death* **3** (of a disease) to attack

affection *n* gentle, lasting love, as of a parent for its child

afflict *v* to cause to suffer in the body or mind

affluent *adj* having plenty of money or other possessions – **-ence** *n*

afford *v* **1** (*usu. with* can, could, able to) to be able to buy: *We can afford a house* **2** to do, spend, give, bear, etc., without serious loss or damage: *Can you afford £5?* **3** *literature* to provide with: *The tree afforded us shelter*

afloat *adv, adj* **1** on or as if on water; floating: *Help me get my boat afloat* **2** on ship; at sea: *How long did you spend afloat?* **3** covered with water;

flooded **4** out of debt: *Lend me some money to keep me afloat*

afraid *adj* **1** full of fear: *Don't be afraid of dogs* **2** worried about possible results: *Don't be afraid of asking for help* **3** *polite* sorry for something that has happened or is likely to happen: *I am afraid I've broken your pen*

¹**after** *adv* following in time or place: *We arrived soon after*

²**after** *prep* **1** following in time, place, or order; behind; later than: *We shall leave after breakfast* **2** in the manner or style of: *A painting after the great master* **3** in accordance with: *a man after my own heart* **4** in search of; with a desire for: *The policeman ran after the thief* **5** with the name of: *The boy was named after his uncle*

³**after** *conj* at a later time than (when): *I found your coat after you had left*

⁴**after** *adj* **1** later in time: *He grew weak in after years* **2** in the back part, esp. of a boat: *the after deck*

afternoon *adj, n* **1** (of) the period between midday and sunset **2** a rather late period: *the afternoon of her life*

afterwards *adv* later; after that

again *adv* **1** once more: *Please say that again* **2** in addition **3** **now and again** sometimes (but not very often)

against *prep* **1** in an opposite direction to: *We sailed against the wind* **2** in opposition to: *He was against the* new motorway **3** next to; touching: *She leant against the wall*

¹**age** *n* **1** the period of time a person has lived or a thing has existed: *What is your age?* **2** one of the periods of life: *At 40 a man has reached middle age* **3** an advanced or old period of life: *bent with age* **4** the particular time of life at which a person becomes able or not able to do something: *people under age are not allowed to drink* **5** all the people living at a particular time: *This age doesn't know what poverty is* **6** *esp. spoken* a long time: *It's been ages/an age since we met* **7** (**be/come**) **of age** (to be or reach) the particular age, usu. 18 or 21, when a person becomes responsible in law for his own actions, and is allowed to vote, get married, etc.

²**age** *v* **aged, aging** *or* **ageing 1** to make or become old **2** to make or become fitter for use with the passage of time: *The wine aged well*

agenda *n* **-das** *or* **-da** a list of the subjects to be considered at a meeting

agent *n* **1** a person who acts for another, esp. one who looks after or represents the business affairs of a person or firm **2** a person who makes money by bringing people into touch with others or the products of others **3** a person or thing that works to produce a result: *Rain and sun are the agents which help plants to grow*

aggravate *v* **-vated, -vating 1** to make

more serious or dangerous: *The lack of rain aggravated the already serious lack of food* **2** *esp. spoken* to annoy – **-tion** *n*

aggressive *adj* **1** *offensive* always ready to quarrel or attack: *He is very aggressive* **2** not afraid of opposition: *A successful businessman must be aggressive* – ~**ly** *adv* – ~**ness** *n*

agile *adj* able to move quickly and easily – ~**ly** *adv* – **-ility** *n*

agitate *v* **-tated, -tating 1** to shake (a liquid) or move (the surface of a liquid) about **2** to cause anxiety to **3** to argue strongly in public or to act for or against some political or social change – **-tation** *n*

ago *adj* back in time from now; in the past: *He left 10 minutes ago*

agony *n* **-nies** very great pain: *He lay in agony until the doctor arrived*

agree *v* **agreed, agreeing 1** to accept an idea, opinion, etc., esp. after argument; approve: *He agreed to my idea* **2** to have or share the same opinion, feeling, or purpose

agreeable *adj* **1** to one's liking: *agreeable weather* **2** ready to agree: *Are you agreeable?*

agreement *n* **1** the state of having the same opinion, feeling, or purpose: *We are in agreement* **2** an arrangement or promise of action, as made between people, groups, businesses, or countries: *You have broken our agreement by not doing the work* **3** the use of matching forms (e.g. in number, gender,

person, or case) of noun, adjective, verb, etc., in a sentence

agriculture *n* the art or practice of farming, esp. of growing crops – **-tural** *adv* – **-tur(al)ist** *n*

ahead *adv, adj* **1** in or into a forward position; in or into the future: *One man went ahead to clear the road. / The days ahead will be busy* **2 ahead of a** in advance of **b** better than **3 get ahead** to do well

¹**aid** *v* to give support to

²**aid** *n* **1** support; help: *He went to the aid of the hurt man* **2** a person or thing that helps: *A dictionary is an important aid in learning a new language*

¹**aim** *v* **1** to point or direct (a weapon, remark, etc.) towards some object, esp. with the intention of hitting it: *He aimed the gun carefully* **2** to direct one's efforts: *I aim to be a writer*

²**aim** *n* **1** the act of directing a weapon, remark, etc.: *The hunter took aim* **2** the desired result of one's efforts; purpose: *What is your aim in working so hard?*

¹**air** *n* **1** the mixture of gases which surrounds the earth and which we breathe: *The fresh air made him feel hungry* **2** the sky or the space above the ground: *He jumped into the air* **3** the sky as something through which to fly **4** the general character or appearance of something; appearance of, or feeling caused by, a person or place: *an air of excitement at the meeting* **5** that part

of a piece of music that is easily recognized and remembered; tune **6 clear the air a** to make the air in a place fresh again, as by opening the windows **b** to get rid of misunderstanding, doubt, etc., by stating the facts clearly **7 in the air** *esp. spoken* **a** (of stories, rumours, etc.) being passed on from one person to another **b** not fully planned or settled **8 into thin air** *esp. spoken* completely out of sight or reach

²**air** *v* **1** (of clothes, sheets, beds, etc.) to dry or become dry by putting in a place that is warm or dry **2** to make or become fresh by letting in air: *We aired the room by opening the windows* **3** to make known to others, esp. in a noisy manner: *They tired of him airing his knowledge*

aircraft *n* **-craft** a flying machine of any type, with or without an engine

airport *n* a place where aircraft can land and take off, which has several buildings, and which is regularly used by paying passengers

airs —also **airs and graces** *n offensive* (esp. of a woman) unnatural manners or actions that are intended to make people think one is more important than one really is (esp. in the phrases **give oneself airs, put on airs**)

ajar *adv, adj* (of a door) not quite closed

¹**alarm** *n* **1** a warning of danger, as by ringing a bell or shouting: *Raise the alarm!* **2** any apparatus, such as a bell, noise, flag, by which a warning

is given **3** sudden fear and anxiety as caused by the possibility of danger

²**alarm** *v* **1** to excite with sudden fear and anxiety **2** to make conscious of danger

album *n* **1** a book whose pages have little or no writing and which is used for collecting photographs, stamps, etc. **2** LONG-PLAYING RECORD

alcohol *n* **1** the pure colourless liquid present in wine, beer, spirits, etc. that can make one drunk **2** the drinks containing this- **3** any of a class of chemical substances of which the alcohol in wine is one – ~**ic** *adj* – ~**ically** *adv*

¹**alert** *adj* watchful and ready (to meet danger): *He is an alert boy* –~**ly** *adv* –~**ness** *n*

²**alert** *n* **1** a warning to be ready for danger **2** the period in which people remain especially watchful for danger

³**alert** *v* to warn: *The doctor alerted me to the dangers of smoking*

algebra *n* a branch of mathematics in which symbols and letters are used instead of numbers – ~**ic(al)** *adj* – ~**ically** *adv*

alibi *n* **-s** an argument that a person charged with a crime was in another place at that time and that he therefore could not have done it: *Have you an alibi?*

¹**alight** *v* **alighted** *or* **alit** *esp. written* to get off at the end of a journey; come down from the air

²**alight** *adj* **1** on fire; in flames **2** having the lights on

¹**alike** *adj* being (almost) the same: *The 2 brothers are very alike*

²**alike** *adv* in (almost) the same way; equally

alive *adj* **1** having life **2** active: *Although old he is still very much alive* **3** still in existence: *The argument was kept alive by the politicians* **4 alive with** covered with or full of (living things)

alkali *n* **-lis** *or* **-lies** *technical* any of various substances that form chemical salts when combined with acids – ~**ne** *adj*

¹**all** *adj* the complete amount, quantity, or number of; the whole of

²**all** *adv* **1** completely: *The table was all covered with papers* **2** to a very great degree; much: *With help we will finish all the sooner* **3** for each side: *The score is 3 all* **4 all along** *esp. spoken* all the time **5 all but** almost **6 (not) all there** *esp. spoken* (not) having a good quick mind **7 all the same** *esp. spoken* even so **8 all the same to** *esp. spoken* not making any difference or causing any worry to **9 all told** counting everyone or everything **10 all up (with)** *esp. spoken* at an end; ruined

³**all** *pron* **1** everybody or everything: *He gave all he had* **2 all in all** *esp. spoken* considering everything **3 all of** fully: *It'll cost all of £5* **4 all that** *esp. spoken* so very: *Things aren't all that good* **5 (not) at all** (not) in any way: *I do not agree at all* **6 for**

all in spite of **7 for all one knows, cares, etc.** *esp. spoken* as far as one knows, cares, etc. **8 it was all one could do (not) to** *esp. spoken* it was very difficult to **9 once and for all** for the last time

allergy *n* **-gies 1** a condition of being unusually sensitive to something eaten, breathed in, or touched, in a way that causes pain or suffering **2** *esp. spoken* a strong dislike (for) – **-gic** *adj*

alley *n* **alleys 1** a narrow street or path between buildings in a town **2** a path in a garden or park, esp. one bordered by trees or bushes **3** a long narrow piece of ground, or floor, along which heavy balls are rolled in order to knock over skittles

alliance *n* **1** the act of allying or the state of being allied **2** a close agreement or connection between countries, groups, families, etc.

allow *v* **1** to permit **2** to make possible (for): *Your gift allows me to buy a car* **3** to give, esp. money or time

allowance *n* **1** something, esp. money, provided regularly or for a special purpose: *an allowance of £5,000 a year* **2** money taken off the cost of something, usu. for a special reason **3** the taking into consideration of facts that may change something, esp. an opinion **4** share

¹**alloy** *n* **alloys** a metal made by mixing together 2 or more different metals

²**alloy** *v* **alloyed, alloying** to mix (one metal) with another

all right *adv, adj* **1** safe or healthy: *Is the driver all right?* **2** *esp. spoken* (in a way that is) acceptable, satisfactory, or unobjectionable: *He mended my radio all right* **3** Yes; I/we agree **4** beyond doubt: *He's ill all right*

¹**ally** *v* **allied, allying** to join or unite, as by political agreement or marriage: *The small country allied itself to the stronger power*

²**ally** *n* **allies 1** a country that is joined to another by political agreement, esp. one that will provide support in war **2** a person who helps or supports one

almighty *adj* **1** having the power to do anything: *God Almighty* **2** *esp. spoken* very big, strong, great, etc.: *an almighty crash*

almost *adv* very nearly

¹**alone** *adj* only: *He alone knows the secret*

²**alone** *adv* without others: *He lived alone*

¹**along** *prep* in the direction of the length of; following the course of: *We walked along the road*

²**along** *adv* **1** forward; on: *My roses are coming along nicely* **2** with others or oneself: *I took my sister along* **3** **all along** all the time **4** **along with** together with

aloud *adv* **1** in a voice that may be heard: *He read the poem aloud* **2** in a loud voice: *to cry aloud*

alphabet *n* the set of letters used in writing any language, esp. when arranged in order −∼**ical** *adj* −∼**ically** *adv*

already *adv* by or before a stated, suggested, or expected time: *When we got there he had arrived already*

also *adv* as well; too: *I also bought a present*

alter *v* to make or become different: *This shirt must be altered* −∼**able** *adj*

alteration *n* **1** the act of making or becoming different **2** a change; something changed

¹**alternative** *adj* (of 2 things) that may be used, had, done, etc., instead of another; other −∼**ly** *adv*

²**alternative** *n* something that may be taken or chosen instead of one or several others: *There are several alternatives to your plan*

although *conj* in spite of the fact that; though

¹**altogether** *adv* **1** completely: *not altogether bad* **2** considering all things

²**altogether** *n* **in the altogether** *humour* nude

aluminium *n* a light, easily shaped, silver-white metal that is an element

always *adv* **1** at all times; at each time: *She always looks cheerful* **2** for ever

am *short form* **'m** − *1st person sing. pres. tense of* BE

¹**amateur** *n* **1** a person who paints pictures, performs plays, takes part in sports, etc., for enjoyment and without being paid for it **2** a person

without experience or skill in a particular art, sport, etc.

²**amateur** *adj* **1** of, by, or with amateurs: *amateur football* **2** being an amateur or amateurs: *an amateur actor* **3** lacking skill: *His performance was amateur*

amaze *v* **amazed, amazing** to fill with great surprise: *Your knowledge amazes me* −~**ment** *n*

amazing *adj* causing great surprise or wonder because of quantity or quality −~**ly** *adv*

ambassador −*fem.* **ambassadress** *n* a minister of high rank representing his country in another country −~**ship** *n* −~**ial** *adj*

ambiguous *adj* **1** able to be understood in more than one way; of unclear meaning: *an ambiguous reply* **2** uncertain; unclear − **-guity** *n* −~**ly** *adv* −~**ness** *n*

ambition *n* **1** strong desire for success, power, riches, etc.: *That politician is full of ambition* **2** that which is desired in this way: *A big house is my ambition*

ambitious *adj* **1** having a strong desire for success, power, riches, etc. **2** showing or demanding a strong desire for success, great effort, great skill, etc.: *an ambitious attempt* −~**ly** *adv* −~**ness** *n*

ambulance *n* a motor vehicle for carrying sick or wounded people, esp. to hospital

¹**ambush** *v* to attack from a place where one has hidden and waited

²**ambush** *n* **1** a surprise attack from a place of hiding **2** the place where the attackers hide

amen *interj* (used at the end of a prayer or hymn) may this become true; so be it

amendment *n* **1** the act of improving or changing: *Your plan needs some amendment* **2** a change made in or suggested for a law, statement, etc.

amends *n* something done to repair or pay for some unkindness, damage, etc.: *Make amends for your rudeness*

amiable *adj* of a pleasant nature; friendly − **-bility** *n* − **-bly** *adv*

amid −also **amidst** *prep literature* in the middle of; among

ammunition *n* bullets, bombs, explosives, etc., esp. things fired from a weapon

among −also **amongst** *prep* **1** in the middle of; surrounded by: *I live among the mountains* **2** in a group consisting of: *She is among my most welcome visitors*

amount *n* a quantity or sum: *Large amounts of money*

amphibious *adj* able to live or move both on land and in water

ample *adj* **1** enough or more than is necessary: *We have ample money* **2** with plenty of space; large: *an ample garden* − **-ply** *adv*

amputate *v* **-tated, -tating** to remove (part of the body) by cutting off, esp. for medical reasons: *to amputate a leg* − **-tation** *n*

amuse *v* **amused, amusing 1** to satisfy or excite the sense of humour: *Your story amuses me* **2** to cause to spend time in a pleasant manner: *She amused the child for hours*

amusement *n* **1** the state of being amused; enjoyment **2** something that causes one's time to pass in an enjoyable way: *Big cities have many amusements*

an *indef article* (the form of the indefinite article used before a word that starts with a vowel sound) : *an apple / an hour*

anaesthetic *n* a substance that produces an inability to feel pain, heat, etc., either in a limited area (**local anaesthetic**) or in the whole body, together with unconsciousness (**general anaesthetic**) –anaesthetic *adj*

analyse *v* **-lysed, -lysing** to examine carefully (esp. by dividing into parts) in order to find out about

anarchy *n* **1** absence of government or control **2** lawlessness and social and political disorder caused by this **3** absence of order – **-chic, -chical** *adj* – **-chically** *adv*

anatomy *n* **-mies 1** the scientific study of the bodies and parts of animals **2** the body or parts of a person or animal **3** the dissection of a body or part of an animal to study the way it is built – **-ist** *n* – **-ical** *adj* – **-ically** *adv*

ancestor –*fem.* **ancestress** *n* a person, esp. one living a long time ago, from whom another is descended – **-tral** *adj*

¹**anchor** *n* **1** a piece of heavy metal, usu. a hook with 2 arms, for low-

ering into the water to keep a ship from moving **2** a person or thing that provides strong support and a feeling of safety **3 weigh anchor** to pull up the anchor and move off

²**anchor** *v* **1** to stop sailing and lower an anchor to keep a ship from moving **2** to fix or be fixed firmly

¹**ancient** *adj* **1** in or of times long ago: *ancient Rome* **2** having existed since a very early time **3** *often humour* very old

²**ancient** *n* a person, esp. a Roman or Greek, who lived in times long ago

and *conj* **1** as well as; too **2** (used to express result or explanation): *Water the seeds and they will grow* **3 and so forth** and more of the same kind or in the same manner

angel *n* **1** a messenger and servant of God, usu. represented as a person with large wings dressed in white **2** a spirit that watches and guards one **3** a person, esp. a woman, who is very kind, beautiful, etc. – ~**ic** *adj* – ~**ically** *adv*

¹**anger** *n* a fierce feeling of displeasure, usu. leading to a desire to hurt or stop the person or thing causing it

²**anger** *v* to make angry

¹**angle** *n* **1** an amount of turning, measured in degrees, and shown in diagrams by two straight lines that meet at a point **2** a corner, as of a building or piece of furniture **3** *esp. spoken* a point of view: *Look at it from my angle* **4 at an angle** not

upright or straight; sloping or turning away,

²**angle** *v* **angled, angling 1** to turn or move at an angle **2** *often offensive* to represent (something) from a particular point of view: *She angles her reports to please her editor*

angling *n* the sport of catching fish with a hook and line – **-gler** *n*

angry *adj* **angrier, angriest 1** filled with anger **2** stormy –**angrily** *adv*

anguish *n* very great pain and suffering, esp. of mind: *She was in anguish over her missing child* –~**ed** *adj*

¹**animal** *n* **1** a living creature having senses and able to move itself when it wants to **2** all this group except human beings **3** a person considered as lacking a mind and behaving like a wild non-human creature **4** a mammal

²**animal** *adj* **1** of, concerning, or made from animals **2** *usu. offensive* concerning the body: *animal desires*

ankle *n* **1** the joint between the foot and the leg **2** the thin part of the leg just above the foot

anniversary *n* **-ries 1** a day which is an exact year or number of years after something has happened: *the anniversary of the day I met you* **2** a ceremony, feast, etc., held on this day

announce *v* **announced, announcing 1** to make known publicly or clearly: *They announced the date of their wedding* **2** to state in a loud voice (the name of a person or thing on arrival, as of people at a party or aircraft at an airport) **3** to read (news) or introduce (a person or act) on the radio, television, etc. –~**r** *n*

announcement *n* a statement saying what has happened or what will happen

annoy *v* **annoyed, annoying** to cause trouble; make a little angry, esp. by repeated acts: *These flies are annoying me* –~**ance** *n*

¹**annual** *adj* (happening, appearing, etc.) every year or once a year, esp. about the same date –~**ly** *adv*

²**annual** *n* **1** a plant that lives for only one year or season **2** a publication produced once a year having the same title but containing different items

anonymous *adj* **1** with name unknown **2** without the writer's name: *an anonymous letter* – **-mity** *n* –~**ly** *adv*

¹**another** *adj* **1** a second: *another piece of cake* **2** different from the first or other

²**another** *pron* **1** one more of the same sort: *She has taken another of my books* **2** a person other than oneself: *Is it brave to die for another?*

¹**answer** *n* **1** a reply, as to a question or polite greeting **2** a reply in the form of action: *In answer to my shouts people ran to help* **3** a reply to an argument or charge **4** something which is discovered as a result esp. of thinking, using figures, etc.: *Having all the figures she found the*

answer quickly: it was 279 **5** a piece of usu. written work to show knowledge or ability, as in an examination

²**answer** *v* **1** to give an answer (to) **2** to do something as a reply (to): *I answered with a smile* **3** to attend or act in reply to (a sign, such as a telephone ringing, a whistle, etc.): *I telephoned this afternoon, but nobody answered* **4** to act or move in reply; obey: *The dog answers to his name* **5** to be satisfactory for: *This tool will answer our needs* **6** to be as described in; to fit: *He answers the description you gave* **7** to reply to (a charge or argument)

ant *n* a small insect living on the ground in well-ordered groups and famous for hard work

antarctic *adj, n* (of or concerning) the most southern part of the world

anthology *n* **-gies** a collection of poems, or of other writings, often on the same subject, chosen from different books or writers

anticipate *v* **-pated, -pating 1** *sometimes considered bad usage* to expect: *We are not anticipating trouble* **2** to do something before: *We anticipated our competitors by buying the land* **3** to see (what will happen) and act as necessary, often to stop someone doing something: *We anticipated where they would try to cross* **4** to provide for the probability of (something) happening **5** to make use of, deal with, or consider before the right or

proper time: *Do not anticipate your earnings by spending too much* – – **pation** *n*

anticlimax *n* **1** something unexciting coming after something exciting: *To be back in the office after a holiday is an anticlimax* **2** *often humour* a sudden change from something noble, serious, exciting, etc., to something foolish, unimportant, or uninteresting

anticlockwise *adj, adv* in the opposite direction to the hands of a clock

¹**antique** *adj esp. written or literature* old and therefore valuable

²**antique** *n* a piece of old furniture, jewellery, etc., that is becoming rare and valuable

antiseptic *n, adj* (a chemical substance) able to prevent flesh, blood, etc., from developing disease, esp. by killing bacteria

anxiety *n* **-ties 1** fear or an example of this, esp. as caused by uncertainty **2** a cause of this **3** *esp. spoken* a strong wish to do something: *anxiety to please*

anxious *adj* **1** feeling anxiety; fearful: *He was anxious for his safety* **2** causing anxiety or worry **3** having a strong wish to do something; eager – **~ly** *adv*

¹**any** *adj, pron* **1** one or some of whatever kind: *Choose any you like* **2** one, some, or all, of whatever quantity; an unstated number or amount: *Have you got any money?* **3** none at all: *I haven't any money* **4** of the usual or stated kind: *This*

isn't any ordinary fish **5** the smallest or least possible amount or degree of: *It isn't any use* **6** no matter which, what, where, how, etc.: *Any room will do* **7** *esp. spoken* a, an, or one: *This car hasn't any engine!* **8** as much as possible: *He will need any help he can get* **9** in **any case** also **at any rate**– whatever may happen **10** unlimited or unmeasured in amount, number, etc.: *I have any number of things I must do today*

²**any** *adv* in any degree; at all: *Do you feel any better?*

anybody –also **anyone** *pron* **1** any person **2** a person of importance: *If you want to be anybody you must work hard* **3 anybody's guess** *esp. spoken* a matter of uncertainty

anyhow *adv esp. spoken* **1** without any regular order; in a careless manner: *His clothes were thrown down just anyhow* **2** in any case **3** (used to show a change of subject): *John's a good friend of mine. Well anyhow, I left the next morning*

¹**anything** *pron* **1** any one thing; something: *Is there anything in that box?* **2** no matter what: *Anything will do to keep the door open* **3** a thing of any kind, esp. something important or serious: *I was cut but it wasn't anything* **4 anything but** not at all; far from **5 as easy/fast/strong, etc., as anything** *sl* very easy/fast/strong, etc. **6 if anything** if there is any difference **7 like anything** *sl* (used to add force to a verb): *We ran like*

anything **8 or anything** (suggests that there are other possibilities): *If he wants to call me or anything, I'll be here*

²**anything** *adv* at all: *Is this box anything like what you need?*

anyway *adv esp. spoken* in any case: *I shall go and see him anyway*

anywhere *adv* **1** (in, at, or to) any place: *Did you go anywhere yesterday?* **2** in, at, or to no matter what place: *Sit anywhere*

apart *adv* **1** separate; away: *The buildings are miles apart* **2** to pieces: *He tore the chicken apart and began to eat* **3** in or into a state of separation, independence, disconnection: *If I see the 2 boys apart I don't know which is which* **4 apart from** without considering

apathy *n* lack of feeling or interest in something or everything; lack of desire or ability to act in any way

¹**ape** *n* **1** a large monkey without a tail or with a very short tail (such as a gorilla or chimpanzee) **2** *usu. offensive* a person who copies the behaviour of others

²**ape** *v* **aped, aping** to copy

apologize, -ise *v* **-gized, -gizing** to express sorrow, as for a fault or causing pain: *I apologized to her for stepping on her foot*

apology *n* **-gies 1** a statement expressing sorrow for a fault, causing trouble or pain, etc. **2** a defence or explanation of a belief, idea, etc.: *Shelley's 'Apology for Poetry'* **3** *esp. spoken* a very poor example of something: *This is an apology for a meal*

appalling *adj* **1** causing fear; shocking, terrible **2** *esp. spoken* of very bad quality: *appalling food* −~**ly** *adv*

apparatus *n* **-tuses** *or* **-tus 1** a set of instruments, machines, tools, materials, etc., that work together or are needed for a particular purpose **2** a group of parts that work together inside a body: *The breathing apparatus includes the nose, throat, and lungs*

apparent *adj* **1** easily seen or understood **2** not necessarily true or real; seeming: *Their apparent grief turned to laughter*

apparently *adv* it seems (that); as it appears

¹**appeal** *n* **1** a strong request for help, support, mercy, etc.: *an appeal for forgiveness* **2** power to move the feelings; attraction; interest **3** a call to a higher court to change the decision of a lower court **4** (esp. in sports) a call from a player for a decision from the referee or umpire

²**appeal** *v* **1** to make a strong request for help, support, etc.; beg: *He appealed for mercy* **2** to please, attract, or interest: *She appeals to me* **3** to call on a higher court to change the decision of a lower court **4** (esp. in sports) to call for a decision, as from the referee

appear *v* **1** to come into sight: *A car appeared over the hill* **2** to seem; look: *He appears to want to leave* **3** to come to a certain place, esp. in view of the public, as for attention or sale: *His book will be appearing in the shops soon* **4** to be present officially as in a court of law: *He had to appear before the committee* **5** to be found; exist

appearance *n* **1** the act of appearing, as to the eye, mind, or public **2** that which can be seen; look: *He had an unhealthy appearance* **3 put in/ make an appearance (at)** to attend , esp. for a short time only

appendix *n* **-dixes** *or* **dices 1** also **vermiform appendix−** a short wormlike organ leading off the bowel, and having little or no use **2** something added, esp. information at the end of a book

appetite *n* **1** a desire or wish, esp. for food: *Don't spoil your appetite* **2** a desire to satisfy any bodily want: *sexual appetites* **3 whet someone's appetite** to make someone eager for more of something

applaud *v* **1** to praise (a play, actor, etc.) esp. by clapping **2** to express strong agreement with

applause *n* loud praise, esp. by clapping

apple *n* **1** a hard round fruit with white juicy flesh and usu. a red, green, or yellow skin that grows on a tree of the rose family **2 the apple of someone's eye** *esp spoken* the person or thing most liked

appliance *n* an apparatus, or tool for a particular purpose, often one on a larger machine

application *n* **1** the putting to use **2** the quality of being useful or suitable: *That rule has no application to this case* **3** a request or act of requesting, esp. officially and in writing **4** the putting of one thing onto another, esp. medicine onto the skin **5** careful and continuous attention or effort: *He worked with great application*

apply *v* **applied, applying 1** to request something, esp. officially and in writing **2** to bring or put into use: *Apply as much force as is necessary* **3** to put on or next to: *Apply medicine to his wound* **4** to have an effect; be directly related: *This rule does not apply* **5** to cause to work hard or with careful attention

appoint *v* **1** to put in or choose for a position, job, or purpose: *to appoint a new teacher* **2** to set up or make by choosing: *to appoint a committee* **3** *esp. written* to arrange; decide: *Let's appoint a day to meet*

appointment *n* **1** the agreement of a time and place for meeting or such a meeting: *He will only see you by appointment* **2** (the choosing of someone for) a position, job, or office: *the appointment of a chairman*

appreciate *v* **-ated, -ating 1** to be thankful for: *I appreciate your help* **2** to understand and enjoy the good qualities of: *Do you appreciate good wine?* **3** to understand fully (the worth or amount of) **4** to increase in value: *This house has appreciated (in value)*

appreciation *n* **1** judgment, as of the quality, worth, or facts of something **2** a written account of the worth of something **3** grateful feelings: *He showed no appreciation of my advice* **4** rise in value, esp. of land or possessions

¹apprentice *n* a person who is under an agreement to serve, usu. for low wages, a person skilled in a trade, in order to learn that person's skill

²apprentice *v* **-ticed, -ticing** to make or send as an apprentice: *apprenticed to an electrician*

¹approach *v* **1** to come near or nearer (to): *We approached the camp* **2** to speak to, esp. about something for the first time: *Did he approach you about a loan?* **3** to begin to consider or deal with (something non-material): *He approached the idea with caution*

²approach *n* **1** the act of approaching: *the approach of winter* **2** a means or way of entering: *All approaches were blocked* **3** a speaking to someone for the first time, esp. in order to begin close personal relations: *making approaches to strangers* **4** a method of doing something: *That player's approach to music is quite new*

¹appropriate *v* **-ated, -ating 1** to set aside for some purpose: *The government appropriated a large sum for building works* **2** to take for oneself; steal: *The minister appropriated government funds*

²**appropriate** *adj* correct or suitable: *His bright clothes were not appropriate for a funeral* –~**ly** *adv* –~**ness** *n*

approval *n* **1** the act of approving **2** official permission **3 on approval** also *esp. spoken* **on appro**–(of goods) to be returned without payment if not found satisfactory

approve *v* **approved, approving** to agree officially to –**approvingly** *adv*

approve of *v prep* to consider good, right, wise, etc.: *I don't approve of wasting time*

approximate *adj* nearly correct but not exact –~**ly** *adv*

April *n* the 4th month of the year

apt *adj* **1** having a tendency to do something; likely: *This shoe is apt to slip* **2** clever and quick to learn and understand: *an apt student* **3** exactly suitable: *an apt remark* –~**ly** *adv* –~**ness** *n*

aptitude *n* natural ability or skill, esp. in learning

aquarium *n* **-iums** *or* **-ia 1** a glass container for fish and other water animals **2** a building (esp. in a zoo) containing many of these

arbitrary *adj* **1** of power that is uncontrolled and used without considering the wishes of others: *The arbitrary decisions of the factory owners angered the workers* **2** *often offensive* decided by or based on personal opinion or chance rather than reason: *My choice was quite arbitrary* – **-rily** *adv* – **-riness** *n*

¹**arch** *n* **1** a curved top sometimes with a central point resting on 2 supports **2** something with this shape, esp. the middle of the bottom of the foot

²**arch** *v* to make into or form the shape of an arch

³**arch** *adj* amused, gay, or intended to attract; coy: *an arch smile* – ~**ly** *adv*

archaeology *n* the study of the buried remains of ancient times, such as houses, pots, tools, and weapons – **-gical** *adj* – **-gically** *adv* – **-gist** *n*

archaic *adj* belonging to the past –~**ally** *adv*

architect *n* a person who plans new buildings and sees that they are built properly

architecture *n* **1** the art and science of building, including its planning, making, and ornamentation **2** the style or manner of building, esp. as belonging to a particular country or period of history – **-tural** *adj* – **-turally** *adv*

arctic *adj* **1** of or concerning the most northern part of the world **2** very cold

arduous *adj* needing much effort; difficult –~**ly** *adv* –~**ness** *n*

are *short form* **'re** *pres. tense of* BE **a** *(2nd person sing.)*: *You are my cousin* **b** *(1st, 2nd, and 3rd person pl.)*: *We/you/they are friends*

area *n* **1** a particular space or surface **2** a part of the world **3** the measure of a surface: *the area of a rectangle* **4** a subject or specialist field of ideas or work

arena *n* **1** an enclosed area for public shows, sports, etc. **2** a scene or place of activity, esp. of competition

argue *v* **argued, arguing 1** to reason strongly in defence of one's opinions **2** *literature* to show; suggest: *The way he spends money argues him to be a rich man* **3** to give reasons to prove or try to prove **4** to disagree in words; quarrel

argument *n* **1** a reason given to support or disprove something: *There are many arguments against smoking* **2** the use of reason to persuade someone: *We must settle this by argument not by fighting* **3** a disagreement; quarrel

arise *v* **arose, arisen 1** to come into being; happen **2** *old use* to get up; stand up

aristocracy *n* **-cies 1** the people of the highest social class, esp. from noble families **2** the best or most powerful members of any group or class, in any activity **3** government by people of the highest social rank

aristocrat *n* **1** a member of an aristocracy **2** the finest example of a group or type −~**ic** *adj* −~**ically** *adv*

arithmetic *n* **1** the science of numbers **2** the adding, subtracting, multiplying, etc., of numbers −~**al** *adj* −~**ally** *adv*

¹**arm** *n* **1** either of the 2 upper limbs of a human being or other 2 legged animal **2** something that is shaped like or moves like an arm **3** the part of a garment that covers the arm **4** the part of a chair on which the arm rests **5 at arm's length** at a safe distance away **6 with open arms** gladly and eagerly −~**less** *adj*

²**arm** *v* **1** to supply with or have weapons or armour **2** to supply what is needed for a purpose

armchair *n* a chair with arms

armour *n* **1** protective metal covering on fighting vehicles, ships, and aircraft, and as worn by fighting men in former times **2** vehicles with such covering **3** a protective covering of plants or animals

arms *n* **1** weapons **2** COAT OF ARMS **3 bear arms** *literature* to serve as a soldier **4 lay down one's arms** to surrender **5 take up arms** *literature* **a** to get ready to use weapons **b** to become a soldier **6 under arms** (of soldiers) armed **7 up in arms** very angry and ready to argue or fight

army *n* **armies 1** the military forces of a country that fight on land **2** a large body of people trained for war **3** any large group, esp. one with some purpose: *an army of workers/ants*

arose *past tense of* ARISE

¹**around** *adv* **1** on all sides; about; in every direction **2** near in time, number, etc.; about

²**around** *prep* **1** on all sides of; all round; surrounding **2** round: *driving around Yorkshire*

arrange *v* **arranged, arranging 1** to set in order **2** to plan in advance; prepare

arrangement *n* **1** the act of putting into or of being put into order **2**

something that has been put in order **3** something arranged, planned, or agreed in a particular way **4** the act of making an agreement or settlement **5** the setting out of a piece of music **6** the result of this: *an arrangement for piano*

¹**arrest** *v* **1** to seize (someone) in the name of the law **2** to bring to an end; stop **3** to catch and fix (esp. somebody's attention)

²**arrest** *n* **1** the act of arresting or of being arrested **2** *technical* the act of stopping or the state of being stopped **3** **under arrest** held prisoner by the police

arrival *n* **1** the act of arriving **2** a person or thing that arrives or has arrived

arrive *v* **arrived, arriving 1** to reach a place or position, esp. the end of a journey: *arrive home / arrive at a decision* **2** to happen; come **3** (of a baby) to be born **4** to win success: *Now that his books were sold in every shop he felt that he had arrived*

arrogant *adj* proud and self-important in a rude way −∼**ly** *adv* − **-ance** *n*

arrow *n* a thin straight pointed stick that is shot from a bow

arson *n* the criminal act of setting fire to property −∼**ist** *n*

art *n* **1** the making or expression of something beautiful, such as painting **2** things produced in this way (esp. in the phrase **work of art**) **3** fine skill esp. in such making or expression: *the art of painting well / the art of making friends*

artery *n* **-ries 1** a blood vessel that carries blood from the heart to the rest of the body **2** a main road, railway, river, etc.

¹**article** *n* **1** a particular or separate thing or object, esp. one of a group **2** a piece of writing in a newspaper, magazine, etc. **3** the English words 'a" or 'an" (**indefinite article**) and 'the" (**definite article**) or the words that do the same work in other languages

²**article** *v* **-cled, -cling-** to place under agreement to train under someone in a profession: *I am articled to a firm of lawyers*

artificial *adj* **1** made by man; not natural **2** insincere; unreal −∼**ly** *adv* −∼**ity** *n*

artillery *n* **1** large guns **2** the part of the army using such weapons

artist *n* **1** a painter; someone who practises one of the other arts **2** a person who shows inventive skill in his work **3** an actor, singer, or other performer

artistic *adj* **1** of, concerning, or typical of art or artists **2** made with skill and imagination; beautiful **3** liking what is well done in art −∼**ally** *adv*

¹**as** *adv* **1** to the same degree or amount; equally: *Paul runs fast, but I run just as fast* **2** when considered in the stated way: *Britain as seen by a foreigner*

²**as** *conj* **1** (used to link parts of a comparison) *He can run as fast as I can. / She likes him as much as Paul* (='as much as Paul does" or

'as much as she likes Paul'') / *He works in the same office as my brother* **2** (used to introduce a reason, result, purpose, or example) *I can't come tonight as I'm going to a concert. / He was so careless as to leave his coat in Geneva. / Jane brought her camera so as to photograph the procession. / Such animals as lions and tigers / Animals such as lions and tigers are kept in the zoo* **3** while: *She dropped her programme as she stood up* **4 as it were** in a manner of speaking: *He is my best friend, my second self, as it were* **5 as of right** by right: *All the money is yours as of right* **6 as yet** up to now; so far

³**as** *pron* **1** in accordance with what: *David, as you know, is a scientist. / It is just as you like* **2** in accordance with the way in which: *He is quite good, as boys go*

⁴**as** *prep* **1** like **2** in the state, character, condition, job, etc. of being: *The kitten uses that box as a bed. / I saw Oliver as Romeo*

ascend *v esp. written* **1** to move upwards; rise **2** to climb **3 ascend the throne** to become king or queen

¹**ash** *n* a common forest tree that produces black buds, or its hard wood

²**ash** *n* the powdery remains left after something has burnt

ashamed *adj* **1** feeling shame, guilt, or sorrow **2** unwilling to do something through fear of feeling shame or of being laughed at: *He was ashamed to ask such a simple question* **–~ly** *adv*

ashore *adv* on, onto, or to the shore or land

¹**aside** *adv* to or towards the side; out of the way: *She stepped aside to let him pass. / Joking aside, we really must do something*

²**aside** *n* **1** words spoken by an actor to the audience, not to the other characters **2** a remark not intended to be heard by everyone present

ask *v* **1** to request (information) **2** to make a request for or to **3** to demand; expect **4** to invite

asleep *adj* **1** sleeping **2** (of an arm or leg) unable to feel; numb **3 fall asleep a** to go to sleep **b** *polite* to die

aspire *v* **aspired, aspiring** to direct one's hopes and efforts to some important aim

aspirin *n* **-rin** *or* **-rins** (a tablet of) a medicine that lessens pain and fever

ass *n* **1** any of a family of animals including the donkey, which are like horses but smaller and with longer ears **2** *esp. spoken* a stupid foolish person

assassin *n* a person who murders (a ruler or politician)

assassinate *v* **-ated, -ating** to murder (a ruler, politician, etc.) **– -ation** *n*

¹**assault** *n* **1** a sudden violent attack **2** *law* (the threat of) an unlawful attack with blows against another person

²**assault** *v* to attack suddenly and violently

assemble *v* **-bled, -bling 1** to gather or collect together **2** to put together

assembly *n* **-blies 1** a group of people esp. for a special purpose **2** a meeting together of people **3** a law-making body

assert *v* **1** to state or declare forcefully **2** to make a claim to; defend in words **3** to show, esp. forcefully **4** **assert oneself a** to act in a way that shows one's power, control, etc. **b** to behave in a way that attracts notice

assess *v* **1** to decide the amount or value of **2** to judge the quality or worth of – ~ment *n*

asset *n* a valuable possession, quality, or skill –opposite **liability**

assist *v* to help or support – ~ance *n*

assistant *n* a person who helps another, as in a job

association *n* **1** a society of people joined together for a particular purpose **2** the act of joining or the state of being joined with somebody or something **3** the act of connecting things, esp. in the mind

assorted *adj* of various types mixed together

assortment *n* a group of mixed things; mixture

assume *v* **assumed, assuming 1** to take as a fact without proof; suppose **2** to take upon oneself: *to assume new duties*

assurance *n* **1** also **self-assurance**– strong belief in one's own ability **2** a trustworthy statement; promise **3** insurance: *life assurance*

assure *v* **assured, assuring 1** to promise; try to persuade **2** to make (oneself) certain **3** to insure, esp. against death

astonish *v* to produce surprise or wonder in (someone)

astonishment *n* great surprise or wonder

astrology *n* the art of understanding the supposed influence that the heavenly bodies have on our lives – -ger *n* – -gical *adj* – -gically *adv*

astronomy *n* the scientific study of the sun, moon, stars, etc. – -mer *n*

at *prep* **1 a** in a certain place in time or space: *at home / at Christmas* **b** on a point on a scale: *It melts at 90°. / at 60 pence each* **2** towards, intending, or intended to hit: *Those remarks were aimed at me* **3** as a sign or result of feelings caused by: *I laughed at his silliness* **4** in the field or area of: *good at French*

ate *past tense of* EAT

athlete *n* a person skilled at games needing strength and speed

athletics *n* a branch of sport involving running, jumping, and throwing

atlas *n* a book of maps

atmosphere *n* **1** the mixture of gases that surrounds any heavenly body, esp. the earth **2** the air **3** the feeling produced by the surroundings

atom *n* **1** the smallest piece of an element that still has the same qualities and can combine with other substances **2** *esp. spoken* a very small bit

atom bomb –also **atomic bomb** *n* a bomb whose very powerful explosion is caused by splitting an atom and setting free its force

atomic *adj* **1** of or concerning an atom or atoms **2** working by atomic energy – ~**ally** *adv*

atomic energy *n* also **nuclear energy–** the powerful force that is given out when the middle part (nucleus) of an atom is changed, as by being split

atrocity *n* **-ties 1** great evil, esp. cruelty **2** a very evil, esp. cruel, act **3** *esp. spoken* something that is very displeasing or ugly – **-cious** *adj* – **-ciously** *adv*

attach *v* to fix; fasten; join

¹attack *v* **1** to bring violence (on), esp. with weapons **2** to speak or write strongly against **3** to harm, esp. by a continuing action: *The disease attacked his bones* **4** to begin with eagerness: *He attacked the food as if he had not eaten for a week* – ~**er** *n*

²attack *n* **1** violence intended to harm **2** writing or words intended to hurt or damage **3** a sudden period of illness, usu. serious: *a heart attack*

¹attempt *v* to make an effort at; try

²attempt *n* **1** an effort made to do something **2 attempt on someone's life** an effort to murder someone

attend *v* **1** to pay attention **2** to be present at **3** to look after; give help; serve

attendance *n* **1** the act of attending: *a doctor in attendance on the sick man* **2** the act of being present, esp. regularly: *attendance at school* **3** the number of people present

attention *n* **1** the act of fixing the mind, esp. by watching or listening **2** particular care, notice, or action **3** a military position in which a person stands straight and still: *to stand at attention*

attentive *adj* **1** taking careful notice; listening carefully **2** careful to fulfil the wishes of another – ~**ly** *adv* – ~**ness** *n*

attitude *n* **1** the position or manner of standing of the body **2** a manner of feeling and behaving **3** judgment; opinion

attract *v* **1** to cause to like, admire, notice, or turn towards **2** to draw towards one **3** to draw by unseen forces

attraction *n* **1** the act of attracting **2** something which attracts **3** *technical* (in science) the force by which bodies tend to approach each other

attractive *adj* **1** having the power to attract **2** having good looks – ~**ly** *adv* – ~**ness** *n*

audience *n* **1** the people listening to or watching a performance, speech, show, etc. **2** a formal meeting between somebody powerful and somebody less important: *The queen allowed him an audience of 20 minutes*

August *n* the 8th month of the year

aunt –also (*esp. spoken*) **auntie, aunty**

n **1** the sister of one's father or mother, the wife of one's uncle, or a woman whose brother or sister has a child **2** a woman who is a friend of a small child or its parents

authentic *adj* known to be what it is claimed to be; real; genuine −∼**ally** *adv* −∼**ity** *n*

author *n* **1** the writer of a book, newspaper article, play, poem, etc. **2** the originator or maker of anything, esp. an idea or plan

authority *n* **-ties 1** the ability, power, or right to control and command **2** a person or group with this power or right, esp. in public affairs **3** right or official power, esp. for some stated purpose **4** a person, book, etc., whose knowledge or information is dependable, good, and respected

autobiographical −also **autobiographic** *adj* of or concerning the facts of one's own life, esp. as written in a book −∼**ly** *adv*

¹autograph *n* a person's handwriting, esp. his signature

²autograph *v* to write one's signature on (a book, letter, etc. that one has written)

¹automatic *adj* **1** (of a machine) able to work without human help **2** done without thought, esp. as a habit **3** certain to happen −∼**ally** *adv*

²automatic *n* something, such as certain weapons, cars, etc., in which some parts work automatically

autumn *n* the season between summer and winter −∼**al** *adj* −∼**ally** *adv*

available *adj* **1** able to be got, obtained, used, etc. **2** able to be visited or seen − **-ability** *n* − **-ably** *adv*

avenue *n* **1** a road between 2 rows of trees **2** a wide street in a town **3** the way to a result (often in the phrase **explore every avenue**)

¹average *n* **1** the amount found by adding together several quantities and then dividing by the number of quantities: *The average of 3, 8, and 10 is 7* **2** a level or standard regarded as usual or ordinary −**average** *adj*

²average *v* **-raged, -raging 1** to be or come to an average **2** to do, get, or have as a usual quantity **3** to calculate the average of

aviation *n* **1** the art or science of flying aircraft **2** the aircraft industry

avoid *v* **1** to escape: *I avoided being punished* **2** to keep away from, esp. on purpose −∼**able** *adj* −∼**ance** *n*

await *v* **1** to wait for **2** to be in store for; be ready for

¹awake −also **awaken** *v* **awoke** *or* **awaked, awaked** *or* **awoken 1** to wake **2** to make or become conscious or active

²awake *adj* **1** having woken; not asleep **2** conscious (of) **3 wide awake a** not at all sleepy **b** not easily deceived

¹award *v* **1** to give officially as a prize **2** to give by a decision in a court of law

²**award** *n* **1** something given officially, esp. a prize **2** a decision, or that which is given by a decision, in a court of law **3** a sum of money given to a student so that he can afford to study

aware *adj* having knowledge or consciousness − ∼**ness** *n*

away *adv* **1** from this or that place; to, at, or in another place **2** to an end; to nothing: *The water boiled away* **3** continuously: *He sawed away at the thick branch till at last it was cut through*

awful *adj* **1** terrible; shocking **2** *esp. spoken* very bad: *awful weather* **3** *literature & old use* causing feelings of respect mixed with fear and wonder − ∼**ness** *n*

awkward *adj* **1** clumsy **2** not well made for use; difficult to use; causing difficulty **3** (of a person) difficult to deal with **4** embarrassing − ∼**ly** *adv* − ∼**ness** *n*

¹**axe** *n* **axes** **1** a tool with a heavy metal blade on the end of a long handle used to cut wood **2** *esp. spoken* (in the phrases **give/get the axe**) sudden ending, esp. because of lack of money, of **a** one's employment **b** a plan **3** **have an axe to grind** *esp. spoken* to have private and often selfish reasons for one's actions

²**axe** *v* **axed, axing** to remove suddenly from a job, a list of plans for completion, etc.

axle *n* the rod which passes through the centre of a wheel

¹**baby** *n* **babies** **1** a very young child, esp. one who has not learnt to speak **2** a very young animal or bird **3 a** the youngest of a group **b** a small member of a group **4** a person who behaves like a baby **5** *sl esp. US* a person, esp. a girl or woman: *I've got a gun here, baby, so hand over your money*

²**baby** *v* **babied, babying** *esp. spoken* to treat like a baby; give a great deal of care or attention to

baby-sit *v* **-sat, -tt-** to take care of children while their parents are out − ∼**ter** *n*

bachelor *n* an unmarried man − ∼**hood** *n*

¹**back** *n* **1** the part of the body of a human or animal down the middle of which runs the spine **2** the less important side or surface (of an object) **3** (of a building) the side opposite to the main entrance **4** (of a vehicle) **a** the inside part behind the driver **b** the outside surface opposite to the usual direction of movement **5** the furthest part (from the point towards which a group of people are facing or moving) **6** (of a chair) the part that one leans against when sitting **7** (of a book or newspaper) the last part; end **8** (in games like football) a player or position that defends the area near the team's own goal **9 at the back (of)** behind **10 back to back** with the backs facing each other **11 break the back of** to do most of; do the worst part of (something that must

be done) **12 be glad to see the back of someone** *esp. spoken* to be glad when someone goes away **13 have/ with one's back to the wall** (to be) in a bad state of affairs, that is hard to get out of **14 put one's back into** to work very hard at **15 put someone's back up** *esp. spoken* to annoy someone **16 turn one's back on** to avoid; go away from (esp. when one should stay) −∼**less** *adj*

²**back** *adv* **1** towards or at the back: *to tie one's hair back* **2** to or at a place or time where something or someone was before: *Put the book back on the shelf* **3** (of a clock) so as to show an earlier time

³**back** *adj* **1** long past **2** (of money) owed from an earlier time: *back pay/rent* **3** at the back: *back door*

⁴**back** *v* **1** to go or cause to go backwards: *The car backed through the gate* **2** to support and encourage, often with money **3** to bet money on **4** to be or make the back of: *curtains backed with a plastic material* **5** *technical* (of the wind) to change direction anti-clockwise

background *n* **1** the scenery or ground behind something, e.g. in a painting or photograph **2** a position as unnoticeable as possible: *to remain in the background* **3** the conditions existing when something happens or happened: *The election took place against a background of widespread unemployment* **4** a person's family, experience, and education

backing *n* **1** material or moral help **2** something that is used to make the back of an object **3** (esp. in popular music) the music that is played by those other than the main performer or performers

backlash *n* **1** a sudden violent backward movement after a forward one **2** a movement against a growing belief or practice, esp. against a political or social development

backward *adj* **1** directed towards the back, the beginning, or the past **2** returning: *the backward journey* **3** behind in development **4** unsure of oneself; shy −∼**ly** *adv* −∼**ness** *n*

backwards *adv* **1** away from one's front; towards the back **2** with the back first: *walking backwards* **3** with the back where the front should be; back to front **4 bend/fall over backwards** to try as hard as possible or almost too hard

bacon *n* **1** salted or smoked meat from the back or sides of a pig, often sold in thin slices **2 bring home the bacon** *sl* to succeed, esp. in providing for one's family **3 save one's bacon** *esp. spoken* to have a narrow escape

bacteria *n sing.* **-rium** very small living things, each consisting of a single cell, and some of which cause disease − **-rial** *adj*

¹**bad** *adj* **worse, worst 1** not of acceptable quality; poor **2** unfavourable **3** decayed: *bad fish* **4** morally wrong **5** not suitable for a purpose: *very bad light in this room* **6** unpleasant:

bad news **7** harmful: *Smoking is bad for your health* **8** not healthy: *bad teeth* **9** not feeling healthy or happy **10** serious; severe: *a bad cold / a bad defeat* **11** incorrect: *bad grammar* **12** (of language or a word) not used in polite society **13 in bad faith** dishonestly; without intending to carry out a promise **14 feel bad about** *esp. spoken* to be sorry or ashamed about **15 go bad** to become unfit to eat **16 have/get a bad name** to lose or have lost people's respect **17 (It's/That's) too bad** *esp. spoken* I'm sorry: *Too bad you couldn't come last night* – ~**ness** *n*

²**bad** *n* **1** that which is bad **2 go to the bad** to begin living in an immoral or evil way

badge *n* a sign worn to show a person's employment, rank, membership of a group, etc.

¹**badger** *n* a grey burrowing animal that has a white face with 2 black stripes, and is active at night

²**badger** *v* to ask again and again

badly *adv* **worse, worst 1** in a bad manner **2** by a great deal: *badly beaten in the race* **3** a great deal; very much

baffle *v* **-fled, -fling** to bring to a halt by confusing: *The examination question baffled me completely and I couldn't answer it* – **-ling** *adj* – **-lingly** *adv* – ~**ment** *n*

¹**bag** *n* **1** a container made of soft material , opening at the top **2** the quantity of usu. small birds or animals shot or caught on any one occasion **3** a bagful **4 in the bag** *sl* as desired: *Don't worry. We've got the match in the bag*

²**bag** *v* **-gg- 1** to put into a bag or bags **2** *esp. spoken* to kill or catch (animals or birds): *We bagged a rabbit* **3** *sl* to take or keep : *Try to bag seats at the back for us* **4** *esp. spoken* to hang loosely, like a bag: *His trousers bagged at the knees*

baggage *n* **1** luggage army equipment such as tents, beds, etc. **3** *humour* a good-for-nothing young woman

¹**bait** *v* **1** to provide (a hook or trap) with bait **2** to make (an animal or a person) angry intentionally: *bear baiting*

²**bait** *n* **1** food used to catch fish or animals **2** something that attracts attention or causes desire **3 rise to the bait a** (of a fish) to take bait near the surface of the water **b** (of a person) to respond to something offered as bait, either by being attracted or by becoming angry

bake *v* **baked, baking 1** to cook in an oven **2** to harden by heating

baker *n* a person who bakes bread and cakes, esp. professionally

¹**balance** *n* **1** an instrument for weighing things by making the amounts in 2 hanging pans equal **2** a weight or influence on one side equalling that on the other **3** a state where all parts have their proper weight **4** money or something else remaining or left over: *a bank balance* **5 in the balance** uncertain(ly)

6 off balance unsteady or unsteadily
7 on balance all things considered
²**balance** *v* **-anced, -ancing 1** to consider or compare **2** to be or cause
to be steady, esp. in a difficult position **3** to be or cause to be of equal
weight, importance, or influence to
(something/each other) **4** to have
no more money going out than
coming in: *My accounts balance for
the first time this year!*
balcony *n* **-nies 1** a platform built out
from an upper window of a building
2 the seats upstairs in a theatre or
cinema
bald *adj* **1** with little or no hair **2**
plain; without ornament −~**ness** *n*
¹**ball** *n* **1** a round object used in play;
anything of a round shape **2** a ball
as thrown or kicked in cricket, football, etc. **3** a rounded part of the
body: *the ball of the foot* **4 on the
ball** *esp. spoken* showing up-to-date
knowledge
²**ball** *n* **1** a large formal occasion for
dancing **2** *sl* a very good time
ballet *n* **1** a dance in which a story is
told without speech or singing **2**
the music for such a dance **3** the
art of a ballet dancer
¹**balloon** *n* **1** a bag of light material
filled with hot air or a light gas **2**
a small rubber bag that can be
blown up, used as a toy **3** anything
shaped like this, esp. the space
round the words spoken by cartoon
figures **4 the balloon goes up** the
action starts

²**balloon** *v* to get bigger or rounder
like a balloon being blown up
¹**ballot** *n* **1** a paper used to vote **2** the
number of votes recorded
²**ballot** *v* to decide by secret voting
ballpoint −also **biro, ballpoint pen** *n*
a pen having a small steel ball that
rolls ink onto the paper
bamboo *n* **1** a tall plant of the grass
family **2** the hard hollow jointed
stems of this plant
ban *v* **-nn-** to forbid, esp. by law −**ban**
n
banana *n* a long curved yellow-
skinned tropical fruit
¹**band** *n* **1** a thin flat narrow piece of
material, esp. for fastening things
together or forming part of a garment: *hatband* **2** a stripe **3** any of
several areas of like shape into
which a larger whole can be
divided, such as a band of radio
waves
²**band** *v* to put a band or bands on
³**band** *n* **1** a group of people formed
for some common purpose **2** a
group of musicians, esp. one that
plays 'popular" music
¹**bandage** *n* a strip of material for
binding round a wound
²**bandage** *v* **-daged, -daging** to bind
with a bandage
bandit *n* an armed robber −~**ry** *n*
¹**bang** *v* **1** to strike sharply **2** to thump
or slam noisily **3** to make a sharp
loud noise
²**bang** *n* **1** a sharp blow **2** a sudden
loud noise
³**bang** *adv esp. spoken* right; directly;

exactly: *We came bang up against more trouble*

⁴bang *n esp. US* a fringe cut straight across the forehead

banger *n* **1** a sausage **2** a noisy firework **3** an old unreliable car

banish *v* **1** to send away, usu. out of the country, as a punishment **2** to stop thinking about: *Banish that thought from your mind* –~**ment** *n*

banister *n* a handrail guarding the edge of stairs or a landing

¹bank *n* **1** land along the side of a river, lake, etc. **2** a mound of earth, sand, snow, etc. **3** a mass of clouds

²bank *v* (of a car or aircraft) to move with one side higher than the other, esp. when making a turn

³bank *n* a row, esp. of oars, in an ancient boat

⁴bank *n* **1** a place in which money is kept and paid out on demand, and where related activities go on **2** a place where something is held ready for use **3** a supply of money in a game of chance or the person in charge of it

bank note *n* a piece of paper money issued for public use

¹bankrupt a person who is unable to pay his debts

²bankrupt *v* to make bankrupt or very poor

³bankrupt *adj* **1** unable to pay one's debts **2** no longer able to produce anything good **3** completely without (good things) –~**cy** *n*

banner *n* **1** a flag **2** a long piece of cloth on which a sign is painted, usu. carried between 2 poles

¹banquet *n* a dinner in honour of a special person or occasion, esp. one at which speeches are made

²banquet *v* to take part in a banquet

baptism *n* **1** a Christian ceremony in which a person is touched or covered with water to show that he has joined the Church **2** **baptism of fire a** a soldier's first battle **b** any unpleasant first experience of something –~**al** *adj*

baptize, -ise – **-tized, -tizing 1** to perform the ceremony of baptism on **2** to give a name to at baptism

¹bar *n* **1** a long piece of wood or metal used as a fastening or barrier **2** something that blocks things off or makes them difficult or impossible to do **3** a slab of solid material: *a bar of soap* **4** an underwater bank across the mouth of a river, entrance to a harbour, etc. **5** a narrow band of colour or light **6** (in music) **a** a group of notes **b** the downward lines marking these off in writing **7** a counter or a room with a counter where alcoholic drinks are sold **8** **behind bars** in prison **9** **the prisoner at the bar** the person being tried in a court of law

²bar *v* **-rr- 1** to close with a bar **2** to keep in or out by barring a door, gate, etc. **3** to block (movement or action): *to bar the way* **4** not to allow: *Guns are barred in Alice's restaurant* **5** to mark with a band or broad line

barbarous *adj* **1** uncivilized **2** very cruel **3** showing many mistakes in the use of language – ~**ly** *adv*

barber *n* a person who cuts men's hair and shaves them

¹**bare** *adj* **1** naked; uncovered **2** empty: *a bare room* **3** not more than; only: *A bare word would be enough* – ~**ness** *n*

²**bare** *v* **bared, baring** to take off a covering; bring to view

barely *adv* **1** in a bare way **2** only just; hardly

¹**bargain** *n* **1** an agreement, esp. one to do something in return for something else **2** something bought cheaply

²**bargain** *v* to talk about the conditions of a sale, agreement, or contract

¹**barge** *n* **1** a large flat-bottomed boat for carrying heavy goods on a canal or river **2** a large rowing boat used on ceremonial occasions

²**barge** *v* **barged, barging** to move about quickly but clumsily

¹**bark** *v* **1** to make the sound that dogs make **2** (of a gun) to sound when fired **3** to speak in a sharp loud voice: *The officer barked out an order*

²**bark** *n* **1** the sound made by a dog **2** a sound like this **3** a voice like this, or words spoken in such a voice

³**bark** *n* the strong outer covering of a tree

⁴**bark** *v* **1** to take the bark off **2** to knock the skin off (esp. in the phrase **bark one's shin**)

barley *n* a plant grown for food and making beer and spirits

barn *n* a farm building for storing crops

barracks *n* **barracks** buildings that soldiers live in

barrel *n* **1** a round wooden container with curved sides and a flat top and bottom **2** a tube-shaped part of something: *a gun barrel*

barren *adj* **1** (of female animals) unable to bear young **2** (of trees or plants) bearing no fruit **3** (of land) having poor soil **4** useless; empty: *a barren argument* – ~**ness** *n*

barrier *n* something placed in the way in order to control people or things moving forward

¹**base** *n* **1** the bottom of something, on which it stands **2** the starting point of something: *The base of the thumb is where it joins the hand* **3** a centre from which a start is made in an activity, often one where supplies are kept **4** a military camp **5** a line on which a geometrical figure stands **6** *technical* the number in relation to which others are built up: *Ordinary numbers use base 10, but many computers work to base 2* **7** the number around which logarithms are built **8** the main part of a mixture **9** (in chemistry) a substance which combines with an acid to form a salt **10** (in the game of baseball) any (esp. the first 3) of the 4 points which a player must touch in order make a run

²**base** *adj esp. in literature* dishonourable – ~**ly** *adv* – ~**ness** *n*

baseball *n* a game played with a bat and ball between 2 teams of 9 players each, on a large field of which the centre is 4 bases that a player must touch in order to score a run

basement *n* rooms in a house below street level

base on – also **base upon** *v prep* **based, basing** to give (something) a reason or starting point in: *One should always base one's opinions on facts*

basic *adj* more necessary than anything else, and on which everything else rests or is built

basin *n* 1 a shallow container for water 2 a round container for food 3 the area of country from which a river collects its water 4 the deep part of a harbour 5 a wide part of a canal with moorings

basket *n* 1 a container made of woven sticks or other such material 2 an open net fixed to a metal ring high up off the ground, through which the ball mush be thrown in basketball

basketball *n* a game in which each team of 5 players tries to throw a large ball through the other team's basket

bastard *n* 1 a child of unmarried parents 2 *sl* a person (usu. a man) that one strongly dislikes 3 *sl* a man; fellow

¹**bat** *n* 1 any of several types of wooden stick used for hitting a ball in various games 2 a sharp blow

²**bat** *v* -tt- 1 to hit with or as if with a bat 2 (in cricket and baseball) to hit a ball or have a turn to bat –**batter** *n*

³**bat** *n* any of several kinds of flying mouselike animals that are active at night

⁴**bat** *v* 1 to blink quickly 2 **not bat an eyelid** to show no sign of one's feelings

batch *n* a set; group; quantity: *a batch of orders*

¹**bath** *n* 1 an act of washing one's whole body 2 water for a bath 3 also **bathtub**– a container in which one sits to bath 4 *technical* liquid in a container, used for a special purpose

²**bath** *v* 1 to give a bath to 2 to have a bath

bathe *v* **bathed, bathing** 1 to go swimming 2 to pour water or other liquid over , usu. for medical reasons 3 to spread over with (or as if with) light, water, etc.: *bathed in sunlight* –**bathe** *n* – ~**r** *n*

¹**batter** *v* 1 to beat hard and repeatedly 2 to cause to lose shape or be badly damaged by continual hard beating or by continual use

²**batter** *n* a mixture of flour, eggs, and milk, beaten together and used in cooking

battery *n* -ies 1 a number of big guns together with the men who serve them 2 a group of connected electric cells 3 a line of boxes in which hens are kept so that they will lay eggs frequently **4** a large group or set of things: *He faced a battery of cameras* **5** *law* striking another person (esp. in the phrase **assault and battery**)

¹**battle** *n* a fight between enemies or opposing groups; a struggle

²**battle** *v*-**tled, -tling** to fight or struggle

bazaar *n* **1** an Eastern marketplace **2** a sale to get money for some good purpose

be *v pres. tense* **I am, you are, he is, we are, you are, they are,** *(short forms* **I'm, you're, he's, we're, you're, they're,)** *(negative short forms* **I'm not, isn't, aren't)** *past tense* **I was, you were, he was, we were, you were, they were** *(past negative short forms* **wasn't, weren't),** *past part.* **been,** *pres. part.* **being 1** (a helping verb, forming various tenses): *We're going now. / He was bitten by a dog* **2** (a verb which connects the subject of a sentence with another word or other words to give information about the subject): *Horses are animals. / This book is mine. / He will be happy. / The old lady was upstairs* **3** to exist

¹**beach** *n* the shore of the sea or a lake or the bank of a river, esp. one used for swimming and sunbathing

²**beach** *v* to run onto the shore: *to beach a boat*

¹**bead** *n* **1** a small object which can be threaded onto a string or wire and worn with others esp. round the neck, for ornament **2** a small drop of liquid **3 draw a bead (on)** to take aim (at)

²**bead** *v* **1** to ornament with beads **2** to cover with small drops

beak *n* **1** the hard horny mouth of a bird, a turtle, etc. **2** anything shaped like this

¹**beam** *n* **1** a large long heavy piece of wood, steel, or concrete , esp. one used to support a building **2 broad in the beam** *sl* wide across the hips

²**beam** *n* **1** a ray of light **2** radio waves sent out along a narrow path **3** a bright look or smile

³**beam** *v* **1** to send out light; shine **2** to smile brightly and happily **3** (of the radio) to send out in a certain direction

bean *n* **1** any of various climbing plants or the seed or pod it bears, esp. one that can be used as food **2** a seed of certain other plants, from which food or drink can be made: *coffee beans* **3** *esp. spoken* a valueless thing: *not worth a bean* **4** *sl* the smallest possible coin: *I haven't a bean* **5 full of beans** *esp. spoken* active and eager **6 spill the beans** *sl* to tell a secret, usu. unintentionally

¹**bear** *n* **bears** *or* **bear 1** any of various kinds of usu. large and heavy animals with thick rough fur **2** a rough, bad-mannered, bad-tempered man

²**bear** *v* **bore, borne, bearing 1** *esp. written* to carry from one place to another; carry away **2** to support **3**

to have or show **4** to keep (a feeling) in one's mind (in relation to someone) **5** to be suitable for **6** to give birth to **7** to produce (a crop or fruit) **8** to suffer: *to bear pain* **9** to carry (oneself) in a certain way **10** to behave in a certain way **11** to turn in the stated direction **12** to have: *x bears no relation to y* **13 bear in mind** to keep in one's memory

¹**beard** *n* **1** hair on the face below the mouth **2** long hairs on a plant, as on barley −~**less** *adj*

²**beard** *v* to face or deal with (someone) boldly

beast *n* **1** an animal, esp. a large farm animal **2** an unpleasant, cruel person or thing

¹**beastly** *adj* **-lier, -liest** strongly dislikeable: *a beastly person/habit* − **-liness** *n*

²**beastly** *adv esp. spoken* very (esp. unpleasantly or badly)

¹**beat** *v* **beat, beaten** *or* **beat, beating** **1** to hit repeatedly **2** to shape by hitting **3** to hit, move, or cause to move regularly: *to beat a drum / The heart beats* **4** to mix rapidly: *to beat eggs* **5** to defeat; do better than **6 Beat it!** *sl* Go away at once! **7 beat time** to make movements in time with music

²**beat** *n* **1** a single stroke or blow, esp. as part of a series **2** a regular sound produced by or as if by repeated beating **3** time in music or poetry **4** the usual path followed by a policeman on duty

³**beat** *adj sl* very tired

beautiful *adj* **1** having beauty **2** *esp. spoken* very good −~**ly** *adv*

beauty *n* **-ties** **1** qualities that give pleasure to the senses or lift up the mind **2** someone (usu. female) or something beautiful **3** *esp. spoken* someone or something very good (or bad): *Your black eye is a real beauty!*

beaver *n* **1** a broad-tailed animal of the rat family which builds dams across streams **2** its valuable fur **3 eager beaver** a person who is almost too keen on working hard

because *conj* for the reason that: *I do it because I like it*

beckon *v* to make a sign to call (someone)

become *v* **became, become, becoming** **1** to come to be: *He became king* **2** to suit, be suitable to, or be fitting for: *That dress becomes you*

¹**bed** *n* **1** an article of furniture to sleep on **2** a piece of ground prepared for plants **3** a level surface on which something rests; base **4** the bottom of a river, lake, or sea **5** a stretch of rock **6 go to bed with** *esp. spoken* to have sexual relations with

²**bed** *v* **-dd-** **1** to fix on a base (or beneath the surface); embed **2** to plant in a bed or beds

bedroom *n* a room for sleeping in

bee *n* **1** a type of insect that makes honey, often lives in groups, and can sting painfully **2 a bee in one's bonnet** an unreasonably fixed idea

beech *n* a type of tree with smooth

grey trunk, spreading branches, and dark green or copper-coloured leaves

¹beef *n* **1** the meat of farm cattle **2** *esp. spoken* (power of) the muscles

²beef *v sl* to complain

been 1 *past part. of* BE **2 a** gone and come back from: *They have been to India* **b** arrived and left: *Has the postman been?*

beer *n* **1** a type of alcoholic drink made from grain **2** a separate drink or container of this **3** any of several kinds of drink made from plants: *ginger beer*

¹beetle *n* any of several types of insect with hard wing coverings

²beetle *v* **-tled, -tling** *sl* (of people) to move off quickly

beetroot *n* a plant with a large round red root, cooked and eaten as a vegetable

¹before *adv* **1** in advance; ahead **2** at an earlier time; already

²before *prep* **1** in front of: *He stood before her* **2** earlier in time than: *the day before yesterday* **3 before the mast** *literature* on a sailing ship **4 before one's time** too soon to be accepted by people: *Darwin was before his time with his ideas*

³before *conj* **1** earlier than the time when **2** more willingly than: *He'd die of hunger before he would steal*

beg *v* **-gg- 1** to ask for (food, money, etc.) **2** to ask humbly for **3** to allow oneself: *I beg to point out that you are wrong* **4** (of a dog) to sit up with the front legs held against the chest

5 to avoid: *Your answer seems to beg the real question*

¹beggar *n* **1** a person who lives by begging **2** *sl* a fellow

²beggar *v* **1** to make very poor **2 beggar description** to be beyond the powers of language to describe

begin *v* **began, begun, beginning 1** to start **2 to begin with** as the first reason: *We can't go. To begin with, it's too cold*

behalf *n* **on behalf of someone/ someone's behalf** (acting, speaking, etc.) for someone

behave *v* **behaved, behaving 1** to act; bear oneself **2** to act in an acceptable or polite way **3** (of things) to act in a particular way

behaviour *n* way of behaving

¹behind *adv* **1** to the back; at the back; where something or someone was earlier **2** late: *I've got behind with my homework*

²behind *prep* **1** to or at the back or farther side of **2** in support of: *Don't be afraid – we're all behind you!* **3 behind the times** out of date

¹being *n* **1** existence; life **2** the qualities or nature of a thing, esp. a living thing **3** a living thing, esp. a person

²being *adj* **for the time being** for a limited period

belief *n* **1** trust **2** the feeling that something is true or real **3** something believed; an idea which is considered true **4 beyond belief** too strange to be believed

believe *v* **believed, believing 1** to

have a firm religious faith to consider to be true or honest: *to believe
someone* **3** to hold as an opinion;
suppose **−believable** *adj* **−believ-
ably** *adv*

believe in *v prep* **1** to have faith or
trust in (someone) **2** to consider
to be true; consider to exist **3** to
consider (something) to be of worth

bell *n* **1** a round hollow metal vessel,
which makes a ringing sound when
struck **2** the sounding or stroke of
a bell **3** something with the form
of a typical bell **as sound as a bell**
esp. spoken **a** healthy **b** in perfect
condition

bellow *v* **1** to make the loud deep
sound typical of a bull **2** to shout
(something) in a deep voice
−bellow *n*

belly *n* **-lies** **1** *esp. spoken* the part of
the human body which contains
the stomach and bowels **2** something curved or round like this

belong *v* **1** to be suitable: *A telephone
belongs in every home* **2** to be in the
right place: *That chair belongs in
the other room*

belong to *v prep* **1** to be the property
of **2** to be a member of **3** to be
connected with

¹below *adv* **1** in or to a lower place;
on a lower level **2** on or to a deck
lower than the main deck of a ship
3 lower on the same page or on the
following page: *See p.85 below*

²below *prep* in a lower place than; on
a lower level than

¹belt *n* **1** a band worn around the
waist **2** a continuous band of
flexible material used for driving a
machine or for carrying materials
3 an area that has some special
quality: *the Corn Belt*

²belt *v* **1** to fasten with a belt **2** to
fasten (to something) with a belt:
He belted on his sword **3** to hit with
a belt **4** *esp. spoken* to hit very hard:
I belted him in the eye **5** *sl* to travel
fast

bench *n* **1** a long seat for 2 or more
people **2** the seat where a judge sits
in court **3** the judge himself or
judges as a group **4** a long worktable

¹bend *v* **bent, bending** **1** to force or
be forced into or out of a curve or
angle **2** to lean away or cause to
lean away from an upright position
3 to direct (one's efforts) to: *He bent
his mind to the job*

²bend *n* **1** the act or action of bending
or the state of being bent **2** something that is bent, such as a curved
part of a road or stream **3 round
the bend** *sl* mad

¹beneath *adv esp. written* in a lower
position; below

²beneath *prep* **1** in or to a lower position than; below; under and often
close or touching **2** not suitable to
or worthy of

¹benefit *n* **1** advantage; profit **2** money
provided by the government as a
right, esp. in sickness or unemployment

²benefit *v* (of non-living things) to be
useful, profitable, or helpful to

berry *n* **-ries** a small soft fruit

beside *prep* **1** at or close to the side of **2** in comparison with **3 beside the point** having nothing to do with the main point or question **4 beside oneself (with)** almost mad (with trouble or strong emotion)

besides *adv, prep* in addition (to); as well(as) USAGE Compare **beside, besides, except**: **1 Beside** can be used at the end of a sentence: *That's the girl you were*

¹**best** *adj* (*superlative of* GOOD) **1** of the highest quality, moral values, skill, usefulness, etc. **2 the best part of** most of: *I stayed the best part of a week*

²**best** *adv* (*superlative of* WELL) **1** in the best way **2** most **3 as best one can** in the best way one is able

³**best** *n* **1** the best state or part **2** something that is best **3** the greatest degree of good or quality **4** one's greatest, highest, or finest effort, state or performance **5 get the best of (someone)** to defeat (someone) **6 make the best of** to do as much or as well as one can with: *to make the best of a bad state of affairs*

⁴**best** *v* to defeat (someone)

¹**bet** *n* **1** an agreement to risk money on the result of a future event **2** a sum of money so risked

²**bet** *v* **bet** *or* **betted, betting** to risk (money) on the result of a future event

betray *v* **betrayed, betraying 1** to be disloyal or unfaithful to **2** to give away or make known: *Her face betrayed her nervousness* –~**er** *n* –~**al** *n*

¹**better** *adj* (*comparative of* GOOD) **1** of higher quality, moral value, usefulness, etc.: *You're a better man than I am* **2 be better than one's word** to do more than one has promised **3 the better part of** more than half

²**better** *adj* (*comparative of* WELL) completely well; improved in health: *She'll be much better soon*

³**better** *adv* (*comparative of* WELL) **1** in a more excellent, thorough, admirable, etc., way: *She knows the story better than I. / You look better in blue* **2 had better** ought to; should: *You'd better be there*

⁴**better** *v* **1** to improve or cause to improve: *try to better last year's record* **2 better oneself** to educate oneself or earn more money –~**ment** *n*

between *prep* **1** in the space or at the time separating: *I sat between them. / He arrived between 6 and 7 last night* **2** as a connection of: *a train service between Leeds and Liverpool* **3** with a part for each of: *Between us we managed to finish the job*

beverage *n* a liquid for drinking, esp. tea, coffee, milk, etc.

beware *v* to be careful: *Beware of the dog*

bewilder *v* to confuse, esp. by the presence of lots of different things –~**ment** *n*

¹**beyond** *adv* on or to the further side;

further: *Men can travel to the moon and beyond*

²**beyond** *prep* **1** on or to the further side of: *What lies beyond the mountains?* **2** later than: *Don't stay there beyond midnight* **3** out of reach of; much more than: *The fruit is beyond my reach. / His bad behaviour is beyond a joke*

¹**bias** *n* **1** (that which causes) the rolling of a ball in the game of bowls in a curve **2** an influence for or against; prejudice **3** a tendency of mind: *a scientific bias* **4 cut (cloth) on the bias** to cut diagonally across the line of the threads

²**bias** *v* **-s-** *or* **-ss-** to cause to form settled favourable or unfavourable opinions without enough information to judge fairly

Bible *n* **1** (a copy of) the holy book of the Christians, consisting of the Old Testament and the New Testament **2** (a copy of) the holy book of the Jews; the Old Testament – **-lical** *adj* – **-lically** *adv*

bicycle –also **cycle**, (*esp. spoken*) **bike** *n*, *v* **-cled, -cling** (to ride) a 2-wheeled vehicle which one pedals with the feet –**bicyclist** *n*

¹**bid** *v* **bade** *or* **bid, bidden** *or* **bid, bidding 1** to say (a greeting or goodbye) **2** to tell (someone to do something): *Do as you're bidden* –~**der** *n*

²**bid** *v* **bid, bidding 1** to offer (a price): *He bid £5 for an old book* **2** (in playing cards) to declare one's intention of winning (a certain number of tricks): *I bid 2 spades* –~**der** *n*

³**bid** *n* **1** an offer to pay a certain price at a sale or auction **2** an offer to do some work at a certain price; tender: *Bids for building the bridge were invited* **3** (a turn to make) a declaration of the number of tricks a cardplayer says he intends to win

¹**big** *adj* **-gg- 1** of more than average size, weight, importance, etc. **2** doing a great deal of some activity: *a big spender* **3** *literature* (of a woman) pregnant: *big with child* **4 have big ideas** to want to do something important –~**ness** *n*

²**big** *adv sl* **1 talk big** to talk as if one were more important than one really is **2 think big** to plan to do a great deal

bigot *n* a person who thinks strongly and unreasonably that his own opinion is correct –~**ed** *adj* –~**edly** *adv* –~**ry** *n*

¹**bill** *n* the beak of a bird

²**bill** *v* **bill and coo** (of lovers) to kiss and speak softly to each other

³**bill** *n* **1** a plan for a law, written down for a parliament to consider **2** a list of things bought and their price **3** a printed notice **4** *US* a piece of paper money; note: *a 5-dollar bill* **5 fill the bill** to be suitable **6 foot the bill** to pay and take responsibility

⁴**bill** *v* to advertise in printed notices: *billed (to appear) as Hamlet*

billion *adj, n, pron* **billion** *or* **billions 1** the number 1,000,000,000; 10^9

2 the number 1,000,000,000,000; 10^{12} – ~**th** *adj, n, pron, adv*

bin *n* a large wide-mouthed container with a lid for bread, flour, etc., or for waste

¹**bind** *v* **bound, binding 1** to tie; tie together: *Bind the prisoner's hands together. / She bound (up) her hair* **2** to bandage **3** to fasten together and enclose in a cover: *to bind a book* **4** to strengthen or ornament with a band of material: *The dress is bound with ribbon* **5** to stick together: *This dough isn't wet enough to bind properly* **6** to cause to obey esp. by a law or a promise: *I am bound by this agreement* **7** to make or declare it necessary for (someone) to do something: *They bound me to remain silent* **8** to unite: *Many things bind us (together)*

²**bind** *n sl* an annoying state of affairs

bingo *n, interj* **1** a game played by covering numbered squares on a card **2** an expression of joy at a sudden successful result

binoculars *n* a pair of glasses used for looking at distant objects with both eyes

biography *n* **-phies** (the type of literature concerned with) an account of a person's life – **-phic, -phical** *adj* – **-phically** *adv*

biology *n* **1** the scientific study of living things: *to study biology* **2** the scientific facts about the life of a living thing: *the biology of bacteria* – **-gical** *adj: biological studies* – **-gically** *adv* – **-gist** *n*

¹**birch** *n* **1** any of several kinds of tree, with smooth wood and thin branches **2** a rod or bunch of sticks made from its wood, used for caning people

²**birch** *v* to whip or cane as a punishment

bird *n* **1** a creature with wings and feathers **2** *sl* a person, usually a young woman **3** *sl* a rude noise made as a sign of disapproval: *They gave the actor the bird* **4 birds of a feather** people of the same kind **5 early bird** a person who gets up or arrives early **6 kill 2 birds with one stone** to get 2 results with one action

biro *n* **biros** *trademark* a ballpoint: *written in biro*

birth *n* **1** the act or time of being born: *She weighed 8 pounds at birth* **2** the act or fact of producing young (often in the phrase **give birth to**) **3** family origin: *French by birth* **4** beginning; start; origin: *the birth of a new political party*

birthday *n* **-days** the date on which someone was born

biscuit *n* **1** any of many types of flat thin dry sweetened or unsweetened cake **2** pottery, china, etc., after its first heating in the oven but before the glaze is put on **3 take the biscuit** *sl* to be the best/worst thing one has ever seen or heard of

bishop *n* **1** a priest in charge of the other priests in a large area **2** a chess-piece that can be moved any number of squares diagonally

¹bit *n* **1** a metal bar put in the mouth of a horse as part of a bridle and used for controlling its movements **2** a part of a tool for making holes **3 take the bit between its/one's teeth** (of a person) to begin with determination

²bit *n* **1** a small piece, quantity, or amount: *He ate every bit of the pudding. / an interesting bit of news / There's a little bit of time left* **2** a short time: *Wait a bit!* **3 a bit (of)** *esp. spoken* **a** to some degree; rather: *I'm a bit tired tonight / Don't believe all he says – he's a bit of a boaster* **b** at all: *I'm not a bit tired now*

¹bitch *n* **1** a female dog **2** *rude* a woman

²bitch *v sl* to complain: *Don't bitch about the heat*

¹bite *v* **bit, bitten, biting 1** to cut, seize, or attack with the teeth: *My monkey doesn't bite. / The boy bit into the apple* **2** to make or put into the stated condition in this way: *The dog has bitten a hole in my trousers* **3** (of insects) to prick the skin (of) and draw blood: *The mosquitoes are biting me* **4** (of fish) to accept food on a fisherman's hook **5** to take hold of something firmly: *The car's tyres would not bite on the snow* **6 bite one's lips** to try to hide one's anger or displeasure **7 bite someone's head off** to speak to or answer someone angrily **8 bite the dust** *sl* **a** to be killed **b** to be completely defeated

²bite *n* **1** an act of biting **2** a piece bitten off **3** *esp. spoken* something to eat: *He hasn't had a bite (to eat) all day* **4** a wound made by biting, esp. by an animal **5** sharpness; bitterness: *There's a bite in this cold wind*

¹bitter *adj* **1** having a sharp biting taste like beer or black coffee **2** (of cold, wind, etc.) very sharp, biting, etc. **3** causing pain or grief: *a bitter disappointment* **4** filled with, showing, or caused by unpleasant feelings: *bitter enemies* **5 to the bitter end** *esp. spoken* to the very end –~**ly** *adv* –~**ness** *n*

²bitter *n* bitter beer

¹black *adj* **1** of the colour of coal; of the darkest colour; without light: *a black cat* –opposite **white 2** (of coffee) without milk or cream **3** (of a person) of a black-skinned race: *a black scientist* **4** very dirty: *Your hands are black!* **5** (of feelings, news, etc.) very bad: *It's a black day for us* **6** very angry or annoyed: *a black look* **7** *literature* evil: *black-hearted* **8** funny about unpleasant or dangerous people or states of affairs (in the phrases **black humour, black comedy**) –~**ness** *n*

²black *n* **1** the colour that is black: *dressed in black* **2** a person of a black-skinned race **3 in the black** having money in a bank account

³black *v* **1** to make black: *to black someone's eye* **2** (esp. of a trade union) to declare it wrong to work with (goods, a business firm, etc.)

blackberry *n* **-ries** (the edible berry of) various types of bramble −~**ing** *n* to go blackberrying

blackbird *n* any of various types of bird of which the male is black

blackboard *n* a dark smooth surface for writing or drawing on with chalk

blackmail *v* to make (someone) give money by threatening to reveal a secret unles money is paid −**blackmail** *n* −~**er** *n*

blacksmith −also **smith** *n* a metalworker who makes and repairs things made of iron, esp. one who makes horseshoes

bladder *n* **1** a bag of skin inside the body in which waste liquid (urine) collects before it is passed out **2** a bag of skin, leather, or rubber which can be filled with air or liquid

blade *n* **1** the flat cutting part of a knife, sword, razor, or other cutting tool **2** the flat wide part of an oar, a propeller, a cricket bat, etc. **3** a long flat plant leaf, esp of grass

blame *v, n* **blamed, blaming 1** (to give) the responsibility for (something bad): *They blamed the failure on George. / George took the blame* **2 be to blame** to be guilty: *The children were not to blame* −~**less** *adj* −~**lessness** *n* −~**worthy** *adj* −~**worthiness** *n*

¹**blank** *adj* **1** without writing, print, or other marks: *a blank page* **2** expressionless; without interest: *a blank look* −~**ly** *adv* −~**ness** *n*

²**blank** *n* **1** an empty space: *My mind was a complete blank. / Please fill in this blank* **2 draw a blank** to be unsuccessful

blanket *n* **1** a thick covering used esp. on beds to protect from cold **2** a thick covering: *a blanket of mist*

blare *v, n* **blared, blaring** (to make) a sharp, loud, and unpleasant sound: *the blare of car horns*

¹**blast** *n* **1** a quick strong movement of air: *an icy blast of wind* **2** (the powerful rush of air caused by) an explosion: *The blast from the bomb blew out all the windows in the area* **3 (at) full blast** (of work, activity, etc.) fully: *He was working (at) full blast in order to complete the order before the holidays*

²**blast** *v* **1** to break up (esp. rock) by explosions **2** to strike with explosives **3** to cause to dry up and die by heat, cold, lightning, etc: *The icy wind had blasted the new spring growth* **4** to damn −~**ed** *adj*

³**blast** *interj* (used for expressing great annoyance)

¹**blaze** *n* **1** the sudden sharp shooting up of a flame; a big dangerous fire: *The roadside grass became a blaze* **2** brightly shining light or bright colour: *The flowers made a blaze of red* **3** an explosion of angry feeling: *In a blaze of anger he shouted at them* − **-zing** *adj*

²**blaze** *v* **blazed, blazing 1** to (begin to) burn with a bright flame **2** to show very bright colour; shine brightly or warmly

³blaze *n* a white mark, esp. on the front of a horse's head

blazer *n* a jacket, sometimes with the badge of a school, club, etc., on it

bleach *v* to make or become white

bleak *adj* cold and cheerless: *bleak winter weather / Two weeks in hospital seems a bleak prospect* – ~**ly** *adv*

bleat *v, n* 1 (to make) the sound of a sheep, goat, or calf 2 (to make) a weak complaint: *He's always bleating about something*

bleed *v* **bled, bleeding** 1 to lose blood 2 (of the heart) to feel as if wounded by sorrow: *My heart bleeds for the starving children* 3 to draw blood from (esp. as was done by doctors in former times) 4 to make (someone) pay too much money: *The landlord bled them dry for their flat*

¹blend *v* 1 to mix: *Blend the sugar and flour* 2 to produce (tea, coffee, whisky, etc.) from a mixture of several varieties 3 to go well together; harmonize; combine: *The countryside and the houses seem to blend (into each other)*

²blend *n* a product of blending: *a blend of coffee*

bless *v* **blessed** *or* **blest, blessing** 1 to ask God's favour for (sometimes used humorously): *Bless this house / Well, bless my soul!* 2 to make holy: *The priest blessed the bread and wine* 3 to praise or call holy: *Bless the name of the Lord!*

blessing *n* 1 an act of asking or receiving God's help, or protection: *the blessing of the Lord* 2 something one is glad of: *Count your blessings* 3 approval; encouragement: *Father gave his blessing to our holiday plans* 4 **a blessing in disguise** something not very pleasant, which turns out to be a good thing after all

blew *past tense of* BLOW

¹blind *adj* 1 unable to see: *He is blind in one eye* 2 intended for those who cannot see: *a blind school* 3 not understanding or caring: *He is blind to the effect of his actions* 4 careless; thoughtless; uncontrolled: *blind rage* 5 without reason or purpose: *the blind forces of nature* 6 navigating with instruments only, inside an aircraft without looking outside: *a blind landing* 7 in or into which it is difficult to see: *a blind corner* 8 *sl* slightest (esp. in the phrase **not take a blind bit of notice**) 9 **bake blind** to cook (pastry) by itself, a filling being added later 10 **turn a blind eye (to)** to take no notice of 11 **the blind leading the blind** people with little information advising people with even less – ~**ly** *adv* – ~**ness** *n*

²blind *v* 1 to make unable to see: *He was blinded by the smoke* 2 to make unable to notice or understand: *His desire to do it blinded him to all the difficulties*

³blind *n* 1 a covering made of cloth or other material that is fastened above a window and pulled down to cover it 2 a way of hiding the truth by giving a false idea

44

¹**blink** v 1 to shut and open (the eyes) quickly 2 (of distant lights) (to seem) to go rapidly on and off

²**blink** n 1 an act of blinking 2 **on the blink** esp. spoken (of machinery) not working properly

blister n, v 1 (to form) a water-filled swelling under the skin, caused by rubbing, burning, etc.: blisters on my feet / My feet blister easily 2 (to cause) a swelling on the surface of things such as painted wood: The heat blistered the paint –~**ful** adj:the blistering sun –~**ingly** adv

¹**blitz** n 1 a sudden heavy attack, esp. from the air, or a period of such attacks 2 sl a period of great activity for some special purpose: I must have a blitz to get my room tidy

²**blitz** v to make blitz attacks on: London was blitzed during the war

blizzard n a long severe snowstorm

blob n a drop or small round mass

¹**block** n 1 a solid mass or piece of wood, stone, etc. 2 a quantity of things considered as a single whole: a block of seats in a theatre 3 a piece of wood or metal with words or drawings cut into its surface, for printing 4 a large building divided into separate parts (esp. flats or offices) 5 a building or group of buildings between 2 streets: Turn left after 2 blocks 6 something that gets in the way or that stops activity: a road block / a block in the pipes 7 the large piece of wood on which people were beheaded 8 **knock**

someone's block off sl to knock someone's head off

²**block** v to prevent (movement, activity, or success): to block the enemy's advance

bloke n esp. spoken a man; fellow

blond adj, n 1 (fem. **blonde**) (a person) with fair skin and hair 2 (of hair) light-coloured (usu. yellowish)

¹**blood** n 1 red liquid which carries oxygen to all parts of the body and is pumped round by the heart 2 family relationship: of noble blood 3 **bad blood** strong unpleasant feeling: There is bad blood between them 4 **Blood is thicker than water** Relatives are really more important than friends 5 **fresh/new blood** a new person or new people (in a firm, group, etc.): We need an injection of new blood with fresh ideas 6 **in cold blood** cruelly and on purpose: I couldn't kill the mouse in cold blood 7 **make someone's blood boil** to make someone very angry 8 **make someone's blood run cold** to make someone very frightened

²**blood** v to give (someone) a first experience: He's just being blooded at the game

¹**bloody** adj -ier, -iest 1 covered with blood 2 connected with wounding and killing –**bloodily** adv –**bloodiness** n

²**bloody** adj, adv sl not polite (used for giving force to a judgment): It's bloody wonderful! / 'Lend you £5? Not bloody likely!'

¹**bloom** n 1 a flower 2 a covering of

fine powder on ripe grapes, plums, etc. **3 in the bloom of** at the best time of/for: *in the bloom of youth/ beauty*

²**bloom** *v* **1** to produce flowers, come into flower, or be in flower **2** to be or become rich in plant life **3** to be or look healthy: *blooming with health* **4** to develop: *Their friendship bloomed*

¹**blossom** *n* **1** (a mass of) the flowers of a flowering tree or bush: *apple blossom / the blossom on the trees* **2 in blossom a** (esp. of a tree or bush) bearing flowers **b** at a high stage of development: *a friendship in full blossom*

²**blossom** *v* **1** (esp. of a flowering tree or bush) to produce or yield flowers; bloom **2** to develop; grow: *Jane is blossoming out into a beautiful girl*

¹**blot** *n* **1** a mark that spoils or makes dirty: *a blot of ink on the paper* **2** a fault or shameful act: *a blot on one's character* **3 blot on the landscape** something ugly that spoils the look of its surroundings

²**blot** *v* **-tt-** to make blots (on): *This pen blots easily* **2** to dry or remove with or as if with blotting paper

blotting paper *n* special thick soft paper which can take up liquids, used to dry wet ink after writing

blouse *n* a usu. loose garment for women, reaching from the neck to the waist

¹**blow** *v* **blew, blown, blowing 1** to move by a current of air: *The wind has blown my hat off* **2** to send out a strong current of air (esp. from the lungs) **3** to make or give shape to by forcing air into or through: *to blow glass* **4** to sound by forcing air into or through: *The horn blew* **5** (of an electrical fuse) to break or be broken suddenly **6** *sl* to lose or spend: *I blew £10 at cards* **7** *sl* to leave suddenly and quickly: *Let's blow now* **8** *sl* damn: *Well, I'll be blowed!* **9 blow hot and cold (about)** to be for and against in turns **10 blow one's own trumpet/horn** to say good things about oneself **11 blow one's top/stack** *sl* to become violently angry **12 blow someone's mind** *sl* to fill someone with strong feelings of wonder or confusion **13 There she blows!** said on a ship by the first person who sees a whale

²**blow** *n* an act or example of blowing

³**blow** *v literature* to bloom: *a full-blown rose*

⁴**blow** *n* **1** a hard stroke with the hand, a weapon, etc.: *a blow on the head* **2** a shock or misfortune: *It was a great blow when he failed to pass the exam* **3 come to blows** also **exchange blows–** to start fighting **4 strike a blow for** to do something important for: *Strike a blow for freedom*

blow up *v adv* **1** to explode or be destroyed by exploding: *blow up the bridge* **2** to make or be made firm by filling with air: *blow up a balloon/tyres* **3** to enlarge: *blow up* *a photograph* **4** to become suddenly angry

¹blue *adj* **1** of the colour of the clear sky on a fine day: *a blue dress / Your hands are blue with cold* **2** sad, depressed: *I'm feeling rather blue today* **3** **scream/shout blue murder** to complain loudly **4** **till one is blue in the face** unsuccessfully for ever –~**ness** *n* –**bluish** *adj*

²blue *n* (a) blue colour: *dressed in blue*

¹bluff *adj* (of a person or his manner) rough, plain, and cheerful: *He had a bluff way of speaking* –~**ly** *adv* –~**ness** *n*

²bluff *n* a high steep bank or cliff

³bluff *v* **1** to deceive by pretending to be stronger, cleverer, surer of the truth, etc., than one is: *He's only bluffing* **2** to find or make (one's way) by doing this: *He could bluff his way through any difficulty*

⁴bluff *n* **1** the action of bluffing **2** **call someone's bluff** to tell someone who is bluffing to do what he threatens to do, guessing that he will not be able to: *When he threatened to dismiss me I called his bluff*

¹blunder *v* **1** to make a blunder **2** to move awkwardly or unsteadily, as if blind: *He blundered through the dark forest* –~**er** *n*

²blunder *n* a stupid or unnecessary mistake: *to make a blunder*

¹blunt *adj* **1** (of a knife, pencil, etc.) not sharp **2** rough and plain, without trying to be polite or kind:

a few blunt words –~**ness** *n* –~**ly** *adv*

²blunt *v* to make blunt

¹blush *v* **1** to become red in the face, from shame or embarrassment: *She blushed as red as a rose* **2** to be ashamed: *I blush to admit it* –~**ingly** *adv*

²blush *n* **1** a case of blushing **2** **spare someone's blushes** to avoid making someone blush

¹board *n* **1** a thin flat piece of cut wood; plank **2** a stiff flat surface used for a special purpose: *drawing board / chessboard / darts board / bread board / noticeboard* **3** the cost of meals: *board and lodging* **4** a committee or association with a special responsibility: *Our company has 3 women on its board of directors* **5** **above board** completely open and honest **6** **across the board** including all groups or members: *a wage rise of 10 pounds a week across the board* **7** **go by the board** (of plans, arrangements, etc.) to come to no result; fail completely **8** **on board** in or on a ship or public vehicle **9** **sweep the board** to win (nearly) everything

²board *v* **1** to cover with boards or boarding **2** to go on board a ship or public vehicle **3** to get or supply meals and usu. lodging for payment: *She arranged to board some students from the university*

boarder *n* **1** a person who pays to sleep and eat at another person's house; lodger **2** a schoolchild who lives at the school

boast *v* **1** to talk or say proudly or to praise oneself: *He's just boasting* **2** to have cause to be proud of: *This village boasts three shops* –**boast** *n*: *His boast is that he's the best* –**boaster** *n*

¹**boat** *n* **1** a small vessel for travelling on water: *a fishing/sailing/rowing boat* **2** any ship: *Are you going by boat or by air?* **3** **in the same boat** facing the same dangers **4** **rock the boat** to make matters worse

²**boat** *v* to use a small boat for pleasure (often in the phrase **go boating**)

¹**bob** *v* **-bb-** **1** to move quickly and repeatedly up and down, as on water: *The small boat was bobbing on the sea* **2** to curtsy quickly: *She bobbed politely at me*

²**bob** a bobbing movement, esp. a curtsy

body *n* **-ies** **1** the whole of a person or animal as opposed to the mind: *You can imprison my body but not my mind* **2** this without the head or limbs: *a wound on his leg and another on his body* **3** this when it is dead: *Where did you bury his body?* **4** a large amount: *The oceans are large bodies of water* **5** a number of people who do something together: *The House of Commons is an elected body* **6** a person: *Mrs Jones was a dear old body* **7** technical an object; piece of matter: *The sun, moon, and stars are heavenly bodies* **8** full strong quality: *I like a wine with plenty of body* **9** the main part; *The audience sat in the body of the hall*

bog *n* **1** (an area of) soft wet ground **2** *sl* lavatory

¹**boil** *n* a swelling under the skin, that is full of pus and eventually bursts

²**boil** *v* **1** to (make the contents of a vessel) reach or continue to be at the temperature at which liquid changes into a gas: *Peter boiled the kettle* **2** to cook in water at 100°C: *Boil the potatoes for 20 minutes* **3** to cause to reach the stated condition by cooking in water: *soft-boiled eggs* **4** **make someone's blood boil** to make someone very angry

³**boil** *n* **1** an act or period of boiling: *Give the clothes a good boil* **2** boiling point

boiler *n* a container for making hot water, as in a house, or for boiling water, as in a steam engine

bold *adj* **1** daring; courageous; adventurous: *a very bold action* **2** (of the appearance of something) strongly marked; clearly formed: *a drawing done in a few bold lines* **3** **as bold as brass** rude(ly); without respect –~**ly** *adv* –~**ness** *n*

¹**bolt** *n* **1** a round bar with a spiral thread which can fit into a nut or threaded hole to fasten things together **2** a metal bar that slides across to fasten a door or window **3** a quantity of cloth rolled up **4** a short heavy arrow to be fired from a crossbow **5** a thunderbolt

²**bolt** *v* **1** to run away suddenly, as in fear: *The horse bolted* **2** to swallow

hastily: *He bolted (down) his break-fast* **3** to stay or keep in a given state with a bolt: *These 2 parts are bolted together* **4** to fasten with a bolt: *Bolt the door*

³**bolt** *adv* straight and stiffly: *He made the children sit bolt upright*

⁴**bolt** *n* **1** an act of running away **2** **make a bolt for** to try to escape quickly by way of

¹**bomb** *n* **1** a hollow container filled with explosive, or with other chemicals of a stated effect: *a time bomb / a smoke bomb* **2** the atomic bomb, or the means of making and using it: *Has that country got the bomb now?* **3** **(go) like a bomb** *esp. spoken* (to go) **a** (of a vehicle) very fast **b** very successfully **4** **spend/cost a bomb** *esp. spoken* to spend/cost a lot of money

²**bomb** *v* to attack with bombs, esp. by dropping them from aircraft

¹**bond** *n* **1** a paper in which a government or company promises to pay back with interest money that has been invested: *4 1/2% National Savings bonds* **2** a written agreement with the force of law: *enter into a bond* **3** a feeling, likeness, etc., that unites 2 or more people or groups: *bonds of friendship* **4** a state of being stuck together: *This new glue makes a firmer bond* **5** **one's word is (as good as) one's bond** one's spoken promise can be completely trusted

²**bond** *v* to stick together (as if) with

glue: *These 2 substances won't bond together*

¹**bone** *n* **1** (one of) the hard parts of the body, round which are the flesh and skin **2** **all skin and bone** very thin **3** **cut to the bone** to reduce (costs, services, etc.) as much as possible: *The bus service has been cut to the bone* **4** **feel in one's bones** to believe strongly though without proof **5** **make no bones about** to feel no doubt or shame about –~**less** *adj*

²**bone** *v* **boned, boning** to take the bones out of: *Will you bone this joint of meat for me?* –~**d** *adj*

bonfire *n* a large fire built in the open air

bonnet *n* **1** a round head-covering tied under the chin, worn by babies and in former times by women **2** a soft flat hat worn by men, esp. soldiers, in Scotland **3** a metal lid over the front of a car

bonus *n* **1** an additional payment beyond what is usual, or expected: *The workers got a Christmas bonus* **2** anything pleasant in addition to what is expected: *The win on the pools was a real bonus*

¹**book** *n* **1** a collection of sheets of paper fastened or bound together as a thing to be read, or to be written in **2** one of the main divisions or parts of a larger written work (as of a long poem or the Bible) **3** any collection of things fastened together in a cover: *a book of stamps* **4** **make (a) book on** to offer to take

bets on the results of **5 throw the book at** to make all possible charges against

²**book** *v* **1** to arrange in advance to have (something): *You'll have to book up early* **2** to enter charges against, esp. in the police records: *booked on a charge of speeding* –~**able** *adj* –~**ing** *n*

boom *v* **1** to make a deep hollow sound **2** to grow rapidly, esp. in value, importance, etc.: *Business is booming* –**boom** *n*

boomerang *n* a curved stick which flies in a circle and comes back when thrown, used for hunting by Australian natives

¹**boost** *v* **1** to push up from below **2** to increase: *to boost prices* **3** to help to improve: *We need to boost our spirits* **4** *technical* to increase (esp. the supply of electricity or water) in force, pressure, or amount

²**boost** *n* **1** a push upwards **2** an increase in amount **3** an act that brings encouragement: *a boost to our spirits*

¹**boot** *n* **1** a covering of leather, rubber, or canvas for the foot with a part for supporting the ankle **2** an enclosed space at the back of a car for luggage **3** a blow given by or as if by a foot wearing a boot: *The thief gave me a boot in my stomach* **4** *sl* the act of sending someone away rudely, esp. from a job: *He got the boot*

²**boot** *v* **1** to kick **2** also **boot out**– to send away rudely

booze *v,n* **boozed, boozing** *sl* (to drink) an alcoholic drink –**boozy** *adj* –**boozily** *adv* –**booziness** *n*

¹**border** *n* **1** an edge **2** (land near) the dividing line between 2 countries

²**border** *v* **1** to put a border on **2** to be a border to; come close to: *fields bordered by woods* **3** to have a common border with: *France borders Germany*

¹**bore** *v* **bored, boring** to make a round hole or passage in or through something: *bore through solid rock* –~**r** *n*

²**bore** –also **borehole** *n* a hole made by boring esp. for oil, water, etc.

³**bore** *past tense of* BEAR

⁴**bore** *n* a very large wave caused by a tide running up a narrow river

⁵**bore** *n* **1** *offensive* a person who causes others to lose interest, esp. by continual dull talk **2** something which is rather unpleasant: *It's a bore having to go out again*

⁶**bore** *v* to make uninterested –~**dom** *n*

born *adj* **1** brought into existence by or as if by birth: *The baby was born at 8 o'clock* **2** at birth; originally: *born French* / *nobly born*

borne *past part. of* BEAR

borough *n* a town, or a division of a large town, with certain rights and powers of government

borrow *v* **1** to take for a certain time and with intention to return: *to borrow £5 from a friend* **2** to take or copy: *English has borrowed (words)* *from many languages* −~**er** *n* −~**ing** *n*

¹**boss** *n* a round usu. metal ornament which stands out from the surface of something

²**boss** *n* employer; person having control over others

³**boss** *v* to behave like a boss

botany *n* the scientific study of plants − **-nist** *n*

¹**both** *adj* being the 2; having to do with the one and the other: *both shoes*

²**both** *pron* the one as well as the other: *Both of us thought so*

³**both** *conj* **both . . . and . . .** not only . . . but also . . .: *both New York and London have traffic problems*

¹**bother** *v* **1** to cause to be nervous; annoy or trouble, esp. in little ways: *I'm busy: don't bother me* **2** to cause inconvenience to oneself: *Don't bother about it* **3** *sl* (used for adding force to expressions of displeasure): *Bother the lot of you!*

²**bother** *n* **1** (a cause of) trouble or anxiety: *We had a lot of bother finding our way* **2** also *sl* **bovver**− violence or threatening behaviour −~**some** *adj*

¹**bottle** *n* **1** a container, typically of glass or plastic, with a narrow neck and usu. no handle **2** alcoholic drink: *John's on the bottle again!*

²**bottle** *v* **-tled, -tling** to put into or preserve in bottles: *bottling wine*

bottom *n* **1** the base on which something stands; the lowest part, inside or outside: *the bottom of the stairs*

2 the ground under an area of water: *the bottom of the sea* **3** the lowest position or situation: *at the bottom of the class* **4** the far end: *at the bottom of our garden* **5** the part of the body on which one sits **6** the cause: *Who is at the bottom of all this trouble?* **7** **Bottoms up!** *esp. spoken* Finish your drinks! **8** **knock the bottom out of** to take away the necessary support on which something rests: *The bad news knocked the bottom out of market prices* **9** **the top and bottom of it** the truth; the whole of it

bough *n* a branch of a tree

bought *past tense and part. of* BUY

¹**bounce** *v* **bounced, bouncing 1 a** (of a ball) to spring back or up again from the ground **b** to cause (a ball) to do this **2** to jump or cause to jump or spring up and down or move with a springing movement: *She bounced the baby* **3** *sl* (of a cheque) to be returned by a bank as worthless

²**bounce** *n* **1** the act or action of bouncing: *The ball has plenty of bounce* **2** lively, often noisy behaviour: *She has a lot of bounce* −**bouncy** *adj* − **-cily** *adv* − **-ciness** *n*

¹**bound** *adj* going (to): *bound for home*

²**bound** *v* to mark the edges of; keep within a certain space: *London is bounded by the Home Counties*

³**bound** *adj* **1** fastened by or as if by a band; kept close to: *bound to one's job* **2 a** certain: *It's bound to rain*

soon **b** compelled: *I'm bound to blame him* **c** determined: *He's bound to go, and nothing will stop him* **3** (of a book) fastened within covers: *bound in leather*

⁴**bound** *n* a jump or bounce

⁵**bound** *v* to jump or bounce

boundary *n* -ries **1** the limiting or dividing line of surfaces or spaces: *the boundaries of the country* **2** the outer limit of anything: *the boundaries of knowledge* **3** (in cricket) **a** the line which marks the limit of the field of play **b** a hit to or over this line, that is worth 4 (or 6) runs

¹**bouquet** *n* flowers picked and fastened together in a bunch

²**bouquet** *n* the smell of wine, etc.: *a rich bouquet*

bourgeois *n, adj* **bourgeois** *French* **1** (of, related to, or typical of) a member of the middle class **2** *offensive* (a person) very concerned with possessions and good manners

bout *n* **1** a short period of activity **2** an attack of illness: *bouts of fever* **3** a boxing match

¹**bow** *v* **1** to bend forward the head or upper part of the body to show respect or yielding: *Bow to the Queen* **2** to express in this way: *He bowed his thanks* −~**ed** *adj*

²**bow** *n* **1** a movement of bowing **2** **take a bow** to come on stage to receive praise at the end of a performance

³**bow** *n* **1** a piece of wood held in a curve by a tight string and used for shooting arrows **2** a long thin piece

of wood with stretched horsehairs fastened along it, used for playing stringed instruments **3** an ornamental looped knot

⁴**bow** *v* **1** *technical* to bend or curve **2** to play on a musical instrument with a bow

⁵**bow** *n* the forward part of a ship

bowels *n* **1** −also **bowel**− a long pipe from the stomach by which waste matter leaves the body **2** the inner, lower part

¹**bowl** *n* **1** a deep round container for holding liquids, flowers, sugar, etc. **2** anything in the shape of a bowl: *the bowl of a pipe* −~**ful** *n*

²**bowl** *n* **1** a ball for rolling in the game of bowls **2** an act of rolling the ball in the games of bowls or bowling

³**bowl** *v* **1** to roll (a ball) in the games of bowls or bowling **2** to play the games of bowls or bowling **3** (in cricket or rounders) to throw (the ball) towards the batsman **4** (in cricket) to force (a batsman) to leave the field by bowling a ball which hits the wicket **5** to cause to roll: *The wind bowled his hat down the street*

bowling *n* any of various games in which balls are rolled at an object or a group of objects: *tenpin bowling*

bowls *n* an outdoor game in which one tries to roll a big ball as near as possible to a small ball called 'the jack'

¹**box** *n* **boxes** *or* **box** a type of small

52

evergreen tree, often used in hedges

²**box** *n* **1** a container for solids, usu. with stiff sides and a lid: *a shoebox* **2** a small room or enclosed space: *a box at the theatre* **3** (in cricket) a rounded piece of metal or plastic worn by the batsman to protect his genitals **4** *sl* television: *What's on the box tonight?*

³**box** *v* to put in one or more boxes

⁴**box** *v* to fight (someone) or hit with the fists: *They boxed (with) each other* −~**er** *n*

boxing *n* the sport of fighting with the fists

Boxing Day *n* a public holiday on the first weekday after Christmas

¹**boy** *n* **boys 1** a young male person **2** a son, esp. young **3** a person of any age who acts like a boy **4** a male person, of any age, from a given place: *He's a local boy* **5** (now considered offensive) a male servant of a different race **6** *becoming rare* (used in forming phrases for addressing men): *Thank you, dear boy* −~**hood** *n* −~**ish** *adj* −~**ishly** *adv* −~**ishness** *n*

²**boy** *interj sl* (expressing excitement): *Boy, what a game!*

boycott *v* **1** to refuse to do business with: *They're boycotting the shop* **2** to refuse to attend or take part in: *to boycott a meeting* −**boycott** *n*

bra −also **brassiere** *n* a woman's close-fitting undergarment worn to support the breasts

bracelet *n* a band or ring worn round the wrist or arm as an ornament

¹**bracket** *n* **1** a piece of metal or wood put in or on a wall to support something: *a lamp bracket* **2** either of a pair of signs ((-), ⟨-⟩, or {-}) used for enclosing a piece of information

²**bracket** *v* **1** to enclose in brackets **2** to regard as belonging together: *Don't bracket them (together)*

¹**brag** *v* **-gg-** to speak in praise of oneself

²**brag** *n* a type of card game

¹**braid** *v* **1** *esp. US* to plait **2** to ornament with braid

²**braid** *n* **1** *esp. US* a plait **2** a woven band of threads to put on material: *gold braid for a uniform*

¹**brain** *n* **1** *medical* the organ in the upper part of the head, which controls thought and feeling **2** the mind **3** a person with a good mind: *the best brains in the country* **4** **have something on the brain** to think about something continually

²**brain** *v* **1** to kill by knocking out the brains of **2** to hit hard on the head

brainwave *n* *esp. spoken* a sudden clever idea

¹**brake** *n* an apparatus for slowing and bringing to a stop (as of a wheel or car)

²**brake** *v* **braked, braking 1** to cause to slow or stop: *to brake a car* **2** to use a brake

bramble *n* the wild prickly bushes of the rose family ; the wild form of blackberry

¹**branch** *n* **1** an armlike stem growing

from the trunk of a tree or from another stem **2** an armlike part or division of some material thing: *a branch of a river* **3** a division of a non-material thing: *a branch of knowledge*

²**branch** *v* **1** to become divided into branches: *Follow the road until it branches* **2** to form such a division: *the road branches to the right*

¹**brand** *n* **1** a class of goods which is the product of a particular producer **2** a special kind: *his own brand of humour* **3** a piece of burnt or burning wood **4** a mark made (as by burning) usu. to show ownership: *These cattle have my brand on them*

²**brand** *v* **1** to mark with a brand **2** (of bad experiences) to leave a mark on: *Prison has branded him for life* **3** to give a lasting bad name to: *branded as a thief*

brandy *n* **-dies** a strong alcoholic drink usu. made from wine

brass *n* **1** a very hard bright yellow alloy of copper and zinc **2** an object made of this metal, esp. a musical wind instrument **3** (the players of) the set of brass instruments in an orchestra **4** *sl* money **5** *sl* shameless daring: *How did she have the brass?*

¹**brave** *adj* courageous and ready to suffer danger or pain –~**ly** *adv* –~**ry** *n*

²**brave** *v* **braved**, **braving** to meet (danger, pain, or trouble) without showing fear: *St George braved the dragon*

³**brave** *n* a young North American Indian warrior

bread *n* **1** a common food made of baked flour: *a loaf of bread* **2** food generally: *our daily bread* **3** means of staying alive: *to earn one's bread* **4** *sl* money **5** **break bread with** *pompous* to eat with

breadth *n* **1** (the) distance from side to side; width **2** a wide stretch **3** the quality of taking everything or many things into consideration: *breadth of mind* **4** **the length and breadth of** every part of

¹**break** *v* **broke**, **broken**, **breaking** **1** to separate into parts suddenly or violently, but not by cutting or tearing **2** to separate or become separated from the main part in this way **3** to make or become unusable by damage: *He broke his wristwatch* **4** to make or become, suddenly or violently: *The prisoner broke loose* **5** to open the surface of: *to break the skin* **6** to disobey; not keep: *to break the law* **7** to force a way (into, out of, or through): *He broke into the shop* **8** to bring under control: *to break a horse* **9** to do better than: *to break a record in sports* **10** to make known: *to break the news* **11** to interrupt (an activity): *Let's break for a meal* **12** to bring or come to an end: *to break the silence* **13** to come esp. suddenly into being or notice: *as day breaks* **14** to fail as a result of pressure: *His health broke* **15** to change suddenly in direction, level, loudness, etc.: *His voice broke*

when he was 15 **16** to discover the secret of: *She broke their code* **17** (in tennis) to win a game against the server **18 break the back of** to finish the main or the worst part of **19 break camp** to pack up everything and leave a camping place **20 break cover** to run out from a hiding place **21 break the ice** to get through the first difficulties in starting a conversation **22 break new/fresh ground** to make new discoveries **23 break step** to march irregularly **24 break wind** to let out gases from the stomach and bowels

²**break** *n* **1** an opening made by breaking or being broken: *a break in the clouds* **2** a pause for rest: *a coffee break* **3** a change from the usual pattern: *a break from the past* **4** the time of day before sunrise when daylight first appears: *at daybreak* **5** (in cricket) a change of direction of the ball **6** (in snooker and billiards) the number of points made by one player during one continuous period of play **7** (in tennis) a case of winning a game from the server **8** a chance; piece of luck: *Give him a break*

break down *v adv* **1** to destroy; reduce to pieces **2** to defeat or be defeated **3** (of machinery) to fail to work **4** to fail **5** to lose control of one's feelings: *He broke down and wept* **6** to change chemically: *Food is broken down by chemicals* **7** to separate into different kinds

breakfast *n, v* (to eat) the first meal of the day

¹**breast** *n* **1** either of the 2 parts of a woman's body that produce milk, or the smaller similar parts on a man **2** the upper front part of the body between the neck and the stomach **3** *literature* the part of the body where the feelings are supposed to be: *a troubled breast*

²**breast** *v* **1** *literature* to stand up fearlessly against **2** to meet and push aside with one's chest

breath *n* **1** air taken into and breathed out of the lungs: *Let me get my breath back* **2** an act of breathing air in and out once: *a deep breath* **3** a movement of air: *hardly a breath of air* **4** a word about or slight sign of: *a breath of spring in the air* **5** a moment (in the phrases **in one breath, in the same breath, in the next breath**) **6 catch one's breath a** to stop breathing for a moment because of strong feeling **b** to get one's breath **7 draw/take breath** to have a rest **8 hold one's breath** to stop breathing for a time **9 take one's breath away** to make one unable to speak from surprise, pleasure, etc. **10 waste one's breath** to talk uselessly, without effect

breathe *v* **breathed, breathing 1** to take into (and send out of) the lungs (air, gas, etc.) **2** *literature* to live: *the greatest man who ever breathed* **3** to whisper **4** to give or send out (a smell, a feeling, etc.): *He'll breathe new life into the team* **5** (of flowers, wine, cloth, etc.) to take in air **6 breathe down someone's neck** to keep too close a watch on what someone is doing **7 breathe one's last** to die

¹**breed** *v* **bred, breeding 1** (of animals) to produce young **2** to keep for the purpose of producing young: *He breeds cattle* **3** to train; educate; bring up **4** to cause or be the beginning of – ~**er** *n*

²**breed** *n* a kind or class of animal (or plant) usu. developed by man: *a breed of dog*

¹**breeze** *n* a light gentle wind

²**breeze** *v* **breezed, breezing** *esp. spoken* **1** to move swiftly and unceremoniously: *He breezed in and demanded tea* **2** to pass easily: *She breezed through her exams*

¹**brew** *v* **1** to make (beer) **2** to make tea or coffee ready for drinking **3** (esp. of something bad) to prepare or be in preparation or ready to happen: *A storm was brewing*

²**brew** *n* the result of brewing: *Do you like this brew?*

¹**bribe** *v* **bribed, bribing** to influence unfairly by favours or gifts: *He bribed the policeman* – ~**ry** *n*

²**bribe** *n* something offered or given in bribing

brick *n* **1** (a hard piece of) baked clay used for building **2** something in the shape of a brick: *a brick of ice cream* **3** *sl* a very nice trustworthy person **4 drop a brick** *sl* to make a blunder

bride *n* a girl or woman about to be married, or just married – **-dal** *adj*

bridegroom –also **groom** *n* a man about to be married, or just married

¹**bridge** *n* **1** something that carries a road over a valley, river, etc., and is usu. built of wood, stone, iron, etc. **2** the raised part of a ship on which the officers stand when on duty **3** the bony upper part of the nose **4** the part of a pair of spectacles that rests on or above the nose

²**bridge** *v* **bridged, bridging** to build a bridge across

³**bridge** *n* a card game for 4 players

¹**bridle** *n* leather bands on a horse's head for controlling it

²**bridle** *v* **-dled, -dling 1** to put a bridle on **2** bring under control: *Bridle your tongue* **3** to show anger or displeasure, esp. by an upward movement of the head and body

¹**brief** *adj* **1** short, esp. in time: *a brief letter* **2 in brief** in as few words as possible – ~**ly** *adv*

²**brief** *n* **1** a short statement, esp. one giving facts about a law case **2** a set of instructions setting limits to someone's powers or duties: *It's my brief to instruct him*

³**brief** *v* to give last instructions or necessary information to: *Let me brief you before the meeting* – ~**ing** *n*

briefcase *n* a flat case for carrying papers or books, which opens at the top

brigade *n* **1** a part of an army, of about 5,000 soldiers **2** a group of people who have certain duties: *the Fire Brigade*

bright *adj* 1 giving out or throwing back light very strongly 2 strong, clear, and easily seen: *bright red* 3 famous 4 full of life; cheerful: *bright eyes* 5 clever; quick at learning: *a bright child* 6 showing signs of future success: *a bright future* –~**ly** *adv* –~**ness** *n*

brilliant *adj* 1 very bright, splendid, or showy 2 very clever; causing great admiration: *a brilliant speaker* 3 having or showing great skill (esp. in playing a musical instrument): *a brilliant artist* – **-liance** *n* – **-liancy** *n* –~**ly** *adv*

¹**brim** *n* 1 the top edge of a cup, bowl, etc., esp. with regard to the contents: *full to the brim* 2 the bottom part of a hat which turns outwards to give shade or protection against rain

²**brim** *v* **-mm-** to be overflowing: *brimming over with joy*

bring *v* **brought, bringing** 1 to come with or lead: *Bring me the book* 2 to cause or lead to: *Spring rains bring summer flowers* 3 to sell or be sold for: *This old car will bring about £10* 4 *law* to make officially: *bring a charge against* 5 to cause to come: *Her cries brought the neighbours* 6 to cause to reach a certain state: *Bring them together* 7 **bring to book** to force to give an explanation, or to be punished

brink *n* 1 an edge at the top of a cliff or other steep high point 2 a state of dangerous nearness (esp. in the phrases **on/to the brink of**)

brisk *adj* 1 quick and active: *a brisk walker* 2 pleasantly cold and strong: *a brisk wind* –~**ly** *adv* –~**ness** *n*

bristle *n, v* **-tled, -tling** (to stand up like) short stiff coarse hair: *a face covered with bristles / His hair bristled with anger*

British *adj, n* (the people) of Britain –~**er** *n*

brittle *adj* 1 hard but easily broken: *Glass is brittle* 2 easily damaged, hurt, or destroyed: *a brittle friendship* 3 lacking warmth or depth of feeling: *brittle gayness*

broad *adj* 1 wide: *broad shoulders* 2 not limited; general: *broad opinions / a broad general idea* 3 easy to see or understand: *a broad suggestion* 4 full and clear (esp. in the phrase **broad daylight**) 5 (of a local accent or way of speaking) strong: *He spoke broad Scots* 6 (esp. of subjects for laughter) bold and rude: *broad jokes* –~**ly** *adv* –~**ness** *n*

¹**broadcast** *adj* of, related to, or made public by radio (or television) broadcasting

²**broadcast** *n* a single radio (or television) presentation

³**broadcast** *v* **broadcast, broadcasting** 1 to spread around; make widely known: *to broadcast the gossip* 2 to send out or give (as) a radio or television presentation: *The BBC broadcasts every day* –~**er** *n* –~**ing** *n*

¹**broke** *adj sl* completely without money (often in the phrases **flat/ stony broke**)

²**broke** *past tense of* BREAK

¹**broken** *adj* **1** violently separated into smaller pieces **2** damaged or spoilt by breaking: *a broken clock/leg* **3** disobeyed or not fulfilled: *a broken law/promise* **4** brought to an end; crushed: *a broken marriage / a broken spirit* **5** imperfectly spoken or written: *broken English* −~**ly** *adv* −~**ness** *n*

²**broken** *past part. of* BREAK

¹**bronze** *v* **bronzed, bronzing** to give the appearance or colour of bronze to: *bronzed by the sun*

²**bronze** *n* **1** an alloy mainly of copper and tin **2** the dark reddish-brown colour of this **3** a work of art made of bronze

brooch *n* an ornament worn on women's clothes, fastened by a pin

¹**brood** *n* a family of young birds or other young creatures all produced at the same time

²**brood** *v* **1** to sit on eggs as a hen does **2** to continue to think, usu. angrily or sadly (about): *Don't brood about it* −~**er** *n*

³**brood** *adj* kept for giving birth to young: *a brood hen*

¹**brook** *v* to allow or accept without complaining: *He would brook no interruptions*

²**brook** *n* a small stream

brother *n* **1** a male relative with the same parents **2** a male member of the same group: *We must all stand together, brothers!* **3** (a title for) a male member of a religious group, esp. a monk −~**ly** *adj* −~**liness** *n*

brought *past tense and part. of* BRING

brow *n* **1** a forehead **2** the upper part of a slope or a hill

¹**brown** *adj, n* (of) a colour like black mixed with orange which is that of coffee −~**ish** *adj*

²**brown** *v* to make or become brown or browner: *browned by the sun*

¹**browse** *n* a period of time spent in browsing

²**browse** *v* **browsed, browsing** **1** to feed on young plants, grass, etc.: *goats browsing on shrubs* **2** to read here and there in books, esp. for enjoyment: *to browse through some books*

¹**bruise** *v* **bruised, bruising** **1** to cause one or more bruises on: *She bruised her knee* **2** to show one or more bruises: *Soft fruit bruises easily*

²**bruise** *n* a discoloured place where the skin of a human, animal, or fruit has been injured by a blow but not broken

¹**brush** *n* **1** also **brushwood**− small branches broken off from trees or bushes **2** (land covered by) small trees and bushes

²**brush** *n* **1** an instrument for cleaning, smoothing, or painting, made of sticks, stiff hair, nylon, etc.: *a clothesbrush* **2** the tail of a fox **3** an act of brushing: *Give my coat a brush* **4** a light touch in passing: *He felt the brush of her dress*

³**brush** *v* **1** to clean or smooth with a

brush: *to brush the floor* **2** to remove with or as if with a brush: *to brush dirt off*

⁴**brush** *v* **1** to pass lightly over or across; touch lightly in passing: *The breeze brushed his cheek* **2** to move lightly or carelessly: *She just brushed past*

⁵**brush** *n* a short and unimportant involvement: *a brush with the police*

brutal *adj* **1** having or showing no fine or tender human feeling: *a brutal attack* **2** severe: *the brutal truth* – **-tality** *n* – **-tally** *adv*

¹**brute** *adj* like an animal in being cruel or very strong: *brute strength*

²**brute** *n* **1** an animal, esp. a large one: *a brute of a hound* **2** an unfortunate animal: *The horse broke its leg, the poor brute* **3** a rough, cruel, or bad-mannered person, esp. a man –**brutish** *adj* –**brutishly** *adv*

¹**bubble** *v* **-bled, -bling** **1** to form, produce, or rise as bubbles **2** to make the sound of bubbles rising in liquid: *The pot bubbled quietly* **3** (usu. of women) to express a lot of a good feeling: *Mary was bubbling with joy*

²**bubble** *n* **1** a ball of air or gas usu. contained in a liquid shell: *to blow soap bubbles* **2** the sound or appearance of a boiling mixture: *the bubble of the cooking pot* **3** something empty or not lasting –**bubbly** *adj*

¹**bucket** *n* a usu. round open metal or plastic container with a handle, for carrying liquids; pail

²**bucket** *v* **1** *esp. spoken* to pour very hard: *rain bucketing down* **2** to move roughly and irregularly: *The car bucketed down the road*

¹**buckle** *n* a fastener for joining the ends of 2 straps, or for ornament

²**buckle** *v* **-led, -ling** **1** to fasten with a buckle **2** to make or become bent or wavy: *The shock buckled the wheel of my bicycle*

¹**bud** *n* a flower (or leaf) before it opens

²**bud** *v* **-dd-** to produce buds

¹**budget** *n* **1** a plan of how to spend or take in money: *a family/ government budget* **2** the quantity of money stated in either type of plan –~**ary** *adj*

²**budget** *v* to plan spending: *save money by budgeting*

¹**buffet** *n* a blow or sudden shock

²**buffet** *v* to strike sharply or repeatedly

³**buffet** *n* a meal laid out for guests who serve themselves

¹**bug** **1** *US* any small insect **2** *esp. spoken* a germ **3** *sl* an apparatus for listening secretly to conversations **4** a bedbug

²**bug** *v* **-gg-** *sl* to fit with a secret listening apparatus: *The police have bugged my office*

bugle *n* a brass wind instrument, like a trumpet but shorter –~**r** *n*

¹**build** *v* **built, building** to make by putting pieces together: *He built a model ship out of wood* –~**er** *n*

²**build** *n* shape and size, esp. of the human body: *We are of the same build*

building *n* **1** something usu. with a roof and walls that is intended to stay in one place **2** the business of making objects of this sort

bulb *n* **1** a round root of certain plants **2** any object of this shape, esp. the glass part of an electric lamp that gives out light **– ~ous** *adj*

¹bulge *n* a swelling of a surface **–bulgy** *adj* **–bulgily** *adv* **–bulginess** *n*

²bulge *v* **bulged, bulging** to swell out

bulk *n* **1** great size or quantity **2** the main part: *The bulk of the work has been done* **3** roughage

¹bull *n* **1** the male form of cattle **2** the male of the elephant, the whale, and other animals **3 take the bull by the horns** *esp. spoken* to face difficulties without fear

²bull *n* a solemn official letter from the Pope

bulldog *n* any of several types of English dog with a short neck and front legs far apart

bulldozer *n* a powerful machine used for pushing heavy objects, earth, etc., out of the way

bullet *n* a type of shot fired from a gun, usu. long and with a rounded or pointed end

bulletin *n* **1** a short public notice: *the latest bulletin about the President's health* **2** a short news report or printed news sheet

bull's-eye *n* **1** the circular centre of a target that people try to hit when shooting **2** a kind of large hard round sweet **3** a circular window

bully *v* **-lied, -lying** to use one's strength to hurt or frighten (weaker people) **–bully** *n*

¹bump *v* **1** to strike or knock with force or violence **2** to move with much jolting , as of a wheeled vehicle over uneven ground

²bump *n* **1** a sudden forceful blow or shock **2** a raised round swelling

bun *n* **1** a small round sweet cake **2** a mass of hair fastened into a tight round shape, usu. at the back of the head

¹bunch *n* **1** a number of things fastened, held, or growing together: *a bunch of flowers/keys* **2** *esp. spoken* a group

²bunch *v* **1** to form into one or more bunches **2** (of cloth) to gather into folds

¹bundle *n* **1** a number of articles tied, fastened, or held together **2** a number of fine threadlike parts lying closely together, esp. nerves, muscles, etc.

²bundle *v* **-dled, -dling 1** to move or hurry roughly: *They bundled the children off to school* **2** to store in a disordered way

bungalow *n* a house all on one level

bunk bed **–also bunk** *n* either of usu. 2 beds fixed one above the other

bunker *n* **1** a place to store coal **2** (in golf) a sandy hole, from which it is hard to hit the ball **3** a strongly-built shelter for soldiers, esp. underground

¹buoy *n* **buoys** a floating object fastened to the bed of the sea to show ships where there are rocks

²**buoy** v **buoyed, buoying** to keep (someone or something) floating –~**ancy** n –~**ant** adj –~**antly** adv

¹**burden** n esp. written **1** a heavy load **2** a duty hard to do properly

²**burden** v to load or trouble

³**burden** n the main point: the burden of the story

bureaucracy n -cies **1** government officers **2** a group of people like this in a business **3** government by such officers rather than by those who are elected, often supposed to have excessive rules

bureaucrat n a member of a bureaucracy –~**ic** adj –~**ically** adv

burglar n a thief who breaks into houses, shops, etc. –~**y** n

burial n the putting of a dead body into a grave

¹**burn** v **burnt** or **burned, burning 1** to be on fire **2** to shine: a light burning **3** to be unpleasantly hot: the burning sand **4** to experience a very strong feeling: She is burning to tell you the news **5** to hurt, damage, or destroy by fire: He burnt all his papers **6** to use for power, heating, or lighting: ships that burn coal

²**burn** n **1** a hurt place produced by burning: burns on her hand **2** an act of firing the motors on a spacecraft

¹**burrow** n a hole in the ground made by an animal, esp. a rabbit, in which it lives or hides

²**burrow** v to make by digging: to burrow a hole

¹**burst** v **burst, bursting 1** to break suddenly, esp. by pressure from within **2** to come suddenly, often with force: She burst through the door **3** (in the -ing form) to be filled to the breaking point: I am bursting with joy

²**burst** n a sudden outbreak: a burst of laughter

burst out v adv to begin suddenly: They burst out laughing

bury v -ied, -ying **1** to put into the grave **2** to hide away: The dog has buried a bone

¹**bus** n a large passenger-carrying motor vehicle, esp. a public one

²**bus** v -ss- to carry (or travel) by bus

bush n **1** a small low tree **2** wild country in Australia or Africa

business n **1** one's work **2** trade and the getting of money **3** a particular money-earning activity such as a shop **4** a duty: It's a teacher's business to make children learn **5** an affair; event; matter; thing: a strange business –~**man,** –~**woman** n

¹**bust** n **1** the human head, shoulders, and chest, esp. as shown in sculpture **2** a woman's breasts

²**bust** v **busted** or **bust, busting** esp. spoken to break, esp. with force

³**bust** v **busted, busting** sl (of the police) **a** to arrest **b** to raid

¹**busy** adj -ier, -iest **1** working; not free **2** full of work: a busy day –**busily** adv –**busyness** n

²**busy** v -ied, -ying to keep (oneself)

busy: *He busied himself with answering letters*

¹**but** *conj* **1** rather; instead: *not one, but 2!* **2** in spite of this: *tired but happy* **3** except for the fact that: *I was going to write, but I lost your address*

²**but** *prep* except: *no one but me*

³**but** *adv* **all but** almost: *The job is all but finished!*

⁴**but** *n* **ifs and buts** unnecessary doubts: *I'm tired of your ifs and buts*

¹**butcher** *n* a person who kills animals for food or sells meat

²**butcher** *v* **1** to kill (animals) and prepare for sale as food **2** to kill bloodily or unnecessarily −~y *n*

¹**butt** *v* to strike or push with the head or horns: *He butted his head against the wall* −**butt** *n*

²**butt** *n* a person or thing that people make fun of

³**butt** *n* **1** a large, thick, or bottom end of something **2** a cigarette end

⁴**butt** *n* a large barrel for liquids

¹**butter** *n* **1** yellow fat made from milk **2** a substance like butter: *peanut butter* −~y *adj*

²**butter** *v* to spread with butter

¹**butterfly** *n* **-flies** any of several insects with 4 often beautifully-coloured wings

²**butterfly** *n* a way of swimming chest downwards, moving both arms together in a circular motion while kicking the legs up and down

buttock *n* either of the 2 fleshy parts on which a person sits

¹**button** *n* **1** a small usu. round or flat thing fixed to a garment and passed through a buttonhole to act as a fastener **2** a button-like object for starting, stopping, or controlling a machine

²**button** *v* to fasten with buttons

¹**buy** *v* **bought, buying 1** to obtain (something) by giving money (or something else of value) **2** to be exchangeable for: *Our money buys less than it used to*

²**buy** *n esp. spoken* an act of buying

¹**buzz** *v* **1** to make a low hum, as bees do **2** to make a low confused whisper: *The crowd buzzed with excitement* **3** to fly low and fast over: *Planes buzzed the crowd*

²**buzz** *n* **1** a noise of buzzing **2** *sl* a telephone call: *give him a buzz*

¹**by** *prep* **1** near; beside: *standing by the window* **2** by way of; through: *to enter by the door* **3** past: *He walked by me* **4** not later than: *By tomorrow he'll be here* **5** as a result of action on the part of: *written by Shakespeare* **6** in accordance with: *to play by the rules* **7** to the amount of: *His horse won by a nose* **8** using; by means of: *She earned money by writing.* / *We went by air* **9** (in measurements and operations with numbers): *a room 15 feet by 20 feet* / *to divide X by Y* **10** (showing the size of groups that follow each other): *The animals went in 2 by 2* **11** *technical* having (the stated male animal, esp. a horse) as a father: *Golden Trumpet, by Golden Rain out of Silver Trumpet*

²**by** *adv* **1** past: *Please let me by* **2** near: *Do it when nobody is by*

cab *n* **1** a taxi **2** (in former times) a horse-drawn carriage for hire **3** the driver's part of a bus, railway engine, etc.

cabbage *n* a type of large round vegetable with thick green leaves used as food

cabin *n* **1** a small room on a ship usu. for sleeping **2** a small roughly built house

cabinet *n* **1** a piece of furniture with drawers and shelves **2** the most important government ministers, who meet as a group

¹**cable** *n* **1** a thick heavy strong rope, wire, or chain **2** a set of telegraph or telephone wires underground or under the sea **3** a telegraphed message

²**cable** *v* **-bled, -bling** to send by telegraph

cafe, café *n* a small restaurant serving light meals

¹**cage** *n* **caged, caging 1** a framework of wires or bars in which animals or birds may be kept **2** an enclosed area for prisoners **3** (in a mine) the framework in which men and apparatus are raised to or lowered from the surface

²**cage** *v* to put into a cage

¹**cake** *n* **1** a food made by baking flour, eggs, sugar, etc. **2** a round flat piece of food: *a potato cake* **3** a solid block: *a cake of soap*

²**cake** *v* **caked, caking** to cover thickly

calamity *n* **-ties** a terrible event

calculate *v* **-lated, -lating 1** to work out by using numbers **2** to estimate **3** to plan; intend

calculating machine –also **calculator** *n* a simple machine which can carry out number operations

calculation *n* **1** the act of calculating **2** the result of calculating: *His calculation was correct*

calendar *n* **1** a system which names, arranges, and numbers each day of each month of the year **2** a set of tables or sheets showing this system

¹**calf** *n* **calves** the young of the cow or of some other large animals

²**calf** *n* **calves** the fleshy back part of the human leg below the knee

¹**call** *v* **1** to shout; cry out: *He called for help* **2** to make a short visit: *The milkman calls once a day* **3** to telephone or radio to **4** to (try to) cause to come or happen by speaking loudly or by sending an order: *Mother is calling me.* / *The president called an election* **5** to waken (someone) **6** to name: *We'll call the baby Jean* **7** to say that (someone) is: *She called me fat*

²**call** *n* **1** a shout; cry **2** a short usu. formal or business visit **3** a command; summons: *The minister waited for a call to the palace* **4** (in card games) a bid **5** (in sports and games) the decision of the umpire **6** an attempt to telephone someone; telephone conversation **7 at/on call** ready to work at a command: *The nurse is on call tonight*

caller *n* **1** a person who makes a short

visit **2** a person making a telephone call **3** a person who calls out numbers in a game or instructions in a dance

¹**calm** *n* **1** an absence of wind or rough weather **2** a time of peace and quiet —**calm** *adj*

²**calm** *v* to make calm: *The mother calmed her child*

calves *pl.* of CALF

came *past tense of* COME

camel *n* **1** either of 2 large long-necked animals used for riding or carrying goods in desert countries—**a** the Arabian dromedary with one hump **b** the Asian Bactrian camel with 2 humps **2** a light yellow-brown colour

camera *n* **1** an apparatus for taking photographs or filming **2** the part of the television system which changes images into electrical signals **3** **in camera** *esp. written* privately

¹**camouflage** *n* a way of using colouring or shape which makes it difficult to see something: *Many animals have a natural camouflage which hides them from their enemies*

²**camouflage** *v* **-flaged, -flaging** to hide by using camouflage: *The military vehicles were camouflaged*

¹**camp** *n* a place where people live **a** in tents or huts for a short time usu. for pleasure or **b** unwillingly: *a labour camp*

²**camp** *v* **1** to pitch a camp **2** to sleep in a tent —~**er** *n*

¹**campaign** *n* **1** a set of military actions with a purpose **2** a set of actions to obtain a result in politics or business

²**campaign** *v* to take part in a campaign —~**er** *n*

¹**can** *v* **could**, *negative short form* **can't** **1** to know how to: *I can swim* **2** to be able to: *Can you get home in time?* **3** to be allowed to: *In rugby any player can pick up the ball* **4** may; might: *Can this be for me?* **5** will: *Can you hold on, please?*

²**can** *n* a tin in which foods are preserved without air

³**can** *v* **-nn-** to preserve (food) by putting in a can

canal *n* **1** a watercourse dug in the ground **a** to allow ships or boats to travel along it **b** to bring water to or remove water from an area **2** *medical* a narrow passage in the body

¹**canary** *n* **-ies** a type of small yellow bird usu. kept as a pet

²**canary** *n, adj* (having) a bright yellow colour

cancel *v* **-ll-** **1** to give up (a planned activity) **2** to declare that (something) is to be without effect: *She cancelled her order* **3** to mark (a postage stamp) officially to prevent re-use **4** to balance; equal **5** to cross out (writing) **6** *technical* (of both sides of an equation or both numbers of a fraction) to permit division by the same number or quantity: *Will 2xy=4xp cancel by anything?*

cancer *n* **1** (an) abnormal growth in the body that often spreads to other parts **2** (a) spreading evil: *Violence is the cancer of our society* – ~**ous** *adj* – ~**ously** *adv*

candidate *n* **1** a person taking an examination **2** a person who wants, or whom others want, to be chosen for a position

candle *n* a wax stick with a wick which gives light when it burns

¹**cane** *n* **1 a** the hard smooth often hollow stem of certain tall grasses such as bamboo **b** the straight stem of certain fruit-producing plants such as the blackberry **2** the punishment of beating with a cane

²**cane** *v* **caned, caning** to beat with a cane

cannibal *n* **1** a person who eats human flesh **2** an animal which eats the flesh of its own kind – ~**ism** *n* – ~**istic** *adj*

¹**cannon** *n* **cannons** *or* **cannon** a powerful gun fixed to the ground or onto a carriage or to be fired from an aircraft

²**cannon** *v* to strike forcefully; knock

cannot can not

canoe *n, v* **canoed, canoeing** (to travel by) a long light narrow boat, pointed at both ends, and moved by a paddle – ~**ist** *n*

canvas *n* **1** strong rough cloth used for tents, sails, bags, etc. **2** a piece of this used for an oil painting **3 under canvas a** in tents **b** (of a ship) with sails spread

canvass, -vas *v* to go about asking for political support, orders for one's goods, or opinions

¹**cap** *n* **1** a soft flat head-covering **2** this given as a sign of honour: *He has 2 caps for cricket* **3** an often white head-covering sometimes worn by women servants **4** a protective covering for the end of an object: *the cap on the bottle* **5** a small paper container of explosive, usu. used in toy guns

²**cap** *v* **-pp- 1** to put a cap on **2** to give a cap as a sign of honour **3** to improve on (what someone has said or done)

capable *adj* **1** having the power to do **2** clever – **-bly** *adv*

capacity *n* **-ties 1** the amount that something can hold **2** ability; power: *He has a big capacity for enjoying himself* **3** character; position: *speaking in my capacity as minister*

¹**capital** *adj* **1** punishable by death **2** excellent **3** (of a letter) written in its large form (such as A, B, C) rather than its usual form (such as a, b, c)

²**capital** *n* **1** a town which serves as the centre of government **2** wealth, esp. when used to produce more wealth **3** a capital letter

capitalism *n* production and trade based on the private ownership of wealth

¹**capitalist** *n* a person who owns or controls much wealth (capital) and esp. who lends it at interest

²**capitalist** –also **capitalistic** *adj* practising or supporting capitalism

capsule *n* **1** an amount of medicine

in an outer covering, the whole of which is swallowed **2** the part of a spaceship occupied by the pilots and which can be separated after take-off

¹**captain** *n* **1-** the leader of a team or group **2** the person in command of a ship or aircraft **3** a military or naval officer

²**captain** *v* to be captain of; command; lead

captive *adj, n* **1** (a person) taken prisoner esp. in war **2** (one who is) imprisoned: *captive animals* – **-vity** *n*

¹**capture** *n* taking or being taken by force

²**capture** *v* **-tured, -turing 1** to take prisoner **2** to take control of by force from an enemy; win; gain **3** to preserve in an unchanging form on film, in words, etc.

car *n* **1** also **motor car-** a vehicle with 3 or usu. 4 wheels and driven by a motor, esp. one for carrying people **2** a carriage or vehicle on a railway or cable **3** any small vehicle as part of a lift, balloon, airship, etc.

caravan *n* **1** a group of people travelling together through desert areas **2** a covered horse-drawn cart in which people such as gipsies live or travel **3** a vehicle which can be pulled by car, with cooking and sleeping facilities

carbon *n* **1** an element found in a pure form as diamonds or graphite, or in an impure form as coal **2** also **carbon paper-** thin paper coated with carbon used for making copies **3** also **carbon copy-** a copy made using this paper; duplicate

¹**card** *n, v* (to use) a comblike instrument for preparing wool, cotton, etc., for spinning

²**card** *n* **1** also *esp. written* **playing card-** one of a pack of 52 small sheets of stiffened paper marked to show number and suit and used for various games **2 a** a small sheet of stiffened paper usu. with information on it: *a membership card* **b** *esp. spoken* visiting card **3 a** a piece of stiffened paper usu. with a picture on the front and a message inside sent to a person on a birthday, at Christmas, etc.: *a get-well card* **b** a postcard **4** a list of events, esp. at a sports meeting

³**card** *n* stiffened paper

cardboard *n, adj* (made from) a stiff paperlike material used for making boxes, the backs of books, etc.

cardigan *n* a knitted woollen jacket with sleeves

¹**care** *n* **1** worry; anxiety; sorrow; grief **2** charge; keeping; protection; responsibility: *under the doctor's care* **3** serious attention; effort: *Do your work with care!* **4** carefulness in avoiding harm, damage, etc.: *Cross the road with care* **5 care of** also **c/o-** (used when addressing letters to mean) living at the address of: *John Smith, care of Mary Jones, 14, High Street* **6 take into care** to put (esp. a child) into a home

owned by the state to make sure of proper treatment

²care *v* **cared, caring 1** to like; want: *I don't care to play football* **2** to mind; be worried, anxious, or concerned (about): *She didn't care where her son went*

¹career *n* **1** a job or profession which one intends to follow for life **2** the general course of a person's working life: *Churchill's career* **3** fast violent speed: *The horse went at full career*

²career *v* to go at full speed; rush wildly

careful *adj* **1** taking care to avoid danger: *You must be careful crossing the road* **2** showing attention to details: *He's a careful worker* **3** done with care; showing care: *Doctors made a careful examination* **4** *esp. spoken* not wanting to spend money; ungenerous –~**ly** *adv* –~**ness** *n*

careless *adj* **1** not taking care; inattentive: *A careless driver is a danger* **2** not showing care or thought; done without care **3** free from care; untroubled **4** thoughtless; not worried: *He's careless about money* –~**ly** *adv* –~**ness** *n*

caretaker *n* also (*esp. Scots*) **janitor**– a person who looks after a school or other public building and does small repairs, cleaning, etc.

cargo *n* **-goes** (one load of) freight carried by a ship, plane, or vehicle

carpenter *n* a person who makes and repairs wooden objects – **-try** *n*

¹carpet *n* **1** heavy woven material for covering floors **2** a shaped piece of this material, usu. fitted to the size of a particular room

²carpet *v* **1** to cover (as if) with a carpet **2** *esp. spoken* to reprimand (someone): *He was carpeted for bad work*

carriage *n* **1** a wheeled vehicle, esp. horse-drawn **2** a railway passenger vehicle **3** (the cost of) moving goods from one place to another **4** a wheeled support for moving a heavy object, esp. a gun **5** a movable part of a machine: *This printing machine has a carriage which holds and moves the paper* **6** the manner of holding one's head and body; deportment **7 carriage forward** *technical* the cost of carrying (the goods) is to be paid by the receiver **8 carriage paid/free** *technical* the cost of carrying (the goods) has been paid by the sender

carrot *n* a type of vegetable with a fairly long orange-red root

carry *v* **-ried, -rying 1** to bear (someone or something) in one's arms, on one's back, etc., while moving **2** to act as the means by which (a person or thing) is moved from one place to another; transport; convey: *Pipes carry oil across the desert* **3** to bear the weight of (something) without moving: *This pillar carries the whole roof* **4** to keep or hold (something) with one; wear: *In Britain police do not carry guns* **5** to move or hold (oneself) in a certain way **6** to pass from one person to another; spread: *Many serious diseases are carried by insects* **7** to be able to reach a certain distance; transmit; cover space: *Her voice does not carry far* **8** (of a shop) to have (goods) for sale **9** to put (a number) into the next column to the left as when doing addition **10** to contain: *The report carried a serious warning of future trouble* **11** to have as a usual or necessary result: *Such a crime carries a serious punishment* **12** to win the sympathy, support, or agreement of: *The government carried the country and won the election* **13** (esp. of a law or plan) to be approved **14 carry all/everything before one** to be completely successful **15 carry the can** *esp. spoken* to take the blame **16 carry weight (with)** to have influence (with)

¹cart *n* **1** a usu. 2-wheeled vehicle drawn by an animal and used for carrying goods **2** any of various types of small light wooden vehicle with 2 or 4 wheels and moved by hand

²cart *v* **1** to carry in a cart **2** *esp. spoken* to carry as if in a cart, usu. in a disrespectful manner: *The police carted the prisoners off to prison* **3** *esp. spoken* to carry by hand: *Must you cart that bag round all day?*

carton *n* a box made from cardboard for holding goods

cartoon *n* **1** a humorous drawing, often dealing satirically with some-thing in the news **2** also (*esp. written*) **animated cartoon**– a cinema film made by photo-graphing a set of drawings –~**ist** *n*

carve *v* **carved, carving** **1** to cut (usu. wood or stone) in order to make a special shape **2** to cut (cooked meat) into pieces or slices **3** to make or get by hard work: *He carved out a name for himself* –~**r** *n*

¹case *n* **1** an example: *a case of stu-pidity* **2** a particular occasion or state of affairs: *Pauline's stupid, but it's different in the case of Mary; she's just lazy* **3 a** (of diseases) a single example: *This is a case of fever* **b** a person suffering from an illness **4 a** a set of events needing police inquiry **b** a person being dealt with by the police, a social worker, etc. **5** a question to be decided in a court of law **6** the facts and arguments supporting one side in a disagreement or in a question brought before a court: *The police have a clear case against the prisoner* **7** (in grammar) (changes in) the form of a word (esp. of a noun, adjective, or pronoun) showing its relationship with other words in a sentence **8 in case** for fear that; lest; because it may happen that **9 in case of a** for fear that (that stated event) should happen: *We insured the house in case of fire* **b** if (the stated event) should happen: *Break the glass in case of fire*

²case *n* **1** a container in which goods

can be stored or moved **2** a suitcase **3** an outer covering for holding a filling: *a pastry case*

³**case** *v* **cased, casing** to enclose or cover with a case

¹**cash** *n* money in coins and notes

²**cash** *v* to exchange (a cheque or other order to pay) for cash

cashier *n* a person in charge of money receipts and payments in a bank, hotel, shop, etc.

¹**cast** *v* **cast, casting** **1** to throw or drop **2** to throw off; remove: *Every year the snake casts (off) its skin* **3** to give (a vote) **4** to give an acting part to (a person) **5** to make (an object) by pouring hot metal (or plastic) into a mould **6** to make and put into effect (a spell)

²**cast** *n* **1** an act of throwing **2** the actors in a play, moving picture, etc. **3** a stiff protective covering of cloth and plaster, for holding a broken bone in place while it gets better **4** an object cast in a mould **5** general shape or quality: *the noble cast of his head* **6** *becoming rare* a slight squint **7** a small pile of earth left by worms when they make a hole

¹**castle** *n* **1** a strongly-built building made in former times to be defended against attack **2** also **rook**– (in the game of chess) one of the powerful pieces placed on the corner squares of the board at the beginning of each game

²**castle** *v* **-tled, -tling** (in the game of chess) to move the king 2 squares towards either of his own castles and put the castle on the square that the king has moved across

castrate *v* **-trated, -trating** to remove the sex organs of (an animal or person) – **-tration** *n*

¹**casual** *adj* **1** resulting from chance **2** not serious or thorough **3** informal; not for special use **4** not close: *a casual friendship* **5** (of workers) employed for a short period of time – ~**ly** *adv* – ~**ness** *n*

²**casual** *n* a person employed for a short period of time

casualty *n* **-ties** **1** a person hurt or killed in an accident or war **2** a person or thing defeated or destroyed **3** also **casualty ward, department**– a place in a hospital where people hurt in accidents are treated

cat *n* **1** a small animal with soft fur and sharp teeth and claws, often kept as a pet or in buildings to catch mice and rats **2** any of various types of animals related to this, such as the lion or tiger **3 let the cat out of the bag** *esp. spoken* to tell a secret (often unintentionally) **4 rain cats and dogs** *esp. spoken* to rain very heavily

catalogue *n, v* **-logued, -loguing** (to make) a list of places, names, goods, etc. in a special order so that they can be found easily

catapult *n, v* **1** (to use) a small Y-shaped stick with a rubber band fastened between the forks to shoot small stones at objects **2** (to use) a powerful apparatus for helping planes take off from a ship **3** (to use) a machine for throwing heavy stones into the air, used, in former times, as a weapon for breaking down walls

¹**catch** *v* **caught, catching 1** to get hold of; seize **2** to trap (esp. an animal) after chasing or hunting; take **3** to find unexpectedly; come upon suddenly; discover by surprise: *Mother caught me stealing* **4** to be in time for: *to catch the train* **5** to get (an illness) **6** to cause to become hooked, held, fastened, or stuck, accidentally or on purpose **7** to hit (a person or animal); strike: *The blow caught him on the head* **8** to attract (esp. interest or attention) **9** to get or notice for a moment: *I caught sight of my friend in town* **10** to start to burn, work, operate: *The fire caught quickly* **11** to hear; understand: *I didn't catch what you said* **12** (in cricket) to send (a player) off the field by taking and holding a ball knocked off the bat before it touches the ground **13 catch one's breath** to draw in one's breath for a moment from surprise, fear, shock, etc. −∼**er** *n*

²**catch** *n* **1** an act of seizing and holding a ball **2** *esp. spoken* (the amount of) something caught: *Her husband was a good catch. They say he's very rich* **3** a hook or other device for fastening something or holding it shut **4** *esp. spoken* a hidden or awkward difficulty: *That question looks easy, but there's a catch in it*

catch up *v adv* **1** to come up from behind; draw level with **2** to bring or come up to date

caterpillar *n* the wormlike young of the butterfly and other insects

cathedral *n* the chief church of a bishop's see, typically a large building of beautiful design

cattle *n* large 4-legged farm animals, esp. cows

caught *past tense & part. of* CATCH

cauliflower *n* a type of vegetable with green leaves around a large white head of undeveloped flowers

¹**cause** *n* **1** something which produces an effect; a person, thing, or event that makes something happen **2** reason: *Don't complain without (good) cause* **3** a principle or movement strongly supported

²**cause** *v* **caused, causing** to lead to; be the cause of

¹**caution** *n* **1** a spoken warning **2** great care; the act of paying attention or of taking care **3** *old sl* a person or thing whose behaviour causes amusement

²**caution** *v* **1** to warn against possible danger **2** to warn about doing something often with the threat of punishment for repeating it

cautious *adj* careful; paying attention −∼**ly** *adv* −∼**ness** *n*

cavalry *n* soldiers who fight on horseback −∼**man** *n*

cave *n* a deep natural hollow place **a**

underground **b** in the side of a cliff or hill

cavern *n* a large deep cave

¹**cease** *v* **ceased, ceasing** *esp. written* to stop (esp. an activity)

²**cease** *n esp. written* **without cease** continuously

ceaseless *adj esp. written* unending; without ceasing —~**ly** *adv*

ceiling *n* **1** the inner surface of the top of a room **2** *technical* the greatest height at which a plane can fly **3** *technical* the height above ground of the bottom of the lowest clouds

celebrate *v* **-brated, -brating 1** to enjoy oneself on a special occasion **2** to mark (a special occasion) with public or private rejoicings **3** to praise (someone or something) in writing, speech, etc.

celebration *n* **1** the act of celebrating **2** an occasion of celebrating

celebrity *n* **-ties 1** a famous person **2** the state of being famous

cell *n* **1** a small room **a** in a prison **b** in a monastery or convent **2** one of the groups of people in a secret, esp. political, organization **3** one part of a larger whole, as one of the divisions of a honeycomb **4** a device for making electrical current by chemical action **5** a very small division of living matter, with a nucleus

cellar *n* an underground room, usu. used for storing goods

cellophane *n trademark* thin transparent material used for wrapping goods

¹**cement** *n* **1** a grey powder, made from a burned mixture of lime and clay, which becomes like stone when mixed with water and allowed to dry **2** any of various types of thick hard-drying sticky substances used for filling holes, as in the teeth, or joining things

²**cement** *v* to join together or make firm (as if) with cement

cemetery *n* **-teries** a place set aside for the burial of the dead

¹**censor** *n* an official who examines printed matter, films, etc. to remove anything regarded as harmful —~**ship** *n*

²**censor** *v* to examine (books, films, letters, etc.) with the intention of removing anything offensive

census *n* **censuses 1** an official count of a country's total population **2** an official count of anything of importance for governmental planning

cent *n* (a coin worth) 0.01 of any of certain money standards, such as the dollar

centigrade also Celsius— *adj, n* (of, in, or related to) the scale of temperature in which water freezes at 0° and boils at 100°

central *adj* **1** being the centre **2** being at, in, or near the centre **3** chief; main; of greatest importance **4** convenient; easily reached: *Our house is very central for the shops* —~**ly** *adv*

¹**centre** *n* **1** a middle part or point; the exact middle, esp. the point around which a circle is drawn **2** a point, area, person, or thing that is

the most important in relation to an interest, activity, or condition **3** having a moderate position esp. in politics **4** (in sport) a player in a team who plays in or near the middle of the field

²**centre centred, centring** v **1** to have or cause to have a centre **2** to have or cause to have as a main subject **3** to place in or at the centre **4** (in sports) to pass (a ball) to the centre of a field

century n -ries **1** a period of 100 years **2** one of the 100-year periods counted from the supposed year of Christ's birth **3** (in cricket) 100 runs made by one player in one innings

cereal n **1** any kind of grain **2** a plant which is grown to produce grain **3** (any of various types of) food made from grain, esp. eaten at breakfast

ceremonial n **1** the special order and formal rules of ceremony, esp. in religious life **2** a ceremony −**ceremonial** adj

ceremony n -nies **1** a special formal and well-established set of actions used for marking an important private or public, social or religious event **2** the special order and formal behaviour demanded on particular occasions **3 stand on/upon ceremony** to follow formal rules of behaviour

¹**certain** adj **1** sure; established beyond doubt or question **2** sure; having no doubt: *I'm certain she saw me*

²**certain** adj **1** not named or described

but taken as known; some particular: *Certain laws exist to protect customers* **2** some but not a lot of

certainly adv **1** without doubt; surely **2** (as a polite or strong way of answering a question) yes; of course

certainty n -ties **1** the state of being certain; freedom from doubt **2** a clearly established fact

certificate n an official document stating that a certain fact or facts are true: *a birth certificate*

¹**chain** n **1** (a length of) usu. metal rings, connected to one another, used for fastening, supporting, ornamenting, etc. **2** a number of connected things, such as events, shops, mountains, etc.

²**chain** v to limit the freedom of (someone or something) as if with a chain

¹**chair** n **1** a piece of furniture to sit on, which has typically a back, seat, 4 legs, and sometimes arms **2** the office or official seat of someone, such as a chairman, in charge of a meeting **3** the position of professor: *the chair of chemistry*

²**chair** v **1** to be chairman of (a meeting) **2** to lift up and carry (someone), usu. as a sign of admiration

chairman −also **chairperson** (*fem.* **chairwoman**) n -men a person **a** in charge of a meeting **b** who directs the work of a committee, department, etc. −∼**ship** n

¹**chalk** n **1** a type of limestone formed from the shells of very small sea

animals, used for making lime and various writing materials **2** (a piece of) this material, white or coloured, used for writing or drawing –~**y** *adj*

²**chalk** *v* to write, mark, or draw with chalk

¹**challenge** *v* **-lenged, -lenging 1** to call (someone) to compete against one, esp. in a fight, match, etc. **2** to demand official proof of the name and aims of (someone) **3** to question the lawfulness or rightness of (someone or something) **4** to call (a person or thing) to competitive action or effort; test the abilities of (a person or thing) –~**r** *n*

²**challenge** *n* **1** an invitation to compete in a fight, match, etc. **2** a demand usu. by a soldier, to stop and prove who and what one is **3** the quality of demanding competitive action, interest, or thought **4** an expression of doubt about the lawfulness of something

champagne *n* a type of costly French white wine containing a lot of bubbles, usu. drunk on special occasions

¹**champion** *n* **1** a person who fights for, or defends a principle, movement, person, etc. **2** a person or animal unbeaten in competition

²**champion** *v* to fight for, support strongly, or defend (a principle, movement, person, etc.)

³**champion** *adj esp. spoken* very good; better than most

¹**chance** *n* **1** the force that seems to make things happen without cause; luck; good or bad fortune **2** (a) possibility; likelihood that something will happen **3** a favourable occasion; opportunity **4** a risk

²**chance** *v* **chanced, chancing 1** to take place by chance; happen by accident **2** to take a chance with; risk

³**chance** *adj* accidental; unplanned

¹**change** *v* **changed, changing 1** to make or become different **2** to give, take, or put something in place of (something else, usu. of the same kind) **3** to put (different clothes) on oneself **4** to put (fresh clothes or coverings) on a baby, child, bed, etc. **5** to give (money) in exchange for money of a different type **6** to leave and enter (different vehicles) in order to continue or complete a journey **7** to cause the engine of a vehicle to be in a different (higher or lower) gear: *Change into a lower gear when you go up the hill* **8 change gear(s)** to make a change in speed by causing the engine of a vehicle to be in a different gear **9 change hands** to go from the ownership of one person to another

²**change** *n* **1** (an example of) the act or result of changing **2** something different done for variety, excitement, etc. **3 a** a fresh set of clothes **b** something fresh used in place of something old **4** the money returned when the amount given is more than the cost **5** money in small units

changeable *adj* 1 (esp. of the weather) likely to change 2 often changing; variable – **-bly** *adv* –~**ness** *n*

¹channel *n* 1 the bed of a stream of water 2 the deepest part of a river, harbour, or sea passage 3 a narrow sea passage connecting 2 seas 4 a passage for liquids 5 any course or way along which information travels 6 a particular band of radio waves used for broadcasting television; television station or the programmes broadcast by it 7 a way, course, or direction of thought or action

²channel *v* **-ll-** 1 to direct 2 to form a channel in 3 to take or go in a channel

chaos *n* 1 a state of complete disorder and confusion 2 *poetic* the state of the universe before there was any order

chaotic *adj* in a state of complete disorder and confusion; confused –~**ally** *adv*

chapter *n* 1 one of the main divisions of a book, usu. having a number or title 2 a special period in history; number of connected happenings

¹character *n* 1 (in writing or printing systems) a sign, letter, or mark: *Chinese is written in characters* 2 the combination of qualities which makes one thing different from another 3 moral strength; honesty 4 *esp. spoken* a person 5 a person in a book, play, etc. 6 *esp. spoken* an odd or humorous person

²character *adj* 1 (of a person) able to play an unusual, odd, or difficult part in a play 2 (of a part in a play) needing the qualities of such a person

¹charge *v* **charged, charging** 1 to ask in payment 2 to record (something) to someone's debt 3 to rush in or as if in an attack 4 to declare officially and openly (that something is wrong) 5 to command; give as a responsibility: *He charged me to look after his daughter* 6 **a** to load (a gun) **b** *literature* to fill (a glass) 7 to (cause to) take in the correct amount of electricity

²charge *n* 1 the price asked or paid for an article or service 2 care; control; responsibility 3 **a** a person or thing for which one is responsible **b** a duty; responsibility 4 an order; command 5 a spoken or written statement blaming a person for breaking the law, or doing something morally wrong: *The charge was murder* 6 a rushing forceful attack 7 the amount of explosive to be fired at one time 8 (a quantity of) electricity put into a battery or other electrical apparatus 9 **in charge of** responsible for

charity *n* **-ties** 1 the giving of help to the poor 2 an organization that gives this help 3 **charity begins at home** one's first duty is to one's family 4 **(as) cold as charity** unfeeling; unfriendly

¹charm *n* 1 a magic word or act 2 an object worn to keep away evil or bring luck 3 the power or ability to please or win over **4 work like a charm** *esp. spoken* to be a complete success

²charm *v* **1** to please; win over; delight **2** to control or protect (something) as if by magic – ~**ing** *adj* – ~**ingly** *adv* –

¹chart *n* **1** a map, esp. a detailed map of a sea area **2** (a sheet of paper with) information in written or illustrated form: *weather chart*

²chart *v* **1** to make a map or chart of **2** *esp. spoken* to make a rough plan, in writing

¹charter *n* **1** an official document giving rights, freedoms, etc. **2** the practice of hiring or renting buses, planes, etc.: *charter flights*

²charter *v* to hire or rent (a plane, bus, etc.)

¹chase *v* **chased, chasing** to run after; to hunt; to drive away

²chase *n* **1** an act of chasing **2 give chase** to chase

¹chat *v esp. spoken* to talk in a friendly manner

²chat *n esp. spoken* a gossipy conversation

¹chatter *v* **1** to talk rapidly and idly at length **2** (of certain animals and birds) to make rapid speechlike sounds **3** to knock together, esp. through cold or fear – ~**er** *n*

²chatter *n* **1** rapid small talk **2** a rapid knocking sound made by teeth, machines, etc.

¹cheap *n* **on the cheap** *esp. spoken* without paying the full cost

²cheap *adj* **1** low in price ; good value

2 charging low prices **3** needing little effort: *The army won a cheap victory* **4** worth little **5 a** of poor quality; shoddy **b** vulgar **6 dirt cheap** *esp. spoken* at a very low price **7 feel cheap** *esp. spoken* to feel ashamed – ~**ly** *adv* – ~**ness** *n*

¹cheat *n* **1** a dishonest person **2** an example of cheating; deceitful trick **3** a card game in which 2 or more players try to win by cheating

²cheat *v* **1** to trick (someone) **2** to act dishonestly or deceitfully to win an advantage, esp. in a game **3** to escape as if by deception: *The swimmers cheated death in spite of the storm*

¹check *n* **1** a stop; control: *We've kept the disease in check for a year now* **2** something which stops, controls, etc. **3** an examination to make certain that something is correct **4** a standard against which something can be examined **5** a receipt; ticket or object for claiming something **6** a pattern of squares **7** the position of the king in chess when under direct attack

²check *v* **1** to stop; control; hold back **2** to test, examine, or mark to see if correct

¹cheek *n* **1** a fleshy part on either side of the face **2** *esp. spoken* a buttock **3** *esp. spoken* insolence **4 cheek by jowl (with)** in close association or very close together

²cheek *v esp. spoken* to behave disrespectfully towards (someone)

cheeky *adj* **-ier, -iest** *esp. spoken* disrespectful; rude **−cheekily** *adv* **−cheekiness** *n*

¹cheer *n* **1** a shout of praise, encouragement, etc. **2** happiness; gaiety: *He's always full of cheer at Christmas*

²cheer *v* **1** to shout in praise, approval, or support **2** to give encouragement, hope, help, or support to

cheerful *adj* happy; in good spirits; causing happiness; willing **−∼ly** *adv* **−∼ness** *n*

cheese *n* **1** food made from pressed milk solids **2** a usu. large shaped and wrapped quantity of this

¹chemical *adj* of, connected with, used in, or made by chemistry **−∼ly** *adv*

²chemical *n* any substance used in or produced by chemistry

chemist *n* **1** a scientist who specializes in chemistry **2** also *esp. written* **pharmacist−** a person skilled in making medicine or who owns or runs a shop where medicines are sold

chemistry *n* **1** the science which studies elements and compounds **2** the chemical make-up and behaviour of a substance: *the chemistry of lead*

cheque *n* **1** a specially printed order form to a bank to pay money **2** **crossed cheque** a cheque which must be put into a bank account before being paid **3** **blank cheque** a signed cheque given to the person to whom it is payable who writes on it the amount to be paid later

cherry *n* **-ries** a small usu. red round

fruit with a stonelike seed, or the tree on which this grows

chess *n* a game for 2 players, with 16 pieces (**chessmen**) each, which are moved across a square board with 64 black and white squares (**chessboard**), in an attempt to trap the opponent's king

chest *n* **1** the upper front part of the body **2** a large strong box for valuables or goods **3** **get (something) off one's chest** to confess

¹chestnut *n* **1** an edible reddish-brown nut or the tree upon which this grows **2** a reddish-brown horse **3** *esp. spoken* a stale joke or story

²chestnut *adj, n* (having) a deep reddish-brown colour

¹chew *v* **1** to crush (food or tobacco) with the teeth **2** **bite off more than one can chew** *esp. spoken* to attempt more than one can deal with **3** **chew the fat** *esp. spoken* to chat **4** **chew over** to think over (a question, difficulty, etc.) −

²chew the act of chewing

chick *n* **1** the young of a bird, esp. a chicken **2** *sl* a young woman

¹chicken *n* **1** the domestic hen kept to give eggs and meat **2** the cooked meat of the young hen or cock **3** *sl* (*used esp. by children*) a coward **4** **count one's chickens before they're hatched** to base plans on something which has not yet happened

²chicken *adj sl* lacking courage

¹chief *n* **1** a leader; ruler; person with highest rank; head of a party, organization, etc.: *a Red Indian chief / the chief of police* **2** *sl* a boss **3** (used as a humorous but polite form of address by one man to another): '*Where to, Chief?*' *the taxi driver asked me*

²**chief** *adj* highest in rank; most important: *the chief constable/ inspector/justice/crop*

chiefly *adv* **1** mainly; mostly but not wholly: *Bread is chiefly made of flour* **2** above all

chieftain *n* the leader of a tribe, clan, etc.

child *n* **children 1** a baby; boy or girl; son or daughter; descendant **2** *offensive* **a** an adult who behaves childishly **b** an inexperienced person: *a child in money matters* **3** a product; result **4 get someone/be with child** *literature* to make someone/be pregnant

childhood *n* **1** the condition or period of time of being a child **2 second childhood** weakness of mind caused by old age

¹**chill** *v* **1** to make or become cold, esp. without freezing **2** to (cause to) feel cold as from fear

²**chill** *adj* **1** cold: *a chill wind* **2** unfriendly; discouraging: *a chill meeting*

³**chill** *n* **1** an illness marked by shivering **2** an unpleasant coldness: *a chill in the air* a discouraging feeling, often of fear

chilly *adj* **-ier, -iest 1** disagreeably cold **2** unfriendly; discouraging:*He was given a chilly welcome* **–chilliness** *n*

chimney *n* **-neys** a hollow passage often rising above a roof for smoke to be carried off

chin *n* **1** the front part of the face below the mouth **2 (Keep your) chin up!** *esp. spoken* Don't give up

china *n* **1** a hard white substance made by baking fine clay at high temperatures **2** plates, cups, etc., made from this

¹**chip** *n* **1** a small piece of brick, wood, paint, etc., broken off **2** a crack or mark left when a small piece is broken off **3** a flat plastic counter representing money in games of chance **4** a long thin piece of potato cooked in deep fat **5** a tiny set of electronic parts and their connections, produced as a single unit in or on a small slice of material such as silicon, that can replace a larger conventional circuit **6 chip off the old block** *esp. spoken* (usu. said by and about males) a person very like his father

²**chip** *v* **1** to (cause to) lose a small piece from the surface or edge: *This rock chips easily* **2** to cut (potatoes) into small pieces to cook as chips

chirp also chirrup– *v* **1** to make the short sharp sound(s) of small birds or some insects **2** to speak gaily in a way that sounds like this **–chirp** *n*

chirpy *adj* **-ier, -iest** *esp. spoken* (of people) in good spirits; cheerful **–chirpily** *adv* **–chirpiness** *n*

¹**chisel** *n* a metal tool with a sharp edge at the end of a blade, used

for cutting into or shaping wood, stone, etc.

²**chisel** *v* -ll- **1** to cut or shape with a chisel **2** *sl* to get (something) by deceitful or unfair practices – ~**ler** *n*

¹**chocolate** *n* **1** a solid sweet usu. brown substance made from the crushed seeds of the cacao tree **2** a small sweet made with this substance **3** a sweet brown powder from this substance, used for flavouring foods and drinks **4** a drink made from hot milk and this powder

²**chocolate** *adj, n* (having) a usu. dark brown colour

¹**choice** *n* **1** the act of choosing **2** the power, right, or chance of choosing **3** someone or something chosen **4** a variety from which to choose

²**choice** *adj* **1** (esp. of food) of high quality: *choice apples* **2** *literature* well chosen: *He told the story in choice phrases* – ~**ly** *adv* – ~**ness** *n*

choir *n* a group of people who sing together or the part of a church where such a group sits: *a church/ school choir*

¹**choke** *v* **choked, choking 1** to (cause to) struggle to breathe or (cause to) stop breathing because of blocking of or damage to the windpipe **2** to fill (a space or passage) completely: *The roads were choked with traffic. / choked up with anger*

²**choke** *n* **1** the act of choking **2** an apparatus that reduces the amount of air going into a car engine to make starting easier

choose *v* **chose , chosen, choosing 1** to pick out from a number; select **2** to decide: *He chose not to go home*

¹**chop** *v* -pp- **1** to cut by repeatedly striking with or as if with an axe **2** to cut into small pieces **3** to strike (a ball) with a quick downward stroke

²**chop** *n* **1** a quick short cutting blow **2** a short quick downward stroke or blow **3** a slice of meat usu. containing a bone: *lamb chops* **4 get the chop** *sl* to be dismissed from work

chopstick *n* either of a pair of narrow sticks used for eating Chinese food

chore *n* **1** a daily job, esp. in a house **2** a difficult or disliked task: *It's such a chore to do the shopping every day!*

¹**chorus** *n* **1** a group of people who sing together **2** a piece of music for such a group **3** a group of dancers, singers, or actors who play a supporting part in a film or show **4** a piece of music played or sung after each verse of a song **5** something said by many people at one time: *a chorus of shouts* **6** *technical* **a** (esp. in ancient Greek drama) a group of actors who used poetry and music to explain the action **b** (in Elizabethan plays) a person who makes speeches throughout explaining the action

²**chorus** *v* to sing or speak at the same time

chose *past tense of* CHOOSE

chosen *past part. of* CHOOSE

Christ *n* also **Jesus Christ**– the founder of Christianity believed by

Christians to be the son of God and to live forever in heaven

christen *v* **1** to baptise and give a name to (someone esp. a child) **2** to name (esp. a ship) at an official ceremony −~**ing** *n*

¹**Christian** *n* **1** a person who believes in Jesus Christ and his teachings, usu. a member of a Christian church **2** a good person

²**Christian** *adj* **1** believing in Christianity **2** of or related to Christ, Christianity, or Christians **3** having qualities such as kindness, generosity, etc.

Christianity *n* the religion based on the life and teachings of Christ

Christmas *n* **1** also **Christmas Day** − a Christian festival held annually on December 25th in honour of Christ's birth **2** the period just before, and the 12 days just after, this

chronic *adj* **1** (of diseases) continual; lasting a long time: *a chronic cough* **2** (of a sufferer from a disease or illness) seriously suffering from a long-lasting disease or illness: *a chronic alcoholic* **3** *sl* very bad; terrible: *a chronic sense of humour* −~**ally** *adv*

chuckle *v* **-led, -ling** to laugh quietly −**chuckle** *n*

chunk *n esp. spoken* a short thick piece or lump; a fairly large amount

church *n* **1** a building for public Christian worship **2** public Christian worship **3** the profession of the clergy **4** religious power (as compared with state power) **5** Christians everywhere considered as one body

cider, cyder *n* an alcoholic drink made from apple juice

cigar *n* a roll of uncut tobacco leaves for smoking

cigarette *n* a narrow tube of finely cut tobacco rolled in thin paper for smoking

cinder *n* **1** a small piece of partly burned wood, coal, etc. **2** the waste left after metal has been melted from ore ; slag

cinema *n* **1** a theatre in which films are shown **2** also (*esp. US*) **movies** − the art or industry of making moving pictures

¹**circle** *n* **1** a curved line which passes through a set of points which are all the same distance from a centre **2** something having the general shape of this line; ring: *a circle of trees* **3** an upper floor in a theatre, usu. with seats set in curved lines **4** a group of people with common interests: *He has a large circle of friends*

²**circle** *v* **-cled, -cling 1** to draw or form a circle around (something) **2** to move or travel in a circle

circuit *n* **1** a complete route: *the circuit of the old city walls* **2** the complete circular path of an electric current **3** a set of electrical parts for some special purpose: *a television circuit* **4** a regular journey from place to place made by a judge to hear law cases **5** a group of establishments offering the same films, plays, etc.

¹circular *adj* **1** round; shaped like a circle **2** forming or moving in a circle: *circular saw / circular railway* **3** indirect; roundabout

²circular *n* a printed advertisement, paper, or notice for a large number of people

circulate *v* **-lated, -lating 1** to (cause to) move or flow along a closed path: *Blood circulates round the body* **2** to (cause to) spread widely: *The news of defeat quickly circulated* **3** to move about freely: *The prince circulated from group to group at the party*

circulation *n* **1** the flow of gas or liquid around a closed system, esp. of blood through the body **2** the movement of something such as news or money from place to place or from person to person: *His book has been taken out of circulation* **3** the average number of copies of a newspaper, magazine, etc., sold

circumstance *n* **1** a fact, detail, condition, or event which influences what happens: *The police want to consider each circumstance* **2** formal usu. official ceremony (esp. in the phrase **pomp and circumstance**)

circumstances *n* **1** the state of a person's financial affairs: *easy/reduced circumstances* **2** the state of affairs, esp. those beyond one's control: *The circumstances forced me to accept* **3** **in/under no circumstances** never; regardless of events

circus *n* **1** a company of skilled performers and trained animals who give public performances, often in a large tent **2** a public performance by such a group **3** an open space where streets join together: *Oxford Circus* **4** *offensive* a noisy badly behaved group of people **5** (in Ancient Rome) an open space surrounded by seats in which sports, races, etc., took place

cistern *n* a container for storing rainwater or as part of the system which flushes a toilet

citizen *n* **1** a person who lives in a particular city or town, esp. one who has voting or other rights there **2** a member of a particular country by birth or naturalization who may expect protection from it **−~ship** *n*

city *n* **cities 1** a large and important town usu. with a centre for business and amusements, and often having a cathedral **2** the people who live in such a place

civil *adj* **1** of the general population; not military or religious: *civil government / civil marriage* **2** of all citizens: *civil rights / civil liberty* **3** (of law) dealing with the rights of private citizens **4** polite enough to be acceptable: *Keep a civil tongue in your head!*

civilian *n, adj* (a person) not of the armed forces

civilization, -sation *n* **1** an advanced stage of human social development **2** the type of advanced society of a particular time or place: *the civilizations of ancient China and Japan* **3** modern society with all its comforts **4** the act of civilizing or of being civilized

civilize, -lise *v* **-lized, -lizing 1** to (cause to) bring from a lower to a highly developed stage of social organization: *The Romans hoped to civilize the barbarians* **2** *esp. spoken* to (cause to) improve in education and manners: *We should civilize that boy*

civil service *n* **1** all the national government departments except the armed forces, law courts, and religious organizations **2** all the people employed in this: *The civil service ought to obey the elected government*

¹claim *v* **1** to ask for or demand (a title, property, money, etc.) as the rightful owner or as one's right: *Did you claim on the insurance after your car accident?* **2** to declare to be true; maintain

²claim *n* **1** a demand for something as one's own by right: *a claim for money* **2** a right to something: *The poor have a claim to our sympathy* **3** a statement of something as fact: *The government's claim that war was necessary was mistaken* **4** something claimed, esp. an area of land or a sum of money **5 jump a claim** to take land that another person has claimed **–~ant** *n*

clang *v* to (cause to) make a loud ringing sound, as when metal is struck **–clang** *n*

¹clap *v* **-pp- 1** to strike (one's palms) loudly together **2** to show approval by doing this; applaud **3** to strike lightly with the open hand: *He clapped his son on the back* **4** *esp. spoken* to put, place, or send quickly: *The judge clapped the criminal in prison* **5 clap eyes on** *esp. spoken* to see (someone or something): *It's many years since I clapped eyes on him*

²clap *n* **1** a loud explosive sound: *a clap of thunder* **2** the sounds of hands being clapped **3** a light friendly hit

¹clash *v* **1** to come into opposition: *The enemy armies clashed. / Those colours she's wearing clash* **2** (of events) to be inconveniently at the same time: *Her wedding clashed with my examination* **3** to (cause to) make a loud confused noise

²clash *n* **1** a loud confused noise **2** an example of opposition or disagreement: *clash of interests* **3** a fight; battle: *a border clash*

¹clasp *n* **1** a fastener for holding 2 things together **2** a firm handgrip or an embrace

²clasp *v* **1** to seize firmly; embrace **2** to fasten with a clasp

¹class *n* **1** the division of a society into groups of different social and political status: *The nation is divided by the question of class* **2** a social group: *the ruling classes / the upper class* **3** a division of people or things according to rank, behaviour, achievement, quality, etc.: *a first class degree* **4** a grouping of plants or animals **5** a level of quality of travelling conditions on a train, plane, boat, etc.: *(a) first class (ticket) to Birmingham, please* **6** a group of pupils or students taught together or the time during which they are taught **7** *technical* (in statistics) a set of values which are grouped together **8** *esp. spoken* high quality (of people and things)

²class *v* **1** to put into a class; classify **2** to consider: *I class that as wicked-ness*

¹classic *adj* **1** having the highest quality; of the first class **2** serving as a standard, model, or guide; well known, esp. as the best example **3** of or belonging to an established set of artistic or scientific standards

²classic *n* **1** a piece of literature or art, a writer, or an artist of lasting importance: *Shakespeare's plays were classics* **2** a famous event usu. with a long history, esp. (in horse races) one of the 5 chief English flat races

classify *v* **-fied, -fying 1** to arrange or place (animals, plants, books, etc.) into classes **2** to mark or declare (information) secret

¹clatter *v* to (cause to) move with a number of rapid knocking sounds

²clatter *n* **1** a number of rapid short knocks; rattle **2** noise; busy activity: *the busy clatter of the city*

¹claw *n* **1** a sharp usu. curved nail on the toe of an animal or bird **2** something shaped like this (such as a crab's pincers or the forklike end of a **claw hammer**)

²claw *v* to tear, seize, pull, etc., with claws or nails

clay *n* heavy earth, used for making bricks, pots, earthenware, etc., when baked −∼**ey** *adj*

¹clean *adj* **1** not dirty; disease-free; fresh; pure **2** without mistakes; readable: *a clean copy of the report* **3** morally or sexually pure; honourable; free from guilt; fair, sportsmanlike: *a clean life / (esp. spoken) a clean joke / a clean fighter* **4** (of animals) that can lawfully be eaten by Jews according to their religion **5** well-formed; streamlined; even; regular; clear; precise: *the clean shape of the railway engine / a clean cut / a clean style* **6 clean sweep** a complete change or victory **7 come clean** *esp. spoken* to confess −∼**ness** *n*

²clean *adv* **1** all the way: *The bullet went clean through (his arm)* **2** *esp. spoken* completely: *I'm clean out (of food)* **3** *esp. spoken* in a fair way: *Play the game clean*

³clean *v* **1** to make or become clean: *Metal ornaments clean easily* **2** to cut out the bowels and inside parts of the body from (birds, fish, and animals that are to be eaten)

clean out *v adv* **1** to make (the inside of something) clean and tidy **2 a** to take all the money of (someone) by stealing or by winning **b** to steal everything from (a place)

clean up *v adv* **1** to clean thoroughly: *It's your turn to clean (the bedroom) up* **2** to remove by cleaning **3** *esp. spoken* to gain (money) as profit

¹**clear** *adj* **1** bright; transparent: *a clear sky / clear eyes* **2** easily heard, seen, read, or understood **3** thinking without difficulty: *a clear thinker* **4** certain; confident: *She is quite clear about her plans* **5** untroubled: *a clear conscience* **6** free from obstructions: *a clear road* **7** of a pure and even colour: *a clear skin* **8** obvious: *a clear case of murder* **9** complete: *a clear victory* –~**ness** *n*

²**clear** *adv* **1** in a clear manner **2** out of the way: *She jumped clear* **3** *esp. spoken* completely: *He got clear away*

³**clear** *v* **1** to make or become clear **2** to remove from; take away: *Clear the plates away. / We must clear the area of enemy soldiers* **3** to free from blame: *The prisoner was cleared* **4** to pass by or over without touching: *The horse cleared the fence* **5** *esp. spoken* to satisfy the official conditions of: *The car cleared customs* **6** to give official permission to: *The building plans have been cleared* **7** to pass (a cheque) through a clearing house **8** *esp. spoken* to earn (a large amount of money) **9** to repay (a debt) in full **10 clear the air** to remove doubt and bad feeling

clearly *adv* **1** in a clear manner **2** obviously: *clearly a mistake*

clear up *v adv* **1** to explain: *to clear up the mystery* **2** to tidy up; finish: *lots of work to clear up* **3** to come to an end: *I hope your troubles clear up soon*

clergyman –also (*old use*) **cleric** *n* -**men** a Christian priest or minister

clerk *n* a person employed in an office, shop, etc., to keep records, accounts, etc.

clever *adj* **1** quick at learning and understanding **2** skilful, esp. at using the hands or body: *a clever worker* **3** being the result of a quick able mind: *a clever idea* **4** *esp. spoken* (often of an insincere person) appearing able or skilful –~**ly** *adv* –~**ness** *n*

client *n* **1** a person who pays esp. a lawyer for advice, or who gets help from the social services **2** a customer

cliff *n* a high very steep face of rock, ice, earth, etc., esp. on a coast

climate *n* **1** the average weather conditions at a particular place **2** the general temper or opinions of a group of people or period of history: *the moral climate*

¹**climax** *n* **1** that part in a related set of events, ideas, expressions, etc., which is most powerful, interesting, and effective, and which usu. comes near the end **2** (of a play, book, film, etc.) the most important part, usu. near the end

²**climax** *v* to (cause to) reach a climax

¹**climb** *v* **1** to go esp. up, over, or through, esp. by using the hands and feet **2** to go up (esp. mountains) as a sport **3** to rise to a higher point **4** to slope upwards **5** (esp. of a plant) to grow upwards, esp. along a supporting surface **6** *esp.spoken* to get into or out of clothing usu. quickly

²**climb** *n* **1** a journey upwards made by climbing **2** a very steep slope?

cling *v* **clung, clinging** to hold tightly; stick firmly

clinic *n* **1** a building or part of a hospital where a group of people, esp. doctors, give treatment **2** an occasion in a hospital when medical students are taught by looking at ill people

¹**clip** *v* **-pp-** to fasten with a clip

²**clip** *n* **1** a small plastic or usu. metal object for holding things tightly together or in place **2** a magazine in or fastened to a gun, from which bullets and explosive can be rapidly passed into the gun for firing

³**clip** *v* **-pp- 1** to cut with scissors or another sharp instrument **2** to leave out (parts of a word or sentence) when speaking or to shorten in this way **3** to put a hole in (a ticket) **4** *esp. spoken* to strike with a short quick blow

⁴**clip 1** the act of clipping **2** *technical* the quantity of wool cut from a flock of sheep at one time **3** *esp. spoken* a short quick blow **4** *esp. spoken* a fast speed **5** a usu. short extract from a cinema film

clipping *n* a piece cut off or out of something

¹**cloak** *n* **1** a loose outer garment, usu. sleeveless **2** something which covers or hides: *His behaviour was a cloak for his evil intentions*

²**cloak** *v* to hide or cover (ideas, thoughts, beliefs, etc.)

¹**clock** *n* **1** an instrument for measuring and showing time **2** *esp. spoken* a mileometer (instrument in a vehicle recording the distance travelled) or speedometer (instrument showing a vehicle's speed) **3** *sl* someone's face **4** **around/round the clock** all day and night without stopping **5** **put the clock back a** (in countries which change the time at the beginning of winter and summer) to move the hands of a clock back one or 2 hours **b** to set aside modern laws, ideas, etc., and stay with old-fashioned ones

²**clock** *v* **1** to time: *I clocked him while he ran a mile* **2** *sl* to strike

clockwork *n* **1** the machinery that works a clock, or machinery like this that runs from energy stored in a coiled spring, usu. wound up with a key **2** **like clockwork** without trouble

¹**clog** *n* a kind of wooden shoe or one with a thick usu. wooden sole

²**clog** *v* **-gg-** to make or become blocked

¹**close** *v* **closed, closing 1** to shut **2** to make or be not open to the public **3** to stop or cause to stop operation: *This factory is closing (down)* **4** to

bring to an end: *She closed her speech* **5** to bring or come together: *His arms closed tightly round her*

²**close** *n* an end (often in the phrases **bring/come/draw to a close**)

³**close** *n* **1** an enclosed area or space, esp. around a cathedral; courtyard **2** a narrow entrance or passage usu. leading into a courtyard

⁴**close** *adj* **1** near **2 a** near in relationship **b** with deep feeling: *close friends* **3 a** tight **b** narrow; limited **4** thorough: *a close watch* **5** lacking fresh or freely moving air: *close weather* **6** in which the competitors are almost equal; decided by a very narrow margin **7** secretive **8** not generous: *close with money* –~**ly** *adv* –~**ness** *n*

⁵**close** *adv* **1** near: *Don't come so close!* **2 close to home** *esp. spoken* near the (often unpleasant) truth: *What she said was very close to home*

cloth *n* **1** material made from wool, hair, cotton, etc., by weaving, and used for making garments, coverings, etc. **2** a piece of this used for a special purpose: *a tablecloth*

clothes *n* garments

clothing *n often written & technical* garments worn together on different parts of the body

¹**cloud** *n* **1** (a variously-shaped mass of) very small drops of water in the air. **2** a mass of dust, smoke, etc., which floats in the air **3** (an area of) darkness in something otherwise transparent: *There was some cloud in the beer* **4** something that causes unhappiness or fear: *Her death was a cloud on an otherwise happy year*

²**cloud** *v* **1** to cover or become covered with or as if with clouds **2** to make uncertain, confused, etc.: *Age clouded his memory* **3** to make or become less transparent or darker

cloudy *adj* **-ier, -iest 1** full of clouds; overcast **2** not clear or transparent **3** uncertain –**cloudiness** *n*

¹**clown** *n* **1** a performer, esp. in the circus, who makes people laugh **2** a person who acts stupidly –~**ish** *adj* –~**ishly** *adv* –~**ishness** *n*

²**clown** *v* to behave like a clown

¹**club** *n* **1** a society of people who join together for sport, amusement, etc. **2** *also* **clubhouse–** a building where such a society meets **3** a heavy wooden stick, thicker at one end than the other, used as a weapon **4** a specially shaped stick for striking a ball in certain sports, esp. golf **5** a playing card with one or more 3-leafed figures printed on it in black **6 in the club** *sl* expecting a baby

²**club** *v* **-bb-** to beat with a club

clue *n* something that helps to find an answer to a question, difficulty, etc.

clumsy *adj* **-sier, -siest 1** awkward in movement or action **2** done or made awkwardly –**clumsily** *adv* –**clumsiness** *n*

clung *past tense and past part. of* CLING

¹**cluster** *n* a group of things of the same kind growing or being close together

²**cluster** *v* to gather or grow in clusters

¹**clutch** *v* to hold tightly

²**clutch** *n* **1** the fingers or hands in the act of clutching **2** the act of clutching **3** an apparatus, as in a car, which allows working parts to be connected or disconnected

³**clutch** *n* a number of eggs laid by a bird, esp. a hen, at one time, or the group of chickens born from these

¹**coach** *n* a large enclosed 4-wheeled horse-drawn carriage, used esp. in former times or in official ceremonies **2** a bus used for long-distance travel or touring **3** a railway carriage **4** a person who trains sportsmen for games, competitions, etc. or someone employed privately to train a student for an examination

²**coach** *v* **1** to train or teach (a person or group) **2** to act as a coach

coal *n* **1** a black or dark brown mineral mined from the earth, which can be burned to give heat, and from which gas, coal tar, etc., can be made **2** a flaming, burning, or already burnt piece of this mineral

coarse *adj* **1** not fine **2** having a rough surface: *coarse cloth* **3** rough in manner: *coarse behaviour* –~**ly** *adv* –~**ness** *n*

¹**coast** *n* **1** the land next to the sea **2** an area bordering the sea –~**al** *adj*

²**coast** *v* to keep moving after effort has ceased, esp. to travel down a hill without using any power

¹**coat** *n* **1** an outer garment with long sleeves, usu. worn for warmth **2** an animal's fur, wool, hair, etc. **3** a covering spread over a surface: *a coat of paint*

²**coat** *v* to cover with a coat: *coated in dust*

coat of arms *n* a group of patterns or pictures, usu. painted on a shield or shield-like shape, used by a noble family, town council, etc., as their special sign

cobbler *n* **1** a shoemender **2** a careless workman

cobweb *n* a very fine network of sticky threads made by a spider to catch insects

¹**cock** *n* **1** a fully-grown male bird, esp. a chicken **2** a tap, valve, etc., for controlling flow in a pipe **3** the hammer of a gun **4** the position of a gun's hammer when drawn back for firing **5** *sl* (used by men to men): *Excuse me, cock*

²**cock** *v* **1** to set (the hammer of a gun) in position for firing **2** to cause (parts of the body) to stand up: *The horse cocked its ears* **3** to tilt

³**cock** *n* **1** the act of cocking **2** a slight slope

cockerel *n* a young cock

Cockney *n* **-neys** a Londoner, esp. one from the East End

cockpit *n* the part of a plane or racing car in which the pilot and copilot sit

cocktail *n* **1** a mixed alcoholic drink **2** a small quantity of specially prepared seafood eaten at the start of a meal

cocky *adj* **-ier, -iest** *esp. spoken* too sure of oneself –**cockiness** *n*

cocoa *n* **1** a dark brown powder made by crushing the cooked seeds of the cacao tree, used for giving foods and drinks a sweet chocolate flavour **2** a drink made from hot milk or water mixed with this powder

coconut *n* **1** a large brown hardshelled nut with hard white flesh and a hollow centre filled with a milky juice **2** the flesh of this eaten raw as food

¹**cod** –also **codfish** *n* **cod** *or* **cods** a type of large edible North Atlantic sea fish

²**cod** *v* **-dd-** *sl* to make a fool of

¹**code** *n* **1** a system of using words, letters, numbers, etc., to keep messages secret **2** a system of signals used instead of letters and numbers in a message that is to be broadcast, telegraphed, etc. **3** a body of established social customs: *a code of behaviour* **4** a collection of laws

²**code** –also **encode** *v* **coded, coding** to translate into a code

coffee *n* **1** a brown powder made by crushing the dark beans of the coffee tree, used for making drinks or flavouring food **2** a drink made by adding hot water and/or milk to this powder

coffin *n* the box in which a dead person is buried

coherent *adj* easily understood; consistent –~**ly** *adv*

¹**coil** *v* to wind into a ring or spiral: *Coil the rope up*

²**coil** *n* **1** a connected set of rings into which a rope, wire, etc., can be

wound **2** a single one of these rings **3** *technical* **a** an electrical apparatus made by winding a continuous piece of wire into some shape, used for carrying an electric current **b** 2 parts like this in a car that use induction to produce a high-voltage spark

¹**coin** *n* a piece of metal, usu. flat and round, made by a government for use as money

²**coin** *v* **1** to make (coins) from metal **2** to invent (a word or phrase) –~**er** *n*

coincide *v* **-cided, -ciding** **1** to happen at the same time **2** to be in agreement: *My beliefs and yours don't coincide*

coincidence *n* **1** a combination of chance events that seem planned **2** the condition or fact of coinciding – **-dental** *adj* – **-dentally** *adv*

¹**cold** *adj* **1** having a low temperature **2** not feeling warm **3** *esp. spoken* (in games) still a long way from finding an object, the answer, etc. **4** *esp. spoken* unconscious, esp. as the result of a blow (esp. in the phrase **out cold**) **5** unkind **6** cooked but not eaten hot –~**ly** *adv* –~**ness** *n*

²**cold** *n* **1** the absence of heat; low temperature; cold weather **2** an illness, esp. of the nose and/or throat, common in winter **3** (**out**) **in the cold** *esp. spoken* seemingly unwanted

¹**collapse** *v* **-lapsed, -lapsing** **1** to fall or drop down or inwards suddenly **2** to fold into a shape that takes

up less space **3** to fall helpless or unconscious **4** to fail completely **5** *medical* (of a lung or blood vessel) to fall into a flattened mass

²**collapse** *n* **1** (an example of) falling down or inwards **2** (an example of) completely breaking down: *the collapse of the pound* **3** (an example of) completely losing strength and/or will: *a nervous collapse*

¹**collar** *n* **1** the part of a shirt, dress, or coat that stands up or folds down round the neck **2** a close-fitting ornamental neck band **3** a leather or metal band round an animal's neck **4** a round leather object put round the shoulders of a horse to help it pull a vehicle or other object **5** *technical* a band or coloured marking round the neck **6** any of various ring-like machine parts

²**collar** *v* **1** *esp. spoken* to seize **2** *sl* to take without permission

colleague *n* a fellow worker, esp. in a profession

collect *v* **1** to gather together **2** to gather (objects) as a hobby, for study, etc. **3** to call for and take away **4** to regain control of (oneself, one's thoughts, senses, etc.) **5** to obtain payment of (money): *The government collects taxes*

collection *n* **1** the act of collecting **2** the emptying of a post-box by a postman **3** a group of objects collected as a hobby, for study, etc. **4** a sum of money collected, esp. at a religious service **5** a pile of material, dirt, etc., often unwanted

college *n* **1** a school for higher education **2** a body of teachers and students forming a separate part of certain universities **3** any of certain large public or private schools **4** *technical* a body of people with a common profession, purpose, etc.: *the Royal College of Nurses*

collide *v* **-lided, -liding 1** to meet and strike (together) violently **2** to disagree strongly

collision *n* (an example of) colliding

colonel *n* an officer of middle rank in the army or American air force

colony *n* **-nies 1** a country or area under the control of a distant country and often settled by people from that country **2** a group of people of the same nationality, profession, etc., living together: *the French colony in Saigon* **3** a group of the same kind of plants or animals growing or living together in close association **4** all the bacteria growing together as the descendants of a single cell

colossal *adj* very large in size or quantity −∼**ly** *adv*

¹**colour** *n* **1** the quality which allows the eyes to see the difference between (for example) a red and a blue flower of the same size and shape **2** red, blue, green, black, brown, yellow, white, etc. **3** (a) substance used for giving one of these special qualities to something: *The artist painted in watercolours* **4** the complexion **5** details or behaviour of a place, thing, or

person, that excite: *the life, noise, and colour of the market* **6 give/lend colour to** to make appear likely or true **7 off colour** *esp. spoken* rather ill

²**colour** *v* **1** to cause to have colour or a different colour esp. with a crayon or pencil **2** to take on or change colour **3** to give a special effect or feeling to: *Personal feelings coloured his judgment* **4** to become red in the face

colourful *adj* **1** full of colour or colours; bright **2** likely to excite the senses or imagination: *a colourful event*

column *n* **1** a pillar used in a building as a support or ornament or standing alone as a monument **2** anything looking like a pillar: *a column of smoke* **3** one of 2 or more divisions of a page, lying side by side and separated by a narrow space, in which lines of print are arranged **4** an article by a particular writer, that regularly appears in a newspaper or magazine **5** many rows of people, vehicles, etc., following behind the other **6** a list of numbers arranged one under the other

¹**comb** *n* **1** a toothed piece of bone, metal, plastic, etc., used for cleaning, tidying, and straightening the hair or worn in a woman's hair for ornament **2** a thing like this in shape or use, such as an object used for carding wool, cotton, etc. **3** an

act of combing **4** the red growth of flesh on a cock's head

²**comb** *v* **1** to clean or arrange (esp. the hair) with a comb **2** to search thoroughly

¹**combat** *v* **-tt-** to fight

²**combat** *n* (a) struggle between 2 men, armies, ideas, etc.

combination *n* **1** combining or being combined **2** a number of people or things united in a common purpose **3** the list of special numbers or letters needed to open a type of lock **4** something that results from 2 or more things, esp. chemicals, being combined **5** *technical* one of the sets into which a list of numbers, letters, etc., can be arranged

¹**combine** *v* **-bined, -bining** to come, bring, or act together

²**combine** —also **combine harvester** *n* a machine that reaps, threshes, and cleans grain

come *v* **came** , **come, coming** **1** to move towards the speaker or a particular place **2** to arrive in the course of time: *Uncle's birthday is coming soon* **3** to reach: *The water came to my neck* **4** to be (in a place in a set): *Monday comes after Sunday* **5** to happen or begin: *In time I came to love her* **6** to happen as a result of the stated cause **7** to become: *The buttons came unfastened* **8** to be offered, produced, etc.: *Milk comes from cows* **9 come full circle** to end at the place where one started **10 come home to** *esp. spoken* to be fully understood by **11**

come and go to change **12 come unstuck** to meet with failure **13 how come** *esp. spoken* how did it happen (that) **14 to come** in the future

comedian *n* **1** an actor who **a** tells jokes or does amusing things **b** acts in funny plays or films **2** *esp. spoken* a person who amuses others **3** a person who cannot be taken seriously

come down *v adv* **1** to be passed on from one period of history to another: *This song comes down to us from the 10th century* **2** to be reduced in price **3** to lose position, respect, or rank **4** to fall **5** to leave a big city for the country **6** to leave university (esp. Oxford or Cambridge) **7 come down to earth** to return to reality

comedy *n* **-dies 1** an amusing play, film, or other work which ends happily **2** an event, activity, or type of behaviour in real life that is amusing **3** the amusing quality of a play, film, book, person's behaviour, etc.

come round *v adv* **1** also **come to–** to regain consciousness **2** to change sides or opinions: *to come round to our way of thinking* **3** to happen regularly: *Birthdays come round too quickly when one is older* **4** to become calmer after being angry: *Leave him alone and he'll soon come round*

¹**come to** *v prep* **1** to concern: *When it comes to politics I know nothing* **2** to reach all the way to: *The water came to my waist* **3** to amount to: *The bill came to £5.50* **4** to enter the mind of: *Suddenly the words came to me* **5 come to heel a** (of a dog) to follow closely just behind the owner **b** (of a person) to obey **6 come to oneself a** to regain self-control **b** *literature* to regain consciousness **come to pass** *usu. written* to happen

²**come to** *v adv* COME ROUND

¹**comfort** *n* **1** the state of being free from suffering **2** help, kindness, etc., given to a person who is suffering: *a word of comfort to a dying man* **3** a person or thing that gives strength or hope, or that makes grief or pain easier: *He was a great comfort to me when I was ill* – ~**less** *adj*

²**comfort** *v* to give comfort to – ~**er** *n*

comfortable *adj* **1** giving comfort: *a comfortable chair* **2** not experiencing too much pain, grief, anxiety, etc.: *My mother is comfortable after her operation* – **-bly** *adv*

¹**comic** *adj* intended to amuse

²**comic** *n* **1** *esp. spoken* a person who is amusing, esp. a professional comedian **2** a magazine for children containing stories told in drawings

comma *n* the mark (,) used in writing and printing, for showing a short pause

¹**command** *v* **1** to direct with the right to be obeyed; order: *Our leader is not fit to command us* **2** to deserve

and get: *This man is able to command respect* **3** *esp. written* to be in a position to use: *to command great wealth* **4** to be in a position to control: *This fort commands the valley*

²**command** *n* **1** an order: *All his commands were obeyed* **2** control: *The army is under the king's command* **3** a division of the army, air force, etc., under separate control: *pilots of the Southern Air Command* **4** a group of officers with the power to give orders: *the German High Command* **5** the ability to use: *a good command of French*

commando *n* **-dos** *or* **-does** a member of a small fighting force trained to make quick attacks into enemy areas

commence *v* **-menced, -mencing** *esp. written* to begin — ~**ment** *n*

¹**comment** *n* an opinion, explanation, or judgment: *What comments have you about my son's behaviour?*

²**comment** *v* to make a remark; give an opinion: *The king does not comment on election results*

commentary *n* **-ries** **1** a written collection of opinions, explanations, judgments, etc., on a book, event, person, etc. **2** a description spoken during an event, match, etc.

commentator *n* a broadcaster who gives a commentary

commerce *n* the buying and selling of goods, esp. between different countries

¹**commercial** *adj* **1** of, related to, or used in commerce **2 a** likely to produce profit: *Oil has been found in commercial quantities* **b** desiring to make a big profit without regard for other considerations: *This musician only makes commercial records* **3** (of television or radio) paid for by charges made for advertising — ~**ly** *adv*

²**commercial** *n* an advertisement on television or radio

commit *v* **-tt-** **1** to do (something bad or unlawful) **2** to order to be placed under the control of another, esp. in prison or in a mental hospital: *He was found guilty and committed* **3** to promise to a certain cause, position, opinion, or course of action: *The government can't commit any more money to the Health Service* **4 commit oneself** to make one's opinions known **5 commit to memory** *esp. written* to memorize

committee *n* a group chosen to do a particular job or for special duties

¹**common** *adj* **1** belonging to or shared equally by 2 or more; united: *a common desire to defeat the enemy* **2** found or happening often and in many places: *Rabbits and foxes are common in Britain* **3** ordinary: *the common man* **4** coarse in manner — ~**ness** *n*

²**common** *n* an area of open grassland which people are free to use: *the village common*

commonly *adv* usually

Common Market —also (*technical & usu. written*) **European Com-**

munity a West European political and economic organization to encourage trade and friendly relations between its member states

common sense *n* practical good sense and judgment

Commonwealth *n* **1** an organization of independent states formerly part of the British Empire, to encourage trade and friendly relations among its members **2** the official title of some countries or states: *The Commonwealth of Puerto Rico* **3** England from 1649 to 1660, esp. under Cromwell

communicate *v* **-cated, -cating 1** *esp. written* to make known **2** *esp. written* to pass on (a disease, heat, movement, etc.) **3** *esp. written* to share or exchange opinions, news, information, etc.: *Has the Minister communicated with the President?*

communication *n* **1** the exchange of information, news, or ideas **2** something communicated

communism *n* a classless social and political system in which the means of production are owned and controlled by the state or the people as a whole, and the goods and wealth produced shared according to the principle 'from each according to his ability, to each according to his needs' – **-ist** *n* – **-istic** *adj*

community *n* **-ties 1** a group of people living together and/or united by shared interests, religion, nationality, etc. **2** *technical* a group of plants or animals living together in the same surroundings, usu. dependent on each other **3** *technical* a group of men and/or women who lead a shared life of prayer and work according to a set of religious rules **4** the public: *A politician serves the community*

commuter *n* a person who makes a regular journey between home and work, esp. by train

companion *n* **1** a person who spends time with another **2** a person hired to help, live with, or travel with another esp. older or ill person **3** either of a matching pair of things **4** *technical* (used in some British titles of honour): *Benjamin Britten C.H. (Companion of Honour)*

companionship *n* the relationship of companions

company *n* **-nies 1** companionship: *I was grateful for Jean's company* **2** companions **3** a body of (usu. about 120) soldiers, usu. part of a larger group **4** the officers and men of a ship **5** a group of people combined together for business or trade; firm: *a bus company* **6** the members of such a group whose names do not appear in a firm's official name (in the phrase **and Company**): *Robinson and Company*

comparatively *adv* to a certain degree

compare *v* **-pared, -paring 1** to examine or judge (one thing) against another: *If you compare the handwritings you'll find many similarities* **2** to show the likeness of (one thing) with another: *It's* *impossible to compare Buckingham Palace and my house*

comparison *n* 1 comparing 2 a statement of the points of likeness and difference between 2 things 3 likeness: *There is no comparison between frozen and fresh food*

compartment *n* one of the parts into which an enclosed space is divided: *His maps are in a small compartment in the front of his car*

compass *n* 1 an instrument for showing direction, usu. with a freely-moving magnetic needle which always points to the north 2 any of several other instruments used for this purpose 3 a V-shaped instrument for drawing circles, measuring distances on maps, etc.

compel *v* -ll- to make do something by or as if by force: *The rain compelled us to stay indoors* −**compelling** *adj* −**compellingly** *adv*

compensate *v* -sated, -sating to provide with a balancing effect for some loss or something lacking; make a suitable payment for loss: *Many firms compensate their workers if they are hurt at work* − -**sation** *n* − -**satory** *adj*

compete *v* -peted, -peting to try to win something in competition: *John competed for a place in the final*

competition *n* 1 the act of competing:*He was in competition with 10 others for the job* 2 a test of strength, skill, etc.: *a horticultural competition* 3 the struggle to gain advan-tage, profit, or success: *keen competition for first place* 4 the person or people against whom one competes − -**itive** *adj* − -**itively** *adv* − -**itiveness** *n*

competitor *n* a person, team, firm, etc., competing with another or others

complain *v* to express feelings of annoyance, pain, unhappiness, grief, etc. −~**er** *n* −~**ing** *adj* −~**ingly** *adv*

complaint *n* 1 a statement expressing annoyance, dissatisfaction, grief, etc. 2 a cause or reason for complaining 3 something, such as an illness, causing pain or discomfort: *a chest complaint*

¹**complete** *adj* 1 whole and in order: *John's birthday did not seem complete without his father* 2 finished: *When will work on the railway be complete?* −~**ness** *n*

²**complete** *v* -pleted, -pleting to make whole or perfect: *I need one more stamp to complete my collection* −~**ly** *adv* − -**tion** *n*

complexion *n* the natural colour and appearance of the skin, esp. of the face

complicated *adj* 1 consisting of many connected parts: *a complicated machine* 2 difficult to understand or deal with −~**ly** *adv* −~**ness** *n*

compose *v* -posed, -posing 1 to make up; form: *The teacher asked what water was composed of* 2 to write (music, poetry, etc.) 3 to make calm, quiet, etc.: *Jean soon composed herself*

composition *n* **1** the act of putting together parts to form something **2** a result of this, such as a piece of music or art or a poem **3** a short piece of writing done as an educational exercise **4** something consisting of a mixture of various substances

¹**compound** *v* **1** to put together to form a whole: *He compounded various substances into an effective medicine* **2** to add to or increase (something bad): *Our mistakes were compounded by those of others*

²**compound** *adj* **1** (of a single whole) consisting of 2 or more separable parts, substances, etc. **2** (of a word or sentence) consisting of 2 or more main parts: *'Childcare' is a compound word consisting of 'child' and 'care'*

³**compound** *n* **1** a combination of 2 or more parts, substances, etc., esp. a chemical consisting of 2 different elements combined in such a way that it usu. has qualities different from those of the substances from which it is made **2** a compound word or sentence

comprehend *v esp. written* to understand – – -**hensibility**

¹**comprehensive** *adj* **1** thorough; broad **2** of or related to education in a comprehensive –~**ly**

²**comprehensive** *n* a school where pupils of all abilities and from all social classes are taught from the age of 11

¹**compromise** *n* **1** the act of settling a difference of opinion by each side yielding some of its demands and agreeing to some of the demands of the other **2** an agreement reached in this way: *a compromise between comfort and economy*

²**compromise** *v* -**mised**, -**mising** **1** to settle a difference of opinion by taking a middle course **2** to make open to dishonour, danger, etc.: *John felt compromised by his friendship with the criminal*

compulsory *adj* put into force by the law, orders, etc.: *Education is compulsory in Britain* – -**rily** *adv*

computer *n* an electric calculating machine that can store and recall information and make calculations at very high speeds

comrade *n* **1** a close companion, esp. one who shares difficult work or troubles **2** (esp. used as a title in Communist countries) a citizen; fellow member of a union, political party, etc.

conceal *v* to hide; keep from being known –~**ment** *n*

concede *v*-**ceded**, -**ceding** **1** to admit as true, just, or proper, often unwillingly **2** to give as a right; yield: *The champion conceded 10 points* **3** to end a game or match by admitting defeat

conceit *n* also **conceitedness**– too high an opinion of one's own abilities, value, etc. – ~ed *adj* – ~edly *adv*

conceive *v* -**ceived**, - **ceiving** 1 *technical* to become pregnant with: *Our first child was conceived in March* 2 to think of; consider: *Scientists first conceived the idea of the atomic bomb in the 1930s*

¹**concentrate** *v* -**trated**, -**trating** 1 to keep or direct (all one's thoughts, efforts, attention, etc.): *Concentrate on your work* 2 to come or bring together in or around one place: *The crowds concentrated in the centre of the town* 3 *technical* to strengthen by reducing the per cent of water in a solution

²**concentrate** *n* a concentrated form of something: *orange juice concentrate*

concentration *n technical* 1 the act of concentrating; close or complete attention 2 the measure of the amount of a substance contained in a liquid: *What is the concentration of salt in sea water?*

¹**concern** *v* 1 to be about: *This story concerns a good girl and a wicked fairy* 2 to be of importance or interest to; have an effect on 3 to make unhappy or troubled 4 to worry; interest: *A doctor should concern himself with your health*

²**concern** *n* 1 a matter of interest or importance to someone: *Your homework isn't my concern* 2 serious care or interest: *a nurse's concern for a sick man* 3 worry 4 a business – ~ed *adj* – ~edly *adv*

concerning *prep* about

concert *n* 1 a musical performance by a number of singers or musicians or both 2 **in concert** working together; in agreement

conclude *v* -**cluded**, -**cluding** 1 *esp. written* to come or bring to an end: *We concluded the meeting* 2 to arrange or settle 3 to come to believe after consideration of known facts – -**clusion** *n*

¹**concrete** *adj* 1 *technical* existing as something real or solid: *Beauty is not concrete but a window is* 2 particular; definite: *a concrete proposal* – ~**ly** *adv*

²**concrete** *n* a building material made by mixing sand, small stones, cement, and water

³**concrete** *v* -**creted**, -**creting** to cover with concrete

condemn *v* 1 to express strong disapproval of 2 to state the punishment for, esp. one of death or long imprisonment: *The prisoner was condemned to death* 3 to declare officially unfit for use: *This house is condemned* – ~**ation** *n*

¹**condition** *n* 1 a state of being or existence: *the condition of weightlessness* 2 general health or fitness: *to improve your condition by running* 3 a disease 4 something stated as necessary for something else: *She will join us on one condition: that we divide the profits*

²**condition** *v esp. technical* to train: *conditioned by upbringing*

¹**conduct** *n* 1 *esp. written* behaviour 2

direction of the course of (a business, activity, etc.)

²**conduct** *v* **1** *esp. written* to behave (oneself): *Your children conduct themselves well* **2** to direct the course of (a business, activity, etc.) **3** to lead or guide (a person, tour, etc.) **4** to stand before and direct the playing of (musicians or a musical work) **5** to act as the path for (electricity, heat, etc.): *Plastic won't conduct electricity*

conductor *n* **1** a person who directs the playing of a group of musicians **2** a person employed to collect fares on a public vehicle **3** a substance that conducts electricity, heat, etc.: *Wood is a poor conductor of heat*

cone *n* **1** a solid object with a circular base and a point at the top **2** a hollow or solid object shaped like this: *ice cream cones* **3** the fruit of a pine or fir, consisting of a number of seed - containing pieces, shaped like this **4** a type of cell in the area at the back of the eye that is sensitive esp. to the different colours in light

conference *n* a meeting held so that opinions on a subject, or subjects, can be exchanged: *A conference of states was held today*

confess *v* **1** to admit (a fault, crime, etc.) **2** *technical* to make (one's faults) known to a priest or God

confession *n* an example of admitting one's crimes, faults, etc. or a religious service at which this is done

confidence *n* **1** faith **2** belief in one's own or another's ability **3** some personal matter told secretly to a person

confident *adj* feeling or showing confidence −∼**ly** *adv*

confidential *adj* **1** to be kept secret: *confidential information* **2** trusted with private matters: *a confidential secretary* −∼**ity** *n* −∼**ly** *adv*

confine *v* **-fined, -fining 1** to enclose within limits **2** *medical* to keep (a woman about to give birth to a baby) in bed: *She was confined on the 20th and gave birth on the 21st*

confirm *v* **1** to support; make certain; give proof of **2** *technical* to admit to full membership of a church −**ation** *n*

confiscate *v* **-cated, -cating** to seize without payment in order to keep, destroy, give to others, etc.: *The teacher confiscated my radio* − −**cation** *n* − **-catory** *adj*

¹**conflict** *n* **1** a war; struggle **2** the meeting of opposing ideas or beliefs: *conflict between religion and science* **3** a disagreement

²**conflict** *v* to be in opposition

confuse *v* **-fused, -fusing 1** to make more difficult to understand **2** to mix up; mislead: *We tried to confuse the enemy* **3** to fail to tell the difference between: *I'm always confusing salt and sugar* −∼**d** *adj* −∼**dly** *adv* − **-fusing** *adj* − **-fusingly** *adv*

confusion *n* **1** disorder: *The room was in complete confusion* **2** the state of being confused

congratulate *v* **-lated, -lating 1** to speak to with praise and admiration for a happy event or something successfully done: *We congratulated him on passing the examination* **2** to have pleasure or pride in for something successfully done: *You can congratulate yourself on your performance* – **-lation** *n* – **-latory** *adj*

conjure *v* **-jured, -juring 1** to cause to appear by or as if by magic **2** to do clever tricks which seem magical, esp. by very quick movement of the hands – ~**r, -juror** *n*

connect *v* **1** to join; unite **2** (of trains, buses, etc.) to be so planned that passengers can change to another or from one to the other: *This flight connects with the New York one* – ~**ed** *adj* – ~**ion** *n*

conquer *v* **1** to take (land) by force **2** to defeat **3** to gain control over (something unfriendly or difficult): *Man has yet to conquer the stars* – ~**or** *n*

conquest *n* **1** the act of conquering: *This land is ours by right of conquest* **2** something conquered

conscience *n* an inner sense that judges one's actions , and makes one feel guilty, good, evil, etc.

conscious *adj* **1** able to understand what is happening: *He is hurt but still conscious* **2** knowing; understanding: *John isn't conscious of his bad manners* – ~**ly** *adv* – ~**ness** *n*

¹**consent** *v* to agree

²**consent** *n* agreement

consequence *n* **1** something that follows from an action or condition **2** *esp. written* importance: *Is it of any consequence to you?*

consequently *adv* as a result

conservation *n* **1** preservation **2** the controlled use of a limited supply of natural things, to prevent waste or loss

conservatism *n* **1** the belief that the established order of society should be kept as it is for as long as possible and then changed only slowly **2** dislike of change, esp. sudden change: *conservatism in matters of language* – **-tive** *adj, n* – **-tively** *adv*

consider *v* **1** to think about: *I'm considering changing my job* **2** to regard as: *I consider it a great honour*

considerable *adj* fairly large or great in amount, size, or degree – **-bly** *adv*

consideration *n* **1** careful thought: *We shall give your request careful consideration* **2** thoughtful attention to the wishes and feelings of others **3** a reason: *A number of considerations led me to refuse*

consistent *adj* continually keeping to the same principles or course of action; having a regular pattern – ~**ly** *adv*

consist of *v prep* to be made up of: *The United Kingdom consists of Great Britain and Northern Ireland*

conspiracy *n* **-cies** a secret plan, or the act of secretly planning, to do something unlawful

¹**constant** *adj* **1** unchanging: *a con-*

stant speed **2** happening all the time: *constant argument* **3** *literature* faithful: *a constant friend* −∼**ly** *adv*

²**constant** *n technical* something, esp. a number or quantity, that never varies

constitute *v* **-tuted, -tuting** *esp. written* to make up: *7 days constitute a week*

constitution *n* **1** the body of laws and principles which govern a country **2** the general condition of a person's body or mind: *He has a weak constitution* **3** the way in which something is made up **4** constituting

construct *v* **1** to make by putting together or combining parts: *to construct a bridge / a difficult sentence to construct* **2** to draw (a geometrical figure) using suitable instruments −∼**ion** *n* −∼**or** *n* −∼**ional** *adj*

constructive *adj* helping to improve or develop something −∼**ly** *adv* −∼**ness** *n*

consult *v* to go to for information, advice, etc. −∼**ation** *n* −∼**ative** *adj*

¹**contact** *n* **1** the condition of meeting, touching or coming together with **2** relationship **3** an electrical part that can be moved to touch or not touch a like part, thus completing or interrupting an electrical circuit

²**contact** *v* to get in touch with by message, telephone, etc.

contain *v* **1** to have within itself: *Beer contains alcohol* **2** to enclose: *How*

big is the angle contained by these 2 sides?

container *n* **1** a box, barrel, bottle, etc., for holding something **2** a very large usu. metal box in which goods are packed for easy transport

¹**contemporary** *adj* **1** of or belonging to the same time **2** of or belonging to the present: *contemporary furniture*

²**contemporary** *n* **-ries** a person born or living at the same time as another

¹**content** *adj* satisfied; happy −∼**ment** *n* −∼**ed** *adj*

²**content** *v* to make (a person or oneself) happy or satisfied

³**content** *n* happiness; satisfaction

⁴**content** *n* **1** the subject matter of a book, paper, etc. **2** the amount of a substance contained in something: *a high food content*

¹**contest** *v esp. written* to compete for; fight (for) −∼**ant** *n*

²**contest** *n* **1** a struggle or fight **2** a competition: *a beauty contest*

continent *n* any of the 7 main masses of land on the earth: *Africa is a continent* −∼**al** *adj*

continual *adj* repeated; frequent: *He hates these continual arguments* −∼**ly** *adv*

continue *v* **-ued, -uing** to go or cause to go on: *The fighting continued for a week. / The road continues for 5 miles* − **-uation** *n*

continuous *adj* continuing without interruption −∼**ly** *adv*

contraception *n* birth control; the act

or practice of preventing sex from resulting in the birth of a child, and/or the methods for so doing

¹contract *n* **1** a formal agreement, having the force of law, between 2 or more people or groups **2** a signed paper on which the conditions of such an agreement are written **3** *technical* (in the card game bridge) an agreement between partners to try and win a stated number of tricks

²contract *v* **1** to arrange by formal agreement **2** to get (something unwanted): *He contracted a fever* **3** to make or become smaller in size: *Metal contracts as it cools*

contradict *v* **1** to declare to be wrong or untruthful **2** (of a statement, fact, etc.) to be opposite in nature or character to: *Your actions contradict your principles* −~**ion** *n* −~**ory** *adj*

¹contrary *n* **-ries** the opposite

²contrary *adj* difficult to handle or work with; unreasonably keeping to one's own opinions or plans: *Mrs Smith is too contrary to make friends easily* − **-arily** *adv* − **-ariness** *n*

³contrary *adj* completely different; wholly opposed: *contrary opinions*

¹contrast *n* **1** the act of contrasting **2** (a) difference or unlikeness, esp. of colour or brightness

²contrast *v* **1** to compare so that differences are made clear: *The writer contrasts good with evil* **2** to show a difference when compared: *Your*

actions contrast with? your principles

contribute *v* **-uted, -uting 1** to join with others in giving or supplying: *Allan didn't contribute to Jane's present when she left the office* **2** to supply (a written article) to a newspaper, magazine, etc. − **-bution** *n*

¹control *v* **-ll- 1** to have power over **2** to have directing influence over ; direct; fix the time, amount, degree, or rate of: *The pressure of steam is controlled by this button* **3** to test by comparison with a chosen standard: *a controlled experiment* −~**ler** *n*

²control *n* **1** the power to control or influence **2** guidance; the fixing of the time, amount, degree, or rate of an activity; act of controlling **3** *technical* a standard against which a scientific study can be judged

controversy *n* **-sies** (an) argument about something over which there is much disagreement − **-sial** *adj* − **-sially** *adv*

convenience *n* **1** fitness; suitableness: *We bought this house for its convenience* **2** a suitable time: *Please come at your convenience* **3** an apparatus, machine, service, etc., which gives comfort or advantage to its user **4** personal comfort or advantage

convenient *adj* **1** suited to one's needs: *a convenient time* **2** near: *Our house is convenient for the shops* −~**ly** *adv*

conventional *adj* **1** following

accepted practices and customs sometimes too closely **2** (of a weapon) not atomic – ~**ly** *adv*

conversation *n* (an) informal talk in which people exchange news, feelings, etc. – ~**al** *adj* – ~**ally** *adv* – ~**alist** *n*

¹convert *v* **1** to persuade a person to accept a religion, political belief, etc. **2** to change to or into another substance or state, or from one use or purpose to another: *Coal can be converted to gas by burning* **3** (in rugby and American football) to kick (a ball) over the bar of the goalposts – **-version** *n*

²convert *n* a person who has been persuaded to accept a religion, political belief, etc.

convey *v* **-veyed, -veying 1** to take or carry from one place to another: *Wires convey electricity* **2** to make known: *Words convey meaning* – ~**er**, ~**or** *n*

¹convict *v* to give a decision that (someone) is guilty of a crime, esp. in a court of law: *He was convicted of murder*

²convict *n* a person who has been found guilty of a crime and sent to prison, esp. for a long time

convince *v* **-vinced, -vincing** to cause to believe or feel certain – ~**d** *adj*

¹cook *n* a person who prepares and cooks food

²cook *v* to prepare (food) for eating by using heat

cooker *n* **1** an apparatus on or in which food is cooked **2** a fruit intended to be cooked: *These apples are cookers*

¹cool *adj* **1** neither warm nor cold; pleasantly cold **2** calm; unexcited **3** lacking warm feelings; not as friendly as usual – ~**ish** *adj* – ~**ly** *adv* – ~**ness** *n*

²cool *v* to make or become cool – ~**er** *n*

³cool *n* **1** something neither warm nor cold: *the cool of the evening* **2** *sl* calmness of temper: *Try and keep your cool*

cooperate, co-operate *v* **-rated, -rating** to work or act together for a purpose – **-rator** *n*

cooperation, co-op- *n* **1** the act of working together for a purpose **2** willingness to help – **-tive** *adj* – **-tively** *adv*

¹copper *n* **1** a soft reddish metal that is an element, is easily shaped, and allows heat and electricity to pass through it easily **2** *esp. spoken* a coin of low value made of this or of bronze **3** a metal vessel, esp. one in which clothes are boiled – ~**y** *adj*

²copper *n, adj* (having) a reddish-brown colour

¹copy *n* **1** a thing made to be exactly like another **2** a single example of a magazine, book, etc.: *a copy of 'The Times'* **3** *technical* material ready to be printed

²copy *v* **-ied, -ying 1** to make a copy of **2** to follow as a pattern: *Jean always copies the way I dress*

cord *n* **1** (a length of) thick string or

thin rope **2** also **chord**– a part of the body, such as a nerve or number of bones joined together, that is like a length of this in appearance: *the vocal cords* **3** cloth, such as corduroy, with raised lines on the surface

¹**core** *n* **1** the most important or central part of anything: *an apple core* **2 a** a bar of magnetic metal used in an electric motor **b** a tiny ring-shaped piece of magnetic metal (e.g.ferrite) used in computer memories

²**core** *v* **cored, coring** to remove the core from (a fruit) –~**r** *n*

¹**cork** *n* **1** the bark of the cork oak found in Southern Europe and North Africa **2** a round piece of this material (or a substitute) used to seal a bottle

²**cork** *v* to close (the neck of a bottle or other object) tightly with a cork

¹**corn** *n* **1** (the seed of) any of various types of grain plants, esp. wheat **2** also **maize, Indian corn** – *esp US & Australian* (the seed of) a type of tall plant grown for its ears of yellow seeds: sweet corn

²**corn** *v* to preserve (meat) in salt or salty water: *corned beef*

³**corn** *n* a painful area of thick hard skin on the foot, usu. on or near a toe

¹**corner** *n* **1** (the inside or outside of) the point at which 2 lines, surfaces, or edges meet: *the corners of the page* **2** the place where 2 roads or paths meet: *the corner of Smith Street and Beach Road* **3** (in football) a kick taken from the corner of the field: *He scored from a corner*

²**corner** *v* **1** to force into a difficult or threatening position: *The dog cornered the rat* **2** to gain control of (the buying, selling, or production of goods) **3** to turn a corner: *My car corners well*

¹**corporal** *adj esp. written* of, on, or related to the body: *corporal punishment*

²**corporal** *n* a noncommissioned officer of low rank in the army or British air force

corporation *n* **1** a group of people elected to govern a town **2** a body of people permitted by law to act as a single person, esp. for purposes of business: *John works for a large American chemical corporation*

corpse *n* a dead body

¹**correct** *v* **1** to make right; mark the mistakes in **2** to cure of a fault, esp. by punishing: *Mary hates to correct her children* –~**ion** *n* –~**ive** *adj, n*

²**correct** *adj* right: *a correct answer* –~**ly** *adv* –~**ness** *n*

correspond *v* **1** to match: *These goods don't correspond with my order* **2** to exchange letters regularly –~**ence** *n* –~**ent** *adj*

corridor *n* a passage, esp. enclosed

¹**corrupt** *v* to change from good to bad –~**ible** *adj* –~**ibility** *n*

²**corrupt** *adj* **1** immoral; wicked **2** dishonest; open to bribery: *a corrupt judge* –~**ly** *adv* –~**ness** *n*

¹cosmetic *n* a beauty preparation such as a face-cream, body-powder, etc.

²cosmetic *adj* of, related to, or causing increased beauty – ~**ian** *n*

cosmos *n* the universe considered as an ordered system

¹cost *n* **1** the price of making or producing something **2** the amount paid or asked for goods or services **3** something needed, given, or lost, to obtain something: *He saved his daughters at the cost of his own life*

²cost *v* **cost, costing 1** to have (an amount of money) as a price **2** to cause (loss or disadvantage) to: *Your crime will cost you your life*

³cost *v* to calculate the price to be charged for: *The job was costed by the builder at about £150*

costly *adj* **-lier,-liest 1** expensive **2** won at a great loss: *the costliest war in history* – **-liness** *n*

costume *n* **1** the clothes typical of a certain period, country, rank, etc., esp. as worn by an actor or actress **2** *becoming rare* a woman's suit consisting of a matching skirt and short coat – **-mier** *n*

cot *n* a small bed for a young child, usu. with movable sides so that the child cannot fall out

cottage *n* a small house, esp. in the country

cotton *n* **1** a tall plant grown in warm areas for the soft white hair that surrounds its seeds **2** this soft white hair used to make thread, cloth, cotton wool, etc. **3** thread or cloth made from this: *a cotton dress*

¹couch *v* to express in a certain way: *The refusal was couched in friendly language*

²couch *n* **1** a long piece of furniture, usu. with a back and arms, on which more than one person may sit **2** a bed-like piece of furniture on which a person lies to be examined by a doctor

¹cough *v* **1** to push air out from the throat suddenly, with a rough explosive noise, esp. because of discomfort in the lungs or throat during a cold or other infection **2** to clear from the throat by doing this: *She coughed up the bone* **3** to make a sound like a cough

²cough *n* **1** a condition marked by repeated coughing **2** an act or sound of coughing: *She gave a nervous cough*

could *v* *negative short form* **couldn't 1** *past tense of* can: *I could run faster then* **2** (used to say that something would or might be possible): *I could come tomorrow if you like* **3** (in requests) would: *Could you tell me the time, please?* **4** should: *You could at least have met me at the station!* **5** might: *I wrote down the number so that I could remember it*

¹council *n* a group of people appointed or elected to make laws, rules, or decisions or to give advice

²council *adj* of, owned by, or related to a district, borough, or county council

¹counsel *n* **1** advice: *Listen to an old*

man's counsel **2** *law* a lawyer acting for someone in court

²**counsel** *v* **-ll-** *esp. written* to advise

counsellor *n* an adviser

¹**count** *v* **1** to say the numbers in order **2** to name one by one in order to find the whole number in a collection; add up: *Count these apples* **3** to consider: *Count yourself lucky to be alive* **4** to have value or importance: *Skill counts for a lot in this game* –~**able** *adj*

²**count** *n* **1** an act of counting; total reached by counting **2** one of a number of crimes of which a person is accused: *found guilty on all counts*

³**count** *n* (the title of) a European nobleman with the rank of earl

¹**counter** *n* **1** a narrow table or flat surface on which goods are shown or at which people in a shop, bank, etc., are served **2 under the counter** privately, secretly, and often unlawfully

²**counter** *n* **1** a person or machine that counts, esp. an electrical apparatus that records the number of times an event happens **2** a small flat object used in games instead of money

countess *n* **1** (the title of) the wife of an earl or count **2** a noblewoman who holds the rank of earl or count

countless *adj* too many to be counted

count on –also **count upon** *v prep* **1** to depend on; trust **2** to expect; take into account

country *n* **-tries 1** a nation or state with its land or population **2** the people of a nation or state: *The country is opposed to war* **3** land with a special nature: *mining country* **4** the land outside cities or towns; land used for farming or left unused: *a day in the country* / *a country house*

county *n* **-ties** a large area divided from others for purposes of local government

¹**couple** *v* **-pled, -pling 1** to join together **2** (of animals) to mate

²**couple** *n* **1** 2 things of the same kind: *a couple of socks* **2** a man and a woman together, esp. a husband and wife **3** *esp. spoken* a few; several: *I'll have a couple of drinks*

coupon *n* **1** a ticket that shows the right of the holder to receive some payment, service, etc. **2** a printed form on which goods can be ordered, an enquiry made, a competition entered, etc.

courage *n* **1** the ability to control fear in the face of danger, hardship, pain, misfortune, etc.; bravery **2 have the courage of one's convictions** to be brave enough to do or say what one thinks is right **3 take one's courage in both hands** to gather enough courage to do something one is afraid of

courageous *adj* brave; fearless: *It was courageous of you to save the drowning man* –~**ly** *adv* –~**ness** *n*

¹**course** *n* **1** movement from one point to another; continuous movement in space or time: *During the course*

of the flight drinks will be served **2** the path over which something moves: *The ship was blown off course* **3** an area of land or water on which a race is held or certain types of sport played **4** a plan of action **5** a set of lessons on one subject or a group of subjects **6** a set of events of a planned or fixed number, as of medical treatment **7** any of the several parts of a meal **8 a matter of course** that which one expects to happen **9 in due course** without too much delay **10 of course** certainly; naturally; as everyone knows or must agree **11 run/take its/their course** (of an illness, state of affairs, number of events, etc.) to continue to its natural end **12 stay the course** to continue something through to the end in spite of difficulties

²**course** *v* **coursed**, **coursing** to flow or move rapidly: *Tears coursed down his cheeks*

¹**court** *n* **1** a room or building in which law cases can be heard and judged **2** the judge, law officials, and people attending, gathered together to hear and judge a law case **3** the officials, noblemen, servants, etc., who attend a king or queen **4** an area, or part of an area, specially prepared and marked for various ball games, such as tennis **5** also **courtyard** –an open space wholly or partly enclosed by buildings

²**court** *v* **1** to pay attention to **a** an influential person whose favour one seeks **b** a woman a man hopes to marry **2** to try to obtain (a desired state): *The teacher courted popularity by giving his pupils very little work* **3** to risk (something bad), often foolishly or without enough thought: *to court danger/defeat*

courteous *adj* polite and kind **–~ly** *adv* **–~ness** *n*

courtesy *n* **-sies 1** polite behaviour; good manners **2** a polite or kind action or expression **3 by courtesy of** because of the kindness of or permission given by (someone) usu. without payment

cousin *n* **1** the child of one's uncle or aunt **2** a person or thing of a closely related type

¹**cover** *v* **1** to place or spread something upon, over, or in front of (something) **2** to hide; conceal **3** to be or lie on the surface of; spread over: *Dust covered the furniture* **4** to have as a size: *The town covers 5 square miles* **5** to travel (a distance): *I want to cover 100 miles by dark* **6** to watch for possible trouble: *The police are covering all roads out of town* **7** to report the details of as for a newspaper: *I want a reporter to cover the trial* **8** to be enough money for: *Will £10 cover the cost of a new skirt?* **9** to protect as from loss; insure **10** to protect (a person) by aiming a gun at an enemy: *You run out the back while I cover you from the window* **11** to keep a gun aimed at (someone): *The police had the criminal covered* **12** (of a gun, castle, etc.) to command; control:

This fort covers the harbour entrance **13** to act in place of (someone who is absent): *Will you cover for John today, Jean?* **14** to include; consist of; take into account: *The talk covered the history of medicine*

²**cover** *n* **1** anything that protects by covering, esp. a piece of material **2** a lid; top **3** the outer front or back page of a magazine or book **4** a cloth used on a bed to make it warmer: *Do you need some more covers on your bed?* **5** shelter or protection: *The flat land gave the soldiers no cover* **6** insurance against loss, damage, etc. **7** something that hides or keeps something secret: *This business is a cover for unlawful activity* **8** **under separate cover** in a separate envelope

¹**cow** *n* **1** the fully-grown female form of cattle, elephants, and certain other large animals **2** *offensive sl* a woman

²**cow** *v* to conquer or bring under control by violence or threats: *The natives were cowed by the army*

coward *n* a person unable to face danger, pain, or hardship because he lacks courage —~**ly** *adj* —~**ice** *n* —~**liness** *n*

cowboy *n* **1** a man, usu. working on horseback, employed to look after cattle, esp. in the western US and Canada **2** *sl* a wild irresponsible fellow

¹**crab** *n* a type of edible sea animal with a broad roundish flattened shell-covered body and 5 pairs of legs

²**crab** *v* **-bb-** *esp. spoken* to complain in a bad-tempered way

¹**crack** *v* **1** to make or cause to make a sudden explosive sound: *The whip cracked* **2** to break or cause to break, esp. after a blow, without dividing into separate parts: *The vase cracked when dropped* **3** to break or cause to break open **4** to change or cause to change suddenly or sharply in direction, level, loudness, etc.: *His voice cracked with grief* **5** *esp. spoken* to tell (a joke) in a clever or amusing way **6** to lose control or effectiveness: *Is John about to crack up?* **7** to strike or cause to strike with a sudden blow **8** to discover the secret of: *to crack a code* **9** *esp. spoken* to open for drinking **10** *technical* to separate into simpler compounds: *Oil is cracked by heating under pressure* **11** **cracked up to be** *esp. spoken* believed to be **12** **get cracking** also **get weaving** —*esp. spoken* to get down to work without delay

²**crack** *n* **1** a loud explosive sound: *a crack of thunder* **2** a narrow space: *The door opened just a crack* **3** a split caused by a sharp blow **4** a sudden sharp blow **5** *esp. spoken* an attempt: *He made a crack at writing* **6** a clever quick forceful joke, reply, or remark **7** a sudden change in the level or loudness of the voice **8** **at the crack of dawn** at the first light of day

cracker *n* **1** a small thin unsweetened

biscuit **2** a paper toy which bangs when its ends are pulled, used esp. at Christmas

¹**crackle** *v* **-led, -ling** to make or cause to make small sharp sudden repeated sounds: *The fire crackled*

²**crackle** *n* the noise of repeated small sharp sounds

¹**cradle** *n* **1** a small (rocking) bed for a baby **2** the place where something begins: *Greece was the cradle of democracy* **3** any of various frameworks used for supporting or holding something

²**cradle** *v* **-dled, -dling** to hold gently

¹**craft** *n* **1** a job or trade needing skill, esp. with one's hands **2** all the members of a particular trade or profession as a group

²**craft** *n* **craft** a small boat, aircraft, or spacecraft

crafty *adj* **-ier, -iest** cleverly deceitful –**craftily** *adv* –**craftiness** *n*

¹**cramp** *n* severe pain from the sudden tightening of a muscle

²**cramp** *n* a frame or tool with a movable part which can be screwed tightly in place, used for holding things together

³**cramp** *v* **1** to fasten tightly with a cramp **2** to prevent the natural growth or development of

¹**crane** *n* **1** a machine for lifting and moving heavy objects **2** a type of large tall fish-eating bird with very long legs, beak, and neck

²**crane** *v* **craned, craning** to stretch out (one's neck) esp. to get a better view

¹**crash** *v* **1** to have or cause to have a sudden, violent, and noisy accident **2** to move violently and noisily: *The elephant crashed through the forest* **3** to make or cause to make a sudden loud noise **4** (in the world of business and money matters) to fail suddenly **5** *sl* to spend the night in a particular place; sleep –**crash** *adv*

²**crash** *n* **1** a sudden loud noise **2** a violent vehicle accident **3** a sudden severe business failure

¹**crawl** *v* **1** to move slowly with the body close to the ground, or on the hands and knees **2** to go very slowly: *The traffic crawled along* **3** to be completely covered by worms, insects, or other such animals or to have a sensation of being covered by them: *That apple is crawling with worms* **4** *esp. spoken* to try to win the favour of someone of higher rank by being too nice to them

²**crawl** *n* **1** a very slow movement **2** also **Australian crawl** – a rapid way of swimming while lying on one's stomach, moving first one arm and then the other over one's head, and kicking the feet up and down

crayon *n,v* (to draw with) a stick of coloured wax or chalk

crazy *adj esp. spoken* **-zier, -ziest 1** mad; foolish **2** very fond (of) or interested (in): *She's crazy about dancing* – **-zily** *adv* – **-ziness** *n*

creak *v,n* (to make) the sound of a badly-oiled door when it opens

—**creaky** *adj* —**creakily** *adv* —**creakiness** *n*

¹cream *n* **1** the edible thick fatty slightly yellowish liquid that separates from and rises to the top of milk when left to stand **2** food made of or containing a sweet soft smooth substance, like this **3** a preparation made thick and soft like cream, esp. used for softening and improving the skin or as a medicine: *face cream* **4** the best part of anything: *the cream of society* —**creamy** *adj* —**creaminess** *n*

²cream *adj, n* (having) the yellowish-white colour of cream

³cream *v* **1** to beat (food) until creamy **2** to prepare (a vegetable, meat, etc.) with cream or a creamy liquid: *creamed potatoes*

¹crease *n* **1** a line made on cloth, paper, etc., by crushing, folding, or pressing **2** a line marked on the ground to show special areas or positions in certain games

²crease *v* **creased, creasing** to make a line or lines appear on (a garment, paper, cloth, etc.) by folding, crushing, or pressing: *Don't sit for too long or you'll crease your new dress*

create *v* **-ated, -ating 1** to cause (something new) to exist; produce (something new): *We've created a beautiful new house from an old ruin* **2** to appoint to a special rank or position: *He was created Prince of Wales* **3** *esp. spoken* to be noisily angry: *Will you stop creating and go to sleep?*

creation *n* **1** the act of creating **2** something produced by man's invention or imagination: *an artist's creation* **3** the universe, world, and all living things

creature *n* **1** an animal of any kind **2** (*used in expressions of feeling*) a person: *She was a poor creature* **3** a strange or terrible being: *creatures from outer space*

¹credit *n* **1** belief; trust; faith: *This story is gaining credit* **2** public attention; approval: *I got no credit for my work* **3** a cause of honour: *You're a credit to your team* **4** a system of buying goods or services when they are wanted and paying for them later **5** a period of time during which the full price of an article bought under this system must be paid: *six months' credit* **6** the quality of being likely to repay debts and be honest with money: *His credit is good* **7** (the amount of) money in a person's account, as at a bank **8** (esp. in the US) a measure of a student's work, esp. at a university, often equal to one hour of class time a week

²credit *v* to believe

¹creep *v* **crept, creeping 1** to move slowly and quietly (with the body close to the ground) **2** to grow along the ground or a surface: *a creeping plant* **3** to have an unpleasant sensation, as of worms, insects, etc., moving over the skin: *His ghost story made my flesh creep*

²**creep** *n* **1** *sl* an unpleasant person who tries to win the favour of a person of higher rank, esp. by praising insincerely **2** the slow movement of loose soil, rocks, etc.

cremate *v* **-mated, -mating** to burn (a dead person) at a special funeral ceremony −**cremation** *n*

crest *n* **1** a showy growth of feathers on top of a bird's head **2** the top of something, esp. of a mountain, hill, or wave **3** a special ornamental picture used as a personal mark on letters or envelopes −~**ed** *adj adj*

¹**crew** *n* **1** all the people working on a ship, plane, etc. (except the officers) **2** a group of people working together: *a stage crew*

²**crew** *v* to act as the crew

¹**cricket** *n* a type of small brown insect, the male of which makes loud short noises by rubbing its leathery wings together

²**cricket** *n* an outdoor game played with a ball, bat, and wickets, by 2 teams of 11 players each −~**er** *n*

cried *past tense and past part. of* CRY

cries *3rd person sing. pres. tense of* CRY

crime *n* **1** an offence which is punishable by law; unlawful activity in general **2** *esp. spoken* a shame: *It's a crime the way he treats her*

criminal *n* a person who carries out a crime or crimes −**criminal** *adj* −~**ly** *adv*

¹**crimson** *adj, n* (having) a deep slightly purplish red colour

²**crimson** *v* to become or make crimson

¹**cripple** *n* a person partly or wholly unable to use one or more of his limbs, esp. the legs

²**cripple** *v* **-pled, -pling 1** to hurt or wound in such a way that use of one or more of the limbs is made difficult or impossible **2** *esp. spoken* to make useless; weaken seriously

crisis *n* **-ses 1** the turning point in a serious illness, at which there is a sudden change for better or worse **2** a turning point in the course of anything: *a political crisis*

¹**crisp** *adj* **1** hard; dry; easily broken **2** firm; fresh: *a crisp apple* **3** (of style, manners, etc.) quick; clear **4** (of the air, weather, etc.) cold; dry; fresh −~**ly** *adv* −~**ness** *n*

²**crisp** *v* to make or become crisp, esp. by cooking or heating −~**y** *adj* −~**iness** *n*

³**crisp** −also **potato crisp** *n* a thin piece of potato cooked in very hot fat, dried, and usu. sold in packets

critic *n* **1** a person skilled in forming and expressing judgments about the good and bad qualities of something, esp. art, music, etc. **2** a person who finds fault with someone or something

critical *adj* **1** finding fault; judging severely **2** marked by careful attention and judgment: *a critical thinker* **3** very serious: *a critical illness* **4** of or related to the work of a critic **5** *technical* (in science) of, being, or related to a fixed value as of pressure, temperature, etc. at which a substance changes suddenly – ~ly *adv*

criticism *n* **1** the act of forming and expressing judgments about the good or bad qualities of anything, esp. artistic work **2** such a judgment **3** unfavourable judgment or opinions; disapproval

criticize, -ise *v* **-cized, -cizing 1** to find fault with; judge severely: *The teacher criticized my answer* **2** to make judgments about the good and bad points of: *Would you like to read and criticize my new book?*

croak *v,n* **1** (to make) a deep low noise such as a frog makes **2** (to speak with) a rough voice as if one has a sore throat

crockery *n* cups, plates, pots, etc., esp. made from baked clay

crocodile *n* **-diles** *or* **-dile 1** any of several types of large reptile that live on land and in lakes and rivers in the hot wet parts of the world, the skin of which is used as leather **2** a line of people, esp. schoolchildren, walking in pairs

crooked *adj* **1** not straight; bent **2** *esp. spoken* dishonest – ~ly *adv* – ~ness *n*

¹**crop** *n* **1** a plant or plant product such as grain, fruit, or vegetables grown or produced by a farmer **2** the amount of such a product produced and gathered in a single season or place: *a good crop* **3** a baglike part of a bird's throat where food is stored and partly digested **4**

also **hunting crop, riding crop** – a short riding whip consisting of a short fold of leather fastened to a handle **5** the handle of a whip **6** a very short haircut

²**crop** *v* **-pp- 1** (of an animal) to bite off and eat the tops of (grass, plants, etc.) **2** to cut (a person's hair or a horse's tail) short **3** to plant with a crop **4** to bear a crop: *The beans have cropped well this year*

¹**cross** *n* **1** an upright post with a shorter bar crossing it near the top **a** on which Christ and others were nailed by their hands and feet and left to die in ancient times **b** which is worn round the neck as a sign of Christian faith **c** which is built on graves or public places to remind people of the dead **2** any of various representations of this, used for ornament, in art, heraldry, etc. **3** an ornament of this shape worn as an honour; a medal, esp. for military bravery **4** this shape as the sign of the Christian faith or religion **5** an example of sorrow or suffering as a test of one's patience or goodness: *Everyone has his own cross to bear* **6** a figure or mark formed by one straight line crossing another, as X **7** an animal or plant that is a mixture of breeds: *a* **tiglon** *is a cross between a lion and a tiger* **8** a combination of 2 different things **9** an act of crossing the ball in soccer **10 on the cross** diagonally; from corner to corner

²**cross** *v* **1** to go, pass, or reach across

2 to lie or pass across each other: *Our letters crossed in the post* **3** to place or fold across each other: *Jean sat with her legs crossed* **4** to oppose (someone or his plans, wishes, etc.) **5** to draw a line across **6** to draw 2 lines across (a cheque) to show that it must be paid into a bank account **7** to make a movement of the hand forming a cross on (oneself) as a religious act **8** to cause (an animal or plant) to breed with one of another kind **9** (in soccer) to kick (the ball) across the field towards the centre, esp. towards the goal

³**cross** *adj* angry; bad-tempered –~**ly** *adv* –~**ness** *n*

crossroads *n* **crossroads 1** a place where 2 or more roads cross **2** a point at which an important decision must be taken

cross-section *n* **1** (a drawing of) a surface made by cutting across something, esp. at right angles to its length **2** a typical or representative example of the whole: *a cross-section of British society*

crouch *v* to lower the body close to the ground by bending the knees and back –**crouch** *n*

¹**crow** *n* **1** any of various types of large shiny black birds with a loud hoarse cry **2 as the crow flies** in a straight line

²**crow** *v,n* **1** (to make) the loud high cry of a cock **2** (to make) wordless sounds of happiness or pleasure (esp. of a baby)

¹**crowd** *v* to fill or come together in large numbers: *Shoppers crowded into the store*

²**crowd** *n* **1** a large number of people gathered together **2** a particular social group **3** people in general

crowded *adj* **1** completely full of people **2** uncomfortably close together –~**ness** *n*

¹**crown** *n* **1** an ornamental head covering made of gold with jewels in, worn by a king or queen as a sign of royal power **2** a circle of flowers or leaves worn on the head as a sign of victory, honour, or rank **3** a decoration of this shape used in art, ornaments, coat of arms, etc. **4** the governing power of a kingdom that has limited the personal political power of its king or queen: *Crown land actually belongs to the state* **5** the rank of king or queen **6** the top or highest part of anything, as of the head, hat, mountain, etc. **7** a British coin worth 25 pence, used in former times as money but now made only on ceremonial occasions to be kept not spent **8** the part of the tooth which can be seen **9** the most perfect point of anything

²**crown** *v* **1** to give royal power to by solemnly placing a crown on the head of **2** to place a circle of flowers or leaves on someone's head as a sign of victory **3** to complete worthily: *Success crowned his efforts* **4** *esp. spoken* to hit (someone) on the head

crucial *adj* of deciding importance –~**ly** *adv*

cruel *adj* 1 liking to cause pain or suffering ; unkind; merciless 2 painful; causing suffering: *a cruel wind* –~**ly** *adv* –~**ness** *n*

cruelty *n* -**ties** also **cruelness** – the state or quality of being cruel

¹**cruise** *v* **cruised, cruising** 1 to sail in an unhurried way searching for enemy ships or for pleasure 2 (of a car, plane, etc.) to move at a practical rather than high speed

²**cruise** *n* a sea voyage for pleasure

crumb *n* 1 a very small piece of dry food, esp. bread or cake 2 a small amount: *crumbs of knowledge*

¹**crumble** *v* -**bled, -bling** 1 to break into very small pieces 2 to decay; come to ruin: *Her hopes crumbled to nothing*

²**crumble** *n* 1 a cooked dish of sweetened fruit covered with a mixture of flour, fat, and sugar 2 the mixture of flour, fat, and sugar cooked in this dish

crumple *v* -**pled, -pling** 1 to make or become full of creases by pressing, crushing, etc. 2 *esp. spoken* to fall down; lose strength: *The enemy crumpled under our attacks*

¹**crush** *v* 1 to press with great force so as to break, hurt, or destroy the natural shape or condition 2 to press tightly: *The people crushed through the gates* 3 to destroy completely, esp. by using force: *to crush all opposition* 4 to crumple

²**crush** *n* 1 uncomfortable pressure caused by a great crowd of people 2 a drink made by crushing the juice from fruit 3 *esp. spoken* a strong foolish and short-lived liking or love for someone

crust *n* 1 the hard usu. brown outer surface of baked bread 2 a piece of bread with this on one side 3 the baked pastry on a pie 4 a hard outer covering (as of earth or snow)

¹**cry** *v* **cried, crying,** *3rd person sing. pres. tense* **cries** 1 to produce tears from the eyes with or without sounds expressing grief, sorrow, sadness, etc. 2 to make loud sounds expressing fear, sadness, or some other feeling: *The boy cried out with pain* 3 (of certain animals and birds) to make one's natural sound 4 to make known by shouting out

²**cry** *n* **cries** 1 any loud sound, sometimes expressing fear, pain, etc. 2 a loud call; shout 3 a period of crying 4 a general public demand or complaint: *a cry for lower taxes* 5 a call to action: *a battle cry* 6 the natural cry of certain animals or birds 7 **in full cry a** (of a group of dogs) making loud noises as they hunt an animal **b** (of a person) eagerly demanding or attacking

¹**cuckoo** *n* -**oos** 1 a type of grey European bird that lays its eggs in other birds' nests 2 the call of this bird

²**cuckoo** *adj sl* stupid; mad; foolish

culprit *n* the person guilty or believed to be guilty of a crime or offence

cultivate *v* -**vated, -vating** 1 to prepare (land) for the growing of crops 2 to plant, grow, and raise (a crop) **3** to improve or develop by careful attention, training, or study: *to cultivate a love of art* **4** to encourage the growth of friendship with or the good will of

culture *n* **1** artistic and other activity of the mind and the works produced by this **2** a state of high development in art and thought existing in a society and represented at various levels in its members: *a man of little culture* **3** the arts, customs, beliefs, and all the other products of human thought made by a people at a particular time **4** development and improvement of the mind or body by education or training **5** the practice of raising animals and growing plants or crops **6** (a group of bacteria produced by) the practice of growing bacteria for scientific or medical use − **-ral** *adj* − **-rally** *adv*

cunning *adj, n* (showing or having) cleverness in deceiving −~**ly** *adv*

¹**cup** *n* **1** a small round container, usu. with a handle, from which liquids are drunk **2** also **cupful** − the amount held by one cup **3** a specially shaped ornamental vessel, usu. made of gold or silver, given as a prize in a competition **4** a specially prepared drink of wine or other alcoholic drink: *cider cup*

²**cup** *v* **-pp-** to form (esp. the hands) into the shape of a cup

cupboard *n* a set of shelves enclosed by doors, where articles may be stored

¹**cure** *v* **cured, curing 1** to bring health to (a person) in place of disease or illness, esp. by medical treatment: *This medicine should cure you* **2** to make (a disease, illness, etc.) go away, esp. by medical treatment **3** to remove (something bad): *Government action to cure unemployment* **4** to preserve (food, skin, tobacco, etc.) by drying, hanging in smoke, covering with salt, etc.

²**cure** *n* **1** a course of medical treatment **2** a drug or medicine that cures an illness, disease, etc.: *a cure for the common cold* **3** something that cures something bad − **-rable** *adj*

curiosity *n* **-ties 1** the desire to know or learn **2** a strange, interesting, or rare object, custom, etc.

curious *adj* **1** eager to know or learn **2** having or showing too much interest in other people's affairs **3** odd; strange; peculiar: *a curious state of affairs* **4** interesting because rare; unusual −~**ly** *adv*

¹**curl** *v* **1** to twist into or form a curl or curls: *I'm going to have my hair curled* **2** to move in a curve or spiral: *Smoke curled above the fire*

²**curl** *n* **1** a small lock of twisted hair **2** something with the shape of the lines on a screw **3** the state of having this shape or being in masses of this type

curly *adj* **-lier, -liest** having curls −**curliness** *n*

currant *n* 1 a small dried seedless grape 2 any of various types of small bushes or the small fruits in bunches on them: *a blackcurrant bush*

currency *n* -cies 1 common use; general acceptance 2 the particular type of money in use in a country: *German currency*

¹**current** *adj* 1 belonging to the present time: *current fashions* 2 commonly accepted: *This word is no longer in current use* −~**ly** *adv*

²**current** *n* 1 a continuously moving mass of liquid or gas, esp. flowing through slower-moving liquid or gas 2 flow of electricity 3 a general tendency: *the current of public opinion*

¹**curse** *n* 1 a word or sentence asking God, heaven, a spirit, etc., to bring down evil on someone or something 2 the evil called down in this way: *Our tribe is under a curse* 3 a cause of misfortune, evil, etc.: *Foxes can be a curse to farmers* 4 a word or words used in swearing

²**curse** *v* **cursed, cursing** 1 to call down God's anger, evil, etc., upon (someone) 2 to swear (at)

¹**curtain** *n* 1 a piece of hanging cloth that can be drawn to cover a window or door or to divide a room 2 a sheet of heavy material drawn across or lowered in order to conceal or reveal a stage 3 something that covers, hides, etc.: *a curtain of smoke*

²**curtain** *v* to provide (a window, house, etc.) with a curtain

curtsy, curtsey *v* -sied, -sying; -seyed, -seying (of a woman or girl) to bend the knees and lower the head and shoulders as an act of respect −**curtsy, curtsey** *n*

curve *v* **curved, curving** to bend round with no sharp angles −**curve** *n*

¹**cushion** *n* 1 a bag filled with a soft substance on which a person can lie, sit, etc. 2 something like this in shape or purpose: *Hovercrafts ride on a cushion of air*

²**cushion** *v* 1 to lessen the force of: *Nothing can cushion the blow* 2 to protect from hardship or sudden change: *The princess led a cushioned life* 3 to provide with a cushion or cushions

custom *n* 1 an established social practice 2 regular support given to a shop by its customers 3 the habitual practice of a person: *His custom was to get up early and have a cold bath*

customer *n* 1 a person who buys from a shop or trader 2 *sl* a person one has to deal with: *an odd customer*

customs *n* 1 taxes paid on goods entering or (less often) leaving a country 2 the government organization to collect these taxes 3 a place where travellers' belongings are searched when leaving or entering a country

¹**cut** *v* **cut, cutting** 1 to make an opening in, separate, or remove (something) with a sharp edge or

instrument: *to cut a cake* **2** to make with a sharp instrument: *to cut a hole* **3** to shorten with a sharp instrument: *Your nails need cutting* **4** to grow (a tooth) **5** to interrupt (a supply of gas, electricity, etc.): *The water was cut for 2 hours yesterday* **6** to make (esp. a public service) smaller, less frequent, etc.: *cutting train services* **7** to remove, so as to improve: *All sex and violence were cut from the picture before it was shown* **8** to hurt the feelings of: *His cruel remark cut me deeply* **9** to be absent on purpose from: *to cut school* **10** to bring down a tree with an axe, saw, etc. **11** to gather in (corn, wheat, etc.) **12** to divide (a pile of playing cards) in 2 before dealing **13** to cross: *The line AC is cut by line PQ at point Z* **14** to make (a ball) spin by striking: *cut the ball to the right* **15** to stop filming: *'Cut!' shouted the director* **16** to walk across rather than round (a corner) **17** to make (a record) **18 cut and run** *sl* to escape by running

²**cut** *n* **1** the result of or something obtained by cutting **2** a reduction: *cuts in government spending* **3** the style in which clothes are made: *I don't like the cut of his new suit* **4** a stroke with a sword, knife, etc. **5** an act of removing a part: *Before this play is broadcast several cuts must be made* **6** a share: *The government takes a 50% cut of oil profits* **7** a quick sharp stroke in cricket,

tennis, etc. **8 a cut above** of higher quality or rank than

cutlery *n* knives and other cutting instruments, esp. those used when eating

cut-price *adj* cheap; reduced

¹**cycle** *n* **1** a number of related events happening in a regularly repeated order: *the cycle of the seasons* **2** the time needed for this to be completed: *a 50-second cycle* **3** a bicycle or motorcycle

²**cycle** **cycled, cycling** to bicycle – -**list** *n*

cynic *n* *sometimes offensive* a person who thinks that all men act in their own interests, who sees little good in anything, and who shows this by making unkind remarks –~**al** *adj* –~**ism** *n* –~**ally** *adv*

dad –also **daddy** *n* *esp. spoken* a father

daffodil *n* a type of yellow flower of early spring

dagger *n* **1** a short pointed knife used as a weapon **2** also **obelisk**– a sign (+) used in printing to draw attention to something

¹**daily** *adj, adv* (happening, appearing, etc.) once every day

²**daily** *n* -**lies** **1** a newspaper sold every day except Sunday and perhaps Saturday **2** also **daily help** – *esp. spoken* a woman servant who comes in to clean a house daily

¹**dainty** *n* -**ties** an especially nice piece of food, usu. small and sweet, like a little cake

²**dainty** *adj* -**tier, -tiest** **1** small and delicate **2** not easy to please, esp.

about food: *a dainty eater* – **-tily**
adv – **-tiness** *n*

dairy *n* **-ies** **1** (on a farm) a place
where milk is kept and butter and
cheese are made **2** a farm where
milk, butter, and cheese are produced **3** a shop where milk, butter,
etc. are sold – ~**ing** *n*

daisy *n* **-sies** a very common type of
small wild or garden flower, yellow
in the centre and white round it

¹dam *n* the mother of a 4-legged
animal

²dam *n* a wall or bank built to keep
back water

³dam *v* **-mm-** **1** to build a dam across:
to dam the river **2** to keep back by
means of a dam: *to dam up the
water*

¹damage *n* **1** harm; loss: *The storm
caused great damage* **2** *sl* the price
(esp. in the phrase **What's the
damage?**)

²damage *v* **-aged, -aging** to cause
damage to

¹damn *v* **1** (esp. of God) to send to
punishment without end after
death **2** to declare to be very bad:
The newspapers all damned the play

²damn –also **damnation** *interj sl* (an
expression of anger)

¹damp –also **dampness** *n* wetness

²damp *v* to make damp

³damp *adj* rather wet: *a damp room*
– ~**ly** *adv*

¹dance *v* **danced, dancing** **1** to move
to music **2** to move quickly up
and down: *The waves danced in the
sunlight* –**dancer** *n*

²dance *n* **1** an act of dancing **2** (the
name of) a set of movements per-
formed to music, usu. including leg
movements: *The waltz is a beautiful
dance* **3** a party for dancing: *to go
to a dance* **4** a piece of music for
dancing: *The band played a slow
dance*

dandruff *n* a common disease in
which bits of dead skin form among
the hair

danger *n* **1** the possibility of harm:
The sign says 'Danger! Falling rocks'
2 a cause of danger: *the dangers of
smoking* – ~**ous** *adj* – ~**ously** *adv*

dangle *v* **-gled, -gling** to hang or swing
loosely: *he dangled the keys on his
chain*

¹dare *v* **dared, daring** *pres. tense negative short form* **daren't** **1** to be
brave or rude enough (to): *I don't
know how you dare to say such
things!* **2** to be brave enough to
face: *He dared many dangers* **3** to
challenge: *He dared me to jump*

²dare *n* a statement that someone is
not brave enough to do something

daring *adj* **1** very brave **2** unusual;
new: *a daring idea* **3** shocking: *a
daring film* – ~**ly** *adv* – ~**daring** *n*

¹dark *adj* **1** without light **2** tending
towards black **3** evil **4** sad;
unfavourable: *look on the dark side*
5 secret; hidden: *He kept his plans
dark* – ~**ly** *adv* – ~**ness** *n*

²dark *n* **1** the absence of light: *to see
in the dark* **2** a dark colour

darken *v* to make or become dark

darling *n, adj* (a person) who is very much loved

¹**dart** *n* **1** a small sharp-pointed object to be thrown, shot, etc., as a weapon or in games **2** a quick movement in a direction: *He made a dart for the door* **3** a fold made to make a garment fit better, and held together by sewing

²**dart** *v* **1** to move suddenly and quickly **2** to throw out suddenly: *He darted an angry look at his enemy*

¹**dash** *v* **1** to run quickly: *I must dash to catch a train* **2** to strike with great force: *The waves dashed the boat against the rocks* **3** to break by throwing with great force **4** to destroy or ruin (hopes, spirits, etc.): *The angry letter dashed my hopes* **5** damn: *Dash it all*

²**dash** *n* **1** a sudden quick run **2** (the sound of) liquid striking: *the dash of the waves against the ship* **3** a small amount of something mixed or added: *a dash of pepper* **4** a mark (–) used in writing and printing **5** a long sound used in sending messages by telegraph: *The message consisted of dots and dashes* **6 cut a dash** to have a strong effect that makes people remember your appearance and style

data *n* facts; information

¹**date** *n* a small brown sweet fruit with a long stone or the palm tree which produces this fruit

²**date** *n* **1** time shown by the number of the day, the month, and the year **2** a period in history: *This Greek dish is of very early date* **3** an arrangement to meet at a particular time and place **4 out of date** old fashioned

³**date** *v* **dated, dating** to know the date of: *I can't date that old house exactly* **2** to write the date on: *Please date your letters* **3** to seem no longer in fashion: *This music is beginning to date* –**datable, dateable** *adj*

daughter *n* **1** someone's female child **2** something thought of as a daughter: *French is a daughter language of Latin* –~**ly** *adj*

dawdle *v* -**dled, -dling** *esp. spoken* to spend time doing nothing; move very slowly –~**r** *n*

¹**dawn** *v* (of the day, morning, etc.) to begin to grow light

²**dawn** *n* **1** the time of day when light first appears before the sun rises **2** the beginning or first appearance: *the dawn of civilization*

day *n* **days 1** a period of light: *I can see by day, but not by night* **2** a period of 24 hours **3** a period of time: *In my day things were different* **4** a struggle or competition: *We've won the day* **5 call it a day** to finish working for the day **6 pass the time of day** to have a short conversation

daze *v* **dazed, dazing** to make unable to think or feel clearly: *After the accident John was dazed* –**daze** *n* –~**dly** *adv*

dazzle *v* -**zled, -zling 1** to make unable to see by throwing a strong light in the eyes **2** to cause wonder to: *She* *was dazzled by her success* **–dazzle** *n*

¹**dead** *adj* **1** no longer alive or without life **2** unable to feel: *It's so cold that my fingers feel dead* **3** not in use: *a dead language* **4** without the necessary power, movement, or activity: *The television's been dead since the storm* **5** very tired **6 a** (of a ball) out of play **b** (of a ball) unable to bounce **c** (of ground where ball games are played) on which the ball does not roll fast **7** (of sounds or colours) dull **8** complete: *a dead stop* **–~ness** *n*

²**dead** *n* **in the dead of** in the quietest period of

³**dead** *adv* completely: *She stopped dead. / dead certain* **2** directly: *dead ahead*

deadline *n* a date or time before which something must be done

¹**deadly** *adj* **-lier, -liest 1** likely to cause death: *a deadly disease* **2** aiming to destroy: *a deadly enemy* **3** highly effective: *a deadly argument against his plan* **4** very great; total: *deadly seriousness* **5** like death in dullness: *a deadly conversation* **6** making it impossible for the spirit or soul to advance further (esp. in the phrase **the seven deadly sins**) **– -liness** *n*

²**deadly** *adv* **1** suggesting death: *deadly pale* **2** very: *deadly serious*

deaf *adj* **1** unable to hear **2** unwilling to listen: *deaf to all my prayers* **–~ness** *n*

¹**deal** *n* **1** a quantity or degree: *a great*

deal of support **2** the giving out of cards to players in a game

²**deal** *v* **dealt, dealing 1** to give as one's share of something: *It's my turn to deal the cards* **2** to strike (in the phrase **deal someone a blow**)

³**deal** *n* **1** an act of dealing **2** *esp. spoken* treatment received: *a raw deal* **3** an arrangement to the advantage of both sides: *to do a deal*

dealer *n* **1** a person who deals cards **2** a person in a business: *a used-car dealer*

dealing *n* method of business; manner of behaving: *plain honest dealing*

deal with *v prep* **1** to do business with: *I've dealt with this shop for 20 years* **2** to take action about: *Children are tiring to deal with* **3** to be concerned with: *This book deals with the troubles in Ireland*

¹**dear** *adj* **1** much loved **2** (used at the beginning of a letter) **3** precious: *Life is dear to him* **4** costly **–~ness** *n*

²**dear** *n* a person who is loved

dearly *adv* **1** with much good feeling: *I should dearly love to go to Scotland* **2** at a high price: *He paid dearly for his experience*

death *n* **1** the end of life **2** the cause of loss of life or destruction:*If you go out you'll catch your death of cold*

¹**debate** *n* a meeting in which a question is talked over by people or groups, each expressing a different point of view: *a debate in Parliament*

²**debate** *v* **debated, debating 1** to

argue about **2** to consider the arguments for and against: *I debated the idea in my mind* – **-table** *adj* –~**r** *n*

debt *n* **1** something owed: *a debt of £10* **2** the state of owing: *in debt* **3 debt of honour** a debt that a gentleman will pay although the law does not force him to

debut *n French* **1** a first public appearance: *The singer made his debut as Mozart's Don Giovanni* **2** a formal entrance into society by a young woman

decade *n* a period of 10 years

decay *v* **decayed, decaying 1** to go or cause to go bad: *Sugar can decay the teeth* **2** to lose health, power, etc. **–decay**

deceit *n* **1** dishonesty **2** something that deceives; a trick

deceitful *adj* dishonest –~**ly** *adv* –~**ness** *n*

deceive *v* **deceived, deceiving** to cause (someone) to accept as true or good what is false or bad **–deceiver** *n*

December *n* the 12th and last month of the year

decent *adj* **1** fitting; proper: *decent behaviour* **2** rather good: *quite a decent meal* **–decency** *n* –~**ly** *adv*

decide *v* **decided, deciding 1** to arrive at an answer or make a choice about: *to decide where to go* / *They decided to fly* **2** to bring to a clear end: *One blow decided the fight*

¹decimal *adj* having to do with the number 10 –~**ly** *adv*

²decimal –also **decimal fraction**– *n* a number like .5, .375, .06, etc.

decision *n* **1** a choice or choosing: *Whose decision was it?* **2** the quality of being able to make choices with firmness

deck *n* **1** a floor built across a ship **2** a surface like this, such as the floor of a bus **3** *esp US* a pack of cards

declaration *n* **1** the act of declaring: *a declaration of war* **2** something declared: *a written declaration of all the goods you bought abroad*

declare *v* **declared, declaring 1** to make known publicly or officially: *Jones was declared the winner* **2** to state with great force **3** to make a full statement of (property for which money may be owed to the government): *Have you anything to declare?* **4** (of the captain of a cricket team) to end the innings before all the team are out **5** (in the game of bridge) to say which type of card will be trumps **–declarable** *adj* **–declaratory** *adj*

¹decline *v* **declined, declining 1** to slope downwards **2** to move from a better to a worse position: *The old man's health declined rapidly* **3** to refuse, usu. politely **4** (in grammar) to give the different forms of (a noun, pronoun, or adjective)

²decline *n* a period of deterioration

decorate *v* **-rated, -rating 1** to provide with something ornamental:*streets decorated with flags* **2** to paint the walls or outside of a house **3** to give (someone) an official mark of honour, such as a medal – **-ation** *n*

¹**decrease** *v* **decreased, decreasing** to make or become less: *Our sales are decreasing* –opposite **increase**

²**decrease** *n* **1** decreasing or being decreased **2** the amount by which something decreases

dedicated *adj* (esp. of people) very interested in or working hard for an idea, purpose, etc. –~**ly** *adv*

deed *n* **1** something done on purpose: *good deeds* **2** *law* a paper that proves and records an agreement

¹**deep** *adj* **1** going far down or in **2** not near the surface **3** wide: *a deep border* **4** going a stated amount in an understood direction: *cars parked 3 deep* **5** difficult to understand or get to know: *deep scientific principles / a deep person* **6** mysterious and strange: *a deep dark secret* **7** able to understand things thoroughly: *a deep mind* **8** strong; difficult to change: *deep feelings* **9** (of a colour) strong and full but not bright **10** (of a sound) low –~**ly** *adv* –~**ness** *n*-

²**deep** *adv* **1** to a great depth **2** late: *deep into the night*

deep freeze *n* a freezer

deer *n* **deer** any of several types of grass-eating fast 4-footed animal, of which the males often have wide branching horns

¹**defeat** *v* **1** to beat; win a victory over **2** to cause to fail: *It was lack of money that defeated their plan*

²**defeat** *n* defeating or being defeated

¹**defect** *n* a fault: *defects in a machine* –~**ive** *n*

²**defect** *v* to desert a political party, group, or movement, esp. in order to join an opposing one –~**or** *n* –~**ion** *n*

defence *n* **1** defending: *the defence of one's country* **2** means used in defending: *Mountains are a defence against the wind* **3** a speech or arguments defending oneself, esp. in a court of law **4** the lawyers who defend someone in court **5** the part of a team that tries to defend its own goal –~**less** *adj*

defend *v* **1** to protect against attack **2** to play at (a position) so as to keep an opponent from winning **3** to show the rightness of, by argument **4** to act as a lawyer for **5** to oppose attack: *He's better at defending than attacking*

defensive *adj* **1** that defends: *defensive weapons* **2** seeming to expect attack: *I wonder why he's so defensive about his wife?* –~**ly** *adv* –~**ness** *n*

defiance *n* **1** defiant behaviour **2** **in defiance of** in open disregard for

defiant *adj* fearlessly refusing to obey –~**ly** *adv*

define *v* **defined, defining** **1** to give the meaning(s) of (a word or idea) **2** to explain the qualities, nature, etc., of: *to define the position of the government* **3** to show the limits of: *a clearly defined shape outside the window*

definite *adj* **1** having clear limits **2** undoubted: *a definite success* **3** firm and willing to act: *definite behaviour*

definitely *adv* 1 in a definite way 2 without doubt: *He is definitely coming*

defy *v* **defied, defying** *3rd person sing. pres. tense* **defies** 1 to show no fear of nor respect for: *to defy the law* 2 to dare; challenge: *I defy you to give me one good reason* 3 to remain unreachable by: *It defies description*

degree *n* 1 a step or stage in a set rising in order from lowest to highest: *getting better by degrees* 2 *technical* any of various measures: *Water freezes at 32 degrees Fahrenheit (32°F) or 0 degrees Centigrade (0°C). / an angle of 90 degrees (90°)* 3 a title given by a university 4 *esp. old use* a rank in society: *a lady of high degree*

¹**delay** *n* 1 delaying or being delayed 2 an example of being delayed: *delays on roads because of heavy traffic*

²**delay** *v* **delayed, delaying** 1 to put off until later 2 to make late 3 to act slowly

delete *v* **deleted, deleting** to cut out (esp. something written): *Delete his name from the list* – **-tion** *n*

¹**deliberate** *adj* 1 carefully planned: *taking deliberate action* 2 on purpose: *That shooting was not accidental, but deliberate* 3 (of speech, thought, or movement) slow; careful – ~**ly** *adv* – ~**ness** *n*

²**deliberate** *v* **-rated, -rating** to consider (difficult questions) carefully,

often in meetings with other people – **-ative** *adj*

delicate *adj* 1 needing careful handling: *a delicate piece of china* 2 needing tact: *a delicate subject* 3 easily yielding to illness: *a delicate child* 4 very pleasing but not strong: *delicate colours* – ~**ly** *adv*

delicious *adj* pleasing; delightful – ~**ly** *adv* – ~**ness** *n*

¹**delight** *n* 1 a high degree of pleasure 2 something that gives great pleasure

²**delight** *v* 1 to give great pleasure 2 to take great pleasure in doing something: *She delights in cooking lovely meals*

delightful *adj* highly pleasing – ~**ly** *adv*

deliver *v* 1 to set free 2 to hand over 3 to help in the birth of 4 to say; read aloud 5 to send (something aimed or guided) to the intended place: *deliver a blow*

¹**deluge** *n* 1 a great flood 2 very heavy rain

²**deluge** *v* **deluged, deluging** 1 to cover with a great flood 2 to pour out a great flood of things over (someone): *The minister was deluged with questions*

delusion *n* 1 deceiving or being deceived 2 a false belief – **-sive** *adj*

¹**demand** *n* 1 a claim 2 the desire for goods or services: *Oil is in great demand these days*

²**demand** *v* 1 to claim as if by right: *I demand my money!* 2 to need

urgently: *This work demands your attention*

democracy *n* **-cies 1** government by the people or their representatives **2** a country governed by its people or their representatives **3** social equality

democratic *adj* **1** of, related to, or favouring democracy **2** favouring and practising social equality $-\sim$**ally** *adv* – **-ratization** *n*

demolish *v* to destroy; tear down – **-ition** *n*

demonstrate *v* **-strated, -strating 1** to show clearly **2** to prove or make clear, esp. by reasoning **3** to show the value or use of, esp. to a possible buyer **4** to arrange or take part in a public march or show of strong feeling – **-tion** *n*

den *n* **1** the home of a wild animal **2** a centre of secret or unlawful activity

denial *n* **1** the act or a case of denying **2** a statement denying something

denied *past tense and past part. of* DENY

denies *3rd person sing. pres. tense of* DENY

dense *adj* **1** closely packed together: *a dense crowd* **2** stupid $-\sim$**ly** *adv* $-\sim$**ness** *n*

¹**dent** *n* a hollow place on a surface made by a blow or pressure: *a dent in one's car*

²**dent** *v* to show or cause to show one or more dents

dental *adj* of or related to teeth

dentist –also (*esp. written*) **dental sur-**

geon *n* a person professionally trained to treat teeth $-\sim$**ry** *n*

deny *v* **denied, denying,** *3rd person sing. pres. tense* **denies 1** to declare untrue; refuse to believe **2** to disclaim connection with: *He denied his country* **3** to refuse to give or allow: *He denied his children love* **4 deny oneself** to go without pleasure

depart *v* **1** *esp. written* to leave; go away **2** *polite* also **depart this life**– to die $-\sim$**ed** *adj* $-\sim$**ure** *n*

department *n* **1** any important division of a government, business, school, etc. **2** (in various countries) a political division rather like a British county **3** *esp. spoken* an area of activity or responsibility: *Advertising is my department* $-\sim$**al** *adj*

dependence *n* **1** the quality or state of being dependent, esp. being influenced or supported by a person or thing **2** trust **3** a need; reliance: *dependence on sleeping pills*

dependent *adj* that depends on

depend on –also **depend upon** *v prep* **1** to trust; rely on: *My children depend on me* **2** to vary according to: *Our picnic depends on the weather*

¹**deposit** *v* **1** to put down or let fall: *Deposit the sand here* **2** to place (money) in a bank, safe, etc

²**deposit** *n* **1** something deposited: *gold deposits* **2** a part payment of money, made so that the seller will not sell the goods to anyone else **3** an act of depositing

depress *v* **1** to push down; lower **2** to

cause to sink to a lower level or position: *Does mass unemployment depress wages?* **3** to lessen the activity or strength of **4** to sadden; discourage **–depressing** *adj* **–depressingly** *adv* **–depressed** *adj*

depression *n* **1** an act of pressing down or the state of being pressed down **2** a part of a surface lower than the other parts **3** an area where the air pressure is low in the centre and higher towards the outside: *A depression usually brings bad weather* **4** sadness and hopelessness **5** a period of reduced business activity and high unemployment

depth *n* **1** deepness: *The lake's depth is 30 feet* **2 out of/beyond one's depth** beyond one's ability to understand **3 in depth** done with great thoroughness

deputy *n* **-ties 1** a person appointed to act for another **2** a member of parliament in certain countries, such as France **3** (in the US) a person appointed to help a sheriff

derelict *adj* left to decay

derive from *v prep* **derived, deriving from 1** to obtain from **2** to come from **–derivable** *adj* **–derivation** *n*

descend *v* to come, fall, or sink from a higher to a lower level; go down: *in descending order of importance*

descendant *n* a person or other living thing that has another as grandfather or grandmother, great-grandfather, etc.

descent *n* **1** a downward movement; going down **2** family origins: *She is*

of German descent **3** a sudden attack or visit

describe *v* **described, describing 1** to give a picture of in words **2** to draw or move in the shape of: *to describe a circle*

description *n* **1** the act of describing **2** something that describes: *a good description of life* **3-** a sort or kind (esp. in the phrases **of that description; of every description; of all descriptions**) – **-tive** *adj* – **-tively** *adv* – **-tiveness** *n*

¹**desert** *n* a large, sometimes sandy, piece of land where there is very little rain and less plant life than elsewhere

²**desert** *v* **1** to leave empty or leave completely **2** to leave in a difficult position: *My friends have deserted me!* **3** to leave (military service) without permission **–deserter** *n* **–desertion** *n*

deserve *v* **deserved, deserving** to be worthy of; be fit for: *The best player deserved to win* **–deservedly** *adv* **–deserving** *adj*

¹**design** *v* **1** to draw or plan out **2** to intend; mean: *a book designed for colleges* **–~er** *n*

²**design** *n* **1** a plan, drawing, or pattern of how to do or make something **2** the arrangement of parts of a product: *This machine is of bad design* **3** purpose; intention; plot

desirable *adj* **1** worth having, doing, or desiring: *For doctors it is desirable to know about medicine* **2** causing desire, esp. sexual desire – **-bility** *n* – **-bly** *adv*

¹desire *v* **desired, desiring 1** *esp. written* to wish or want very much **2** to wish to have sexual relations with –**desirous** *adj*

²desire *n* **1** a strong wish, often for sexual relations: *his desire for Cleopatra / my desire to return* **2** something or someone desired

desk *n* a table, often with drawers, at which one reads, writes, etc.

¹despair *v* to lose all hope

²despair *n* **1** complete lack or loss of hope **2** the cause of this feeling (esp. in the phrase **the despair of**)

despatch *n, v* dispatch

desperate *adj* **1** ready for any wild act: *a desperate criminal* **2** wild or dangerous; done as a last attempt **3** (of a state of affairs) very difficult and dangerous –**~ly** *adv* – **-ation** *n*

despise *v* **despised, despising** to regard as worthless, bad, etc.

dessert *n* the sweet dish in a meal served after the main dish

destination *n* a place to which someone or something is going; end of a journey

destiny *n* **-nies 1** fate; that which must happen **2** that which seems to decide man's fate, thought of as a person or a force

destroy *v* **destroyed, destroying 1** to tear down or apart; ruin; wreck **2** to kill (esp. a tame animal)

destruction *n* **1** the act of destroying or state of being destroyed **2** that which destroys: *Pride was her destruction*

¹detail *n* a small point or fact or group of such points: *an eye for detail*

²detail *v* **1** to appoint to some special duty: *He detailed them to look for water* **2** to give a lot of facts about

detain *v* **1** to keep (a person) from leaving **2** to delay

detect *v* to find out; notice: *I detected anger in his voice* –**detector** *n*

detective *n* a policeman who hunts out information on crimes

detention *n* **1** the act of detaining or state of being detained **2** being kept in school after school hours as a punishment

deter *v* **-rr-** to discourage or prevent from acting (as by threats)

deteriorate *v* **-rated, -rating** to make or become worse – **-ration** *n*

determination *n* **1** firm intention **2** strong will; firmness **3** the act of determining

determine *v* **-mined, -mining 1** to form a firm intention in the mind: *He determined to go* **2** to decide **3** to limit; control **4** to find out and fix exactly: *to determine the moon's position*

deterrent *n, adj* (something) that deters – **-rence** *n*

detest *v* to dislike strongly –**~able** *adj* –**~ably** *adv* –**~ation** *n*

develop *v* **1** to make or become larger, more complete, more active, etc.: *to develop a business/one's mind/an illness* **2** to think out or present fully: *to develop an idea* **3** (in photography) to make or become visible on a film or photographic paper **4** to bring out the economic possibilities of (land, water, etc.)

development *n* **1** the act of developing or the state of being developed **2** the amount or result of such developing: *the great development of his chest muscles* **3** a developed piece of land, esp. one with houses **4** a new event or piece of news

device *n* **1** an instrument; invention; tool **2** something (such as a special phrase) which is intended to produce a particular artistic effect in a work of literature **3** a drawing, esp. one used by a noble family as its special sign **4** a plan or trick **5 leave someone to his own devices** to leave (someone) alone, without help

Devil *n* the strongest evil spirit; Satan

devil *n* **1** an evil spirit or person **2** a high-spirited person, ready for adventure **3** *esp. spoken* (in expressions of strong feeling) fellow; man; boy: *You lucky devil!* **4** *sl* (used to give force to various expressions): *What the devil happened?* **5 go to the devil** to be ruined **6 Go to the devil!** *sl* Go away at once! **7 the very devil** very difficult or painful – ~**ish** *adj* – ~**ishness** *n*

devoted *adj* loyal, loving, or fond (of) – ~**ly** *adv*

devote to *v prep* **devoted, devoting to** to give completely to: *He has devoted his life to helping the blind*

devour *v* **1** to eat up quickly and

hungrily **2** (of a feeling) to possess (a person) completely

dew *n* small drops of water which form on cold surfaces overnight – **dewy** *adj* – **dewily** *adv* – **dewiness** *n*

diabolic – also **diabolical** *adj* of or coming from the devil; wicked or cruel – ~**ally** *adv*

diagonal *n, adj* **1** (in the direction of) a straight line joining 2 opposite corners of a 4-sided flat figure **2** (any straight line) which runs in a sloping direction – ~**ly** *adv*

diagram *n* a plan, figure, or drawing, often showing an arrangement of parts – ~**matic** *adj*

¹**dial** *n* **1** the face of an instrument such as a clock showing time, speed, etc. **2** the plate on the front of a radio, used to find a particular station **3** the wheel on a telephone with holes for the fingers, which is moved round when one makes a telephone call

²**dial** *v* **-ll-** to call (a number, person, or place) on a telephone with a dial

dialect *n* a separate form of a language, spoken in one part of a country – ~**al** *adj*

dialogue *n* a conversation, usu. in a book or between people with different views

¹**diamond** *n* **1** a very hard, valuable jewel, usually colourless **2** an ornament set with one or more of these jewels: *Shall I wear my diamonds tonight?* **3** a figure with 4 straight sides of equal length that stands on

one of its points **4** a playing card with such figures in red **5** (in baseball) **a** the area of the field inside the 4 bases **b** the whole playing field **6 rough diamond** a kind person with rough manners

²**diamond** *adj* indicating the 60th yearly return of some important date: *diamond jubilee*

diary *n* **-ries 1** (a book containing) a daily record of a person's life **2** a book with separate spaces for each day of the year, in which one writes down things to be done

¹**dice** *n* **dice 1** a small 6-sided block, with a different number of spots from 1–6 on the various sides **2** any game of chance played with these

²**dice** *v* **diced, dicing 1** to play dice (with someone, for money, etc.) **2** to cut (food) into small square pieces: *diced carrots* **3 dice with death** to take great risks

¹**dictate** *v* **-tated, -tating 1** to say (words) for someone else to write down: *She dictated a letter* **2** to state (demands, conditions, etc.) with the power to enforce – **-tation** *n*:*The teacher gave us a French dictation*

²**dictate** *n* an order which should be obeyed

dictator *n* a ruler who has complete power – ~**ial** *adj*

dictionary *n* **-ries 1** a book that lists words in alphabetical order, with their meanings **2** a book like this that gives, for each word, one or more words in another language with approximately the same meaning: *a German-English dictionary* **3** a book like this with words from a special subject

did *1st, 2nd, and 3rd person sing. and pl. past tense of* DO

¹**die** *v* **died, dying 1** to stop living **2** to cease: *The day is dying in the west* **3** (of knowledge, ideas, etc.) to become lost and forgotten

²**die** *n* **1** a metal block used for pressing or cutting metal, plastic, etc., into shape **2** an instrument used for making a screw or bolt **3** *old or US sing. of* dice

diesel engine –also **diesel** *n* an engine in which heavy oil is exploded by hot air

¹**diet** *n* **1** a person's usual food and drink **2** a limited list of food, eaten for one's health, to lose weight, etc. (often in the phrases **be/go on a diet**) –**dietary** *adj*

²**diet** *v* to live on a diet

difference *n* **1** a way of being unlike **2** an amount of unlikeness: *The difference between 5 and 11 is 6* **3** a disagreement **4 split the difference** to agree on an amount halfway between

different *adj* **1** unlike; not of the same kind **2** separate; other: *They go to different schools* **3** *esp. spoken* unusual – ~**ly** *adv*

difficult *adj* **1** not easy; hard to do, understand, etc. **2** (of people) hard to get along with; not easily pleased

difficulty *n* **1** the quality of being

difficult; trouble **2** something difficult; a trouble: *money difficulties*

¹**dig** *v* **dug** , **digging 1** to break up and move (earth): *dig a garden* **2** to make (a hole) by taking away earth **3** to bring to light; uncover **4** *sl* to like or understand: *Do you dig jazz?* **5 dig someone in the ribs** to touch someone with one's elbow, as to share a joke −∼**ger** *n*

²**dig** *n esp. spoken* **1** a quick push: *Give him a dig!* **2 a** an ancient place being uncovered by archaeologists **b** the digging up of such a place

¹**digest** *n* a greatly shortened written account; summary

²**digest** *v* **1** to change into a form that the body can use: *Sugar digests easily* **2** to think over and understand −∼**ible** *adj* −∼**ibility** *n*

digestion *n* power to digest food: *a weak digestion*

digit *n* **1** any numeral from 0 to 9 **2** a finger or toe −∼**al** *adj*

dignify *v* **-fied**, **-fying** to give dignity to − **-fied** *adj*

dignity *n* **-ties 1** true nobleness of character **2** calm and formal behaviour **3** a high rank, office, or title **4 beneath one's dignity** below one's moral or social standard **5 stand on one's dignity** to demand proper respect

dilute *v* **diluted, diluting** to make (a liquid) weaker or thinner: *He diluted the paint with oil* −**dilution** *n* −∼**d** *adj*

¹**dim** *adj* **-mm- 1** (of a light) not bright **2** not easy to see **3** (of eyes) not

able to see clearly **4** *esp. spoken* (of people) stupid **5 take a dim view of** *esp. spoken* to think badly of −∼**ly** *adv* −∼**ness** *n*

²**dim** *v* **-mm-** to make or become dim

din *n* a loud, continuous, and unpleasant noise

dine *v* **dined, dining 1** *esp. written* to eat dinner **2** to give a dinner for (often in the phrase **wine and dine**) −**diner** *n*

dinner *n* **1** a day's main meal, eaten either at midday or in the evening **2** a formal evening meal, for a special occasion

dinosaur *n* any of several types of large long-tailed reptiles that lived in very ancient times

¹**dip** *v* **-pp- 1** to put into a liquid for a moment and then take out **2** to put (an animal) quickly into a chemical liquid that kills insects **3** to drop or lower slightly, often just for a moment: *to dip a car's headlights*

²**dip** *n* **1** *esp. spoken* a quick swim **2** a slope down; slight drop in height **3** the act of dipping: *Give the sheep a dip* **4** any liquid used for dipping: *a savoury dip*

diplomacy *n* **1** the art and practice of conducting relations between nations **2** skill at dealing with people − **-mat** *n* − **-matic** *adj* − **-matically** *adv*

¹**direct** *v* **1** to tell (someone) the way (to a place) **2** to control and manage (the way something is done) **3** to order: *The policeman directed the crowd to leave* **4** to write the address

on (a letter) **5** to aim (attention, remarks, etc.)

²**direct** *adj* **1** straight **2** leading from one point to another without stopping and without anything coming between: *a direct flight / a direct result* **3** honest and easily understood **4** exact: *He's the direct opposite of his brother* –~**ness** *n*

³**direct** *adv* in a straight line; without stopping or turning aside

direction *n* **1** control: *under my direction* **2** the course on which or point to which a person or thing moves or is aimed

¹**directly** *adv* **1** in a direct manner: *directly opposite the church* **2** at once **3** *esp. spoken* soon

²**directly** *conj esp. spoken* as soon as

director *n* **1** a person who directs an organization **2** a member of the board of directors who run a company **3** a person who directs a play or esp. a film, instructing the actors, cameramen, etc. –~**ship** *n*

dirt *n* **1** unclean matter, esp. in the wrong place **2** soil; loose earth **3** nasty talk or writing about sex; pornography **4** *esp. spoken* nasty talk about people **5 dirt cheap** *esp. spoken* very cheap

¹**dirty** *adj* **-ier, -iest 1** not clean or making not clean: *a dirty job* **2** *esp. spoken* unpleasantly concerned with sex: *dirty stories* **3** *esp. spoken* (of the weather) rough and unpleasant **4 do the dirty on someone** *sl* to treat someone in a mean way **5 give someone a dirty look** *esp.*

spoken to look at someone in a nasty way –**dirtily** *adv*

²**dirty** *v* **-ied, -ying** to make or become dirty

disability *n* **-ties** the state of being disabled or something that disables

disable *v* **-bled, -bling** to make (a person) unable to use his body properly –~**ment** *n*

disadvantage *n* **1** an unfavourable condition or position: *His bad health is a disadvantage* **2** loss; damage; harm –~**ous** *adj* –~**ously** *adv*

disagree *v* **-greed, -greeing** to have different opinions or meanings; differ –~**ment** *n*

disappear *v* **1** to go out of sight **2** to cease to exist; become lost –~**ance** *n*

disappoint *v* **1** to fail to fulfil the hopes of: *I'm sorry to disappoint you* **2** to defeat (a plan or hope) –~**ed** *adj* –~**edly** *adv* –~**ing** *adj* –~**ingly** *adv* –~**ment** *n*

disapprove *v* **-proved, -proving** to have a bad opinion (of): *He disapproves of my going out to work* – -**proval** *n* – -**provingly** *adv*

disaster *n* a sudden great misfortune – -**trous** *adj* – -**trously** *adv*

disc *n* **1** something round and flat **2** a gramophone record **3** a flat piece of strong elastic substance (cartilage) between the bones (vertebrae) of one's back

¹**discipline** *n* **1** training of the mind and body, usu. according to rules **2** control, order, or obedience: *disci-*

pline in the classroom **3** punishment **4** a branch of learning, such as history or mathematics – **-plinary** *adj*

²**discipline** *v* **-plined, -plining 1** to train, esp. in order to control **2** to punish

disclose *v* **-closed, -closing** to make known; uncover: *to disclose the truth*

discotheque –also (*esp. spoken*) **disco** *n* a club where people dance to pop records

discourage *v* **-aged, -aging 1** to take away courage from: *Defeat discourages me* **2** to try to prevent, esp. by showing dislike – **-agingly** *adv* –~**ment** *n*

discover *v* to find out or find, esp. for the first time: *Columbus discovered America in 1492* –~**able** *adj* –~**er** *n* –~**y** *n*

discuss *v* to talk about or over; consider –~**ion** *n*

disease *n* an illness caused by infection or unnatural growth –~**d** *adj*

¹**disgrace** *v* **-graced, -gracing** to bring shame or disgrace on

²**disgrace** *n* **1** shame; loss of respect **2** a cause of shame and loss of respect: *Your shirt is a disgrace!* **3 be in disgrace** *esp. spoken* (esp. of a child) to be regarded with disapproval because of something one has done

¹**disguise** *v* **-guised, -guising 1** to change the appearance of, so as to hide the truth: *She disguised herself as a man* **2** to hide (the real state of things)

²**disguise** *n* **1** something worn to hide who one really is **2 in disguise a** disguised **b** hidden but real: *His illness became a blessing in disguise, when he married his nurse*

¹**disgust** *n* a strong dislike caused by an unpleasant sight, sound, etc.

²**disgust** *v* to cause a feeling of disgust in

¹**dish** *n* **1** a large, flat, and often round plate from which food is served **2** prepared food of one kind: *Cake is his favourite dish* **3** any object shaped like a dish **4** *esp. spoken (said by men)* a pretty girl

²**dish** *v* *esp. spoken* to ruin (a person or his hopes)

dishonest *adj* not honest –~**ly** *adv* –~**y** *n*

¹**dislike** *v* **-liked, -liking** not to like

²**dislike** *n* **1** a feeling of not liking **2 take a dislike to** to begin to dislike

dismay *v, n* **-mayed, -maying** (to fill with) a feeling of fear and hopelessness

dismiss *v* **1** *esp. written* to send away (from employment) **2** to allow to go: *to dismiss a class* **3** to put away (a subject) from one's mind **4** (of a judge) to stop (a court case) **5** (in cricket) to end the innings of (a player or team) –~**al** *n*

disobedient *adj* not obeying –~**ly** *adv* – **-ence** *n*

disobey *v* **-beyed, -beying** to fail to obey

¹**disorder** *v* to put into disorder; confuse

²**disorder** *n* **1** lack of order; confusion

2 a riot 3 a slight disease or illness: *a stomach disorder*

¹**dispatch, despatch** *v* 1 to send off: *dispatch letters* 2 to finish quickly: *We soon dispatched the cake* 3 to kill

²**dispatch, despatch** *n* 1 2 a government message, or one sent to a newspaper by one of its writers 3 speed and effectiveness: *with great dispatch*

dispense *v* **dispensed, dispensing** 1 to deal out; give out 2 to mix and give out (medicines) according to a doctor's prescription −**dispenser** *n*

¹**display** *v* **displayed, displaying** to show

²**display** *n* **displays** 1 the act or action of displaying 2 a collection of things displayed 3 **on display** being shown publicly

disposable *adj* that can be freely used or thrown away: *disposable cups*

dispose of *v prep* to get rid of; finish with

dispose to *v prep* to give a certain feeling or tendency to: *He is disposed to anger*

disposition *n* 1 a general tendency of character 2 a general feeling: *We felt a disposition to leave*

disprove *v* **-proved, -proving** to prove to be false

¹**dispute** *v* **disputed, disputing** 1 to argue about or contest (something) 2 to disagree about; doubt 3 to resist: *Our soldiers disputed the enemy advance* −**disputation** *n* −**disputatious** *adj* −**disputatiously** *adv*

²**dispute** *n* 1 an argument or quarrel 2 **in dispute (with)** in disagreement (with) 3 **in/under dispute** being argued about

disqualify *v* **-fied, -fying** to make or declare unfit or unable: *Her youth disqualifies her from office*

dissolve *v* **-solved, -solving** 1 to make or become liquid by putting into liquid: *Dissolve the salt in water* 2 to break up or end: *He dissolved the meeting* 3 to waste away, fade away, or disappear: *His strength dissolved* 4 to lose one's self-control because of strong feeling: *to dissolve in/into tears* − **-soluble** *adj*

distance *n* 1 separation in space or time: *What is the distance to London?* 2 a distant point or place 3 **go the distance** (in sports, esp. boxing) to keep running, fighting, etc., till the end of the match

distant *adj* 1 separate in space or time; far off; away 2 coming from or going to a distance: *a distant journey* 3 not closely related: *distant relations* 4 not friendly −~**ly** *adv*

distil *v* **-ll-** 1 to make (a liquid) into gas and then make the gas into liquid, as when separating alcohol from water 2 to separate in this way: *to distil alcohol from potatoes* −~**lation** *n*

distinct *adj* 1 different: *a distinct political party* 2 clearly seen, heard, smelt etc.: *a distinct smell* −~**ly** *adv* −~**ness** *n*

distinction *n* 1 difference 2 the quality

of being unusual, esp. unusually good: *a writer of distinction* **3** a special mark of honour

distinguish *v* **1** to recognize, see, hear, etc.: *I can distinguish them at a distance* **2 3** to set apart as different: *Elephants are distinguished by their trunks* **4** to win (oneself) honour

distinguished *adj* marked by excellence or fame

¹**distress** *n* **1** great suffering, sorrow, or embarrassment; pain or great discomfort **2** a state of danger: *sailors in distress*

²**distress** *v* to cause distress to

distribute *v* **-uted, -uting 1** to divide among several: *to distribute books to students* **2** to spread out; scatter **3** to give out or deliver **4** to supply (goods), esp. to shops – **-tribution** *n* – **-tributional** *adj*

district *n* a part of a country, city, etc.; area: *a postal district*

disturb *v* **1** to change the usual condition of: *Wind disturbed the water* **2** to break in upon or interrupt (an activity, person, etc.) **3** to cause to become anxious **4 disturb the peace** *law* to cause public disorder

disturbance *n* **1** an act of disturbing or the state of being disturbed: *The police charged 5 men with causing a disturbance* **2** something that disturbs

¹**ditch** *n* a long narrow not very deep V- or U-shaped trench

²**ditch** *v sl* to get rid of; leave suddenly: *He ditched the hat in the lake*

¹**dive** *v* **dived, diving 1** to jump down or go down swiftly, esp. into water: *He dived off the cliff* **2** to move quickly and suddenly into some place, activity, etc.: *to dive into a doorway* **3** to put one's hand quickly into something, esp. in order to get something out

²**dive** *n* **1** an act of diving **2** *esp. spoken* a not very respectable pub, meeting place, etc.

diver *n* a person who dives, esp. one who works at the sea bottom in special dress with a supply of air

divert *v* **1** to turn aside or away from something: *They diverted the river* **2** to amuse; entertain **−diversion** *n* **−diversionary** *adj*

divide *v* **divided, dividing 1** to separate into parts, groups, shares, different directions, etc.: *to divide a cake / The road divides at the river* **2** to find out how many times one number contains or is contained in another number: *15 divided by 3 is 5* **3** to be an important cause of disagreement between: *I hope this will not divide us* **4** to vote by separating into groups for and against: *Parliament divided on the question*

¹**divine** *adj* **1** of, related to, or being God or a god **2** *esp. spoken* very very good **−~ly** *adv*

²**divine** *v* **divined, divining 1** to discover or guess (the unknown, esp. the future) by or as if by magic **2** to find or look for (water or minerals) under ground **−diviner** *n*

division *n* **1** separation or dividing **2** one of the parts or groups into which a whole is divided **3** a large military or naval group, esp. one able to fight on its own **4** something that divides or separates **5** disagreement **6** the act of finding out how many times one number is contained in another: *the division of 15 by 3* **7** a vote in Parliament in which all those in favour go to one place and all those against go to another

¹**divorce** *n* **1** a complete end of a marriage declared by a court of law **2** a separation

²**divorce** *v* **divorced, divorcing 1** to end a marriage between (a husband and wife) or to (a husband or a wife): *The court divorced them* **2** to separate: *It is hard to divorce love and duty*

dizzy *adj* **-zier, -ziest 1** having an unpleasant feeling that things are going round and round **2** causing this feeling (esp. in the phrase **a dizzy height**) **3** having a pleasant feeling of excitement and lightness **4** *esp. spoken* silly **–dizzily** *adv* **–dizziness** *n*

¹**do** *v* **did, done, doing,** *3rd person sing. pres. tense* **does,** *pres. tense negative* **don't, doesn't,** *past tense negative* **didn't 1** (a helping verb, used to make negative statements and orders): *He didn't come. / Don't go yet* **2** (a helping verb, used to form questions): *Did he arrive in time?* **3** (a helping verb used to give extra force, and often said with emphasis): *He did come, after all! / Not only did he come, but he*

brought his sister, too **4** (a helping verb which takes the place of a verb already just used, or about to be used as an answer): *'What are you doing?' 'I'm cooking.' / He likes skating and so does she*

²**do** *v* **1** (with actions and nonmaterial things): *to do woodwork / a lesson / to do 80 miles an hour* **2** (with action nouns ending in *-ing*): *He does the cooking* **3** (with certain nonmaterial expressions): *I did my best to help him. / I used to do business with him. / Those who do good will find peace* **4** (with people and nonmaterial things) to give or provide with: *That picture doesn't do her justice* **5** (with people) to be enough for: *'Will £5 do you?' 'It will do me nicely'* **6** to cheat: *You've been done!* **7** *esp. spoken* to punish; hurt **8** to serve: *The barber will do you next* **9** to perform as or copy the manner of: *Olivier did 'Othello' last night* **10** to arrange: *to do one's hair* **11** to clean: *to do one's teeth* **12** to cook: *I do fish very well* **13** to prepare: *Do us a report* **14** to behave; act: *Do as you're told!* **15** to be suitable: *Will £5 do?* **16** (in the *-ing*-form) happening: *What's doing tonight?* **17 That will do!** That's enough! **18 do one's own thing** *sl* to do what is personally satisfying **19 How do you do?** *polite* (a form of words used when introduced to someone: in later meetings, say 'How are you?') **20 make do (with something)** also **make (something) do–** *esp. spoken*

to use (something) even though it may not be perfect or enough **21 That does it!** (an expression showing that enough, or too much has been done) **22 What do you do?** What is your work?

¹**dock** n a common broad-leafed plant that grows by the roadside

²**dock** v to take away a part of: *to dock a man's wages*

³**dock** n a place where ships are loaded or repaired

⁴**dock** v to bring to, come to, or remain at a dock

⁵**dock** n the place in a law court where the prisoner stands

¹**doctor** n **1** a person holding one of the highest degrees given by a university **2** a person whose profession is to attend to sick people

²**doctor** v esp. spoken **1** to give medical treatment to **2** to repair **3** to change for some purpose, often dishonestly: *doctoring the election results* **4** to make (an animal) unable to breed

document v,n (to prove with one or more of) a paper that gives information or support for an argument: *Can you document your claim?* −∼**ary** adj

¹**dodge** v dodged, dodging **1** to move suddenly aside, esp. to avoid **2** esp. spoken to avoid by a trick or dishonesty −∼**r** n: *a tax dodger*

²**dodge** n **1** an act of avoiding by a sudden movement **2** esp. spoken a clever way of avoiding something or of tricking someone

does 3rd person sing. pres. tense of DO

¹**dog** n **1** a common 4-legged flesh-eating animal, esp. any of the many varieties used by man as a companion or for hunting, working, etc. **2** the male of this animal and of certain animals like it, esp. the fox and the wolf **3** esp. spoken a fellow: *a gay dog* **4** lead a dog's life esp. spoken to have a life with many troubles **5 Let sleeping dogs lie** Leave alone things which may cause trouble **6 not have a dog's chance** esp. spoken to have no chance at all **7 top dog** esp. spoken the person on top, who has power **8 treat someone like a dog** esp. spoken to treat someone very badly

²**dog** v **-gg-** to follow closely (like a dog); pursue

doing pres. part. of DO

dole n **1** something doled out **2 go/be on the dole** esp. spoken to start to receive/to receive money from the government because one is unemployed

dole out v adv **doled, doling out** to give small amounts of (money, food, etc.) (to people in need)

doll n **1** a small figure of a person, esp. for a child to play with **2** sl a young woman or girl, esp. one with charm or one who dresses too finely

dollar n **1** any of various standards of money, used in the US, Canada, Australia, New Zealand, Hong Kong, etc. It is worth 100 cents and its sign is $ **2** a piece of paper, coin, etc., of this value

dome *n* a rounded top, esp. on a building or room −~**d** *adj*

¹**domestic** *adj* **1** of the house or family **2** liking home life **3** of one's own country −~**ally** *adv*

²**domestic** *n* a domestic servant, usu. female

dominate *v* **-nated, -nating 1** to have power (over), control (over), or the most important place (in): *She dominates her sisters.* / *Sports dominate in that school* **2** to be higher than: *The mountain dominated the town*

donate *v* **donated, donating** to make a gift of, esp. for a good purpose − **-tion** *n*

done 1 finished: *Have you done with the scissors?* **2** past part. of DO

donkey *n* **-keys 1** a type of animal of the horse family, but smaller and with longer ears; ass **2** a stupid or stubborn person

¹**doom** *n* a terrible fate, such as unavoidable destruction: *to meet one's doom*

²**doom** *v* to cause to experience something unavoidable and unpleasant, such as death or failure

door *n* **1** a movable flat surface that opens and closes the entrance to a building, room, or piece of furniture: *the kitchen/cupboard door* **2** a doorway **3** any entrance: *This agreement opens the door to peace* **4** (in certain fixed phrases) house; building: *My sister lives only 2 doors away.* / *The salesman went from door to door* **5 answer the door** to go and open the door to see who has knocked or rung **6 at death's door** *literature* near death **7 by the back door** secretly or by a trick **8 out of doors** outdoors **9 show someone the door** to make it clear that someone is not welcome and should leave **10 show someone to the door** to go politely to the door with someone who is leaving

doorbell *n* a bell provided for visitors to a house to ring for attention

doorway *n* **-ways** an opening for a door

¹**dose** −also **dosage**− *n* **1** a measured amount (esp. of medicine) given or to be taken at one time **2** anything (usu. unpleasant) that has to be taken or borne: *a dose of hard work*

²**dose** *v* **dosed, dosing** *often offensive* to give a dose, esp. of medicine, to

¹**dot** *n* **1** a small usu. round spot: *a dot on the letter i* **2** a short sound or flash forming part of a letter when sending messages, esp. by telegraph **3 on the dot** *esp. spoken* at the exact time **4 the year dot** *sl, often offensive* a very long time ago

²**dot** *v* **-tt- 1** to mark with a dot **2** to cover with or as if with dots: *a lake dotted with boats* **3** to hit sharply

¹**double** *adj* **1** having or made up of 2 parts that are alike: *double doors* **2** for 2 people, animals, etc.: *a double bed* **3** having 2 different qualities: *a double purpose*

²**double** *n* **1** something that is twice another in quantity, strength, speed, or value: *I paid £2 for this*

and Mr. Smith offered me double (= £4) for it **2** an alcoholic drink of spirits, with twice the amount usu. sold **3** a person who looks like another: *He is my double* **4** an actor or actress of similar build or appearance who takes the place of another in a film for some special, esp. dangerous, purpose **5 at the double** (esp. of soldiers) at a rate between walking and running **6 double or quits** the decision (in a game where money is risked) to risk winning twice the amount one has already won, or losing it all **7 on the double** *esp. spoken* very quickly

³**double** *adv* **1** twice (the amount, size, or quality): *10 is double 5* **2** **2** together

⁴**double** *v* **-led, -ling 1** to multiply (a number or amount) by 2: *Sales doubled in 5 years* **2** to make a sudden sharp turn: *He doubled (back) on his route* **3** to sail round by changing direction quickly **4** to fold or bend sharply or tightly over

¹**doubt** *v* **1** to be uncertain (about) **2** to mistrust: *I doubt his honesty* **3** to consider unlikely: *I doubt that he'll come* −~**er** *n*

²**doubt** *n* **1** a feeling of uncertainty of opinion **2** a feeling of mistrust or disbelief: *I have doubts about him* **3 without doubt** it is certain

doubtful *adj* **1** full of doubt; not trusting **2** uncertain **3** not probable **4** of questionable honesty, value, etc.: *a doubtful fellow* −~**ly** *adv*

doubtless *adv* **1** without doubt **2** probably

dough *n* **1** flour mixed with other dry materials and water for baking **2** *sl, esp. US* money

dove *n* **1** any of various types of pigeon; soft-voiced bird often used as a sign of peace **2** *esp. US* a politician in favour of peace

¹**down** *adv* **1** towards or into a lower position: *Lift that box down from the shelf* **2** to or into a sitting or lying position **3** in or towards the south: *down in London* **4** to or towards a point away from the speaker, though not always a point at a lower level: *Walk down to the shop with me* **5** (with verbs of fixing or fastening) firmly; safely: *Stick down the envelope* **6** on paper; in writing: *'Did you write down the number?' 'I have it down somewhere.'* **7** (of money to be paid at once) in cash: *You can buy this car for £30 down and £5 a week for 3 years* **8** to the moment of catching, getting, or discovering: *The men hunted the lion down* **9** into silence: *The speaker was shouted down* **10** to a state of less activity, force, power, etc.: *Please turn the radio down* **11** in our family for 300 years **12 down under** *esp. spoken* in or to Australia or New Zealand

²**down** *adj* **1** in a low position, esp. lying on the ground: *The telephone wires are down!* **2** directed or going down **3** being at a lower level: *Sales are down* **4** being in a state of

reduced or low activity or spirits **5** *esp. spoken US* finished: *8 down and 2 to go* **6 down for** entered on the list for (a race, school, etc.) **7 down on** *esp. spoken* having a low opinion of or dislike for

³**down** *prep* **1** to or in a lower or descending position; along; to the far end of: *He ran down the hill* **2** to or in the direction of the current of: *to go down the river*

⁴**down** *n* **have a down on someone** *esp. spoken* to have a low opinion of, or feel dislike for, someone

⁵**down** *v* **1** to knock to the ground or defeat **2** to swallow quickly (esp. a liquid) **3 down tools** (of workers) to stop working, esp. to strike

⁶**down** *n* fine soft feathers, hair, etc.

¹**downhill** *adv* **1** towards the bottom of a hill **2** towards a worse state (esp. in the phrase **go downhill**)

²**downhill** *adj* **1** sloping towards the bottom of a hill **2** *esp. spoken* easy: *The hardest part is over; the rest is downhill*

downstairs *adj, adv* on or to a lower floor and esp. the main or ground floor of a building: *to come downstairs* —**downstairs** *n*

doze *v* **dozed, dozing** to sleep lightly —**doze** *n*

dozen —*abbrev.* **doz.** *adj, n* **dozen** *or* **dozens 1** a group of 12 **2 dozens of** *esp. spoken* lots of

¹**drag** *n* **1** the action or an act of dragging **2** something that is dragged along over a surface **3** something or someone that makes

it harder to go forwards **4** the force of the air that acts against the movement of an aircraft **5** *sl* something dull and uninteresting: *Your party was a drag* **6** *sl* an act of breathing in cigarette smoke **7** *sl* woman's clothing worn by a man

²**drag** *v* **-gg- 1** to pull (a heavy thing) along: *dragging a tree along* **2** to cause to come or go unwillingly **3** to move along too slowly: *He dragged behind the others* **4** to look for something by pulling a heavy net along the bottom of (a body of water): *to drag the lake for a body*

dragon *n* an imaginary fire-breathing animal in children's stories

¹**drain** *v* **1** to flow or cause to flow off gradually or completely **2** to make or become gradually dry or empty of fluid, energy, etc.: *Let the glasses drain* **3** to carry away the surface water of: *They want to drain the land* **4** to empty by drinking the contents of **5** to make weak and tired by using up the forces of body, mind, or feelings

²**drain** *n* **1** a pipe, tube, etc., that drains matter away **2** something that empties or uses up

drama *n* **1** a play **2** plays as a form of literature **3** an exciting or dangerous group of events: *the drama of international politics*

dramatic *adj* **1** of or related to drama **2** exciting **3** catching the imagination by unusual appearance or effects: *a dramatic woman* —~**ally** *adv*

drank *past tense of* DRINK

drastic *adj* strong, sudden, and often violent or severe: *drastic changes* –~**ally** *adv*

¹**draught** *n* **1** a current or flow of air **2** an act of swallowing liquid or the amount of liquid swallowed at one time **3** the depth of water needed by a ship to float **4 on draught** (esp. of beer) from a barrel **5** a small round piece used in playing draughts

²**draught** *adj* **1** (of animals) used to pull loads: *a draught horse* **2** from a barrel: *draught beer*

draughts *n* a game for 2, each with 12 round pieces, on a board of 64 squares

¹**draw** *v* **drew** , **drawn, drawing 1** to pull a cart: *drawn by a horse* **2** to cause to go in a stated direction: *to draw someone aside* **3** to attract: *drawn towards him* **4** to cause to come **5** (of people) to take (a breath) in **6** to cause (blood) to flow **7** to bring or pull out, esp. with effort: *to draw a tooth* **8** to remove the bowels from: *to draw a chicken* **9** to collect (liquid) in a container: *to draw water from the well* **10** (of a ship) to need (a stated depth of water) in order to float **11** to get, receive, or take: *to draw money from a bank* **12** to bend (a bow) ready to shoot an arrow **13** to pull out (a weapon) for use **14** to end a game, battle, etc. without either side winning **15** to make pictures with a pencil, pen, etc. **16 a** to make with

a pencil, pen, etc. **b** to make a picture of in this way **17** to prepare (esp. a cheque) properly: *to draw a cheque on one's bank* **18** to produce or allow an air current: *The chimney draws well* **19 draw the/a line** to fix a border against some activity or between 2 areas: *to draw the line at stealing* **20 draw the curtain** to close or open the curtain

²**draw** *n* **1** an act or example of drawing: *He picked a winning number on the first draw* **2** a state of affairs in which neither side wins: *The game was a draw* **3** a person or thing that attracts

drawer *n* a sliding boxlike container with an open top (as in a desk)

¹**drawn** *adj* **1** twisted: *a face drawn with sorrow* **2** (of games, battles, etc.) ended with neither side winning

²**drawn** *past part. of* DRAW

¹**dread** *v* to fear greatly

²**dread** *n* a great fear or cause of such fear: *a dread of heights*

dreadful *adj* **1** causing great fear; terrible: *dreadful pain* **2** unpleasant –~**ness** *n*

¹**dream** *n* **1** a group of thoughts, images, or feelings experienced during sleep **2** a similar experience when awake **3** a state of mind in which one has such an experience and does not pay much attention to the real world **4** something not real but hoped for: *Her dream is a new bicycle* **5** *esp. spoken* a thing or

person notable for beauty or excellence: *Their new house is a dream*

²dream *v* **dreamed** *or* **dreamt**, **dreaming 1** to have (a dream) about something **2** to imagine

dregs *n* **1** bitter bits in a liquid that sink to the bottom **2** the most worthless part of anything: *the dregs of society*

drench *v* to make thoroughly wet

¹dress *v* **1** to put clothes on **2** to provide with clothes **3** to make or choose clothes for: *The princess is dressed by a famous dressmaker* **4** to put on special formal clothes for the evening **5** to arrange, finish, clean, or otherwise prepare: *to dress stone* **6** to clean and put medicine and a protective covering on (a wound) **7** to decorate: *to dress a Christmas tree* **8** to arrange goods interestingly in (esp. a shop window) **9 dressed to kill** *esp. spoken* wearing very showy clothes

²dress *n* **1** clothing, esp. outer clothing or that worn on special occasions **2** a woman's or girl's outer garment that covers the body from shoulder to knee or below

³dress *adj* **1** related to or used for a dress **2** (of clothing) suitable for a formal occasion: *a dress shirt* **3** requiring or permitting formal dress

dressing *n* **1** a usu. liquid mixture for adding to a dish, esp. a salad **2** material used to cover a wound

dressing gown *n* a long loose coat,

worn before or after sleeping or bathing

drew *past tense of* DRAW

¹dribble *v* **-bled, -bling 1** to flow or let flow little by little: *Saliva dribbled from his lip. / The baby is dribbling* **2** to move (esp. a ball) by a number of short kicks or strokes with foot, hand, or stick

²dribble *n* **1** a small slowly-moving stream or flow **2** a very small or unimportant quantity

dried *past tense and past part. of* DRY

¹drift *n* **1** a movement or tendency without visible purpose and usu. slow: *the government's aimless drift* **2** a mass of matter blown up by wind: *snow drifts* **3** earth, sand, stones, and rock left by running water or a glacier **4** the general meaning of a conversation, book, etc.

²drift *v* **1** to float or be driven along as if by wind, waves, etc.: *They drifted out to sea* **2** to pile up under the force of wind or water

¹drill *v* **1** to make (holes) with a drill **2** to make holes in: *to drill someone's teeth* **3 a** to train (soldiers) in military movements **b** to practise military movements under instruction **4** to instruct by repeating: *Drill them in sums*

²drill *n* **1** a tool or machine for making holes **2** training and instruction, esp. by means of repetition **3** *esp. spoken* the correct way of doing something effectively: *What's the drill here?*

¹**drink** *v* **drank** , **drunk, drinking 1** to swallow (liquid) **2** to take in: *drinking air into his lungs* **3** to give or join in (a toast) **4** to use alcohol, esp. too much **5** to bring to a stated condition by taking alcohol: *He drank himself to death*

²**drink** *n* **1** a liquid suitable for swallowing **2** the habit or an act of drinking alcohol: *Have another drink!*

¹**drip** *v* **-pp- 1** to fall or let fall in drops: *Water is dripping from the roof* **2** to overflow: *a voice dripping with sweetness*

²**drip** *n* **1** the action of falling in drops **2** (an apparatus for holding) liquid put into a blood vessel at a slow rate **3** *sl* a dull and unattractive person

¹**drive** *v* **drove, driven, driving 1** to force, usu. to go or do something: *to drive trade away / Steam drives the engine* **2** to guide and control (a vehicle): *She drives well* **3** to take in a vehicle as stated: *Can you drive me to the station?* **4** (of a vehicle) to perform in the stated way: *This car drives well* **5** to produce by opening a way: *to drive a tunnel* **6** (esp. of rain) to move along with great force **7** to collect (esp. snow) into large heaps

²**drive** *n* **1** a journey in a vehicle **2** an act of hitting a ball, the distance a ball is hit, or the force with which it is hit **3** a driveway **4** a strong well-planned effort by a group for a particular purpose: *a membership* *drive* **5** a competition of the stated type, esp. a card game: *a whist drive* **6** an important need which causes a person to act: *the sex drive* **7** a forceful quality of character that gets things done **8** the apparatus by which a machine is set or kept in movement: *This car has front-wheel drive*

driveway *n* **-ways** a usu. private road through a park or to a house

droop *v* **1** to hang or bend downwards **2** to weaken: *His spirits drooped* **−droop** *n*

¹**drop** *n* **1** the amount of liquid that falls in one small mass **2** the smallest possible amount of liquid **3** a small round sweet **4** a fall: *a long drop into the hole* **5** that which is dropped: *a drop of food from an aircraft* **6 get the drop on someone** *sl* to get quickly into a more favourable position than someone

²**drop** *v* **-pp- 1** to fall or let fall suddenly or in drops **2** to let fall or lower: *to drop a handkerchief / to drop one's voice* **3** to go lower; become less: *Prices dropped* **4** *esp. spoken* to let (someone) get out of a vehicle: *Drop me at the corner* **5** to leave out, esp. from a team: *I've been dropped for Saturday's match* **6** to give up: *He's dropped his old friends* **7** *drug-users' sl* to take (drugs) **8** to come or go informally: *Drop in and see us* **9** to get further away from a moving object by moving more slowly than it: *Our car dropped behind* **10 drop**

someone a line/note to write a short letter to someone

drought *n* a long period of very dry weather

drove *past tense of* DRIVE

drown *v* 1 to die by being under water too long 2 to kill by holding under water too long 3 to cover completely or make thoroughly wet, usu. with water 4 to cause (oneself) to become very active in something: *He drowned himself in work* 5 to cover up (a sound) by making a loud noise

¹**drug** *n* 1 a medicine or material used for making medicines 2 a habit-forming substance

²**drug** *v* **-gg-** to add drugs to, or give drugs to, esp. so as to produce unconsciousness: *to drug a sick man*

¹**drum** *n* 1 a circular musical instrument whose tight skinlike surface is struck by hand or with a stick 2 a sound like that of such an instrument 3 a piece of machinery or a large container shaped like a drum

²**drum** *v* **-mm-** 1 to beat or play a drum 2 to make drum-like noises: *He drummed on the table with his fingers*

¹**drunk** *adj* 1 under the influence of alcohol: *drunk and disorderly* 2 overcome with success or joy

²**drunk** *n offensive* a person who is drunk

³**drunk** *past part. of* DRINK

¹**dry** *adj* **drier, driest** 1 not wet 2 (of parts of the earth) emptied of water: *a dry lake* 3 no longer giving milk

4 without tears or other liquid substances from the body: *dry sobs* 5 having or producing thirst: *I am feeling very dry* 6 (esp. of bread) without butter or not fresh 7 (of alcoholic drinks, esp. wine) not sweet 8 without rain or wetness 9 not allowing the sale of alcoholic drink: *a dry state* 10 dull and uninteresting: *The book was as dry as dust* 11 amusing without appearing to be so; quietly ironic: *dry humour* **–dryly, drily** *adv* **–dryness** *n*

²**dry** *v* **dried, drying** 1 to make or become dry: *Dry your hands* 2 to preserve (food) by removing liquid: *dried fruit*

¹**duck** *n* **ducks** *or* **duck** 1 (*masc.* **drake**)– a swimming bird with short legs and short neck, some wild, some kept for food 2 the meat of this bird 3 *esp. spoken* a person one likes: *She's a sweet old duck* 4 (in cricket) the failure to make any runs

²**duck** *v* 1 to lower (one's head or body) quickly, esp. so as to avoid being hit 2 to push under water: *He ducked his head in the stream* 3 *esp. spoken* to try to avoid (a difficulty or something unpleasant): *He tried to duck out of going* **–duck** *n*

¹**due** *adj* 1 owed or owing as a debt or right 2 proper: *drive with due care* 3 payable 4 expected; supposed (to): *The next train is due at 4 o'clock*

²**due** *n* something that rightfully belongs to someone (esp. in the phrase **give someone his due**)

³**due** *adv* (*before* north, south, east, *and* west) directly; exactly

¹**duel** *n* **1** a fight with guns or swords, between 2 people **2** a struggle or argument between any 2 opposed people, groups, or animals

²**duel** *v* **-ll-** to fight a duel with (another person or each other)

due to *prep* because of; caused by: *His illness was due to bad food*

dug *past tense and past part. of* DIG

¹**dull** *adj* **1** (of colour or surfaces) not bright, strong, or sharp **2** (of sound) not clear; low **3** (of weather, the sky, etc.) cloudy; grey **4** (of the senses) not of good quality **5** (of pain) not clearly felt **6** slow in understanding: *dull children* **7** uninteresting; unexciting: *The company was very dull* −~y *adv* −~**ness** *n*

²**dull** *v* to make or become dull: *This will dull the pain*

dumb *adj* **1** unable to speak: *We were struck dumb* **2** unwilling to speak: *to remain dumb despite torture* **3** *esp. spoken* stupid −~**ly** *adv* −~**ness** *n*

dummy *n* **-mies 1** an object made to look like and take the place of a real thing **2** something like a human figure made of wood or wax and used to make or show off clothes **3** a rubber thing for sucking, put in a baby's mouth to keep it quiet

¹**dump** *v* **1** to drop or unload in a heap or carelessly **2** *sl* to get rid of suddenly **3** to sell (goods) in a foreign country at a very low price

²**dump** *n* **1** a place for dumping some-

thing (such as waste material) **2** (a place for) a stored supply of military materials **3** *offensive* a dirty and untidy place: *This town's a real dump*

dunce *n* a slow learner; stupid person

dungeon *n* a close dark prison, usu. underground, beneath a castle

¹**duplicate** *adj* consisting of 2 that are exactly alike: *a duplicate key*

²**duplicate** *n* something that is exactly like another; copy

³**duplicate** *v* **-cated, cating 1** to copy exactly **2** to make again; make double − **-cation** *n*

during *prep* all through, or at some point in the course of: *Let us go on a picnic one day during the holidays*

dusk *n* the time when daylight is fading; darker part of twilight, esp. at night

¹**dust** *n* **1** powder made up of very small pieces of waste matter **2** finely powdered earth: *In the summer we have a great deal of dust* **3** powder made up of small pieces of some substance: *gold dust* **4** *literature* the earthly remains of bodies once alive **5 throw dust in someone's eyes** *esp. spoken* to deceive someone −~**less** *adj*

²**dust** *v* **1** to clean the dust from; remove dust **2** to cover with dust or fine powder: *to dust a cake with sugar*

dustbin *n* a container with a lid, for holding refuse

dusty *adj* **-ier, -iest** covered with dust

duty *n* **duties 1** what one must do

either because of one's job or because one thinks it right: *It's my duty to help you* **2** a type of tax: *customs duties*

¹**dwarf** *n* **1** a person, animal, or plant of much less than the usual size **2** a small imaginary manlike creature in fairy stories

²**dwarf** *v* **1** to prevent the proper growth of **2** to cause to appear small by comparison: *The new building dwarfs all the shops*

dwell *v* **dwelt** *or* **dwelled, dwelling** *esp. written* to live

dwindle *v* **-dled, -dling** to become gradually fewer or smaller

¹**dye** *n* a vegetable or chemical substance, usu. liquid, used to colour things

²**dye** *v* **dyed, dyeing** to give or take (a stated) colour by means of dye: *She dyed the dress (red)* **-dyer** *n*

dynamic *adj* **1** *technical* of force or power that causes movement **2** (of people) full of power and activity **-~ally** *adv*

¹**dynamite** *n* **1** a powerful explosive used in mining **2** *esp. spoken* something or someone that will cause great shock, surprise, admiration, etc.: *That news story is dynamite*

²**dynamite** *v* **-mited, -miting** to blow up with dynamite

¹**each** *adj* every one separately: *Give a piece to each child*

²**each** *pron* every one separately

³**each** *adv* for or to every one

each other **-**also **one another** *pron* (means that each of 2 or more does something to the other or others): *The kittens were chasing each other*

eager *adj* keen; full of interest or desire: *He listened with eager attention* **-~ly** *adv* **-~ness** *n*

eagle *n* **1** any of various types of very large strong birds of prey with hooked beaks and very good eyesight **2** (in golf) an act of hitting the ball into the hole, taking 2 strokes fewer than is average for that particular hole

¹**ear** *n* **1** the organ of hearing in man and animals **2** attention or notice: *She has the minister's ear* **3** keen recognition of sounds, esp. in music and languages: *an ear for music* **4 all ears** *esp. spoken* listening attentively **5 by ear** to play (music) from memory of the sound alone **6 out on (one's) ear** *sl* suddenly thrown out of a place or dismissed from a job **7 up to (one's) ears in** *esp. spoken* deep in or busy with **8 wet behind the ears** *sl* immature and without experience

²**ear** *n* the head of a grain-producing plant such as corn or wheat, used for food

¹**early** *adv* **-lier, -liest 1** before the usual, arranged, or expected time **2** towards the beginning of a period

²**early** *adj* **1** arriving, developing, happening, etc., before the usual, arranged, or expected time **2** happening towards the beginning of the day, life, a period of time, etc. **3** happening in the near future: *I hope for an early answer* **- -liness** *n*

earn *v* **1** to get (money) by working **2** to get (something that one deserves) because of one's qualities: *He earned the title of 'The Great'* –~**er** *n*

¹earnest *n* seriousness: *It is snowing in real earnest* (=very hard)

²earnest *adj* determined and serious: *an earnest attempt* –~**ly** *adv* –~**ness** *n*

earnings *n* **1** money which is earned by working **2** money made by a company: profit

¹earth *n* **1** the world on which we live **2** the earth's surface as opposed to the sky **3** soil in which plants grow **4** also (*abbrev.*) **E–** the wire which connects a piece of electrical apparatus to the ground **5** the hole where certain wild animals live, such as foxes **6 down to earth** direct and practical **7 on earth** *esp. spoken* (used for giving force to an expression): *What on earth is it?*

²earth *v* to connect a piece of electrical apparatus to the ground

earthquake *n* a sudden shaking of the earth's surface, which may cause great damage

¹ease *n* **1** the state of being comfortable and without worry: *a life of ease* **2** the ability to do something without difficulty: *to jump over with ease* **3 ill at ease** uncomfortable and nervous **4 (stand) at ease** (*used esp. as a military command*) (to stand) with feet apart

²ease *v* **eased, easing 1** to take away (pain or worry) **2** to make more comfortable **3** to make looser **4** to become less difficult: *Their relationship has eased* **5** to cause (something) to move as stated, by using care: *I eased the drawer open with a knife*

easily *adv* **1** without difficulty **2** without doubt: *She is easily the prettiest here*

¹east *adv* towards the east

²east *n* **1** (to, facing, or in) the direction in which the sun rises **2** one of the 4 main points of the compass, which is on the right of a person facing north **3** (of wind) (coming from) this direction: *The wind is in the east*

Easter *n* the yearly feast-day when Christians remember the death of Christ and his rising from the grave

eastern *adj* of or belonging to the east part of the world or of a country

¹easy *adj* **-ier, -iest 1** not difficult **2** comfortable and without worry: *He leads a very easy life* **3 (of) easy virtue** *old use* (of) low sexual morals **4 I'm easy** *esp. spoken* I'll willingly accept what you decide **5 on easy terms** (when buying a car, furniture, etc.) (to pay) a little at a time instead of all at once –**easiness** *n*

²easy *adv* **1 easier said than done** harder to do than to talk about **2 easy does it** Do it less quickly and/or with less effort!; relax! **3 go easy** work less hard **4 go easy on** (someone) to be less severe with (someone) **5 go easy on** (something) not to use too much of it **6**

stand easy (*used esp. as a military command*) stand more comfortably than when at ease

eat *v* **ate, eaten, eating 1** to take into the mouth and swallow **2** to use regularly as food: *Tigers eat meat* **3** to have a meal: *What time do we eat?* **4 be eaten up with** (jealousy, desire, etc.) to be completely and violently full of **5 eat one's words** to take back what one has said; say that one is sorry for having said something

¹**echo** *n* **-oes** a sound sent back or repeated, as from a wall of rock or inside a cave

²**echo** *v* **echoed, echoing 1** to come back or cause to come back as an echo **2** to copy or repeat

¹**eclipse** *n* **1** the disappearance, complete or in part, of the sun's light when the moon passes between it and the earth, or of the moon's light when the earth passes between it and the sun **2** the loss of fame, success, etc.: *Once a famous actress, she is now in eclipse*

²**eclipse** *v* **eclipsed, eclipsing 1** (of the moon or earth) to cause an eclipse (of sun or moon) **2** to do or be much better than; to make (someone or something) lose fame and appear dull by comparison **3** make dark or troubled: *Our happiness was eclipsed by the news*

economic *adj* **1** connected with trade, industry, and wealth; of or concerning economics: *The country is in a bad economic state* **2** profitable:

She let her house at an economic rent

economics *n* **1** the science of the way in which industry and trade produce and use wealth **2** the principles of making profit, saving money, and producing wealth – **-mist** *n*

¹**economy** *n* **-mies 1** (an example of) the careful use of money, time, strength, etc. **2** an economic system

²**economy** *adj* **1** cheap or big (and good value): *economy prices/size* **2** intended to save money: *In our school we had an economy drive to save energy*

¹**edge** *n* **1** the thin sharp cutting part of a blade, a tool, etc.; cutting line where 2 sides meet **2** the narrowest part along the outside of a solid **3** a border: *the edge of the cliff* **4 have the edge on** be better than **5 on edge** nervous **6 set someone's teeth on edge** to give an unpleasant feeling to someone

²**edge** *v* **edged, edging 1** to place an edge or border on **2** to move little by little **3** (in cricket) to hit (the ball) off the edge of the bat

edible *adj* fit to be eaten; eatable **–edibility** *n* **–~s** *n*

educate *v* **-cated, -cating** to teach; train the character or mind of: *He was educated at a very good school* **– -tor** *n*

education *n* **1** (the results of) teaching or the training of mind and character **2** a field of knowledge dealing

143

with how to teach effectively: *a college of education*

¹**effect** *n* 1 a result 2 a result produced on the mind or feelings 3 **in effect a** in operation: *The old system will remain in effect until May* **b** for all practical purposes: *She is, in effect, the real ruler* 4 **take effect a** to come into operation **b** to begin to produce results: *The medicine quickly took effect* 5 **to ... effect** with ... general meaning: *He called me a fool, or words to that effect*

²**effect** *v esp. written* to cause, produce, or have as a result: *I will effect my purpose*

effective *adj* 1 having a desired effect; producing the desired result: *an effective method* 2 actual; real – ~**ly** *adv*

efficient *adj* working well and without waste – ~**ly** *adv* – -**ency** *n*

effort *n* 1 the use of strength; trying hard with mind or body: *He can lift the box without effort* 2 a show of strength: *At least make an effort* 3 the result of trying: *Finishing the work in one day was an effort*

egg *n* 1 a rounded object containing new life, which comes out of the body of a female bird, snake, etc. 2 (the contents of) this when used for food 3 the seed of life in a woman or female animal, which joins with the male seed to make a baby 4 **a bad egg** a worthless and dishonest person

eight *adj, n, pron* 1 the number 8 2 a

rowing-boat for racing that holds 8 men –**eighth** *adj, n, pron*

eighteen *adj, n, pron* the number 18 – ~**th** *adj, n, pron, adv*

eighty *adj, n, pron* **-ties** the number 80 –**eightieth** *adj, n, pron, adv*

¹**either** *adj* 1 one or the other of 2 2 one and the other of 2; each: *He had a policeman on either side of him*

²**either** *pron* one or the other of

³**either** *conj* (used before the first of 2 or more choices separated by *or*)

⁴**either** *adv* (*used with negative expressions*) also: *I haven't read it and my brother hasn't either*

¹**elaborate** *adj* full of detail; carefully worked out: *an elaborate machine* – ~**ly** *adv* – ~**ness** *n*

²**elaborate** *v* **-rated, -rating** to add more detail to (something) – **-tion** *n*

elastic *adj* 1 which springs back into the original shape after being stretched: *an elastic band* 2 not stiff or fixed; able to be changed to fit all cases: *elastic rules* –**elastic** *n* – ~**ity** *n*

¹**elbow** *n* 1 the joint where the arm bends, esp. the outer point of this 2 the part of a garment which covers this arm joint 3 an L-shaped joint shaped like this arm joint, in a pipe, chimney, etc. 4 **out at elbow(s) a** badly dressed and poor-looking **b** (of a garment) worn out and with holes in it

²**elbow** *v* to push with the elbows: *He elbowed me out of the way*

¹**elder** *n* also **elder tree–** a type of small tree, with white flowers and red or black berries (**elderberry**)

²**elder** *adj* **1** (esp. in a family) the older of 2 people: *my elder brother* **2** older than another person (esp. a son) of the same name

³**elder** *n* **1** the older of 2 people **2** a man who holds an official position in some Christian churches

elderly *adj* (of a person) getting near old age: *My father is getting elderly now*

eldest *adj, n* (a person, esp. in a family, who is) oldest of 3 or more

¹**elect** *adj* elected to or chosen for an office but not yet officially placed in it

²**elect** *v* **1** to choose (someone) by voting **2** to decide (to do something), esp. about the future: *He elected to become a doctor*

election *n* (an example of) the choosing of representatives to fill a position, esp. a political office, by vote

electric *adj* **1** being, using, or producing electricity: *an electric spark* **2** produced by electricity **3** very exciting: *His speech had an electric effect upon the listeners* *–*~**ally** *adv*

electrical *adj* **1** concerned with electricity **2** using electricity in some way: *electrical apparatus* *–*~**ly** *adv*

electricity *n* **1** the power which is produced by friction, by a battery, or by a generator, and which gives us heat, light, and sound, and drives machines **2** electric current

electron *n* a 'bit' of negative electricity moving round one 'bit' of positive electricity (PROTON) inside an atom

elegant *adj* having the qualities of grace, style, beauty, and fashion: *an elegant woman* *–*~**ly** *adv* – **-ance** *n*

element *n* **1** a quality or amount which can be noticed: *There is an element of truth in what you say* **2** the heating part of a piece of electrical apparatus **3** *old use* any of the 4 substances earth, air, fire, and water, from which (it was believed) everything material was made **4** any of more than 100 substances that consist of atoms of only one kind and that in combination make up all other substances: *Both hydrogen and oxygen are elements, but water is not*

elementary *adj* **1** (of a question) simple and easy to answer **2** concerned with the beginnings, esp. of education and study

elephant *n* **-phants** *or* **-phant** the largest 4-footed animal now living, with 2 long curved tusks and a long nose called a trunk with which it can pick things up

eleven *adj, n, pron* **1** the number 11 **2** a complete team of 11 players in football, cricket, etc. *–*~**th** *adj, n, pron, adv*

eliminate *v* **-nated, -nating 1** to remove or get rid of **2** to show that (a possibility) does not exist and so need not be considered – **-nation** *n*

elm *n* also **elm tree–** any of several

types of tall broad-leaved tree or its hard heavy wood

else *adv* **1** besides; in addition: *Who else did you see?* **2** in or at a different place, time, or way; apart from that mentioned: *When else can we meet?* **3 or else** or otherwise: *He must pay £100 or else go to prison*

elsewhere *adv* at, in, or to another place: *We must look elsewhere*

embarrass *v* **1** to cause to feel ashamed or socially uncomfortable **2** to cause to feel anxious about money: *He was embarrassed by debts* – ~**ingly** *adv*

embarrassment *n* **1 a** the act of embarrassing **b** the state of being embarrassed **2** a difficulty about money **3** a person or thing that embarrasses

¹**embrace** *v* **embraced, embracing** **1** to take and hold (another or each other) in the arms as a sign of love **2** (of things) to contain or include: *This book embraces many subjects* **3** *esp. written* to make use or take willingly: *He embraced my offer to employ him* **4** to become a believer in: *He embraced the Muslim religion*

²**embrace** *n* the act of embracing

embroider *v* **1** to do ornamental work with needle and thread on (cloth) **2** to improve (a story) by adding imaginary details

¹**emerald** *n* a bright green precious stone

²**emerald** *adj, n* (of) the colour of an emerald; clear bright green

emerge *v* **emerged, emerging** **1** to come or appear (from/out of some-where): *The sun emerged from behind the clouds* **2** to become known as a result of inquiry – **-gence** *n*

emergency *n* **-cies** an unexpected and dangerous happening which must be dealt with at once

emigrate *v* **-grated, -grating** to leave one's own country in order to go and live in another – **-tion** *n*

emotion *n* **1** a strong instinctive feeling: *Love, hatred, and grief are emotions* **2** strength of feeling: *His voice shook with emotion* – ~**less** *adj* – ~**lessly** *adv* – ~**lessness** *n*

emotional *adj* **1** having feelings which are strong or easily moved **2** (of words, literature, music, etc.) **a** showing strong feeling **b** able to cause strong feeling **3** with regard to the emotions: *emotional difficulties* – ~**ly** *adv*

emperor *n* (*fem.* **empress**) the head of an empire

emphasis *n* **-ses** special force given to certain words or details, in speaking, writing, etc., to show their importance – **-atic** *adj* – **-atically** *adv*

emphasize, -ise *v* **-sized, -sizing** to place emphasis on

empire *n* a group of countries under one government, usu. ruled by an emperor

employ *v* **employed, employing** **1** to use or take on as a paid worker: *The firm employs about 100 men* **2** to use: *The police sometimes have to* *employ force* **3** to spend time: *She employs her free time in sewing*

employee *n* a person who is employed

employer *n* a person who employs others

employment *n* **1** the state of being employed **2** the act of employing

¹**empty** *adj* **-ier, -iest** **1** containing nothing or nobody: *an empty cup* **2** *esp. spoken* hungry **3** *offensive* without sense or purpose; meaningless: *empty promises* **–emptily** *adv* **–emptiness** *n*

²**empty** *v* **-tied, -tying** **1** to make empty: *They emptied the bottle* **2** (of a place, a container, etc.) to send or move its contents somewhere else: *The room emptied very quickly*

³**empty** *n* **-ties** a container or vehicle that has been emptied: *He took all the empties* (=empty bottles) *back to the shop*

enable *v* **-bled, -bling** **1** to make (a creature) able (to do something): *a bird's wings enable it to fly* **2** to give (someone) the power or right (to do something)

enclose *v* **enclosed, enclosing** **1** to surround with a fence or wall so as to shut in **2** to put (esp. something sent with a letter) inside: *I enclose a cheque for £50.00* **– -sure** *n*

¹**encounter** *v* **1** to meet or be faced by (something bad, esp. a danger or a difficulty) **2** to meet unexpectedly

²**encounter** *n* a sudden meeting (usu. either unexpected or dangerous)

encourage *v* **-aged, -aging** to give courage or hope to (someone); urge

(someone) on to fresh efforts – **-agingly** *adv* **–~ment** *n*

encyclopaedia, -pedia *n* a book or set of books dealing with every branch of knowledge, or with one particular branch, in alphabetical order

¹**end** *n* **1** the point(s) where something stops **2** the furthest point from here: *He's down at the end of the garden* **3** the latest point in time: *the end of the year* **4** a little piece that is left over: *cigarette ends* **5** an aim or purpose: *saving money to a particular end* **6** death: *a peaceful end* **7** a particular part of a business **8** **at a loose end** having nothing to do **9** **at an end** finished **10** **end on** with the narrow sides hitting each other **11** **end to end** with the narrow sides touching each other **12** **go off the deep end** to lose control of oneself; become angry **13** **keep one's end up** to go on facing difficulties bravely and successfully **14** **make (both) ends meet** to get just enough money for one's needs **15** **no end of** *esp. spoken* an endless amount of **16** **on end a** (of time) continuously **b** upright

²**end** *v* to finish

¹**endeavour** *v* to try

²**endeavour** *n* an effort; attempt

ending *n* the end, esp. of a story, film, play, or word: *a happy ending*

endless *adj* **1** never finishing: *The journey seemed endless* **2** *technical* (of a belt, chain, etc.) circular; with the ends joined **–~ly** *adv*

endurance *n* the state or power of enduring: *Long-distance runners need great endurance*

endure *v* **endured, enduring** **1** to bear (pain, suffering, etc.) **2** *esp. written* to last: *His books will endure for ever* **3** to remain alive: *They can not endure much longer–* – **-durable** *adj* – **-ring** *adj* – **-ringly** *adv*

enemy *n* **-mies** **1** a person who hates or dislikes another person; one of 2 or more people who hate or dislike each other: *His behaviour made him many enemies* **2** someone or something that wants to harm, or is against (someone or something): *The army advanced to meet the enemy*

energetic *adj* full of energy – ~**ally** *adv*

energy *n* **-gies** **1** (of people) the quality of being full of life: *Young people usually have more energy than the old* **2** the power one can use in working: *to devote all one's energies to a job* **3** the power which does work and drives machines: *atomic/electrical energy*

engage *v* **engaged, engaging** **1** to arrange to employ: *engage a new secretary* **2 a** (of machine parts) to lock together: *This wheel engages with that wheel and turns it* **b** to cause (machine parts) to do this **3** to take up (time, attention, etc.) **4** to attack: *They engaged the enemy (in battle)*

engaged *adj* **1** (of people) busy **2** (of a telephone line) in use **3** (of seats, tables, etc.) reserved **4** having agreed to marry: *Edward and I have got engaged*

engagement *n* **1** an agreement to marry **2** a promise to meet a person, or to do something: *I can't come because I have an engagement* **3** a battle

engine *n* **1** a piece of machinery with moving parts which changes power (from steam, electricity, oil, etc.) into movement **2** also **locomotive**– a machine which pulls a railway train **3** FIRE ENGINE

¹engineer *n* **1** a person who designs machines, roads, bridges, harbours, etc.: *an electrical/a civil/mining engineer* **2** a skilled person who controls an engine or works with machines

²engineer *v* **1** to plan and make as an engineer does: *The road is very well engineered* **2** to cause by planning: *His enemies engineered his ruin*

engineering *n* **1** the science of an engineer **2** the result of engineering: *The Queen admired the engineering of the new railway*

¹English *adj* belonging to England

²English *n* **1** the people of England **2** the language of England **3** **the Queen's/King's English** good correct English

enjoy *v* **enjoyed, enjoying** **1** to get happiness from **2** to possess or use (something good): *He has always enjoyed very good health* **3** **enjoy oneself** to experience pleasure – ~**ment** *n*

enlarge *v* **enlarged, enlarging** to make or grow larger: *This photograph should enlarge well*

enormous *adj* very large indeed – ~**ness** *n*

¹**enough** *adj* as much or as many as may be necessary: *enough seats / enough money*

²**enough** *adv* **1** to the necessary degree: *warm enough to swim* **2 fair enough** all right; satisfactory **3 sure enough** as expected: *He said he would come, and sure enough he came*

³**enough** *pron* a quantity or number which satisfies need: *I have enough to do*

enquire *v* **enquired, enquiring** to inquire

enquiry *n* **-ries** an inquiry

ensure *v* **ensured, ensuring** to make (something) certain (to happen)

enter *v* **1** to come or go into: *to enter a room* **2** to come in: *Please do not enter without knocking* **3** to become a member of: *to enter the army* **4** to write down (names, amounts, etc.) in a book

enterprise *n* **1** a plan to do something daring or difficult **2** the courage that is needed for this **3** the way of carrying on business: *private enterprise* **4** an organization, esp. a business firm

entertain *v* **1** to give a party (for): *He does his entertaining in restaurants* **2** to amuse: *A teacher should entertain as well as teach* **3** to be willing to think about (an idea, doubt, etc.)

entertaining *adj* amusing: *an entertaining story* – ~**ly** *adv*

entertainment *n* **1** the act of entertaining **2** (a) public amusement: *A cinema is a place of entertainment*

enthusiasm *n* a strong feeling of interest and admiration: *his enthusiasm for Eastern music* – **-ast** *n* – **-astic** *adj* – **-astically** *adv*

entire *adj* with nothing left out; complete: *an entire set of Shakespeare's plays* – ~**ly** *adv*

¹**entrance** *n* **1** an opening by which one enters **2** the act of entering: *The actor made only 2 entrances*

²**entrance** *v* **entranced, entrancing** to delight greatly – **entranced** *adj*

entry *n* **entries 1** the act of coming or going in **2** the right to enter: *a street with a 'No Entry' sign* **3** the act or result of writing something down on a list **4** a person, thing, or group entered in a race or competition

envelope *n* a covering which contains something, esp. the cover of a letter

envious *adj* feeling or showing envy: *She was envious of her sister's beauty* – ~**ly** *adv*

environment *n* **1** the conditions which influence development: *Children need a happy home environment* **2** the air, water, and land in which man lives: *new laws to prevent the pollution of the environment* – ~**al** *adj* – ~**ally** *adv*

¹**envy** *n* a feeling one has towards someone when one wishes that one had his qualities or possessions

²envy *v* **envied, envying** to feel envy for or of

¹epidemic *adj* very common in one place for a time: *Violence is reaching epidemic levels*

²epidemic *n* a large number of cases of the same infectious disease at the same time

¹equal *adj* **1** (of 2 or more) the same in number, value, etc.: *Cut the cake into 6 equal pieces* **2** (of a person) having enough strength, ability, etc.: *Bill is quite equal to running the office* **3 on equal terms** (meeting or speaking) as equals

²equal *n* a person that is equal (to another or to oneself)

³equal *v* **-ll- 1** (of sizes or numbers) to be the same (as): *'x=y' means that x equals y* **2** to be as good, clever, etc. (as): *None of us can equal her*

equality *n* being equal

equally *adv* **1** to an equal degree: *both equally pretty* **2** in equal shares: *They shared the work equally*

equator *n* an imaginary line drawn round the world halfway between its north and south poles – ~**ial** *adj* – ~**ially** *adv*

equip *v* **-pp-** to provide with what is necessary: *He equipped himself to go sailing*

equipment *n* **1** the things needed: *office equipment* **2** equipping

erase *v* **erased, erasing** to rub out or remove (esp. a pencil mark) – ~**r** *n*

errand *n* a short journey made to get something or to carry a message

erratic *adj* changeable without reason; irregular – ~**ally** *adv*

error *n* **1** a mistake; something done wrongly **2** being wrong in behaviour or beliefs

¹escape *v* **escaped, escaping 1** to reach freedom: *The prisoners have escaped* **2** (of liquids or gases) to find a way out: *gas escaping from the pipe* **3** to avoid (an evil): *escaped death* **4** to be unnoticed by: *Nothing escaped his attention*

²escape *n* **1** the act of escaping: *The thief made his escape* **2** a case of escaping by a liquid or gas: *an escape of gas* **3** something that frees one from dull reality: *She reads love stories as an escape*

¹escort *n* **1** a person or people who go with another: *The prisoner travelled under police escort* **2** a man who takes a woman out for the evening

²escort *v* to go with (someone) as an escort

especially *adv* **1** to a particularly great degree: *I love Italy, especially in summer* **2** specially: *This crown was made especially for the King*

espionage *n French* spying; the work of finding out political secrets

Esq., also **Esquire** *n* (used as a title of politeness usu. written after a man's name): *Peter Jones, Esq.*

¹essay *v* **essayed, essaying** to try (to do something): *to essay a task*

²essay *n* **essays** a piece of writing,

usu. short and on one subject −~**ist** *n*

³**essay** *n* an attempt or effort: *She made her first essays at cooking*

¹**essential** *adj* **1 a** necessary: *Food and drink are essential to life* **b** forming the central part of: *Her most essential quality is kindness* **2** technical of an essence: *essential oils*

²**essential** *n* **1** something that is necessary **2** something that forms the essence (of something): *the essentials of grammar*

establish *v* **1** to set up (an organization) **2** to place in a position: *He established his son in business* **3** to make certain of: *to establish the truth of a story* **4** to make (a rule) **5** to cause people to believe in (a claim, fact, etc.): *She established her fame as an actress*

estate *n* **1** a piece of land in the country, usu. with a large house on it **2** a piece of land on which buildings have all been built together in a planned way **3** the whole of a person's property, according to the law **4** *old use* (esp. of France before the Revolution) social or political class: *The 3 estates of the realm (*=country*) were the lords, the priests, and the common people*

estate agent *n* a person whose business is to sell and buy houses and land −**estate agency** *n*

¹**estimate** *v* -mated, -mating **1** to calculate the value of something: *I estimate her age at 35* **2** to calculate the cost of doing a job − **-tor** *n*

²**estimate** *n* **1** a calculation (of the value, degree, or quality of something): *My estimate of her character was wrong* **2** an offer to do a job for a certain price: *We got 2 or 3 estimates before having the roof repaired*

estimation *n* judgment or opinion: *He has lowered himself in my estimation*

etc., also **et cetera** *adv Latin* and the rest; and so on

eternal *adj* going on for ever: *Rome has been called the Eternal City* −~**ly** *adv*

Eucharist *n* (the bread and wine taken at) the Christian ceremony based on Christ's last supper on Earth −~**ic** *adj*

¹**even** *adj* **1** flat, level: *Cut the bushes even with the fence* **2** unchanging: *an even temperature* **3** equal: *He won the first game and I won the second, so now we're even* **4** (of a number) that can be divided exactly by 2: *2,4,6,8, etc. are even numbers* −~**ly** *adv* −**evenness** *n*

²**even** *adv* **1** (*used before the surprising part of a statement)* which is more than might be expected: *Even John doesn't go out in the summer (*so certainly nobody else does). / *John doesn't go out even in the summer* (so certainly not in the winter) **2** indeed; and one might almost say: *He looked pleased, even delighted*

3 still; yet: *It's even colder than yesterday*

evening *n* **1** the end of the day and early part of the night **2** a party, performance, etc., happening in the evening: *a musical evening*

event *n* **1** a happening: *the chief events of 1977* **2** a race, competition, etc., arranged as part of a day's sports: *The next event will be the 100 yards race* **3 at all events** in spite of everything: *She had a terrible accident, but at all events she wasn't killed* **4 in any event** whatever may happen: *I'll probably see you but in any event I'll telephone* **5 in the event of (something)** if (something) happens: *He asked his sister to look after his children in the event of his death*

eventually *adv* in the end: *He worked so hard that eventually he made himself ill*

ever *adv* **1** at any time: *Have you ever been to Paris?* **2** at any time before: *faster than ever* **3** (used for giving force to an expression): *I pulled as hard as ever I could* **4** always: *the ever-increasing population* **5 ever so/such** *esp. spoken* very **6 for ever** forever

every *adj* **1** each, counted one by one (of more than 2): *I enjoyed every minute of it* **2** once in each: *He comes every day* **3** as much as possible: *She made every attempt* **4** all the others: *Every other girl but me got a prize!*

everybody –also **everyone** *pron* every person

everything *pron* all; the whole, made up of a number of things: *Everything is ready for the party*

everywhere *adv* in, at, or to every place: *I've looked everywhere*

evidence *n* **1** (esp. in science or law) words or things which prove a statement or make a matter more clear: *Can you show me any evidence for your statement?* **2 in evidence** able to be seen and noticed: *Mrs Jones was much in evidence at the party* **3 turn Queen's/King's evidence** (of a criminal) to speak against another criminal in a lawcourt

evident *adj* clear because of evidence: *It's evident that you are tired* **–~ly** *adv*

¹evil *adj* **-ll-** very bad; wicked; harmful: *evil thoughts* **–evilly** *adv*

²evil *n* (a) great wickedness or misfortune: *'Deliver us from evil'* (prayer)

¹exact *v* *esp. written* to demand and obtain by force, threats, etc.: *He exacted obedience from the children* **–~ion** *n*

²exact *adj* correct and without mistakes: *the exact time* **–~ness, ~itude** *n*

exactly *adv* **1** with complete correctness: *The train arrived at exactly 8 o'clock* **2** just; quite: *The doctor told him not to smoke, but he did exactly the opposite* **3** I agree!: *'We need a drink.' 'Exactly! Let's have one'*

exaggerate *v* **-rated, -rating** to make (something) seem larger, better, worse, etc., than in reality: *It was a rabbit, not a lion; you're exaggerating as usual!* –~**d** *adj* –~**dly** *adv*

examination *n* **1** also (*esp. spoken*) **exam** a test of knowledge **2** (an act of) examining: *a medical examination / the examination of the witnesses*

examine *v* **-ined, -ining 1** to look at closely, in order to find out something: *The doctor examined her carefully* **2** to ask (a person) questions, in order to measure knowledge or find out something **--iner** *n*

example *n* **1** something taken from a number of things of the same kind, which shows a general rule: *Her rudeness was a typical example of her usual bad manners* **2** a person, or behaviour, that is worthy of being copied: *Mary's courage is an example to us all* **3 make an example of someone** to punish someone so that others will be afraid to behave as he did

exceed *v* **1** to be greater than: *The cost will not exceed £50* **2** to do more than: *exceeding the speed limit*

exceedingly *adv* very: *exceedingly kind*

excel *v* **-ll-** to be very good; be better than: *She excels as a teacher*

excellent *adj* very good; of very high quality – **-ence** *n* –~**ly** *adv*

¹**except** *v* to leave out: *You will all be punished; I can except no one* –~**ed** *adj Everyone enjoyed walking home,*

John excepted; he grumbled all the way –~**ing** *prep*

²**except** –also **excepting** *prep*- but not; leaving out: *all the questions except for the last one / I like her except when she's angry*

³**except** *conj* apart from: *She can do everything except cook*

exception *n* **1** (a case of) excepting or being excepted: *You will all be punished. I can make no exceptions* **2 take exception (to)** to be made angry (by) **3 with the exception of** except; apart from

exceptional *adj* unusual, often in a good sense –~**ly** *adv*

¹**excess** *n* **1** the fact of exceeding, or an amount by which something exceeds **2** something more than is reasonable: *an excess of anger* **3 in excess of** more than: *to spend in excess of one's income*

²**excess** *adj* additional; more than usual: *excess postal charges*

excessive *adj* too much; too great –~**ly** *adv*

¹**exchange** *n* **1** exchanging: *He gave me an apple in exchange for a cake* **2** also **telephone exchange**– a central place where all the telephone wires are joined so that people may speak to each other **3** a place where businessmen meet to buy and sell goods: *the Corn Exchange / the Stock Exchange*

²**exchange** *v* **exchanged, exchanging 1** to give and receive (something in return for something else): *John exchanged hats with Peter* **2 exch-**

ange contracts to complete the first stages in buying or selling a house **3 exchange words/blows** to quarrel/fight –~**able** *adj*

excite *v* **excited, exciting 1** to cause (someone) to lose calmness and to have strong feelings, often pleasant: *The story excited the little boy very much* **2** to cause to happen by raising strong feelings: *The king's cruelty excited a rising of the people* **3** to make active: *Strong coffee excites your nerves*

excitement *n* being excited

excluding *prep* not including: *30 people, excluding me*

excursion *n* a short journey for pleasure

¹**excuse** *v* **excused, excusing 1** to forgive for a small fault: *Please excuse my bad handwriting* **2** to make (bad behaviour) seem less bad: *Nothing will excuse his cruelty to his children* **3** to free (someone) from a duty: *Can I be excused from football practice?*

²**excuse** *n* the reason given when asking to be forgiven: *Have you any excuse to offer for coming so late?*

execute *v* **-cuted, -cuting 1** to carry out (an order or piece of work) **2** *law* to carry out the orders in (a will) **3** to kill as a lawful punishment: *executed for murder*

execution *n* **1** the carrying out of an order or piece of work **2** the act of carrying out the orders in a will **3** (a) lawful killing as a punishment: *Executions used to be held in public*

¹**executive** *adj* concerned with making and carrying out decisions: *a man of great executive ability*

²**executive** *n* a person or group in an executive position

¹**exercise** *n* **1** (a) use of any part of the body or mind so as to strengthen and improve it: *get more exercise* **2** a question or set of questions to be answered by a pupil for practice **3** the use of a power or right (esp. in the phrase **the exercise of**) **4** a movement made by soldiers, naval ships, etc., to practise fighting

²**exercise** *v* **-cised, -cising 1** to give or take exercise **2** to use (a power or right): *exercise patience*

exert *v* to use (strength, skill, etc.) ~**ion** *n*

¹**exhaust** *v* **1** to tire out **2** to use up completely: *My patience is exhausted*

²**exhaust** *n* **1** also **exhaust pipe**– the pipe which allows unwanted gas, steam, etc., to escape from an engine or machine **2** the gas or steam which escapes through this pipe

¹**exhibit** *v* **1** to show in public **2** to show other people that one possesses (a feeling, quality, etc.) –~**or** *n*

²**exhibit** *n* something exhibited

exhibition *n* **1** a public show of objects **2** an act of exhibiting **3** money given by a school or university to a specially deserving student **4 make an exhibition of oneself** to behave foolishly in public

¹**exile** *n* 1 unwanted absence from one's country, often for political reasons 2 a person who has been forced to leave his country

²**exile** *v* **exiled, exiling** to send into exile

exist *v* 1 to live or be real: *The Roman Empire existed for several centuries* 2 (of a person) to continue to live, esp. with difficulty: *so poor they can hardly exist*

existence *n* 1 existing: *the existence of God* 2 life; way of living

exit *n* 1 a way out 2 an act of leaving, esp. of an actor: *Make your exit through the door at the back of the stage*

exorbitant *adj* (of cost, demands, etc.) unreasonably great: *exorbitant prices* – **-tance** *n* –~**ly** *adv*

expand *v* to make or grow larger –~**able** *adj* –**expansion** *n*

expect *v* 1 to think (that something will happen or that one will receive something): *I expect he'll pass the examination* 2 to wait for 3 to believe and hope (that someone will do something): *The officer expected his men to do their duty* 4 to suppose; think: *'Who broke that cup?' 'I expect it was the cat.'* 5 **be expecting** to be pregnant

expedition *n* (the persons, vehicles, etc., going on) a journey

expel *v* **-ll-** 1 to force out: *to expel air from one's lungs* 2 to dismiss officially (from a school, club, etc.)

expend *v* to spend or use up (esp. time, care, etc.)

expense *n* 1 cost 2 **at someone's expense a** with someone paying the cost **b** (esp. of a joke or trick) against someone: *He tried to be clever at my expense* 3 **spare no expense** to try hard without considering cost

expensive *adj* costing a lot of money –~**ly** *adv*

¹**experience** *n* 1 knowledge or skill which comes from practice rather than from books 2 something that happens to one and has an effect on the mind: *Our journey by camel was quite an experience*

²**experience** *v* **-enced, -encing** to undergo as an experience

¹**experiment** *n* (a) trial made in order to learn or prove something –~**al** *adj* –~**ally** *adv*

²**experiment** *v* to make an experiment –~**ation** *n*

expert *adj, n* (a person) with special knowledge or training –~**ly** *adv* –~**ness** *n*

expire *v* **expired, expiring** 1 to come to an end: *My season ticket will expire this week* 2 *literature* to die

explain *v* 1 to give the meaning (of something): *Explain what this word means* 2 to be the reason for; account for –~**er** *n*

explanation *n* 1 explaining 2 something that explains: *The only explanation for his behaviour is that he's mad*

explode *v* **exploded, exploding** 1 to blow up or burst 2 to show sudden violent feeling: *to explode with anger*

explore *v* **explored, exploring 1** to travel into or through (a place) for the purpose of discovery **2** to examine carefully in order to learn more: *explored the possibilities* –**explorer** *n* – **-ration** *n*

explosion *n* **1** (a loud noise caused by) an act of exploding **2** a sudden bursting out: *explosions of laughter* **3** a sudden increase

¹**explosive** *adj* **1** that can explōde **2** that can cause people to explode: *The question of race today is an explosive one* –~**ly** *adv* –~**ness** *n*

²**explosive** *n* an explosive substance

¹**export** *v* to send (goods) out of a country for sale –~**able** *adj* –~**ation** *n* –~**er** *n*

²**export** *n* **1** exporting **2** something that is exported: *the chief exports of Australia* **3** ˈ**invisible exports** money brought into a country in other ways than by the sale of goods

expose *v* **exposed, exposing 1** to uncover: *to expose one's skin to the sun* **2** to leave (a baby) to die of cold and hunger out of doors **3** to make known (a secretly guilty person or action): *I threatened to expose him* **3** to uncover (a film) to the light, when taking a photograph

¹**express** *adj* **1** (of a command, wish, etc.) clearly stated **2** (of an intention or purpose) special: *I came with the express purpose of seeing you* **3** going or sent quickly: *an express letter*

²**express** *n* **1** also **express train** – a fast train: *the 9.30 express to London*

2 a service given by the post office, railways, etc., for carrying things faster

³**express** *v* **1** to show (a feeling, opinion, or fact) in words or in some other way: *She expressed her thanks* **2** to press (oil, juice, etc.) out: *juice expressed from oranges*

⁴**express** *adv* by express: *sent the parcel express*

expression *n* **1** expressing: *They greeted him with many expressions of pleasure* **2** the showing of feeling: *She sings with much expression* **3** a word or phrase: *'To kick the bucket' is a slang expression meaning 'to die'* **4** a look on a person's face **5** (in mathematics) a collection of terms separated from each other by + and -: $x^2 + 4$ *is an expression*

extend *v* **1** (of space, land, or time) to reach, stretch, or continue **2** to make longer or greater: *to extend one's garden* **3** to stretch out (a part of one's body) **4** to give or offer (help, friendship, etc.): *to extend a warm welcome to him*

extension *n* **1** extending or of being extended **2** a part which is added to make anything longer, wider, or greater **3** any of many telephone lines which connect the central board to various rooms or offices **4** **University Extension** teaching and examining students who cannot attend a university all the time

extensive *adj* covering a large surface **2** large in amount: *extensive damage* –~**ly** *adv* –~**ness** *n*

extent *n* 1 the length or area to which something extends: *the full extent of the Sahara desert* 2 (a) degree: *I agree with you to some extent*

exterior *n* the outside: *the exterior of the house* –**exterior** *adj*

¹**extra** *adj, adv* beyond what is usual

²**extra** *n* 1 something added, for which an extra charge is made 2 a film actor who has a small part in a crowd scene: *We need 1,000 extras for the big scene when they cross the Red Sea* 3 a special edition of a newspaper 4 a run in cricket not made off the bat

extraordinary *adj* 1 very strange 2 more than ordinary: *a girl of extraordinary beauty* 3 as well as the ordinary one(s): *There will be an extraordinary meeting next Wednesday* – **-rily** *adv*

¹**extreme** *adj* 1 at the very beginning or very end 2 the greatest possible: *extreme heat* 3 going beyond the usual limits: *extreme opinions*

²**extreme** *n* 1 an extreme degree: *Sometimes he eats too much and sometimes nothing. He goes from one extreme to the other* 2 **go/be driven to extremes** to act too violently

extremely *adv* very

¹**eye** *n* 1 the organ of sight, of which there are 2 at the front of the human head 2 the front part of this organ, with the coloured parts which can be seen: *Her children have blue eyes* 3 the power of seeing: *To the painter's eye, this would be a beautiful scene* 4 the

hole in a needle through which the thread passes 5 the dark spot on a potato, from which a new plant can grow 6 the calm centre of a storm, esp. of a hurricane 7 a small link of metal into which a hook fits for fastening: *Her dress fastens with hooks and eyes* 8 **catch someone's eye a** (of things) to be noticed **b** to draw someone's attention to oneself 9 **get/keep one's eye in** (esp. in cricket and other ball games) to get/keep, through practice, the ability to judge the speed and direction of a ball 10 **have an eye for** to have the ability to see, judge, and understand clearly 11 **in the eye/eyes of the law** according to the law; as the law sees it 12 **more than meets the eye** more than actually appears or is seen 13 **one in the eye for** *esp. spoken* a disappointment or defeat for 14 **see eye to eye** to agree completely – **~less** *adj*

²**eye** *v* **eyed, eyeing** *or* **eying** to look at closely or with desire: *She eyed me jealously*

eyebrow *n* 1 the line of hairs above each of the 2 human eyes 2 **raise one's eyebrows** to express surprise, doubt, displeasure, or disapproval

eyelash *n* any of the small hairs of which a number grow from the edge of each eyelid in humans and most hairy animals

eyelid *n* either of the pieces of covering skin which can move down to close each eye

eyesight *n* the power of seeing

fable *n* **1** a short story that teaches a moral or truth, esp. a story in which animals or objects speak **2** a story about great people who never actually lived; legend; myth **3** a false story or account

fabric *n* **1** cloth made by threads woven together in any of various ways **2** framework, base, or system: *the fabric of society* **3** the walls, roof, etc., of a building

fabulous –also *(esp. spoken)* **fab** *adj* **1** (nearly) unbelievable: *a fabulous amount* **2** *esp. spoken* very good or pleasant; excellent **3** existing or told about in fables: *fabulous creatures*

¹face *n* **1** the front part of the head from the chin to the hair **2** a look or expression **3** a position of respect (esp. in the phrases **lose** *or* **save one's face**) **4** part of the surface of a solid, contained between edges **5** the front, upper, outer, or most important surface of something **6** the surface of a rock, either on or below the ground, from which coal, gold, diamonds, etc., are dug: *The miners work at the face for 7 hours each day* **7** the style or size of a letter as used by a printer **8 fly in the face of** to act in opposition to, on purpose **9 have the face** to be bold or rude enough to **10 in the face of** against (something which opposes) **11 on the face of it** judging by what one can see; apparently **12 put a good/bold face on something** to behave or make it appear as if

things are better than they are **13 set one's face against** to oppose strongly

²face *v* **faced, facing 1** to have or turn the face or front towards or in a certain direction **2** to meet or oppose firmly and not try to avoid: *He faced up to his difficulties* **3** to need consideration or action by: *The difficulty that faces us is the number of those in need* **4** to cover or partly cover (esp. the front part of) with a different material

facilities *n* means to do things; that which can be used: *One of the facilities is a large library*

fact *n* **1** something that has actual existence or an event that has actually happened or is happening; something true; information regarded as true: *The detective asked for for facts, not opinions* **2** *law* deed; crime: *an accessory after the fact* **3 as a matter of fact, in fact** really the truth is that

factor *n* **1** any of the forces, conditions, influences, etc., that act with others to bring about a result: *His manner is a factor in his success* **2 a** (in arithmetic) a number which, when multiplied by one or more numbers, produces a given number: *2, 3, 4, and 6 are all factors of 12* **b** (in algebra) an expression which will divide into a given expression

factory *n* **-ries** a building or group of buildings where goods are made, esp. in great quantities by machines

fade *v* **faded, fading 1** to lose or cause to lose strength, colour, freshness, etc.: *Cut flowers soon fade* **2** to disappear or die gradually: *The shapes faded (away) into the night* **3** (in film or sound mixing, as in cinema or broadcasting) to change the strength of (sound or vision) slowly

fail *v* **1** to be (judged in a test to be) unsuccessful (in) **2** to decide that (somebody) has not passed an examination **3** to not produce the desired result; not perform or do: *Last year the crops failed* **4** to be of little or no use when needed: *His friends failed him when he needed money* **5** to lose strength; become weak **6** (of a business) to be unable to continue

failure *n* **1** lack of success; failing **2** a person, attempt, or thing that fails **3** (an example of) the state of being unable to perform: *(a) heart failure* **4** inability of a business to continue

¹**faint** *adj* **1** weak and about to lose consciousness: *He felt faint* **2** performed in a weak manner; lacking strength, courage, or spirit: *faint praise* **3** lacking clearness, brightness, strength, etc.: *faint sound* –~**ly** *adv* –~**ness** *n*

²**faint** *v* to lose consciousness, as because of loss of blood, heat, or great pain

³**faint** *n* an act or condition of fainting

¹**fair** *adj* **1** free from dishonesty or injustice: *a fair businessman* **2** that is allowed to be done, given, etc., as under the rules of a game: *It is not fair to kick another player in football* **3** fairly good, large, fine, etc. **4** not stormy; fine; clear **5** having a good clear clean appearance or quality: *a fair copy of a report* **6** (esp. of a person's skin or hair) light in colour; not dark **7** (of women) *esp. old use* beautiful; attractive –~**ness** *n*

²**fair** *adv* in a just or honest manner or according to the rules; fairly: *to play fair*

³**fair** *n* **1** a funfair **2** a market, esp. one held at a particular place at regular periods **3** a very large show of goods, advertising, etc.: *a book fair*

fairly *adv* **1** in a manner that is free from dishonesty, injustice, etc.: *He told the facts fairly* **2** in a manner that is allowed or according to certain rules **3** for the most part; rather; quite: *He paints fairly well* **4** completely; plainly

fairy *n* **-ries** a small imaginary figure with magical powers and shaped like a human

fairy tale –also **fairy story** *n* **1** a story about fairies and other magical people **2** a story or account that is hard to believe, esp. one intended to deceive –**fairy-tale** *adj*

faith *n* **1** strong belief; trust, which may go beyond reason or proof: *He has faith in my ability* **2** word of honour; promise: *I kept/broke faith with them* **3** the condition of being sincere; loyalty: *to act in good faith* **4** belief and trust in and loyalty to God **5** something that is believed in strongly, esp. a system of religious belief; religion

faithful *adj* **1** full of or showing loyalty: *a faithful friend* **2** believing strongly in religion **3** sure to do what has been promised or what is expected: *faithful worker* **4** true to the facts or to an original: *faithful account* **5** loyal to one's (marriage) partner by having no sexual relationship with anyone else **−~ness** *n*

faithfully *adv* **1** with faith **2** exactly: *I copied the letter faithfully* **3 yours faithfully** the usual polite way of introducing one's name at the end of a letter

¹fake *v* **faked, faking 1** to make or change (esp. a work of art) so that it appears better, more valuable, etc. **2** to pretend: *She faked illness* **−faker**

²fake *n* a person or thing that is not what he or it looks like: *The painting looked old but was a recent fake*

³fake *adj* made and intended to deceive

¹fall *v* **fell, fallen, falling 1** to descend or go down freely, as by weight or loss of balance; drop: *The clock fell off the shelf* **2** to come down from a standing position, esp. suddenly: *He fell to his knees* **3** to become lower in level, degree, or quantity: *Their voices fell* **4** to come or happen, as if by descending: *Night fell quickly* **5** to pass into a new state or condition; become: *fall asleep* **6** to hang loosely: *His hair falls over his shoulders* **7** to drop down wounded or dead, esp. to die in battle **8** to be defeated or conquered: *The city fell (to the enemy)* **9** to lose power or a high position **10** to slope in a downward direction: *The land falls towards the river* **11** (of the face) to take on a look of sadness, disappointment, shame, etc., esp. suddenly **12 fall over backwards/oneself to do something** to be very eager or too eager to do something

²fall *n* **1** the act of falling: *He suffered a fall* **2** (the quantity of) something that has fallen: *a fall of rocks* **3** a decrease in quantity, price, demand, degree, etc. **4** the distance through which anything falls **5** the defeat of a city, state, etc.; surrender or capture

false *adj* **1** not true or correct **2** declaring what is untrue; deceitful **3** not faithful or loyal **4** not real: *false teeth* **5** made or changed so as to deceive **−~ly** *adv* **−~ness** *n* **−falsity** *n*

falsehood *n* **1** an untrue statement **2** the telling of lies

fame *n* the condition of being well known and talked about **−~d** *adj*

¹familiar *n* a close friend

²familiar *adj* **1** generally known, seen, or experienced; common: *a familiar sight* **2** having a thorough knowledge (of): *I am familiar with that book* **3** informal; easy: *He wrote* *in a familiar style* **4** too friendly for the occasion

¹**family** *n* **-lies 1** any group of people related by blood or marriage, esp. a group of 2 grown-ups and their children **2** children: *Have you any family?* **3** all those people descended from a common ancestor **4** a group of things related by common characteristics, esp. a group of plants, animals, or languages **5 in the family way** *esp. spoken* pregnant

²**family** *adj* suitable for children as well as older people: *a family film*

famine *n* (a case of) very serious lack of food: *Many people die of famine every year*

famous *adj* very well known

¹**fan** *n* any of various instruments meant to make a flow of air, esp. cool air

²**fan** *v* **-nn- 1** to cause air, esp. cool air, to blow on (something) with or as if with a fan **2** to excite to activity with or as if with a fan **3** to spread like a fan: *The soldiers fanned out across the hillside*

³**fan** *n* a very keen follower or supporter

¹**fancy** *n* **-cies 1** imagination, esp. in a free and undirected form **2** the power of creating imaginative ideas and expressions, esp. in poetry **3** an image, opinion, or liking not based on fact or reason: *I've taken a fancy to that silly hat*

²**fancy** *v* **-cied, -cying? 1** to form a picture of; imagine **2** to believe without being certain **3** to have a liking for; wish for: *I fancy that girl*

³**fancy** *adj* **-cier, -ciest** more ornamental, brightly coloured, expensive, or finer than ordinary everyday (things) **–fancily** *adv*

fantastic *adj* **1** odd, strange, or wild in shape, meaning, etc.; not controlled by reason or related to reality: *fantastic dream/story/fears* **2** very great or large **3** *esp. spoken* very good; wonderful **–~ally** *adv*

¹**far** *adv* **farther** *or* **further** , **farthest** *or* **furthest 1** at or to a great distance: *to travel far from home* **2** a long way; very much: *far too busy* **3 as/so far as** to the degree or distance that **4 how far** to what degree or distance **5 in as/so far as** to the degree that **6 So far, so good** Things are satisfactory up to this point, at least

²**far** *adj* **farther** *or* **further, farthest** *or* **furthest 1** also **farther–** more distant of the 2: *the far/farther side of the street* **2 a far cry** a long way

farce *n* **1** a (type of) light humorous play full of silly things happening **2** an occasion or set of events that is a silly and empty show **–farcical** *adj* **–farcically** *adv*

¹**fare** *v* **fared, faring** *rare* to get on; succeed: *I fared quite well in the exam*

²**fare** *n* **1** the price charged to carry a person, as by bus, train, or taxi **2** a paying passenger, esp. in a taxi **3** food, esp. as provided at a meal

farewell *n, interj* goodbye

¹**farm** *n* an area of land, together with

its buildings, concerned with the growing of crops or the raising of animals

²**farm** *v* to use (land) for growing crops, raising animals, etc.

farmer *n* a man who owns or plans the work on a farm

farther *adv, adj* (comparative of FAR) at or to a greater distance or more distant point; further

farthest *adv, adj* (*superlative of* FAR) most far

fascinate *v* -nated, -nating to charm powerfully; be very interesting to: *I'm fascinated with/by Buddhist ceremonies* – -ting *adj* – -tingly *adv*

Fascism *n* a political system in which all industrial activity is controlled by the state, no political opposition is allowed, nationalism is strongly encouraged, and socialism violently opposed

fascist *n, adj* (a supporter) of Fascism

¹**fashion** *n* **1** the way of dressing or behaving that is considered the best at a certain time **2** a manner; way of making or doing something: *He behaves in a very strange fashion* **3 after a fashion** not very well

²**fashion** *v* to shape or make (something into or out of something else) usu. with one's hands or with only a few tools

¹**fast** *adj* **1** quick; moving quickly **2** firm; firmly fixed: *The colours aren't fast and may wash out* **3** (of a photographic film) suitable for being exposed for a very short time **4** (of a clock) showing a time that is later

than the true time **5** allowing quick movement: *the fast lane of the motorway* **6 make fast** to tie firmly: *Make the boat fast*

²**fast** *adv* **1** quickly **2** firmly; tightly: *to stick fast*

³**fast** *v* to eat no food, esp. for religious reasons

⁴**fast** *n* an act or period of fasting: *He broke his fast by drinking some milk*

fasten *v* to make or become firmly fixed or closed: *He fastened (up) his coat*

fastener *n* something that fastens things together

fastening *n* something that holds things shut, esp. doors and windows

¹**fat** *adj* -tt- **1** (of creatures and their bodies) having (too) much fat **2** (of meat) containing a lot of fat **3** thick and well-filled **4-** (esp. of land) producing plentiful crops **5 a fat lot of** *sl* no; not any: *A fat lot of good/of use that is!* – ~ness *n*

²**fat** *n* **1** the material under the skins of animals and human beings which helps to keep them warm **2 a** this substance considered as food **b** vegetable oil in a solid form used in the same way

fatal *adj* **1** causing or resulting in death **2** very dangerous and unfortunate

fatally *adv* **1** so as to cause death **2** as was very unfortunate

fate *n* **1** the imaginary cause beyond human control that is believed to decide events **2** an end or result, esp. death: *They met with a terrible fate*

father *n* a male parent – ~**less** *adj*

¹**fault** *n* 1 a mistake or imperfection 2 a bad point, but not of a serious moral kind, in someone's character: *Your only fault is carelessness* 3 technical (in geology) a crack in the earth's surface, where one band of rock has slid against another 4 (in games like tennis) a mistake in a service, which may lose a point 5 **at fault** in the wrong

²**fault** *v* 1 to find a fault in 2 (of rocks) to break and form a fault

faulty *adj* -ier, -iest (esp. of machines, apparatus, etc.) having faults –**faultily** *adv*

¹**favour** *n* 1 encouragement and approval; willingness to be kind 2 unfairly generous treatment; (too much) sympathy for one person as compared to others: *She always favours her son* 3 a kind act that is not forced or necessary: *Will you do me a favour and phone for me?* 4 a badge or coloured ribbon worn to show that one belongs to a political party, supports a football team, etc. 5 **in favour of a** believing in or choosing; on the side of **b** (of a cheque) payable to

²**favour** *v* 1 to regard or treat with favour 2 (of conditions) to make pleasant and easy 3 (of a child) to look like (a parent): *He favours his father with his brown eyes*

favourable *adj* 1 (of a message, answer, etc.) saying what one wants to hear 2 (of conditions) advantageous; favouring – -**rably** *adv*

¹**favourite** *n* 1 something or someone that is loved above all others 2 someone who receives too much favour: *A teacher shouldn't have favourites* 3 (in horseracing) the horse in each race that is expected to win

²**favourite** *adj* being a favourite: *his favourite son*

¹**fear** *n* 1 the feeling that one has when danger is near: *to be without fear* 2 danger 3 *old use* great respect (in the phrase **the fear of God**) 4 **No fear!** *esp. spoken* (in answer to a suggestion that one should do something) Certainly not! 5 **without fear or favour** with justice

²**fear** *v esp. written* 1 to be afraid of 2 to be afraid (for the safety of someone or something) 3 **I fear** (*used when telling bad news*) I'm sorry that I must now say

fearful *adj* 1 (making someone) afraid: *a fearful storm* 2 very great; frightful: *a fearful waste of time!* – ~**ly** *adv* – ~**ness** *n*

fearless *adj* without fear – ~**ly** *adv* – ~**ness** *n*

¹**feast** *n* 1 a splendid esp. public meal; a specially good or grand meal: *The king gave/held a feast* 2 a day kept in memory of some happy religious event

²**feast** *v* to provide for someone, or have, a specially good or grand meal: *We feasted on chicken and coconuts*

feat *n* a clever esp. bodily action, showing strength, skill, or courage: *His leap was quite a feat*

¹feather *n* **1** one of the many parts of the covering which grows on a bird's body **2 a feather in one's cap** a deserved honour that one is proud of

²feather *v* **1** to put feathers on: *to feather arrows* **2** to cover with feathers (esp. in the phrase **tar and feather**) **3** to make the blade of an oar lie flat on the surface of the water **4 feather one's nest** to make oneself rich, esp. dishonestly, through a job in which one is trusted

¹feature *n* **1** a (typical or noticeable) part or quality **2** any of the noticeable parts of the face **3** a special long article in a newspaper: *a front-page feature on coalmining* **4** a full-length cinema film with an invented story portrayed by actors

²feature *v* **-tured, -turing 1** to include as a special feature: *a new film featuring Dustin Hoffman* **2** to be present as a feature: *Fish features largely in their diet*

February *n* **-ries** the 2nd month of the year

fed up *adj esp. spoken* unhappy, tired, and discontented, esp. about something dull one has had too much of

fee *n* a sum of money paid for professional services to a doctor, lawyer, private school, etc.

feeble *adj* **-bler, -blest** weak; with little force **-feebly** *adv* **-~ness** *n*

¹feed *v* **fed, feeding 1** to give food to **2** (of animals or babies) to eat: *The horses fed quietly* **3** to put, supply, or provide, esp. continually: *to feed the wire into the hole*

²feed *n* **1** a meal taken by an animal or baby **2** food for animals: *hen feed* **3** the part of a machine through which the machine is supplied: *a blockage in the petrol feed*

¹feel *v* **felt, feeling 1** to get knowledge of by touching with the fingers: *Feel the quality of the cloth* **2** to experience (the touch or movement of something) **3** to experience (a condition of the mind or body); be consciously: *Do you feel hungry yet?* **4** to believe, esp. for the moment (something that cannot be proved): *She felt that he no longer loved her* **5** to (be able to) experience or suffer from sensations **6 feel free to do something** to be welcome to do something

²feel *n* **1** the sensation caused by feeling something: *This cloth has a warm woolly feel* **2** an act of feeling **3 get the feel of** to become used to and skilled at

¹feeling *n* **1** a consciousness of (something felt in the mind or body): *a feeling of shame/thirst* **2** a belief or opinion, not based on reason **3** the power to feel sensation: *He lost all feeling in his toes* **4** excitement of mind; emotion; understanding: *He played the piano with feeling*

²**feeling** *adj* showing strong feelings: *a feeling look* –~**ly** *adv*

¹**fell** *v* **1** to cut down (a tree) **2** *esp. written* to knock down (a person)

²**fell** *past tense of* FALL

fellow *n* **1** *esp. spoken* a man **2** a member of a society connected with some branch of learning **3** a high-ranking member of an Oxford or Cambridge college **4** someone with whom one shares a (stated) activity or spends time in a (stated) place: *We were schoolfellows*

fellowship *n* **1** a group or society **2** the position of **a** a fellow of a college **b** a paid research worker at a university **3** the condition of being friends through sharing or doing something together; companionship

¹**felt** *n* thick firm cloth made of wool, hair, or fur, pressed flat: *a felt hat*

²**felt** *past tense and past part. of* FEEL

¹**female** *n* a female person or animal

²**female** *adj* **1** of the sex that gives birth to young **2** (of plants or flowers) producing fruit **3** *technical* having a hole made to receive a part that fits into it: *a female plug*

¹**feminine** *adj* **1** of or having the qualities suitable for a woman **2** (in grammar) in a class of words that are not masculine or neuter: *'She" is a feminine pronoun* – **-nity** *n*

²**feminine** *n* the class of feminine words

¹**fence** *n* **1** a wall made of wood or wire, dividing 2 areas of land **2** someone who buys and sells stolen goods **3 sit on the fence** *usu. offen-*sive to avoid taking sides in an argument, in order to see where one's own advantage lies

²**fence** *v* **fenced, fencing 1** to fight with a sword as a sport **2** to avoid giving an honest answer to a question **3** to put a fence round

¹**ferry** *v* **-ried, -rying** to carry on or as if on a ferryboat

²**ferry** –also **ferryboat** *n* **-ries** a boat that goes across a river or any other narrow stretch of water, carrying people and things

fertile *adj* **1** producing many young, fruits, or seeds: *Some fish are very fertile: they lay 1,000's of eggs* **2** (of land) which produces or can produce good crops **3** (of living things) able to produce young **4** inventive; full of suggestions, ideas, etc.: *a fertile imagination*

festival *n* **1** also **festivity**– public gaiety and feasting **2** a time regularly marked out for this; a (religious) feast: *Christmas is one of the Christian festivals* **3** a time of the stated entertainment or at the stated place: *a pop festival*

fetch *v* **1** to go and get and bring back: *Fetch the doctor!* **2** *esp. spoken* to be sold for **3** to attract; bring: *a story that fetched the tears to one's eyes*

fever *n* **1** a medical condition caused by many illnesses, in which the sufferer suddenly develops a very high temperature **2** any of a group of (stated) diseases that cause this:

yellow fever **3** an excited state: *in a fever of impatience*

feverish *adj* **1** having or showing a slight fever **2** caused by fever

few *adj, pron, n* **1** (*of plurals; used without* a, *to show the smallness of the number)* not many; not enough: *who has fewest mistakes?* **2** (*of plurals; used with* a) a small number, but at least some: *Can you stay a few days longer?* **3 few and far between** rare; not happening often **4 quite a few** also **a good few** a fair number (of)

fiancé –(*fem* **fiancée**) *n French* a man to whom a woman is engaged

fibre *n* **1** one of the thin thread-like parts that form many animal and plant growths such as wool, wood, or muscle. Some plant fibres are spun and woven into cloth **2** a mass of these, used for making cloth, rope, etc. **3** a (type of) thread made chemically for weaving: *man-made fibre* **4** coarse matter in food **5** (of mind or morals) **a** quality **b** strength

fiction *n* **1** stories or novels about things that did not really happen, or imagined accounts of real events, as compared to other sorts of literature like history or poetry **2** an invention of the mind; an untrue story

¹fidget *n esp. spoken* someone, esp. a child, who fidgets

²fidget *v* **1** to move one's body around restlessly, so as to annoy people:

children fidgeting in church **2** to make nervous and restless

¹field *n* **1** a stretch of land on a farm marked off in some way or surrounded by a fence or wall, and used for animals or crops **2** any open area where **a** the stated game is played **b** the stated substance is mined: *an oilfield* **c** the stated activity is practised: *an airfield* **d** the surface is of the stated kind: *a field of snow* **3** a branch of knowledge or activity: *the field of art* **4** the place where practical operations happen, as compared to places where they are planned or studied, such as offices, factories, and universities **5** (in physics) the area in which the (stated) force is felt: *a gravitational field* **6** (in horse-racing) all the horses in the race except the favourite

²field *v* **1** (in cricket and baseball) to catch or stop (a ball that has been hit) **2** to be (a member of) the team whose turn it is to do this because they are not batting **3** to put into operation; produce (an army, team, etc.)

fierce *adj* **1** angry, violent, and cruel **2** (of heat, strong feelings, etc.) very great –~**ly** *adv* –~**ness** *n*

fiery *adj* **-ier, -iest 1** flaming and violent; looking like fire: *fiery red hair* **2** quickly moved to anger or violent action

fifteen *adj, n, pron* **1** the number 15 **2** a complete team of 15 players in rugby union football – ~**th** *adj, n, pron, adv*

fifth *adj, n, pron, adv* 5th

fifty *adj, n, pron* -**ties** the number 50 – -**tieth** *adj, n, pron, adv*

¹**fight** *v* **fought, fighting 1** to use violence against (another or others) as in a battle **2** to use argument against (someone, or each other): *He and his wife are always fighting* **3** to take part in (a war, battle, etc.) **4** to try to prevent; stand against: *to fight a fire*

²**fight** *n* **1** a battle; an occasion of fighting **2** also **fighting spir·it** – the power or desire to fight: *There's no fight left in him*

¹**figure** *n* **1** (the shape of) a whole human body, as shown in art or seen in reality **2** the human shape, considered from the point of view of being attractive: *exercises to improve one's figure* **3** an important person (of the stated kind): *a political figure* **4** any of the number signs from 0 to 9: *Write the number in words and in figures* **5** (used before the number of a map, drawing, etc. in a book) **6** a line drawing such as a square, circle, or diagram, used in study or for explaining something

²**figure** *v* -**ured,** -**uring 1** to take part: *Roger figured as chief guest* **2** *US esp. spoken* to consider; believe: *I figured you'd want tea* **3** **That figures!** That seems reasonable and what I expected

¹**file** *v, n* **filed, filing** (to rub or cut with) a steel tool with a rough face, used for rubbing down, smoothing, or cutting through hard surfaces: *a nail file*

²**file** *v* **1** to put (papers or letters) in a file **2** *law* to send in or record officially: *to file an application*

³**file** *n* **1** any of various arrangements of drawers, shelves, boxes, or cases, for storing papers in an office **2** a collection of papers on one subject, stored in this way **3** a collection of related data treated as a unit in a computer

⁴**file** *v, n* (to move in) a line of people one behind the other (often in the phrase **in single file**)

¹**fill** *v* **1** to make or become full **2** to enter or cause to enter (a position) **3** to put a filling into (a tooth) **4** to fulfil; meet the needs or demands of: *to fill a prescription*

²**fill** *n* a full supply; the quantity needed to fill something; as much as one can or wants to take

¹**film** *n* **1** a thin skin of any material: *plastic film* **2** (a roll of) the prepared substance on which one takes photographs or makes cinema pictures **3** a story or subject which is photographed and projected onto a screen to give the effect of movement

²**film** *v* to make a cinema picture (of)

¹**filter** *n* **1** an apparatus containing paper, sand, etc., through which liquids can be passed so as to make them clean **2** a (coloured) glass that reduces the quantity or changes the

quality of the light admitted into a camera or telescope

²**filter** *v* **1** to send through a filter **2 a** (of a group) to move slowly **b** (of an idea) to become gradually known **3** (of traffic in Britain) to turn left, when traffic going right or straight ahead must wait until a red light changes to green

filth *n* **1** very nasty dirt **2** words, curses, etc., that are very rude or vulgar −∼**y** *adj* −∼**ily** *adv* −∼**iness** *n*

fin *n* **1** any of the winglike parts that a fish uses in swimming **2** a part shaped like this, on a man-made object such as a car, aircraft, or bomb

¹**final** *adj* **1** last; coming at the end **2** that cannot be changed: *I won't go, and that's final!*

²**final** *n* **1** the last and most important in a set of matches **2** the last edition of a daily newspaper **3** the last and most important examination in a college course

finally *adv* **1** at last **2** so as not to allow further change: *It's not finally settled yet*

¹**finance** *n* (the science of) the control of (esp. public) money − **-cial** *adj* − **-cially** *adv*

²**finance** *v* **financed, financing** to provide money for

¹**find** *v* **found, finding** **1** to discover, esp. by searching; get (someone or something that was hidden or lost) **2** to learn or discover (a fact that was not known) **3** to discover (someone or something) to be, by chance or experience: *When we arrived, we found him in bed* **4** (of things) to reach; arrive at: *The bullet found its mark* **5** to know that (something) exists or happens **6** *law* to decide (someone) to be: *'How do you find him?' 'We find him not guilty, my lord'* **7** to provide: *The cook gets £30 a week and all found* (=food, shelter, etc. all provided)

²**find** *n* something good or valuable that is found

¹**fine** *n* an amount of money paid as a punishment

²**fine** *v* **fined, fining** to take money from as a punishment −**finable, fineable** *adj*

³**fine** *adj* **1** beautiful and of high quality; better than most of its kind **2 a** very thin: *fine hair* **b** in very small grains or bits: *fine sugar* **3** (of weather) bright and sunny; not wet **4?** (of a person or conditions) healthy and comfortable: *This flat's fine for 2 people* **5** delicate; to be understood only with an effort: *fine points of an argument* **6** (of work) delicate and careful; on a small scale: *fine sewing* **7** (of words) too grand and perhaps not true: *That's all very fine, but what about me?* **8** terrible: *Your shoes are in a fine muddy state* −∼**ness** *n*

⁴**fine** *adv* **1** so as to be very thin or in very small bits **2** very well: *It suits me fine* **3** **cut/run it fine** *esp. spoken* to allow only just enough time and no more

¹finger *n* **1** one of the 5 movable parts with joints at the end of each human hand **2** one of 8 such parts (as opposed to the thumbs) **3** the part of a glove that is made to fit one of these parts **4 keep one's fingers crossed** to hope for the best **5 pull one's finger out** *sl* to start working hard

²finger *v* to feel or handle with one's fingers

fingerprint *n* the mark of a finger, as used in the discovery of crime

¹finish *v* **1** to reach or bring to an end; reach the end of (an activity): *What time does the concert finish? / We finished up in Paris* **2** to put the last touches or polish to (something that one has made): *to finish off a dress*

²finish *n* **1** the end or last part, esp. of a race **2** the appearance or condition of having been properly finished, with paint, polish, etc.: *the beautiful finish of old French furniture*

fir *n* also **firtree–** a straight tree with needleshaped leaves that bears seeds in cones

¹fire *n* **1** the condition of burning; flames and great heat **2** a heap of burning material, lit on purpose for cooking, heat, etc.: *to sit round the fire* **3** a piece of gas, or electrical, apparatus for warming a room, with the flames or red-hot wires able to be seen **4** shooting by guns; firing: *Hold your fire* (=don't shoot) strong feeling and excitement: *The boy is full of fire* **6 catch fire** to begin to burn **7 fire and sword** burning and killing in war **8 hang fire** (of events) to develop too slowly **9 open/cease fire** to start/stop shooting **10 play with fire** to take great risks **11 set on fire** also **fire, set fire to–** to light (something not really meant to burn) **12 under fire** being shot at: *to show courage under fire* **13 would go through fire and water** would face great hardship and danger

²fire *v* **fired, firing 1** (of a person or a gun) to shoot off bullets: *She fired her gun at them* **2** to send off with speed and force: *A rocket was fired at the moon. / He fired questions at the boys* **3** to set on fire **4** to bake (clay pots, dishes, etc.) in a special oven **5** *esp. spoken* to dismiss from a job; sack: *Get out! You're fired!* **6** to excite: *He was fired with the desire to visit China*

fire brigade *n* an organization for preventing and putting out fires

fire engine *n* a special vehicle that carries firemen and fire-fighting apparatus to a fire

fire escape *n* a set of metal stairs leading down outside a building to the ground, by which people can escape in case of fire

fireplace *n* the opening for a fire in the wall of a room, with a chimney above it

firework *n* a small container filled with an explosive chemical powder that burns to produce a show of light and noise, or explodes with a loud noise

¹firm *adj* **1** strong; solid; hard **2** (in business, esp. of money) not tending to become lower in value: *The pound stayed firm against the dollar* **3** steady: *Is that chair firm enough?* **4** staying strong; not changing or yielding: *a firm belief/believer / a firm hold* – ~**ly** *adv* – ~**ness** *n*

²firm *v* to make or become firm: *The jelly firmed quickly*

³firm *n* a business company

⁴firm *adv* firmly

¹first *adj, n, pron* **1** the person, thing, or group to do or be something before any others: *Ann was the first to arrive* **2** a British university examination result of the highest quality: *He got a first* **3** **at first** at the beginning **4** **the first** the slightest

²first *adv* **1** before anything else **2** for the first time: *when we first met*

first aid *n* treatment to be given by an ordinary person to a person hurt in an accident or suddenly taken ill

first-class *adj* of the highest or best quality: *first-class work*

¹fish *n* **fish** *or* **fishes 1** a creature whose blood changes temperature according to the temperature around it, which lives in water and uses its fins and tail to swim **2** part of one of these, when used as food **3** any fairly large creature that lives in water, such as a whale **4** **drink like a fish** to drink too much

alcohol **5** **like a fish out of water** uncomfortable because one is in a strange place, among strangers, etc.

²fish *v* **1** to try to catch fish; to search (for something under water) as with a hook: *to fish for trout* / *Why are you fishing around in your pockets?* **2** to catch fish in (a piece of water): *This river has been fished too much* **3 a** *esp. spoken* to try to attract admiring words **b** to enquire indirectly: *fishing for information*

fisherman *n* **-men** a man who catches fish, for sport or for his living

fishmonger *n* someone who sells fish in a shop

fist *n* the hand with the fingers closed in tightly

¹fit *n* **1** the appearance of the signs of slight illness in a sudden way, for a short time: *a fit of coughing* **2** a period of loss of consciousness with strange, uncontrolled movements of the body: *to have fits* **3** a sudden violent feeling: *in a fit of anger* **4** **by/in fits and starts** continually starting and stopping; not regularly

²fit *adj* **-tt- 1** right and suitable: *a meal fit for a king* **2** in good health; strong in bodily condition: *He runs to keep fit* **3** **fit to burst** *esp. spoken* (as if) about to explode: *laughing fit to burst* **4** **fit to drop** *esp. spoken* (as if) about to fall on the ground **5** **see/think fit to do** to decide to do (esp. something foolish)

³fit *v* **-tt- 1** to be the right size or shape (for): *The lid fits badly* **2** to make clothes the right size and shape for: *It's difficult to fit him—he's so fat* **3** to provide, and put correctly into place: *to fit new locks on the doors* **4** to be suitable (for): *His behaviour doesn't fit his new position* **5** to make suitable: *Her height fitted her for netball* **6 fit the bill** to be just what one wants

⁴fit *n* the way in which something fits: *This coat's a beautiful fit*

five *adj, n, pron* the number 5

¹fix *v* **1** to fasten firmly (into the stated position): *Fix the door open* **2** to agree on; arrange: *We've fixed the date for the wedding* **3** to protect (colours or photographic film) from the effects of light, by chemical treatment **4** to cook, prepare, or put in order: *Let me fix you a drink!* **5** to use unfair or illegal influence on (someone or something) so as to make sure of a desired result: *Can they fix the judge?* **6** *sl* to deal with; get even with (someone): *I'll fix George*

²fix *n* **1** *esp. spoken* an awkward or difficult position **2** *drug-users' sl* an injection (of the stated drug) **3** a decision on one's position in space (as when on a ship) reached by looking at the stars, taking measurements, etc.

fixture *n* **1** something necessary, such as a bath, that is fixed into a building and sold with it **2** a match or sports competition taking place on an agreed date

¹flag *n* any of various types of plant with blade-like leaves, such as the wild iris. They grow in wet places

²flag —also **flagstone** *n* a flat square of stone for a floor or path

³flag *n* **1** a square or oblong piece of cloth, usu. with a pattern or picture on it and fastened by one edge to a flagpole or rope: *to fly the flag of Norway* **2 show the white flag** to yield; show that one is cowardly or afraid **3 under the flag (of)** serving or protected (by)

⁴flag *v* **-gg-** to cause (a car or train) to stop by waving one's arm or a flag at the driver

⁵flag *v* to be or become weak and less alive or active: *his flagging interest in the subject*

flair *n* a natural ability to do some special thing: *a flair for writing*

¹flake *n* **1** a light leaflike little bit of something soft: *flakes of snow* **2** a thin flat broken-off piece of something hard: *a flake of rock*

²flake *v* **flaked, flaking** to fall off in flakes: *The paint's beginning to flake off*

¹flame *n* **1** (a tongue of) red or yellow burning gas: *The sticks burst into flames* **2 in flames** burning: *a city in flames* **3 old flame** someone with whom one used to be in love

²flame *v* **flamed, flaming** to become red, bright, etc. by or as if by burning: *The candles flamed brighter*

¹flap *n* **1** the sound of flapping **2** a light blow given by flapping **3** a wide flat thin part of anything that hangs down, esp. so as to cover an opening: *the flap of a tent* **4** *esp. spoken* a state of excited anxiety: *Don't get in a flap*

²**flap** *v* **-pp- 1** to wave slowly up and down or to and fro, making a noise: *The bird flapped its wings. / The sail flapped in the wind* **2** *esp. spoken* to be excited and anxious

¹**flare** *v* **flared, flaring** to burn with a bright flame, but uncertainly or for a short time

²**flare** *n* **1** a flaring light: *a sudden flare as she lit the gas* **2** something that provides a bright light out of doors, as a signal at an airfield

¹**flash** *v* **1** (of a light) to appear or exist for a moment: *The lightning flashed* **2** to make a flash with; shine for a moment (at): *She flashed a smile at him* **3** to move very fast: *The days flashed by* **4** to show for a moment: *to flash a message on the screen* **5** (of an idea) to come suddenly: *It flashed through his mind that she might be a spy* **6** *sl* to show the sexual parts, esp. on purpose to shock others

²**flash** *n* **1** a sudden quick bright light: *flashes of lightning* **2** one movement of a light or flag in signalling **3** a first short news report, received by telegraph, radio, etc. **4** (in photography) the method or apparatus for taking photographs in the dark **5 flash in the pan** a sudden success that offers no promise for the future, because it will not be repe-

ated **6 in a/like a flash** very quickly, suddenly, or soon

flask *n* **1** a narrow-necked bottle, as used by scientists in the laboratory **2** a flat bottle for carrying alcohol or other drinks in the pocket or fastened to one's belt, saddle, etc. **3** also **thermos, thermos flask, vacuum flask–** a bottle having 2 thin glass walls between which a vacuum is kept, used for keeping the contents either hot or cold **4** the amount of liquid that a flask contains

¹**flat** *adj* **-tt- 1** parallel with the ground; smooth and level: *The earth is round, not flat* **2** having a broad smooth surface and little thickness: *flat cakes* **3** (of beer and other gassy drinks, or their taste) having lost the gas **4** dull; uninteresting: *Everything seems so flat since Robert left* **5** (in music) lower than the true note **6** (in music) half a note lower than (in the phrases **A flat, B flat, C flat,** etc.) **7** complete; firm; with no more argument: *She gave me a flat refusal* **8** (of a tyre) without enough air in it **9** (of the feet) not having proper arches **10** (of a battery) needing to be connected with a supply of electric current and charged **11** *esp. spoken* (after an expression of time, showing surprise at its shortness) exactly; and not more: *I got dressed in 3 minutes flat!* **12 fall flat** (of an idea or plan) to fail; have no effect **–~ness** *n*

²**flat** *n* **1** a low level plain, esp. near water: *mud flats* **2** the flat part or side: *I hit him with the flat of my hand* **3** a movable upright piece of wooden or canvas stage scenery, representing esp. the wall of a room **4** (the sign, ♭, for) a flat note in music **5 on the flat** on level ground

³**flat** *adv* **1** *esp. spoken* completely: *He's flat broke* **2** (in music) lower than the true note

⁴**flat** –also **apartment** *n* a set of rooms esp. on one floor, including a kitchen and bathroom, usu. one of many such sets in a building or block

flatly *adv* **1** in a dull level way: *It's hopeless, he said flatly* **2** completely; firmly (in phrases like **flatly refuse**)

flatter *v* **1** to praise too much or insincerely in order to please **2** to make feel important, beautiful, clever, etc.: *She was flattered at the invitation* **3** to make (someone) look too beautiful: *a flattering photograph* **4 flatter oneself** to have the pleasant though perhaps mistaken opinion –~**er** *n*

¹**flavour** *n* **1** a taste; quality that only the tongue can experience: *a strong flavour of cheese* **2** the quality of tasting good or pleasantly strong –~**less** *adj*

²**flavour** *v* to give flavour to: *to flavour with chocolate*

¹**flaw** *n* a small sign of damage, such as a mark or crack, that makes an object not perfect: *a flaw in a plate* –~**less** *adj* –~**lessly** *adv*

²**flaw** *v* to make a flaw in

flee *v* **fled, fleeing** **1** to escape (from) by hurrying away **2 flee the country** to go abroad for safety

¹**fleet** *n* **1** a number of ships, such as warships in the navy **2** a group of buses, aircraft, etc., under one control

²**fleet** *adj literature* fast; quick: *a fleet-footed runner* –~**ly** *adv* –~**ness** *n*

flesh *n* **1** the soft substance, including fat and muscle, that covers the bones and lies under the skin **2** the meat of animals used as food **3** the soft edible part of a fruit or vegetable **4** man's body as opposed to his mind or soul: *The spirit is willing but the flesh is weak* **5 flesh and blood a** human beings: *sorrows more than flesh and blood can bear* **b** relatives **6 go the way of all flesh** to die **7 one's pound of flesh** the exact amount of what is owed to one, esp. when this will cause the person who owes it great pain or trouble **8 in the flesh** in real life

flew *past tense of* FLY

¹**flex** *v* to bend and move (one of one's limbs, muscles, etc.) so as to stretch and loosen, esp. in preparation for work

²**flex** *n* (a length of) bendable electric wire in a protective covering, used for connecting an electrical apparatus to a supply

flexible *n* **1** that can bend or be bent easily **2** that can change or be changed to be suitable for new needs, changed conditions, etc. – **-ibly** *adv* – **-ibility** *n*

flicker *v* **1** to burn unsteadily; shine with an unsteady light: *The candle flickered out* **2** to move backwards and forwards quickly and unsteadily: *Shadows flickered on the wall* **–flicker** *n*

¹flight *n* **1** the act of flying: *a bird's first flight from the nest* **2** the distance covered or course followed by a flying object **3** a trip by plane: *Did you have a good flight?* **4** the aircraft making a journey: *flight Number 447 to Geneva* **5** a group of birds or aircraft flying together: *a flight of pigeons* **6** a set (of stairs, as between floors)

²flight *n* the act of running away or fleeing

¹flimsy *adj* **-sier, -siest 1** (of material) light and thin **2** (of an object) easily broken or destroyed; lacking strength – **-sily** *adv* – **-siness** *n*

²flimsy *n* **-sies** a very thin sheet of typing paper, used esp. when several copies of something are made

¹fling *v* **flung, flinging 1** to throw violently **2** to move (part of oneself) quickly or violently: *She flung back her head proudly* **3** **fling oneself into** to begin (an activity) with great interest or force

²fling *n* **1** an act of flinging; throw **2** a short wild time of satisfying one's own desires (in the phrase **have one's/a fling**)

¹float *n* **1** a piece of wood or other light object that floats, used on a fishing line or to support the edge of a fishing net **2** an air-filled container used instead of wheels by planes that land on water **3** a large flat vehicle on which special shows, ornamental scenes, etc., are drawn in processions **4** a sum of money collected in advance and kept for use if an unexpected need arises

²float *v* **1** to stay or cause to stay at the top of liquid or be held up in air without sinking: *Wood floats on water* **2** to move easily and lightly as on moving liquid or air: *The logs float down the river* **3** to establish (a business, company, etc.) by selling shares **4** to suggest: *The idea was first floated before the war* **5** to vary freely in exchange value from day to day: *the floating pound* **– ~er** *n*

¹flock *n* **1** a group of sheep, goats, or birds **2** a crowd; large number of people **3** the group of people who regularly attend a church

²flock *v* to gather or move in large crowds

flog *v* **-gg- 1** to beat severely with a whip or stick, esp. as a punishment **2** *sl* to sell or try to sell **3** **flog a dead horse a** to waste one's time with useless efforts **b** to keep repeating something already understood or accepted

¹flood *n* **1** the covering with water of a place that is usu. dry **2** a large flow: *a flood of complaints*

²flood *v* **1** to fill or become covered with water: *The river flooded the valley* **2** to overflow **3** to arrive or go in such large numbers as to be difficult to deal with: *Requests flooded in after the advert* **4** to cover or spread into completely: *The room was flooded with light*

¹floor *n* **1** the surface on which one stands indoors; surface nearest the ground **2** (of the sea, a cave, etc.) the bottom **3** a level of a building; storey **4** a level area specially prepared for a particular purpose: *a dance floor* **5** the part of a parliament or council building where members sit and speak **6 take the floor** to start dancing, as at a party or in a dance hall **7 wipe the floor with** to defeat totally

²floor *v* **1** to provide with a floor: *floored with boards* **2** to knock down: *He floored his attacker* **3** *esp. spoken* to beat; defeat or make helpless with surprise or confusion: *I was floored by his argument*

flounder *v* **1** to move with great difficulty, esp. making violent efforts not to sink: *He floundered through the deep snow* **2** to struggle or lose control when speaking or doing something

flour *n, v* (to cover with) powder made from grain, esp. wheat, used for making bread, pastry, cakes, etc. –~**y** *adj*

¹flourish *v* **1** to wave in the hand and so draw attention to (something): *He flourished his letter in his mother's face* **2** to grow healthily; be successful; be well: *a flourishing business* **3** to be alive or producing results at a certain time in history: *Chaucer flourished at the end of the 14th century* –~**ingly** *adv*

²flourish *n* **1** a showy fancy movement or manner that draws people's attention to one: *He opened the door with a flourish* **2** a curve or ornament in writing

¹flow *v* **1** (of liquid) to run or spread smoothly; pour: *The stream flowed rapidly* **2** to move along smoothly without pause: *The cars flowed in a steady stream* **3** (of hair, cloth, etc.) to fall loosely and gracefully **4** (of the tide) to rise; come in

²flow *n* **1** a pouring out: *a flow of oil* **2** the movement or rate of flowing **3** a supply of gas, electricity, etc. **4** the rise of the tide

¹flower *n* **1** the part of a plant, often beautiful and coloured, that produces seeds or fruit **2** a plant that is grown for the beauty of this part **3** *in literature* the best part: *the flower of youth* –~**less** *adj*

²flower *v* **1** (of a plant) to produce flowers **2** to develop; come to be in its best state: *His genius flowered*

flown *past part. of* FLY

flu *n esp. spoken* influenza

fluent *adj* **1** speaking, writing, or playing music in an easy smooth manner: *He is fluent in 5 languages* **2** (of speech, writing, etc.) expressed readily and without pause – **-ency** *n* –~**ly** *adv*

¹fluid *adj* **1** having the quality of flowing, like liquids, air, gas, etc.;

not solid **2** unsettled; not fixed: *fluid ideas* −∼**ity** *n*

²**fluid** *n* **1** a liquid **2** *technical* a fluid substance

flung *past tense and past part. of* FLING

¹**flutter** *v* **1** (of a bird, an insect with large wings, etc.) to move the wings quickly and lightly without flying **2** to fly by doing this **3** (of wings) to move quickly and lightly **4 a** (of a thin light object) to move quickly in the air: *The flag fluttered in the wind* **b** to cause (a thin light object) to do this: *She fluttered her hand-kerchief* **5** to move in a quick irregular way: *She fluttered her eyel-ids*

²**flutter** *n* **1** a fluttering movement **2** a state of excited interest: *His arrival put the girls in a flutter* **3** *esp. spoken* a gamble or bet, taken in a light way: *to have a flutter on the horses* **4** *technical* a shaking movement that causes a fault in the action of a machine, esp. as **a** in a record player, causing faulty high sounds

¹**fly** *v* **flew, flown, flying 1** to move through the air by means of wings or a machine **2** to control and guide (an aircraft, helicopter, etc.) in flight **3** to carry or send in an air-craft: *He's flying his car to Europe* **4** to use (a particular airline) for travelling by **5** to cross (a stretch of water) by flying: *to fly the English Channel* **6** to be carried along in the air: *Clouds were flying across the sky* **7** (of something fixed at one end) to wave or float in the air **8 a**

to raise in the air on the end of a thread, rope, etc.: *to fly a kite* **b** to show (a flag) ceremonially in this way **9** to pass rapidly; hurry: *Time flies* **10** *esp. spoken* to leave in a hurry: *I'm late; I must fly* **11** to move suddenly and with force: *The window flew open* **12** to escape (from); flee **13 the bird has flown** the person needed or wanted has gone away or escaped **14 let fly (at) a** to attack with blows or words **b** to shoot **15 make the dust/feathers/ fur/sparks fly** to cause a quarrel or a fight

²**fly** *n* **flies 1** any of several types of small insect with 2 wings (esp. the housefly) **2** any of several types of flying insect: *a butterfly* **3** a copy of a winged insect made of thread, feather, or silk wound round a hook used for catching fish **4 there are no flies on someone** someone is not a fool and cannot be tricked

¹**foam** *n* **1** a whitish mass of bubbles on the surface of a liquid or on skin **2** a chemical substance in this form, such as one used in controlling dangerous fires −**foamy** *adj*

²**foam** *v* to produce foam: *The mad dog was foaming at the mouth*

¹**focus** *n* **-cuses** *or* **-ci 1** (in mathem-atics) a point from which lines are drawn to any points on a curve in such a way that the lengths of these lines are related to each other by some law **2** the point at which beams of light or heat, or waves of sound meet after their direction has

been changed **3** the central point; centre of interest: *to be a focus of attention* **4 in (to)/out of focus** (not) having or giving a clear picture because the lens is (is not) correctly placed —**focal** *adj*

²**focus** *v* -s- *or* -ss- **1** to bring into a focus: *to focus one's mind on work* **2 a** to arrange the lens in (an instrument) so as to obtain a clear picture **b** to make (a picture) clear by doing this

foetus *n* **1** *technical* a young creature inside the mother, esp. at a later stage when all its parts have been developed for use at birth **2** a young human in the early stages of development inside the mother, esp. before it is recognizable as a baby or able to live separately —**foetal** *adj*

¹**fog** *n* **1** very thick mist **2** mistiness on a photographic plate or film, or on a print from such a film **3 in a fog** *esp. spoken* in a state of mind in which something cannot be understood

²**fog** *v* -gg- **1** to make or become difficult to see through because of a misty covering: *Steam has fogged my glasses* **2** to make or become unclear owing to fog: *Light has fogged this film*

foggy *adj* -gier, -giest **1** not clear because of fog; very misty **2** unclear: *I've only a foggy idea what it was all about* —**foggily** *adv* —**fogginess** *n*

¹**fold** *n* **1** a sheltered corner of a field where farm animals, esp. sheep, are kept for protection, surrounded by a fence or wall **2 return to the fold** to come back home or to return to one's religion

²**fold** *v* **1** to turn or press back one part of (something, esp. paper or cloth) and lay on the remaining part; bend into 2 or more parts: *She folded the tablecloth* **2** to bend (a limb) close to the body: *The cat folded its tail round its front feet* **3** to press (a pair of limbs) together: *He folded his arms* **4** to wrap: *Fold a piece of paper round the flowers* **5** to be able to be bent back; close up: *Does this table fold?* **6** *esp. spoken* to fail: *The business has folded (up)*

³**fold** *n* **1** a part of a thin flat material laid over another part: *The curtain hung in heavy folds* **2** a mark made by folding; a crease: *to iron folds out of a dress* **3** a hollow part inside something folded **4 a** a bend in a valley **b** a hollow in a hill **5** *technical* a bend in the bands of rock and other material that lie one under the other beneath the surface of the earth

¹**folk** *n* **1** people **2** people of one race or nation, or sharing a particular kind of life

²**folk** *adj* of, connected with, or being music or any other art that has grown up among working or country people as an important part of their way of living and belongs to a particular area, trade, etc., or that has been made in modern times as a copy of this

follow *v* 1 to come, arrive, go, or leave after; move behind in the same direction 2 to go in the same direction as: *Follow the river* 3 to come next in order or on a list: *May follows April* 4 to carry on (a certain kind of work): *He follows the trade of baker* 5 to keep in sight or pay attention to: *He followed the speaker's words closely* 6 to understand clearly: *I can't follow his line of reasoning* 7 to take a keen interest in: *He follows all the cricket news* 8 to accept and act according to: *Will you follow my advice?* 9 to be or happen as a necessary effect or result (of): *Disease often follows war* **10 as follows** as now to be told: *The results are as follows.....* **11 to follow** as the next dish; as the next thing to eat

follower *n* an admirer or supporter of some person, belief, or cause

folly *n* **-lies** 1 foolishness 2 an unwise act, habit, etc.: *the follies of youth* 3 a building of strange or fanciful shape, that has no particular purpose, esp. as built only to be looked at

fond *adj* 1 loving in a kind, gentle, or tender way: *He signed the letter, 'With fondest love, Cyril'* 2 foolishly loving: *A fond mother may spoil her child* 3 foolishly trusting or hopeful: *He has a fond belief in his own cleverness* 4 having a great liking or love (for) −~**ly** *adv* −~**ness** *n*

food *n* 1 **a** something that living creatures or plants take into their bodies to give them strength and help them to develop and to live **b** something solid for eating: *We get food there, but never anything to drink* 2 an edible substance 3 subject matter (for an argument or careful thought)

¹**fool** *n* 1 a person whom one considers to be silly; person lacking in judgment or good sense 2 (in former times) a servant at the court of a king or noble, whose duty was to amuse his master; jester 3 a dish made of cooked soft fruit, pressed into a liquid and beaten up with cream 4 (**the**) **more fool you** I think you were a fool

²**fool** *v* 1 to deceive; trick 2 to speak or behave in a silly way: *Can't you stop fooling?*

foolish *adj* unwise; without good sense −~**ly** *adv* −~**ness** *n*

¹**foot** *n* **feet** 1 the movable part of the body at the end of the leg, below the ankle, on which a man or an animal stands 2 (*pl. sometimes* **foot**) (a measure of length equal to) 12 inches or about ·305 metres 3 the bottom part; base: *the foot of the page* 4 the lower end (of anything) where feet lie: *the foot of the bed* 5 manner of walking; step: *fleet of foot* 6 the part of a stocking or sock that covers the foot 7 a division of a line in poetry, in which there is usu. a strong beat and one or 2 weaker ones: *In the line 'The way/was long/the wind/was cold', the words between each pair of upright lines*

make up a foot **8** soldiers who march and fight on foot; infantry **9 a foot in both camps** a position not completely favouring one side or the other, so that each thinks it has one's support **10 a foot in the door** a beginning of influence, favour, etc. **11 fall on one's feet** *esp. spoken* to come out of a difficult state of affairs without harm; have good luck **12 find one's feet** to become used to new or strange surroundings; settle in **13 get a foot in** *esp. spoken* to get a chance to be in **14 get/have cold feet** to be too nervous to do something, esp. losing courage just before something **15 keep one's feet** to be able to remain standing; not fall **16 my foot** *esp. spoken* I don't believe it **17 put a foot wrong** to say or do anything wrong **18 put one's best foot forward a** to walk as fast as possible **b** to make one's best effort **19 put one's feet up** *esp. spoken* to rest by lying down or sitting with one's feet supported on something **20 put one's foot down a** *esp. spoken* to speak and act firmly on a particular matter **b** *sl* to drive very fast **21 put one's foot in it** *esp. spoken* to say the wrong thing or make an awkward mistake **22 set foot in/on** to enter; visit

²**foot** *v esp. spoken* to pay (a bill)

football *n* **1** any of several games for 2 teams in which a ball is kicked and/or thrown about a field in an attempt to get goals, esp. **a** soccer **b** rugby **2** any of several types of large ball filled with air, usu. made of leather, used in these games —~**er** *n*

footing *n* **1** a firm placing of the feet; room or a surface for the feet to stand on: *She lost her footing and fell* **2** a sure position; base: *Is this business on a firm footing?* **3** a special condition or quality of relationship suited to a certain state of affairs: *The army is now on a peacetime footing* **4** an accepted place in some group

footpath *n* a narrow path or track for people to walk on

footstep *n* **1** a mark or sound of a person's step **2** the distance covered by one step **3 follow in the footsteps of** to follow an example set by (someone else in the past)

¹**for** *prep* **1** that is/are intended to belong to, be given to, or be used in connection with: *a present for Mary* **2** in order to reach, get, or have: *We set off for London* **3** at/on/in (the time of): *She's coming for Christmas* **4** representing; taking the place of; instead of; corresponding to: *Red is for danger. / I'll do it for you* **5** in favour of; in support of: *They work hard for charity* **6** as regards; in regard to: *an ear for music* **7** because of: *You look better for your holiday* **8** in spite of: *For all his efforts, he didn't succeed* **9** considering how little: *For all the good we've done we might as well have left it as it was* **10** at

the price of: *a pen for 50 pence* **11** as the price of: *50 pence for a pen / a bad mark for every mistake* **12** (of time or distance) the length of; over the space of; during: *We ran for 2 miles. / He stayed for a week* **13** *used with a noun/pronoun and in the object form and a verb in the infinitive to make a phrase which could be expressed as a clause: The bell rang for the lesson to begin* (=in order that it should begin) **14** *usu. offensive* **that's ... for you!** as you must agree, that's what . . . is like **15** **there's ... for you!** that's the complete opposite of . . .: *He just grabbed the money and left- — there's gratitude for you!*

²**for** *conj esp. written* because: *We must start early, for we have a long way to go*

forbid *v* **-bade** *or* **-bad, -bidden, -bidding** **1** to command not to do something: *I forbid you to use my car* **2** to command that (something) must not be done: *Smoking is forbidden in the concert hall* **3** **God forbid (that)** I very much hope it will not happen (that)

forbidden *adj* **1** not allowed; against the teachings of religion **2** that may not be used, entered, or visited by ordinary people: *the forbidden city*

¹**force** *n* **1** natural or bodily power; active strength: *the force of the explosion* **2** fierce or uncontrolled use of strength; violence: *The thief took the money from the old man by*

force **3** *technical* (measurement of) a power that changes or may produce change of movement in a body on which it acts or presses: *The force of gravity makes things fall to earth* **4** a person, thing, belief, action, etc., that has a strong enough influence to cause widespread changes in a way of living, or that has uncontrollable power over living things: *the forces of evil / the forces of nature* **5** strong influence on the mind: *I was persuaded by the force of his argument. / force of habit* **6** a group of people banded together or trained for some kind of action, esp. military action: *land and sea forces / the police force* **7** **in force** in large numbers: *The police were there in force* **8** **in(to) force** (of a rule, order, law, etc.) in(to) effect, use, or operation **9** **join forces (with)** to unite (with) for a purpose

²**force** *v* **forced, forcing** **1** to make (an unwilling person or animal) do something; drive: *The rider forced his horse on through the storm* **2** to push using force: *We had to force the window open* **3** to produce by unwilling effort; produce with difficulty or against nature: *forced laughter* **4** to hasten the growth of (a plant) by the use of heat **5** **force one's/someone's/the pace** to take or cause to take faster or too fast action

forecast *n, v* **-cast** *or* **-casted, -casting** (to make) a statement of future events, based on some kind of knowledge or judgment: *The weather forecast*

forefront *n* the most forward place; leading position: *in the forefront of the fighting*

foreground *n* **1** the nearest part of a scene in a view, a picture, or a photograph **2** the most important or noticeable position: *She likes to keep herself in the foreground*

forehead *n* the part of the face above the eyes and below the hair

foreign *adj* **1** to, from, of, in, being, or concerning a country or nation that is not one's own or not the one being talked about: *foreign travel / I can't understand him; he must be foreign* **2** having no place (in); having no relation (to): *Love is foreign to his nature* **3** coming or brought in from outside; not belonging; harmful

foreigner *n* a person belonging to a country other than one's own

foreman *n* **-men 1** (fem. **forewoman**)— a skilled and experienced workman who is put in charge of other workers **2** the leader of the jury who speaks for the rest and reports to the court what they have decided

foremost *adj* **1** most important; leading **2** furthest forward; first

foresee *v* **-saw, -seen, seeing** to form an idea or judgment about (the future); expect: *We should have foreseen this trouble* –~**able** *adj*

forest *n* **1** (a large area of land thickly covered with) trees and bushes, either growing wild or planted for some purpose **2** a large number of upright objects close together: *a forest of hands*

foretell *v* **-told, -telling** to tell (what will happen in the future)

forever, for ever *adv* **1** for all time: *We left our old home forever* **2** continually: *He's forever mending his motorbike*

¹**forfeit** *n* what must be lost or forfeited for something

²**forfeit** *v* to have (something) taken away from one because some agreement or rule has been broken, or as a punishment, or as the result of some action: *You have forfeited your chance of getting your money back* –~**ure** *n*

forgave *past tense of* FORGIVE

¹**forge** *n* **1** (a building or room containing) a large apparatus with a fire inside, used for heating and shaping metal objects **2** a large apparatus that produces great heat inside itself, used for melting metal, making iron, etc.

²**forge** *v* **forged, forging 1** to form by heating and hammering **2** to make a copy of (something) in order to deceive: *a forged passport*

³**forge** *v* to move with a sudden increase of speed and power: *The racehorse forged ahead*

forget *v* **-got, -gotten, -getting 1** to fail to remember: *I forget where to go* **2** to fail to remember to bring, buy, etc., (something): *Don't forget the cases* **3** to stop thinking about (something): *'I'm sorry I broke your* *teapot.' 'Forget it.'* **4** to fail to give attention to: *He forgot his old friends when he became rich* **5 forget one-self** to lose one's temper or self-control

forgive *v* **-gave, -given, -giving** to say or feel that one is no longer angry about and/or wishing to give punishment to (someone) for (something): *I'll never forgive you*

¹**fork** *n* **1** a metal or plastic instrument for holding or carrying food to the mouth, having a handle at one end with 2 or more points at the other **2** a wooden-handled farm or gardening tool with 2 or more metal points at one end used for breaking up the soil **3** a place where something long and narrow divides, or one of the divided parts: *a fork in the road* **4** one of the 2 parallel metal points at the front of a bicycle, motorcycle, etc., between which the wheel is fixed

²**fork** *v* **1** to lift, carry, move, etc., with a fork **2** (of something long and narrow) to divide, esp. into 2 parts **3** to take the (left or right) fork of a road

forked *adj* **1** having one end divided into 2 or more points: *a forked tongue* **2** that divides into 2 or more parts at a point

¹**form** *n* **1** shape; appearance; body: *She has a tall graceful form* **2** a general plan or arrangement; kind or sort: *Different countries have different forms of government* **3** the way in which a work of art is put together: *a master of form* **4** ceremony; rule or custom: *a form of marriage* **5** *esp. spoken* behaviour of the stated type in relation to what is- expected: *Schoolboys often think it bad form to tell a teacher of another boy's wrong-doing* **6** (esp. in sport) condition of skill, fitness, and standard of performance: *The footballer's been out of form* **7** spirits: *Tom is in fine form* **8** a way in which a word may be written or spoken as a result of variations in spelling or pronunciation, according to some rule: *There are 2 forms of the past of 'to dream': 'dreamed' and 'dreamt'* **9** a printed paper divided by lines into separate parts, in each of which answers to questions must be written down **10** a long wooden seat, usu. without a back **11** a class in a British school, and in some American schools

²**form** *v* **1** to take shape; appear; develop: *Steam forms when water boils* **2** to take the shape of: *The buildings formed a hollow square* **3** to make: *Eskimoes form igloos out of blocks of ice* **4** to develop as a result of thought, effort, experience, or training: *form a friendship* **5** to make according to rule: *to form a correct sentence* **6** to make up; gather together; arrange: *forming a club* **7** to be; be the substance of **8** to stand or cause to stand or move in a certain order: *The soldiers formed into a line*

formal *adj* **1** ceremonial; according to

custom: *a formal dinner party* **2** stiff in manner and careful about correctness of behaviour: *He's very formal with everybody* **3** having a set or regular shape: *a formal garden* **4** unreal; belonging to appearance only: *There's only a formal likeness between the 2 brothers* −~**ly** *adv*

former *adj esp. written* **1** of an earlier period: *a former judo champion* **2** the first of 2 people or things just spoken about: *Of swimming and football he much preferred the former*

formerly *adv* in earlier times: *This painting was formerly owned privately, but now it belongs to the nation*

formula *n* **-las** *or* **-lae** **1** *technical* a general law, fact, etc., expressed shortly by means of a group of letters, numbers, etc.: *The chemical formula for water is* H_2O **2** a list of the substances used in making something, such as a of how they are to be mixed: *the secret formula for a new rocket fuel* **3** a combination of things, events, etc., which will lead almost unavoidably to the stated result: *Drinking and driving is a formula for trouble* **4** a combination of suggestions, plans, etc., that can be agreed on by both sides: *The employers and the union leaders have agreed an acceptable formula for wages*

fort *n* **1** a strongly made building used for defence at some important place **2 hold the fort** to look after everything while someone is away

forth *adv esp. Bible or literature* forward: *from this day forth*

fortieth *adj, n, pron, adv* 40th

fortnight *n* 2 weeks

fortunate *adj* having or bringing good fortune; lucky

fortunately *adv* by good chance; luckily: *Fortunately the train was on time for once*

fortune *n* **1** fate; chance, esp. as an important influence on one's life; luck: *She had the good fortune to be free from illness* **2** whatever happens in the future to a person by chance, good or bad: *Through all his changing fortunes, he never lost courage* **3** success; good luck: *Fortune smiled on him* **4** wealth; a great amount of money, possessions, etc.

forty *adj, n, pron* **-ties** the number 40

¹**forward** *adj* **1** directed towards the front; advancing: *a forward movement* **2** near, at, or belonging to the front: *the forward part of the train* **3** particularly or unusually advanced or early in development: *a forward child* **4** (esp. of a young person) unpleasantly sure of oneself, too bold, often in sexual matters **5** ready and eager: *He's always forward with help* **6** getting on fast (with work, study, plans, etc.): *How far forward are your plans?* **7** advanced; modern: *very forward in one's thinking* −~**ly** *adv* −~**ness** *n*

²**forward** −also **forwards** *adv* **1**

towards the front in the direction one is facing: *Take 2 steps forward* **2** towards the future: *We look forward and try to plan wisely* **3** to an earlier time: *They moved the meeting forward from the 20th to the 18th* **4** into a noticeable position: *The lawyer brought forward some new reasons* **5** also **on–** (of a clock) so as to show a later time

³**forward** *n* one of the attacking players in teams of various sports (such as soccer, rugby, and hockey)

⁴**forward** *v* **1** to send forward or pass on (letters, parcels, etc.) to a new address **2** *esp. written* to send: *We are forwarding you our catalogue* **3** to help advance the development of – ~**ing** *n*

fought *past tense and past part. of* FIGHT

¹**foul** *adj* **1** evil-smelling or evil-tasting; unclean; impure: *a foul-tasting medicine* **2** (of a pipe, chimney, etc.) blocked with dirt or waste matter, so that liquid, smoke, etc., cannot pass freely **3** *technical, esp. sailing* (of a rope, chain, etc.) twisted; knotted; mixed up in disorder **4** (of weather) rough; stormy **5** evil; cruel; shameful: *Murder is a foul deed* **6** (of language) full of curses **7** *esp. spoken* very bad; unpleasant: *I've had a foul morning* **8** (in sport) against the rules: *He struck his opponent a foul blow* –~**ly** *adv* –~**ness** *n*

²**foul** *n* (in sport) an act that is against the rules

³**foul** *v* **1** to make or become dirty, impure, or blocked with waste matter: *The dog's fouled the path* **2** (in sports, esp. football) to be guilty of a foul: *Smith ran into Jones and fouled him* **3** *sailing* (of a boat) to run against (another) **4** (of a rope, chain, etc.) to get mixed up or twisted with (something)

¹**found** *v* **1** to build or start building (something large): *The castle is founded on solid rock* **2** to begin the development of; establish: *This company was founded in 1724* **3** to start and support by supplying money: *The rich man founded a hospital*

²**found** *v* **1** to melt (metal) and pour into a hollow mould **2** to make (something) of metal in this way

³**found** *past tense and past part. of* FIND

foundations –also **foundation** *n* **1** the solid stonework, brickwork, etc., first set in holes dug deep in the earth, to support the walls of a building: *to lay the foundations of a new hospital* **2** the base; that by which things are supported, or on which they are based: *He laid the foundations of his success by study and hard work*

¹**founder** *n* a person who founds something: *Mohammed was the founder of the Muslim religion*

²**founder** *v* **1** (of a ship) to fill with water and sink **2** to come to nothing; fail: *The plan foundered for lack of support*

fountain *n* **1** (an apparatus of pipes,

sometimes hidden inside beautiful stone figures or bowls set in an ornamental lake or smaller piece of water in a garden, or other open space, producing) a stream of water that shoots straight up into the air **2** a flow, esp. rising straight into the air: *A fountain of water shot from the pipe* **3** the place where something begins or is supplied: *The ruler was respected as the fountain of honour*

four *adj, n, pron* **1** the number 4 **2** (esp. in games of cards) a set or group of 4: *to make up a four for cards* **3** (in cricket) 4 runs, usu. gained by hitting the ball to the edge of the field **4** a 4 man rowing-boat for racing **5. . . and four** . . . pulled by 4 horses: *a coach and four*

fourteen *adj, n, pron* the number 14 – ~**th** *adj, n, pron*

fourth *adj, n, pron adv* 4th

fowl *n* **fowls** *or* **fowl 1** a farmyard bird, esp. a hen **2** *old use & poetic* a bird

¹fox *n* **1** (fem. **vixen**)– **a** any of several types of small doglike flesh-eating wild animal with a bushy tail, esp. **b** a type of European animal with reddish fur, preserved in Britain to be hunted and often said to be clever and deceiving **2** the skin of this animal, used as fur on clothing **3** *esp. spoken, usu. offensive* a person who deceives others by means of clever tricks: *He's a sly old fox*

²fox *v esp. spoken* **1 a** to deceive cleverly; trick **b** to be too difficult for someone to understand: *The ques-*

tion foxed me completely **2** to pretend

fraction *n* **1** a very small piece or amount: *She spends only a fraction of her earnings* **2** (in mathematics) a division or part of a whole number: *1/3 and 5/8 are fractions*

¹fracture *n technical, esp. medical or written* the act or result of breaking or cracking something, esp. a bone

²fracture *v* **-tured, -turing** *technical esp. medical or written* to break or crack: *He fell and fractured his upper arm*

fragile *adj* **1** easily broken, damaged, or destroyed: *This vase is fragile* **2 a** slight in body or weak in health: *The old lady looks very fragile* **b** *usu. humour* not in a good condition of health and spirits; weak: *'I'm feeling rather fragile after all that beer last night,'* *he said* – **-gility** *n*

¹fragment *n* **1** a small piece broken off: *She dropped the bowl and it broke into fragments* **2** an incomplete part, esp. of a work of art

²fragment *v* **1** to break into fragments **2** to cause to be made up of incomplete parts, esp. not understandable: *The interruption fragmented his argument*

frail *adj* **1** not strongly made or built: *That bridge is too frail to take a man's weight* **2** weak or slight: *Her frail hands could hardly hold a cup*

¹frame *v* **framed, framing 1** to surround with a solid protecting edge or border: *to frame a picture in wood* **2** to act as a setting or background to: *A hat framed her pretty face* **3** to build; make: *Forts are framed for defence* **4** to give shape to (words, sentences, ideas, etc.); express: *An examiner must frame his question clearly* **5** *esp. spoken* to cause to seem guilty of a crime by means of carefully planned but untrue statements or proofs: *He was framed by the real criminals*

²**frame** *n* **1** the main supports over and around which something is stretched or built: *Some small boats are made of skins stretched over a wooden frame* **2** the hard solid parts which are fitted together to make something: *a bicycle frame* **3** the form or shape of a human or animal body: *a man with a powerful frame* **4** a firm border or case into which something is fitted or set, or which holds something in place: *a window frame* **5** a setting; background; surroundings: *The trees make a pleasant frame to the house* **6** —also **cold frame** a large wooden box set in the ground and having a sloping glass roof that can be raised or lowered, used for protecting and growing young plants **7** one of a number of small photographs making up a cinema film **8** a complete stage of play in games such as snooker and bowling

framework *n* **1** a supporting frame; structure **2** a plan or system: *the framework of modern government*

¹**frank** *adj* free and direct in speech; open in manner; plain and honest −~**ness** *n* −~**ly** *adv*

²**frank** *v* to print a sign on a letter to show that the charge for posting has been paid

fraud *n* **1** (an act of) deceitful behaviour for the purpose of gain, which may be punishable by law **2** *offensive* a person who pretends or claims to be what he is not: *People who tell your future by means of a pack of cards are frauds* **3** *offensive* a thing which is not, or does not do, what is claimed for it

¹**freak** *n* **1** a living creature of unnatural form **2** *esp. spoken* a person with rather strange habits or ideas **3** a peculiar happening: *By some strange freak, snow fell in Egypt a few years ago* **4** a sudden strange wish or change of mind **5** *sl* a fan: *a film freak*

²**freak** *adj* unnatural in degree or type; very unusual: *a freak storm*

¹**free** *adj* **1** moving about at will; not tied up, bound, or held in prison: *The prisoner wished to be free again* **2** owing no service or duty to anyone; not in the power of anyone; independent **3** self-governing; not controlled by the state; having a form of government that respects the rights of private people: *Britain is a free country* **4** without payment of any kind; given away: *a free gift* **5** not controlled or limited in any way or not accepting any control, esp. by rule or custom: *He gave me free access to his library* **6** (esp. of

bodily action) natural; graceful: *free movement to music* **7** not fixed onto anything; not set in position; loose: *the free end of a flag* **8** not busy: *The doctor will be free soon* **9** not being used; not kept for anybody: *Can you find a free space to park the car?* **10** (of a way or passage) open; not blocked **11** generous; full in quantity: *She's free with her money* **12** *offensive* too friendly; lacking in respect: *The boy's manner is rather free to his teachers* **13** without (someone or something unwanted); safe from: *The old lady is never free from pain* **14 a** without making or asking payment of: *free of charge* **b** clear of; no longer troubled by: *You'll be glad when you're free of her* **15** not prevented in any way; allowed: *She'll be free to enjoy herself soon* **16** (in chemistry) not combined with any element; pure

²**free** *adv* **1** in a free manner: *Don't let the dog run free* **2** without payment: *Babies travel free on buses* **3** in a loose position; so as to be no longer joined: *He pushed the window until it swung free*

³**free** *v* **freed, freeing 1** to set free **2** to make (a slave) free **3** to move or loosen (a person or thing when prevented from moving): *It took half an hour to free the trapped man* **4** to take away from (a person or animal) anything uncomfortable, inconvenient, difficult, unwel-come, etc.: *Can you free me from duty for an hour?*

freedom *n* **1** the state of being free: *The master gave the slave his freedom* **2** certain rights, often given as an honour: *They gave her the freedom of their house* **3** the power to do, say, think, or write as one pleases **4** the condition of being without something harmful or unpleasant: *freedom from pain*

freely *adv* **1** willingly; readily: *I freely admit I was wrong* **2** openly; plainly: *You may speak freely* **3** without any limitation on movement or action: *Oil the wheel; then it will turn more freely* **4** generously: *He gives freely to charity* **5** in great amounts: *to bleed freely*

¹**freeze** *v* **froze, frozen, freezing 1** to harden into ice as a result of great cold **2** to make or become solid at a very low temperature: *She slipped on the frozen mud* **3** to be unable or to make unable to work properly as a result of ice or low temperatures: *The engine has frozen up* **4** (of land, a solid surface, etc.) to become covered with ice and snow **5** (of weather) to be at or below the temperature at which water becomes ice: *It froze hard last night* **6** *esp. spoken* to be, feel, or become very cold: *It's freezing in this room* **7** to make very cold, stiff, or without feeling: *He looks half frozen* **8** to stop suddenly or make or become quite still: *The teacher froze the noisy class with a single look* **9** to

become unfriendly in manner: *They sat in frozen silence* **10** to preserve (food) by means of very low temperatures **11** to fix prices or wages officially at a given level for a certain length of time **12** to prevent (business shares, bank accounts, etc.) from being used, by government order

²**freeze** *n* **1** a period of very cold icy weather **2** a fixing of prices or wages at a certain level

freezer *n* **1** also **deep freeze** – a type of large refrigerator in which frozen food can be stored for a long time **2** also **freezing compartment**– an enclosed specially cold part of a refrigerator for making small ice blocks, storing frozen foods, etc.

¹**frequent** *adj* common; found or happening often; repeated many times; habitual – –~**ly** *adv*

²**frequent** *v esp. written* to be often in (a place, someone's company, etc.)

fresh *adj* **1** in good condition because not long gathered, caught, produced, etc.; not spoilt in taste, appearance, etc., by being kept too long; new **2** (of water) not salt; drinkable **3** (of food) not preserved by added salt, tinning, bottling, freezing, or other means **4** newly prepared; newly cooked: *Let me make you a fresh pot of tea* **5** lately arrived, happened, found, grown, or supplied: *Fresh goods appear in our shops every week* **6** clean: *He put on fresh clothes* **7** (an) other and additional; renewed: *He's making a fresh attempt to pass his examination* **8** (an) other and different: *It's time to take a fresh look at this affair* **9** not tired; young, healthy, and active; strengthened: *The plants look fresh after the rain* **10** (of colour) pure; bright; clear **11** (of skin) clear and healthy **12** (of paint) newly put on; not dry **13** (of air) pure; cool **14** *often technical* (of wind) rather strong; gaining in force **15** *esp. spoken* (of weather) cool and windy **16** (of a person) inexperienced (in): *She's quite fresh to office work* **17** *esp. spoken* (too) bold with someone of the opposite sex: *She's trying to get fresh with my brother* –~**ness** *n*

friction *n* **1** the force which tries to stop one surface sliding over another: *Friction gradually caused the sliding box to slow down and stop* **2** the rubbing, often repeated, of 2 surfaces together, or of one against another **3** unfriendliness and disagreement caused by 2 opposing wills or different sets of opinion, ideas, or natures: *If they have to share a room there'll probably be friction*

Friday *n* **-days** the 6th day of the week

friend *n* **1** a person who shares the same feelings of natural liking and understanding, the same interests, etc., but is not closely related **2** a helper; supporter; adviser; person showing kindness and understanding: *Our doctor's been a good* *friend to us* **3** a person from whom there is nothing to fear **4** a companion: *The dog is a faithful friend of man* **5** *esp. written* a useful quality, condition, or thing: *Bright light is the painter's best friend* **6** a person who is being addressed or spoken of in public: *Friends, we have met here tonight ......* **7 a** a person whose name one does not know, esp. one who is seen regularly or often: *What can I do for you, my friend?* **b** a stranger noticed for some reason, usu. with amusement or displeasure: *Our friend with the loud voice is here again*

friendly *adj* **-lier, -liest 1** acting or ready to act as a friend: *A friendly dog came to meet us* **2** sharing the relationship of friends (with): *Bill is very friendly with Ben* **3** favouring; ready to accept ideas: *This company has never been friendly to change* **4** kind; generous; supporting or protecting; ready to help: *You're sure of a friendly welcome here* **5** not an enemy **6** not causing or containing unpleasant feelings when in competitions, arguments, etc. **– -liness** *n*

friendship *n* the condition of sharing a friendly relationship

fright *n* **1** the feeling or experience of fear **2** an experience that causes sudden fear; shock: *You gave me a fright by knocking so loudly* **3** *esp. spoken* a person who or thing that looks silly, unattractive, or shocking

frighten –also (*literature*) **fright** *v* **1** to fill with fear **2** to influence or drive by fear: *He frightened off his attacker by calling for the police* **– ~ingly** *adv*

frightful *adj* **1** fearful; terrible; shocking: *The battlefield was a frightful scene* **2** *esp. spoken* very bad; unpleasant; difficult: *frightful weather* **– ~ness** *n* **– ~ly** *adv*

¹fringe *n* **1** an ornamental edge of hanging threads, sometimes twisted or knotted, on a curtain, tablecloth, garment, etc. **2** a line of things which borders something: *A fringe of trees stood round the pool* **3** a short border of hair, with the lower edge usu. cut in a straight line, hanging over a person's forehead **4** a border of long hair on part of an animal, or of hairlike parts on a plant **5** the part farthest from the centre; edge: *It was easier to move about on the fringe of the crowd* **6** a group which is only loosely connected with a political or other movement, and may not agree with it on all points

²fringe *v* **fringed, fringing** to act as a fringe to

frog *n* **1** any of several types of small hairless tailless animal, usu. brownish-green, that live in water and on land, have long back legs for swimming and jumping, and croak **2** a fastening to a coat or other garment, often ornamental, consisting of a long button and a circular band for putting it through **3**

a 3-sided horny part in the middle of the bottom of a horse's foot

from *prep* **1** (*showing a starting point in time*) beginning at: *From the moment he saw her, he loved her* **2** (*showing a starting point in place*) having left; beginning at: *a letter from Mary* **3** (*showing a starting point in rank, order, price, number, amount, etc.*): *He rose from office boy to managing director* **4** out of: *Bread is made from flour*

¹**front** *n* **1** the position directly before someone or something: *The teacher called the boy to the front* **2** the surface or part facing forwards, outwards, or upwards **3** the most forward or important position: *the front of the train* **4 a** the most important side of a building, containing the main entrance or facing the street **b** a side of a large important building: *The west front of the church contains some fine old windows* **5** a road, often built up and having a protecting wall, by the edge of the sea, esp. at a resort **6** the manner and appearance of a person: *He always presents a smiling front to the world* **7** a line along which fighting takes place in time of war, together with the part behind it concerned with supplies **8** a combined effort or appearance against opposing forces: *The members of the government formed a united front against the party in opposition* **9** *often humour* a group of people making a combined effort for some purpose: *She worked on the home front* (=in her own country), *helping to produce weapons for the army* **10** a widespread and active political movement: *The People's Front is seeking to gain supporters* **11** a line of separation between 2 masses of air of different temperature: *a cold/warm front* **12** *esp. spoken* a person, group, or thing used for hiding the real nature of a secret or unlawful activity: *The import firm was a front for drug smuggling* **13 in front of a** in the position directly before **b** in the presence of

²**front** *v* (of a building) to have the front towards; face to: *The head post office fronts the railway station*

³**front** *adj* **1** being at, related to, or coming from the front **2** being at the front: *the front row at a concert* **3** at or connected with the front of a building: *the front garden* **4** *esp. spoken* being a front: *They used a front organization to hide their trade in forbidden goods*

frontier *n* **1** the limit or edge of the land of one country, where it meets the land of another country **2** the border between settled and wild country, esp. that in the US in the past: *The frontier in America was rough and lawless in the old days* **3** a border between the known and the unknown: *The frontiers of medical knowledge are being pushed farther back*

¹**frost** *n* **1** weather at a temperature

below the freezing point of water; frozen condition of the ground and/or air: *Frost can kill off a young plant* **2** a period or state of this **3** a white powdery substance formed on outside surfaces from very small drops of water when the temperature of the air is below freezing point: *The grass was covered with frost* **4 of frost** *technical* below the freezing point of water: *There was 5 degrees of frost last night*

²**frost** *v* **1** to make or become covered with frost: *The cold has frosted the windows* **2** to roughen the surface of a sheet of glass so that it is not possible to see through

frosty *adj* **-ier, -iest 1 a** stingingly cold; cold with frost: *a frosty day* **b** covered or seeming to be covered with frost **2** unfriendly; cold: *a frosty greeting* – **-tily** *adv* – **-tiness** *n*

¹**frown** *v* **1** to draw the brows together in anger or effort, so as to show disapproval or to protect the eyes against strong light, causing lines to appear on the forehead **2** (of a thing) to have a dangerous or unfriendly appearance when seen from below: *The mountains frown down on the plain* – ~**ingly** *adv*

²**frown** *n* **1** a serious or displeased look, causing lines on the forehead; act of frowning **2** the lines left on the forehead by this act

froze *past tense of* FREEZE

frozen *past part. of* FREEZE

¹**fruit** *n* **1** an object that grows on a tree or bush, contains seeds, is used for food, but is not usu. eaten with meat or with salt **2** these objects in general, esp. considered as food **3** a type of this object: *Apples, oranges, and bananas are fruit* **4** *technical* a seed-containing part of any plant **5** a result, good or bad: *His failure is the fruit of laziness*

²**fruit** *v* (of a tree, bush, etc.) to bear fruit

fruitful *adj* **1** successful; useful; producing good results: *a fruitful meeting* **2** *old use* (of living things) bearing many young or much fruit – ~**ly** *adv* – ~**ness** *n*

frustrate *v* **-trated, -trating 1** to prevent the fulfilment of; defeat (someone or someone's effort): *The weather frustrated our plans* **2** to cause to have feelings of annoyed disappointment: *2 hours' frustrating delay* – **-ation** *n*

¹**fry** *v* **fried, frying 1** to cook in hot fat or oil **2** *esp. spoken* to have the skin burnt: *We shall fry in this hot sun*

²**fry** *n* **fry** a small fish that has just come out of its egg

¹**fuel** *n* **1 a** (a type of) material that is used for producing heat or power by burning: *Wood, coal, oil, gas, and petrol are different kinds of fuel* **b** material that can be made to produce atomic power **2** something that increases anger or any other strong feeling: *Being asked to work longer hours added fuel to the flames of their discontent*

²**fuel** *v* -ll- to provide with fuel

¹**fugitive** *adj* **1** escaping; running away **2** *esp. literature or written* **a** hard to keep present in the mind: *a fugitive thought* **b** passing rapidly; not lasting, esp. in interest or importance: *The value of most newspaper writing is only fugitive*

²**fugitive** *n* a person escaping from the law, the police, danger, etc.: *a fugitive from justice*

fulfil *v* -ll- **1** to do or perform: *A nurse has many duties to fulfil* **2** to carry out (an order, conditions, etc.); obey **3** to keep or carry out faithfully (a promise, agreement, etc.) **4** to supply or satisfy (a need, demand, or purpose) **5** to make or prove to be true; cause to happen as appointed or predicted: *His belief that the world would end was not fulfilled* **6** to make true; carry out (something wished for or planned, such as hopes, prayers, desires, etc.) **7** to develop and express the abilities, character, etc., of (oneself) fully: *She fulfilled herself as a mother*

fulfilment *n* **1** the act of fulfilling or condition of being fulfilled: *His plans have come to fulfilment* **2** satisfaction after successful effort: *a sense of fulfilment*

¹**full** *adj* **1** (of a container) filled with liquid, powder, etc., as near to the top as is convenient in practice **2** (of a container) filled to the top **3** (of a space) containing as many people, objects, etc., as possible; crowded: *a full train* **4** containing or having plenty (of): *Her eyes were full of tears* **5** *esp. spoken* well fed, often to the point of discomfort; satisfied: *I can't eat any more; I'm full up* **6** complete; whole: *the full truth of the matter* **7** the highest or greatest possible: *He drove at full speed* **8** possessing all the rights or qualities of the stated position: *Only full members are allowed to vote* **9 a** having the mind and attention fixed only (on): *full of her own importance* **b** overflowing (with a feeling, quality, etc.): *full of excitement* **10** (of a part of a garment) wide; flowing; fitting loosely **11** (of a shape, a body, or its parts) **a** round; rounded; fleshy: *full breasts* **b** *polite* fat: *This shop sells dresses for the fuller figure* **12** (of colour, smell, sound, taste, or substance) deep, rich, and powerful: *wine with a full body* **13** *literature* having had one's share and more: *He died full of years and honours*

²**full** *adv* **1** straight; directly: *The sun shone full on her face* **2** very; quite: *They knew full well that he had lied*

³**full** *n* **1** the greatest height, degree, point, etc.: *The tide's at the full* **2 in full** completely: *The debt must be paid in full*

full-scale *adj* **1** large; making use of all known facts, information, etc.: *He's writing a full-scale history of 19th century France* **2** (of an activity) of not less than the usual kind; not shortened, lessened, etc., in any way; total: *a full-scale war* **3**

using all one's powers, forces, etc.: *a full-scale attack*

full stop –also **period, point** *n* a point (.) marking the end of a sentence or a shortened form of a word

fully *adv* **1** quite; at least: *It's fully an hour since he left* **2** completely; altogether: *fully trained*

fumble *v* **-bled, -bling 1** to move the fingers or hands awkwardly in search of something, or in an attempt to do something **2** to handle (something) without neatness or skill; mishandle: *The cricketer fumbled the catch* –~**r** *n*

fumes *n* heavy strong-smelling air given off from smoke, gas, fresh paint, etc., that causes a pricking sensation when breathed in

fun *n* **1** playfulness: *The little dog's full of fun* **2** amusement; enjoyment; pleasure or its cause: *Have fun at the party tonight* **3** amusement caused by laughing at someone else: *He's become a figure of fun* **4 for fun** also **for the fun of it / the thing**– for pleasure; without serious purpose

¹function *n* **1** a special duty (of a person) or purpose (of a thing): *The function of a chairman is to lead and control meetings* **2 a** a public ceremony: *The Queen attends many official functions* **b** *esp. spoken* a large or important gathering of people for pleasure or on some special occasion **3 a** a quality or fact which depends on and varies with another: *The size of the crop is a function of the quality of the soil and the amount of rainfall* **b** *technical* (in mathematics) a relationship in which every member of one set (the domain) is linked with exactly one member (the image) of another set (the range) **c** a variable which depends on another variable according to such a function: *In $X = 5y$, X is a function of y*

²function *v* (esp. of a thing) to be in action; work: *The machine doesn't function properly*

¹fund *n* **1** a store or supply (of non-material things) ready for use as needed: *The speaker had a fund of examples to prove his points* **2** a supply or sum of money set apart for a special purpose: *the school sports fund*

²fund *v* *esp. technical* to provide money for (an activity, organization, etc.): *The work is funded by the government*

¹fundamental *adj* **1** (of a non-material thing) deep; being at the base, from which all else develops: *a fundamental difference between their aims* **2** (of a non-material thing) of the greatest importance; having a greater effect than all others: *a fundamental cause of his success* **3** (of a non-material thing) very necessary: *Fresh air is fundamental to good health* **4** (of a quality) belonging to a person's or thing's deep true character

²fundamental *n* a rule, law, etc., on which a system is based; necessary or important part: *A fundamental of good behaviour is consideration for others*

funeral *n* **1** a ceremony, usu. religious, of burying or burning a dead person **2** a procession taking a dead person to be buried or burned **3** *esp. spoken* a difficulty or unpleasantness that concerns or will concern someone alone: *If you choose to do it, it's your funeral*

funfair *n* **1** a noisy brightly lit show which for small charges offers big machines to ride on, games of skill, and other amusements, esp. one that moves from town to town **2** also **amusement park–** an outdoor area where such a show is held

fungus *n* **-gi** *or* **-guses 1** any of several types of simple fast-spreading plant without flowers, leaves, or green colouring matter, which may be in a large form, (mushrooms, toadstools, etc.), or in a very small form, (mildew, mould, etc.) **2 a** these plants in general, esp. considered as a disease **b** these plants in a large group **3** a disagreeable thing of sudden growth or appearance: *A fungus of ugly little houses sprang up* – **-goid** *adj* – **-gal** *adj*

¹**funnel** *n* **1** a metal chimney for letting out smoke from a steam engine or steamship **2** a tubelike vessel that is large and round at the top and small at the bottom, used in pouring liquids or powders into a vessel with a narrow neck

²**funnel** *v* **-ll- 1** to pass through or as if through a funnel **2** (esp. of something large or made up of many parts) to pass through a narrow space: *The large crowd funnelled through the gates* **3** to form into the shape of a funnel: *He funnelled his hands*

funny *adj* **-nier, -niest 1** amusing; causing laughter **2** strange; hard to explain; unusual: *What can that funny noise be?* **3** *esp. spoken* out of order; not quite correct; rather dishonest: *There's something funny about the telephone; it won't work* **4** *esp. spoken* **a** slightly ill: *She felt a bit funny* **b** slightly mad: *He went rather funny after his wife died* **5** *esp. spoken* deceiving; using tricks; too clever: *Don't get funny with me* – **-niness** *n*

¹**fur** *v* **-rr-** to make or become covered with fur

²**fur** *n* **1** the soft thick fine hair that covers the body of some types of animal, such as bears, rabbits, cats, etc. **2** a hair-covered skin of certain types of animal, such as foxes, rabbits, mink, etc., which has been or will be treated and used for clothing **3** (a garment) made of one or more of these **4** a greyish covering on the tongue **5** a hard covering on the inside of pots, hot-water pipes, etc., caused by lime in heated water

furious *adj* **1** very angry in an uncontrolled way **2** powerful: *a furious blow* **3** wild; uncontrolled: *a furious temper* –~**ness** *n* –~**ly** *adv*

furnace *n* **1** an apparatus in a factory,

in which metals and other substances are heated to very high temperatures in an enclosed space **2** a large enclosed fire used for producing hot water or steam

furnish *v* **1** to put furniture in (a room or building); supply with furniture **2** *esp. written* to supply (what is necessary for a special purpose)

furniture *n* all large or quite large movable articles that are placed in a house, room, or other area, in order to make it convenient, comfortable, and/or pleasant to live in such as beds, chairs, tables, etc.

¹**further** *adv, adj (comparative of* FAR*)* **1** more: *Don't try my patience any further* **2** farther: *too tired to walk any further* **3** later: *There'll be a further performance*

²**further** *v* to help (something); advance; help to succeed: *to further the cause of peace*

furthermore *adv* also; in addition

fury *n* **furies 1** very great anger **2** a state of very great anger: *fly into a fury for the slightest reason* **3** a wildly excited state (of feeling): *a fury of impatience* **4** wild force or activity: *the fury of the storm* **5** *esp. spoken* a fierce angry woman or girl: *Jane's a little fury if she can't get what she wants*

¹**fuse** *n* **1** a long string treated with an explosive powder, or a narrow pipe filled with this powder, used for carrying fire to an explosive article and so causing it to blow up: *He lit the fuse and ran for shelter* **2** an apparatus screwed into a bomb, shell, or other weapon, which causes it to explode when touched, thrown, etc.

²**fuse** *n* **1** a (small container with a) short thin piece of wire, placed in an electric apparatus or system, which melts if too much electric power passes through it, and thus breaks the connection and prevents fire or other damage: *A fuse has blown* **2** *esp. spoken* a failure of electric power, owing to the melting of one of these

³**fuse** *v* **fused, fusing 1** (of metal) to melt or cause to melt in great heat: *Lead fuses at a low temperature* **2** to join or become joined by melting: *Copper and zinc are fused to make brass* **3** to stop or cause to stop working owing to a fuse: *The lights have fused* **4** to unite

¹**fuss** *n* **1** unnecessary, useless, or unwelcome expression of excitement, anger, impatience, etc.: *What a fuss about nothing!* **2** an anxious nervous condition: *to get into a fuss* **3** a show of annoyance probably resulting in punishment: *There's sure to be a fuss when they find the window's broken* **4** unwanted or unnecessary activity; hurry: *What's all this fuss about?*

²**fuss** *v* **1** to act or behave in a nervous, restless, and anxious way over small matters **2** to make nervous

future *adj, n* **1** (belonging to or happening in) the time after the present: *The future is unknown to us* **2**

(expected, planned, arranged, etc., for) the life in front of a person; that which will happen to someone or something: *I wish you a happy future* **3** (in grammar) (being) the tense of a verb that expresses what will happen at a later time: *The future (tense) of English verbs is formed with the help of 'shall" and 'will"* **4** *esp. spoken* likelihood of success: *There's no future in this job*

gadget *n esp. spoken* a small machine or useful apparatus

¹gag *v* **-gg-** **1** to put a gag into the mouth of **2** to prevent from speaking or expressing something **3** *esp. US* to be unable to swallow and start to vomit

²gag *n* **1** something put over or into the mouth to keep it still or esp. to prevent the person from talking or shouting **2** *esp. spoken* a joke or funny story

gaiety *n* **-ties** **1** also **gayness**– the state of being gay **2** joyful events and activities

¹gain *n* **1** the act of making a profit; increase in wealth **2** a profit; increase in amount

²gain *v* **1** to obtain (something useful, necessary, wanted, etc.): *to gain experience* **2** to make (a profit or increase in amount): *The car gained speed* **3** (of a watch or clock) to move too fast and show a time later than the correct time **4** *esp. written* to reach, esp. with effort or difficulty: *We finally gained the summit*

galactic *adj* of or concerning a galaxy

galaxy *n* **-ies** **1** any of the large groups of stars which make up the universe **2** a splendid gathering of people, esp. those famous, beautiful, or clever

gale *n* **1** a weather condition in which a strong wind blows **2** a sudden noise, esp. laughter: *A gale of laughter came from inside*

gallantry *n* **-tries** *literature* **1** (an act of) polite attention paid by a man to a woman **2** (an act of) bravery, esp. in battle —**gallant** *adj*

gallery *n* **-ries** **1** a private room, hall, or building where works of art are shown and usu. offered for sale **2** a public building where paintings (and perhaps other works of art) are shown **3** an upper floor built out from an inner wall of a hall or theatre, from which activities below may be watched, esp. the highest one with the cheapest seats **4** a covered passage, open on one side **5** a long narrow room, such as one used for shooting practice **6** a level underground passage in a mine or joining natural caves

gallon *n* a measure for liquids, 8 pints or 4 quarts (in Britain 4.54, in America 3.78 litres)

¹gallop *n* **1** the fastest movement of a horse, when all 4 feet come off the ground together **2** a ride at this speed **3** a rush

²gallop *v* **1** to go, or cause to go, at a gallop **2** (of a person or animal) to go very fast

gambit *n* **1** (in chess) a set of moves in which a piece is risked for later advantage **2** an action or esp. use of language which is used to produce a future effect, esp. as part of a trick or clever plan

¹**gamble** *v* **-bled, -bling 1 a** to play cards or other games for money; risk money on horse races **b** to risk one's money in business **2** to take the risk that something will go well, or as one wishes, after doing something that depends on it – **-bler** *n*

²**gamble** *n* a risky matter or act

¹**game** *n* **1** a form of play or sport, or one example or type of this **2** a set of things, usu. a board and counters which are used to play such a game indoors **3** a single part of a set into which a match is divided, as in tennis **4** wild animals, some birds and some fish, which are hunted or fished for food, esp. at certain seasons as a sport **5** a trick or secret plan: *What's your game?* **6 fair game a** troublesome animals which can fairly be shot **b** a person who can justly be attacked in words **7 Two can play at that game** You are not the only one that can get advantages by behaving in such a way, I can too!

²**game** *v* **gamed, gaming** to gamble

³**game** *adj* **1** brave and ready for action: *a game fighter* **2** willing: *Who's game for a swim?* –~**ly** *adv*

⁴**game** –also (*esp. spoken*) **gammy** *adj* (of a limb, esp. a human leg) unable

to be used properly because of something wrong

gamekeeper *n* a man employed to raise and protect game, esp. birds, on private land

gammon *n* the meat from the back part and leg of a pig when it has been preserved by smoke or salt

gander *n* **1** a male goose **2** *esp. spoken* a look

gang *n* **1** a group of people working together, such as prisoners or building workers **2** a group of criminals **3** *often offensive* a group of friends who are against other groups

gangster *n* a member of a gang of criminals, esp. those who use guns to threaten and kill

gaol *n*, *v* jail –~**er** *n*

gap *n* **1** an empty space between 2 objects or 2 parts of an object: *a gap in the fence* **2** an amount of distance or difference **3** a lack (of something): *There are gaps in my knowledge*

gape *v* **gaped, gaping 1** to look hard in surprise, esp. with the mouth open **2** to come apart or open: *His shirt gaped open*

¹**garage** *n* **1**- a building in which motor vehicles can be kept **2** a place where petrol can be bought and cars repaired

²**garage** *v* **-aged, -aging** to put in a garage

¹**garden** *n* **1** a piece of land, often near a house, on which flowers and vegetables may be grown **2** a public

park with flowers, grass, paths, and seats

²garden *v* to work in a garden, making plants grow −~**er** *n* −~**ing** *n*

garment *n esp. written* (the name used, esp. by the makers, for) an article of clothing

¹gas *n* **gases 1** (a type of) substance like air, which is not solid or liquid **2** a substance of this type which is burnt in the home to supply heat for the rooms and cooking and formerly for light **3** also **laughing gas**— such a substance, called **nitrous oxide,** used as a general anaesthetic by a dentist while he pulls a tooth out **4** *US esp. spoken* petrol **5** *esp. spoken* unimportant talk **6 step on the gas** to increase the speed (of the car) −~**eous** *adj*

²gas *v* **-ss- 1** to poison with gas **2** to talk a long time about unimportant things

gasp *v* **1** to catch the breath suddenly and audibly esp. because of surprise, shock, lack of air, etc. **2** to say while breathing in this way: *He gasped out the message* −**gasp** *n*

gate *n* **1** a movable frame, often barred, which closes an opening in a fence, wall, etc. **2** either of a pair of large frames as used to control the water level at locks , or to close the road at a level crossing **3** a gateway

gateway *n* **-ways 1** an opening in a fence, wall, etc., across which a gate may be put **2** a way of finding: *Hard work is the gateway to success*

¹gather *v* **1** to come or bring together: *Gather round, and I'll tell you a story* **2** to obtain (information or qualities) bit by bit: *He gathers facts about new cars* **3** to collect or pick: *Gather your toys up* **4** to understand from something said or done: *I didn't gather much from the confused story* **5** to draw (material) into small folds

²gather *n* something produced by gathering: *She made gathers in the skirt*

¹gauge *n* **1** a standard measure of weight, size, etc., to which objects can be compared **2** the thickness of wire or certain metal objects, or the width of the barrel of a gun **3** the distance between the rails of a railway or between the wheels of a train **4** an instrument for measuring size, amount, etc., such as the width of wire, the amount of rain

²gauge *v* **gauged, gauging 1** to measure by means of a gauge **2** to judge the worth, meaning, etc., of

gave *past tense of* GIVE

gay *adj* **gayer, gayest 1** cheerful **2** bright or attractive, so that one feels happy to see it, hear it, etc.: *gay colours/music* **3** only concerned with pleasure: *the gay life* **4** *esp. spoken* homosexual −~**ness** *n*

¹gaze *v* **gazed, gazing** to look steadily −**gazer** *n*

²gaze *n* a steady fixed look

¹gear *n* **1** a set of things collected together, esp. when used for a particular purpose: *climbing gear* **2** an apparatus or part of a machine which has a special use in controlling a vehicle: *steering gear* **3** any of several arrangements, esp. of toothed wheels in a machine, which allows power to be passed from one part to another so as to control the power, speed, or direction of movement **4** *sl* clothes

²**gear** to supply with gears

geese *pl. of* GOOSE

gelignite *n* a very powerful explosive

gem *n* **1** a precious stone, esp. when cut into a regular shape **2** a thing or esp. person of especial value

gene *n* any of several small parts of the threadlike parts (chromosomes) in the nucleus of cells. Each of these parts controls the development of the qualities in a living thing which have inherited from its parents

¹**general** *adj* **1** concerning or felt by everybody or most people: *general anxiety* **2** not limited to one thing, place, etc.: *general education* **3** not detailed; describing the main things only: *Give me a general idea* **4** chief: *Major-General* **5** **general practice** the part of the medical service in which one doctor treats all illnesses; job of a family doctor **6** **in general a** also **as a general rule**— usually **b** (*after a pl. noun*) most: *People in general like her*

²**general** *n* an officer of very high rank in the army or in command of an army

general election *n* an election in which all the voters in the country take part at the same time to choose the members of parliament

generally *adv* **1** usually **2** by most people: *The plan has been generally accepted* **3** without considering details, but only the main points

generate *v* **-rated, -rating 1** *esp. written* to cause to exist **2** *technical* to produce (heat or electricity): *a generating station*

generation *n* **1** the act or action of generating: *Falling water may be used for the generation of electricity* **2** a period of time in which a human being can grow up and have a family, perhaps 25 or 30 years **3** a those who are the same number of steps from an ancestor: *We belong to the same generation* **b** people of roughly the same age group **4** all the members of any developing class of things at a certain stage: *second generation computers*

generator *n* a machine which generates, usu. electricity

generosity *n* **-ties 1** the quality of being generous **2** a generous act

generous *adj* **1** showing readiness to give money, help, kindness, etc. **2** in large amounts: *a generous meal* **-~ly** *adv*

genetics *n* the study of how living things develop according to the effects of those substances passed on in the cells from the parents -- **icist** *n*

genitals – also **genitalia** *n* the outer sex organs **-genital** *adj* **-genitally** *adv*

genius *n* **1** great ability, esp. in producing works of art **2** a person of such ability or of very high intelligence **3** a special ability, sometimes unpleasant in effect: *a genius for mathematics*

gentle *adj* **1** kind and ready to help others **2** soft in movement: *a gentle wind* **3** *old use* high-born – ~**ness** *n* – **-ly** *adv*

gentleman *n* **-men 1** a man who behaves well and can be trusted to act honourably **2** *polite* a man **3** (in former times) a man who had a private income and did not need to work – ~**ly** *adj*

genuine *adj* (of an object or feelings) real – ~**ly** *adv* – ~**ness** *n*

geography *n* the study of the world and its countries, seas, rivers, towns, etc. – **-pher** *n* – **-phical** *adj* – **-phically** *adv*

geology *n* the study of the rocks, soil, etc. which make up the earth, and the way they have formed – **-gical** *adj* – **-gically** *adv* – **-gist** *n*

geometry *n* the study in mathematics of the angles and shapes formed by the relationships of lines, surfaces, and solids in space

germ *n* **1** a very small invisible creature living on food or dirt or in the body, so causing disease **2** a beginning point, esp. of an idea **3** also **germ cell**– a small part or cell of a living thing which can grow into a new plant, animal, etc.

gesture *n,v* **-tured, -turing** (to make) a movement, usu. of the hands, to express a certain meaning or feeling

get *v* **got, getting 1** to receive or experience: *I got a blow on the head* **2 a** to obtain or acquire: *I'll get something to eat* **b** to take, or deal with **3** to reach the start of an activity: *Get moving!* **4** to bring (something) to a start: *I'll get the car going* **5** to (cause oneself to) become: *The food's getting cold* **6** to be; become: *to get trapped* **7** to bring (into a certain state): *I'll get them dressed* **8** to cause to do: *I got him to help* **9** to move to or arrive at: *We got there early* **10** to put or move into or out of the stated place: *Get that cat out of the house* **11** to succeed in (doing): *If I get to see him I'll ask* **12** to catch (an illness) **13** *esp. spoken* to understand: *He never gets the message* **14** *esp. spoken* to annoy or cause strong feeling to: *That gets me where it hurts* **15** *esp. spoken* to hit: *I got him with a potato* **16** *old use* to become the father of; beget **17** to defeat (someone) in an argument: *I'll get him on that point* **18** to come or bring to the stated degree of success: *My son is really getting somewhere* **19 get (something) done a** to cause (something) to be done; have **b** *esp. spoken* to experience (something being done to one) **c** *esp. spoken* to do (something necessary): *I'll just get these dishes washed* **20 get above oneself** to have too good an opinion of oneself **21 get (something or**

someone) **right/wrong** *esp. spoken* to understand (something or someone) correctly/wrongly

ghastly *adj* **-lier, -liest 1** (of a person) very pale and ill-looking **2** causing great fear: *ghastly news* **3** *esp. spoken* very bad: *We had a ghastly time at the party* – **-liness** *n*

ghetto *n* **-tos** a part of a city in which a group of poor people live who are usu. not accepted as full citizens

¹**ghost** *n* **1** (the spirit of) a dead person who appears again **2 the ghost of a** the slightest – ~**ly** *adj* – ~**liness** *n*

²**ghost** *v* to write in someone else's name for money

giant *n* **1** a man who is much bigger than is usual **2** a very big, strong creature in fairy stories in the form of a man, but often unfriendly to human beings and very cruel and stupid **3** a person of great ability: *a giant among writers* **4** something very large: *That packet is a giant* –

gift *n* **1** something which is given freely; present **2** a natural ability to do something: *a gift for music* **3** *sl* something obtained easily, or cheap at the price

gigantic *adj* unusually large in amount or size – ~**ally** *adv*

¹**gill** *n* a measure equal to 1/4 pint or 0·142 litres

²**gill** *n* **1** one of the organs through which a fish breathes by taking in water to pass over them **2** *esp. spoken & humour* the area of skin around the neck and under the ears

gimmick *n esp. spoken* **1** a trick object or part of an object which is used to draw attention **2** a special way of acting or point of appearance which is noticeable: *an advertising gimmick* – ~**y** *adj*

¹**ginger** *n* **1** a plant with a hot strong root which is used in cooking **2** the quality of being active

²**ginger** *adj, n* (of) an orange-brown colour, esp. the least usual colour of human hair

gipsy *n* **-sies 1** a member of a dark-haired race which may be of Indian origin and now travels about in carts, motor vehicles, and caravans, earning money as horse dealers, musicians, fortune tellers, etc. **2** *esp. spoken & sometimes offensive* a person who habitually wanders

giraffe *n* **giraffes** *or* **giraffe** a type of African leaf-eating animal with a very long neck and legs and orangeish skin with dark spots

girder *n* a strong beam, usu. of iron or steel, which supports the smaller beams in a floor or roof or forms the support of one part of a bridge

girl *n* **1 a** a young female person **b** a daughter: *My little girl is ill* **2** *esp. spoken* a woman: *the girls' football team* **3 a** a woman worker: *shop girls* **b** (esp. formerly) a female servant **4** a girlfriend **5 old girl a** *old use* a friendly way of speaking to a woman **b** a female former pupil of a school

¹**give** *v* **gave, given, giving 1** to pass into someone's hands or care: *Give me the baby* **2** to hand (something)

over as a present **3** to pay in exchange: *She gave him a pound for his help* **4** to cause to experience: *The news gave us a shock* **5** to produce: *Cows give milk* **6** to allow to have: *Give me a chance* **7** to be the cause of (someone's illness): *He's given me flu* **8** to set aside (time, thought, strength, etc.) for a purpose **9** to tell in words: *Give me more information* **10** to show: *That clock gives the right time* **11** to offer (a performance or amusement): *We are giving a party* **12** to admit the truth of: *It's too late now. I give you that* **13** to allow (part of one's body) to be used by another person: *She gave him her hand to shake* **14** to do an action: *She gave a shout* **15** to cause to believe because of information given: *I was given to understand that he was ill* **16** to bend or stretch under pressure: *The leather will give with wearing* **17 give it to someone straight** *sl* to scold someone in an angry or direct way **18 give (someone) what for** *sl* to scold severely, or perhaps beat, (someone) **19 give way (to) a** to yield, as in an argument or when driving a car **b** to break **c** to become less useful or important than: *Steam trains gave way to electric trains* **d** to allow oneself to show (esp. a feeling) **20 What gives?** *sl* (showing surprise) What's going on? **–giver** *n*

²**give** *n* the quality of moving (esp. bending, stretching, or loosening)

under pressure: *There is give in leather*

glacier *n* a mass of ice which moves very slowly down a mountain valley

glad *adj* **-dd-** **1** (of people) pleased and happy about something **2** causing happiness: *glad news* **3** *polite* very willing: *I'll be glad to help you* **–~ness** *n* **–~ly** *adv*

glamorous, -ourous *adj* having or causing glamour: *a glamorous job/girl* **–~ly**

glamour *n* **1** charm and beauty with a romantic power of attraction: *the glamour of foreign countries* **2** personal charm which excites admiration and esp. attracts men to women

¹**glance** *v* **glanced, glancing** **1** to give a rapid look: *He glanced at his watch* **2** to flash with reflected light: *The glasses glanced in the firelight* **3 glance one's eye down/over/through, etc.** to give a hurried reading or look

²**glance** *n* **1 a** a rapid look: *One glance told me he was ill* **b** a rapid movement of the eyes **2** a flash of light, usu. from a bright object **3** a blow which slips to the side: *A sudden glance of the sword cut his shoulder* **4 at a glance** with one look; at once

¹**glare** *v* **glared, glaring** **1** to shine with a strong light and/or unpleasantly: *The sun glared out of the blue sky* **2** to look in an angry way

²**glare** *n* **1** a hard, unpleasant effect given by a strong light: *a red glare over the burning city* **2** an angry

look or stare **3** a state which continually draws the attention of the public: *the glare of publicity*

glaring *adj* **1 a** (of light) hard and too bright **b** (of colours) too bright **2** (of mistakes) very noticeable **3** fierce-looking: *glaring eyes* –~**ly***adv*

glass *n* **1** a hard transparent solid material made from sand melted under great heat **2** a collection of objects made of this: *glass and china* **3** an object made of or containing this, and shaped to make things seem larger, esp. a telescope **4** a drinking vessel **5** *esp. spoken* a mirror

glasses –also **eyeglasses** *n* 2 pieces of specially-cut glass usu. in a frame and worn in front of the eyes for improving a person's ability to see

¹**gleam** *n* **1** a shining light, esp. one making objects bright: *the red gleam of the firelight* **2** a sudden flash of light **3** a sudden showing of a feeling or quality for a short time: *A gleam of interest came into his eye*

²**gleam** *v* **1** to give out a bright light **2** (of a feeling) to be expressed with a sudden light: *Amusement gleamed in his eyes*

glee *n* **1** a feeling of joyful satisfaction at something which pleases one: *She danced with glee when she saw the new toys* **2** a song for 3 or 4 voices together –~**ful** *adj*

¹**glide** *v* **glided, gliding 1** to move (noiselessly) in a smooth, continuous manner, which seems effortless: *The boat glided over the river* **2** to use a glider

²**glide** *n* a gliding movement

glider *n* a plane without an engine, or its pilot

gliding *n* the sport of flying gliders

¹**glimmer** *v* to give a very faint, unsteady light

²**glimmer** *n* **1** a faint unsteady light **2** a small sign: *a glimmer of hope*

¹**glimpse** *v* **glimpsed, glimpsing** to have a passing view of: *I glimpsed her among the crowd*

²**glimpse** *n* **1** a quick look at or incomplete view of: *I caught a glimpse of our new neighbour* **2** a moment of understanding: *His worried face gave me a glimpse of his true feelings*

¹**glitter** *v* to shine brightly with flashing points of light

²**glitter** *n* **1** a brightness, as of flashing points of lights: *the glitter of broken glass* **2** attractiveness; glamour –~**ing** *adj*

globe *n* **1** an object in the shape of a round ball **2** such an object on which a map of the earth or sky is painted, and which may be turned on its base **3** a round glass fish bowl

gloom *n* **-ier, -iest 1** darkness **2** a feeling of deep sadness –~**y** *adj* –~**ily** *adv* –~**iness** *n*

glorious *adj* **1** having, or worthy of, great fame and honour: *glorious deeds* **2** beautiful: *a glorious day* **3** *esp. spoken* very enjoyable: *What a glorious party!* –~**ly** *adv*

glory *n* **-ries 1** great fame or success; praise and honour: *The general was* *crowned with glory* **2** beauty **3** special beauty or cause for pride: *That tree is the glory of the garden* **4** praise offered to God: *Glory be to God* **5** happiness in heaven (esp. in the phrases **send to glory, go to glory**)

glossy *adj* **-ier, -iest** shiny and smooth **–glossily** *adv* **–glossiness** *n*

glove *n* a garment which covers the hand, with separate parts for the thumb and each finger

¹glow *v* **1** to give out heat and/or light without flames or smoke: *The hot coals glowed* **2** to show bright strong colours: *glowing flowers* **3** to show redness and heat in the face (and the body), esp. after hard work or because of strong feelings: *glowing with pride*

²glow *n* **1** a light from something burning without flames or smoke **2** brightness of colour **3** the feeling and/or signs of heat and colour in the body and face, as after exercise or because of good health or strong feelings

¹glue *n* a sticky substance which is obtained from animal bones or fish and used for joining things together **–~y** *adj*

²glue *v* **glued, gluing** *or* **glueing** to join with glue

glut *n* a larger supply or quantity than is necessary: *a glut of eggs*

glutton *n* **1** a person who eats too much **2** *esp. spoken* a person who is always ready to do more of some-thing hard or unpleasant **–~ous** *adj* **–~ously** *adv* **–~y** *n*

gnat *n* a type of small stinging flying insect

gnaw *v* **1 a** to keep biting (something hard), esp. until destroyed: *to gnaw a bone* **b** to worry or give pain to: *Grief gnaws my heart* **2** to make (a way) or destroy by doing this

gnawing *adj* painful and/or worrying: *gnawing hunger*

¹go *v* **went, gone, going** **1** to leave the place where the speaker is (so as to reach another): *I must go/be going* **2** to travel or move: *We went by bus* **3** to reach (as far as stated): *The roots go deep* **4** to start an action: *Get going on the work* **5 a** to do (an activity) **b** *esp. spoken* to do (something undesirable): *Don't go saying that!* **6** to be placed, esp. usually placed: *The boxes go there* **7** (of machines) to work (properly) **8** to become (by a natural change, or by changing on purpose): *She's going grey* **9** to remain (in a certain state): *Her complaints went unnoticed* **10** to be sold: *going cheap* **11** to be spent or used: *Half our money goes on food* **12** to cease or disappear: *Summer's going* **13** to be got rid of: *This car must go* **14 a** to die or (sometimes) to become unconscious: *He went out like a light* **b** to be damaged; to weaken or wear out: *My voice has gone* **15** to be or have to be accepted or acceptable: *Anything goes* **16** to happen (in a certain way): *The hours went slowly* **17 a** to be stated, said, or sung in a certain way **b** to have or suit a certain tune: *The tune goes like this* **18** to divide a certain sum so as to give an exact figure: *3 into 2 won't go* **19** to make the stated sound: *The guns went 'boom'* **20** to match or fit: *This paint doesn't go* **21** to make a movement: *When he waved, he went like this* **22** to be sent for consideration: *Your suggestion will go before the committee* **23** to be about to, or be planning to, travel (to a place): *We are going to France* **24** to lose one's usual powers of control as in illness, when confused or mad: *He's really let himself go* **25** (of people) to work or move, esp. with unusual effort or result: *Her tongue goes 19 to the dozen* **26** to be on average or in general (in cost, quality, etc.): *She was a good cook, as cooks go* **27** to state or do up to or beyond a limit: *It's quite good, as far as it goes* **28 be going** to be present for use, sale, or enjoyment: *Is there any food going?* **29 be going to (do or happen)** (showing a future action or happening as certain, decided on, or impossible to avoid): *It's going to rain* **30 from the word go** from the beginning **31 go a long way** also **go far– a** (of money) to buy a lot **b** (of a person) to succeed **32 go and a** *esp. spoken* to go in order to **b** *esp. spoken* (expresses surprise): *She went and won first prize!* **33 go it alone** to act independently **34 3, 6, etc., months gone**

esp. spoken having been pregnant for 3, 6 months, etc.

¹**go-ahead** *n* permission to act: *to get the go-ahead*

²**go-ahead** *adj* (of people) active in using new methods

goal *n* **1** one's aim or purpose; a place or object one wishes to obtain or reach: *His goal is a place at University* **2** (in games like football) the place where the ball, puck, etc. must go for a point to be gained, or the point thus gained

goalkeeper –also (*esp. spoken*) **goalie** *n* the player in a football team who is responsible for preventing the ball from getting into his team's goal

goat *n* **1** a type of 4-legged animal related to the sheep, which also gives milk and a hairy sort of wool, which can climb steep hills and rocks and eat almost anything **2** *sl* a man who is very active sexually

god *n* **1** (*fem.* **god·dess**) a being (one of many) which is worshipped, as one who made or rules over (a part of) the life of the world **2** a person or thing to which too great importance is given

God *n* **1** the being who in the Christian, Jewish, and Muslim religions is worshipped as maker and ruler of the world **2 God forbid/grant that** May it not happen/happen that **3 God (alone) knows** *esp. spoken* It's impossible to say

godchild *n* **-children** (in the Christian religion) the child for whom one

205

takes responsibility by making promises at a baptism

godparent *n* the person (**godfather** or **godmother**) who makes promises to help a Christian newly received into the church at a baptismal ceremony

¹**going** *n* **1** the act of leaving: *Our going was delayed* **2** the act or speed of travel: *slow going* **3** the condition or possibility of travel: *The mud made it heavy going*

²**going** *adj* **1** in existence: *He's the biggest fool going* **2** as charged at present: *the going rate* **3** working; in operation: *The store is a going concern*

gold *n* **1** a valuable soft yellow metal that is an element used for making coins, jewellery, etc. **2** coins or objects made of this metal generally **3** the colour of this metal **4** kindness, gentleness in behaviour, etc. (esp. in the phrases **heart of gold, as good as gold**)

golden *adj* **1** made of gold **2** of the colour of gold **3** very fortunate or favourable: *a golden opportunity*

goldfish *n* **goldfish** a small fish which is kept as a pet in glass bowls, and in ornamental pools

golf *n,v* (to play) a game in which people drive small hard balls into holes with special clubs, trying to do so with as few strokes as possible —~**er** *n*

gone *past part. of* GO

gong *n* **1** a round piece of metal hanging from a frame, which when struck with a stick gives a deep ringing sound, as used in Eastern music or to call people to meals **2** *sl* a medal

¹**good** *adj* **better**, **best** **1** having the right qualities: *a good play* **2** suitable; favourable: *The weather's good* **3** morally right: *to do a good deed* **4** (of people) kind; helpful **5** (esp. of children) well-behaved **6** suitable for its purpose: *a good idea* **7** enjoyable: *a good story* **8** useful to the health or character: *Milk is good for you* **9** (of food) fresh **10** strong; in good condition; working well: *You need good shoes for hill-walking* **11** having the ability to do something: *good at languages* **12** worthy of respect: *my good man* **13** of a higher standard or quality than average **14** effective in use (usu. over a period of time): *The ticket is good for one month* **15** safe from loss of money: *a good risk* **16** large in size, amount, etc: *a good distance* **17** at least or more than: *a good mile away* **18** (in expressions of feeling): *Good gracious!* **19** (in greetings): *Good morning/afternoon/evening/day* **20 a good deal/few** quite a lot **21** complete; thorough: *Have a good look* **22 All in good time** (it will happen) at a suitable later time; be patient **23 as good as** almost (the same thing as) **24 good and .....** *esp. spoken esp. US* very; completely **25 good for** likely to produce (an effect or money) **26 in good time** early **27 It's a good thing** It's fortunate **28**

make good to be successful, esp. wealthy **29 make something good a** to pay for; make up; repair **b** to put into effect: *make good a promise*

²**good** *n* **1** that which is right and useful in accordance with religious beliefs or moral standards: *an influence for good* **2** that which causes gain or improvement: *I work for the good of my family* **3** good people generally: *Christians believe the good go to heaven when they die* **4 do someone good** to improve someone, esp. in health or behaviour **5 for good (and all)** for ever **6 no good/not much good (doing something/to someone)** useless **7** (an amount) **to the good** with a profit of (an amount)

goodbye *interj, n* (an expression used when leaving, or being left by, someone)

goodness *n* **1** the quality of being good **2** the best part, esp. (of food) the health-giving part **3** (used in expressions of surprise and annoyance): *My goodness!*

goods *n* **1** possessions which can be moved, not houses, land, etc. **2** heavy articles which can be carried by road, train, etc. **3** articles for sale **4 deliver the goods** to produce in full what is expected

goose *n* **geese 1** (*male* **gander**) any of a family of large web-footed birds **2** the white bird of this family that is kept on farms **3** the meat of this bird **4** a silly person, esp. female

gooseberry *n* **-ries 1** the small round green edible fruit of a bush **2 play gooseberry** to be present with a man and woman who would rather be alone

gorgeous *adj esp. spoken* **1** delightful: *This cake is gorgeous* **2** very beautiful –~**ly** *adv* –~**ness** *n*

gorilla *n* a tailless animal which is the largest of the manlike apes, is very strong, and lives in Africa

gospel *n* a set of instructions or teachings

Gospel *n* any of the 4 accounts of Christ's life and teaching in the Bible

¹**gossip** *n* **1** talk or writing, not necessarily correct, about other people's actions and private lives **2** a person who likes to gossip

²**gossip** *v* to talk or write gossip

got *past tense and past part. of* GET

govern *v* **1** to rule: *We have a queen, but it is Parliament that governs* **2** to control or guide (actions and feelings): *Don't let fear govern your decision* **3** to determine the nature of: *The tides are governed by the movements of the moon*

government *n* **1** governing: *The king was not suited to government, and ruled badly* **2** the people who rule –~**al** *adj*

governor *n* **1** a person or one of a group controlling certain types of organization: *a prison governor* **2** (esp. in former times) a person who rules over a state or province on behalf of the central government **3**

the elected head of an American state – ~**ship** *n*

gown *n* **1** *old use or US* a long dress: *an evening gown* **2** a loose outer garment, usu. black, worn for special ceremonies by judges, teachers, etc. **3** a loose garment worn for some special purpose: *a dressing gown*

¹**grab** *v* **-bb-** to seize with a sudden, rough movement, esp. for a selfish reason: *He grabbed the coin and ran off*

²**grab** *n* a sudden attempt to seize something

¹**grace** *n* **1** effortless and attractive **2** kindness: *She had the grace to say that he was right* **3** a delay allowed as a favour, as for payment, work, etc.: *I'll give you a week's grace to finish the work* **4** a prayer before or after meals, giving thanks to God **5** the mercy (of God): *By the grace of God the ship survived the storm* **6** a way of speaking to or of a duke, duchess, or archbishop: *Your/His/Her Grace* **7 in someone's good graces** in someone's favour

²**grace** *v* **graced, gracing** to ornament; give pleasure, by one's/its presence: *Fine furniture graced the rooms*

graceful *adj* **1** (of shape or movement) attractive to see **2** suitably and pleasantly expressed – **-fully** *adv*

gracious *adj* **1** polite, kind and pleasant, esp. to those who have no claim on one's attention: *She was gracious enough to show us round her home* **2** used in speaking of royal persons: *Her Gracious Majesty* **3** having those qualities made possible by wealth: *gracious living* – ~**ly** *adv* – ~**ness** *n*

¹**grade** *n* **1** a degree of rank or quality **2** a mark for the standard of a piece of schoolwork

²**grade** *v* **graded, grading** to separate into levels: *potatoes graded according to size*

gradual *adj* happening slowly and by degrees – **-ually** *adv* – ~**ness** *n*

grain *n* **1** a seed of rice, wheat, etc. **2** crops from plants which produce such seeds **3** a piece of a substance which is made up of small hard pieces: *a grain of sand* **4** the arrangement of the threads or fibres in wood, flesh, rock, and cloth, or the pattern these make **5** a small measure of weight, used for medicines (1/7000 of a pound or 0·648 gram)

gram, gramme *n* a measure of weight, 1/1000 of a kilogram

grammar *n* **1** (the study and practice of) the rules by which words change their forms and are combined into sentences **2** a book which teaches these rules

gramophone *n becoming rare* RECORD PLAYER

¹**grand** *adj* **1** splendid in appearance: *a grand view* **2** important, or thinking oneself so: *a very grand lady* **3** *esp. spoken* very pleasant: *a grand party* **4** complete (esp. in the phrase **the grand total**) – ~**ly** *adv* – ~**ness** *n*

²**grand** *n esp. spoken* GRAND PIANO

grandchild *n* **-children** the child (**grandson** or **granddaughter**) of someone's son or daughter

granddaughter *n* the daughter of someone's son or daughter

grandfather *n* the father of someone's father or mother

grandmother *n* the mother of someone's father or mother

grandparent *n* the parent (**grandfather** or **grandmother**) of someone's father or mother

grand piano *n* **-os** a large piano with strings set across, not upright

grandson *n* the son of someone's son or daughter

grandstand *n* a large group of raised seats, sometimes roofed, from which to watch sports matches, races, etc.

granite *n* a hard type of grey rock, used for building and making roads

¹**grant** *v* **1** to give, esp. what is requested: *He granted them leave to go* **2** to admit to (the truth of): *I grant you that she's a good player*

²**grant** *n* a sum of money given by the state to a person or an organization, for a special purpose: *Students often have to live on a small grant*

grape *n* a small round juicy fruit, usu. green or dark purple, which grows in bunches and is used for making wine

graph *n* a drawing showing the relationship between 2 variables

¹**grasp** *v* **1** to take or keep a firm hold of, esp. with the hands **2** to succeed in understanding: *I grasped the main points*

²**grasp** *n* **1** a firm hold: *I kept her hand in my grasp* **2** reach: *Success is within his grasp* **3** control; power: *in the grasp of a wicked man* **4** understanding: *work beyond my grasp*

¹**grass** *n* **1** various kinds of common low-growing green plants with blade-like leaves **2** land covered by grass **3** any of various types of green plant with tall straight stems and flat blades **4** *sl* a person (often a criminal) who informs the police about criminals

²**grass** *v* **1** to cover (land) with grass **2** *sl* (esp. of a criminal) to inform the police about the action of criminals

grasshopper *n* a type of jumping insect which makes a sharp noise by rubbing parts of its body together

grassy *adj* **-sier, -siest** covered with growing grass

¹**grate** *n* the bars and frame which hold the fuel in a fireplace

²**grate** *v* **grated, grating 1** to rub (usu. food) on a hard rough surface so as to break into small pieces: *grated cheese* **2** to make a sharp unpleasant sound: *The key grated in the lock*

grateful *adj* feeling or showing thanks to another person **–~ly** *adv* **–~ness** *n*

gratitude *n* gratefulness

¹**grave** *n* the place in the ground where a dead person is buried

²**grave** *adj* **1** serious in manner: *His face was grave* **2** important and

needing attention and (often) worrying: *The sick man's condition is grave* –~**ly** *adv*

¹**gravel** *n* a mixture of small stones with sand, used on the surface of roads or paths

²**gravel** *v* –ll– to cover with gravel

gravity *n* **1 a** seriousness of manner: *to behave with gravity* **b** worrying importance **2** the natural force by which objects are attracted to each other, esp. that by which a large mass pulls a smaller one to it: *Anything that is dropped is pulled by gravity towards the centre of the earth*

gravy *n* –vies **1** the juice which comes out of meat as it cooks **2** this juice thickened to serve with meat and vegetables

¹**graze** *v* **grazed, grazing 1** (of animals) to feed on grass **2** to cause (animals) to feed on grass: *We can't graze the cattle till summer* **3** to use (land) for grazing

²**graze** *v* **1** to touch lightly while passing: *The plane's wing seemed to graze the treetops* **2** to break the surface of (esp. the skin) by rubbing against something: *She grazed her knee*

³**graze** *n* a surface wound

¹**grease** *n* **1** animal fat when soft after being melted **2** a thick oily substance

²**grease** *v* **greased, greasing** to put grease on

greasy *adj* –ier, –iest **1** covered with grease or containing it: *greasy food/hair* **2** slippery: *The roads are greasy* –**greasily** *adv* –**greasiness** *n*

¹**great** *adj* **1** of excellent quality or ability: *the great men of the past* **2** important: *a great occasion* **3** large in amount or degree: *a great many* **4** (of people) unusually active in the stated way: *He's a great talker* **5** (*usu. before another adj. of size*) big **6 great with child** *Bible* pregnant –~**ness** *n*

²**great** *n* important people: *He has connections with the great*

greatly *adv* to a large degree: *greatly to be feared*

greed *n* strong desire to obtain a lot or more than is fair, esp. of food, money, or power: *greed for gold* –~**y** *adj* –~**ily** *adv* –~**iness** *n*

¹**green** *adj* **1** of a colour between yellow and blue, which is that of leaves and grass **2** young or unripe: *Green apples are sour* **3** young and/or inexperienced and therefore easily tricked **4** pale in the face, as from sickness, fear, etc. **5** (esp. of memories) fresh, in spite of the passing of time **6** also **green with envy**– very jealous –**greenness** *n* ~**ish** *adj*

²**green** *n* **1** (a) green colour **2** a smooth stretch of grass, for a special purpose, as for playing a game or for the general use of the people of a town: *a village green / a bowling / putting green*

greengrocer *n* a shopkeeper who sells vegetables and fruit

greenhouse *n* a building with glass

roof and sides and often heated, used to protect growing plants

greet *v* **1** to welcome with words, actions, or an expression of feeling: *She greeted him with a loving kiss* **2** to come suddenly to the eyes, ears, etc.: *Complete disorder greeted us*

greeting *n* **1** a form of words or an action used on meeting someone: *She didn't return my greeting* **2** a good wish: *Christmas greetings*

grenade *n* a small bomb which can be thrown by hand or fired from a gun

grew *past tense of* GROW

¹**grey** *adj* **1** of a colour like black mixed with white which is that of ashes and of rain clouds **2** having grey hair: *She's going grey* **3** (of the face) pale because of sudden fear or illness **4** dull, colourless – ~**ness** *n* – ~**ish** *adj*

²**grey** *n* (a) grey colour

³**grey** *v* **greyed, greying** (esp. of hair) to become grey

grief *n* **1** great sorrow, esp. at the death of a loved person **2** a cause of sorrow or anxiety: *His behaviour was a grief to his mother*

grievance *n* a report of or cause for complaint, esp. of unjust treatment: *The workers met to discuss their grievances*

grieve *v* **grieved, grieving 1** to suffer from grief, esp. over a loss: *grieving for her dead husband* **2** to cause grief to

grievous *adj* **1** very seriously harmful: *a grievous mistake* **2** (of wounds, pain, etc.) severe **3 grievous bodily harm** *law* hurt done to a person's body in an attack, for which the attacker may be charged in a court of law – ~**ly** *adv* – ~**ness** *n*

¹**grill** *v* **1** to cook (something) under or over direct heat **2** *sl* to question severely and continuously: *He was grilled for hours by the police*

²**grill** *n* **1** the cooking apparatus used for grilling food **2** meat cooked this way **3** a restaurant which serves mainly grilled foods

grim *adj* **-mm- 1** cruel, hard, or causing fear: *a grim expression* **2** determined in spite of fear: *a grim smile* **3** *esp. spoken* unpleasant; not cheerful: *I've had a grim day* – ~**ly** *adv* – ~**ness** *n*

¹**grin** *v* **-nn-** to make a grin: *to grin with pleasure*

²**grin** *n* a wide smile which shows the teeth

¹**grind** *v* **ground, grinding 1** to crush into small pieces or a powder by pressing between hard surfaces: *She grinds her coffee beans* **2** to rub (esp. the teeth) together or against something, so as to make a noise **3** to make smooth or sharp by rubbing on a hard surface: *to grind the knives and scissors* **4** to press upon with a strong twisting movement: *He ground his knee into the man's stomach* – ~**er** *n*

²**grind** *n* **1** hard uninteresting work: *He finds study a real grind* **2** a long

steady tiring effort of movement, such as a race

grip [1] *v* **-pp-** **1** to take a very tight hold (of): *She gripped my hand* **2** to attract and hold (someone's attention): *The strange stories gripped the hearers*

grip [2] *n* **1** a very tight forceful hold **2** control: *He kept a firm grip on his children* **3** power of understanding or doing: *I played badly; I seem to be losing my grip* **4 a** something which grips: *a hair grip* **b** a handle to be gripped **5 come/get to grips with** to deal seriously with (something difficult)

grit [1] *n* **1** small pieces of a hard material, usu. stone: *Grit is spread on icy roads to make them less slippery* **2** *sl* determination; lasting courage **—gritty** *adj*

grit [2] *v* **-tt- grit one's teeth** to become more determined

groan [1] *v* **1** to make a groan or talk in a groaning way **2** to suffer: *The people groaned under the taxes*

groan [2] *n* **1** a rather deep loud sound of suffering, worry, or disapproval **2** a sound caused by the movement of wood or metal parts heavily loaded: *The chair gave a groan when the fat woman sat down*

grocer *n* a shopkeeper who sells dry and preserved foods, like flour, sugar, rice, and other things for the home, such as matches and soap

grocery *n* **-ies** the shop or trade of a grocer

groom [1] *n* **1** a person who is in charge of horses **2** a bridegroom

groom [2] *v* **1** to take care of (horses), esp. by rubbing, brushing, and cleaning **2** to take care of the appearance of (oneself), by dressing neatly, keeping the hair tidy, etc. **3** (of animals) to clean the fur and skin of: *Monkeys groom each other* **4** to prepare (someone) for a special position or occasion: *grooming her for stardom*

groove [1] *n* a long narrow path or track made in a surface, esp. to guide the movement of something: *The cupboard door slides along a groove*

groove [2] *v* **grooved, grooving** to make grooves in

grope *v* **groped, groping** **1** to try to find something, or to make one's way, by feeling with the hands without being able to see: *He groped in his pocket for his ticket* **2** to search with uncertainty of success: *groping after the truth* **3** *sl* to feel over the body of (a person) so as to get sexual pleasure **—grope** *n* **— -pingly** *adv*

gross [1] *adj* **1** unpleasantly fat **2** (of people's speech & habits) rough, impolite, and offensive: *shocked by his gross words* **3** *law* clearly wrong in law; inexcusable **4** total: *The gross weight of the box of chocolates is more than the weight of the chocolates alone* **—~ly** *adv* **—~ness** *n*

gross [2] *n* the whole; the greater part

gross [3] *v* to gain as total profit or earn as a total amount: *The company grossed £2,000,000 last year*

⁴gross *n* **gross** *or* **grosses** a group of 144; 12 dozen

grotesque *adj* **1** strange and unnatural so as to cause fear or be laughable: *a grotesque monster* **2** concerning the strange and unnatural, esp. in art –~**ly** *adv* –~**ness** *n*

¹ground *n* **1** the surface of the earth: *The branch fell to the ground* **2** soil; earth: *The ground is dry* **3** a piece of land used for a particular purpose: *a football ground* **4** a background: *The curtains have white flowers on a blue ground* **5** a base for argument, study, etc. **6 get off the ground** to make a successful start **7 give ground** to yield; retreat **8 go to ground** (esp. of a fox or criminal) to go into hiding

²ground *v* **1 a** (of a boat) to strike against the bottom or the ground **b** to cause (a boat) to do this **2** to cause (a pilot or plane) to come to or stay on the ground: *aircraft grounded because of thick mist* **3** to base: *I ground my argument on experience*

³ground *past tense and past part. of* GRIND

groundless *adj* (of feelings, ideas, etc.) without base or good reason –~**ly** *adv* –~**ness** *n*

grounds *n* **1** small bits of solid matter which sink to the bottom of a liquid, esp. coffee **2** a reason (esp. in the phrase **on (the) grounds**) **3** land surrounding a large building, such as a country house or hospital

4 a large area used for a particular purpose: *fishing grounds*

¹group *n* **1** a number of people or things placed together **2** a number of people of the same interests, beliefs, age, race, etc. **3** a set of things or organizations connected in a particular way: *blood group A*

²group *v* to form into groups: *We can group animals into several types*

grovel *v* **-ll- 1** to lie or move flat on the ground, esp. in fear or obedience: *The dog grovelled at his feet* **2** to be shamefully humble and eager to please: *He grovels to anyone important*–~**ler** *n*

grow *v* **grew, grown, growing 1** (of living things or parts of them) to increase in size by natural development: *Grass grows after rain* **2** (of plants) to exist and be able to develop: *Cotton grows wild here* **3** to cause to or allow to grow: *He grows vegetables* **4** to increase in numbers, amount, etc.: *The village is growing into a town* **5** to become (gradually): *The noise grew louder*

growl *v* **1** (usu. of animals) to make a deep rough sound in the throat to show anger or give warning **2** to make a sound like this: *growling thunder* –**growl** *n* –**growler** *n*

¹grown-up *adj* fully developed: *She has a grown-up daughter*

²grown-up *n esp. spoken* a fully grown and developed person

growth *n* **1** the act or rate of growing and developing: *Trees take many years to reach their full growth* **2**

increase in numbers or amount: *a sudden growth in membership of the club* **3** something which has grown **4** a lump produced by an unnatural and unhealthy increase in the number of cells in a part of the body

¹**grudge** –also **begrudge** *v* **grudged, grudging** to give or allow unwillingly

²**grudge** *n* a cause for dislike, esp. of another person, real or imagined: *She has a grudge against me*

gruff *adj* **1** (of the human voice) deep and rough **2** (of behaviour) rough; unfriendly or impatient, esp. in one's manner of speaking – –~**ly** *adv* – –~**ness** *n*

¹**grumble** *v* **-bled, -bling** to express discontent: *He has nothing to grumble about* – **-bler**

²**grumble** *n* a complaint

¹**grunt** *v* **1** to make short deep rough sounds in the throat, as if the nose were closed: *a grunting pig* **2** (of human beings) to make such sounds, esp. when dissatisfied, in pain, or tired

²**grunt** *n* a sound like that of a pig

¹**guarantee** *n* **1** a written statement by the maker of an article agreeing to repair or replace it within a certain time if it is faulty **2** an agreement to be responsible for the fulfilment of someone else's promise, esp. for paying a debt **3** something of value given to someone to keep until the owner has fulfilled a promise, esp. to pay **4** something that happens which makes something else certain

²**guarantee** *v* **-teed, -teeing 1** to give a guarantee **2** to promise: *I guarantee you'll enjoy yourself*

¹**guard** *n* **1** a state of watchful readiness to protect or defend (esp. in the phrase **on guard**) **2** a position for defence, esp. in a fight: *He got in under his opponent's guard* **3** a person or group whose duty is to guard: *a prison guard* **4** a member of a group of special soldiers, originally those who guarded the king or queen: *a Horse Guard* **5** a railway official in charge of a train **6** an apparatus which covers and protects: *a mudguard*

²**guard** *v* **1** to defend; keep safe, esp. by watching for danger: *The dog guarded the house* **2** to watch (a prisoner) in order to prevent escape **3** to control

guardian *n* **1** someone that guards **2** *law* a person who looks after another's child esp. after the parents' death – –~**ship** *n*

guerrilla, guerilla *n* a member of an unofficial fighting group which attacks the enemy in small groups unexpectedly

¹**guess** *v* **1** to form (a judgment) or risk giving (an opinion) without knowing or considering all the facts: *Guess how much it cost* **2** to get to know by guessing: *She guessed my thoughts*

²**guess** *n* **1** an attempt to guess **2** an opinion formed by guessing

guest *n* 1 a person who is in someone's home by invitation 2 a person who is invited out and paid for at a theatre, restaurant, etc.: *Come to the concert as my guests* 3 a person who is lodging in a hotel, or as a **paying guest** in someone's home 4 a person who is invited to perform: *a guest singer*

guidance *n* help; advice

¹**guide** *n* 1 something or somebody that shows the way, esp. someone whose job is to show a place to tourists 2 something which influences or controls a person's actions or behaviour: *Don't take your friend's experience as a guide* 3 also **guide book**– a book which gives a description of a place, for the use of visitors 4 an instruction book

²**guide** *v* **guided, guiding** 1 to show the way: *He guided the man home* 2 to control (the movements of) 3 to influence strongly: *Be guided by your feelings*

guilt *n* 1 the fact of having broken a law: *His guilt is proved* 2 responsibility for something wrong; blame 3 the knowledge or belief that one has done wrong: *His face showed guilt* –~**less** *adj* –~**lessly** *adv* –~**lessness** *n*

guilty *adj* **-ier, -iest** 1 having broken a law or disobeyed a moral or social rule: *guilty of murder* 2 feeling or showing guilt: *I have a guilty conscience about losing your letter* –**guiltily** *adv* –**guiltiness** *n*

guitar *n* 1 a 6-stringed musical instrument played by plucking, having a long neck, and a wooden body like a violin but larger 2 any of a number of other musical instruments like this, such as one (an **electric guitar**) with a solid body and a sound that is increased electrically

gulf *n* 1 a large deep stretch of sea partly enclosed by land: *the Persian Gulf* 2 a deep hollow place in the earth's surface: *A great gulf opened before us* 3 a great area of division, esp. between opinions

¹**gulp** *v* 1 to swallow hastily: *Don't gulp your food* 2 to make a sudden swallowing movement as if surprised or nervous

²**gulp** *n* 1 the action of gulping 2 a large mouthful

¹**gum** *n* either of the 2 areas of flesh in which the upper and lower sets of teeth are fixed

²**gum** *n* 1 any of several kinds of sticky substance obtained from the stems of some plants 2 a substance used to stick things together 3 a hard transparent jelly-like sweet 4 a sweet plastic substance to be chewed but not swallowed

³**gum** *v* **-mm-** to stick with gum

gun *n* 1 a weapon from which bullets or shells are fired through a barrel 2 a tool which forces out and spreads a substance by pressure: *a grease gun* 3 **jump the gun a** to start running in a race before the signal to start has been given **b** to start before getting permission

gunpowder *n* an explosive material in powder form

¹**gush** *v* **1** to flow out in large quantities, as from a hole or cut: *Oil gushed from the broken pipe* **2** to express admiration, pleasure, etc., in a great flow of words, foolishly or without true feeling – ~**ing** *adj* – ~**ingly** *adv*

²**gush** *n* **1** a (sudden) flow: *The wound re-opened in a gush of blood* **2** a sudden rush (of words) **3** a sudden show (of strong feeling): *a gush of enthusiasm*

gust *n* a sudden strong rush of air, or of rain, smoke, etc., carried by wind

¹**gutter** *n* **1** a small ditch between a road and the pavement to carry away rainwater **2** an open pipe fixed at the lower edge of a roof to carry away rainwater **3** the lowest poorest social conditions

²**gutter** *v* (of a candle) to burn unevenly

gymnasium *n* **-ums** *or* **-a** a hall with wall bars, ropes, etc., for climbing, jumping, etc.

gymnast *n* a person who trains and is skilled in bodily exercises – ~**ic** *adj* – ~**ically** *adv*

gymnastics *n* the training of the body by exercises

habit *n* **1** customary behaviour: *It's my habit to get up early* **2** a special kind of clothing, esp. that worn by monks and nuns

habitual *adj* **1** usual: *his habitual greeting* **2** by habit: *a habitual thief* – ~**ly** *adv*

had –*short form* **'d 1** *past tense of* HAVE **2** *past part. of* HAVE

haemorrhage *n* a flow of blood, esp. a long or large and unexpected one

haggle *v* **-gled, -gling** to argue over fixing a price

¹**hail** *n* **1** water frozen into little hard balls **2** a number of things which strike suddenly with violence: *a hail of bullets*

²**hail** *v* (of hail) to fall

³**hail** *v* **1** to call out to by name or in greeting: *An old friend hailed me* **2** to recognize as important by calling out (a title): *They hailed him king*

hair *n* **1** a fine threadlike growth from the skin of a person or animal **2** a mass of such growths, such as that on the human head **3 get in (someone's) hair** *esp. spoken* to annoy (someone) **4 split hairs** to concern oneself with unimportant differences – ~**less** *adj*

hairbrush *n* a brush used to smooth the hair and get out dirt

haircut *n* **1** an occasion of having the hair cut **2** the style the hair is cut in

hairdresser *n* a person who cuts, sets, or changes the colour of hair (esp. women's) – **-sing** *n*

hairy *adj* **-ier, -iest 1 a** (not usu. describing the hair on the head) having a lot of hair: *a hairy chest* **b** having a rough surface like hair **2** *sl* exciting in a frightening way: *a hairy drive* – **-riness** *n*

¹**half** *n* **halves 1** either of the 2 equal parts into which something is or

could be divided; 1/2; 50% **2** either of 2 parts or periods of time into which something is divided: *Neither side scored in the first half* **3 by halves** incompletely: *Better not do it at all than do it by halves* **4 go halves (in/on something)** *esp. spoken* to share (the cost of something)

²**half** *n* **halfs** *or* **halves** something which has 1/2 the value or quantity of something, such as a coin, ticket, weight, or measure: *Give me a penny for 2 halfs*

³**half** *pron* either of the 2 parts of a thing or group: *Half of them are here*

⁴**half** *adj* being 1/2 in amount: *half a minute*

⁵**half** *adv* **1** partly: *half cooked* **2 half 7, 8, 9,** etc. (of time) 7.30, 8.30, 9.30, etc.

half-brother *n* a brother related through one parent only

half-hearted *adj* showing little effort and no real interest – ~**ly** *adv* – ~**ness** *n*

halfpenny *n* **halfpennies** *or* **halfpence** **1** (in Britain, before 1971) a coin, 2 of which made an old penny; 1/2d **2** also **half p-** (in Britain, after 1971) a very small coin, 2 of which make a new penny; 1/2p

half-sister *n* a sister related through one parent only

half time *n* the period of time between 2 parts of a game

halfway *adj, adv* at the midpoint between 2 things

hall *n* **1** a large room in which meetings, dances, etc., can be held **2** the passage just inside the entrance of a house, from which the rooms open

hallucination *n* something apparently seen which is not really there, often as the result of a drug or a mental illness – **-atory** *adj*

¹**halt** *v* to stop: *The train was halted by the signal*

²**halt** *n* **1** a stop or pause (esp. in the phrase **come to a halt**) **2** a small railway station: *a country halt*

halve *v* **halved, halving 1** to divide into halves **2** to reduce to half

¹**ham** *n* **1** preserved meat from a pig's leg **2** an actor whose acting is unnatural, with extreme gestures and a booming way of speaking **3** a person who receives and/or sends radio messages using his own apparatus

²**ham** *v* **-mm-** to act (a part on stage) unnaturally or wildly

hamburger *n* a flat circular cake of minced meat, esp. as eaten in a bread roll

¹**hammer** *n* **1** a tool with a heavy head for driving nails into wood, or for striking things to break or move them **2** something made to hit something else, as in a piano, or part of a gun **3** a small bone in the ear **4 come under the hammer** to be sold by auction **5 throwing the hammer** a sport in which competitors throw a metal ball on the end of a wire as far as possible

²**hammer** *v* **1** to strike with a hammer **2** to hit repeatedly

hammock *n* a long piece of cloth or net which can be hung up by the ends to form a bed

¹**hamper** *v* to cause difficulty in activity: *The snow hampered my movements*

²**hamper** *n* a large basket with a lid

¹**hand** *n* **1** the movable parts at the end of the arm, including the fingers **2** a pointer or needle on a clock or machine **3** handwriting: *He writes a clear hand* **4** a set of playing cards held by one person in a game **5** (in squash and badminton) the period of play from the time a player becomes server until he becomes receiver **6** a measure equal to 0.1 metres, used in measuring a horse's height at the shoulder **7** a sailor on a ship **8** a workman **9** encouragement given by clapping the hands (in the phrases **give a (good, big) hand to, get a (big, good) hand) 10** quality of touch (esp. in the phrases **have a light/heavy hand) 11** help (esp. in the phrases **give/lend a hand to) 12** control (esp. in the phrases **get/become out of hand) 13 at first hand** when known through direct experience **14 at hand** near in time or place **15 bring up by hand** to feed (an animal that has no mother) so that it can live and grow **16 get/keep one's hand in** to get used to an activity by practising **17 get the upper hand** to get control or power **18 have one's hands full** to be very busy **19 on every hand** in all directions **20 on the one/other hand** as one point in the argument/as an opposite point: *I want to go to the party, but on the other hand I ought to be studying* **21 out of hand** (esp. of decisions not to do something) at once and without further thought **22 throw in one's hand** to accept defeat **23 turn one's hand to** to begin to practise (a skill)

²**hand** *v* **1** to give from one's own hand into someone else's: *Hand me that book* **2 hand it to (someone)** to admit (someone's) success, esp. in something mentioned next

handbag *n* a small bag for a woman's money and personal things

handful *n* **1** an amount which is as much as can be held in the hand **2** a small number: *a handful of people* **3** a living thing that is difficult to control: *That child is quite a handful*

¹**handicap** *n* **1 a** a disability: *Blindness is a great handicap* **b** disadvantage: *Being small is a handicap in this crowd* **2** a race, sport, or game in which the stronger competitors are disadvantaged by weights, running further than others, etc.

²**handicap** *v* **-pp- 1** to cause to have a disadvantage **2** (of a disability) to prevent (someone) from acting and living in the usual way: *physically handicapped*

handkerchief *n* **-chiefs** *or* **chieves** a piece of cloth or thin soft paper for drying the nose, eyes, etc.

¹**handle** *n* **1** a part of an object for holding it or for opening it **2 fly off the handle** *esp. spoken* to lose one's temper

²**handle** *v* **-dled, -dling 1** to feel or move with the hands **2** to deal with; control **3** to treat: *Handle children kindly* **4** to use (goods) in business, esp. for sale **5** (of a car, boat, etc.) to obey controlling movements in the stated way **—handleable** *adj*

handshake *n* an act of shaking each other's right hand as a greeting or farewell between 2 people

handsome *adj* **1 a** (esp. of men) good-looking **b** (esp. of women) attractive with a firm, large appearance **2** generous: *a handsome present* **—~ly** *adv*

handwriting *n* writing done by hand

handy *adj* **-ier, -iest 1** useful and simple to use **2** clever in using the hands: *handy with her needle* **3** near: *The shops are handy* **— -dily** *adv* **— -diness** *n*

¹**hang** *v* **hung, hanging 1** to fix at the top so that the lower part is free: *to hang curtains* **2** to be in such a position: *The curtains hang well* **3** to keep (certain types of meat) in this position until ready to be eaten **4** to show (a set of paintings) publicly **5 a** to fix (wallpaper) on a wall **b** to fix (a door) in position on its hinges **6** *esp. spoken* damn (esp. in the phrases **I'll be hanged, Hang it!**) **7 hang fire** to stop happening or continuing: *Our plans must hang fire for a time*

²**hang** *v* **hanged, hanging** to kill or die, as in punishment for a crime, by dropping with a rope around the neck

³**hang** *n* **1** the shape or way something hangs: *I don't like the hang of this coat* **2 get/have the hang of** *esp. spoken* to be able to understand, use, or work

hangar *n* a big shed where planes are kept

hanger *n* a hook and crosspiece to fit inside the shoulders of a dress, coat, etc., to keep its shape when hung up

hangover *n* the feeling of headache, sickness, etc., the day after drinking too much alcohol

happen *v* **1** to take place **2** to have the good or bad luck (to) **3** to be true by or as if by chance: *It so happened that I saw him yesterday*

happening *n* an event

happy *adj* **-pier, -piest 1** feeling or giving pleasure **2** suitable: *not a very happy remark* **3** *polite* pleased: *I'll be happy to meet him* **4** (of wishes) joyful (esp. in phrases like **Happy New Year, Happy Birthday**) **— -pily** *adv* **— -piness** *n*

harass *v* **1** to trouble continually **2** to make repeated attacks against: *They harassed the enemy*

¹**harbour** *n* an area of sheltered water where ships are safe from rough seas

²**harbour** *v* **1** to give protection to, esp. by giving food and shelter to (someone bad): *Harbouring crimi-*

nals is an offence in law **2** to keep in the mind: *to harbour a secret wish* –~**er** *n*

¹**hard** *adj* **1** which cannot easily be broken, pressed down, bent, etc. **2** difficult (to do or understand): *hard questions* **3 a** forceful: *a hard push* **b** needing or using force of body or mind: *hard work* **4** full of difficulty: *a hard life* **5** (of people, punishments, etc.) not gentle: *a hard woman* **6** (in English pronunciation) **a** (of the letter *c*) pronounced as *k* rather than *s* **b** (of the letter *g*) pronounced as in *get* rather than as in *rage* **7** (of water) which contains lime, preventing soap from mixing properly with the water **8** (of a drug) being one on which a user can become dependent so that he will be ill if he does not take it **9** unpleasant to the senses, esp. because too bright or too loud: *her hard voice*

²**hard** *adv* **1** with great effort: *Think hard and work hard* **2** heavily: *It's raining hard* **3 be hard done by** to be unfairly treated **4 be hard put to it** to have great difficulty **5 die hard** (of habits) to be lost with difficulty **6 hard at it** working with all one's force in some activity

hardly *adv* **1** almost not: *I could hardly wait* **2** not reasonably: *I can hardly ask him for more money*

hardship *n* something that causes suffering, such as lack of money, hard work, etc.

hardware *n* **1** goods for the home and garden, such as pans, tools, etc. **2** machinery used in war **3** machinery which makes up a computer

hardy *adj* **-dier, -diest 1** strong; able to bear cold, hard work, etc. **2** (of plants) able to live through the winter above ground – **-diness** *n*

¹**hare** *n* **hares** *or* **hare** an animal with long ears, a divided upper lip, a short tail and long back legs which make it able to run fast. It is larger than a rabbit, and does not live in a hole

²**hare, hair** *v* **hared, haring** *esp. spoken* to run very fast: *He hared off down the road*

¹**harm** *n* damage; wrong: *He means no harm* –~**ful** *adj* –~**fully** *adv* –~**fulness** *n*

²**harm** *v* to hurt; damage: *Getting up early won't harm you!*

harmless *adj* that cannot cause harm –~**ly** *adv* –~**ness** *n*

harmony *n* **-nies 1** notes of music combined together in a pleasant sounding way **2** peacefulness: *My cat and dog live in perfect harmony* – **-nious** *adj* – **-niously** *adv* – **-niousness** *n*

¹**harness** *n* **1** the leather bands used to control a horse or fasten it to a cart **2** something of this type, such as the straps fastened round a baby's body to support or confine it

²**harness** *v* **1** to put a harness on or fasten with a harness **2** to use (a natural force) to produce useful power: *harness a river to make electricity*

harp *n* a large musical instrument

with strings running from top to bottom of an open 3-cornered frame, played by stroking or plucking the strings with the hands – ~**ist** *n*

harsh *adj* **1** unpleasant to the senses: *a harsh light* **2** showing cruelty or lack of kindness – ~**ly** *adv* – ~**ness** *n*

¹**harvest** *n* **1** the gathering of the crops **2** the time of year when crops are picked

²**harvest** *v* to gather (a crop)

has –*short form* **'s** *3rd person sing. pres. tense of* HAVE

haste *n* quick urgent movement or action: *Make haste!* (=hurry!)

hasten *v* **1** to move or happen faster: *He hastened home* **2** to be quick to say, because the hearer may imagine something else has happened: *I hasten to say that he is not hurt*

hasty *adj* **-ier, -iest 1** done in a hurry: *a hasty meal* **2** too quick in acting or deciding, esp. with a bad result: *a hasty temper* – **-tily** *adv* – **-tiness** *n*

have –*short form* **'ve** *v* **had, having 1** (a helping verb, forming the perfect tense): *I've been reading. / Have you finished?* **2** also **have got**– to possess, or contain as a part: *She has blue eyes. / This coat has no pockets* **3** to receive or take: *I had a letter today. / He had a hot bath* **4** to enjoy or experience: *We're having a party* **5** to allow: *I can't have you running up and down all day* **6 a** to

cause to be done: *I had my hair cut* **b** to experience: *I had my car stolen* **7 had better** ought to **8 have to** also **have got to**– must: *I have to go now*

haven *n* a place of calm and safety

havoc *n* widespread damage or confusion: *His ideas are causing havoc in the office*

¹**hawk** *n* **1** any of many types of bird, often large, which catch other birds and small animals with their claws for food, and are active during the day **2** a person who believes in using force – ~**ish** *adj* – ~**ishness** *n*

²**hawk** *v* to sell (goods) in the street or at the doors of houses – ~**er** *n*

hay *n* **1** grass which has been cut and dried, esp. for cattle food **2 make hay a** to dry grass in the sun **b** to make use of chances: *"Make hay while the sun shines"* (=while conditions are favourable) –**haymaker** *n* –**haymaking** *n*

haystack –also **hayrick** *n* a large pile of hay built for storing

¹**hazard** *n* a danger: *a health hazard*

²**hazard** *v* to risk: *I hazarded a guess*

hazardous *adj* containing risks or danger – ~**ly** *adv* – ~**ness** *n*

haze *n* **1** light mist or smoke: *a haze of cigarette smoke* **2** a feeling of confusion or uncertainty: *a haze of tiredness*

hazy *adj* **-ier, -iest 1** misty; rather cloudy **2** unclear: *I'm rather hazy about the details* – **-zily** *adv* – **-ziness** *n*

¹**he** *pron* (*used as the subject of a sen-*

tence) **1** that male person or animal: *Be careful of that dog–he sometimes bites* **2** (with general meaning): *Everyone should do what he considers best*

²**he** *n* a male animal: *Is your dog a he?*

¹**head** *n* **1 a** the part of the body which contains the eyes, ears, nose and mouth, and the brain–in man on top of the body, in other animals in front **b** (in man) the part of the head above and behind the eyes: *My head aches* **2** the end where this part rests: *at the head of the bed* **3** the mind or brain: *a good head for figures* **4** a ruler or leader, esp. a headmaster: *the head of a firm* **5** the front side of a coin which often bears a picture of the ruler's head (esp. in the phrase **heads or tails?**) **6** a person or creature: *3 head of cattle* **7** a part at the top of an object which is different or separate from the body: *the head of the nail* **8** the white centre of a boil or pimple on the skin when it is about to burst **9** the top or front: *the head of the queue* **10** also **headland**– an area of land running out into the sea: *Beachy Head* **11** the top part of some plants, when several leaves or flowers grow together there: *heads of lettuce* **12** the white foam on the top of drinks such as beer **13 a a** body of water at a certain height, from which it may fall to produce power to work machinery **b** the pressure or force produced by falling water or by a quantity of steam **14 above/over someone's head** beyond someone's understanding **15 bite someone's head off** *esp. spoken* to answer severely **16 bang one's head against a brick wall** to keep making an effort without getting any result **17 a bring something to a head** to cause to reach a point where something must be done **b come to a head** to reach this point **18 bury one's head in the sand** to avoid facing some difficulty **19 give someone his head** to allow someone freedom to do as he likes **20 go to someone's head a** to intoxicate someone **b** to make someone too proud, or conceited **21 head over heels a** turning over in the air head first **b** completely: *head over heels in love* **22 keep one's head above water** to be able to live on one's income **23 not be able to make head or tail of** to be unable to understand

²**head** *adj* chief: *the head cook*

³**head** *v* **1** to be at the front or in charge of **2** to strike (a ball) with the head **3** to move in a certain direction: *heading home*

headache *n* **1** a pain in the head **2** *esp. spoken* a great difficulty – **-achy** *adj*

headfirst –also **headlong** *adj, adv* **1** with the rest of the body following the head **2** in foolish haste

heading *n* a title at the top of a piece of writing

headlight –also **headlamp** *n* a

powerful light on the front of a vehicle

¹headline *n* **1** the heading in large letters above a newspaper report **2** a main point of the news, as read on radio or television

²headline *v* **-lined, -lining** to give a headline to

headmaster *–fem.* **headmistress** *n* the teacher in charge of a school

headquarters *n* **-ters** the office or place where the people work who control a large organization

headway *n* forward movement against a difficulty: *making headway*

heal *v* to make or become healthy, esp. to grow new skin *–~er n*

health *n* **1** the state of being well, without disease **2** the condition of the body: *in poor health* **3** (before drinking) (a wish for a toast to) someone's success and continued freeedom from illness (esp. in the phrases **drink a health, your health!**)

healthy *adj* **-ier, -iest 1** strong, not often ill **2 a** likely to produce good health **b** good for the mind or character: *That book is not healthy reading for a child* **3** showing good health: *a clear healthy skin* **–healthily** *adv* **–healthiness** *n*

¹heap *n* **1** a pile or mass of things one on top of the other **2** *esp. spoken* a lot: *a heap of trouble*

²heap *v* to pile up **2** to collect or gain in large amounts: *He heaped up great wealth*

hear *v* **heard, hearing 1** to receive and understand by using the ears: *I can hear knocking* **2** to be told: *I heard that he was ill* **3** to give a hearing (esp. to a case in court): *The judge heard the case* **4 won't/wouldn't hear of** to refuse to allow **5 Hear! Hear!** (a shout of agreement)

hearing *n* **1** the sense by which one hears sound: *Her hearing is getting worse* **2** the distance at which one can hear; earshot: *Don't talk about it in his hearing* **3** listening: *At first hearing I didn't like the music* **4** a chance to be heard explaining one's position: *Try to get a hearing* **5** *law* a trial of a case before a judge

heart *n* **1** the organ inside the chest which forces the blood through the blood vessels and round the body **2** the same organ thought of as the centre of the feelings: *He has a kind heart* **3** something shaped like this organ **4** a playing-card with one or more figures of this shape printed on it in red: *the Queen of Hearts* **5** the centre (of something large, and of certain leafy vegetables): *Let's get to the heart of the matter* **6** courage, strength of mind (esp. in the phrases **take heart, lose heart**) **7 after one's own heart** just of the type one likes **8 at heart a** in reality: *He's dishonest at heart* **b** in one's care: *I have your health at heart* **9 by heart** by memory: *to learn by heart* **10 eat one's heart out** to be very troubled **11 from the bottom of one's heart** with real feeling **12 have one's heart in** to be interested in: *I tried to learn music but I didn't have my heart in it* **13 heart and soul** with all one's feelings or agreement **14 have one's heart in one's mouth** to feel very afraid or worried **15 in one's heart of hearts** in one's most secret feelings: *In my heart of hearts I knew it wasn't true* **16 take (something) to heart** to feel the effect of something deeply and take suitable action **17 wear one's heart on one's sleeve** to show one's feelings **18 with all one's heart** with deep feeling

heartbroken –also **broken hearted** *adj* deeply hurt in the feelings

hearth *n* **1** the area round the fire in one's home, esp. the floor of the fireplace **2** the home: *hearth and home*

hearty *adj* **-ier, -iest** **1** warm-hearted: *a hearty greeting* **2** strong and healthy (esp. in the phrase **hale and hearty**) **3** (of meals) large **4** too cheerful, esp. when trying to appear friendly – **-tily** *adv* **--tiness** *n*

¹**heat** *v* to make or become warm or hot: *Heat some milk*

²**heat** *n* **1** the quality or quantity of being warm or cold: *Measure the heat of the water* **2 a** hotness; warmth: *heat from the fire* **b** hot weather: *I can't think in this heat* **3** a state of excitement: *in the heat of the argument* **4** a state of sexual excitement happening regularly to certain female animals: *Our dog is on heat* **5** *technical* the force produced by the movement of groups of atoms **6** a part of a race or competition whose winners compete against other winners until there is a small enough number for a final

heater *n* a machine for heating air or water, by burning gas, oil, electricity, etc.

heather *n* a plant which grows as a small bush on open windy moors and has pink, purple, or sometimes white flowers

heating *n* a system for keeping rooms and buildings warm

¹**heave** *v* **heaved, heaving** **1** to pull and lift **2** to rise and fall regularly: *His chest heaved after the race* **3** *esp. spoken* to throw: *Heave a brick through the window* **4** to give out (a sad sound): *He heaved a loud groan*

²**heave** *v* **hove, heaving** (of a ship) to move in the stated direction or manner: *Another ship hove alongside*

³**heave** *n* **1** a pull or throw **2** an upward movement or set of such movements at regular times: *the heave of waves*

heaven *n* **1** the place where God or the gods are believed to live; place of complete happiness where the souls of good people supposedly go after death **2** the sky **3** great happiness or a very happy place: *I was in heaven at the news*

heavenly *adj* **1** of, from, or like heaven; in or belonging to the sky: *The sun, moon, and stars are* **heavenly bodies** **2** *esp. spoken* wonderful: *What heavenly weather!*

¹heavy *adj* **-ier, -iest 1** of a certain weight, esp. of a weight that makes moving or lifting difficult **2** of unusual force or amount: *heavy rain* **3** serious; full of hard work: *This book is heavy reading. / I've had a heavy day* **4** sad: *heavy news* **5 a** feeling or showing difficulty or slowness in moving: *a heavy sleeper* **b** difficult to do or move in: *The soil makes heavy walking* **6** (of food) rather solid **7** (of weather) **a** still, without wind, dark, etc. **b** (at sea) stormy, with big waves **8** *esp. spoken* **a** severe (towards): *a teacher who is heavy on his pupils* **b** using in large quantities: *This car is heavy on oil* **9 make heavy weather of something** to make something more difficult than it really is — **-vily** *adv* — **-viness** *n*

²heavy *n* **-ies** a serious usu. male part in a play, esp. a bad character

¹hedge *n* **1** a row of bushes or small trees acting as a fence **2** a protection: *a hedge against inflation*

²hedge *v* **hedged, hedging 1** to make a hedge round (a field) **2** to refuse to answer directly **3 hedge one's bets** to protect oneself against loss by supporting more than one side in a competition or struggle

hedgehog *n* a small insect-eating animal which comes out only at night. It rolls itself into a ball and sticks up sharp spines when made afraid

¹heel *n* **1** the back part of the foot **2** the part of a shoe, sock, etc., which covers this, esp. the raised part of a shoe underneath the foot: *to wear high heels* **3 at/on one's heels** very closely behind **4 bring to heel** to force to obey one **5 cool one's heels** also **kick one's heels**— to be made to wait for some time unwillingly **6 turn on one's heel** to turn round suddenly **7 under someone's heel** in someone's power

²heel *v* **1** to put a heel on (a shoe) **2** (esp. of a dog) to move along at someone's heels **3** (in rugby) to send (the ball) back with the heel to another player of one's own team, esp. from the scrum

height *n* **1** the quality or degree of being tall or high: *to measure the height of the tower* **2** (a point at) a fixed or measured distance above another point: *at a height of 10 feet above the ground* **3** a high position or place: *from a great height* **4** the main point; highest degree: *the height of the summer*

heir *n* *—fem.* **heiress** the person who has the lawful right to receive the property or title of an older member of the family who dies

held *past tense and past part. of* HOLD

helicopter *n* a type of aircraft which is made to fly by a set of large fast-turning metal blades, and which can land in a small space, take off vertically, and stay still in the air

¹hell *n* **1** (esp. in the Christian and Muslim religions) a place where the souls of the wicked are said to be punished after death **2** a place or state of great suffering **3** *sl* (a swear word, used in anger or to strengthen an expression) devil: *a hell of a good car* **4 for the hell of it** *esp. spoken* for fun **5 hell for leather** *esp. spoken* very fast **6 like hell a** *esp. spoken* very much: *He worked like hell to get it built* **b** *sl* not at all: *Like hell he paid! I did!* **7 play hell with** *esp. spoken* **a** to cause damage to (something) **b** to be very angry with

²hell *interj sl* (an expression of strong anger or disappointment)

hello —also **hallo, hullo** *interj, n* **-los 1 a** (the usual word of greeting) **b** (the word used for starting a telephone conversation): *Hello, is Mrs. Brown there?* **2** (an expression of surprise): *Hello! What's happening now?* **3** (a call for attention to a distant person): *Hello! Is anybody there?*

helmet *n* a covering to protect the head, as formerly used by men wearing armour, and now as worn for protection by soldiers, motorcyclists, policemen, firemen, etc.

¹help *v* **1** to do part of the work for; be of use to **2** to encourage or produce favourable conditions for: *Trade helps industry to develop* **3** to avoid; prevent; change: *I couldn't help crying* **4** to serve food or drink to: *'Can I have a drink?" 'Help yourself!"* **5 more than one can help** as little as is possible or necessary

²help *n* **1** the act of helping; aid **2** something or somebody that helps: *You're a good help to me* **3** a person, esp. female, employed to do housework: *The new help left after a week*

helpful *adj* willing to help; useful –~**ly** *adv* –~**ness** *n*

helping *n* a serving of food

helpless *adj* unable to look after oneself or to act without help: *a helpless child* –~**ly** *adv* –~**ness** *n*

¹hem *n* the edge of a piece of cloth when turned under and sewn down, esp. the lower edge of a skirt or dress

²hem *v* **-mm-** to make a hem on

hen *n* **1** the female chicken often kept for its eggs on farms **2** a female bird of which the male is the cock: *a hen pheasant*

hence *adv* **1** for this reason or from this origin: *The town was built on the side of a hill: hence the name Hillside* **2** *esp. written or old use* from here or from now: *2 miles hence*

¹her (*possessive form of* SHE) belonging to her: *her dress*

²her *pron* (*object form of* SHE): *Can you see her?*

herb *n* any of several plants whose leaves, stems, or seeds are used to flavour food or to make medicine

¹herd *n* **1** a group of animals of one kind which live and feed together: *a herd of elephants* **2** *offensive* people generally, thought of as acting all alike with no person having his own opinions: *the herd instinct*

²herd *v* **1** to group together: *They herded into the corner* **2** to look after or drive in a herd: *The farmer herded the cows into the field*

here *adv* **1** at, in, or to this place: *Come here!* **2** at this point of time: *I came to a difficulty– here I stopped* **3** (used for introducing something or somebody): *Here is the news....* **4 here and there** scattered about **5 here goes**! now I'm going to have a try (to do something difficult) **6 here, there, and everywhere** in every place **7 Here you are** Here's what you want **8 neither here nor there** not connected with the matter being talked about

heresy *n* **-sies 1** the fact of holding a contrary belief, esp. in official religion **2** such a belief, or an act or statement which shows it

heretic *n* a person who favours heresy or is guilty of a heresy –~**al** *adj* –~**ally** *adv*

heritage *n* **1** something which one receives by right from an older member of the family **2** a condition of life, such as that of one's family or social group, into which one is born

hermit *n* **1** (esp. in former times) a holy man who lived alone, thinking and praying **2** a person who avoids other people

hero –*fem.* **heroine** *n* **-roes 1** a person remembered for bravery, strength, or goodness, esp. for an act of courage under difficult conditions **2** the most important character in a play, poem, story, etc.

heroic *adj* **1** showing the qualities of

a hero **2** large or grand: *a heroic manner* –~**ally** *adv*

heroism *n* **1** the quality of being a hero **2** great courage: *an act of heroism*

herring *n* **-ring** *or* **-rings 1** an edible fish which swims in large shoals in the sea **2 red herring** a fact or point which draws attention away from the main point

hers *pron* (*possessive form of* SHE) that/those belonging to her: *The sheep are hers*

herself *pron* **1** (*reflexive form of* SHE): *She cut herself* **2** (*strong form of* SHE): *She herself said so* **3** *esp. spoken* (in) her usual state of mind or body: *She's more herself today*

hesitate *v* **-tated, -tating** to pause in doubt during or before an action – **-tating** *adj* – **-tatingly** *adv* – **-tion** *n*

¹hide *v* **hid, hidden, hiding 1** to put or keep out of sight; make or keep secret: *You're hiding some important facts* **2** to place oneself so as to be unseen: *I'll hide behind the door*

²hide *n* an animal's skin, esp. when used for leather

³hide *n* a place from where a person may watch animals, esp. birds, without being seen by them

¹high *adj* **1 a** (not usu. of living things) reaching some distance above ground: *a high wall* **b** at a point well above the ground: *high in the sky* **2** important; chief: *high office in the government* **3** showing goodness: *high principles* **4** near the top of the set of sounds which the ear can hear: *a very high voice* **5** above the usual level, rate of movement, etc.: *the high cost of food* **6** (of time) at the most important or mid-point of: *It's high time we went* **7** (of food) not fresh **8** *esp. spoken* **a** drunk **b** under the effects of drugs **9 hold one's head high** to show pride and courage, esp. in difficulty

²**high** *adv* **1** to or at a high level in position, movements or sound: *They climbed high* **2** to or at a high or important degree esp. of social movement: *He's risen high in the world* **3 high and dry** without help: *He left me high and dry* **4 high and low** everywhere

³**high** *n* **1** a high point: *The price reached a new high* **2** *esp. spoken* a state of great excitement and often happiness produced by or as if by a drug

highland *adj, n* (of) a mountainous area

¹**highlight** *n* **1** *technical* the area on a picture or photograph where most light appears to fall **2** an important detail which stands out from the rest: *the highlights of the competition*

²**highlight** *v* to pick out as an important part

highly *adv* **1** to a high degree; very: *highly pleased* **2 a** very well: *highly paid* **b** very much: *highly salted*

Highness *n* (a title used of or to certain royal persons): *Your Highness*

hijack *v* to take control of (a vehicle or aircraft) by force of arms, to

obtain money or political aims —**hijack** *n* —~**er** *n* —~**ing** *n*

¹**hike** *v* **hiked, hiking** to go on a hike —**hiker** *n* —**hiking** *n*

²**hike** *n* a long walk in the country, such as one taken by a group of people for a whole day

hill *n* **1** a raised part of the earth's surface, not so high as a mountain, and not usu. so bare **2** the slope of a road or path

hilt *n* **1** the handle of a sword, or of a knife used as a weapon **2 up to the hilt** completely: *She's up to the hilt in trouble*

him *pron* (*object form of* HE): *I met him yesterday*

himself *pron* **1** (*reflexive form of* HE): *He hurt himself* **2** (*strong form of* HE): *He told me so himself* **3** *esp. spoken* (in) his usual state of mind or body: *He doesn't seem himself today*

¹**hind** *n* **hinds** *or* **hind** a female deer, esp. of the red deer family

²**hind** *adj* (usu. of animals' legs) belonging to the back part

hinder *v* **1** to stop (someone from doing something): *You're hindering me in my work* **2** to prevent: *You're hindering my work*

hindrance *n* **1** the act of hindering **2** something or somebody that hinders

hindsight the ability to see how and why something happened, esp. to know that it could have been prevented

¹**hinge** *n* **1** a metal part which joins 2

objects together and allows the first to swing around the usu. fixed second, such as one joining a door to a post **2** the point on which something else depends: *The home is the hinge on which family life turns*

²**hinge** *v* **hinged**, **hinging** to fix on hinges: *The cupboard door is hinged so it opens on the left*

¹**hint** *n* **1** a small or indirect suggestion **2** a small sign: *a hint of summer in the air* **3** useful advice: *helpful hints*

²**hint** *v* to suggest indirectly: *I hinted that I was dissatisfied*

¹**hip** –also **rose hip** *n* the red fruit of the rose

²**hip** *n* the fleshy part of either side of the human body above the legs

hippopotamus –also (*esp. spoken*) **hippo** *n* **-muses** *or* **-mi**, **hippos** a large African animal with a thick hairless skin, which lives near water

¹**hire** *n* hiring or being hired

²**hire** *v* **hired**, **hiring 1** to get the use of for a special occasion by payment **2** to employ for a time for payment

hire purchase –also (*esp. spoken*) **the never never** *n* a system of payment for goods by which one pays small sums of money with interest regularly after receiving the goods

his *adj, pron* **1** that/those belonging to him: *That's not mine, it's his* **2** (with general meaning): *Everyone must do his best*

¹**hiss** *v* **1** to make a sound like a continuous 's' **2** to say in a sharp whisper: *to hiss a warning* **3** also

hiss at– to show disapproval and dislike of

²**hiss** *n* a hissing sound

history *n* **-ries 1** (the chronological study of) past events **2** (the study of) the development of anything in time: *the history of the English Language* **3** a (written) account of history **4** a long story including details of many events: *She told me her life history* **5 make history** to do or be concerned in something important which will be remembered – **-rical** *adj* – **-rically** *adv*

¹**hit** *v* **hit**, **hitting 1** to give a blow to; strike **2 a** to come against with force **b** to cause to do this by accident or on purpose **3** *esp. spoken* to reach: *We hit the main road here* **4** to have a bad effect on: *Inflation hits the housewife's pocket* (= money) **5** (in cricket) to score: *He hit 3 runs* **6 hit the nail on the head** to be exactly right (in saying something) **7 hit the sack** *sl* to go to bed **8 hit (someone) for six** to defeat or surprise (someone) completely by quick action

²**hit** *n* **1** a blow; stroke **2** a move which brings something against another force: *The arrow scored a hit* **3** a successful musical or theatrical performance **4** a remark which causes the desired effect, esp. if unpleasant: *That joke was a nasty hit at me*

hive *n* **1 a** also **beehive**– a place where bees live, like a small hut or box **b** the group of bees who live together

2 a crowded busy place (esp. in the phrase **a hive of industry**)

¹**hoard** *n* **1** a (secret) store, esp. of something valuable **2** a large amount

²**hoard** *v* to store secretly — ~**er** *n*

hoarding *n* **1** a fence round a piece of land, esp. when building is going on **2** a high fence or board on which large advertisements are stuck

hoarse *adj* **1** (of a voice) harsh-sounding, as though the surface of the throat is rough **2** having a voice of this type — ~**ly** *adv* — ~**ness** *n*

¹**hoax** *n* a trick, esp. one which makes someone believe something which is not true

²**hoax** *v* to play a trick on — ~**er** *n*

hobby *n* -**bies** an enjoyable free time activity

¹**hoe** *n* a long-handled garden tool used for breaking up the soil and removing weeds

²**hoe** *v* **hoed, hoeing** **1** to use a hoe **2** to remove or break with a hoe

¹**hog** *n* **hogs** *or* **hog** **1** a castrated male pig kept for meat **2** a dirty person who eats too much

²**hog** *v* -**gg**- *sl* to take and keep (all of something) for oneself

¹**hoist** *v* to raise up by force, esp. when using ropes on board ship

²**hoist** *n* **1** an upward push **2** an apparatus for lifting heavy goods

¹**hold** *v* **held, holding** **1** to keep or support with a part of the body, esp. with the hands **2** to put or keep (a part of the body) in a certain position: *Hold (yourself) still* **3** to keep back or control: *We held our breath in fear* **4** to be able to contain: *How much does the pan hold?* **5** (esp. of an army) to keep in control or in one's possession: *The city is held by the enemy* **6** to possess (money, land, or position) **7** to keep (someone) in (an interested state of mind) **8** to keep in the stated position or condition: *She held them at arm's length* **9** to express one's belief (that); consider **10** to continue: *Can the good weather hold?* **11** (of a ship or aircraft) to follow correctly **12** (of objects) to keep in position and/or support: *The roof was held up by pillars* **13** to make (something) happen: *We were holding a meeting* **14 hold court** to receive admirers in a group **15 hold good** to be true **16 hold hands (with)** to hold the hand (of another) or the hands (of each other), esp. as a sign of love **17 Hold it!** Don't move! **18 hold one's own** to keep one's (strong) position, even when attacked

²**hold** *n* **1** the act of holding; grip (esp. in the phrases **take/get/catch/lay hold of, keep hold of, lose hold of**) **2** something which can be held, esp. in climbing: *Can you find a hold for your hands?* **3** grip; influence; control: *He's got a good hold of his subject*

³**hold** *n* the part of a ship (below deck) where goods are stored

¹**hole** *n* **1** an empty space within something solid **2 a** the home of a small

animal **b** *esp. spoken* a small unpleasant living-place **3** *esp. spoken* a position of difficulty: *I am in rather a hole* **4** (in golf) a hollow place on the green into which the ball must be hit **5 pick holes in something** to criticize something, esp. when it is not really faulty

²**hole** *v* **holed, holing 1** to make a hole in **2** to put (a ball) in a hole in golf: *to hole in one*

¹**holiday** *n* **-days 1** a time of rest from work, a day (often originally of religious importance) or longer **2 on holiday/on one's holidays** having a holiday, esp. over a period of time

²**holiday** *v* **-dayed, -daying** to have a period of holiday

¹**hollow** *adj* **1** having an empty space inside; not solid **2** (of parts of the body) lacking flesh: *hollow cheeks* **3** having a ringing sound like the note when an empty container is struck **4** (of feelings, words, etc.) not real; empty of meaning **5 beat (someone) hollow** *esp. spoken* to defeat (someone) completely – ~**ly** *adv* – ~**ness** *n*

²**hollow** *n* a space sunk into something, esp. into the ground

holly *n* **-lies** a type of small tree with dark green shiny prickly leaves and red berries

¹**holy** *adj* **1** of God and religion: *the Holy Bible* **2** (of a person or life) in the service of God and religion, esp. when leading a pure life **3** *sl* very bad: *He's a holy terror*

²**holy** *n* **holies** a most holy place (only in the phrase **holy of holies**)

¹**home** *n* **1 a** the house where one lives **b** the place where one was born or habitually lives **2** the house and family one belongs to **3** a place where a living thing can be found living and growing wild: *India is the home of elephants* **4** a place for the care of a group of people or animals of the same type, but not a family: *a children's home* **5** (in some games and sports) a place which a player must aim to reach, such as the goal or the finishing line of a race (esp. in the phrase **the home stretch/straight** (=the last part)) **6 at home a** in the house or family **b** ready to receive visitors **7 leave home** to leave one's family to live independently, esp. after an argument – ~**less** *adj* – ~**lessness** *n*

²**home** *adv* **1** to or at one's home **2** as far as possible and/or to the right place: *He drove the nail home*

³**home** *adj* **1** of, related to, or being a home, place of origin, or base of operations: *the home office of an international firm* **2** domestic: *the home country* **3** prepared, done, or intended for use in a home: *home cooking* **4** working, playing, or happening in a home area: *the home team*

⁴**home** *v* **homed, homing** (of birds such as pigeons) to find one's way back to the starting place

homemade *adj* *sometimes offensive*

made at home, not bought from a shop

homesick *adj* feeling a great wish to be at home, when away – ~**ness** *n*

homework *n* **1** studies which must be done at home so as to learn and prepare for what is studied at school **2** preparation done before taking part in an important activity

homosexual *adj, n* (of or being) a person sexually attracted to members of the same sex

honest *adj* **1** trustworthy **2** showing such qualities: *an honest face* **3** direct; not hiding facts – ~**y** *n*

honestly *adv* **1** in an honest way **2 a** really; speaking truthfully **b** (used for expressing strong feeling usu. mixed with disapproval): *Honestly! What a thing to do!*

honey *n* **1** the sweet sticky material produced by bees, eaten on bread **2** *esp. US* darling **3** *esp. US spoken* something excellent

honeycomb *n* **1** a container of beeswax consisting of 6-sided cells in which honey is stored by the bees **2** something like this in shape

¹honeymoon *n* **1** the holiday taken by people recently married **2** a pleasant period of time

²honeymoon *v* to have one's honeymoon – ~**er** *n*

¹honour *n* **1** great respect, often publicly expressed **2** high standards of character or reputation: *to fight for the honour of one's country* **3** a person who brings respect (to): *He's an honour to his parents* **4** (a title

of respect for a judge): *Your/His Honour* **5** (a polite word): *Would you do me the honour of dancing with me?*

²honour *v* **1** to respect by feelings or by an action which shows feelings: *I'm honoured by your presence* **2** to keep (an agreement), often by making a payment, as in giving money for a cheque or bill

honourable *adj* **1** worthy of honour or respect **2** showing good character – **-bly** *adv*

hood *n* **1 a** a covering for the the head and neck usu. fastened on at the back, as to a coat **b** a covering for the head of a hunting bird **2** something like a hood which fits over the top of something else, as over a chimney to keep the wind out **3** a folding cover over a car, pram, etc. **4** *US* the bonnet covering the engine of a car

hoof *n* **hoofs** *or* **hooves 1** the hard foot of certain animals, as of the horse **2 on the hoof** (of a meat animal) before being killed for meat

¹hook *n* **1** a curved piece of metal, plastic, etc., for catching something on or hanging things on **2** something curved or bent like this: *Hook of Holland* **3 a** (in cricket, golf, etc.) a flight of a ball away from a course straight ahead **b** (in boxing) a blow given with the elbow bent **4 be/get off the hook** to be/get out of one's difficulties

²hook *v* **1** to catch with or as if with a hook: *to hook a fish* **2** to hang on or fasten with or as if with a hook **3** to make into the shape of a hook: *He hooked his arm* **4 a** (of a ball) to travel in a hook **b** to hit (a ball) in a hook

hooligan *n* a noisy rough person who fights, breaks things, etc. –~**ism** *n*

¹hoop *n* **1 a** a circular band of wood or metal, esp. round a barrel **b** such a band used as a child's toy **2 a** circular frame, as formerly used to hold women's skirts out, or for animals to jump through at the circus

²hoop *v* to put a hoop on (a barrel)

¹hoot *v* **1** to make or cause to make a hoot **2** *esp. spoken* to laugh very much

²hoot *n* **1** the sound an owl makes **2** the sound made by a car or ship's horn **3** a shout of dislike, unpleasant laughter, etc. **4 not care a hoot/2 hoots** *esp. spoken* not to care at all

¹hop *v* **-pp- 1 a** (of people) to jump on one leg **b** (of small creatures) to jump **2** to cross by hopping **3 Hop it!** *sl* Go away! **4 hopping mad** very angry

²hop *n* **1** an act of hopping; jump **2** *esp. spoken* an informal dance **3** *esp. spoken* a distance travelled by a plane before landing: *It's a short hop from London to Paris* **4 catch someone on the hop** *esp. spoken* to meet someone when he is unprepared

³hop *n* a tall climbing plant with flowers or its seed-cases which

when dried are used for flavouring beer

¹hope *v* **hoped, hoping 1** to wish and expect; desire in spite of doubts **2 hope against hope** to continue to hope when there is little chance of success

²hope *n* **1** the expectation of something happening as one wishes **2** a person or thing that seems likely to bring success: *You're my only hope/last hope*

¹hopeful *adj* **1** (of people) feeling hope **2** giving cause for hope of success –~**ness** *n*

²hopeful *n* a person who seems likely to succeed, or who desires to succeed: *a young hopeful*

hopefully *adv* **1** in a hopeful way **2** *esp. spoken* if our hopes succeed: *Hopefully we'll be there by dinnertime*

hopeless *adj* **1** (not usu. of people) showing lack of hope: *hopeless tears* **2** giving no cause for hope **3** *esp. spoken* useless: *Your work is hopeless* –~**ly** *adv* –~**ness** *n*

horde 1 a large number or crowd: *a horde of children* **2** (in history) a large wandering group of people of a certain nationality, esp. a fighting one

horizon *n* **1** the limit of one's view, where the sky seems to meet the earth or sea **2** the limit of one's thoughts

horizontal *adj, n* (in) the flat position, along or parallel to the ground –~**ly** *adv*

horn *n* **1** a hard pointed growth found in a pair on the top of the heads of cattle, sheep, and goats **2** something like these growths, as on a snail **3** the material that these growths are made of **4** any of a number of musical wind instruments: *the French horn* **5** a warning apparatus, as in a car **6 take the bull by the horns** to face a difficult thing or person – ~**like,** ~**ed** *adj* – ~**less** *adj*

horrible *adj* **1** causing horror **2** *esp. spoken* very unkind, unpleasant, or ugly – **-bly** *adv*

horrid *adj* horrible – ~**ly** *adv* – ~**ness** *n*

horrify *v* **-fied, -fying** to shock; fill with horror – ~**ingly, -fically** *adv* – **-fic** *adj*

horror *n* **1** a feeling of great shock, fear, and dislike **2** the quality of causing this feeling: *the horror of war* **3** an unpleasant person: *He is a little horror* **4 Chamber of Horrors** (in a waxworks display) the room where murderers, torturers, etc., are represented **5 horror film** a film of a popular type in which fearful things happen which could not happen in reality

horse *n* **1** a type of large strong animal with mane, tail, and hooves which men ride on and use for pulling and carrying heavy things **2** VAULTING HORSE **3 dark horse** a person whose abilities are hidden **4 eat like a horse** to eat a lot **5 Hold your horses!** Don't rush hastily into any-

thing **6 put the cart before the horse** to do or put things in the wrong order

horseback *n* **on horseback** (riding) on a horse

horseman –(*fem.* **horsewoman**) *n* **-men** a person who rides a horse, esp. one who rides well – ~**ship** *n*

horsepower –(*abbrev.* **HP**) *n* **horsepower** a measure of the power of an engine, representing the force needed to pull 550 pounds one foot a second

horseshoe *n* **1** also **shoe**– a curved piece of iron nailed under a horse's foot **2** something made in this shape

horticulture *n* the science of growing fruit, flowers, and vegetables – **-tural** *adj* – **-turalist** *n*

¹**hose** *n* (used esp. in shops) stockings or socks

²**hose** –also **hosepipe** *n* (a piece of) rubber or plastic tube which can direct water onto fires, a garden, etc.

³**hose** *v* **hosed, hosing** to use a hose on, esp. for washing

hospitable *adj* showing the wish to attend to the needs of others, esp. by feeding them, asking them into one's home, etc. – **-bly** *adv*

hospital *n* a place where ill people stay and have treatment

hospitality *n* **1** the quality of being hospitable **2** food, a place to sleep, etc., when given to a guest (esp. in the phrase **partake of someone's hospitality**)

¹**host** n a large number

²**host** n 1 a man who receives guests 2 *old use or humour* an innkeeper (note the phrase **mine host**) 3 an animal or plant on which some lower form of life is living as a parasite

³**host** v to act as host at (a party, friendly meeting, etc.)

⁴**host** n the holy bread eaten at Holy Communion

hostage n a person kept by an enemy so that the other side will do what the enemy wants

hostel n a building in which certain types of person can live and eat, such as students, young people working away from home, etc.

hostess n 1 a female host 2 a young woman who acts as companion, dancing partner, etc., in a social club 3 an airhostess

hostile adj 1 belonging to an enemy 2 unfriendly; showing dislike

hostilities n acts of fighting in war

hostility n the state of being unfriendly

hot adj -tt- 1 having a certain degree of heat, esp. a high degree 2 causing a burning taste: *Pepper makes food hot* 3 (of news) very recent 4 excitable: *a hot temper* 5 a *esp. spoken* (of people) (tending to be) sexually excited b *esp. spoken* sexually exciting 6 *sl* (of stolen goods) difficult to pass on, esp. soon after the crime has taken place 7 *esp. spoken* clever, well-informed, and usu. very interested 8 **get hot** (in a guessing game) to get near something hidden or to guess nearly right 9 **get hot under the collar** to get angry 10 **not so hot** *esp. spoken* not very good

hotel n a building where people can stay for payment

hotly adv 1 in anger and with force 2 closely and eagerly (often in the phrase **hotly pursued**)

¹**hound** n 1 a hunting dog, esp. a foxhound 2 a person who is disliked

²**hound** v to chase or worry continually: *Tell him to stop hounding me*

hour n 1 the period of time, 60 minutes, of which 24 make a day 2 a time of day when such a new period starts: *He arrived on the hour* 3 a distance which one can travel in this period of time: *It's only an hour away* 4 a fixed point or period of time: *The hour has come for a serious talk* 5 a certain period of time: *spent happy hours together* 6 a time, esp. an important one like the present 7 **after hours** later than the usual times of work or business 8 **(at) the eleventh hour** (at) the last moment 9 **the small hours** also (*humour*) **the wee hours**– the hours soon after midnight (1, 2, 3 o'clock) 10 **zero hour** the time when something happens, after a certain period of waiting has passed

¹**house** n 1 a a building for people to live in b the people in such a building 2 a building for animals or goods 3 an important family, esp. noble or royal: *the House of Windsor*

4 a a building in which children live at school, with its own name **b** a division of a school, esp. for sports competitions **5 a** a business firm, esp. one controlled by a family and/or one in the business of publishing **b** a large building used for business **6** the people voting after a debate: *The house divided* **7** a theatre, or the people in it **8** a place where people meet for a certain purpose: *a public house* **9 keep house** to do or control the cleaning, cooking and other things usu. done in a house **10 on the house** (usu. of drinks) being paid for by the people in charge, as by the owner of a public house, by a firm, etc. **11 (as) safe as houses** very safe

²**house** *v* **housed, housing 1** to provide with a place to live **2** to provide space for storing

¹**household** *n* all the people living together in a house

²**household** *adj* having the special responsibility of guarding the king or queen, or the royal palace: *household cavalry*

householder *n* a person who owns or is in charge of a house

housekeeper *n* a person who has charge of the running of a house

housekeeping *n* **1** the care, cleaning, cooking, etc., of and for a house and the people who live in it **2** also **housekeeping mon·ey** – an amount of money set aside each week or month by the husband

and/or wife to pay for things needed in the home

housewife *n* **-wives** a woman who works at home for her family, cleaning, cooking, etc. –~**ly** *adj*

housework *n* work done in taking care of a house, esp. cleaning

housing *n* **1** the act or action of providing a place to live **2** the places provided **3** protective covering, as for machinery: *the engine housing*

hover *v* **1** (of birds, certain aircraft, etc.) to stay in the air in one place **2** (of people) to wait around one place –**hoverer** *n*

hovercraft *n* (*trademark*) a sort of boat which moves over land or water by means of a strong force of air underneath

¹**how** *adv* **1** (*in questions*) **a** in what way or by what means: *How can I get to Cambridge?* **b** in what condition, of health or mind: *How is mother?* **c** by what amount; to what degree: *How much does this cost?* **2** (in exclamations): *How they cheered!* **3 How come?** *esp. spoken (in/or as an expression of surprise)* Why is it? How can it be that... **4 How do you do?** also **How d'ye do?** (the phrase used to someone just met or introduced to the speaker) **5 How's that?** (in cricket) (a call suggesting that the batsman is out)

²**how** *conj* the fact that: *Do you remember how he arrived almost at the end of the party?*

¹**however** *conj* in whatever way

²**however** *adv* **1** to whatever degree **2** in spite of this: *It's raining. However, I think we should go*

¹**howl** *v* **1** to make howls **2** to say or express with a howl: *He howled (out) my name* **3** to weep loudly

²**howl** *n* a long loud cry, as in pain, anger, etc., esp. that made by wolves and dogs

hub *n* **1** the central part of a wheel, to which the rim is connected **2** the centre of activity or importance

¹**huddle** *v* **-dled**, **-dling** to crowd together

²**huddle** *n* a crowd of people, or a number of things, close together and not in any order

¹**hug** *v* **-gg-** **1** to hold tightly in the arms **2** to hold on to (an idea) with a feeling of pleasure or safety **3** to go along while staying near: *The boat hugged the coast*

²**hug** *n* the act of hugging

huge *adj* very big **−~ness** *n*

¹**hum** *v* **-mm-** **1** (of bees and certain animals) to make a continuous buzz **2** (of people) to make a buzzing sound esp. as a way of singing **3** (of work being carried out) to be active: *Things are starting to hum* **−hum** *n*

²**hum** *v* **-mm-** **hum and haw** to express uncertainty

¹**human** *adj* **1** of or concerning man **2** showing the feelings, esp. those of kindness, which people are supposed to have: *He seems quite human now*

²**human** **−also human being** *n* a man, woman, or child, not an animal

humane *adj* **1** showing human kindness **2** **humane killer** something which can be used to kill animals painlessly

humanity *n* **1** the quality of being humane or human **2** human beings generally

¹**humble** *adj* **1 a** (of people) low in rank or position **b** (of positions) unimportant **2** having a low opinion of oneself and a high opinion of others **3 your humble servant** a way of ending a letter before signing it, used esp. formerly **− -bly** *adv*

²**humble** *v* **-bled**, **-bling** to make (someone or oneself) humble or lower in position

humid *adj* (of air and weather) containing water

humiliate *v* **-ated**, **-ating** to cause to feel humble or to lose the respect of others **− -ation** *n*

humility *n* the quality of being humble

humorous *adj* funny **−~ly** *adv*

¹**humour** *n* **1** the ability to be amused: *a sense of humour* **2** the quality of causing amusement **3** *becoming rare* a state of mind; mood (only in certain phrases): *in a bad humour* **4** *old use* any of 4 liquids thought in the Middle Ages to be present in the body in varying degrees, and to influence the character

²**humour** *v* to keep (someone) happy by acceptance of (esp.) foolish wishes, behaviour, etc.

¹**hump** *n* **1** a lump or round part which stands out noticeably **2** a

lump on the back, as on a camel **3** *esp. spoken* a feeling of bad temper or dislike of life in general: *It's giving me the hump* **4 over the hump** past the worst part

²**hump** *v* **1** to curve into a hump **2** *esp. spoken* to carry on the back

hundred *adj, n, pron* **-dred** *or* **-dreds** the number 100 – ~**th** *adh, n, pron, adv*

hundredweight – (*abbrev.* **cwt**) *n* **-weight** 112 pounds

hung *past tense and past part. of* HANG

hunger *n* **1** the wish or need for food **2** a strong wish: *hunger for excitement* **3** lack of food

hungry *adj* **-grier, -griest 1** feeling or showing hunger **2** causing hunger (esp. in the phrase **hungry work**) **3** with a strong wish: *We're hungry for news* **4 go hungry** to remain without food – **-grily** *adv*

¹**hunt** *v* **1** to chase in order to kill (animals and birds) either for food or sport **2** to chase foxes on horseback with hounds **3** to search (for)

²**hunt** *n* **1** an act of hunting **2 a** the act of hunting foxes **b** the people who regularly hunt foxes together **3** a search

hunter *n* **1** a person or animal that hunts, usu. wild animals **2** a strong horse used in foxhunting **3** someone who searches too eagerly (esp. for something of advantage to himself): *a fortune hunter*

¹**hurdle** *n* **1** a wooden frame used with others for making fences **2** a frame for jumping over in a race **3** a difficulty to be overcome

²**hurdle** *v* **-dled, -dling** to run a hurdle race – ~**r** *n*

hurl *v* **1** to throw with force **2** to shout out violently: *He hurled curses*

hurricane *n* a violent wind storm, esp. in the West Indies

hurried *adj* done in haste – ~**ly** *adv*

¹**hurry** *v* **-ried, -rying 1** to be or make quick in action, sometimes too quick **2** to send or bring quickly: *A doctor hurried to the accident*

²**hurry** *n* **1** haste; quick activity **2** need for haste

¹**hurt** *v* **hurt, hurting 1** to cause pain and/or injury to (esp. a part of the body) **2** to cause to feel pain **3** to cause pain to (a person's feelings) **4** *esp. spoken* to have a bad effect (on): *It won't hurt to wait a bit*

²**hurt** *n* **1** harm; damage, esp. to feelings **2** injury to the body

¹**husband** *n* the man to whom a woman is married

²**husband** *v esp. written* to save carefully and/or make the best use of: *to husband one's strength*

¹**hush** *v* to be or make silent and/or calm

²**hush** *n* (a) silence, esp. a peaceful one

¹**husky** *adj* **-kier, -kiest 1** (of a person or voice) difficult to hear and breathy **2** (of a person) big and strong – **-kily** *adv* – **-kiness** *n*

²**husky** *n* **-kies** a type of large working dog used by Eskimoes

hut *n* a small building, often made of

wood, esp. one used for living in or for shelter

hydrogen *n* a gas that is an element, without colour or smell, is lighter than air, and burns very easily

hygiene *n* **1** the study and practice of health, esp. by paying attention to cleanliness **2** cleanliness generally

hygienic *adj* **1** causing or keeping good health **2** clean – ~**ally** *adv*

hymn *n* a song of praise, esp. to God

hypnosis *n* (the production of) a sleep-like state in which a person can be controlled by the person who produced it – -**notic** *adj* – -**notically** *adv*

hypnotism *n* the practice of hypnosis – -**tist** *n*

hypocrisy *n* -**sies** the practice of pretending to be something very different from, and usu. better than, what one actually is

hypocrite *n* one who practises hypocrisy – -**critical** *adj* – -**critically** *adv*

hysteria *n* **1** a condition of nervous excitement in which the sufferer laughs and cries uncontrollably and/or shows strange changes in behaviour or bodily state **2** wild excitement, as of a crowd of people – -**ric** *n*

hysterical *adj* **1** in a state of hysteria **2** (of feelings) expressed wildly – ~**ly** *adv*

I *pron* (used as the subject of a sentence) the person speaking: *I'm your mother, aren't I?/am I not?*

¹**ice** *n* **1** water which has frozen to a solid **2** a serving of ice cream **3**

break the ice to begin to be friendly with strangers , or to begin something difficult **4 cut no ice (with someone)** to have little effect (on someone) **6 keep (something) on ice** to keep for later use

²**ice** *v* **iced, icing 1** to make very cold by using ice **2** to cover (a cake) with icing

iceberg *n* a large piece of ice floating in the sea, mostly below the surface

ice cream *n* a sweet frozen mixture , usu. containing milk products and eggs

icicle *n* a pointed stick of ice formed when running water freezes

icy *adj* **icier, iciest 1** very cold **2** covered with ice –**icily** *adv* –**iciness** *n*

idea *n* **1** a picture in the mind **2** a plan **3** an opinion **4** a guess; feeling of probability **5** understanding (esp. in the phrase **no idea**) **6** a suggestion or sudden thought: *What a good idea!* **7 one's idea of** (used for expressing what one likes a lot) **8 The idea!** also **What an idea!**– (an expression of surprise at something strange or silly)

¹**ideal** *adj* **1** perfect **2** expressing perfection unlikely to exist in reality: *the ideal system of government* – ~**ly** *adv*

²**ideal** *n* **1** a perfect example **2** (a belief in) high or perfect standards

identical *adj* the same; exactly alike – ~**ly** *adv*

identification *n* **1** the act of identifying or state of being identified **2**

means (such as an official paper) of proving who one is

identify *v* **-fied, -fying 1** to prove or show the identity of **2** to show or feel to be identical: *I'd identify the 2 tastes*

identity *n* **-ties 1** who or what a particular person or thing is: *Please prove your identity* **2** sameness; exact likeness **3** *esp. spoken* identification

idiot *n* **1** a foolish person **2** *old use or technical* a person of very weak mind usu. from birth −∼**ic** *adj* −∼**ically** *adv*

¹**idle** *adj* **1 a** not working **b** (of time) not used for doing anything **2** lazy **3** of no use; not producing anything good (note the phrase **idle gossip**) −∼**ness** *n* −**idly** *adv*

²**idle** *v* **idled, idling 1** to waste time doing nothing **2** (of an engine) to run slowly because it is disconnected and not being used for useful work −**idler** *n*

idol *n* **1** an image worshipped as a god **2** someone or something admired or loved too much

¹**if** *conj* **1** supposing that; on condition that: *We'll go only if it rains* **2** although: *a pleasant if noisy child* **3** whether: *Did she say if she was coming?*

²**if** *n* **ifs and buts** reasons given for delay

igloo *n* **-loos** an Eskimo house made of hard icy blocks of snow

ignite *v* **ignited, igniting** to start or cause to start to burn

ignition *n* **1** the act or action of igniting **2** the means, or apparatus for, starting an engine by electrically firing the gases from the petrol

ignorance *n* lack of knowledge

ignorant *adj* **1** lacking knowledge **2** *esp. spoken* rude, impolite

ignore *v* **ignored, ignoring** not to take notice of

¹**ill** *adj* **worse, worst 1** not well in health **2** hurt **3** bad: *ill luck*

²**ill** *adv* **1** badly, poorly, cruelly, or unpleasantly: *The child has been ill-treated* **2** scarcely: *I can ill afford it*

³**ill** *n* a bad thing: *the ills of life*

ill-bred *adj* badly behaved or rude

illegal *adj* against the law −∼**ly** *adv* −∼**ity** *n*

illegible −also **unreadable** *adj* which cannot be read − **-bility** *n* − **-bly** *adv*

illiterate *adj, n* unable to read and write −∼**ly** *adv* − **-racy** *n*

illness *n* (a) disease; unhealthy state of the body

ill-treat *v* to be cruel to −∼**ment** *n*

illuminate *v* **-nated , -nating 1** to give light to or to ornament with lights **2** (esp. in former times) to paint with gold and bright colours − **-ation** *n*

illusion *n* **1** the condition of seeing things wrongly **2** a false appearance or idea: *His confidence was an illusion*

illustrate *v* **-trated, -trating 1** to add pictures to (something written) **2** to show the meaning of by giving related examples: *The gift illu-*

strates her generosity – **-tive** adj – -tively adv

illustration n **1** the act of illustrating **2** a picture to go with the words of a book, speaker, etc. **3** an example which explains the meaning of something

image n **1** a picture esp. in the mind **2** a copy: *He's the image of his father* **3** a metaphor or simile; a vivid phrase which suggests a picture to the reader **4** someone's appearance as seen by other people: *Her image was poor*

imaginary adj **1** not real, but produced from pictures in one's mind **2** (of a number) having a square less than 0

imagination n **1** the act of imagining or the ability to imagine **2** the mind: *It's all in your imagination* **3** esp. spoken something only imagined and not real

imaginative adj **1** that shows use of the imagination **2** good at inventing imaginary things or new ideas: *an imaginative child* –~**ly** adv

imagine v **-gined,-gining 1** to form in the mind: *I can imagine the scene clearly* **2** to suppose or have an idea about, esp. mistakenly or without proof: *He imagines that people don't like him*

imitate v **-tated, -tating 1** to take as an example: *You should imitate his way of doing things* **2** to copy the behaviour, appearance, speech, etc., typical of **3** to appear like

something else – **-ation, -ativeness** n – **-ative** adj – **-atively** adv

immaculate adj pure; unspoilt; unmarked; without fault: *immaculate behaviour/shoes* –~**ly** adv

immature adj **1** not fully formed or developed **2** showing a lack of control and good sense in one's behaviour –~**ly** adv – **-turity** n

immediate adj **1** done or needed at once: *an immediate reply* **2** nearest; next: *in the immediate future*

immediately adv, conj at once; as soon as: *immediately I'd eaten*

immense adj very large – **-ensity** n

immensely adv very much

immerse v **immersed, immersing 1** to put deep under water: *immersed in a bath* **2** to cause to enter deeply into an activity: *immersed in work* – **-sion** n

immigrate v **-grated, -grating** to come into a country to make one's life and home there – **-gration** n – **- grant** n

immoral adj **1** not considered good or right: *Stealing is immoral* **2** offensive to society's ideas of what is good or right, esp. in sexual matters; obscene –~**ly** adv –~**ity** n

immortal adj that will not die; that continues for ever –~**ity** n

immune adj **1** unable to be harmed because of special powers in oneself: *immune to disease* **2** protected – **immunity** n

impact n **1** the force of one object hitting another **2** the force of an idea, invention, system, etc.

impartial *adj* fair – ~**ly** *adv* – ~**ity** *n*

impatient *adj* **1** not patient **2** eager: *impatient to see his wife* – ~**ly** *adv* – **-ience** *n*

impede *v* **impeded, impeding** to get in the way of; make (something) difficult to do – **-iment** *n*: *He has a speech impediment*

¹**imperfect** *adj* **1** not perfect **2** of or about the imperfect – ~**ion** *n* – ~**ly** *adv*

²**imperfect** *n* (an example of) the tense of the verb which shows a continuing action in the past

impertinent *adj* rude or not respectful – **-nence** *n* – ~**ly** *adv*

impetus *n* **1** the force of something moving **2** a push forward: *adding impetus to my ideas*

¹**implement** *n* a tool or instrument

²**implement** *v* to carry out or put into practice: *to implement one's ideas*

implore *v* **implored, imploring** to ask earnestly for

imply *v* **implied, implying 1** to express indirectly: *Refusal to answer implies guilt* **2** to cause to be necessary

impolite *adj* not polite – ~**ly** *adv* – ~**ness** *n*

¹**import** *v* to bring in (something) esp. from abroad: *imported silk* – ~**er** *n*

²**import** *n* something brought into a country from abroad or the act of so doing

important *adj* **1** which matters a lot **2** powerful – **-ance** *n* – ~**ly** *adv*

impose *v* **imposed, imposing 1** to establish (an additional payment) officially: *impose taxes* **2** to force the acceptance of **3** to force unwelcome presence on **4** to take unfair advantage, in a way that causes additional work and trouble – **-sition** *n*

impossible *adj* **1** not possible **2** hard to bear; very unpleasant: *He makes life impossible for us* – **-bility** *n* – **-bly** *adv*

impostor *n* someone who deceives by pretending to be someone else

impress *v* **1** to press (something) into something else, or to mark as a result of this pressure: *a pattern impressed on clay* **2** to fill (someone) with admiration: *I was impressed by his performance* **3** to make the importance of (something) clear to: *Impress on him the value of hard work*

impression *n* **1** the act of impressing or state of being impressed **2** a mark left by pressure **3** the image a person or thing gives to someone's mind: *What's your impression of him?* **4** a feeling about the nature of something **5** an attempt to copy, usu. in a funny way, the most interesting points of

impressive *adj* causing admiration by giving one a feeling of size and/or importance – ~**ly** *adv* – ~**ness** *n*

imprison *v* to put in prison or withhold freedom from – ~**ment** *n*

improper *adj* **1** not suitable: *an improper remark* **2** not correct **3** showing thoughts which are not socially acceptable, esp. about sex (esp. in the phrase **an improper suggestion**) – ~**ly** *adv* – **-priety** *n*

improve *v* **improved, improving 1** to make better **2** to get better: *His health's improving* – ~**ment** *n*

improvise *v* **-vised, -vising** to do or make (something) unprepared, usu. because a sudden need has arisen: *He improvised a tune on the piano* – **-visation** *n*

impulse *n* **1** a single push, or a force acting for a short time in one direction along a wire, nerve, etc.: *an electrical impulse* **2** a sudden wish to do something: *She acted on impulse*

impulsive *adj* having or showing a tendency to act on impulse – ~**ly** *adv* – ~**ness** *n*

¹in *prep* **1** (so as to be) contained by (something with depth, length, and height); within: *to live in the house* **2** surrounded by (an area); within and not beyond: *cows in a field* **3** shown or described as the subject of: *a character in a story* **4** (showing employment): *She's in business/in politics* **5** wearing: *dressed in silk* **6** towards (a direction): *in the wrong direction* **7** using to express oneself; with or by means of: *Write it in French* **8** at some time during; at the time of: *in the afternoon* **9** (with lengths of time) **a** during not more than the space of: *He learnt English in 3 weeks* **b** after: *I'll come in an hour* **c** during; for: *My first good meal in a week* **10** (showing the way something is done or happens): *in fun* **11** (showing a relation or pro-portion) per: *a tax of 40p in the £* **12** (showing quantity or number): *in part* (=partly) **13** as to; as regards: *lacking in courage* **14** having or so as to have (a condition): *in danger* **15** as a/an; by way of: *in reply* **16** **in all** together; as the total **17** **in that** because

²in *adv* **1** (so as to be) contained or surrounded; away from the open air, the outside, etc.: *Let's go in there where it's warm* **2** (so as to be) present (esp. at home): *The train isn't in yet* **3** from a number of people, or from all directions to a central point: *Letters have been pouring in* **4 a** (of one side in a game such as cricket) batting: *Our side went in first* **b** (of the ball in a game such as tennis) inside the line **5** (so as to be) fashionable: *Long skirts came in last year*

³in *adj* **1** *sl* fashionable: *This is the in place to go now* **2** burning: *Is the fire still in?*

⁴in *n* **the ins and outs (of something)** the various parts and difficulties to be seen when something is looked at in detail

inability *n* **-ties** lack of power or skill

inaction *n* lack of action or activity – **-tive** *adj* – **-tively** *adv* – **-tivity** *n*

inadequate *adj* **1** not good enough in quality, ability, size, etc.: *I feel inadequate to the occasion* **2** (of a person) not good at looking after oneself, esp. in social life – ~**ly** *adv* – **-acy** *n*

incapable *adj* not able to do something – **-bility** *n* – **-bly** *adv*

incentive *n* **1** an encouragement to greater activity **2** the urge and ability to get things done

¹**inch** *n* **1** a measure of length; 1/12 of a foot (about 0·.025 metres) **2 within an inch of** very near **3 not give/budge an inch** not to change one's opinions at all

²**inch** *v* to move slowly and with difficulty: *I inched (my way) through the hole*

incident *n* **1** an event **2** an event that includes violence: *In a recent incident 2 bombs exploded*

incidental *adj*, *n* **1** (something) happening or appearing irregularly or as a less important part of something important **2** (something, esp. a fact or detail which is) unimportant

incite *v* **incited, inciting** to cause or encourage to a strong feeling or action: *He incited them to anger* – ~**ment** *n*

¹**incline** *v* **inclined, inclining 1** to slope **2** to cause to move downwards: *to incline one's head (in greeting)* **3** to encourage to feel, think, etc. **4** to tend (to); feel drawn (to): *I incline to another point of view* **5** to tend (to); be likely (to show a quality): *I incline to fatness* – **-nation** *n*

²**incline** *n* a slope

include *v* **included, including** to have or put in as a part; contain in addition to other parts: *The price*

includes postage – **-ding** *prep* – ~**d** *adj* – **-usion** *n*

inclusive *adj* **1** containing or including everything (or many things): *an inclusive charge* **2** including all the numbers or dates – ~**ly** *adv*

income *n* money which one receives regularly ,usu. payment for one's work, or interest from investments

incompetent *adj*, *n* (someone) completely unskilful: *an incompetent teacher* – **-ence, -ency** *n* – ~**ly** *adv*

incomplete *adj* not complete; not perfect – ~**ly** *adv* – ~**ness** *n*

incongruous *adj* comparing strangely with what surrounds it – ~**ly** *adv* – ~**ness** *n* – **-uity** *n*

inconsistent *adj* not agreeing with something else/one another; changeable: *Those two remarks are inconsistent* – ~**ly** *adv* – **-ency** *n*

inconvenient *adj* causing difficulty; not what suits one: *an inconvenient time* – ~**ly** *adv* – **-ence** *n*

incorporate *v* **-rated, -rating 1** to include as a part of a group: *The new plan incorporates the old one* **2** to join with one another/someone else in making a company or corporation – **-ration** *n*

incorrect *adj* not correct – ~**ly** *adv* – ~**ness** *n*

¹**increase** *v* **increased, increasing** to make or become larger in amount or number

²**increase** *n* **1** a rise in amount, numbers, etc. **2 on the increase** increasing – **-singly** *adv*

incredible adj too strange or good to be believed; unbelievable: *an incredible excuse* – **-bility** n – **-bly** adv

indebted adj very grateful to (someone) for help given – ~**ness** n

indecisive adj **1** giving an uncertain result: *an indecisive victory* **2** unable to make decisions – ~**ly** adv – ~**ness** n

indeed adv **1** (*said in answer to a speaker who has suggested the answer*) certainly: *'Did you hear the explosion?' 'Indeed I did!'* **2** on the contrary: *'I won't do it!' 'Indeed you will!'* **3** (*used after* very + *adjective or* adverb *to make the meaning even stronger*): *very large indeed*

indefinite adj **1** not clear: *indefinite responsibilities* **2** not fixed, esp. as to time: *at an indefinite date* – ~**ness** n – ~**ly** adv

¹**independent** adj **1** not needing other things or people **2** (of money) belonging to one privately, so that one can live without working **3 a** habitually taking decisions alone **b** the result of taking one's own decisions: *independent work* **4** not governed by another country – **-ence** n – ~**ly** adv

²**Independent** n a person who does not belong to a political party

¹**index** n **-dexes** or **-dices 1** an alphabetical list at the back of a book, of names, subjects, etc., mentioned in it and the pages where they can be found **2** a sign **3** *technical* also

exponent – a number which shows how many times to multiply a number by itself, such as the number 4 in the expression $2^4 = 2 \times 2 \times 2 \times 2 = 16$ **4** the system of numbers by which prices, costs, etc., can be compared to a former level (esp. in the phrase **cost of living index**)

²**index** v **1** to provide with an index **2** to include in an index **3** to prepare an index – ~**er** n

indicate v **-cated, -cating 1** to point out: *He indicated the shop* **2** to make a sign (for): *He indicated that I could leave* **3** to make clear **4** to show the direction in which one is turning in a vehicle **5** to suggest: *The car's failure to start indicates a flat battery* – **-ation** n

indicator n **1** a needle or pointer on a machine showing the measure of some quality, or a substance which shows what is happening in a chemical mixture **2** any of the lights on a car which flash to show which way it is turning **3** something that gives an idea of the presence, absence, nature, quantity, or degree of something else

indifferent adj **1** not interested in; not caring about or noticing: *I was indifferent to the cold* **2** not very good – ~**ly** adv – **-ence** n

indigestible adj **1** (of food) which cannot be easily broken down in the stomach into substances to be used by the body **2** (of facts) which cannot be taken into the mind easily – **-bility** n – **-bly** adv

indigestion *n* illness or pain caused by the stomach being unable to deal with the food which has been eaten

indignant *adj* expressing or feeling surprised anger – **-ation** *n* – ~**ly** *adv*

indirect *adj* 1 not straight; not directly connected 2 not paid directly but through price rises (esp. in the phrase **indirect taxation**) 3 a meaning something which is not directly mentioned: *an indirect remark/answer* b happening in addition to, or instead of, what is directly meant: *the indirect result* – ~**ly** *adv* – ~**ness** *n*

indispensable *adj* that is too important to live without – **-bility** *n* – **-bly** *adv*

¹**individual** *adj* 1 (*often with* each) single; particular; separate 2 suitable for each person or thing only: *Individual attention must be given to every one* 3 (of a manner, style, way of doing things) particular to the person, thing, etc., concerned (and different from others) – ~**ly** *adv*

²**individual** *n* 1 a single being or member of a group, treated separately 2 a person

indoctrinate *v* -nated, -nating *usu. offensive* to put ideas into (someone's) mind – **-nation** *n*

indoor *adj* which is (done, used, etc.) indoors

indoors *adv* to, in, or into the inside of a building

indulge *v* indulged, indulging 1 to yield, perhaps too much, to the desires of (someone), esp. habitually 2 to let oneself have (one's wish to do or have something, etc.) – ~**nt** *adj* – ~**ntly** *adv*

industrial *adj* 1 of industry and the people who work in it: *industrial unrest* 2 having highly developed industries – ~**ly** *adv*

industrious *adj* hard-working – ~**ly** *adv* – ~**ness** *n*

industry *n* -tries 1 (the work of) factories and large organizations generally 2 the private owners and shareholders of such factories and organizations 3 a particular sort of work, usu. employing lots of people and using machinery 4 continual hard work

inefficient *adj* that does not work well so as to produce good results quickly – ~**ly** *adv* – **-ciency** *n*

inept *adj* 1 foolishly unsuitable: *an inept remark* 2 totally unable to do things – ~**ly** *adv* – ~**itude**, ~**ness** *n*

inertia *n* 1 the force which prevents a thing from being moved when it is standing still, and keeps it moving when it is moving 2 the state of being powerless to move or too lazy to move

inevitable *adj* which cannot be prevented from happening; which always happens: *An argument was inevitable* – **-bility** *n* – **-bly** *adv*

inexpensive *adj* not expensive – ~**ly** *adv*

infallible *adj* never making mistakes; always having the right effect: *an infallible cure* – **-bility** *n*

infant *n* a very young child –**infant** *adj*

infantry *n* soldiers who fight on foot –~**man** *n*

infect *v* **1** to put disease into the body of (someone): *The disease infected her eyes* **2** to make impure by spreading into **3** to make (someone else) have feelings of the same type: *She infected them with her laughter*

infection *n* **1** the state or result of being infected, or the action of infecting **2** an illness brought by infection: *suffering from a lung infection*

infectious *adj* **1** (of a disease) which can be spread by infection, esp. in the air **2** *esp. spoken* (of a disease) which can be spread by touch –~**ly** *adj* –~**ness** *n*

infer *v* **-rr-** to draw the meaning from (something): *What can I infer from your letter?* –~**ence** *n* –~**ential** *adj* –~**entially** *adv*

¹**inferior** *adj* **1** *technical* lower in position: *an inferior court of law* **2** (of people and things) not good or less good in quality or value –~**ity** *n*

²**inferior** *n* *often offensive* a person of lower rank, esp. in a job

infernal *adj* **1** of hell: *the infernal powers* **2** *esp. spoken* bad; terrible –~**ly** *adv*

infest *v* to cause trouble to or in, by being present in large numbers: –~**ation** *n*

infinite *adj* **1** without limits or end **2** very large; as much as there is –~**ly** *adv*

infinity *n* **-ties** a limitless or very large amount of time or space

inflammable *adj* **1** also **flammable**– which can be set on fire **2** easily excited or made angry

inflate *v* **inflated, inflating** to fill until swelled with air, gas, etc. – **-atable** *adj*

inflation *n* **1** the act of inflating or state of being inflated **2** the rise in prices thought to be caused by increases in the costs of production or an increase in the money supply

inflict on –also **inflict upon** *v prep* to force (something unwanted or unpleasant) on (someone): *Don't inflict your ideas on me* – **-tion** *n*

¹**influence** *n* **1** power, or a person with the power, to gain an effect on the mind of: *He's a good/bad influence* **2** the power to get things done by use of wealth, position, etc. – **-ential** *adj* **-entially** *adv*

²**influence** *v* **-enced, -encing** to have an effect on; affect

influenza –also **flu** *n* a disease which is like a bad cold but more serious

inform *v* to tell; give information to –~**ant** *n* –~**ative** *adj* –~**atively** *adv*

informal *adj* not formal; casual: *informal clothes* –~**ity** *n* –~**ly** *adv*

information *n* (something which gives) knowledge in the form of facts

ingenious *adj* having or showing cleverness at making or inventing things: *an ingenious idea* – ~**ly** *adv* –**ingenuity** *n*

ingenuous *adj* simple, open, innocent, and inexperienced – ~**ly** *adv* – ~**ness** *n*

ingredient *n* a particular one of a mixture of things, esp. in cooking

inhabit *v* to live in – ~**able** *adj*

inhabitant *n* a person (or sometimes an animal) that lives in a particular place

inherit *v* **1** to receive (property, a title, etc.) left by someone who has died; to take possession of what one has the right to as heir **2** to receive (qualities of mind or body) from one's parents, grandmother or grandfather, etc. – ~**ance** *n*

¹**initial** *adj* which is (at) the beginning of a set: *initial talks* – ~**ly** *adv*

²**initial** *n* a large letter at the beginning of a name, esp. when used alone to represent a person's first name(s) and last name

³**initial** *v* **-ll-** to sign one's name by writing one's initials

¹**initiate** *v* **-ated, -ating 1** to start (something) working **2** to introduce esp. with a special ceremony **3** to introduce to (someone) some secret or mysterious knowledge

²**initiate** *n* a person who is instructed or skilled in some special field

initiative *n* **1** the first movement or act which starts something happening (esp. in the phrase **take the initiative**) **2** the ability to do things in a

way one has worked out for oneself: *I did it on my own initiative*

inject *v* to put (liquid) into with a syringe

injection *n* **1** the act or occasion of injecting **2** the liquid used for this: *a large/small injection*

injure *v* **injured, injuring 1** to hurt (a living thing) **2** to offend: *Did I injure her (feelings)?* – **-rious** *adj* – **-riously** *adv*

injury *n* **-ries 1** harm; damage to a living thing **2** an act that damages or hurts

ink *n* coloured liquid used for writing (or drawing)

¹**inland** *adj* inside a country, not near the coast or other countries: *inland trade*

²**inland** *adv* towards or in the heart of the country

in-laws *n* the father and mother, and sometimes other relatives, of the person someone has married

inn *n* a small hotel or place where one can stay and/or drink alcohol, eat meals, etc.

inner *adj* **1** inside; closest to the centre: *the inner ear* **2** secret, esp. if of the spirit: *an inner meaning*

innings *n* **innings** the period of time during which a cricket team or player bats

¹**innocent** *adj* guiltless; harmless; simple – ~**ly** *adv* – **-cence** *n*

²**innocent** *n* a simple person with no knowledge of evil

innocuous *adj* harmless; not offensive – ~**ly** *adv* – ~**ness** *n*

innovation *n* **1** the introduction of something new **2** a new idea, method, or invention

innuendo *n* **-does** *or* **-dos** a suggestion of something unpleasant which is not stated

inquest *n* an official inquiry usu. to find out the cause of someone's death

inquire, en- *v* **inquired, inquiring** to ask; to seek information: *She inquired after your health* – ~**r** *n*

inquiry, en- *n* **-ies 1** an act of inquiring; a question **2** investigations to find out the reason for something or how something happened

inquisitive *adj* of an inquiring nature – ~**ly** *adv* – ~**ness** *n*

insane *adj* mad – ~**ly** *adv* – **-anity** *n*

inscrutable *adj* (of people and their acts) whose meaning is hidden or hard to find out; mysterious: *an inscrutable smile* – **-bility** *n* – **-bly** *adv*

insect *n* a small creature with no bones and a hard outer covering, 6 legs, and a body divided into 3 parts, such as an ant or fly

insert *v* to put something inside (something else): *to insert a key in a lock* – **insert,** ~**ion** *n*

¹**inside** *n* the area within something else; the part that is nearest to the centre, or that faces away from other people or from the open air

²**inside** *adj* **1** to or on the area within (something else), esp. in a house; facing the inside **2** at or from the heart or centre of the action: *the inside story*

³**inside** *prep* on or to the inside of; within

⁴**inside** *adv* **1** to or in the inside **2** *sl* in prison

insist *v* **1** to declare firmly **2** to order (something to happen): *I insisted on him going* – ~**ence,** ~**ency** *n*

insolent *adj* showing disrespectful rudeness – ~**ly** *adv* – **-solence** *n*

insomnia *n* habitual inability to sleep – ~**c** *n, adj*

inspect *v* **1** to examine (the details of something) **2** to make an official visit to judge the quality of – ~**ion** *n*

inspector *n* **1** an official who inspects **2** a police officer of middle rank – ~**ate,** ~**ship** *n*

inspiration *n* **1** the act of inspiring or state of being inspired **2** something or someone which causes one to feel inspired **3** a good idea – ~**al** *adj*

inspire *v* **inspired, inspiring 1** to encourage ability or feeling in (someone): *You inspire me with admiration* **2** to give unusual power to do good, esp. as from God **3** to be the force which produces (usu. a good result): *His music was inspired by love*

install *v* **1** to settle in an official position, esp. with ceremony **2** to set (an apparatus) up, ready for use **3** to settle somewhere: *I installed myself in front of the fire*

instalment *n* **1** one of several pay-

ments: *the last instalment of my debt*
2 a single part of a book, play, etc.
which appears in regular parts

instance *n* **1** a single fact, event, etc.,
expressing a general idea: *an
instance of bad behaviour* **2 for
instance** for example

¹**instant** *n* a moment of time

²**instant** *adj* **1** happening at once **2**
urgent: *in instant need* **3** which can
be prepared quickly: *instant coffee*
–~ly adv: Come instantly!
–~aneous adj –~aneously adv
–~aneousness n

instead *adv* in place of that: *It's too wet
to walk, we'll go swimming instead*

instead of *prep* in place of: *Will you
go to the party instead of me?*

instinct *n* **1** a force in animals causing
behaviour not based on learning:
Some animals hunt by instinct **2**
natural feelings: *Trust your
instincts –~ive adj –~ively adv*

¹**institute** *v* **-tuted, -tuting** to set up
for the first time (a society, rules,
etc.)

²**institute** *n* a society formed for a
purpose: *a scientific institute*

institution *n* **1** instituting **2** a habit,
custom, etc., which has existed for
a long time: *Marriage is an institution* **3** a large society or organization
4 the building in which such an
organization works *–~al adj*

instruct *v* **1** to teach **2** to order: *I
instructed him to come early –~or
n*

instruction *n* **1** instructing; teaching

2 advice on how to do something:
an instruction book –~al adj

instrument *n* **1** a tool: *medical instruments* **2** an object such as a piano,
horn, etc. played to give music **3**
someone or something used as a
tool: *an instrument of fate*

insufficient *adj* not enough *–~ly adv
– -ciency n*

¹**insult** *v* to offend

²**insult** *n* something which insults

insurance *n* **1** agreement to pay
money in case of misfortune (such
as illness, death, or accident): *life
insurance* **2** money paid to or by an
insurance company as a result of
such an agreement **3** protection:
*Buy a lock as insurance against thi-
eves*

insure *v* **insured, insuring** to protect
by insurance: *My house is insured
against fire*

intact *adj* whole; untouched: *The
clock arrived intact –~ness n*

intake *n* **1** the amount or number
taken in: *a large intake of students*
2 the place in a tube, pipe, etc.,
where fluid is taken in

intellect *n* the ability to reason

¹**intellectual** *adj* **1** concerning the
intellect **2** having reasoning powers
–~ly adv

²**intellectual** *n* a person who lives by
using his mind and is interested in
thinking

intelligence *n* **1** ability to reason and
understand **2** information: *intelligence about enemy planes – -gently
adj – -gently adv*

intend *v* to plan; mean: *I intend to go. / It was intended as a joke*

intense *adj* strong, esp in quality: *intense cold* –~**ly** *adv* – **-sity** *n*

¹**intent** *n* **1** *law* intending to do something bad: *with intent to steal* **2** purpose: *with good intent* **3 to all intents and purposes** very nearly

²**intent** *adj* with attention: *an intent look* –~**ly** *adv* –~**ness** *n*

intention *n* a plan; purpose: *It wasn't my intention to hurt*

intentional *adj* on purpose –~**ly** *adv*

intercede *v* **-ceded, -ceding** to speak in favour of another – **-cession** *n*

¹**interest** *n* **1** a readiness to give attention: *I have no interest in politics* **2** a subject which one gives attention to: *Eating is his only interest* **3** advantage or favour: *It's in your interest to speak out* **4** a share (in a company, business, etc.) **5** money paid for the use of money: *money lent at 6% interest*

²**interest** *v* to cause (someone) to have interest, desire, etc. –~**ing** *adj* –~**ingly** *adv*

interfere *v* **-fered, -fering 1** to get in the way **2** to push oneself into someone else's affairs

interference *n* **1** interfering **2** the noises and activities which spoil the working of electrical apparatus, esp. a radio

interior *adj, n* (the part which is) inside: *interior furnishings*

internal *adj* **1** of or in the inside, esp. of the body **2** not foreign: *internal trade* –~**ly** *adv*

¹**international** *adj* concerned with more than one nation –~**ly** *adv*

²**international** *n* **1** an international sports match **2** a player in such a match

interpret *v* **1** to understand or show the meaning of **2** to put (spoken words) into another language –~**er** *n* –~**ative,** ~**ive** *adj*

interpretation *n* **1** interpreting **2** the performance of the intentions of a musician, writer, etc., by a performer

interrogate *v* **-gated, -gating** to question formally – **-gation** *n* – **-gator** *n*

interrupt *v* **1** to break the flow of (something continuous) **2** to break the flow of speech of (someone) –~**ion** *n*

interval *n* **1** a period between events **2** such a period between the parts of a play, concert, etc. **3** (in music) the difference in pitch between 2 notes **4 at intervals** happening after equal periods or appearing at equal distances: *at 20-minute intervals*

intervene *v* **-vened, -vening 1** to interrupt so as to prevent or cause something: *I intervened and stopped the fight* **2** to come between: *in the intervening years* – **-vention** *n*

¹**interview** *n* **1** a meeting where a person is asked questions, esp. to decide whether to offer him a job or college place **2** such a meeting to discover an important person's actions, points of view, etc.

²**interview** *v* to question in an interview – ~**er** *n*

intestine *n* the tube carrying food away from the stomach – **-tinal** *adj*

¹**intimate** *v* **-mated, -mating** to make known indirectly; suggest – **-mation** *n*

²**intimate** *adj* **1** close in relationship: *intimate friends* **2** personal; private: *intimate beliefs* **3** in a sexual relationship: *They were intimate* **4** resulting from close connection: *intimate knowledge of Spain* – ~**ly** *adv* – **-macy** *n*

³**intimate** *n* a person closely connected with another

intimidate *v* **-dated, -dating** to frighten (someone) into doing what one wants – **-dation** *n*

into *prep* **1** to the inside of: *They broke into his store* **2** so as to be in: *to fall into the water / to get into a temper* **3** so as to be: *to translate it into French* **4** (used when dividing one number by another): *3 into 6 goes twice* **5** *sl* keen on; interested in: *He's into modern music*

intricate *adj* containing much detail and difficult to understand – ~**ly** *adv* – **-cacy** *n*

¹**intrigue** *v* **intrigued, intriguing 1** to interest greatly **2** to make a secret plot

²**intrigue** *n* **1** plotting **2** a plot

introduce *v* **-duced, -ducing 1** to make known for the first time to each other or someone else **2** to bring in for the first time: *They introduced the idea that children should learn*

to drive **3** to bring or put in: *The first notes introduce a new type of music. / to introduce the pipe into the hole* – **-ductory** *adj*

introduction *n* **1** introducing or being introduced **2** an occasion of telling people each others' names **3** an explanation at the beginning of a book or speech **4** the beginning part: *the story's introduction*

intuition *n* **1** the power to know without reasoning **2** a piece of knowledge that results: *an intuition that her friend was ill* – **-tive** *adj* – **-tively** *adv*

invade *v* **invaded, invading 1** to attack and take control of (a country, city, etc.) **2** to enter in large numbers: *Holiday makers invaded the seaside* **3** to enter into and spoil: *to invade someone's privacy* – ~**r** *n*

¹**invalid** *adj* not correct, esp. in law – ~**ly** *adv* – ~**ity** *n*

²**invalid** *n* a person made weak by illness: *my invalid mother* – ~**ism** *n*

invaluable *adj* valuable beyond measure: *invaluable help*

invariable *adj* which cannot vary – **-bly** *adv* – **-bility** *n*

invasion *n* an act of invading

invent *v* **1** to make up or produce (something new): *Bell invented the telephone in 1876* **2** to make up (something untrue): *The whole story was invented* – ~**or** *n*

invention *n* **1** inventing **2** something invented

invert *v* to put in the opposite position, esp. upside down **–inversion** *n*

invest *v* to put (money) into something in order to make more money: *invest £100 in the business*

investigate *v* **-gated, -gating** to examine thoroughly **– -gator** *n* **– -gation** *n*

investment *n* **1** investing **2** something invested or in which one invests: *an investment of £100 in a business*

invisible *adj* **1** that cannot be seen **2** not usually recorded in statements of profit:*invisible earnings/exports* **– -bility** *n* **– -bly** *adv*

invitation *n* **1** inviting **2** a request to be present or take part **3** an encouragement

invite *v* **invited, inviting 1** to ask (somebody) to a social occasion **2** to ask for, esp. politely: *Questions were invited after the meeting* **3** to encourage: *Some shops invite crime by making it easy to steal*

involve *v* **involved, involving 1** to cause (someone) to become connected: *Don't involve me in your mistakes* **2** to include: *This job involves living abroad* **–~ment** *n*

inward *adj* **1** on or towards the inside **2** of the mind or spirit **–~ly** *adv*

inwards *adv* towards the inside

IOU *abbrev. for:* 'I owe you'; a piece of paper admitting a debt

iris *n* **1** a tall yellow or purple flower with large leaves **2** the coloured part of the eye round the pupil

¹iron *n* **1** a useful silver-white metal that is an element **2** a heavy metal object with a handle, pointed at the front and flat underneath, used for making cloth smooth **3** any of the set of 9 golf clubs with metal heads, used for driving a ball short distances

²iron *adj* of great strength; unyielding: *an iron will*

³iron *v* to make smooth with an iron: *I've ironed your shirt*

ironic **–also ironical** *adj* expressing irony; bitterly funny: *an ironic saying* **–~ally** *adv*

irony *n* **-ies 1** use of words in which there is a contrast between what is said and what is meant **2** an event which has the opposite result from what is expected: *life's little ironies*

¹irregular *adj* **1** (of shape) uneven; not level **2** (of time) at unevenly separated points **3** not according to the rules **4** (in grammar) not following the usual pattern: *an irregular verb* **–~ly** *adv*

²irregular *n* a soldier in a non-regular army

irregularity *n* **-ties 1** being irregular **2** something irregular, such as crime or unevenness

irrelevant *adj* not having any connection with something: *Age is irrelevant for this job* **–~ly** *adv* **– -vance, -vancy** *n*

irresistible *adj* too desirable or strong to be resisted: *an irresistible child / an irresistible force* **– -bly** *adv*

irrespective of *prep* without regard to

irresponsible *adj* not thinking of the

effect of one's actions – **-bility** *n* – **-bly** *adv*

irrigate *v* **-gated, -gating** to supply water to (dry land) with canals or pipes – **-gable** *adj* – **-gation** *n*

irritate *v* **-tated, -tating** 1 to annoy 2 *technical* to cause (something living, esp. part of a body) to act when influenced by a force 3 to make sore: *Wool irritates my skin* – **-tant** *n*

irritation *n* 1 irritating or being irritated 2 a sore place

is –*short form* **'s** *3rd person sing. pres. tense of* BE: *He/she/it is welcome. / Father's here. / What is/what's that?*

island *n* 1 a piece of land surrounded by water 2 something standing alone or apart: *an island of pleasure in a dull evening* 3 a raised place in the middle of the road, where people crossing can wait

isle *n poetic* an island

isolate *v* **-lated, -lating** 1 to separate from others: *Floods isolated our village* 2 to separate from others for examination: *They have isolated the virus* – **-lation** *n*

¹**issue** *n* 1 coming or bringing out 2 something given out: *a daily issue of milk* 3 something published again: *today's issue of 'The Times'* 4 an important point: *The real issue is ...* 5 *old use and law* children (esp. in the phrase **die without issue**)

²**issue** *v* **issued, issuing** 1 to bring out (esp. something printed) for public attention 2 to provide officially: *issued the soldiers with guns*

¹**it** *pron* 1 **a** that thing: *'Where's my dinner?' 'The cat ate it'* **b** that person or animal whose sex is unknown or not thought important: *What a beautiful baby–is it a boy?* 2 (*used as a subject in various verb patterns*): *It's raining. / It's Thursday. / It felt funny being called Grandmother. / As it happens, I'm French. / It was Jean who shot the President* 3 **if it weren't/hadn't been for** without the help or influence of 4 **That's it a** That's complete **b** That's right 5 **catch it** *esp. spoken* to get into trouble 6 **have had it** *esp. spoken* to have no further hope of success: *We've had it: the bus left 5 minutes ago*

²**it** *n* 1 the most important person in a game 2 *sl* **a** a very important person: *He thinks he's it* **b** the important point: *This is it–I have to make my mind up*

¹**itch** *v* 1 to feel a soreness which one wants to scratch 2 to cause this soreness: *The wound itches* 3 *esp. spoken* to desire to do something: *I'm itching to go*

²**itch** *n* 1 an itching feeling 2 a strong desire

item *n* a single thing among a set

its *adj* (*possessive form of* IT) belonging to it: *The cat washed its ears*

it's *short form of*: 1 it is: *It's raining* 2 it has: *It's rained*

itself *pron* 1 (*reflexive form of* IT): *The cat's washing itself* 2 (*strong form of*

IT): *We won't buy new tyres when the car itself is so old* **3 in itself** without considering the rest

ivory *n* **-ries 1** a hard white substance, of which elephants' tusks are made **2** the creamy colour of ivory

ivy *n* **ivies** a plant which climbs up walls and has shiny 3- or 5-pointed leaves

¹jab *v* **-bb-** to push (something pointed): *He jabbed his stick into my face*

²jab *n* **1** a push with something pointed **2** a quick straight blow **3** *sl* an injection

jack *n* **1** an apparatus for lifting something heavy, such as a car, off the ground **2** also **knave**– any of the 4 playing cards with a picture of a man and usu. a rank between the 10 and the queen **3** the small white ball at which players aim in bowls

jacket *n* **1** a short coat with sleeves **2** any outer cover: *potatoes in their jackets*

jackpot *n* the biggest amount of money to be won in a game of chance

jagged –also **jaggy** *adj* having a sharp uneven edge – ~**ly** *adv*

¹jail –also **gaol** *n* a prison

²jail –also **gaol** *v* to put in jail

¹jam *v* **-mm- 1** to pack tightly into a small space: *I can't jam another thing into this bag* **2** to push forcefully: *She jammed the lid down on my finger. / He jammed the brakes on* **3** (of parts of machines) to get

stuck **4** to block (radio messages) by broadcasting noise

²jam *n* **1** a mass of people or things jammed together: *a traffic jam* **2 in a jam** *esp. spoken* in trouble

³jam *n* fruit boiled and preserved in sugar, for spreading on bread

January *n* **-ries** the first month of the year

¹jar *v* **-rr- 1** to make an unpleasant sound **2** to give an unpleasant shock to **3** to go badly together: *jarring opinions/colours*

²jar *n* an unpleasant shock

³jar *n* a container like a bottle with a short neck and wide mouth: *2 jars of jam*

¹jaw *n* **1** also **jawbone**– either of the 2 face bones which hold the teeth **2** the appearance of the lower jaw: *a square jaw*

²jaw *v esp. spoken* to talk

jay *n* **jays** any of several noisy brightly-coloured birds of the crow family

jazz *n* **1** any of several types of music originated by black Americans, usu. with a strong beat and some free playing by each musician **2** *sl* nonsense

jealous *adj* **1** fearing to lose what one has; possessive **2** wanting to get what another has: *He is jealous of their success* – ~**ly** *adv* – ~**y** *n*

jeans *n* strong cotton trousers, worn for work and informally

jeep *n* a type of car for travelling over rough ground

jeer v to laugh rudely (at): *The crowd jeered the prisoners* **–jeer** n

jelly n **-lies 1** soft food that shakes when moved, made with gelatine: *orange jelly* **2** fruit juice boiled with sugar and cooled to become a spread for bread: *apple jelly* **3** any material between a liquid and solid state

¹jerk v to move with a jerk: *He jerked his head back*

²jerk n a short quick strong pull or movement

jerky adj **-ier, -iest** with jerks – **-kily** adv – **-kiness** n

jersey n **-seys 1** a sweater **2** fine usu. woollen cloth used esp. for dresses

¹jest n a joke: *in jest*

²jest v esp. written to joke: *a jesting remark* **–jestingly** adv

¹jet n a hard black mineral that can be polished , used in ornaments

²jet v **-tt-** to come or send out in a jet or jets: *The water jetted out*

³jet n **1** a narrow stream of liquid, gas, etc., forced through a small hole: *jets of water* **2** a narrow opening from which this is forced out **3** an aircraft powered by a jet engine

⁴jet v **-tt-** to travel by jet aeroplane

jet engine n an engine that pushes out hot gases behind it, and is used to make aircraft fly

jetty n **-ties** a wall built out into water, for getting on ships or as a protection against the waves

Jew n a person descended from the inhabitants of ancient Israel, or practising their religion **–~ish** adj

jewel n **1** a precious stone, often fitted in an ornament or in the machinery of a watch **2** a person or thing of great value

jeweller n a person who deals in jewels

jewellery, -elry n ornaments with jewels

jigsaw puzzle n a picture made up of irregular pieces to be fitted together

¹jingle v **-gled, -gling** to sound with a jingle

²jingle n **1** a sound as of small bells **2** a simple poem with a very regular beat

job n **1** a piece of work: *Do a better job next time* **2** something hard to do: *It was a job to talk with all that noise* **3** sl a crime, esp. robbery or a beating **4** regular paid employment: *He has a job in a bank* **5 a good/bad job** esp. spoken a good/bad thing: *He's gone, and a good job too!*

¹jockey n **-eys** a person who rides in horse races, esp. professionally

²jockey v **-eyed, -eying 1** to get (someone to do something or into a position) by tricks **2 jockey for position** to try skilfully to get into a good position

¹jog v **-gg-** to shake or push slightly **2** to move slowly and unsteadily: *The carriage jogged along the track* **3** to move along steadily and uneventfully **4** to run slowly and steadily **5 jog someone's memory** to make someone remember **–~ger** n

²jog n **1** a slight shake, push, or knock **2** also **jog trot–** a slow steady run

¹**join** v **1** to fasten; connect: *to join the ends of a rope* **2** to bring together: *to join people in marriage* **3** to take part with: *Will you join me in a drink?* **4** to become a member of: *to join the army* **5** to run into; meet: *Where does the path join the road?*

²**join** n a place where 2 things are joined

¹**joint** n **1** a way of making a join **2** a thing used for making a join **3** a place where things join **4** a large piece of meat **5** *sl* a public place, esp. one of amusement

²**joint** adj shared by 2 or more people: *a joint account with the bank* –~ly adv

³**joint** v to divide (meat) at the joints

¹**joke** n **1** anything said or done to cause amusement **2** a person, thing, or event that is not taken seriously

²**joke** v **joked, joking** to tell or make jokes –**jokingly** adv

joker n **1** a person who jokes **2** *esp. spoken* a person not be taken seriously **3** an·additional playing card, which in some games may have any value

¹**jolly** adj **-lier, -liest 1** merry; happy **2** *esp. spoken* slightly drunk **3** nice; pleasant –**jollily** adv –**jollity, jolliness** n

²**jolly** adv *esp. spoken* very: *a jolly good thing*

³**jolly** v **-lied, -lying** *esp. spoken* to urge gently: *They jollied her into going*

¹**jolt** v to shake or shock

²**jolt** n a sudden shake or shock

¹**jot** n a very small amount: *not a jot of truth*

²**jot** v **-tt-** to write quickly

journal n **1** a diary **2** a periodical

journalism n the work or profession of producing, esp. writing for, newspapers – **-ist** n – **-istic** adj

¹**journey** n **-neys** a trip of some distance

²**journey** v **-neyed, -neying** to travel

joy n **joys 1** great happiness **2** a person or thing that causes joy **3** *esp. spoken* success: *I tried to phone her, but I didn't have any joy*

joyful adj full of joy –~**ly** adv –~**ness** n

jubilee n a period of great rejoicing, esp. to mark or remember some event

¹**judge** v **judged, judging 1** to act as a judge in (a law case) **2** to give a decision about (someone or something), esp. in a competition: *to judge horses* **3** to give an opinion about: *A man should be judged by his deeds*

²**judge** n **1** an official who has the power to decide questions brought before a law court **2** a person with the knowledge, experience, or right to make decisions or give opinions: *I'm no judge of music*

judgment, judgement n **1** an official decision given by a law court **2** an opinion: *to form a judgment* **3** the ability to judge: *a man of weak judgment*

¹**jug** n **1** a pot for liquids with a handle and a lip for pouring **2** *sl* prison

²**jug** *v* **-gg-** to boil in a closed pot: *jugged hare*

juggle *v* **-gled, -gling 1** to keep (several objects) in the air at the same time, throwing them up and catching them **2** to play with (something): *to juggle ideas* **3** to do something dishonest: *Don't juggle with your accounts* –~**r** *n*

juice *n* **1** the liquid part of fruit, vegetables, and meat **2** *sl* anything that produces power, such as electricity, petrol, etc.

juicy *adj* **-ier, -iest 1** full of juice: *a juicy orange* **2** interesting, esp. because providing information: *all the juicy details* – **-ciness** *n*

jukebox *n* a machine which plays records when a coin is put in

July *n* **Julies** the 7th month of the year

¹**jumble** *v* **-bled, -bling** to mix in disorder

²**jumble** *n* a disorderly mixture

jumble sale *n* a sale of used clothes, toys, etc., to get money for some good work

¹**jump** *v* **1** to spring suddenly and quickly: *to jump out of the water* **2** to spring over: *He jumped the stream* **3** to make a quick sudden movement, usu. upwards: *His heart jumped for joy. / Oil prices jumped sharply* **4** *esp. spoken* to travel on (a train) without paying **5** to attack suddenly **6 jump to it** *esp. spoken* to hurry **7 jump the gun** to start something too soon

²**jump** *n* an act of jumping

¹**jumper** *n* a person or horse that jumps

²**jumper** *n* a knitted garment for the upper body, pulled on over the head ; sweater

junction *n* a place of joining or uniting: *a railway junction*

June *n* the 6th month of the year

jungle *n* **1** a thick tropical forest **2** a disorderly mass: *the jungle of tax laws*

junior *adj* **1** younger **2** of lower rank: *a junior minister* –**junior** *n*

¹**junk** *n* **1** *esp. spoken* old useless things **2** *esp. spoken* poor material: *This book is junk* **3** *sl* the dangerous drug heroin ◄

²**junk** *v esp. spoken* to get rid of as worthless

³**junk** *n* a Chinese sailing ship with a flat bottom and rather square sails

jury *n* **juries 1** a group of people chosen to decide questions in a law court **2** a group chosen to judge a competition: *the jury of the Miss World competition*

¹**just** *adj* **1** fair and honest **2** well-deserved: *a just reward* **3** exact: *a just balance* –~**ly** *adv* –~**ness** *n*

²**just** *adv* **1** exactly: *He was sitting just here. / He came just as I was leaving* **2** very near the present or stated time: *They've just arrived. / just after Christmas* **3** almost not: *You only just caught the train* **4** (*esp. spoken*) completely: *That's just perfect!* **5** merely: *just the door squeaking, not a ghost*

justice *n* **1** being just; fairness **2** correctness: *the justice of his remarks* **3** the power of the law: *to bring a criminal to justice*

jut out *v adv* **-tt-** to stick out: *The wall juts out into the road*

¹juvenile *adj* **1** of or for young people: *juvenile books* **2** young and foolish

²juvenile *n esp. written* a young person

kaleidoscope *n* **1** a tube fitted with mirrors and pieces of coloured glass which shows coloured patterns when turned **2** anything with changing colours, patterns, etc.: *The sunset was a kaleidoscope of colours* – **-scopic** *adj* – **-scopically** *adv*

kangaroo *n* **-roos** an Australian animal which jumps along on large back legs and carries its young in a special pocket

keel *n* **1** a long bar along a boat's bottom from which the frame of the boat is built up **2 on an even keel** without any sudden changes; without trouble

¹keen *adj* **1** sharp; cutting **2** (of the mind, feelings, senses, etc.) strong, quick at understanding, etc.: *a keen mind / keen sorrow / keen sight* **3** with eagerness and activity: *a keen struggle for power / She is not keen to come* **4** *esp. spoken* having a strong liking for: *keen on politics* –~**ly** *adv* –**keenness** *n*

²keen *v* to express sorrow loudly, often by a song or cry –**keen** *n*

¹keep *v* **kept, keeping 1** to fulfil: *She kept her promise* **2** to guard; protect:

May God keep you! / *to keep a secret* **3** to take care of: *She kept her sister's children* **4** to own, employ, or have the use of: *to keep a house* **5** to own and take care of, usu. in order to make money: *to keep cows / They keep a shop* **6** to have or hold for some time: *Please keep this until I come back. / The shop keeps all writing needs* **7** to have without the need of returning: *Keep the change* **8** to cause to continue to be: *That kept her warm. / Her illness kept her in hospital. / The tyrant kept the people down* **9** to continue to be: *She kept warm/ studying* **10** to remain fit to eat: *This fish won't keep* **11** to delay: *What kept you?*

²keep *n* **1** a great tower of a castle **2** necessary goods and services (esp. in the phrase **earn one's keep**)

keeper *n* a person who guards, protects, or looks after: *zoo keeper / shopkeeper / doorkeeper / wicket keeper*

keep on *v adv* **1** to continue: *Prices keep on increasing* **2** to continue to have or employ: *I've kept both gardeners on* **3** to talk continuously: *He keeps on about his operation. / Don't keep on at me about it!*

keep up *v adv* **1** to cause to remain high: *She kept up her spirits by singing* **2** to keep in good condition: *keep up a house* **3** to continue: *keep up the good work* **4** to remain the same: *Will the fine weather keep up?* **5** to keep out of bed **6** to remain level: *I had to run to keep up with* *you* **7 keep up with the Joneses** to stay level with one's neighbours socially

¹kennel *n* a small house for a dog

²kennel *v* to keep or put in a kennel

kept *past tense and past part. of* KEEP

kerb *n* a line of raised stones separating the footpath from the road

kernel *n* **1** the part inside the shell of a nut **2** the part of a seed inside its hard covering: *the kernel of a grain of corn* **3** the important or main part of something

kettle *n* a usu. metal pot with a lid, handle, and spout for heating water

¹key *n* **keys 1** a usu. metal instrument for locking or unlocking, winding (a clock), tightening or loosening (a spring), etc. **2** any part in an apparatus that is pressed with the finger: *the keys of a piano/a typewriter* **3** something that explains or helps you to understand: *a key to the grammar exercises* **4** someone or something very important: *a key man* **5** a set of musical notes with a certain starting note: *in the key of C* **6** a winglike seed of certain types of tree (such as the sycamore)

²key *v* **keyed, keying** to make ready or suitable for: *factories keyed to the needs of the army*

khaki *adj, n* **1** a yellow-brown colour **2** cloth of this colour, esp. as worn by soldiers

¹kick *v* **1** to hit with the foot **2** (esp. in rugby) to score by doing this: *kick a goal* **3** to move the feet backwards and forwards **4** *esp. spoken* to make by complaining: *kick up a fuss* −~**er** *n*

²kick *n* **1** an act of kicking **2** *sl* a sharp feeling of excitement: *She drives fast for kicks* **3** *esp. spoken* power to produce an effect: *This wine has a lot of kick*

¹kid *n* **1** a young goat **2** leather made from its skin **3** *esp. spoken* a child

²kid *v* **-dd-** *esp. spoken* **1** to pretend or deceive: *He's not really hurt: he's only kidding* **2 You're kidding!** I don't believe you −**kidder** *n*

kidnap *v* **-pp-** to take (someone) away unlawfully in order to demand money or something else for his safe return −**kidnapper** *n*

kidney *n* **-neys** one of 2 organs in the lower back, shaped like a bent oval, which separate urine from the blood

¹kill *v* **1** to cause to die **2** to destroy: *That mistake killed his chances* **3 kill time** to make time pass by finding something to do −~**er** *n*

²kill *n* **1** the animal(s) killed in hunting **2** the act of killing **3 in at the kill** present at the end of a struggle, competition, etc.

kilogram −also **kilo** *n* 1,000 grams

kilometre *n* 1,000 metres

kilt *n* a short pleated skirt worn by Scotsmen

¹kind *n* **1** a group that are alike; type; sort: *people of many kinds / the only one of its kind* **2** nature or type: *different in size but not in kind* **3 in kind** (of payment) using goods rather than money **4 of a kind a** of the same kind **b** of poor quality: *coffee of a kind*

²kind *adj* helpful; gentle and well-wishing: *Be kind to animals*

kindle *v* **-dled, -dling 1** to set fire to or catch fire **2** to cause to start: *His cruelty kindled hatred in my heart* **3** to show excitement: *When she saw him her eyes kindled*

¹kindly *adj* **-lier, -liest** friendly; sympathetic **– -liness** *n*

²kindly *adv* **1** in a kind manner **2** please: *Kindly put it back* **3 take kindly to** to accept easily: *He didn't take kindly to your remarks*

kindness *n* **1** being kind **2** a kind action

king *n* **1** (the title of) the male ruler of a country, usu. the son of a former ruler **2** a very powerful or outstanding member of a group: *a king among men* **3** (in certain games) **a** a very important piece **b** any of the 4 playing cards with a picture of a king and a rank above the queen **–~ly** *adj* **–~ship** *n*

kingdom *n* **1** a country under a king or queen **2** an area over which someone has control: *The cook's kitchen is her kingdom* **3** any of the 3 great divisions of natural objects: *the animal/plant/mineral kingdom* **4 the Kingdom of God** the rule of God

kiosk *n* **1** a small open hut, often used to sell newspapers **2** a public telephone box

kipper *n* a smoked salted herring cut open

¹kiss *v* **1** to touch with the lips as a greeting or sign of love **2** to express by kissing: *He kissed them goodbye* **3** to touch gently: *The wind kissed her hair* **4 kiss the dust/ground** to show acceptance of defeat **–~able** *adj*

²kiss *n* **1** an act of kissing **2 kiss of life** a method of reviving a drowning person by breathing into his mouth

kit *n* **1** the clothes and other articles of a soldier, sailor, traveller, etc. **2** a set of articles needed for a purpose: *a toy aircraft kit*

kitchen *n* a room used for cooking

kite *n* **1** a type of large hawk that kills small animals **2** a very light frame covered with paper or cloth for flying at the end of a long string

kitten *n* a young cat **–~ish** *adj* **–~ishly** *adv*

¹kitty *n* **-ties** a cat or kitten

²kitty *n* **-ties 1** (in some card games) money put out by all the players at the beginning and taken by the winner **2** *esp. spoken* money collected by a group for an agreed purpose

knack *n* a skill or ability: *He has a knack of making friends*

knead *v* **1** to mix (flour and water for bread) together by pressing with the hands **2** to press in a similar way on (something, such as a muscle)

¹knee *n* **1** the middle joint of the leg **2** the part of a garment that covers the knee

²knee *v* **kneed, kneeing** to hit with the knee

kneel *v* **knelt, kneeling** to go down on the knee(s): *She knelt to pray*

knew *past tense of* KNOW

knickers *n* women's underpants

¹**knife** *n* **knives** a blade fixed in a handle for cutting

²**knife** *v* **knifed, knifing** to strike with a knife used as a weapon

¹**knight** *n* **1** (in former times) a noble soldier on horseback serving a ruler **2** a man given the title 'Sir" by the king or queen of England **3** (in chess) a piece, usu. with a horse's head, that moves 2 squares forward and one to the side –~**hood** *n* –~**ly** *adj*

²**knight** *v* to make (someone) a knight

knit *v* **knitted** *or (rare)* **knit, knitting** **1** to make (clothing) by joining threads into a network by means of long needles: *knit a sock* **2** *technical* to use the commonest stitch in this activity: *Knit one, purl one* **3** to unite closely: *The 2 edges of that broken bone will knit together smoothly* –~**ter** *n*

knitting *n* that which is being knitted

knitwear *n* knitted clothing

knives *pl. of* KNIFE

knob *n* **1** a round handle or control button **2** any round lump: *a knob of butter* –~**bly** *adj*

¹**knock** *v* **1** to strike a blow, usu. making a noise: *Please knock on the door* **2** to hit hard **3** *sl* to express unfavourable opinions about **4** (of an engine) to make a noise because something is mechanically wrong **5** *sl* to surprise greatly; shock

²**knock** *n* **1** a sound caused by knocking **2** a piece of bad luck or trouble **3** *esp. spoken* (in cricket) a player's innings

knock off *v adv* **1** *esp. spoken* to stop work **2** *sl* to steal **3** to reduce a total payment by: *I'll knock £2 off* **4** *esp. spoken* to do or finish quickly

knock out *v adv* **1** (in boxing) to make (one's opponent) unable to rise for 10 seconds **2** *esp. spoken* to surprise **3** (of a drug) to put to sleep **4** to force out of a competition: *Our team was knocked out early*

¹**knot** *n* **1** a lumplike fastening formed by tying **2** a hard mass in wood where a branch has come off a tree **3** a hard mass: *His muscles stood out in knots* **4** a small close group of people **5** a measure of the speed of a ship, about 1,853 metres (about 6,080 feet) per hour

²**knot** *v* **-tt-** to make a knot in or join with knots: *to knot the rope tightly*

¹**know** *v* **knew, known, knowing** **1** to have (information): *I know that is true* **2** to have learnt: *I know how to swim* **3** to have seen, heard, etc.: *I've known him to run faster than that* **4** to experience: *He has known both grief and happiness* **5** to be familiar with (someone): *I've known him for years* **6** to recognize: *She knows good food* **7** **know all the answers** to behave as if one knew everything **8** **you know** (used for adding force to a statement): *You'll have to try harder, you know*

²**know** *n* **in the know** well-informed

knowledge *n* 1 that which is known; understanding: *a knowledge of French* 2 familiarity with: *a good knowledge of London*

knuckle *n* 1 a finger joint 2 **rap over the knuckles a** (to give) a blow on the knuckles **b** (to make) an attack with words

¹**label** *n* 1 a piece of material fixed to something, on which is written what it is, where it is to go, etc. 2 a word or phrase describing a group or class

²**label** *v* **-ll-** 1 to fix a label on 2 to describe as: *His enemies labelled the boy a thief*

laboratory —also **lab** *n* **-ies** a place where a scientist works, with apparatus for examining and testing materials

laborious *adj* needing or showing great effort or difficulty —~**ly** *adv* —~**ness** *n*

¹**labour** *n* 1 work or effort 2 workers, esp. those who use their hands 3 giving birth 4 a piece of work

²**labour** *v* 1 to work, esp. hard 2 to move with difficulty; struggle: *She laboured up the hill*

labourer *n* a worker whose job needs strength rather than skill

labyrinth *n* 1 a network of twisting and crossing passages; a maze 2 something complicated or difficult to understand —~**ine** *n*

¹**lace** *n* 1 a string pulled through holes in neighbouring edges to draw them together: *shoelaces* 2 a netlike ornamental cloth

²**lace** *v* **laced, lacing** 1 to draw together with a lace 2 to pass (a string, thread, etc.) through holes in (something) 3 to add a little alcohol to (weaker drink)

¹**lack** *v* 1 to be without; not have 2 to have less than enough of; need

²**lack** *n* absence or need: *The plants died for lack of water*

lad *n* 1 a boy; youth 2 *esp. N English* a fellow 3 *esp. spoken* a rather bold man

¹**ladder** *n* 1 a frame of 2 bars or ropes of equal length joined by shorter bars that form steps for climbing 2 a fault in a stocking caused by stitches coming undone 3 (in sports such as table tennis) a list of players who play each other regularly to decide who is best

²**ladder** *v* to cause to develop a ladder in a stocking

¹**ladle** *n* a large deep long-handled spoon for lifting liquids out of a container

²**ladle** *v* **ladled, ladling** to serve (food) with or as if with a ladle

lady *n* **ladies** 1 **a** a woman of good social position or good manners **b** a woman in control: *the lady of the house* 2 *polite* a woman

Lady *n* a title put before the name of **a** a woman of noble rank **b** the wife of a knight or the wife or daughter of a nobleman of certain ranks: *Lady Wilson* **c** another title: *Lady President*

¹**lag** *v* **-gg-** to move more slowly: *He lagged behind us*

²**lag** *v* **-gg-** to cover (water pipes and containers) to prevent heat loss

laid *past tense and past part. of* LAY

lain *past part. of* LIE

lair *n* a wild animal's home

¹**lake** *n* a large mass of water surrounded by land

²**lake** –also **crimson lake**– *n* a deep bluish-red colouring matter

¹**lamb** *n* **1** a young sheep **2** its meat **3** *esp. spoken* a young gentle person

²**lamb** *v* (of sheep) to give birth

¹**lame** *adj* **1** not able to walk easily or properly as a result of weakness or accident **2** not easily believed: *a lame excuse* –~**ly** *adv* –~**ness** *n*

²**lame** *v* **lamed, laming** to make lame

¹**lament** *v* to feel or express sorrow –~**ation** *n*

²**lament** *n* **1** a strong expression of sorrow **2** a piece of music expressing sorrow, esp. for a death

lamp *n* an apparatus for giving light

lamppost *n* a pillar supporting a lamp which lights a public area

¹**lance** *n* a long spear used by mounted soldiers in former times

²**lance** *v* **lanced, lancing** to cut (flesh) with a medical instrument usu. to let infection escape

¹**land** *n* **1** the solid dry part of the earth's surface **2** part of the earth's surface all of the same natural type: *forest land / lowland* **3** a country or nation: *war between lands* **4** earth; soil **5** ground owned as property: *You are on my land* **6** ground used for farming **7** **see how the land lies**

to try to discover the present state of affairs

²**land** *v* **1** to come to, bring to, or put on land or water: *The ship landed the goods at Dover. / Our plane landed on the sea* **2** to come, put, arrive, or cause to arrive in a condition or place: *That will land him in prison* **3** to catch (a fish) **4** *esp. spoken* to obtain; gain **5** *esp. spoken* to strike: *I landed a blow on his nose*

landing *n* **1** the level space or passage at the top of stairs **2** arriving or bringing to land **3** a place where people and goods are landed

landlady *n* **-dies 1** a woman who owns and runs a small hotel **2** a female landlord

landlord *n* **1** a person, esp. a man, from whom someone rents property **2** a person, esp. a man, who owns or runs a hotel, pub, etc.

landmark *n* **1** a tall tree, building, etc., by which one can tell one's position **2** something that marks an important point in history or a person's life **3** something marking the limits of a piece of land

¹**landscape** *n* **1** a wide view of scenery **2** a picture of such a scene

²**landscape** *v* **-scaped, -scaping** to improve or arrange (land) with gardens, trees, etc.

landslide *n* **1** a sudden fall of earth or rocks **2** a very large, often unexpected, success in an election

lane *n* **1** a narrow, often winding, road **2** a fixed route used by ships, aircraft, etc. **3** any of the parallel parts into which wide roads are divided

language *n* **1** the system of human expression by words **2** a particular system of words: *the Russian language* **3** any system of signs, movements, etc., used to express meanings: *The movement of a cat's tail is part of its language* **4** words, phrases, style, etc., peculiar to a group or individual: *the poet's/ chemist's language* **5** impolite or shocking words (esp. in the phrases **bad language, strong language**)

lantern *n* **1** a container that protects a light **2** *technical* the top of a building (such as a lighthouse), with windows on all sides

¹lap *n* **1** the front part of a seated person between waist and knees **2** the clothes covering this

²lap *v* **-pp-** **1** (in racing, swimming, etc.) to be at least one lap ahead of (a competitor) **2** to race completely round the track: *He lapped in 2 minutes*

³lap *n* **1** (in racing, swimming, etc.) a single journey round the track **2** one part of a plan or action

⁴lap *v* **-pp-** **1** to drink by taking up with quick tongue movements **2** to hit with little waves and soft sounds

⁵lap *n* **1** an act of lapping a liquid **2** the sound of lapping, as of waves

lapel *n* the part of a coat front below the neck that is folded back on each side

¹lapse *n* **1** a small fault or mistake of memory, behaviour, etc. **2** a gra-

dual passing away: *after a lapse of several years*

²lapse *v* **lapsed, lapsing** **1** to pass gradually: *to lapse into silence* **2** to fail in correct behaviour, duty, etc. **3** (of business agreements, rights, etc.) to come to an end

larder *n* a room or cupboard for food

large *adj* **1** more than usual in size, number, or amount; big **2 at large a** (esp. of dangerous people or animals) free; uncontrolled **b** as a whole: *The country at large is hoping for changes* **–~ness** *n*

largely *adv* **1** to a great degree; chiefly: *largely desert land* **2** in great quantity

¹lark *n* *esp. spoken* something done for a joke

²lark *n* any of several small light brown birds with long pointed wings, esp. the skylark

laser *n* an apparatus that produces a very powerful beam of light that has various uses including cutting materials, sending messages, and making fine measurements

¹lash *v* **1** to strike with or as if with a whip **2** to move violently or suddenly: *The cat's tail lashed about* **3** to attack violently with words **4** to tie firmly

²lash *n* **1** the thin striking part of a whip **2** a stroke with a whip **3** a sudden movement **4** violent beating: *the lash of the waves* **5** *old use* an official whipping **6** an eyelash

lass –also **lassie** *n Scots & N English* **1** a young girl or woman **2** a girlfriend

¹lasso –also **lariat** *n* **-sos** a rope with one end that can be tightened in a noose for catching horses and cattle

²lasso *v* **-soed, -soing** to catch with a lasso

¹last *adj, pron* **1** (the one or ones) after all others: *He was the last to arrive. / the last post* **2** the one before now; most recent: *the last election / last Thursday*

²last *adv* **1** after all others **2** at the time in the past nearest to now: *When did we last meet?*

³last *v* **1** to continue: *Our holiday lasts 10 days. / a lasting sorrow* **2** to be enough for: *This food will last them 3 days*

latch *n* **1** a simple fastening for a door, gate, etc., worked by dropping a bar into a slot **2** a spring lock for a house door

¹late *adv* **1** after the expected time **2** towards the end of a period **3 of late** recently

²late *adj* **1** arriving, developing, happening, etc., after the expected time **2** happening towards the end of a period **3** happening or existing recently: *the late government* **4** recently died: *her late husband* **5** just arrived; fresh: *some late news* –~**ness** *n*

lately *adv* recently

Latin *n, adj* **1** (of) the language of ancient Rome **2** (a member) of any nation that speaks a language that comes from Latin

latitude *n* **1** the distance north or south of the equator measured in degrees **2** freedom in action, expression, etc.

latter *adj esp. written* **1** nearer to the end; later: *the latter years of his life* **2** the second of 2 people or things just spoken of: *Did he walk or swim? The latter seems unlikely*

¹laugh *v* to express amusement, happiness, disrespect, etc., by making explosive sounds, usu. while smiling

²laugh *n* **1** the act or sound of laughing **2** *esp. spoken* something done for a joke

laughter *n* the act or sound of laughing

¹launch *v* **1** to set (a boat) into the water **2** to send (a modern weapon or instrument) into the sky or space **3** to throw with great force **4** to begin (an activity, plan, etc.)

²launch *n* a large usu. motor-driven boat for use on rivers, harbours, etc.

launching pad also launching site *n* a base from which rockets are launched

laundry *n* **-dries 1** a place where clothes are washed and ironed **2** clothes, sheets, etc., needing washing or just washed

lavatory –also (*esp. spoken*) **lav** *n* **-ries 1** a large seatlike bowl connected to a drain, used for getting rid of the body's waste matter **2** a room or building containing this

lavender *n* **1** a plant with small sweet-smelling pale purple flowers **2** the dried flowers and stems of this plant used for giving stored clothes, sheets, etc., a pleasant smell **3** pale purple

lavish *adj* **1** very generous or wasteful: *a lavish spender* **2** produced in great quantity: *lavish praise* –~**ly** *adv* –~**ness** *n*

law *n* **1** a rule supported by government power that members of society must follow **2** the whole body of such rules in a country: *The law forbids stealing* **3** the whole body of these rules and the way they work: *to study law* **4** an accepted rule of behaviour: *the laws of cricket* **5** a statement of what always seems to happen in certain conditions: *Boyle's law is a scientific principle* **7** *esp. spoken* the police or a policeman **8 be a law unto oneself** to do what one wishes, regardless of laws **9 go to law** to begin a law case **10 lay down the law** to give an opinion or order firmly

lawful *adj* **1** recognized or allowed by law: *a lawful marriage* **2** obeying the law –~**ly** *adv* –~**ness** *n*

¹**lawn** *n* a stretch of smooth ground covered with closely cut grass

²**lawn** *n* fine smooth material, as used in summer dresses, handkerchiefs, etc.

lawyer *n* a person (esp. a solicitor) whose business is the law

¹**lay** *v* **laid, laying 1** to place, put, or set: *Lay it on the table. / to lay bricks* **2** to place knives, forks, etc., on, ready for a meal (esp. in the phrase **lay the table**) **3** to cause to settle: *The rain laid the dust* **4** (of birds, insects, etc.) to produce (an egg or eggs): *The hens aren't laying* **5** to bet (esp. money) on the result of some happening **6** to put into a particular condition, esp. of weakness, helplessness, etc.: *The country was laid in ruins* **7** to make (a claim, charge, etc.) in an official way: *to lay claim to a title* **8** to cover or spread over: *He laid mats on the floor* **9 lay hold of** to catch and hold firmly

²**lay** *n* **lays** the manner or position in which something lies

³**lay** *past tense of* LIE

¹**layer** *n* **1** a thickness of some material laid over a surface: *Cover them with a layer of earth* **2** a bird that lays eggs **3** a plant stem that has been fastened partly under the ground, to root and become a separate plant

²**layer** *v* **1** to make a layer of; put down in layers **2** to fasten (a stem) down and cover with earth

layman *n* **-men 1** a person who is not a priest **2** a person not trained in a particular subject, as compared with those who are

layout *n* **1** the planned arrangement of a town, building, etc. **2** the way in which printed matter is set out on paper

lazy *adj* **lazier, laziest 1** disliking activity **2** encouraging inactivity: *a lazy afternoon* – **-zily** *adv* – **-ziness** *n*

¹**lead** *v* **led, leading 1** to show (some-

body) the way; guide **2** to be the means of reaching a place: *The path leads to the village* **3** to direct, control, or govern (an army, people, etc.) **4** (esp. in sports) to be ahead **5** to start or open a game, esp. of cards, with: *She led her highest card* **6** to experience; pass: *He led a hard life*

²**lead** *n* **1** a guiding example **2** a clue, hint **3** the front place in a race, competition, etc. **4** the distance by which a person or thing is in front: *Our product has a good lead over our competitor's* **5** (in card games) the right to play the first card **6** the chief acting part in a play or film **7** the opening part of a newspaper article **8** also **leash–** a length of leather, chain, etc., tied to a dog to control it **9** a wire that carries electrical power **10 take the lead** to start an action or take control

³**lead** *n* **1** a soft heavy metal that is an element, used for waterpipes, to cover roofs, etc. **2** a thin rope with a weight on one end lowered from a ship to measure the water's depth **3** graphite (a black form of carbon), esp. used in pencils

leader *n* **1** a person or thing that leads, esp. one that directs a group, movement, etc. **2** the first violin player of an orchestra

leading *adj* **1** most important; chief **2** guiding or controlling

leaf *n* **leaves 1** one of the usu. flat green parts of a plant that grow from a stem or branch **2** any thin flat object, such as a book page, a sheet of gold, a removable part of a tabletop, etc. **3 turn over a new leaf** to start again, with better behaviour

leafy *adj* **-ier, -iest** covered with leaves

¹**league** *n old use* about 3 miles or 5 kilometres

²**league** *n* **1** a group of people, countries, etc., joined together for protection or for some aim **2** a group of sports clubs or players that play matches amongst themselves **3 in league (with)** working together, often for a bad purpose

³**league** *v* **leagued, leaguing** to unite in a league

¹**leak** *v* **1** to let through or pass through a leak **2** to make known (secret information)

²**leak** *n* **1** a small accidental hole through which something flows **2** the liquid, gas, etc., that escapes through such a hole **3** an accidental spreading of secret information **4** *sl* an act of passing water from the body

¹**lean** *v* **leant** *or* **leaned, leaning 1** to rest in a sloping position: *She leaned against his shoulder* **2** to rest (something) in a sloping position: *Lean it against the wall* **3 lean over backwards** to make every possible effort

²**lean** *adj* **1** without much fat: *lean meat / a lean man* **2** producing or having little value **–~ness** *n*

³**lean** *n* the lean part of meat

¹**leap** *v* **leapt** *or* **leaped, leaping 1** to spring; jump **2** to pass, rise, etc.,

rapidly: *The idea leaped into his mind*

²**leap** *n* **1** a sudden jump **2** a sudden increase in number, quantity, etc.

leap year *n* a year, every 4th year, in which February has 29 days instead of 28

learn *v* **learned** *or* **learnt, learning 1** to gain knowledge (of) or skill (in): *I'm learning French. / to learn quickly* **2** to memorize: *Learn this list of words* **3** to become informed: *She'll learn of my success* **4 learn one's lesson** to suffer so much from doing something that one will not do it again −~**er** *n*

learning *n* deep knowledge gained by study

¹**lease** *n* a written agreement by which an owner gives the use of a property to somebody for a period in return for rent

²**lease** *v* **leased, leasing** to give or take (property) on a lease

¹**least** *adj* (superlative of LITTLE) **1** smallest in size, amount, etc. **2** slightest: *I haven't the least idea*

²**least** *n* **1** the smallest thing, amount, etc.: *Giving him food was the least we could do* **2 at least** if nothing else **3 at the least** not less than

³**least** *adv* **1** in the smallest amount, degree, etc.: *when we least expected it* **2 least of all** especially not **3 not least** partly; quite importantly: *Trade has been bad, not least because of increased costs*

leather *n* animal skin treated to preserve it

¹**leave** *v* **left, leaving 1** to go away or go away from: *The car left the road. / We must leave early* **2** to cease to remain in or with: *I am leaving England/my wife* **3** to allow to remain: *The window was left open* **4** to allow to remain undone, untaken, etc.: *Leave that work for now* **5** to give into the care of someone: *I'll leave buying the tickets to you* **6** to give (through a will) after the death of the giver **7** to have left over: *2 from 8 leaves 6*

²**leave** *n* **1** permission **2** permission to be absent, esp. from army service **3** time spent in such an absence **4** a holiday **5 take leave of** to say goodbye to

leaves *pl. of* LEAF

¹**lecture** *n* **1** a talk in front of people, esp. as a method of teaching **2** a long solemn scolding

²**lecture** *v* **-tured, -turing** to give a lecture (to)

led *past tense & past part. of* LEAD

ledge *n* a narrow flat shelf

leek *n* an onion-like vegetable with a long white fleshy stem

¹**left** *adj* **1** on or belonging to the side of the body that usu. contains the heart **2** on, by, or in the direction of one's left side **3** belonging to or favouring the left in politics

²**left** *n* **1** the left side or direction **2** the left hand **3** political parties that favour the equal division of wealth and property and generally support the workers rather than the employers

³**left** *adv* towards the left

⁴**left** *past tense and past part. of* LEAVE

left-handed *adj* **1** using the left hand rather than the right **2** made for use by a person who does this – ~**ly** *adv* – ~**ness** *n*

leg *n* **1** a limb on which an animal walks and which supports its body **2** that part of this limb above the foot **3** the part of a garment that covers the leg **4** one of the supports on which a piece of furniture stands **5** that part of a cricket field behind and to the left of a right-handed batsman facing the bowler **6 leg before wicket** a way in which a batsman can be out, by (usu. accidentally) stopping a ball that would have hit the wicket with his leg

legal *adj* **1** allowed or made by law; lawful **2** of, concerning, or using the law – ~**ly** *adv* – ~**ity** *n*

legend *n* **1** an old story about great deeds of ancient times, sometimes a true tale to which marvellous events have been added later **2** the words or phrase on a coin **3** a famous person or act, esp. in a particular area of activity – ~**ary** *adj*

legible *adj* (of handwriting or print) that can be read, esp. easily – -**bility** *n* – -**bly** *adv*

legislation *n* **1** the act of making laws **2** a body of laws

legitimate *adj* **1** according to law or another body of rules or standards **2** born of parents who are married to each other – ~**ly** *adv* – -**macy** *n*

leisure *n* time when one is free from employment or other duties; free time – ~**d** *adj*

leisurely *adj*, *adv* without haste – -**liness** *n*

lemon *n* **1** a type of fruit like an orange but with a light yellow skin and sour juice **2** light bright yellow

lemonade *n* also **fizzy lemonade**– a yellow drink tasting of lemons and containing bubbles of gas

lend *v* **lent, lending 1** to give (someone) the use of (something, such as money or a car) for a limited time **2** to give out (money) for profit, esp. as a business – ~**er** *n*

length *n* **1** the measurement from one end to the other or of the longest side of something **2** the measure from one end to the other of a horse, boat, etc., used in stating distances in races **3** a piece of something, esp. of a certain length or for a particular purpose **4** the amount of time from the beginning to the present or to the end **5 at length a** after a long time; at last **b** for a long time; in many words

lengthen *v* to make or become longer

lengthy *adj* -**ier, -iest 1** very long **2** (esp. of speeches and writings) of too great a length – -**ily** *adv* – -**iness** *n*

lenient *adj* **1** merciful in judgment; gentle **2** allowing less than the highest standards of work, behaviour, etc. – -**ience** *n* – ~**ly** *adv*

lens *n* **1** a piece of transparent material, curved on one or both sides, which makes a beam of light passing through it bend, spread out, become narrower, etc., used in glasses for the eyes, cameras, microscopes, etc. **2** a similar structure found behind the black opening (pupil) in front of the eye, which helps the eye to form a picture on its light-sensitive area (retina)

lent *past tense and past part. of* LEND

Lent *n* the 40 days before Easter, during which many Christians give up some of their usual pleasures

leopard –(*fem.* **leopardess**) *n* **leopards** *or* **leopard** a type of large meat-eating catlike animal, yellowish with black spots, found in Africa and Southern Asia

¹**less** *adj, pron* (*comparative of* LITTLE) **1** a smaller amount (than); not so much (of): *I was given less cake and fewer biscuits than she had. / Can we have a bit less noise/less of that noise?* **2 none the less** but all the same; in spite of everything; nevertheless

²**less** *adv* **1** not so; to a smaller degree (than): *Jane's less beautiful than Susan* **2** not so much: *Try to shout less*

³**less** *prep* not counting; minus: *Now I owe you 90p; that's £1 for the concert ticket less the 10p I lent you yesterday*

lessen *v* to make or become less

lesson *n* **1** the period of time a pupil or class studies a subject, esp. as one of many such periods **2** something taught to or learned by a pupil, esp. in school **3** the part of a subject taught or studied at one time **4** something from which one should learn **5** a short piece read from the Bible during religious services

lest *conj esp. written* **1** in order that .... not; in case: *I obeyed her lest she should be angry* **2** for fear that

¹**let** *n* **1** *esp. law* anything that prevents something from being done (in the phrase **without let or hindrance**) **2** (in games such as tennis) a stroke that must be played again, esp., in tennis, when a service hits the top of the net on its way over

²**let** *v* **let, letting** **1** to allow (to do or happen) **2** (the named person) must, should, may: *Let each man decide for himself* **3** to give the use of (a room, a building, land, etc.) in return for regular payments **4 let alone** even less: *The baby can't walk, let alone run* **5 let blood** *medical* to purposely draw blood, so as to cure someone **6 let's** *esp. spoken* I suggest that we should; why not ....: *Let's go swimming on Saturday*

³**let** *n* **1** an act of renting a house or flat to (or from) someone **2** a house or flat that is (to be) rented

let down *v adv* **1** to make (a garment) longer **2** to cause (someone) to be disappointed; fail to keep a promise to (someone) **3 let one's hair down** *esp. spoken* to behave informally; enjoy oneself freely

lethal *adj* able or certain to kill

let off *v adv* **1** to cause (something) to explode or be fired **2** to excuse (someone) from punishment

letter *n* **1** a written or printed message sent usu. in an envelope **2** one of the signs in writing that represents a speech sound

lettuce *n* **1** a type of garden plant with large closely packed pale green leaves **2** these leaves, used in salads

¹**level** *n* **1** a smooth flat surface, esp. a wide area of flat ground **2** a position of height: *The garden is arranged on 2 levels* **3** general standard, quality, or degree **4** an instrument used by surveyors to measure differences in height

²**level** *v* **-ll-** **1** to make or become flat and even **2** to raise or lower to the same height everywhere or to the height of something else **3** to knock or pull down to the ground **4** to make or become equal in position, rank, strength, etc.

³**level** *adj* **1** having a surface which is the same height above the ground all over **2** flat; smooth **3** equal in position or standard **4** steady and unvarying

⁴**level** *adv* so as to be level

¹**lever** *n* **1** a bar used for lifting or moving something heavy . One end is placed under or against the object, the other end is pushed down hard, and the bar turns on a fixed point (fulcrum) **2** any part of a machine working in the same way

²**lever** *v* to move (something) with a lever – ~**age** *n*

liable *adj* **1** likely to, esp. from habit or tendency **2** responsible, esp. in law, for paying for something **3** likely to suffer in law – **-bility** *n*: *His liability to lose his temper lost him many friends. The business failed because its assets were not so great as its liabilities*

liar *n* a person who tells lies

¹**liberal** *adj* **1** willing to understand and respect the ideas and feelings of others **2** favouring some change, as in political or religious affairs **3** favouring a wide general knowledge, the broadening of the mind, and wide possibilities for self-expression **4** giving or given freely and generously

²**liberal** *n* a person with wide understanding, who is in favour of change – ~**ism** *n*

liberate *v* **-rated, -rating** **1** to set free; allow to escape **2** *technical* to cause or allow (gas) to escape from a chemical substance – **-rator** *n*

liberation *n* setting free or being set free

liberty *n* **-ties** **1** freedom from oppressive government or foreign rule **2** freedom from control, service, being shut up, etc. **3** freedom of speech or behaviour which is taken without permission and is sometimes regarded as rude: *'I allowed myself the liberty of reading your letters.' 'What a liberty!'*

librarian *n* a person who is in charge

of or helps to run a library – ~**ship** *n*

library *n* **-ies 1** a (part of a) building which contains books that may be looked at or borrowed, by the public (**public library**) or by members of a special group **2** a collection of books

licence *n* **1** an official paper giving permission to do something, usu. in return for a fixed payment: *a dog licence* **2** permission given, esp. officially, to do something **3** freedom of action, speech, thought, etc. **4** misuse of freedom, esp. in causing harm; uncontrolled behaviour **5** the freedom claimed by an artist to disobey the rules of his art or to change the facts in order to improve a work of art

license, -cence *v* to give official permission to or for

¹**lick** *v* **1** to move the tongue across (a surface) in order to taste, clean, make wet, etc. **2** (esp. of flames or waves) to pass lightly or rapidly over or against (a surface) **3** *esp. spoken* to beat or defeat – ~**ing** *n*

²**lick** *n* **1** the act of licking **2** a small amount (of cleaning, paint, etc.) **3** *esp. spoken* speed: *running down the hill at a great lick*

lid *n* **1** the removable top of a box or other hollow container **2** an eyelid

¹**lie** *v* **lay, lain, lying 1** to be in a flat resting position on a surface, as on the ground or a bed **2** to be in a described place, position, or direction: *The town lies to the east* **3** lie

in state (of a dead body) to be placed in a public place so that people may honour it **4 lie low** to be in hiding

²**lie** *v* **lied, lying** to tell a lie

³**lie** *n* an untrue statement purposely made to deceive

lieutenant *n* **1** a person who acts for, or in place of, someone in a higher position; deputy **2** an officer of low rank in the navy, British army, etc.

life *n* **lives 1** the active force that makes those forms of matter (animals and plants) that grow through feeding and produce new young forms like themselves, different from all other matter (stones, machines, objects, etc.) **2** matter having this active force **3** the state or period in which animals and plants are alive **4** the condition of existence, esp. of a human being **5** the period between birth and death, between birth and a certain point in somebody's life, or between a certain point in somebody's life and their death: *I had been a coward all my life. / a life member* **6** the period for which a machine, organization, etc., will work or last **7** living things in general: *plant life* **8** existence as a collection of widely different experiences **9** spirit; strength; force; cheerfulness **10** also **life imprisonment**– the punishment of being put in prison for a length of time which is not fixed **11** also **life story**– a biography **12** using a living person as the subject of painting, drawing, etc.: *life class-es*

lifetime *n* the time during which a person is alive

¹**lift** *v* 1 to raise or rise from one level and hold or move to another level 2 (esp. of clouds, mist, etc.) to move upwards, melt, or disappear 3 to take and use; steal

²**lift** *n* 1 the act of lifting, rising, or raising 2 a lifting force, such as an upward pressure of air on the wings of an aircraft 3 (*US* **elevator**)– an apparatus in a building for taking people and goods from one floor to another 4 a free ride in a vehicle

¹**light** *n* 1 the natural force that is produced by or redirected from objects and other things, so that we see them 2 something that produces such force and causes other things to be seen, such as a lamp or torch 3 something that will set something else, esp. a cigarette, burning: *Can you give me a light, please?* 4 brightness, as in the eyes, showing happiness or excitement 5 the bright part of a painting 6 the condition of being publicly seen or known (in the phrases **come/bring to light**) 7 the way in which something is regarded: *look at the matter in a new light*

²**light** *adj* 1 having light; not dark; bright 2 not deep or dark in colour; pale

³**light** *v* **lit** *or* **lighted, lighting** 1 to start or cause to start to burn 2 to cause to give light; give light to: *We lit the candle and the candle lit the room* 3 to make or become bright with pleasure or excitement

⁴**light** *adj* 1 of little weight; not heavy 2 small in amount 3 easy to bear or do; not difficult or tiring: *light punishment* 4 (of sleep) from which one wakes easily; not deep 5 (of food) easily digested 6 (of wine and other alcoholic drinks) not very strong 7 (of books, music, plays, actors, etc.) having the intention of amusing only; not deep in meaning 8 (of soil) easily broken up; loose; sandy 9 (of cake, bread, etc.) full of air; well risen; not heavy –~**ness** *n*

⁵**light** *adv* without much luggage: *I travel light*

¹**lighter** *n* a large flat-bottomed boat used for loading and unloading ships

²**lighter** *n* 1 something that lights or sets on fire 2 also **cigarette lighter**– an instrument that produces a flame for lighting cigarettes

light-hearted *adj* cheerful; happy

lighthouse *n* a tower with a powerful flashing light that guides ships or warns them of dangerous rocks

lightly *adv* 1 with little weight or force; gently 2 to a slight or small degree: *lightly cooked?*

¹**lightning** *n* a powerful flash of light in the sky usu. followed by thunder

²**lightning** *adj* very quick, short, or sudden: *a lightning visit*

¹**like** *v* **liked, liking** 1 to be fond of; find pleasant 2 to wish: *I'd like to*

see you – **-king** *n: to have a liking for sweets*

²**like** *adj* the same in many ways; alike

³**like** *prep* **1** in the same way as; having the same qualities as; typical of **2** for example: *There are several people interested, like Mr Jones and Dr Simpson* **3 feel like** to wish to have **4 look like** to seem probably

⁴**like** *n* something of the same kind, quality, or value: *I've never seen its like anywhere else*

⁵**like** *conj esp. spoken* in the same way as: *Do you make bread like you make cakes?*

likelihood *n* the fact or degree of being likely

¹**likely** *adj* **-lier, -liest 1** probable; expected **2** suitable to give results: *a likely plan*

²**likely** *adv* probably

lilac *n* **1** a type of tree with pinkish purple or white flowers giving a sweet smell **2** a purple colour like these flowers

lily *n* **-ies** any of several types of plant with large flowers of various colours, but esp. the one with clear white flowers

limb *n* **1** a leg, arm, or wing of an animal **2** a large branch of a tree –~**less** *adj*

¹**lime** *n* **1** also **quicklime–** a white substance obtained by burning limestone, used in making cement **2** the substance (**slaked lime**) made by adding water to this

²**lime** *v* **limed, liming** to add lime to (fields, land, etc.) to control acid substances

³**lime** –also **lime tree, linden** *n* a type of tree with yellow sweet-smelling flowers

⁴**lime** *n* **1** a type of tree which bears a fruit like a small green lemon **2** the fruit of this tree **3** also **lime-juice–** a drink made from this fruit, which is often used to flavour other drinks

limelight *n* a lot of attention from the public

limestone *n* a type of rock containing mainly calcium (the material in bones)

¹**limit** *n* the farthest point or edge of something

²**limit** *v* to keep below or at a certain point or amount –~**ation** *n*

limited *adj* **1** small in amount, power, etc. **2** (of a company) having to pay back debts only up to a fixed limit

¹**limp** *v* to walk with an uneven step, one leg moving less well than the other –**limp** *n: The operation cured his limp*

²**limp** *adj* lacking strength or stiffness –~**ly** *adv* –~**ness** *n*

¹**line** *v* **lined, lining** to make or be an inner covering for

²**line** *n* **1** a piece of string, wire, or thin cord **2** a thin mark with length but no width, which can be drawn on a surface **3** a cord with a hook at the end, used for fishing **4** a limit or edge marked by a drawn line **5** a row **6** a queue **7** a set of people following one another in time, esp.

a family **8** a row of words in a poem **9** a railway track **10** a system for travelling by or moving goods by road, railway, sea, or air: *an airline / a shipping line* **11** *technical* the equator **12** a business, profession, trade, etc. **13** an area of interest (esp. in the phrase **in one's line**) **14** a type of goods: *a new line in hats*

³**line** *v* **1** to mark with lines or wrinkles **2** to form rows along

linen *n* **1** a type of cloth made from the stems of the plant flax **2** sheets and bedclothes, tablecloths, etc.

liner *n* a large passenger ship

linger *v* to delay going; be slow to disappear −∼**er** *n* −∼**ing** *adj* −∼**ingly** *adv*

lining *n* material covering or for covering the inner surface of a garment, box, etc.

¹**link** *n* **1** something which connects 2 other parts **2** one ring of a chain

²**link** *v* **1** to join or connect **2** to be joined −∼**age** *n*

linoleum −also **lino, oilcloth** *n* a material used esp. as a floor-covering, made up of strong cloth coated with a mixture of linseed oil and other substances

lion −(*fem.* **lioness**) *n* **lions** *or* **lion** a type of large animal of the cat family which lives mainly in Africa. The male has a thick mane over the head and shoulders

lip *n* **1** one of the 2 edges of the mouth **2** this area with the ordinary skin around there, esp. round the top below the nose **3** the edge (of a hollow vessel or opening) **4 a stiff upper lip** a lack of expression of feeling

¹**liquid** *adj* **1** (esp. of something which is usu. solid or gas) in the form of a liquid **2** (of money in banks, not coin) which can be obtained as coin (esp. in the phrase **liquid assets**) **3** (of sounds) clear and flowing, with pure notes

²**liquid** *n* (a type of) substance not solid or gas, which flows and has no fixed shape: *Water is a liquid*

liquorice, licorice *n* a sweet black substance produced from a plant, as used in medicine and sweets

¹**list** *n* a set of names of things written one after the other, so as to remember them

²**list** *v esp. written* to write in a list

³**list** *v* (esp. of a ship) to lean or slope to one side

⁴**list** *n* a leaning position, esp. of a ship

listen *v* to give attention in hearing −∼**er** *n*

lit *past tense and past part. of* LIGHT

literal *adj* **1** exact: *a literal account of a conversation* **2** giving one word for each word (as in a foreign language) **3** following the usual meaning of the words −∼**ly** *adv:to translate literally* −∼**ness** *n*

literary *adj* **1** of or concerning literature **2** producing or studying literature **3** more typical of literature, esp. that of former times, than of ordinary speech or writing

literate *adj* able to read and write −~**ly** *adv*

literature *n* 1 written works which are of artistic value 2 printed material, esp. giving information

litre *n* a measure of liquid equal to about 1 3/4 pints

¹**litter** *n* 1 things thrown away, esp. paper scattered untidily 2 straw used as an animal's bed 3 a bed with handles for carrying a person 4 a group of young animals born at the same time to one mother

²**litter** *v* to cover or scatter untidily

¹**little** *adj* 1 small 2 short 3 young

²**little** *adv* **less, least** 1 to only a small degree: *a little known fact* 2 not at all: *They little thought that they were being watched*

³**little** *adj, pron, n* **less, least** 1 not much; not enough 2 a small amount, but at least some: *She speaks a little French* 3 **make little of a** to treat as unimportant **b** to understand little

¹**live** *v* **lived, living** 1 to be alive; have life 2 to continue to be alive 3 to have one's home; dwell 4 to keep oneself alive: *live on fruit*

²**live** *adj* 1 alive; living 2 (of lighted coal or wood) still burning 3 having power which can be used in an explosion and flames when it hits something hard: *a live bomb* 4 carrying free electricity which can shock anyone who touches it 5 (of broadcasting) seen and/or heard as it happens

lively *adj* **-lier, -liest** full of quick movement, thought, etc. − **-liness** *n*

¹**liver** *n* a large organ in the body which produces bile and cleans the blood

²**liver** *n* a person who lives in the stated way: *an evil liver*

livid *adj* 1 blue-grey, as of bruises 2 (of the face) very pale 3 *esp. spoken* very angry −~**ly** *adv*

¹**living** *adj* alive now

²**living** *n* earnings used to buy what is necessary to life: *to make a living in industry*

living room −also **sitting room** *n* the main room in a house where people can do things together, usu. apart from eating

lizard *n* any of several types of reptile, with a rough skin, 4 legs, and a long tail

¹**load** *n* 1 an amount being carried, or to be carried, esp. heavy 2 the amount which a certain vehicle can carry 3 the power of an electricity supply

²**load** *v* 1 to put a full load on or in (something) 2 to put a charge or film into (a gun or camera)

¹**loaf** *n* **loaves** 1 bread shaped and baked in one large piece 2 *sl* one's head and mind 3 food moulded in a solid piece: *meat loaf*

²**loaf** *v esp. spoken* to waste time, esp. by not working −~**er** *n*

¹**loan** *n* 1 something which is lent 2 an amount of money lent 3 the act of lending

277

²**loan** *v esp. US* to give (someone) the use of; lend

loath, loth *adj* unwilling

loathe *v* **loathed, loathing** to feel hatred or great dislike for – **-thing** *n*

loathsome *adj* which causes great dislike; very unpleasant –~**ly** *adv* –~**ness** *n*

¹**lobby** *n* **-bies** 1 a hall or passage, which leads from the entrance to the rooms inside a building 2 (in the House of Commons) one of 2 passages where members go to vote for or against something 3 a group of people who unite for or against an action, so that those in power will change their minds: *the clean air lobby*

²**lobby** *v* **-bied, -bying** 1 to meet (a member of parliament) in order to persuade him/her to support one's actions and needs 2 to be active in bringing about a change in the law in this way

lobster *n* 1 a type of 8-legged sea animal with a pair of powerful pincers the flesh of which can be eaten 2 the flesh of this as food

¹**local** *adj* 1 of or in a certain place, esp. the place one lives in 2 *technical* concerning only a particular part, esp. of the body: *a local infection*

²**local** *n esp. spoken* 1 a person who lives in the place he is in 2 a pub near where one lives, esp. which one often drinks at

locate *v* **located, locating** 1 to find or learn the position of 2 to fix or set in a certain place –~**d** *adj*

location *n* 1 a place or position 2 an appropriate place away from a film studio, where one or more scenes are made

¹**lock** *n* a small piece of hair

²**lock** *n* 1 an apparatus for closing and fastening something by means of a key 2 the part of a gun which fires it 3 a stretch of water closed off by gates so that the level can be raised or lowered to move boats up or down a slope 4 a hold which wrestlers may use to prevent the opponent from moving 5 (in a machine) the state of being stopped:*in the lock position* 6 the degree to which a steering wheel can be turned 7 **lock, stock, and barrel** completely

³**lock** *v* 1 to fasten with a lock 2 to put in a place and lock the entrance: *lock the car in the garage* 3 to become fixed or blocked: *I can't control the car; the wheels have locked* –~**able** *adj*

¹**locomotive** *adj technical* concerning or causing movement

²**locomotive** *n esp. written* a railway engine

locust *n* a type of insect of Asia and Africa like a grasshopper, which flies from place to place in large groups, often destroying crops

¹**lodge** *v* **lodged, lodging** 1 to stay, usu. for a short time and paying rent 2 to settle firmly in a position

3 to make (a statement) officially: *to lodge a complaint*

²**lodge** *n* **1** a small house near the entrance to a large house **2** a small house for hunters, sportsmen, etc., to stay in while crossing wild country **3** a room for a porter, as in a block of flats or a college **4** (the meeting place of) a local branch of freemasons **5** *technical* a beaver's home

lodger *n* a person who pays rent to stay in somebody's house

lodging *n* a place to stay

¹**loft** *n* **1** a room under the roof of a building; attic **2** a room over a stable, where hay is kept

²**loft** *v* (esp. in cricket and golf) to hit (a ball) high – ~**ed** *adj*

lofty *adj* -**ier**, -**iest 1 a** of unusually high quality of thinking, feeling, desires, etc. **b** showing belief of being better than other people **2** *poetic* high – -**ily** *adv* – -**iness** *n*

¹**log** *n* **1** a thick piece of wood from a tree **2** an official written record of a journey, as in a ship, plane, or car **3** an apparatus which measures the speed of a ship

²**log** *v* -**gg**- to record in a log

logarithm –also *esp. spoken* **log** *n* the power to which a given base, such as 10, must be raised to give a stated number: *The logarithm of 100 is 2 because 10² = 100* – ~**ic** *adj* – ~**ically** *adv*

logic *n* **1** the science of reasoning by formal methods **2** a way of reasoning – ~**al** *adj* – ~**ally** *adv*

loiter *v* to move about with frequent stops – ~**er** *n*

lone *adj* without (other) people

lonely *adj* -**lier**, -**liest 1** alone: *a lonely life in the country* **2** unhappy because of being alone or without friends **3** (of places) without people – -**liness** *n*

¹**long** *adj* **1 a** measuring a good deal from one end to the other **b** covering a great distance or time **2** covering a certain distance or time **3** which seems to last more than is wished

²**long** *adv* (for) a long time

³**long** *n* **1 before long** after a short period of time; soon **2 for long** for a long time

⁴**long** *v* to want very much – ~**ing** *n*, *adj* – ~**ingly** *adv*

longitude *n* the position on the earth east or west of a meridian, usu. measured, from Greenwich

long-playing record also **album, LP**– *n* a larger type of record which turns fairly slowly and plays for a long time (perhaps ¹/₂ an hour each side)

longwinded *adj* (of a person or a way of speaking) saying too much esp. slowly and dully – ~**ly** *adv* – ~**ness** *n*

¹**look** *v* **1** to give attention in seeing; use the eyes **2** to seem by expression or appearance

²**look** *n* **1** an act of looking **2** an expression, esp. in the eyes **3** an appearance

look after *v prep* to take care of (someone or something)

look forward to *v adv prep* to expect to feel pleasure in (something about to happen)

look into *v prep* to examine the meaning or causes of

lookout *n* **1** a future possibility **2** the act of keeping watch **3** a place to watch from **4** a person who keeps watch **5** **one's own lookout** a state of affairs one must take care of for oneself, without others' help **6** **on the lookout for** searching for

look out *v adv* **1** to take care **2** to keep watching (for) **3** to choose from one's possessions: *to look out a party dress*

¹loom *n* a frame or machine for weaving thread into cloth

²loom *v* **1-** to come into sight without a clear form, esp. in a fearsome and unfriendly way **2** to appear great and very worrying in the mind

¹loop *n* **1** the shape made by a piece of string, wire, rope, etc., when curved back on itself **2** something having this shape, esp. one used as a handle or fastening: *Carry the parcel by this loop of string* **3** a piece of loop–shaped metal or plastic fitted inside a woman to prevent her from having children **4** a circular path made by an aircraft in flight **5** a set of commands in a computer program that are repeated until a certain condition is met

²loop *v* **1** to make, make into, or form a loop or loops **2** to pass through a loop, esp. in order to fasten: *Loop that end of the rope through this and knot it* **3** to fasten with a loop of string, rope, etc.

loophole *n* **1** a way of escaping or avoiding something, esp. one provided by a rule or agreement written without enough care **2** a small opening in a castle wall, esp. for shooting arrows through

¹loose *adj* **1** not tied up, shut up, etc.; free from control **2** not bound together, as with string or in a box **3** not firmly fixed; not tight **4** (of clothes) not fitting tightly, esp. because too big **5** made of parts that are not tight together **6** not exact **7** having many sexual adventures: *a loose woman* **8** not well controlled: *She has a loose tongue and will tell everybody* **9** careless, awkward, or not exact: *Loose play lost them the match* **10** (of the bowels) allowing waste matter to flow naturally, or more than is natural **11** not given a fixed purpose **12** **at a loose end** having nothing to do — ~**ly** *adv* — ~**ness** *n*

²loose *v* **loosed, loosing** **1** to let loose; untie; make free **2** **a** to cause (an arrow) to fly **b** to fire (a gun, weapon, etc.) **3** to free from control

³loose *adv* in a loose manner; loosely

⁴loose *n* **on the loose** free, esp. having freedom from the control of the law or freedom to enjoy oneself

loosen *v* **1** to make or become less firm, fixed, tight, etc. **2** to make or become less controlled or more easy and free in movement **3** to set free; unfasten

¹loot *n* goods taken away unlawfully, as by invading soldiers or by thieves

²loot *v* to take loot (from) —~**er** *n*

¹lord *n* **1** a man who rules people; ruler; master **2** a nobleman of high rank **3** a powerful person in a particular industry **4 as drunk as a lord** very drunk

²lord *v* **lord it** (**over someone**) to behave like a lord (to someone), esp. in giving orders

lorry —also **truck** *n* **-ries** a large motor vehicle for carrying goods

lose *v* **lost, losing 1** to come to be without, as through carelessness; fail to find **2** to fail to win, gain, or obtain **3** to cause the loss of **4** to come or cause to come to be without (money) **5** to have less of **6** to have taken away or cease to possess, as through death, destruction, ruin, or time: *She lost her parents recently* **7** to free oneself from: *to lose one's fear of water* **8** to fail to hear, see, or understand: *His voice was soft and I lost some of his words* **9** to fail to use; waste: *The doctor lost no time in getting the sick man to hospital* **10** to fail to keep: *I've lost interest in that subject* **11** to be too late for; miss: *We just lost the train* **12** to give all one's attention to something so as not to notice anything else: *He lost himself in the book* **13** (of a watch or clock) to work too slowly by (an amount of time) **14** to cause (oneself) to miss the way

loss *n* **1** the act or fact of losing possession **2** the harm, pain, damage, etc., caused by losing something **3** a failure to keep or use **4** a failure to win or obtain **5** a person, thing, or amount that is destroyed or taken away **6** a failure to make a profit **7 at a loss a** at a price lower than the original cost **b** unable or uncertain what to do, think, or say; confused

lost *adj* **1** no longer possessed **2** that cannot be found **3** unable to find the way **4** not used, obtained, or won **5** destroyed, ruined, killed, drowned, etc.: *Sailors lost at sea* **6 a** no longer belonging to: *My son was lost to me when he married* **b** no longer possible for (somebody) **c** not noticing: *He was lost to the world in this task* **7** having no influence on

¹lot *n* **1** a great quantity, number, or amount **2** the whole quantity, number, or amount: *Give me the lot* **3** a group of people or things of the same type; amount of a substance or material **4 a lot/lots** much; a great deal

²lot *n* **1** an article or a number of articles sold together **2** a building (and its grounds) where films are made **3** *sl* person; character: *He was always a bad lot* **4** one of several objects used for coming to a decision by chance **5** the use of such objects to make a choice or decision: *decide by drawing lots* **6** the decision or choice made in this way: *The lot fell to/on me* **7** share **8** one's way of life; fortune; fate

lottery *n* **-ries 1** an arrangement in which people buy tickets, a few of which are picked by chance to win prizes **2** something whose result or worth is uncertain or risky

¹loud *adj* **1** being or producing much sound; not quiet; noisy **2** attracting attention by being unpleasantly noisy or colourful –~**ly** *adv* –~**ness** *n*

²loud *adv* loudly; in a loud way

loudspeaker –also **speaker** *n* an apparatus that turns electrical current into sound

¹lounge *v* **lounged, lounging 1** to stand or sit in a leaning lazy manner **2** to pass time in a lazy manner, doing nothing –~**r** *n*

²lounge *n* **1** an act or period of lounging **2** a comfortable sitting room in a house or hotel

lour –also **lower** *v* **1** to look in a dissatisfied bad-tempered manner; to frown **2** (of the sky or weather) to be dark and threatening

¹love *n* **1** a strong feeling of fondness for another person **2** warm interest and enjoyment and attraction (to): *love of music* **3** the object of such interest and attraction **4** a person who is loved also (*bad usage or humour*) **luv**– (a friendly word of address) **6** *esp. spoken* a person or thing that one loves or likes very much: *Isn't that puppy a love!* **7**

(in tennis) the state of having no points **8** **no love lost between** no friendship between

²love *v* **loved, loving 1** to feel love, desire, or strong friendship (for) **2** to have a strong liking for; take pleasure in **3** to have sex with

lovely *adj* **-lier, -liest 1** beautiful, attractive, etc., esp. to both the heart and the eye **2** *esp. spoken* very pleasant: *a lovely meal* – **-liness** *n*

lover *n* **1** a man in love with or having a sexual relationship with a woman outside of marriage **2** a person who is very keen on something

¹low *v* *esp. in literature* to moo

²low *adj* **1** not measuring much from the base to the top; not high **2** being not far above the ground, floor, base, or bottom **3** being or lying below the general level of height **4** being near or at the bottom of a supply or measure **5** on the ground, as after a blow, or dead: *I laid him low with my gun* **6** lacking in strength; weak: *He is low with flu* **7** lacking spirit; unhappy **8** small in size, degree, amount, worth, etc. **9** regarding something as of little worth; unfavourable: *I have a low opinion of that book* **10** near the bottom in position or rank **11** not worthy, respectable, good, etc. **12** cheap: *a low price* **13** for a slow or slowest speed: *Use a low gear when driving slowly* **14** hidden; unnoticed: *The escaped prisoner lay low* **15** not greatly developed; simple:

low plant life **16** not loud; soft – ~**ness** *n*

³**low** *adv* **1** in or to a low position, point, degree, manner, etc. **2** near the ground, floor, base, etc.; not high **3** (in music) in or with deep notes **4** quietly; softly **5 run low** to become less than enough

⁴**low** *n* **1** a point, price, degree, etc., that is low **2** an area of low pressure in the air

¹**lower** *v* to lour

²**lower** *adj* in or being the bottom part

³**lower** *v* **1** to make or become smaller in amount, price, degree, strength, etc. **2** to move or let down in height **3** to bring (someone, esp. oneself) down in rank, worth, or opinion, as by doing something not worthy or wrong; to disgrace

¹**lowly** *adv* **1** in a low position, manner, or degree **2** in a manner that is not proud

²**lowly** *adj* **-lier, -liest 1** low in rank, position, or degree **2** not grand or proud; simple; humble – **-liness** *n*

loyal *adj* true to one's friends, group, country, etc.; faithful – ~**ly** *adv*

loyalty *n* **-ties 1** the quality of being loyal **2** a connection which binds a person to someone or something to which he is loyal

Ltd *abbrev. (used after the name of a limited liability company) for:* limited: *M.Y. Dixon and Son, Ltd, Booksellers*

lubricate *v* **-cated, -cating 1** to put oil or an oily substance into (the moving parts of a machine) to make

them work more easily **2** to make smooth and able to move or be moved easily – **-cation** *n* – **-cator** *n*

luck *n* **1** that which happens, either good or bad, to a person in the course of events by, or as if by, chance; fate; fortune **2** success as a result of chance; good fortune **3 be down on one's luck** to have bad luck, esp. to be without money **4 worse luck** unfortunately

lucky *adj* **-ier, -iest** having, resulting from, or bringing good luck – **-kily** *adv* – **-kiness** *n*

luggage *n* the cases and bags of a traveller

lukewarm *adj* **1** (esp. of liquid) not much hotter than cold **2** showing hardly any interest; not eager

lullaby *n* **-bies** a song to help children go to sleep

¹**lumber** *v* to move awkwardly

²**lumber** *n* **1** useless or unwanted articles, such as furniture, stored away somewhere **2** *esp. US* timber

³**lumber** *v* *esp. spoken* to cause difficulty to (someone), esp. by giving unwanted responsibility: *I'm lumbered with Mary's puppy for the weekend*

luminous *adj* **1** giving light; bright **2** easily understood; clear – ~**ly** *adv* – **-nosity** *n*

¹**lump** *n* **1** a mass of something solid without a special size or shape **2** a hard swelling on the body **3** *esp. spoken* a heavy awkward person **4** a small square-sided block (of sugar) **5** *esp. spoken* the group of workers

in the building industry who are not employed on a continuous contract, but only as and when needed **6 lump in the throat** a tight sensation in the throat caused by unexpressed pity, sorrow, etc.

²**lump** *v* to form into lumps

³**lump** *adj* **1** not divided into parts; all together **2** being in the form of lumps

⁴**lump** *v* **lump it** *esp. spoken* to accept bad conditions without complaint (often in the phrase **like it or lump it**)

¹**lunatic** *n* **1** *old use or offensive* a person suffering from an illness of the mind **2** a wildly foolish person

²**lunatic** *adj* wildly foolish

¹**lunch** –also (*esp. written*) **luncheon** *n* a meal eaten at midday

²**lunch** *v* to eat lunch

lung *n* either of the 2 breathing organs in the chest of man or certain other creatures (mammals, birds, reptiles, and some others)

lurk *v* **1** to wait in hiding, esp. for an evil purpose **2** to move quietly as if having done wrong and not wanting to be seen **3** to exist unseen

lush *adj* **1** (of plants, esp. grass) growing very well, thickly, and healthily **2** *esp. spoken* comfortable, esp. as provided by wealth

lust *n* **1** strong sexual desire, esp. when uncontrolled or considered wrong **2** strong usu. evil desire; eagerness to possess: *lust for power*

luxury *n* **-ries 1** great comfort, as provided without worry about the cost **2** something that is not necessary and not often had or done but which is very pleasant

lying *pres. part. of* LIE

lynch *v* (esp. of a crowd of people) to attack and put to death, esp. by hanging, (a person thought to be guilty of a crime), without a lawful trial

macaroni *n* a food made of thin tubes of pasta

¹**machine** *n* **1** a man-made instrument or apparatus which uses power (such as electricity) to perform work **2** a group of people that controls the activities of a political party

²**machine** *v* **machined, machining 1** to make or produce by machine, esp. in sewing and printing **2** to produce according to exact measurements by use of a cutting machine: *The edge must be machined down to 0·03 millimetres*

machinery *n* **1** machines in general **2** the working parts of an apparatus **3** a system or organization by which action is controlled

mackintosh –also (*esp. spoken*) **mack, mac** *n* a raincoat

mad *adj* **-dd- 1-** suffering from a disorder of the mind **2** (of a dog) suffering from a disease (rabies) which causes wild and dangerous behaviour **3** very foolish and careless of danger **4** filled with strong feeling, interest, etc. **5** *esp. spoken* angry **6 like mad** *esp. spoken* very hard, fast, loud, etc.

madam *n* 1 (a respectful way of addressing a woman) 2 a (young) female who likes to give orders: *She's a little madam, she won't do anything I suggest* 3 a woman who is in charge of a house of prostitutes

maddening *adj* 1 causing much pain or worry 2 *esp. spoken* very annoying – ~ly *adv*

¹**made** *past tense and past part. of* MAKE

²**made** *adj* 1 sure of success: *When you find gold you're made for life* completely suited: *a night made for love*

madly *adv* 1 in a wild way as if mad 2 *esp. spoken* very (much)

madness *n* 1 the state of being mad 2 behaviour that appears mad

magazine *n* 1 a sort of book with a paper cover and usu. large-sized pages, which contains writing, photographs, and advertisements, and which is sold every week or month 2 a storehouse or room for arms, explosives, bullets, etc. 3 the part of a gun, or similar weapon, in which ammunition is placed before firing 4 the place where the film is kept away from the light in a camera

¹**magic** *n* 1 the system of trying to control events by calling on spirits, secret forces, etc. 2 *technical* the system of thought which imagines that images or parts of objects have a power over the objects themselves 3 the art employed by a conjurer who produces unexpected results by tricks 4 a a strange influence or power b a charming and/or mysterious quality

²**magic** *adj* caused by or used in magic

magical *adj* of strange power, mystery, or charm – ~ly *adv*

magician *n* 1 (in stories) a person who can make strange things happen by magic 2 a person who does magic tricks; conjurer

magistrate *n* an official who has the power to judge cases in the lowest courts of law – -acy *n*

magnet *n* 1 any object which can draw iron towards it either naturally or because of an electric current being passed through it 2 a person or thing which draws or attracts (people) – ~ic *adj* – ~ically *adv* – ~ism *n*

magnificent *adj* great, grand, generous, etc. – -cence *n* – ~ly *adv*

magnify *v* -fied, -fying to make (something) appear larger than in reality – -fier *n*

magnifying glass *n* a glass lens, with a frame and handle, which makes what is seen through it look bigger

magpie *n* a type of noisy black and white bird of the crow family which often takes small bright objects

maid –also **maidservant** *n* 1 a female servant 2 *literature & old use* an unmarried girl

¹**maiden** *n* 1 *literature* an unmarried girl 2 also **maiden over–** (in cricket) an over in which no runs are made

²**maiden** *adj* 1 fresh; not used before 2 first; not done before: *the maiden*

flight of an aircraft **3** (of a woman) unmarried: *a maiden aunt*

maiden name *n* the family name a woman has before marriage

¹**mail** *n* **1** the postal system directed and worked by the government **2** letters and anything else sent or received by post, esp. those travelling or arriving together **3** also **mail train–** (esp. in names) a train which carries mail: *the Irish Mail*

²**mail** *v esp. US* to post

³**mail** *n* armour made of metal plates or rings

mailbag *n* a bag made of strong cloth for carrying mail in trains, ships, etc.

mail order *n* a method of selling goods in which the buyer chooses them from a catalogue at home and his order is posted to him

¹**main** *n* **1 a** a chief pipe supplying water or gas, or a chief wire carrying electricity into a building: *a gas main* **2** *poetic* the sea **3 in the main** on the whole; usually; mostly

²**main** *adj* **1** chief; first in importance or size **2 by main force** *esp. literature* by all the strength of the body

mainland *n* a land mass, considered without its islands

mainstream *n* the usual way of thinking or acting in a subject

maintain *v* **1** to continue to have, do, etc., as before **2** to support with money **3** to keep in existence **4** to keep in good condition, by repairing and taking care of **5** to state as true; argue for (an opinion) – ~**able** *adj*

maintenance *n* **1** the act of maintaining **2** money given to wives and/or children by a husband who does not live with them

maize *n* American corn

majesty *n* greatness; a show of power, as of a king or queen – **-tic** *adj* – -**tically** *adv*

Majesty *n* **-ties** (a title for addressing or speaking of a king or queen)

¹**major** *adj* **1** greater in degree, size, etc. **2** *old public school* being the elder of 2 brothers of the stated name in the same school: *Brown major* **3** (in music) based on or being a scale with 4 semitones between the first and third notes **4** (of an operation) more than usually risky

²**major** *n* **1** a middle ranking officer in the army or American airforce **2** *esp. written & law* a person who has reached the age (now 18 in Britain) at which he is fully responsible in law for his actions

¹**majority** *n* **-ties 1** the greater number or part; a number or part that is more than half **2** the difference in number between a large and smaller group (e.g. of votes) **3** *law* the state or time when one has, in law, reached the grown–up state **4 in the majority** (one of) the greater number of people or things

²**majority** *adj* reached by agreement of most, but not all, of the members of a group

¹**make** *v* **made, making 1** to produce by work or action **2** to tidy (a bed that has just been slept in) **3** to put into a certain state, position, etc.: *Too much food made him ill* **4** to earn, gain, or win: *He makes a lot of money in his job* **5** to force or cause (a person to do something/a thing to happen): *The pain made him cry out* **6** to represent as being, doing, happening, etc.; cause to appear as: *This photograph makes her look very young* **7** to calculate (and get as a result): *What time do you make it?* **8** to add up to; come to (an amount) as a result: *2 and 2 make 4* **9** to be counted as (first, second, etc.) **10** to have the qualities of: *This story makes good reading* **11** to travel (a distance) or at (a speed): *The train was making 70 miles an hour* **12** to arrive at or on: *We just made the train* **13** to form (into or from): *The navy has made a man of him* **14** to put forward for consideration or acceptance (a suggestion of payment or a gift): *Let me make you a present of it* **15** *esp. written* to be about (to): *He made to speak, but I stopped him* **16** *esp. spoken* to give the particular qualities of; complete: *It's the bright paint which really makes the room* **17 make as if to** to be about to: *He made as if to speak* **18 make believe** to pretend **19 make it a** to arrive in time **b** *esp. spoken* to succeed **20 make love (to) a** to have sex (with) **b** *esp. old use* to show that one is in love (with) **21 make one's way** to go **22 make or mar/break** which will cause success or complete failure: *a make or break decision/plan*

²**make** *n* **1** the type to which a set of (man-made) objects belongs, esp. the name of the makers **2 on the make** *sl* **a** searching for personal profit or gain **b** trying to obtain a sexual experience with someone

make out *v adv* **1** to see or understand with difficulty **2** to write in complete form: *to make out a list* **3** *esp. spoken* to succeed (in business or life generally) **4** to have a (esp. friendly) relationship: *How did you make out with your new employer?* **5** *esp. spoken* to claim or pretend (that someone or something is so), usu. falsely: *He makes out he's younger than me* **6** to argue as proof: *I'm sure we can make out a case for allowing you another holiday*

maker *n* **1** one of the people (esp. a firm) who make something **2** God: *The old man died and went to meet his Maker*

makeshift *adj* used at the time because there is nothing better

make-up *n* **1** the combination of qualities (in a person's character) **2 a** powder, paint, etc., worn on the face **b** an appearance produced by the use of this **c** the art of using this to prepare the face for working under bright lights on stage

make up *v adv* **1** to become friends again after (a quarrel) **2** to use special paint and powder on the face of (someone or oneself) so as to change or improve the appearance **3** to invent (a story, poem, etc.), esp. in order to deceive **4** to prepare (a drug), esp. according to a doctor's note **5** to make (an amount or number) complete **6** to produce (something) from (material) by cutting and sewing **7** to arrange ready for use: *make up a bed*

malady *n* **-dies** *esp. written* **1** something that is wrong with a system or organization **2** *old use* an illness

¹**male** *adj* **1** of the sex that does not give birth to young **2** suitable to or typical of this sex, rather than the female sex **3** (of a part of a machine) made to fit into a hollow part

²**male** *n* a male person or animal

malice *n* **1** the wish, desire, or intention to hurt **2 with malice aforethought** *law* (of a criminal act) planned before it was done

malicious *adj* feeling or expressing malice −~**ly** *adv*

malt *n* grain, usu. barley, which has been kept in water for a while, then dried, and is used for preparing drinks, like beer

mammal *n* an animal which is fed when young on milk from the mother's body

¹**mammoth** *n* a kind of hairy elephant, larger than the modern one, which lived on earth during the early stages of human development

²**mammoth** *adj* very big

¹**man** *n* **men 1** a fully-grown human

male **2** a human being **3 a** men in general: *Man is taller than woman* **b** the human race: *Man lives in a changing world* **4 a** a husband: *They had been man and wife for 50 years* **b** *esp. spoken* a husband or lover : *waiting for her man to come out of prison* **5** a fully-grown working male or a soldier of low rank: *He is in charge of several men at work* **6** a male person with courage, firmness, etc.: *The army will make a man of you* **7** the right male person: *Here's the man for the job* **8** any of the objects moved in a board game **9 as one man** with the agreement of everyone **10 man about town** a (rich) man who spends all his time at social gatherings, in clubs etc. **11 the man in the street** the average person, who represents general opinion **12 man of God** a priest **13 man of my/your/his word** a keeper of promises **14 man of the world** a man of wide experience −~**like** *adj* −~**ly** *adj*: *The boy walked with a manly stride* −~**liness** *n*

²**man** *v* **-nn-** to provide with people for operation: *Man the guns*

manage *v* **-aged, -aging 1 a** to control (esp. a business) **b** to deal with or guide, esp. skilfully **2** to succeed in dealing with (a difficult movement or action) **3** to succeed in living, esp. on a small amount of money **4** *esp. spoken* to succeed in taking or using: *I can't manage another mouthful*

management *n* **1** the act of managing

esp. a business or money **2** skill in dealing with (usu.) a person (esp. in the phrase **more by luck than management**) **3** the people in charge of a firm, industry, etc., considered as one body

manager *n* **1** (*fem.* **manageress**) a man who controls a business **2** a person who makes arrangements: *She had to be a good manager to live on so little money*

mane *n* the long hair on the back of a horse's neck, or around a lion's face

¹**mangle** *v* **-gled, -gling** to tear to pieces; crush

²**mangle** *n* a machine with rollers which presses water from clothes, sheets, etc.

manhood *n* **1** the condition or period of time of being a man **2** the good qualities of a man, such as courage **3** the sexual powers of a man

mania *n* **1** a very forceful disorder of the mind **2** a desire so strong that it seems mad: *a mania for fast cars* **3** a strong unreasonable desire

maniac *n* **1** a person (thought to be) suffering from mania of some kind: *a sex maniac* **2** a wild thoughtless person – ~**al** *adj* – ~**ally** *adv*

manifesto *n* **-tos** *or* **-toes** a (written) statement making public the intentions of a group of people, esp. of a political party: *the Labour party manifesto*

manipulate *v* **-lated, -lating** **1** to handle (esp. a machine), usu. skilfully **2** to use (someone) for one's own purpose by skilfully influencing, often unfairly or dishonestly – **-lative** *adj* – **-lation** *n*

mankind *n* the human race, both men and women

manner *n* **1** *esp. written* the way in which anything is done or happens **2** a personal way of behaving towards other people: *a very rude manner* **3** a way or style of writing, painting, building, etc., typical of one or more persons, of a country, or of a time in history **4 all manner of** every sort of **5 in a manner of speaking** if one may express it this way **6 not by any manner of means** not at all

manners *n* **1** (polite) social practices or habits: *table manners* **2** social behaviour; ways of living (esp. of a nation): *the manners and customs of the ancient Egyptians*

¹**manoeuvre** *n* **1** the planned moving of (part of) an army or of warships; a set of such moves for training purposes **2** a skilful move or clever trick, intended to deceive, to gain something, etc.

²**manoeuvre** *v* **-vred, -vring** **1 a** to cause (a soldier or ship) to perform one or more manoeuvres **b** (of a soldier or ship) to perform one or more manoeuvres **2** to move (to a position) esp. skilfully: *It was difficult to manoeuvre the table into the room* – **-vrer** *n*

manslaughter *n* *law* the crime of killing a person, unlawfully but not intentionally

mantelpiece *n* a frame around a fireplace, esp. the part on top (**mantelshelf**) where one can put ornaments

¹**manual** *adj* of or using the hands −∼**ly** *adv*

²**manual** *n* a (small) book giving information about something

¹**manufacture** *n* the act of manufacturing

²**manufacture** *v* **-tured, -turing 1** to make by machinery, esp. in large quantities **2** to invent (an untrue story, reason, etc.) −∼**r** *n*

¹**manure** *n* animal waste which is put on the land to improve the crops

²**manure** *v* **manured, manuring** to put manure on

manuscript *n* **1** the first or only copy of a book or piece of writing, esp. written by hand **2** a handwritten book, of the time before printing was invented

many *adj, pron, n* −see MORE, MOST **1** a great number (of): *Were there many people at the play?* **2 in so many words** in exactly those words **3 many's the time, day, etc., (that)** there have been many times, days, etc., (that) **4 one too many for (someone)** clever enough to beat (someone)

¹**map** *n* **1** a representation of the earth's surface , showing the shape of countries, the position of towns, the height of land, etc. **2** a plan of the stars in the sky or of the surface of the moon or a planet **3** a representation showing the position or state of anything **4 (put something)**

on the map *esp. spoken* (to cause something to be) considered important

²**map** *v* **-pp- 1** to make a map of **2** *technical* to represent the pattern of (something) on something else

marathon *n* **1** a running race of about 26 miles, esp. at the Olympic Games **2** any prolonged activity that tests one's power

marble *n* **1** a hard limestone used for building, sculpture, gravestones, etc. and usu. showing an irregular colouring **2** *literature* **a** a smooth and white quality **b** a hard and cold quality **3** a small hard ball of glass used by children in the game of marbles

¹**march** *v* **1** to walk with a regular step like a soldier **2** to force to walk (away): *The mother marched her child up to bed* −∼**er** *n*

²**march** *n* **1** the act of marching **2** the distance covered while marching: *It was a day's march from the city to the camp* **3** regular movement forward **4** a piece of music played in regular time that can be marched to **5** marching by a large number of people to make ideas or dissatisfactions public: *a hunger march* **6 on the march a** moving forward **b** moving ahead and improving: *Science is on the march* **7 steal a march on (someone)** to gain advantage over (someone) by acting quickly

March *n* the third month of the year

mare *n* a female horse

margarine –also *esp. spoken* **marge** *n* a food prepared from animal and/or vegetable fats used instead of butter

margin *n* 1 one or both sides of a page near the edge, where there is no writing or printing 2 the area on the outside edge of a larger area: *the margin of the stream* 3 an amount above what is necessary, esp. for success 4 (in business) the difference between the buying and selling price

¹**marine** *adj* 1 of, near, living in, found in, or obtained from the sea 2 of ships and their goods and trade at sea, esp. concerning the navy

²**marine** *n* 1 the ships of a country which carry goods or travellers (only in the phrases **merchant/mercantile marine**) 2 a soldier who serves on a naval ship or in the navy

mariner *n technical* or *poetic* a sailor or seaman

marital *adj* of or concerning (the duties of) marriage –~**ly** *adv*

¹**mark** *n* 1 a spot, line, or cut that spoils the natural colour or appearance of something 2 an object or sign serving as a guide 3 an action or sign showing a feeling, quality, or condition: *a mark of respect* 4 a spot on the face or body by which a person or animal can be recognized 5 a figure or printed or written sign which shows something 6 a figure, letter, or sign which represents a judgment of quality in another's piece of work,

behaviour, performance in a competition, etc. 7 the object or place one aims at 8 the suitable level of quality (in the phrases **up to/below the mark**) the starting place, esp. for a race: *The runners were all quick off the mark* 10 a sign, usu. a cross, made by a person who cannot write his name 11- (esp. with numbers) a particular type of a machine: *The Mark 4 gun is stronger than the old Mark 3* 12 (**give someone**) **full marks** (**for** (**doing**) **something**) to admire (an action or quality) 13 (**fall**) **wide of the mark a** (to be) far from the subject **b** (to be) far from being correct 14 **make one's mark** (**on**) to gain success, fame, etc., (in) by showing one's best qualities 15 **not** (**quite**) **up to the mark** not (very) well (in health) 16 **On your marks, get set, go!** (used for starting a race)

²**mark** *v* 1 to make a mark on, esp. one that spoils the appearance 2 to receive an unwanted mark, causing a spoiled appearance 3 to show (by position) 4 to cover with marks, esp. on the body 5 **a** to give a mark of quality: *He marked the work 10 out of 10* **b** to record the presence, absence, etc., of 6 to show (the qualities of): *She has the qualities that mark a good nurse* 7 (in football, hockey and such games) to stay in close attention on (an opponent) 8 to pay attention to 9 to be a sign of 10 **mark time a** to make the movements of marching while remaining in the same place

b to spend time on work, business, etc., without advancing

¹market *n* **1** a building, square, or open place for buying and selling goods **2** a gathering of people to buy and sell on certain days at such a place: *market day* **3** an area, country, or countries, where there is a demand for goods: *a world market* **4** demand for goods: *There's no market for hot ice cream* **5** (the state of) trade in certain goods, esp. the rate of buying and selling: *There's great activity in the tea market* **6 in the market (for)** ready to buy **7 on the market** (of goods) for sale **8 play the market** to buy and sell business shares to try to make a profit

²market *v* to offer for sale – ~**able** *adj* – ~**ability** *n* – ~**er** *n*

market place *n* **1** an open area where a market is held **2** the place where goods are sold to the public (as opposed to where they are made, sent out, etc.)

market research *n* the study of what people buy and why, usu. done by firms to try to increase sales

marksman –(*fem.* **markswoman**) *n* -**men** a person who can hit the right mark easily, usu. with a gun – ~**ship** *n*

marmalade *n* a type of jam usu. made from oranges

¹maroon *n* (in former times) a slave of black West Indian origin, who has run away from his master

²maroon *v* **1** to put (someone) off a ship in a deserted place **2** to leave (one or more people) alone, with no means of getting away

³maroon *n, adj* (of) a very dark red-brown colour

marriage *n* **1** the union of a man and woman by a ceremony in law **2** the state of being so united

married *adj* **1** having a husband or wife **2** having as or like a husband/wife: *He's married to his work* **3** of the state of marriage

marrow *n* **1** the soft fatty substance in the centre of bones **2** the most important and necessary part **3** also **vegetable marrow**– a type of dark green vegetable which can grow very big

marry *v* -**ried**, -**rying 1** to take (a person) in marriage **2** (of a priest or official) to perform the ceremony of marriage for (2 people) **3** to cause to take in marriage

marsh *n* (a piece of) land that is all or partly soft and wet, because of its low position

martial *adj* of or concerning war, soldiers, etc. – ~**ly** *adv*

¹martyr *n* **1** a person who dies or suffers for his beliefs **2** *esp. spoken* a person who gives up his own wishes or chance of gain or who accepts something unpleasant in order to please others: *John likes to make a martyr of himself*

²martyr *v* to put to death, or cause to suffer greatly, for a belief

¹marvel *n* **1** a wonder; wonderful thing or example **2** *esp. spoken* a person or thing that causes surprise: *You're a marvel to work so hard at your age*

²**marvel** *v* -ll- to wonder; feel great surprise

marvellous *adj* wonderful, esp. because surprisingly good −~**ly** *adv*

mascot *n* an object, animal, or person thought to bring good fortune

¹**masculine** *adj* **1** of or having the qualities suitable for a man **2** (in grammar) in a class of words that are not feminine or neuter: *'He' is a masculine pronoun*

²**masculine** *n* the class of masculine words

¹**mask** *n* **1** a covering for (part of) the face which hides or protects it **2** a covering like a face, often of paper, as worn by some actors and in some tribal religious and magical ceremonies **3** an appearance which hides the truth or reality; any form of pretending: *a mask of loyalty* −~**ed** *adj*

²**mask** *v* **1** to cover with a mask **2** to hide (esp. feelings)

¹**masquerade** *n* **1** a masked ball **2** something pretended; hiding of the truth

²**masquerade** *v* -raded, -rading to pretend (to be) − -**rader** *n*

¹**mass** *n* a piece of music written specially for all the main parts of the Mass

²**mass** *n* **1** a quantity or heap (of matter) **2** *esp. spoken* a large number (of people or things) **3** (in science)

the amount of matter in a body, measured by the power used in changing its movement

³**mass** *v* to gather together in large numbers

⁴**mass** *adj* of or for a mass, esp. of people: *a mass murderer*

Mass *n* (used in the Catholic and Orthodox churches) the Eucharist

massacre *v* -cred, -cring **1** to kill (a number of people) without mercy **2** *esp. spoken* to defeat severely −**massacre** *n*

massage *v* -saged, -saging to treat (a person's body) by pressing and rubbing to take away pain or stiffness −**massage** *n*

massive *adj* **1** of great size; strong and heavy **2** (of qualities and actions) great; powerful −~**ly** *adv* −~**ness** *n*

mass media *n* the modern means of giving news and opinions to large numbers of people, esp. radio and television

mass-produce *v* -duced, -ducing to produce (goods) in large numbers to the same pattern − -**duction** *n*

mast *n* **1** a long upright pole for carrying flags or sails on a ship **2** an upright metal framework for radio and television aerials

¹**master** *n* **1** a man in control of people, animals, or things **2** (*fem.* **mistress**)− a man who is the head of a house and family **3** also **master mariner**− a man who commands a ship carrying goods or people, or a large fishing boat **4** (*fem.* **mistress**)−

esp. written and old use a male teacher **5** a man who employs workmen or servants **6** a skilled workman with his own business: *a master builder* **7** a man of great skill in art or work with the hands

²**master** *adj* chief; most important: *the master bedroom*

³**master** *v* **1** to gain control over **2** to gain as a skill

masterpiece –also **masterwork** *n* a piece of work, esp. art, which is the best of its type or the best a person has done

¹**mat** *n* **1** a piece of rough strong material used for covering part of a floor **2** a very small rug or piece of carpet **3** a small piece of material used for putting under objects on furniture **4** a knotted mass, esp. of hair

²**mat** *v* **-tt-** to (cause to) become knotted in a thick mass: *matted hair*

³**mat** also **matt** *adj* of a dull, not shiny, surface: *mat paint*

¹**match** *n* **1** a person who is equal in strength, ability, etc., (to another) **2 a** something like or suitable to something else: *We can't find a match for this ornament* **b** a number of things suitable together: *The hat and shoes are a perfect match* **3** *esp. old use* **a** a person considered as a possible husband or wife **b** a marriage **4** a game or sports event where teams or people compete

²**match** *v* **1 a** to be equal to (a person) (in a quality): *You can't match him in good looks* **b** to find an equal

for: *This hotel can't be matched for friendliness* **2** to be like or suitable for use with (something else) **3** to find something like or suitable for use with **4** to cause to compete (with)

³**match** *n* a short thin stick with a head covered by chemicals which catch fire when rubbed or struck against a rough surface

¹**mate** *n* **1** a fellow workman or friend **2** (not in the navy) a ship's officer in command after the captain **3** a helper to a skilled workman: *a builder's mate* **4** one of a male–female pair, usu. of animals

²**mate** *v* **mated, mating** to form (into) a pair, esp. of animals, for sexual union: *Birds mate in the spring*

¹**material** *adj* **1 a** of or concerning matter or substance, not spirit: *The storm did a great deal of material damage* **b** of the body, rather than the mind or soul: *She's too poor to satisfy her family's material needs* **2** important and necessary: *We must make a material change in our plans* **3** *law* concerning information necessary for a just decision: *material evidence* –~**ly** *adv*

²**material** *n* **1** anything from which something is or may be made **2** woven cloth from which clothes may be made **3** knowledge of facts from which action may be taken or a (written) work may be produced: *collecting material for a book* **4** people considered for what they may become after training or devel-

opment: *no officer material among these recruits*

mathematics –also (*esp. spoken*) **maths** *n* the study or science of numbers – **-ical** *adj* – **-ically** *adv* – **-ician** *n*

matron *n* **1** (the title of) a woman in charge of a hospital who has control over the work of all the nurses and other staff, but not over doctors (now officially called a **senior nursing officer**) **2** (the title of) a woman who is in charge of domestic and medical arrangements for children to live in a school **3** *esp. literature or old use* an older married woman, esp. one of quiet careful behaviour

¹**matter** *n* **1** the material which makes up the world and everything in space which can be seen or touched, as opposed to thought or mind **2** a subject itself as opposed to the form in which it is spoken or written about: *subject matter* **3** a (business) affair; subject to which one gives attention **4** a trouble or cause of pain, illness, etc. **5** written material: *reading matter*

²**matter** *v* to be important: *It doesn't matter if I miss my train; technical* to form and give out pus

mattress *n* a large bag, usu. filled with wool, hair, feathers, rubber, or metal springs, on which one sleeps

¹**mature** *adj* **1 a** fully grown and developed **b** typical of a fully developed mind, controlled feelings, etc.; sensible **2** (of cheese, wine, etc.) ready to be eaten or drunk; ripe **3** carefully decided –~**ly** *adv*

²**mature** *v* **matured, maturing** to become or cause to become mature – **-ration** *n*

mauve *adj, n* (of) a pale purple colour

maximum *n, adj* **-ma** *or* **-mums** (being) the largest number, amount, etc.: *He smokes a maximum of 10 cigarettes a day*

may *v negative short form* **mayn't 1** to be in some degree likely to: *He may come or he may not* **2** to have permission to: *May I come in?* **3** I/we hope very much that: *May there never be another world war!* **4** (*expressing purpose*) can: *Sit here, so that I may see your face more clearly* **5 may as well** to have no strong reason not to: *There's nothing on TV, so you may as well switch it off*

May *n* **Mays** the 5th month of the year

maybe *adv* perhaps: *'Will they come?' 'Maybe not'*

mayor *n* the chief person of a city or town –~**al** *adj*

mayoress *n* the wife or chosen companion of a male mayor, or a lady who is a companion to a woman mayor and is present with her at ceremonial occasions

maze *n* an arrangement in lines with a central point reached by twists and turns, some of them blocked, so that it is difficult to get into the centre and out again

me *pron* (*object form of* I): *He bought*

me a drink. / That's me on the left of the photograph

meadow *n* **1** grassland on which cattle, sheep, etc., may feed **2** a field of grass for animals to eat, esp. grass which is cut and dried to make hay

¹**meal** *n* **1** an amount of food eaten at one time **2** the occasion of eating a meal

²**meal** *n* grain which has been crushed into a powder

¹**mean** *adj* **1** ungenerous; unwilling to share or help **2** unkind; unpleasant **3** (esp. of abilities) poor; bad: *He's no mean cook* –~**ly** *adv* –~**ness** *n*

²**mean** *v* **meant, meaning 1** to represent (a meaning): *What does this word mean?* **2** to intend (to say): *She said Tuesday, but meant Thursday* **3** to be determined about/to act on: *I mean what I say* **4** to intend (to be) because of abilities, fate, etc.: *He is meant to be a great man* **5** to be a sign of: *The dark clouds mean rain* **6** to be of importance by (a stated amount): *His work means everything to him* **7** **be meant to** to have to; be supposed to: *You're meant to leave a tip*

meaning *n* **1** the idea which is intended to be understood: *Explain the meanings of these foreign words* **2** importance or value: *the meaning of life*

meaningless *adj* without meaning or purpose –~**ly** *adv* –~**ness** *n*

means *n* **means 1** a method or way (of doing): *The quickest means of travel is by plane* **2** money, income, or wealth, esp. large enough for comfort **3** **by all means** certainly; please do

meantime *n* the time between 2 events: *They go to town on Saturdays, and in the meantime shop in the village*

meanwhile –also *esp. spoken* **meantime** *adv* **1** in the meantime: *They'll be here soon. Meanwhile, we'll have some coffee* **2** during the same period of time: *Eve was cutting the grass, and Adam was meanwhile planting roses*

measles *n* an infectious disease in which the sufferer has a fever and small red spots on the face and body

¹**measure** *n* **1** a system for calculating amount, size, weight, etc. **2** an amount in such a system **3** an instrument or apparatus used for calculating amount, length, weight, etc., esp. a stick or container **4** a certain amount **5** true amount or quality: *There are no words to express the full measure of my gratitude* **6** an action taken to gain a certain end: *If he refuses to pay I shall take measures against him* **7** a musical bar or poetic pattern of sounds which are repeated (metre)

²**measure** *v* **-sured, -suring 1** to find the size, length, amount, degree, etc., (of) in standard measurements **2** to consider carefully (the effect of) **3** to be of a certain size

measurement *n* **1** the act of measuring **2** a length, height, etc., found by measuring

meat *n* **1** the flesh of animals, apart from fish and birds, which is eaten **2** the flesh of animals, including birds but not fish, as opposed to their bones **3** *old use* food (esp. in the phrase **meat and drink**) **4** valuable matter, ideas, etc.: *There was no real meat in his speech*

mechanic *n* a person who is skilled in using, repairing, etc., machinery

mechanical *adj* **1** of, connected with, moved, worked, or produced by machinery **2** (of people or their acts) as if moved by machinery – ~**ly**

mechanics *n* **1** the science of the action of forces on objects **2** the science of making machines **3** the ways of producing or doing: *the mechanics of printing*

mechanism *n* **1** the different parts of a machine arranged together, and the action they have **2** the arrangement and action which parts have in a whole: *the mechanism of the brain* – -**istic** *adj* – -**istically** *adv*

medal *n* a round flat piece of metal, or a cross, with a picture and/or words on it, which is usu. given as an honour for a special achievement, in memory of an important event, etc.

media *n* the newspapers, television, and radio; mass media

¹medical *adj* **1** of or concerning medicine and treating the sick **2** of the treatment of disease by methods other than operation – ~**ly** *adv*

²medical *n* *esp. spoken* a medical examination (of the body)

medicine *n* **1** a substance used for treating disease **2** the science of treating and understanding disease

mediocre *adj* of medium quality or ability but usu. not good enough – -**crity** *n*

meditate *v* -**tated**, -**tating** **1** to think seriously or deeply **2** to fix the attention on one matter, having cleared the mind of thoughts, esp. for religious reasons and/or to gain peace of mind **3** to plan or consider carefully – -**tation** *n* – -**tative** *adj* – -**tatively** *adv*

¹medium *n* -**dia** *or* -**diums** **1** a method for giving information; form of art: *The theatre is his favourite medium* **2** a substance in which objects or living things exist, or through which a force travels: *A fish in water is in its natural medium* **3** a middle position: *a happy medium*

²medium *n* -**diums** a person who claims to have power to receive messages from the spirits of the dead

³medium *adj* of middle size, amount, quality, value, etc.

meek *adj* gentle in nature; yielding to others' actions and opinions – ~**ly** *adv* – ~**ness** *n*

¹meet *v* **met**, **meeting** **1** to come together (with), by chance or arrangement **2** to find or experience **3** to come together or close:

The cars met head-on **4** to get to know or be introduced (to) for the first time: *Come to the party and meet some interesting people* **5** to join at a fastening point: *My skirt won't meet round my middle* **6** to gather together **7** to touch, (as if) naturally: *Their lips met* **8** to answer, esp. in opposition **9** to be there at the arrival of: *The taxi will meet the train* **10** to pay **11** to satisfy

²**meet** *n* a gathering of men on horses with hounds to hunt foxes

meeting *n* **1** the coming together of people, by chance or arrangement **2** a gathering of people, esp. for a purpose

¹**melancholy** *n* sadness, esp. over a period of time and not for any particular reason – **-cholic** *adj*

²**melancholy** *adj* **1** sad **2** causing sadness: *melancholy news*

melody *n* **-dies 1** the arrangement of music in a pleasant way **2** a song or tune **3** the part which forms a clearly recognizable tune in a larger arrangement of notes – **-dic** *adj*

melon *n* any of a few kinds of fruit which are large and rounded, with very juicy edible flesh inside a firm skin

melt *v* **1** to become or cause (a solid) to become liquid **2** to make or become gentle, sympathetic, etc. **3** to disappear or cause to disappear **4** (of a colour, sound, or sensation) to become lost (in another) by moving gently into or across **5 melt**

in the mouth (of solid food) to be soft or tender when eaten

member *n* **1** a person belonging to a club, group, etc. **2 a** a part of the body, such as an organ or limb **b** the male sexual organ

membership *n* **1** the state of being a member of a club, society, etc. **2** all the members of a club, society, etc.

memorable *adj* **1** which is worth remembering **2** noticeable; special – **-bly** *adv*

memorial *n* **1 a** an object, such as a stone monument, in a public place in memory of a person, event, etc. **b** a custom which serves the same purpose: *a memorial service* **2** a historical record: *memorials of a past age*

memory *n* **-ries 1** the ability to remember events and experience **2** an example of remembering **3** the time during which things happened which can be remembered

men *pl. of* MAN

¹**menace** *n* **1** something which suggests a threat or brings danger **2** *esp. spoken* a troublesome person or thing

²**menace** *v* **-aced, -acing** *esp. written* to threaten – **-acingly** *adv*

¹**mend** *v* **1** to repair (a hole, break, fault, etc.) in (something) **2** to improve: *mend one's ways* **3** *esp. spoken* to regain one's health – ~**er** *n*

²**mend** *n* **1** a part mended after breaking or wearing **2** a patch or sewn repair in material **3 on the**

mend *esp. spoken* getting better after illness

mental *adj* 1 of the mind 2 done only in or with the mind 3 concerning disorders or illness of the mind: *a mental hospital* 4 *bad usage* mad – ~**ly** *adv*

mentality *n* -**ties** 1 the abilities and powers of the mind 2 character; habits of thought

¹**mention** *n* 1 the act of mentioning: *He made no mention of her wishes* 2 a short remark about something 3 *esp. spoken* a naming of someone, esp. to honour them: *He was given a mention in the list of helpers*

²**mention** *v* 1 to tell about in a few words, spoken or written 2 to say the name of: *He mentioned a useful book*

menu *n* a list of dishes , esp. in a restaurant

¹**mercenary** *n* -**ries** a soldier who fights for the country that pays him, not for his own country

²**mercenary** *adj* influenced by the wish to gain money or other reward

¹**merchandise** *n* things for sale; goods for trade

²**merchandise** *v* -**dised, -dising** to try to persuade people to buy (goods)

merchant *n* a person who buys and sells goods

merciful *adj* 1 showing mercy 2 by the kindness of God or fortune – ~**ly** *adv* – ~**ness** *n*

merciless *adj* showing no mercy – ~**ly** *adv* – ~**ness** *n*

mercury – also **quicksilver** *n* a heavy silver-white metal that is an element, which is liquid at ordinary temperatures and is used esp. in scientific instruments such as thermometers

mercy *n* -**cies** 1 willingness to forgive, not to punish 2 kindness or pity towards those who suffer or are weak 3 *esp. spoken* a fortunate event 4 **at the mercy of** powerless against

mere *adj* nothing more than

merely *adv* only and nothing else

merge *v* **merged, merging** 1 to become lost in or part of something else/each other 2 (of firms or companies) to combine

meridian *n* 1 an imaginary line drawn on maps from the north pole to the south over the surface of the earth 2 *technical* midday, when the sun reaches its highest point

¹**merit** *n* the quality of deserving praise, reward, etc.; personal worth

²**merit** *v usu. written* to deserve; have a right to

merry *adj* -**rier, -riest** 1 cheerful, esp. laughing 2 causing laughter and fun: *a merry joke* 3 *esp. spoken* rather drunk – -**rily** *adv* – -**riness** *n*

mess *n* 1 a state of disorder or untidiness 2 *esp. spoken* a person whose appearance, behaviour, or thinking is in a disordered state 3 dirty material, esp. passed from an animal's body 4 *esp. spoken* trouble 5 a place to eat, esp. for soldiers or other members of the armed forces

message *n* 1 a spoken or written piece

of information passed from one to another **2** the important or central idea: *the message of this book*

messenger *n* a person who brings a message

Messrs *n* (used chiefly in writing as the *pl.* of Mr., esp. in the names of firms): *Messrs Ford and Dobson, piano repairers*

met *past tense and past part. of* MEET

¹metal *n* any usu. solid shiny mineral substance of a group which can all be shaped by pressure and used for passing an electric current, and which share other properties: *Copper and silver are both metals*

²metal *v* **-ll-** to cover (a road) with a surface of broken stones

metallic *adj* **1** of, like, or containing metal **2** with a ringing quality (of sound): *a sharp metallic note*

metaphor *n* (the use of) a phrase which describes one thing by stating another thing with which it can be compared (as in *the roses in her cheeks*) without using the words "as" or "like" –~**ical** *adj*: *We didn't really mean he had green fingers, it was a metaphorical phrase*

meteor *n* any of various small pieces of matter in space that form a short-lived line of light if they fall into the earth's atmosphere

meteoric *adj* **1** of or concerning a meteor **2** like a meteor, esp. in being very fast or in being bright and short-lived: *a meteoric rise to fame* –~**ally** *adv*

meteorology *n* the study of weather conditions and their causes – **-gical** *adj* – **-gist** *n*

meter *n* a machine which measures the amount used: *a gas meter*

method *n* **1** a way or manner (of doing) **2** (the use of) an orderly system or arrangement: *to use method rather than luck*

methodical *adj* careful; using an ordered system –~**ly** *adv* very small

¹metre *n* (any type of) regular arrangement of notes or esp. words (as in poetry) into strong and weak beats

²metre *n* (a measure of length equal to) 39.37 inches

metric *adj* concerning the system of measurement based on the metre

metric system *n* a system of weights and measures, in which the standard measures are the kilogram for weight and the metre for length

mice *pl. of* MOUSE

¹microfilm *n* (a length of) film for photographing something in a very small size

²microfilm *v* to photograph (something) using microfilm

microphone –also *esp. spoken* **mike** *n* an instrument for carrying or recording sound (as in radio, telephones, etc.) or in making sounds louder

microprocessor *n* a small computer in or on a chip, used esp. to control appliances

microscope *n* an instrument that makes very small near objects seem larger

midday *n* the middle of the day; 12 o'clock noon

¹**middle** *adj* in or nearly in the centre; at the same distance from 2 or more points, or from the beginning and end of something

²**middle** *n* 1 the central part, point, or position 2 *esp. spoken* the waist or the part below the waist

Middle Ages *n* the period in European history between about AD 500 and 1500

middle class *adj, n* (of) the social class to which people belong who are neither noble, very wealthy, etc., nor manual workers

midget *n* 1 a very, or unusually, small person 2 very small, compared with others of the same kind

midnight *n* 12 o'clock at night

midst *n literature or old use* the middle part or position

midway *adj, adv* (that is) halfway or in a middle position

¹**might** *v negative short form* **mightn't** 1 to be or have been in some small degree likely to: *He might come or he might not / Did you see that car nearly hit me? I might have been killed* 2 *polite* (in questions) to have permission to; be allowed to: *'Might I come in?' 'Yes, you may'* 3 **a** (expressing purpose) could: *I wrote down his telephone number, so that I might remember it* **b** (with words expressing hope, wish, or fear) would: *The prisoner had hopes that he might be set free* 4 ought to; should: *You might at least say*

'thank you' when someone helps you 5 (in reported speech) may: *He told us that he might come, but he might not. / He asked whether he might leave it with her. / He said he feared she might not live much longer. / He said I might go if I wished* 6 **might as well** may as well

²**might** *n* power; strength; force

¹**mighty** *adj* **-ier, -iest** 1 *often literature or Bible* having great power or strength; very great 2 *literature* appearing strong and powerful because of great size 3 **high and mighty a** *offensive* considering oneself important **b** of high rank and great power

²**mighty** *adv esp. spoken* very

migrate *v* **migrated, migrating** 1 to move from one place to another, esp. for a limited period 2 (of birds and fish) to travel regularly from one part of the world to another, according to the seasons of the year – **-atory** *adj*

migration *n* 1 the act of migrating 2 a movement of many people, birds, etc., in a body from one part of the world to another

¹**mild** *adj* 1 (of a person, his nature, temper, etc.) gentle; soft 2 not hard or causing much discomfort or suffering; slight: *a mild fever* 3 (of food, drink, etc.) not strong or bitter in taste: *a mild cheese* – ~**ness** *n*

²**mild** *n* a type of beer that has a mild taste

mildly *adv* 1 in a mild manner 2 slightly

mile *n* **1** (a measure of length or distance equal to) 1,609 metres or 1,760 yards **2** *esp. spoken* a very long way; a great deal: *There's no one within miles of him as a cricketer*

milestone *n* **1** a stone at the side of a road, on which is marked the number of miles to the next town **2** an (important) date, time, or event in a person's life, or in history: *The invention of the wheel was a milestone in the history of man*

¹**militant** *adj* having or expressing a readiness to fight or use force; taking an active part in a war, fight, or struggle: *A few militant members of the crowd started throwing stones at the police* – **-cy** *n* –~**ly** *adv*

²**militant** *n* a militant person

military *adj* of, for, by, or connected with soldiers, armies, or war –**military** *n*

¹**milk** *n* **1** a white liquid produced by human or animal females for the feeding of their young, and (of certain animals, such as the cow and goat) drunk by human beings or made into butter and cheese **2** a whitish liquid or juice obtained from certain plants and trees: *coconut milk* **3 in milk** (esp. of a cow) in a condition to produce milk

²**milk** *v* **1** to take milk from (a cow, goat, or other animal) **2** to get money, knowledge of a secret, etc., from (someone or something) by clever or dishonest means

milkman *n* **-men** a man who goes from house to house each day to deliver milk

¹**mill** *n* **1** also **flourmill**– (a building containing) a machine for crushing corn or grain into flour **2** a factory or workshop, esp. in the cotton industry **3** a small machine in which a stated material can be crushed into powder: *a coffee mill*

²**mill** *v* **1 a** to crush (grain) in a mill **b** to produce (flour) by this means **2** to press or roll (a metal) in a machine **3** to mark (the edge of something made of metal, esp. a coin) with regularly placed lines

milligram *n* 1,000th of a gram

millilitre *n* 1,000th of a litre

millimetre *n* 1,000th of a metre

million *adj, n, pron* **million** *or* **millions** the number 1,000,000; 10^6 –~**th** *adj, n, pron, adv*

millionaire *n* a person who has 1,000,000 pounds or dollars; very wealthy man

¹**mimic** *n* **1** a person who copies, or who is good at copying another's manners, speech, etc., esp. in a way that causes laughter **2 a** an animal that copies the actions of people **b** a bird that can copy the human voice

²**mimic** *adj* **1** not real; pretended **2** giving protection by being like something else: *the mimic colouring of zebras*

³**mimic** *v* **-ck-** **1** to copy (someone or something), esp. in order to make people laugh **2** to appear so like (something else) as to deceive

people into thinking it is the real thing

¹mince *v* **minced, mincing 1** to cut (esp. meat) into very small pieces **2** *offensive* to walk taking unnaturally short steps, esp. (of a man) in a womanlike way **3 mince matters/one's words** to speak of something bad or unpleasant using soft language, and avoiding plain direct words

²mince *n* minced meat

¹mind *n* **1** thoughts; a person's way of thinking or feeling **2** the quality which gives the ability to think or feel; intellect: *He has a very sharp mind* **3** a person who thinks, esp. one with a good brain and the ability to lead, to control, etc. **4** intentions: *Nothing was further from my mind* **5 call/bring to mind** to remember **6 have a good mind to** *esp. spoken* to have a strong wish to; be very near a decision to **7 in one's right mind** not mad; able to think rightly **8 make up one's mind** to reach a decision **9 put someone in mind of someone or something** to cause someone to remember, esp. because of a likeness in appearance, character, manners, etc. **10 speak one's mind** to express plainly one's thoughts and opinions, even if unpleasant to hear **11 to one's mind** in one's opinion; according to the way in which one thinks

²mind *v* **1** to be careful (of); pay close attention (to): *Mind the holes in the road.* / *Mind you read the* questions carefully before you begin **2** to have a reason against or be opposed to (a particular thing); be troubled by or dislike: *I don't mind if you go home early* **3** to take care or charge of; look after: *He stayed at home and minded the baby* **4** *dialect esp. Scots* to remember: *I mind the time when we were in Edinburgh together* **5 never mind a** do not feel sorry, sad, or troubled **b** it does not matter (about); it is not important **6 never you mind** *esp. spoken* it is not your business, and you are not to be told **7 would you mind** *polite* please: *Would you mind making a little less noise?*

¹mine *adj old use, poetic* (before a vowel sound or *h*, or often a noun) my: *Mine eyes have seen the glory of the coming of the Lord.* / *Mine host* / *mother mine*

²mine *pron* (Possessive form of I) that/those belonging to me: *That bag's mine; it has my name on it*

³mine *n* **1** a hole, usu. under the ground, from which coal, gold, tin, and other mineral substances are dug: *a tinmine* **2** a person from whom or thing from which one can obtain a great deal (of something, esp. information or knowledge): *a mine of information about the history of the village* **3** a metal case containing explosives, that is placed just below the ground or on or below the surface of the sea and is exploded from far away or when something strikes it **4** (a passage dug underground beneath an enemy position, containing) an explosive

⁴**mine** *v* **mined, mining** 1 to dig or work a mine in (the earth) 2 to obtain by digging from a mine 3 to lay mines in or under 4 to destroy by mines 5 to dig a mine under: *to mine the castle walls*

minefield *n* 1 a stretch of land or water in which mines have been placed 2 something that is full of hidden dangers

miner *n* a worker in a mine

¹**mineral** *n* any of various esp. solid substances that are formed naturally in the earth (such as stone, coal, salt, etc.)

²**mineral** *adj* of, connected with, containing, or having the nature of minerals; belonging to the class of minerals: *Salt is a mineral substance*

mingle *v* **-gled, -gling** *esp. in literature* 1 to mix (with another thing or with people) 2 to mix (different things) together

miniature *n* 1 a very small painting of a person 2 a very small copy or representation of anything: *The child has a collection of miniature farm animals*

minimum *n* **-ma** *or* **-mums** the least, or the smallest possible, quantity, number, or degree

¹**minister** *n* 1 a person in charge of a particular department of the government 2 a person of lower rank than an ambassador, who represents his government in a for-

eign country 3 a clergyman usu. belonging to the Presbyterian or Nonconformist Church – ~**ial** *adj* – ~**ially** *adv*

ministration *n* (a) giving of help and service, esp. by a priest – **-trant** *n*

ministry *n* **-tries** 1 a government department led by a minister or the building in which the department works: *the Ministry of Defence* 2 the office, position or period of office of a minister 3 the group of ministers forming a government 4 priests, considered as a body 5 the priests' profession: *Our son wants to enter the ministry*

¹**minor** *adj* 1 lesser or smaller in degree, size, etc. 2 3 *old public school* being the younger of 2 boys (usu. brothers) of the stated name (esp. at the same school): *Simkins minor* 4 (in music) based on a minor key: *a symphony in F minor*

²**minor** *n law* a person who has not yet reached the age at which he is fully responsible in law for his actions

minority *n* **-ties** 1 the smaller number or part; a number or part that is less than half: *Only a minority want an election now* 2 a small part of a population which is different from the rest in race, religion, etc. 3 *law* the state or time when one has not yet, in law, reached the age of full responsibility

¹**mint** *n* 1 a place where official coins are made 2 *esp. spoken* a large amount (of money) 3 **in mint condi-**

tion (of a coin, postage stamp, etc.) in perfect condition

²**mint** *v* to make (a coin)

³**mint** *n* any of several types of small plant, which have leaves with a particular smell and taste, used in preparing drinks and food

mint sauce *n* a sauce made of finely-chopped mint leaves mixed with vinegar and sugar, served with lamb

¹**minus** *prep* **1** made less by (the stated figure or quantity): *17 minus 5 leaves 12* **2** being the stated number of degrees below the freezing point of water: *The temperature was minus 10 degrees* **3** *esp. spoken* without: *He was minus 2 front teeth after the fight*

²**minus** *n* also **minus sign** – a sign (−) used for showing **a** that the stated number is less than zero **b** that the second number is to be taken away from the first

minuscule *adj* very small

¹**minute** *n* **1** one of the 60 parts into which an hour is divided **2** *esp. spoken* a very short space of time: *I'll be ready in a minute* **3** one of the 60 parts into which a degree of angle is divided: *The exact measurement of this angle is 80 degrees 30 minutes*

²**minute** *v* **minuted, minuting** to make a note of (something) in the minutes of a meeting

minutes *n* a written record of business done, decisions taken, etc., at a meeting

miracle *n* **1** an act or happening (usu. having a good result), that cannot be explained by the laws of nature **2** a wonderful surprising unexpected event **3** a wonderful example (of a quality, ability, etc.)

miraculous *adj* very wonderful; caused, or seeming to be caused, by powers beyond those of nature –~**ly**

¹**mirror** *n* **1** a shiny or polished surface that reflects images that fall on it **2** a true faithful representation (of something): *the mirror of public opinion*

²**mirror** *v* to show, as in a mirror

misadventure *n* **1** *esp. in literature* (an accident; event caused by) bad luck **2 death by misadventure** *law* the death or killing of a person by accident

misbehave *v* **-haved, -having** to behave (oneself) badly or improperly –~**d** *adj* – **-viour**

miscalculate *v* **-lated, -lating** to calculate wrongly – **-lation** *n*

miscellaneous *adj* of several kinds or different kinds; having a variety of sorts, qualities, etc. –~**ly** *adv* –~**ness** *n*

mischief *n* **1** bad, but not seriously bad, behaviour or actions, as of children, probably causing trouble, and possibly damage or harm **2** troublesome playfulness **3** *esp. spoken* a person, esp. a child, who is often troublesomely playful **4** damage, harm, or hurt done by a person, animal, or thing

mischievous *adj* **1** having or showing a liking for mischief **2** *offensive* causing harm, often with intention – ~**ly** *adv* – ~**ness** *n*

misdirect *v* **1** to direct (someone) wrongly **2** to address (a letter, parcel, etc.) wrongly **3** to use (one's strength, abilities, etc.) for a wrong purpose – ~**ion** *n*

miser *n* *offensive* a person who loves money and hates spending it – ~**ly** *adj* – ~**liness** *n*

miserable *adj* **1** very unhappy **2** causing unhappiness, discomfort, etc.: *miserable conditions* **3** very poor (in quality) or very small or low (in degree or amount): *a miserable failure*

misery *n* **-ries** **1** great unhappiness or pain and suffering (of body or of mind) **2** *offensive esp. spoken* a person who is always unhappy and complaining, esp. one who does not like others to enjoy themselves

misfire *v* **-fired, -firing** **1** (of a gun) to fail to send out the bullet when fired **2** (of a car engine) to produce irregularly, or to fail to produce, the flash that explodes the petrol mixture **3** (of a plan, joke, etc.) to fail to have the desired or intended result – **misfire** *n*

misfit *n* a person who does not fit well and happily into his social surroundings or the position he holds

misfortune *n* **1** bad luck, often of a serious nature **2** a very unfortunate condition, accident, or event

misgiving *n* a feeling or feelings of doubt, fear (of the future), and/or distrust

misguide *v* **-guided, -guiding** to lead or influence (someone) into a wrong or foolish course of action – ~**d** *adj* – ~**dly** *adv*

misjudge *v* **-judged, -judging** to judge (a person, action, time, distance, etc.) wrongly – ~**ment** *n*

mislay *v* **-laid, -laying** to lose by putting (something) in a place and forgetting where

mislead *v* **-led, -leading** to cause (someone) to think or act wrongly or mistakenly; guide wrongly, sometimes with the intention to deceive: *Her appearance misled him* – ~**ingly** *adv*

¹**miss** *v* **1** to fail to hit, catch, find, meet, touch, hear, see, etc. (something or someone): *The falling rock just missed my head. / He arrived too late and missed the train* **2** to avoid or escape from (something unpleasant) by such a failure: *I was lucky to miss the traffic accident* **3** to discover the absence or loss of (someone or something): *She didn't miss her bag till she got home* **4** to feel or suffer from the lack of (something): *Give the beggar a coin; you won't miss it* **5** to feel sorry or unhappy at the absence or loss of (someone or something): *He missed his dog which had died*

²**miss** *n* a failure to hit, catch, hold, etc., that which is aimed at

³**miss** *n* **1** (a form of address used) **a** (by pupils to) a woman teacher **b**

(esp. by shopkeepers, servants, etc., to) an unmarried woman **c** (by anyone to) a waitress, girl working in a shop, etc. **2** **technical** a girl whose dress size is between that of a child and a woman

Miss *n* **1** (a title placed before the name of) an unmarried woman or a girl: *Miss Brown* **2** (a title placed before) the name of a place or a type of activity which a young unmarried woman has been chosen to represent, usu. for reasons of beauty: *Miss England 1982*

missile *n* **1** a rocket which can be aimed at a distant object **2** *esp. written* an object or weapon thrown by hand or shot from a gun or other instrument: *The angry crowd threw bottles and other missiles at the players*

missing *adj* not to be found; not in the proper or expected place; lost

mission *n* **1** a group of people, esp. a country's representatives, who are sent abroad for a special reason: *a British trade mission to Russia* **2** the duty or purpose for which these people are sent: *The mission was to sell more cars* **3 a** a building or offices where the work of these people is planned or carried out **b** a building or group of buildings in which a particular form of religion is taught, medical services are given, poor people are helped, etc. **4** the particular work for which one believes oneself to have been sent

into the world: *Nursing is her mission in life*

missionary *n* **-ries** a person sent usu. to a foreign country, to teach and spread his religion

¹**mist** *n* **1** thin fog **2** a film, esp. one formed of small drops of water, through which it is hard to see clearly: *the mist of her tears* **3** something that makes understanding or good judgment difficult

²**mist** *v* to cover with mist

¹**mistake** *v* **-took, -taken, -taking 1** to have a wrong idea about (someone or something); understand wrongly **2** not to recognize (someone or something)

²**mistake** *n* a wrong thought, act, etc.; something done, said, believed, etc., as a result of wrong thinking or understanding, lack of knowledge or skill, etc.: *a spelling mistake*

mistaken *adj* **1** (of a person) wrong; having understood incorrectly **2** (of a statement, idea, etc.) misunderstood **3** (of an action, idea, etc.) incorrect; not well-judged; based on wrong thinking, lack of knowledge, etc.: *She trusted him , in the mistaken belief that he was honest* –~**ly**

mistress *n* **1** a female master: *a new English mistress* **2** a woman with whom a man has a sexual relationship, usu. not a socially acceptable one

mistrust *v* not to trust; distrust –**mistrust** *n*

misunderstand *v* **-stood 1** to understand wrongly; put a wrong meaning on (something said, done, etc.) or on something said by (someone) **2** to fail to see or understand the true character or qualities of (someone): *His wife misunderstands him*

misunderstanding *n* **1** the act of misunderstanding **2** an example of this: *Her poor French often leads to misunderstandings when she visits France* **3** a disagreement less serious than a quarrel

¹**mix** *v* **1** to combine so as to form a whole, of which the parts have no longer a separate shape, appearance, etc., or cannot easily be separated: *You can't mix oil and water* **2** to prepare (such a combination): *His wife mixed him a hot drink* **3** to be or enjoy being in the company of others: *He mixes well in any company* **4** **mix it** *esp. spoken* to fight roughly

²**mix** *n* **1** a combination of different substances: *cake mix* **2** a group of different things, people, etc.

mixed *adj* **1** of different kinds **2** of or for both sexes: *a mixed school* **3** combining people of 2 or more races or religions: *a mixed marriage*

mixture *n* **1** a set of substances mixed together, which keep their separate qualities while combined: *cough mixture* **2** a combination: *a mixture of sadness and humour*

¹**moan** *n* **1** a low sound of pain, grief, or suffering **2** sounds that give the idea of sadness: *the moan of the*

wind **3** a complaint, expressed in a discontented voice: *She always has some moan or another*

²**moan** *v* **1** to make a moan **2** to express with moans: *The prisoner moaned out a prayer for mercy* **3** to complain –~**er** *n*

¹**mob** *n* **1** a large noisy esp. violent crowd **2** the common people **3** a group of lawbreakers –**mob** *adj*

²**mob** *v* **-bb-** **1** (of a group) to attack: *The large bird was mobbed by all the smaller birds* **2** (of a group of people) to crowd around from interest or admiration: *When he left the hall the party leader was mobbed by his supporters*

mobile *adj* **1** movable; not fixed **2** driven from place to place in a vehicle: *a mobile library* **3** changing quickly, as of a person's face – **-ility** *n*

¹**mock** *v* **1** to laugh at (someone or something) when it is wrong to do so; speak or act as if one is not serious, esp. when one should be: *He went to church only to mock* **2** to copy in such a way that the person or thing copied is laughed at: *He made the boys laugh by mocking the way the teacher spoke* –~**er** *n* –~**ingly** *adv*

²**mock** *n* **make a mock of** make a mockery of

³**mock** *adj* not real or true; like something real: *a mock battle*

mockery *n* **-ries** **1** laughing at something that should not be laughed at **2** a person or thing deserving to be laughed at **3** something not worthy of respect or consideration: *The medical examination was a mockery; the doctor hardly looked at the child*

¹**model** *n* **1** a small representation or copy **2** a person or thing almost exactly like another: *She's a perfect model of her aunt* **3** a person or thing worthy to be copied: *This pupil's work is a model of neatness* **4** a person employed to wear clothes and to show them to possible buyers **5** a person employed to be painted by an artist **6** an article which is one of a number of articles of a standard pattern: *The car industry's always producing new models*

²**model** *v* **-ll- 1 a** to make in a soft substance: *to model pots in clay* **b** to make a model of **2** to act as a model **3** to show (an article of clothing) as a model: *A girl was chosen to model the silk dress*

³**model** *adj* **1** being a small copy: *model cars* **2** deserving to be copied: *a model mother*

¹**moderate** *adj* **1** of middle degree, power, or rate **2** within sensible limits **3** of only average quality: *This pupil has only moderate ability* **4** not favouring extreme political or social ideas – ~**ly** *adv*

²**moderate** *v* **-rated, -rating** to make or become less

moderation *n* **1** reduction in force, degree, rate, etc. **2** the ability of keeping one's desires within reasonable limits ; self-control **3 in moderation** within sensible limits

¹**modern** *adj* **1** of the present time; not ancient **2** new and different from the past **3** (of a language) in use today – ~**ity** *n*

²**modern** *n* a person living in modern times or with modern ideas

modernize, -ise *v* **-ized, -izing 1** to make suitable for modern use **2** to become modern – **-ization** *n*

modest *adj* **1** having a lower opinion than is probably deserved, of one's own ability, successes, etc.; hiding one's good qualities **2** not large in quantity, size, value, etc. **3** avoiding anything improper or impure – ~**ly** *adv* – ~**y** *n*

modify *v* **-fied, -fying 1** to change , esp. slightly **2** to make less hard to accept or bear: *to modify one's demands* **3** (in grammar) (of a word) to describe or limit the meaning of (another word): *The adverb 'quietly' modifies the verb 'talk' in the phrase 'to talk quietly'* – **-fication** *n*

moist *adj* **1** slightly wet **2** (esp. of food) not unpleasantly dry – ~**ly** *adv* – ~**ness** *n*

moisture *n* water, or other liquids, in small quantities or as steam or mist

molecule *n* the smallest part of any substance that can be separated from the substance without losing its own chemical form and qualities, and consists of one or more atoms – **-lar** *adj*

moment *n* **1** a period of time too short to measure **2** the time for doing something: *Choose your moment to ask him* **3** *esp. written* importance:

a matter of great moment **4** *technical* (a measure of) the turning power of a force

momentary *adj* lasting for a very short time – **-rily** *adv*

momentum *n* **-ta** *or* **-tums 1** *technical* the quantity of movement in a body, measured by multiplying its mass by the speed at which it moves: *As the rock rolled down ,it gathered momentum* **2** the force gained by the development of events: *The struggle is gaining momentum every day*

monarch *n* a king, queen, etc. – ~**ic,** ~**ical** *adj*

monarchy *n* **-chies 1** rule by a king or queen **2** a state ruled by a king or queen

monastery *n* **-teries** a building in which monks live according to religious rules

Monday *n* **-days** the second day of the week

monetary *adj esp. technical* of or connected with money

money *n* **1** metal coins, or paper notes with their value printed on them, used in buying and selling **2** wealth: *Money doesn't always bring happiness* –~**less** *adj*

mongrel *n* an animal, esp. a dog, whose parents were of mixed or different breeds

monk *n* a member of an all-male group united by a promise to give their lives to a religion and living together in a monastery –~**ish** *adj*

monkey *n* **-keys 1** any of several types of long-tailed active tree-climbing animals, belonging to that class most like man **2** *esp. spoken* a child who plays annoying tricks

¹mono –also (*esp. written*) **monophonic** *adj* using a system of sound recording, broadcasting, or receiving in which the sound appears to come from one direction only when played back: *a mono record*

²mono *n* **-os** *esp. spoken* mono sound production

monopolize, -lise *v* **-lized, -lizing 1** to have or get complete unshared control of **2** to take wholly for oneself, not allowing others to share – **-list** *n* – **-lization** *n*

monopoly *n* **-lies 1** a right or power of only one person or one group to provide a service, trade in anything, produce something, etc. **2** possession or control not shared by others **3** *trademark* a game in which the winner obtains all the pretended money, property, etc.

monotonous *adj* dull; lacking variety – **-ny,** ~**ness** *n* –~**ly** *adv*

monster *n* **1** an unusually large animal, plant, or thing: *a monster aircraft* **2** a creature that is unnatural in shape, size, or qualities, and usu. frighteningly ugly: *a sea monster* **3** a person so evil as to cause strong hatred, fear, etc.: *The judge told the murderer that he was a monster*

monstrous *adj* **1** of unnaturally large size, strange shape, etc. **2** so bad as to cause strong hatred: *monstrous cruelty* −∼**ly** *adv*

month *n* one of the 12 named divisions of the year

¹**monthly** *adj, adv* (happening, appearing, etc.) once a month

²**monthly** *n* **-lies** a magazine appearing once a month

monument *n* **1** a building, gravestone, statue, etc. that preserves the memory of a person or event **2** a building or place considered worthy of preservation for its historic interest or beauty **3** an outstanding example (of): *His actions are a monument to foolishness*

monumental *adj* **1** of or intended for a monument **2** very large and of lasting worth **3** very great in degree: *monumental efforts*

moo *v,* **mooed, mooing; moos** (to make) the noise a cow makes

mood *n* **1** a state of the feelings: *a happy mood* **2** a bad-tempered state of feeling: *He's in one of his moods*

moody *adj* **-ier, -iest 1** having changeable moods **2** bad-tempered, or unhappy, esp. without reasons −**moodily** *adv* −**moodiness** *n*

moon *n* **1** the body which moves round the earth once every 28 days, and can be seen in the sky at night **2** a body that moves round a planet other than the earth **3** *esp. poetic* a month: *many moons ago* −∼**less** *adj*

¹**moonlight** *n* the light from the moon

²**moonlight** *v* **-lighted, -lighting** *esp.*

spoken to have a second job besides a regular one −∼**er** *n*

¹**moor** *n* a wide, open, often raised area covered with rough grass or bushes, that is not farmed because of its bad soil

²**moor** *v* to fasten (a boat) to land, the sea bed, etc. by means of ropes, an anchor, etc.

moot point −also **moot question** *n* an undecided point

¹**mop** *n* **1** a tool for washing floors, made of a long stick with either threads of thick string, or a sponge, on one end **2** a tool like this for washing dishes **3** *esp. spoken* a thick mass (of unbrushed hair), standing up from the head

²**mop** *v* **-pp-** to clean or wipe with a mop

¹**moral** *adj* **1** concerning good or evil, right or wrong **2** based on the idea of what is right (compared with what is lawful): *moral courage* **3** pure in matters of sex **4** able to recognize the difference between right and wrong **5** teaching that which is right in behaviour: *a moral lesson*

²**moral** *n* a good lesson in behaviour that can be learnt from a story or happening

morale *n* one's state of mind with regard to confidence, strength of spirit, etc.: *The trapped men kept up their morale by singing*

morals *n* rules of behaviour, esp. in matters of sex

morbid *adj* **1** having an unhealthy

interest in unpleasant subjects, esp. death **2** *medical* diseased – ~**ity** *n* – ~**ly** *adv*

¹**more** *adj, pron, n* (*comparative of* MANY, MUCH) **1** a greater number, quantity, or part (of): *There are more cars on the roads in summer than in winter.* / *50 is more than 40* **2** an additional or further number, amount, or quantity (of): *I've given you all you asked for; what more d'you want?* / *I have to write 2 more letters* **3 more or less a** nearly: *The work's more or less finished* **b** about: *The repairs will cost £50, more or less*

²**more** *adv* **1** to a greater degree: *His illness was more serious than we thought.* / *He seems to care more for his dogs than for his children* **2** oftener or longer: *You ought to practise more* again (in the phrases **any more, once more, no more**): *The old man doesn't travel any more.* / *The teacher said he'd repeat the question once more* **4 no more** neither: *He can't afford it, and no more can I* **5 the more ..., the more/less ...** to the degree that ..., to an equal/less degree ...: *The more angry he became, the more she laughed at him*

moreover *adv* in addition; besides: *The price is too high, and moreover, the house isn't in a suitable position*

morning *n* **1** the first part of the day, from sunrise usu. until the midday meal **2** the part of the day from midnight until midday: *2 o'clock in the morning*

¹**mortal** *adj* **1** that must die; not living for ever **2** human; of human beings **3** causing death: *a mortal wound* **4** (of an enemy) having a lasting hatred **5** (of a fight) continuing until death or complete defeat: *mortal combat* **6** (of danger, fear, etc.) so great as to fill the mind with thoughts of death **7** *esp. spoken* very great: *It's a mortal shame*

²**mortal** *n esp. in literature* a human being (as compared with a god, a spirit, etc.)

mortality *n* **1** the number or rate of deaths from a certain cause: *a high mortality from this disease* **2** being mortal

mortally *adv* **1** in a manner that causes death: *mortally wounded* **2** very greatly: *mortally afraid*

¹**mortgage** *n* **1** an agreement to have money lent, esp. so as to buy a house, with the house or land belonging to the lender until the money is repaid **2** the amount lent on a mortgage

²**mortgage** *v* **-gaged, -gaging** to give the right to the ownership of (a house, land, etc.) in return for money lent

mosque *n* a building in which Muslims worship

mosquito *n* **-toes** any of several types of small flying insect that prick the skin and then drink blood, one of which can cause the disease malaria

moss *n* (any of several types of) a small flat green or yellow flowerless plant that grows in a thick furry mass on a wet surface – ~**y** *adj*

¹**most** *adj, pron* (*superlative of* MANY, MUCH) **1** greatest in number, quantity, or degree: *The money should be shared among those who have the most need of it.* / *Which is most–10, 20, or 30?* **2** nearly all: *Most of his time is spent travelling* **3 for the most part** nearly completely; in almost all cases

²**most** *adv* **1** to the greatest degree: *the most comfortable hotel* / *You can help me most by peeling the potatoes* **2** very; quite: *It's most annoying*

³**most** *n* **1** the greatest amount: *the most we could afford* **2 at (the) most** not more than: *She's at most 25 years old* **3 make the most of** to get the greatest gain from

mostly *adv* mainly

moth *n* **1** any of several types of quite large winged insects, related to the butterfly but not so brightly coloured, which fly mainly at night and are attracted by lights **2** an infection of clothes by young moths which eat wool, fur, etc.

¹**mother** *n* **1** a female parent **2** one's own female parent **3** a female head of a group of nuns **4** a cause: *Hunger is often the mother of crime* – ~**less** *adj*

²**mother** *v* **1** to care for (someone) like a mother **2** to give birth to

mother-in-law *n* **-s-in-law** the mother of a person's husband or wife

¹**motion** *n* **1** the state of moving: *The train was in motion* **2** a single movement **3** a suggestion formally put before a meeting, which is the subject of arguments for and against **4** an act of emptying the bowels

²**motion** *v* to signal by means of a movement: *She motioned to the waiter*

¹**motive** *n* a reason for action – ~**less** *adj*

²**motive** *adj technical* (of power, force, etc.) causing movement: *the motive power that turns this wheel*

¹**motor** *n* **1** a machine that changes power, esp. electrical power, into movement **2** a car

²**motor** *adj* **1** driven by an engine: *a motor mower* **2** of, for, or concerning vehicles driven by an engine: *the motor industry* **3** *technical* of, related to, or being a nerve that causes a muscle to move

³**motor** *v becoming rare* to travel by car – ~**ist** *n*

motorbike *n* a motorcycle

motorboat *n* a small ship driven by an engine or electric motor

motorcycle *n* a large heavy bicycle with an engine – **-clist** *n*

motorway *n* **-ways** a very wide road esp. for fast long-distance vehicles

motto *n* **-tos 1** a few words taken as the guiding principle of a person, a school, etc. **2** an amusing or clever short saying

¹**mould** *n* loose earth, esp. good soft

soil rich in decayed vegetable substances

²**mould** *n* **1** a hollow vessel having a particular shape, into which a melted substance is poured, so that when the substance hardens, it takes this shape **2** *esp. in literature* (a person's) nature considered as having been shaped by family type, education, etc.: *He's made in his father's mould*

³**mould** *v* **1** to shape or form (something solid) **2** to shape or form (character, behaviour, etc.)

⁴**mould** *n* a soft woolly growth on substances which have been left a long time in warm wet air

mouldy *adj* **-ier, -iest 1** covered with or smelling of mould **2** *sl* bad in quality −**mouldiness** *n*

mound *n* **1** a small hill **2** a large pile: *a mound of letters*

¹**mount** *v* **1** to get on (a horse, a bicycle, etc.) **2** to go up; climb **3** to provide (someone) with a horse or other animal, a bicycle, etc., to ride on **4** to rise in level: *The temperature mounted into the 90s* **5** to fix on a support or in a surrounding substance: *He mounted the photograph on paper* **6** to prepare or begin (an attack) **7** to prepare and produce (a play) for the stage **8** *technical* (of a male animal) to get up on (a female animal) for sex **9 mount guard** to be on guard duty

²**mount** *n* **1** an animal on which one rides **2** something on which or in which a thing is fixed

mountain *n* **1** a very high hill **2** a very large amount: *a mountain of dirty clothes to wash*

mountainous *adj* **1** full of mountains: *mountainous country* **2** very large or high: *mountainous waves*

mourn *v* to grieve; be sorrowful

mourning *n* **1** grief, esp. for a death **2** the clothes worn to show grief at a death

mouse *n* **mice 1** any of several types of small furry animal with a long tail, rather like a small rat **2** a quiet person who is easily frightened

moustache *n* hair on the upper lip

¹**mouth** *n* **1** the opening on the face through which an animal or human being eats and makes sounds **2** an opening: *the mouth of the cave* **3 keep one's mouth shut** *esp. spoken* to avoid speaking ; keep silent

²**mouth** *v* to say, esp. repeatedly without understanding or sincerity: *He crept into the corner, mouthing curses*

mouthful *n* as much (food or drink) as fills the mouth

mouthpiece *n* **1** the part of a musical instrument, a telephone, etc. that is held in or near the mouth **2** a person, newspaper, etc. that expresses the opinions of others: *This newspaper is the mouthpiece of the government*

¹**move** *v* **moved, moving 1** to change or cause to change place or position **2** to change or cause to change: *The government's opinions on this matter haven't moved* **3** *esp. spoken*

to travel, run, etc., very fast: *That car was really moving* **4** (in games such as chess) to change the position of (a piece) **5** to change (one's place of living or working): *to move house* **6** to cause (a person) to have feelings **7** to cause to act: *I felt moved to speak* **8** (of work, events, etc.) to go forward: *Work on the new building is moving quickly* **9** to lead one's life (esp. among people of a certain class): *She moves in the highest circles of society* **10** to put forward (a suggestion) **11** to empty (the bowels) −−∼**r** *n*

²**move** *n* **1** a movement **2** an act of going to a new home, office, etc. **3** (in games such as chess) an act of moving a piece from one square to another **4** a step in a course of action: *a move to stop the war* **5 get a move on** *esp. spoken* to hurry up

movement *n* **1** moving; activity **2** a particular act of moving **3** a group of people united for a particular purpose: *the trade union movement* **4** a general feeling directed towards something new: *the movement towards greater freedom for women* **5** a main division of a musical work, esp. of a symphony **6** the moving parts of a machine, esp. a clock or watch

moving *adj* **1** causing strong feelings, esp. of pity: *a moving story* **2** that moves; not fixed −−∼**ly** *adv*

mow *v* **mowed, mown** *or* **mowed, mowing** to cut (grass, corn, etc.), or cut that which grows in (a field or other area), with a mower or other tool

mower *n* **1** a machine for mowing, esp. (a **lawnmower**) one for cutting grass in gardens **2** a person who mows

Mr *also* (*rare*) **Mister** *n* **1** a title for a man who has no other **2** a title for certain people in official positions: *Mr Chairman* **3** used before the name of a place, sport, etc., to form a title for a man representing that thing: *Mr Baseball*

Mrs *n* **1** a title for a married woman who has no other **2** used before the name of a place, sport, etc., to form a title for a married woman representing that thing: *Mrs 1982 in her modern kitchen*

Ms *n* a title for a woman who does not wish to call herself either 'Mrs' or 'Miss'

¹**much** *adj, pron, n* **−see** MORE, MOST **1** a large quantity, amount, or part (of): *far too much work* / *I haven't read much of it* **2 I thought as much** I expected that **3 make much of a** to treat as important **b** to understand a lot: *I couldn't make much of that book* **c** to treat with a show of fondness **4 not much of a** not a very good: *not much of a day (=bad weather)*

²**much** *adv* **1 a** frequently: *Do you go there much?* **b** to a great degree: *I don't like that idea much* **2** by a large degree: *much worse* **3 much more/less** and even more/less: *I can hardly walk, much less run*

mud *n* very wet sticky earth

muddle *v* **-dled, -dling 1** to put into disorder **2** to confuse in the mind: *I get muddled when they give orders so quickly* –**muddle** *n* –~**r** *n*

muddy *adj* **-dier, -diest 1** covered with mud **2** (of colours) like mud: *a muddy brown* **3** not clear: *muddy thinking* – **-diness** *n*

¹**mug** *n* **1** a round drinking vessel with straight sides and a handle, not usu. with a saucer **2** *sl* the face **3** *esp. spoken* a foolish person easily deceived

²**mug** *v* **-gg-** to rob with violence, as in a dark street –**mugger** *n* –**mugging** *n*

¹**multiple** *adj* including many different parts, types, etc.

²**multiple** *n* a number which contains a smaller number an exact number of times: *3×4=12; so 12 is a multiple of 3*

multiplication *n* **1** the combining of 2 numbers by adding one of them to itself as many times as the other states; the process of forming the product of 2 numbers by repeated addition: *2×4=8 is an example of multiplication* **2** increasing in number

¹**multiply** *v* **-plied, -plying 1** to combine by multiplication: *to multiply 2 numbers together* **2** to increase: *to multiply one's chances of success* **3** to breed: *When animals have more food, they generally multiply faster*

²**multiply** *adv* in a multiple way

multitude *n* **1** a large number: *a multitude of thoughts* **2** *old use & Bible* a large crowd **3** ordinary people, not well educated: *The multitude may laugh at his music, but we know better*

mumble *v* **-bled, -bling** to speak unclearly

municipal *adj* concerning a town under its own government: *municipal affairs* –~**ly** *adv*

¹**murder** *n* **1** the crime of killing a person unlawfully **2** *esp. spoken* a very difficult or tiring experience

²**murder** *v* **1** to kill unlawfully, esp. on purpose **2** to ruin (language, music, etc.) by a bad performance –~**er** *n* –~**ess** *n*

murderous *adj* **1** likely to cause death **2** violent **3** of or like murder –~**ly** *adv* –~**ness** *n*

¹**murmur** *n* **1** (speech with) a soft low sound: *a murmur of voices / the murmur of the stream* **2** a complaint: *He obeyed without a murmur*

²**murmur** *v* **1** to make a soft sound, esp. to speak in a quiet voice **2** to complain in private –~**ing** *n*

muscle *n* (one of) the pieces of elastic material in the body which can tighten to produce movement –~**d** *adj*

muscular *adj* **1** of muscles: *the muscular system* **2** having big muscles: *a muscular body* –~**ly** *adv*

museum *n* a building where interesting objects are kept and usu. shown to the public

¹**mushroom** *n* **1** any of several types

of fungus, some of which are edible
2 anything which develops fast

²**mushroom** *v* **1** to spread in the shape of a mushroom: *The smoke mushroomed into the sky* **2** to develop fast **3** to gather mushrooms: *mushrooming in the woods*

music *n* **1** the arrangement of sounds in pleasant patterns and tunes **2** a written set of notes: *a sheet of music* **3 face the music** to admit to blame and accept the punishment

¹**musical** *adj* **1** of music **2** skilled in music: *a musical child* **3** pleasant to hear — **-ly** *adv*

²**musical** *n* a musical play or film with spoken words, songs, and often dances

musician *n* a performer, writer, or student of music

Muslim —also **Moslem** *n, adj* (a person) of the religion started by Mohammed

¹**must** *v 3rd person sing.* **must** *negative short form* **mustn't** **1** to have to because it is necessary: *I must leave at 6* **2** to be, do, etc., very probably: *I must look funny in this hat!*

²**must** *n esp. spoken* something necessary: *Warm clothes are a must in the mountains*

mustard *n* **1** a yellow-flowered plant with seeds from which a hot-tasting powder can be made **2** a thick mixture of this powder with water, eaten with food

mutilate *v* **-lated, -lating** **1** to damage; cripple: *Her arm was mutilated in the accident* **2** to spoil: *You've muti-*

lated the story by making such big changes — **-tion** *n*

¹**mutiny** *n* **-nies** the taking of power from the person in charge, esp. from a ship's captain — **-nous** *adj*

²**mutiny** *v* **-nied, -nying** to take part in a mutiny — **-neer** *n*

¹**mutter** *v* to speak (usu. angry or complaining words) in a low voice —~**er** *n*

²**mutter** *n* a sound of muttering

mutton *n* the meat from a sheep

mutual *adj* **1** equally shared by each one: *mutual interests* **2** equally so, one towards the other: *mutual enemies* —~**ity** *n* —~**ly** *adv*

my *adj* (*possessive form of* I) **1** belonging to me: *my car / my mother* **2** a cry of surprise, pleasure, etc.: *My! What a clever boy you are*

myself *pron* **1** (*reflexive form of* I): *I cut myself in the kitchen* **2** (*strong form of* I): *I had to do the shopping myself* **3** *esp. spoken* (in) my usual state of mind or body: *I feel more myself today*

mysterious *adj* **1** not easily understood **2** secret **3** suggesting mystery —~**ly** *adv* —~**ness** *n*

mystery *n* **-ries** **1** something which cannot be easily explained **2** a strange secret quality: *stories full of mystery* **3** a religious teaching that is beyond human understanding

myth *n* **1** an ancient usu. religious or magical story, which explains natural or historical events **2** a false story or idea: *the myth that elephants never forget* —~**ical** *adj*

¹nag *n* a horse

²nag *v* **-gg-** **1** to try to persuade by continuous complaining **2** to worry or annoy continuously: *a nagging headache* –~**ger** *n*

³nag *n esp. spoken* a person who has the habit of nagging

¹nail *n* **1** a thin piece of metal with a point at one end and a flat head at the other for hammering into a piece of wood or other material **2** a fingernail or toenail **3 hard as nails** *esp. spoken* **a** without any tender feelings **b** physically tough **4 hit the nail on the head** *esp. spoken* to do or say something exactly right

²nail *v* to fasten with a nail or nails

naive, naïve *adj* **1** having or showing no experience (as of social behaviour), esp. because one is young **2** believing too readily what anyone says or what is most favourable –~**ly** *adv*

naked *adj* **1** (of a person's body) not covered by clothes: *He was naked to the waist* **2** not covered by the usual covering: *a naked hillside* (= without trees) **3** not hidden; plain to see: *the naked truth* **4** (of the eye) without any instrument to help one see: *too small to see with the naked eye* –~**ly** *adv* –~**ness** *n*

¹name *n* **1** the word or words that someone or something is called by **2** a usu. offensive title for someone: *to call someone (nasty) names* **3** fame; reputation **4 in name only** in appearance or by title but not in fact **5 in the name of** by the right or power of

²name *v* **named, naming** **1** to give a name to: *They named the baby John* **2** to identify: *Can you name all the plants in the garden?* **3** to choose or appoint; specify: *We've named August 23rd for our wedding day*

namely *adv* that is to say: *Only one person can do the job, namely you*

namesake *n* one of 2 or more people with the same name

narrate *v* **-rated, -rating** *esp. written* to tell (a story); describe (an event or events) in order

¹narrative *n* **1** that which is narrated: *a narrative of last week's events* **2** the act of narrating

²narrative *adj* **1** telling a story or having the form of a story: *a narrative poem* **2** of or concerning storytelling: *the narrative art*

¹narrow *adj* **1** small from one side to the other, esp. in comparison with length or with what is usual **2** limited; restricted **3** almost not enough or only just successful: *a narrow escape* –~**ness** *n*

²narrow *v* **1** to decrease in width: *to narrow her eyes* **2** to limit; restrict

narrowly *adv* **1** hardly; only just: *One car narrowly missed hitting the other one* **2** in a narrow way or form or within narrow limits **3** in a thorough and usu. doubting way

nasty *adj* **-tier, -tiest** *esp. spoken* **1** ugly; unpleasant **2** harmful; dangerous – **-tily** *adv* – **-tiness** *n*

nation *n* **1** a large group of people

living in one area and usu. having an independent government **2** a large group of people with the same language and culture: *the Indian nations in the western United States* – ~**al** *adj* – ~**ally** *adv*

nationalism *n* **1** (too great) love of and pride in one's country **2** desire by a people or nation to form an independent country – -**list** *n, adj* – -**listic** *adj* – -**listically** *adv*

nationalize, -ise *v* -**ized, -izing** (of a central government) to buy or take control of (a business, industry, etc.) – -**ization** *n*

¹**native** *adj* **1** belonging to or being the place of one's birth: *her native language* **2** (of a person) belonging to a country from birth: *a native Englishman* **3** growing, found, etc., in a place; not brought in from another place: *a' house built of native stone* **4** *often offensive and becoming rare* of or concerning the original people, esp. the non-Europeans, of a place: *a native village*

²**native** *n* **1** someone who was born (in a place) **2** someone who lives in a place all the time or has lived there a long time **3** *often offensive and becoming rare* someone who belongs to an earlier or original people, esp. the non-Europeans, living in a place: *The government of the island treated the natives badly* **4** a plant or animal living naturally in a place

¹**natural** *adj* **1** of, concerning, or being what is or happens ordinarily in the world, esp. **a** not caused, made, or controlled by people: *the natural mineral wealth of a country* **2** expected from experience; usual: *It's natural to shake hands with someone you've just met* **3** not looking or sounding different from usual: *Try to look natural for your photograph* **4** belonging to someone from birth; not learned: *natural charm* **5** (of a person) not needing to be taught; having a skill or quality already in oneself: *a natural musician* **6** (of a family member) actually having the stated relation even if not in law: *John was adopted as a baby: he never knew his natural parents* **7** (of a note in music) not sharp or flat: *Don't sing C sharp, sing C natural!* – ~**ness** *n*

²**natural** *n* *esp. spoken* someone or something well suited or certain to succeed: *The horse is a natural to win the next race* **2** (in music) **a** a note which is not raised or lowered by a sharp or flat; a white note on the piano: *a piece of music played only on the naturals* **b** also **natural sign** – the sign showing that a note is not raised or lowered

naturalist *n* a person who studies plants or animals

naturally *adv* **1** by nature **2** without trying to look or sound different from usual **3** of course; as one could have expected: *'Did you win the game?' 'Naturally.'*

nature *n* **1** the qualities which make someone or something different from others; character **2** type; kind; sort: *ceremonies of a solemn nature* **3** the whole world, esp. as something lasting and not changed by people: *the beauties of nature / a struggle against nature*

naughty *adj* **-tier, -tiest** bad in behaviour; not obeying a parent, teacher, set of rules, etc. **a** (of children or their actions): *It's naughty to pull your sister's hair* **b** humour (of grown-up people): *It was naughty of Father to stay out so late* – **-tily** *adv* – **-tiness** *n*

nauseate *v* **-ated, -ating 1** to cause to feel sick: *a nauseating smell* **2** to be hateful to (someone); sicken

nautical *adj* of or concerning sailors, ships, or the practice of sailing – ~**ly** *adv*

naval *adj* of, concerning, or belonging to a navy or ships of war

navigate *v* **-gated, -gating 1** to direct the course of (a ship, plane, vehicle, etc.) **2** to go by sea, air, etc. from one side or end to the other of (a place) – **-ation** *n*

navy *n* **navies** the organization, including ships, people, buildings, etc., which makes up the power of a country for war at sea

¹**near** *adj, adv, prep* not far from in distance, time, degree, quality, etc.; close (to): *the near future / a house near the river / It's not exactly right, but it's near enough*

²**near** *adj* **1** closely related: *Only near relatives were invited to the wedding* **2** (of one of 2 things) **a** left-hand:

the near front wheel of a car / the pony's near foreleg – opposite **off b** closer: *the near bank of the river* – ~**ness** *n*

³**near** *v* to come closer (to)

nearby *adj, adv, prep* near; within a short distance (from): *a football match being played nearby / in a nearby field*

nearly *adv* almost; not quite or not yet completely: *The job's nearly finished. / I nearly beat him at chess last night*

neat *adj* **1** showing care in appearance; tidy: *neat handwriting* **2** liking order and good arrangement: *Cats are neat animals* **3** simple and exact; elegant: *a neat description* **4** clever and effective: *a neat trick* **5** *esp. spoken* (of alcoholic drinks) without ice or water or other liquid: *I like my whisky neat* – ~**ly** *adv* – ~**ness** *n*

necessarily in a way that must be so; unavoidably: *Good-looking food doesn't necessarily taste good*

necessary *adj* **1** that must be had or obtained; needed: *Food is necessary for life* **2** that must be; determined or fixed by the nature of things: *Death is the necessary end of life*

necessity *n* **-ties 1** the condition of being necessary, needed, or unavoidable; need **2** something that is necessary: *Food and clothing are necessities of life* **3** the condition of being poor or in need: *He was forced by necessity to steal a loaf of bread*

¹**neck** *n* **1** the part of the body between

the head and shoulders **2** this part of the body of an animal, used as food **3** the part of a garment for this part of the body **4** the part of something which is shaped like this part of the body: *the neck of a bottle* **5 get it in the neck** *esp. spoken* to be severely scolded or punished **6 neck and neck** *esp. spoken* (of 2 horses, people, etc., in competition) equal in position **7 risk one's neck** to endanger one's life **8 up to one's neck in** also **up to one's ears in**– *esp. spoken* deeply concerned in: *up to my neck in debt*

²**neck** *v esp. spoken* to kiss, caress, etc.

necklace *n* a string of jewels, beads, pearls, etc., on a chain of gold, silver, etc., worn round the neck as an ornament

¹**need** *n* **1** the condition of lacking or wanting something necessary or very useful: *children's need for milk* **2** what must be done; obligation: *No need to go yet: it's still early* **3** *esp. written* something necessary to have: *supply all our needs* **4** *esp. written* the state of not having enough food or money; poverty: *illness, need, and other troubles of the world* **5 if need be** if it's necessary: *I must finish this job! I'll work all night if need be*

²**need** *v negative short form* **needn't 1** to have a need for; want for some useful purpose; lack; require: *Children need milk. / My shirt needs a button. / This job needs a lot of care, attention, and time. / You* *didn't need to tell him the news; it just made him sad* **2** to have to: *We needn't go yet; the show doesn't start for an hour. | Need you go so soon? | You needn't have told him the news; he knew it already*

¹**needle** *n* **1** a long metal pin used in sewing for pulling thread, with a sharp point at one end and a hole in the other end for the thread **2** a thin pointed object that seems to look like this: *a pine needle* **3** any of various thin rods with points or hooks used in working with wool or other cloth: *knitting needles* **4** (in a record player) the very small pointed jewel or piece of metal which touches a record as it turns and picks up the sound recorded on it **5 needle in a haystack** something very small which is hard to find in a big place

²**needle** *v* **-dled, -dling** *esp. spoken* to annoy by repeated unkind remarks; tease

needless *adj* not needed; unnecessary –~**ly** *adv*

¹**negative** *adj* **1** declaring 'no': *a negative answer / negative expressions like 'not at all'* **2** without any active, useful, or helpful qualities: *negative advice that only tells you what not to do* **3** showing the lack of what was looked for, hoped for, or expected: *The test for bacteria was negative* (=none were found) **4** (of or in electricity) of the type that is based on electrons **5** (of a photograph or film) showing dark places in nature

as light and light places as dark **6 a** (of a number or quantity) less than zero: *a negative profit* (=a loss) **b** of or concerning such a quantity: *the negative sign* (=the sign −) −~**ly** *adv*

²**negative** *n* **1** a statement saying or meaning 'no'; a refusal or denial: *The answer to my request was a strong negative* **2** one of the words and expressions 'no', 'not', 'nothing', 'never', 'not at all', etc. **3** a negative photograph or film

¹**neglect** *v* **1** to give no or too little attention or care to **2** to fail (to do something), esp. because of carelessness or forgetfulness: *Don't neglect to lock the door*

²**neglect** *n* **1** the action of neglecting **2** the condition or fact of being neglected: *an old person living in unhappy neglect*

negligent *adj* **1** not taking or showing enough care **2** showing little effort; careless in a usu. pleasant way: *to dress with negligent grace* −~**ly** *adv* − **-gence** *n*

negligible *adj* too slight or unimportant to make any difference or to be worth any attention − **-bly** *adv*

negotiate *v* **-ated, -ating 1** to talk with another person or group in order to settle a question; try to come to an agreement **2** to produce (an agreement) or settle (a piece of business) in this way: *The trade union negotiated a new contract* **3** to deal with: *a player negotiating a*

hard piece of music − **-ation** − **-ator** *n*

Negress *n technical or not polite* a Negro woman

Negro *n* **-es** *technical or not polite* **1** a person belonging to a division of mankind, with black or dark skin, living in Africa south of the Sahara **2** a descendant of such people, living in the US or elsewhere

neighbour *n* one of 2 or more people that live near one another

neighbourhood *n* **1** a group of people and their homes forming a small area within a larger place such as a town: *a quiet neighbourhood* **2** the area around a point, place, or amount (esp. in the phrase **in the neighbourhood (of)**): *He paid in the neighbourhood of £500 for the car*

¹**neither** *adj, pron* not one and not the other of 2: *'Which of the books did you like?' 'Neither (of them)! They were both dull.' / Neither book was exciting; they were both dull*

²**neither** *conj* (used before the first of 2 or more choices separated by 'nor') not either: *He neither ate, drank, nor smoked; he liked neither the meal nor the cigarettes*

³**neither** *adv* also not: *'I can't swim!' 'Neither can I!'*

nephew 1 the son of one's brother or sister **2** the son of one's wife's or husband's brother or sister

¹**nerve** *n* **1** any of the threadlike parts of the body which form a system to carry feelings and messages to and from the brain **2** strength or control

of mind: *a man of nerve* **3** rude or disrespectful boldness **4** any of the stiff lines on a leaf or an insect's wing **5 strain every nerve** to try as hard as possible

²**nerve** *v* **nerved, nerving** to give courage to

nervous *adj* **1 a** excited and anxious; worried **b** of or resulting from this kind of condition: *a nervous smile* **c** (of a person) easily excited and worried **2** of or related to the nervous system of the body, or to the feelings: *a nervous disease* **3** slightly afraid; timid: *nervous of going too near the wild animals* −~**ly** *adv* −~**ness** *n*

nervous system *n* the system in animals (=the brain, spinal cord, and nerves) which receives and passes on feelings, messages, and other such information from inside and outside the body

¹**nest** *n* **1** a hollow place built or found by a bird for a home and a place to hold its eggs **2** the settled and protected home of any of certain other animals or insects: *an ants' nest* **3** a protected place for hiding or evil activity: *a nest of crime* **4** a group of like objects which fit closely into or inside one another: *a nest of tables*

²**nest** *v* **1** to build or use a nest **2** to fit closely inside another thing or each other: *nested cooking pots*

¹**net** *n* **1** a material of strings, wires, threads, etc. twisted, tied, or woven together with regular equal spaces

between them **2** any of various objects made from this, such as **a** a large piece spread out under water to catch fish **b** a carrier for goods **c** a length dividing the 2 sides of the court in tennis, badminton, etc. **d** the goal in football, hockey, etc. **3** a trap made from this: *a butterfly net* **4** *technical* a flat drawing which, when folded, forms a solid **5** a piece of material in a frame, used (as by firemen) for catching someone falling or jumping

²**net** *v* **-tt- 1** to catch in or as if in a net: *netted no fish large enough to keep* **2** to cover with a net: *Net the fruit trees to protect them from birds*

³**net** *adj* **1** (of an amount) when nothing further is to be subtracted: *net profit* (=after tax, rent, etc. are paid) **2** when everything has been considered; final: *The net result of the tax changes was to make the rich even richer* **3** (of a price) not allowed to be made lower: *The price of the book is £3 net*

⁴**net** *v* **-tt-** to gain as a profit

¹**nettle** *n* any of various wild plants which may sting and make red marks on the skin

²**nettle** *v* **-tled, -tling** to annoy (someone); make (someone) angry or impatient

network *n* **1** a system of lines, tubes, wires, etc., that cross or meet one another: *Britain's railway network* **2** a group or system whose members are connected in some way **3** a group of radio or television stations in different places using many of the same broadcasts

neuter *adj* **1** (in grammar) in a class of words that are not masculine or feminine: *'It' is a neuter pronoun* **2** (of plants or animals) with no or undeveloped sexual organs: *Worker bees are neuter*

¹neutral *adj* **1** in a position in between opposite or different choices; with no qualities of the stated kind, as of something **a** very weak or colourless: *trousers of a neutral colour that look good with any colour of socks* **b** (in chemistry) neither acid nor base **c** with no electrical charge **2** being or belonging to a country which is not fighting or helping either side in a war **3** without any feelings on either side of a question: *I'm neutral in this argument: I don't care who wins* **4** (in a car or other machine) of or concerning the position of the gears in which no power is carried from the engine to the wheels – ~**ity** *n* – ~**ly** *adv*

²neutral *n* the neutral position of the gears in a car or other machine

neutron *n* a very small piece of matter like a proton that is part of the centre of an atom and carries no electricity

never *adv* **1** not ever; not at any time: *I've never met him and I hope I never will* **2** not: *Never fear! / This shirt will never do! / Never mind about the washing-up – I'll do it later* **3 Never mind** *esp. spoken* Don't worry, it does not matter

nevertheless *adv* in spite of that; yet: *I can't take your advice. Nevertheless, thank you for giving it. / He's stupid, but I like him nevertheless*

new *adj* **1** having begun or been made only a short time ago or before: *a new government / new fashions* **2** not used by anyone before: *We sell new and used furniture* **3 a** being found or becoming known only now or recently: *a new star* **b** being in the stated position only a short time: *the new nations of Africa* **4** different from the earlier thing or things ; fresh: *to learn a new language / a new day* **5** taken from the ground early in the season: *small new potatoes* – ~**ness** *n*

news *n* **1** what is reported, esp. about a recent event or events; new information: *news of the election results* **2** any of the regular reports of recent events broadcast on radio and television

newsagent *n* a person in charge of a shop selling newspapers and magazines

newspaper *n* also (*esp. spoken*) **paper**– a paper printed and sold to the public usu. daily or weekly, with news, notices, etc.

next *adj, adv* **1** without anything coming between: *the next house* **2** following nearest in time: *next week / What happened next?*

next door *adv* in or being the next building: *the neighbours next door* –**next-door** *adj*

¹next to *prep* **1** also **next**– in the

closest place to: *I don't like wool next to my skin* **2** closest in order, degree, etc. to: *Next to riding, I like swimming best*

²**next to** *adv esp. spoken* almost: *The speech said next to nothing*

nib *n* the pointed usu. metal piece fitting on the end of a pen, with a crack for ink to flow to the point

¹**nibble** *v* **-bled, -bling 1** to eat with small bites: *Aren't you hungry? You're only nibbling at your food* **2** to show interest; show signs of accepting something

²**nibble** *n esp. spoken* **1** an act of nibbling at something **2** a very small amount of food

nice *adj* **1** good, esp. **a** kind: *How nice of you to do that!* **b** well done or made: *a nice piece of work* **c** pleasant; pleasing: *How nice to see you!* **2** showing or needing careful understanding; delicate: *a nice point of law* **3** *offensive & esp. spoken* bad; wrong: *You're a nice friend: you won't even lend me £5!* –~**ly** *adv* –~**ness** *n*

¹**nickname** *n* a name used informally instead of one's own name, usu. given because of one's character or as a short form of the **real name**

²**nickname** *v* **-named, -naming** to give (someone) a nickname

nicotine *n* a chemical which is poisonous alone and which provides the taste and effect of tobacco

niece *n* **1** the daughter of one's brother or sister **2** the daughter of one's wife's or husband's brother or sister

night *n* **1** the dark part of each day **2** any of various parts of this period, such as **a** the evening: *Saturday is our cinema night* **b** the period after bedtime: *sleep well all night* **3 have a good/bad night** to sleep well/ badly **4 make a night of it** *esp. spoken* to spend all or most of the night in enjoyment **5 night and day** also **day and night**– *esp. spoken* all the time

nightingale *n* any of several European birds related to the robin, known for their beautiful song

nightmare *n* **1** an unpleasant and terrible dream **2** a bad, fearful, or terrible experience or event: *Driving on that ice was a nightmare* – **-marish** *adj* – **-marishly** *adv* – **-marishness** *n*

nil *n* **1** nothing; zero **2** (in a sport) a total of no points

nimble *adj* **1** quick, light, and neat in movement; agile: *nimble fingers* **2** quick in thinking or understanding: *a nimble imagination* – ~**ness** *n* – **-bly** *adv*

nine *adj, n, pron* **1** the number 9 **2** (in the game of golf) the first or last half of a course of 18 holes **3 nine times out of ten** *esp. spoken* almost always

nineteen *adj, n, pron* the number 19 –~**th** *adj, adv, n, pron*

ninety *adj, n, pron* **-ties** the number 90 – **-tieth** *adj, n, adv, pron*

ninth *adj, adv, n, pron* 9th

¹nip *v* **-pp-** **1** to catch (something or someone) in a tight sharp hold between 2 points or surfaces: *The dog nipped the postman on the leg* **2** to cut off by this means: *to nip off the corner of the page with scissors* **3** *esp. spoken* to go quickly; hurry: *I'll nip out and buy a newspaper* **4 nip in the bud** to do harm to (something), esp. so as to keep from succeeding

²nip *n* **1** a coldness or cold wind: *a nip in the air* **2** the act or result of nipping

³nip *n esp. spoken* a small amount of a strong alcoholic drink

nitrogen *n* a gas that is an element without colour or smell, that forms most of the earth's air, and that is found in all living things

¹no *adv* **1** (in an answer expressing refusal or disagreement): *'Will you come to the match?' 'No, thanks.'* / *'Is it raining?' 'No, it's snowing'* **2** not any: *I'm afraid he's no better today* **3** (after *or*) not: *You'll have to do it, whether or no*

²no *adj* **1** not a; not one; not any: *no flowers in the garden* / *no sugar* / *I have no umbrella* **2** not any.... allowed: *No smoking* / *No bicycles against this wall*

nobility *n* **-ties 1** (in certain countries) the group of people of the highest social rank, who have titles **2** the quality or condition of being noble in rank **3** also **nobleness**– the quality or condition of being noble in character or appearance

¹noble *adj* **1** of high quality, esp. morally; worthy; unselfish **2** admirable in appearance; grand: *a noble-looking horse* **3** of a high social rank with a title: *a noble family* **4** (of metals like gold and silver) not chemically changed by air **–nobly** *adv*

²noble –also **nobleman** (*fem.* **noblewoman**) *n* a person belonging to the class of the nobility; peer

¹nobody –also **no one** *pron* not anybody; no person: *Nobody called while you were out.* / *She likes nobody and nobody likes her*

²nobody *n* **-ies** a person of no importance: *I want to be famous! I'm tired of being a nobody*

¹nod *v* **-dd- 1** to bend (one's head) forwards and down, esp. to show agreement or give a greeting or sign **2** to let one's head drop in falling asleep while sitting down: *I nodded off in the meeting and didn't hear what was said* **3** to bend downwards or forwards: *flowers nodding in the wind*

²nod *n* an act of nodding

noise *n* **1** meaningless unwanted sound, esp. **a** the sound heard in any public place **b** unwanted sound which keeps wanted sounds on radio, telephones, etc., from being heard clearly **2** an unmusical sound that is difficult to describe or strange: *What's wrong with my car? The engine makes funny noises* **–~less** *adj* **–~lessly** *adv* **–~lessness** *n*

noisy *adj* **-ier, -iest** making or full of noise: *a very noisy office* **−noisily** *adv* **−noisiness** *n*

nomad *n* **1** a member of a tribe which travels about: *the nomads of the desert* **2** a person who travels with no fixed aim **−~ic** *adj* **−~ically** *adv*

nominate *v* **-nated, -nating 1** to suggest (someone) for election to a position **2** to appoint (someone) to such a position **− -tion** *n*

noncommittal *adj* not expressing a clear opinion or a clear intention or promise to do something **−~ly** *adv*

¹**none** *pron* **1** no amount or part: *None of that money on the table is mine* **2** not one: *None of my friends ever come to see me* **3 have none of** *esp. written* to take no part in, not allow, or not accept: *I'll have none of your stupid ideas!* **4 none other** (*used for expressing surprise*) no one else: *'It's none other than Tom! We thought you were in Africa!'*

²**none** *adv* **1 none the** in no way: *He spent 2 weeks in hospital but he's none the better for it* **2 none the wiser** not knowing about or not discovering a fact, secret, trick, etc.; unaware: *If we take only one piece of cake, mother will be none the wiser* **3 none too** not very or not at all: *The service in this restaurant is none too fast*

nonentity *n* **-ties 1** a person without much ability, character, or import-ance **2** the condition of being unimportant

nonsense *n* **1** speech or writing with no meaning or that goes against good sense **2** foolish behaviour: *a strict teacher who would stand no nonsense* **3** humorous and fanciful poetry usu. telling a rather meaningless story: *Edward Lear's wonderful nonsense*

nonstop *adv* without a pause or interruption: *Fly nonstop to New York! / music playing nonstop all night* **−nonstop** *adj*

noon *n* the middle of the day; 12 o'clock in the daytime

no one *pron* nobody

noose *n* **1** a ring formed by the end of a cord, rope, etc., which closes more tightly as it is pulled **2** a rope with such a ring in it, used to hang a person; death by hanging

nor *conj* **1** (used between the 2 or more choices after *neither*): *just warm, neither cold nor hot* **2** (used before the 2nd, 3rd, etc., choices after *not*) and/or not: *The job cannot be done by you nor me nor anyone else* **3** and also not: *I don't want to go, nor will I (=and I won't). / We have many enemies; nor can we be sure of all our friends*

normal *adj* **1** according to what is expected, usual, or average **2** (of a person) developing in the expected way; without any disorder in mind or body: *a normal child* **3** *technical* at right angles; perpendicular **4** *technical* (of a chemical solution) of

the strength of 1 gram per litre
−∼**ity** *n*

normally *adv* 1 in a normal way or to a normal degree 2 in the usual conditions; ordinarily

¹**north** *adv* towards the north: *Edinburgh is a long way north of London*

²**north** *n* 1 (the direction of) one of the 4 main points of the compass, which is on the left of a person facing the rising sun 2 (of a wind) (coming from) this direction: *a cold north wind*

¹**northeast** *adv* towards the northeast

²**northeast** *n* 1 (the direction of) the point of the compass which is half-way between north and east 2 (of a wind) (coming from) this direction: *a northeast wind*

northerly *adj* 1 towards or in the north: *the northerly shore* 2 (of a wind) coming from the north: *a cold northerly wind*

northern *adj* of or belonging to the north part of anything: *The northern half of the Earth is called the Northern hemisphere*

north pole *n* 1 (the lands around) the most northerly point on the surface of the earth, or of another planet 2 the point in the sky to the north, around which stars seem to turn

northward *adj* going towards the north: *in a northward direction*

northwards *adv* towards the north: *They travelled northwards*

¹**northwest** *adv* towards the northwest

²**northwest** *n* 1 (the direction of) the point of the compass which is half-way between north and west 2 (of a wind) (coming from) this direction: *a northwest wind*

¹**nose** *n* 1 the part of the face above the mouth, which in human beings stands out from the face, through which air is breathed, and which is the organ of smell 2 *esp. spoken* this organ regarded as representing too great interest in things which do not concern one: *Keep your nose out of my affairs!* 3 **a** the sense of smell: *a dog with a good nose* **b** the ability to find or recognize things: *Follow your nose and see what you can find out* 4 the front end of something, such as a car, plane, tool, or gun 5 **lead (someone) by the nose** *esp. spoken* to control (someone) completely 6 **pay through the nose** *esp. spoken* to pay a great deal too much money 7 **turn up one's nose at** to consider (something) not good enough to eat, take part in, etc.

²**nose** *v* **nosed, nosing** 1 to push with the nose 2 to move or push (oneself, a vehicle, etc.) ahead slowly or carefully

nostalgia *n* fondness for something formerly known or for some period in the past − **-gic** *adj* − **-gically** *adv*

nostril *n* either of the 2 openings at the end of the nose, through which air is drawn

nosy, nosey *adj* **-ier, -iest** *offensive & esp. spoken* interested in things that do not concern one −**nosiness**

not *adv* 1 (used for changing a word or

expression to one with the opposite meaning): *I will not pay that bill! / It's a cat, not a dog. / Not everyone likes that book. / (pompous) It's a not unwelcome piece of news* (= it is very welcome) **2** (used in place of a whole expression): *Are you coming or not? / Is she in? If not, could I speak to her sister?* **3 not a** (used before a noun) no: *'How much did this cost?' 'Not a penny!'* **4 Not at all** (an answer to polite praise or thanks): *'Thanks for your trouble.' 'Not at all: I enjoyed it'* **5 not to say** *esp. spoken* and almost; or perhaps even: *He sounded impolite, not to say rude*

¹**notable** *adj* worthy of notice; remarkable, important, or excellent – **-bility** *n*

²**notable** *n* a person of high rank, fame, or importance

¹**notch** *n* **1** a V-shaped cut in a surface or edge **2** a degree; step: *a good book, several notches above anything else by this writer*

²**notch** *v* **1** to make a notch in **2** *esp. spoken* to win or record (a victory or gain): *The team notched up their 3rd victory in a row*

¹**note** *v* **noted, noting 1** to pay attention to and remember: *Please note that this bill must be paid within 10 days* **2** to recognize; observe: *You may have noted that my address has changed* **3** to call attention to; show: *The newspaper does not note what happened next*

²**note** *n* **1 a** a musical sound, usu. of a particular length and pitch **b** a written sign for any of these sounds **2 a** a quality of voice: *a note of anger in what he said* **b** any quality; element: *a note of carelessness in the way she acted* **3** a record or reminder in writing: *Make a note of how much money you spend* **4** a remark added to a piece of writing (as at the side or bottom of a page, or at the end) **5** a short letter **6** a piece of paper money: *a pound note* **7 compare notes** to exchange one's experiences and opinions **8 mental note** something fixed in the mind or to be remembered **9 of note** of fame or importance: *a musician of note*

notebook *n* a book of plain paper in which notes may be written

noted *adj* well-known; famous: *a town noted for its cheeses*

notepaper *n* paper suitable for writing letters

¹**nothing** *pron* **1** no thing; not any thing: *There's nothing in the box. / Nothing's left. / I got it for nothing. / All that work was for nothing! He doesn't want it. / It's nothing serious* **2 not... for nothing** *esp. spoken* not without some (stated or understood) reason: *'What delicious food!' 'I didn't go to cookery classes for nothing!'* **3 to say nothing of** without even considering

²**nothing** *n* a thing or person with no value or importance

¹**notice** *n* **1 a** a warning or information about something to happen: *Can you be ready at short notice?* **b**

formal instruction that a person will no longer live or work in a place **2** attention: *Take particular notice of the road signs* **3** a usu. short written statement of information or instruction **4** a review: *The new play got mixed notices* **5 until further notice** *esp. written* from now until another change is made: *This office will close at 5 o'clock until further notice*

²**notice** *v* **noticed, noticing** to pay attention (to) with the eyes, other senses, or mind: *Did you notice whether I locked the door?*

notice board *n* a board on a wall for notices

notify *v* **-fied, -fying** to tell (someone), esp. formally

notion *n* an idea, belief, or opinion (in someone's mind): *I haven't the faintest notion what you're talking about*

notorious *adj* widely and unfavourably known: *a notorious thief* – ~**ly** *adv*

nought *n* (the figure) 0; zero

noun *n* a word naming a person, thing, quality, action, etc., that can be used as the subject or object of a verb. Nouns are marked *n* in this dictionary

nourish *v* **1** to give good health or growth: *nourishing food* **2** to keep alive: *to nourish a dislike* – ~**ment** *n*

¹**novel** *adj* new, esp. clever or strange: *a novel suggestion*

²**novel** *n* a long written story, usu. in prose , about invented people:

Dickens wrote many novels – ~**ist** *n*: *the famous novelist Dickens*

novelty *n* **-ties 1** the state or quality of being novel **2** something new and unusual: *Hard work was no novelty to him* **3** an unusual cheap small object: *a novelty toy*

November *n* the 11th month of the year

novice *n* **1** a person without experience ; beginner: *a novice at swimming* **2** a member of a religious group training to become a monk or nun

¹**now** *adv* **1** at this time; at present: *We used to live in Bristol but now we live in Bath* **2** (used to attract attention): *Be careful, now!* **3** calculating from or up to the present: *He's been dead for years now*

²**now** *n* the present moment: *Now's the time for action*

nowadays *adv* (esp. in comparisons with the past) in these modern times; now: *We used to drive a lot, but nowadays petrol costs too much*

nowhere *adv* **1** not anywhere; (in/at/ to) no place: *nowhere to be found / The old lady went nowhere* **2** (to/at) no purpose or result: *That will get you nowhere*

nuclear *adj* **1** of, concerning, or being a nucleus **2** of, concerning, or using atomic energy, or the atom bomb: *nuclear physics*

nucleus *n* **-clei 1** an original or central point, part, or group inside a larger thing, group, organization, etc.: *100 books as the nucleus of a new* *library* **2** the central part of an atom, made up of neutrons and protons **3** a part in or near the centre of many cells of living matter that acts as a control centre and contains the genes

¹nude *adj* not wearing clothes; naked: *nude swimming* **–nudity** *n*

²nude *n* a usu. female nude person, esp. in a photograph or work of art **2** a work of art showing a nude person, often a woman **3** the state of being nude: *in the nude*

¹nudge *v* **nudged**, **nudging** to touch or push gently: *nudged her to say it was time to go*

²nudge *n* a slight push

nuisance *n* a person, state of affairs, etc., that annoys: *Don't make a nuisance of yourself. / What a nuisance! I've forgotten my ticket*

¹numb *adj* unable to feel anything: *numb with cold* **–~ness** *n* **–~ly** *adv*

²numb *v* to make numb: *fingers numbed with cold*

¹number *n* a member of the system used in counting and measuring; a written symbol for one of these, or a digit: *Let* x *be a number from 1 to 10. / page numbers in the right-hand corners* **2** (*before one of these, usu. written* No., *or* no.) (having) the stated size, place in order, etc.: *a number 9* (=size 9) (*shoe*) / *We live at no. 107 Church Street* **3** (a) quantity or amount: *Members are few in number* **4** a group: *Their numbers were increased by new*

members **5** a (copy of a) magazine printed at a particular time; issue **6** a piece of music: *She sang several numbers from the musical* **7** **opposite number** a person with the same position in another organization, team, etc.

²number *v* **1** to reach as a total; be ... in number: *The books in the library number in the thousands* **2** to include or be included; count: *He numbers among the best writers* **3** to give a number to: *number the seats*

numeral *adj*, *n* (a sign) that represents a number

numerous *adj* **1** many: *numerous books* **2** of large number: *Those birds have become more numerous lately* **–~ly** *adv* **–~ness** *n*

nun *n* a woman member of a religious order who swears to serve God by obedience, owning nothing, and not marrying

¹nurse *n* **1** a person who cares for sick, hurt, or old people **2** *also* **nursemaid–** a woman employed to take care of a young child

²nurse *v* **nursed**, **nursing 1** to give (a baby) milk from the breast **2** to act as or be a professional nurse **3** to take care of as or like a nurse: *He nursed her back to health* **4** to take care of someone suffering from: *This disease is very hard to nurse* **5** to use carefully so as to preserve: *nursed a drink all evening* **6** to hold (esp. a bad feeling) in the mind: *nursed a grudge*

nursery *n* **-ries 1** a child's bedroom or playroom **2** a place where small children are looked after for a short time **3** a place where young plants and trees are grown for sale or replanting

nut *n* **1 a** a dry fruit with a kernel surrounded by a hard shell **b** this seed, which is eaten **2** a block, usu. of metal, with a threaded hole for screwing onto a bolt **3** *sl* a foolish or mad person: *He's crazy, he's a nut!* **4** *sl* a person with a strong particular interest: *She's a Marlon Brando nut* **5** *sl* one's head: *You must be off your nut* (=mad)! **6** a small lump of coal **7 a hard/tough nut to crack** a difficult question, person, etc. **8 do one's nut** *sl* to be very worried and/or angry

nutrition *n* **1** providing or being provided with food; nourishment **2** the study of how the body uses food

nylon *n* a strong man-made elastic material, often made into cloth or thread

oak *n* **1** any of several types of large tree with hard wood, common in northern countries **2** the wood of this

oar *n* a pole with a wide flat blade, used for rowing a boat

oasis *n* **-ses** a place with trees and water in a desert

oath *n* **1** a solemn promise, or the form of words used in making this **2** an expression of strong feeling using religious or sexual words improperly **3 be on/under oath** *law*

to have made a solemn promise to tell the truth

oatmeal *n* crushed grains of oats used for making cakes and breakfast food

oats *n* **1** a type of edible grain **2** oatmeal

obedient *adj* doing what one is ordered to do; willing to obey –~**ly** *adv* --**ence** *n*

obey *v* **obeyed, obeying** to fulfil the order of: *Obey your teachers*

¹**object** *n* **1** a thing **2** something or someone that attracts attention: *an object of interest/of fear* **3** purpose; aim **4** (in grammar) word(s) saying to whom or to what a preposition is most directly related (**object of a preposition**), who is concerned in the results of an action (**indirect object of a verb**), or to whom or to what something has been done (**direct object of a verb**), as shown, in that order, as follows: *In* **Rome** *John gave* **Mary** *a* **book 5 no object** not a difficulty: *Money is no object*

²**object** *v* to be against something or someone: *Do you object to smoking?* –~**ion** *n* –~**or** *n*

obligation *n* **1** a duty **2 under an obligation** in moral debt

oblige *v* **obliged, obliging 1** to make it necessary (to do something): *I feel obliged to say 'No'* **2** *polite* to do (someone) a favour: *Could you oblige me by opening the window?* **3 (I'm) much obliged (to you)** *polite* (I'm) very grateful (to you)

obliterate *v* **-ated, -ating** to remove all signs of; destroy --**ation** *n*

oblivion *n* the state of having forgotten or being forgotten

oblivious *adj* not noticing – ~**ly** *adv* – ~**ness** *n*

oblong *adj, n* (a figure) with 4 straight sides at right angles, longer than it is wide

obscene *adj* indecent – ~**ly** *adv* – **-nity** *n*

¹**obscure** *adj* **1** hard to understand **2** not well known – ~**ly** *adv* – **-rity** *n*

²**obscure** *v* **obscured, obscuring** to hide; make difficult to see

observe *v* **observed, observing** **1** to see and notice; watch carefully: *They were observed entering the bank* **2** to act in accordance with (law or custom, esp. religious) **3** to make a remark; say – **-vable** *adj* – **-vably** *adv* – **-vant** *adj* – **-vation** *n* – ~**r** *n*

obsess *v* to fill the mind continuously

obsession *n* a fixed idea from which the mind cannot be freed – **-ive** *adj*

obsolete *adj* no longer used; out of date

obstacle *n* something which blocks the way

obstinate *adj* **1** not easy to persuade or defeat **2** not willing to obey – ~**ly** *adv* – **-nacy** *n*

obstruct *v* to block: *obstruct a road/a plan* – ~**ion** *n* an obstruction in the road

obtain *v* to get – ~**able** *Is that record still obtainable?*

obvious *adj* easy to understand; clear – ~**ly** *adv*

¹**occasion** *n* **1** a particular time: *on that occasion* **2** a proper time for something: *A birthday is no occasion for tears* **3** a special event **4** the direct cause of other events **5 have (no) occasion to** to have (no) reason to

²**occasion** *v* to cause: *Your behaviour has occasioned (us) a lot of trouble*

occasional *adj* **1** not regular in time **2** written or intended for a special occasion – ~**ly** *adv*

occupation *n* **1** taking possession of; having in one's possession **2** a job; employment **3** a way of spending time – ~**al** *adj*

occupy *v* **-pied, -pying** **1** to take and hold possession of **2** to hold (an enemy's country, town, etc.) **3** to be in during a particular period of time: *occupy a bed/a taxi* **4** to fill: *occupy space/a position/time* – **-pant** *n* – **-pancy** *n*

occur *v* **-rr-** **1** to happen **2** to exist: *Such plants don't occur here*

occurrence *n* happening: *a rare occurrence*

occur to *v prep* to come to mind: *It's just occurred to me*

ocean *n* **1** the mass of water that covers most of the earth **2** a sea; part of this mass – ~**ic** *adj*

o'clock *adv* (in telling time) exactly the hour stated: *It's 9 o'clock*

October *n* the 10th month of the year

octopus *n* **-puses** a deep-sea creature with 8 long snakelike limbs

odd *adj* **1** strange; unusual **2** not part of a set: *an odd shoe* **3** occasional:

odd job / *odd moments* **4** (after numbers) with rather more: *20-odd years* **5** (of a whole number) not exactly divisible by 2: *1, 3, 5, etc., are odd* –~**ly** *adv*

odds *n* **1** the probability of something happening: *heavy odds against winning* **2 at odds (with)** in disagreement (with) **3 it/that makes no odds** it/that makes no difference; has no importance **4 lay odds** to offer odds **5 long odds** odds that are strongly against (for example 100 to 1) **6 short odds** odds that are not strongly against (for example, 2 to 1)

odds and ends –also (*sl*) **odds and sods** *n* small articles of different types without much value

odour *n* a smell –~**less** *adj* –**odorous** *adj*

of *prep* **1** (about qualities, possessions, etc.) belonging to: *the roots of your hair* **2** made from **3** containing: *a bag of potatoes* **4** (that is) one or some from the whole or all: *several of my friends* **5** made or done by: *the shooting of the hunters* / *the plays of Shakespeare* **6** that is/are: *a friend of mine* **7** done to: *the shooting of the deer* **8** connected or concerned with: *the results of the experiment* **9** that is: *the city of New York* **10** about: *stories of adventure* **11** that has: *a woman of great charm* **12** in relation to: *east of Suez* **13** (*linking certain words in their own particular relationships with the words that complete the meaning of*

the phrase): *a lover of good music* (=*one who loves*) / *He died of fever*

¹off *adv* **1** away; aside: *drive off* **2** in or into a state of being disconnected or removed: *The handle came off.* / *with his shoes off* **3** so as not to be in use: *Turn the light/taps off* **4** to or at a (stated) distance away: *2 miles off* / *several years off* **5** so as to separate: *cut off* **6** to, into, or resulting in a state of nonexistence, completion, or discontinuance: *kill off* **7** away or free from regular work: *have Monday off* **8 better/worse off** in a better/worse condition: *You'd be better off with a bicycle* **9 right/ straight off** at once **10 well/badly off** rich/poor

²off *prep* **1** not on; away from *Keep off the grass* **2** from (a support): *Take the curtains off their hooks* **3** away from, as when subtracting: *cut a piece off* **4** to or at a (stated) distance away from: *The ship was blown off course.* / *We're going off the subject* **5** (esp. of a road) leading from: *a street off the High Street* **6** in the sea near: *an island off the coast* **7** (of a person) no longer keen on or fond of; no longer taking (esp. medicine): *He's off his food.* / *Bill's off drugs now*

³off *adj* **1** (of food) no longer good to eat or drink: *That fish smells off* **2** (of dishes in a restaurant) no longer being served (of behaviour) not what one has a right to expect: *I thought it was a bit off, not even*

answering my letter! **4** *technical* (of part of a horse or vehicle) being the right hand one of a pair of things **5** not going to happen after having been arranged: *The party's off* **6** (of the runners in a race) started **7** (esp. of electrical apparatus) not in use **8** (of a time) unfortunate; quiet and dull: *one of his off days / during the off season* **9** being the half of a cricket field to the right of a (right handed) batsman as he faces the bowler

offence *n* **1** a wrong; crime **2** something unpleasant **3** cause for hurt feelings: *give/cause offence to someone / take offence at something*

offend *v* **1** to do wrong **2** to cause displeasure to: *Her words offended me* −~**er** *n*

¹**offensive** *adj* **1** causing offence **2** attacking −~**ly** *adv* −~**ness** *n*

²**offensive** *n* **1** a continued attack **2** **take the offensive** to attack

¹**offer** *v* **1** to hold out for acceptance or refusal: *She offered me £10,000 for that book* **2** to express willingness: *offer to go*

²**offer** *n* **1** a statement offering (to do) something **2** that which is offered: *an offer of £5*

office *n* **1** a place where business, or written work connected with a business, is done **2** a place where a service is provided: *a ticket office* **3** a government department: *the Foreign Office* **4** employment and special duties: *the office of president*

5 a position of some importance, esp. in government: *in/out of office*

officer *n* **1** a person in a position of command in the armed forces **2** a person who holds a position of some importance, esp. in government, a business, or a group **3** a policeman

¹**official** *n* a person who works in government −~**dom** *n*

²**official** *adj* of or about a position of trust, power, and responsibility: *an official position*

often *adv* **1** (at) many times: *how often?* **2** usually: *Children often dislike homework*

¹**oil** *n* any of several types of liquid used for burning, for making machines run easily, or for cooking −**oily** *adj*

²**oil** *v* to put or rub oil on or into

ointment *n* a substance (often medicinal) containing oil or fat, to be rubbed on the skin

¹**okay, OK** *adv, adj esp. spoken* **1** all right: *That car goes okay now* **2** (asking for, or expressing, agreement): *Let's go there, okay?*

²**okay, OK** *v, n* **okayed, OKed; okaying, OKing** *esp. spoken* (to give) approval or permission

old *adj* **1** advanced in age: *How old are you? / 16 years old* **2** having lived, been in use, or continued for a long time:*old people/shoes/ friends* **3** former: *He got his old job back* **4** known for a long time: *the same old story* **5** (used for making a phrase stronger): *any old time / any old thing*

old-fashioned *adj* (of a type that is) no longer common: *old-fashioned ideas*

omen *n* a sign that something is going to happen in the future: *a good/bad omen*

ominous *adj* being a bad sign: *ominous black clouds* −∼**ly** *adv*

omit *v* -**tt**- to leave not included or not done −**omission** *n*

omnibus *n* **1** a book containing several works, esp. by one writer: *a Dickens omnibus* **2** *old use* a bus

¹**on** *prep* **1** also **upon**− (so as to be) touching; above and touching: *something on the table / a ring on my finger* **2** also **upon**− attached to **3** also **upon**− towards: *on my right / to march on Rome* **4** also **upon**− about: *a book on breeding rabbits* **5 a** during; at the time of: *on Tuesday / on June 1st* **b** also **upon**− at or directly after the event of: *on his appointment as manager* **6** also **upon**− by means of; using: *travel on the train / live on potatoes* **7** in a state of: *on purpose / on holiday*

²**on** *adv* **1** continuously: *He worked on right through lunchtime* **2** further; forward: *Shall we go on?* **3** so as to be in use: *Switch the radio on / Put the alarm on for 7 o'clock* **4** so as to fasten to something: *sew the button on* **5** (of a clock) forward **6 not on** *esp. spoken* impossible to do: *You can't refuse now − it's just not on!*

³**on** *adj* **1** in use; working properly: *Is the gas on? / The radio's on but it isn't working* **2** happening or about to happen; performing or being performed: *There's a new play on tonight. / Is the match still on?* (= is it now taking place? *or* will it take place as arranged?) **3** being the half of a cricket field to the left of a (right-handed) batsman as he faces the bowler

¹**once** *adj* **1** on one occasion: *I've done it once* **2** some time ago: *He once knew her* **3 all at once** suddenly **4 at once a** without delay: *Do it at once!* **b** at the same time: *Don't all speak at once!* **5 once (and) for all** for the last time **6 once or twice** several times; a few times **7 once upon a time** some time ago

²**once** *n* on one occasion: *Do it just this once*

³**once** *conj* from the moment that: *Once printed, this dictionary will be very popular!*

¹**one** *adj, n* **1 a** the number 1: *twenty-one / one o'clock* **b** a: *one/a thousand* (=1,000) */ one/a litre of wine* **c** (in the phrase **one of**): *one of your friends* **2** a certain: *one Sunday* **3** (esp. before past or future times) some: *one day soon* **4** the same: *of one mind* **5** (the) only necessary and desirable: *the one person for this job* **6** (*as opposed to* another, the other, etc.) a particular example or type (of): *He can't tell one tree from another* **7 a one** a bold amusing person: *Oh, you are a one!* **8 a right**

one a fool **9 be one up (on someone)** to have the advantage (over someone) **10 one and the same** the very same

²**one** *pron* **1** (*used instead of a noun phrase that means a single thing or person*): *I haven't a pen; can you lend me one?* **2** any person: *One should do one's duty*

oneself *pron* **1** (*reflexive form of* ONE): *One can't enjoy oneself if one is too tired* **2** (*strong form of* ONE): *One can often make better cakes oneself than the kind the baker sells* **3 to oneself** for one's own private use

onion *n* a round white vegetable, strong smelling, much used in cooking

¹**only** *adj* having no others in the same group

²**only** *adv* and nothing or no one else: *I had only 5 pence. / I only touched it! / Only the goalkeeper can handle the ball*

³**only** *conj* but: *You may go, only come back*

onto *prep* to a position or point on: *He jumped onto/on the horse*

onward *adj* directed or moving forward

onwards *adv* forward in time or space: *from today onwards / moving onwards across the desert*

opaque *adj* **1** not allowing light to pass through **2** hard to understand — **-acity** *n* **−~ly** *adv* **−~ness** *n*

¹**open** *adj* **1** not shut **2** not enclosed: *open fields* **3** not blocked: *An open river is one without ice* **4** not covered: *an open boat* **5** not fastened: *an open shirt* **6** not finally decided or answered: *an open question* **7** not closed to new ideas or experiences: *an open mind* **8** not filled: *The job is still open* **9** not hidden: *open hatred* **10** not hiding anything; honest: *Let's be open with each other* **11** ready for business: *The bank isn't open yet* **12** ready for use: *She kept her bank account open* **13** that anyone can enter: *an open competition* **14** spread out; unfolded: *The flowers are open* **15** (of a cheque) not crossed

²**open** *v* **1** to make or become open **2** to spread out or unfold: *to open a book* **3** to start or cause to start **4** to start or cause to start the usual activities: *to open a new hospital* **5** to make or make usable (a passage) by unblocking it **6 open fire** to start shooting

³**open** *n* **1** the outdoors **2 in(to) the open** (of opinions, secrets, etc.) in(to) general knowledge

¹**opening** *n* **1** the act or an act of becoming or causing to become open **2** a hole or clear space **3** a favourable set of conditions (for): *a business opening* **4** an unfilled position in an organization

²**opening** *adj* first: *opening words*

openly *adv* **1** not secretly **2** in a way suggesting willingness to try new ideas **−openness** *n*

opera *n* a musical play in which many or all of the words are sung **−~tic** *adj* **−~tically** *adv*

operate *v* **-rated, -rating 1** to (cause to) work: *to operate a machine/a factory* **2** to produce effects: *The new law doesn't operate in our favour* **3** to be in action: *That business operates in several contries* **4** *medical* to cut the body in order to set right or remove a diseased part

operation *n* **1** (a state of) working; the way a thing works **2** a state in which effects can be produced: *When does the law come into operation?* **3** an (esp. military) action or code name for this: *the army's operations / Operation Sunshine* **4** a thing (to be) done **5** also **op–** *medical* an act of operating **6** *technical* the use of a rule to get one mathematical expression or figure from others

operator *n* **1** a person who works a machine, apparatus, etc. **2** a person who works a telephone switchboard **3** *often offensive* a person whose operations are successful but perhaps unfair: *a clever/smooth operator*

opinion *n* **1** that which a person thinks about something **2** that which people in general think about something **3** professional judgment or advice

opponent *n* a person who takes the opposite side

opportunity *n* **-ties** a favourable moment or occasion (for doing something)

oppose *v* **opposed, opposing 1** to be, act, or set in action against **2 be opposed to** to oppose

¹**opposite** *n* a person or thing that is as different as possible (from another): *Black and white are opposites*

²**opposite** *adj* **1** as different as possible from **2** facing: *the houses opposite*

³**opposite** –also **opposite to** *prep* facing: *the houses opposite ours*

opposition *n* **1** the act or state of being opposed to or fighting against **2** the political parties, esp. the largest, opposed to the government **3** *technical* a situation when the sun, the earth, and one of the outer planets are in a straight line

oppress *v* **1** to rule in a hard and cruel way **2** to cause to feel ill or sad: *oppressed by the heat* –~**ion,** ~**iveness** *n* – ~**ive** *adj* –~**ively** *adv* – ~**or** *n*

optic *adj* of or belonging to the eyes or the sense of sight –~**al** *adj* –~**ally** *adv*

optician *n* a person who makes and sells glasses (for the eyes)

optimism *n* the belief that things will end well; a hopeful feeling about life – **-mist** *n* – **-mistic** *adj* – **-mistically** *adv*

option *n* **1** the freedom to choose or something chosen or offered for choice: *You have no option* **2** the right to buy or sell something at a stated future time

optional *adj* which may be freely chosen–or not chosen –~**ly** *adv*

or *conj* **1** (*after a negative*) and not: *He never smokes or drinks* **2** (used in a list of possibilities): *Venice or Florence or Rome* **3** if not; otherwise: *Wear your coat or you'll be cold* **4** (*used when giving a preferred word*) that is: *This medicine, or rather drug, has a violent effect*

oral *adj* **1** spoken, not written **2** *esp. medical* of, about, or using the mouth – ~**ly** *adv*

¹**orange** *n* a type of very common round bitter-sweet fruit from hot areas

²**orange** *adj* of a colour between red and yellow

³**orange** *n* (an) orange colour

oration *n* a formal and solemn public speech

orator *n* a public speaker

¹**orbit** *n* **1 a** the path of one heavenly body round another **b** the path of a man-made object round the earth or another heavenly body **c** the path of an electron around the central part of an atom **2** the area within which one person or thing can have an effect upon others – ~**al** *adj*

²**orbit** *v* to move in an orbit round

orchard *n* a place where fruit trees grow

orchestra *n* a large group of people who play music together on stringed, woodwind, brass, and percussion instruments – ~**l** *adj*

ordeal *n* **1** a difficult or painful experience **2 trial by ordeal** (in former times) judging a person by giving him a painful, frightening, and dangerous experience, and considering his behaviour

¹**order** *n* **1** the state in which things are neatly arranged in place: *I tried to bring some order to the bookshelf* **2** fitness for operation: *out of order* **3** the sequence in which a group of people, objects, etc., are arranged: *alphabetical order* **4** the condition in which laws and rules are obeyed **5** a command or direction or something to be done **6** a request (as to a tradesman) to supply goods **7** the goods supplied in accordance with such a request: *collect an order* **8** a paper that allows the holder to be paid money, to see a house that is for sale, etc. **9** the way things in general usually happen or are happening at a particular time in history **10** kind; sort: *something of that order* **11** (in biology) a division, used in putting animals, plants, etc., in groups according to relationship, which has a rank below the class and above the family **12** a group, social class, or rank in a society **13** a group of people who have all received any of several special honours given for service, bravery, etc., or the medal, ribbon, etc., worn as the sign of such an honour: *the Royal Victorian Order* / *wearing his orders* **14** a society of people who lead a holy life **15** *technical* (in mathematics) the number of columns or rows in a square arrangement (matrix) of these **16 in order that** so that **17 in order to** with the purpose or intention of: *He sent a telegram in order to warn them* **18 of/in the order of** about; about as much or

as many as **19 Order! Order!** (-spoken to call someone to order)

²**order** *v* **1** to give an order; command: *They ordered him to stop* **2** to give an order that (something) should be done or made: *order an attack* **3** to command (someone or something) to go: *I shall order you out of the hall!* **4** (of a doctor) to advise (something) as necessary **5** to ask for (something) to be brought, made, etc., in return for payment **6** to arrange, direct: *We must order our affairs better*

¹**orderly** *adj* **1** well-arranged **2** of a tidy nature and habits **3** peace-loving and well-behaved – **-liness** *n*

²**orderly** *n* **-lies 1** a soldier who attends an officer **2** an attendant in a hospital

ordinarily *adv* **1** in an ordinary way **2** usually

ordinary *adj* not unusual; common – **-ariness** *n*

organ *n* **1** a part of an animal or plant that has a special purpose **2** an organization, usu. official, that has a special purpose **3** newspapers, radio, etc., considered as able to have an effect on what people think **4** any of several musical instruments whose sound is like the largest and oldest of them, which sounds by forcing air through pipes, is played from a keyboard, and is often found in churches **5** any of certain other instruments

using air to produce music, such as a mouth organ

organism *n* **1** a living being **2** a whole made of specialized parts each of which is necessary

organization, -sation *n* **1** the arrangement of parts to form an effective whole **2** a group of people with a special purpose – ~**al** *adj* – ~**ally** *adv*

organize, -ise *v* **-ized, -izing** to form (parts) into a whole – ~**r** *n* – ~**d** *adj*

orgy *n* **orgies** a wild unrestrained party – **-giastic** *adj*

Orient *n* Asia; the (Far) East – ~**al** *adj, n*

origin *n* **1** a starting point **2** parents and conditions of early life: *a woman of noble origin(s)*

¹**original** *adj* **1** first; earliest **2** new; of a new type: *an original idea/ invention* **3** able to be new or different from others: *an original thinker* **4** not copied: *an original painting* – ~**ity** *n*

²**original** *n* **1** (usu. of paintings) that from which copies can be made **2** the language in which something was originally written: *studying Greek to read Homer in the original*

originally *adv* **1** in the beginning **2** in a new or different way

¹**ornament** *n* **1** that which is added to decorate something **2** an object possessed for its beauty – ~**al** *adj* – ~**ally** *adv*

²**ornament** *v* to add ornament to – ~**ation** *n*

¹orphan *n* a person (esp. a child) lacking one or both parents

²orphan *v* to cause to be an orphan

orphanage *n* a place where orphan children live

orthodox *adj* 1 generally or officially accepted 2 holding accepted opinions – ~y *n*

ostensible *adj* seeming or pretended – -bly *adv*

ostrich *n* 1 a type of very large African bird with long legs and a long neck, which runs very quickly but cannot fly 2 a person who refuses to accept unpleasant reality

other *adj, pron* the remaining (one or ones) of a set; what is or are left as well as that or those mentioned; additional (ones); not the same (ones): *Where's my other glove?* | *John and the others are here.* | *I haven't brought many cakes. Could you get some others?* | *Think of others/other people as well as yourself*

otherwise *adv* 1 differently 2 apart from that: *My mother still has a cold, but otherwise we're all well* 3 if not: *We'll go early, otherwise we may not get a seat*

ought *v* 1 should: *She ought to look after her children better* 2 will probably: *Prices ought to come down soon*

ounce –*abbrev.* **oz** *n* 1 1/16 of a pound in standard measure 2 1/12 of a pound in the measure used for gold and silver 3 (even) a small amount: *if you had an ounce of sense*

our *adj* (*possessive form of* WE) belonging to us: *She's our daughter, not yours*

ours *pron* (*possessive form of* WE) that/those belonging to us: *Ours are on the table*

ourselves *pron* 1 (*reflexive form of* WE): *We saved ourselves by jumping off* 2 (*strong form of* WE): *We built the house ourselves* 3 *esp. spoken* (in) our usual state of mind or body

¹out *adv* 1 in or to the open air, the outside, etc.: *He put his tongue out* 2 away from home, a building, etc. 3 away from a central point: *Spread out all over the room* 4 completely: *I'm tired out* 5 a (of one side or player in a game such as cricket) no longer allowed to bat b (of the ball in a game such as tennis) outside the line 6 no longer fashionable 7 (of a flower) fully open and ripe 8 no longer lit: *The fire's gone out* 9 on strike: *The railwaymen came out on Monday* 10 (of the tide) low 11 **out of** *technical* born to (the stated animal, esp. a horse)

²out *v* to become known: *The truth will out*

³out *adj* 1 used for sending something away: *the out tray* 2 impossible: *That's completely out* 3 incorrect: *He's badly out in his calculations* 4 no longer lit or burning

⁴out *prep esp. spoken* out of: *He went out the door*

outbound *adj* (going) away, esp. overseas

outbreak *n* a sudden appearance of something bad

outburst *n* a sudden powerful expression of feeling or activity

outcome *n* a result

outcry *n* a public show of anger

outdated —also **out-of-date** *adj* no longer in general use

outdoor —also **out-of-door** *adj* existing, happening, done, or used not in a building

outdoors *adv, n* (in) the open air

outer *adj* on the outside further from the centre

outfit *n* **1** everything, esp. clothes, needed for a particular purpose **2** a group of people, esp. if working together

outgrow *v* **-grew, -grown, -growing** to grow more than, or too much for

outlandish *adj* strange and unpleasing —~**ly** *adv* —~**ness** *n*

¹**outlaw** *n* a criminal

²**outlaw** *v* **1** to declare (someone) to have lost the protection given by law **2** to declare (something) unlawful

outlet *n* **1** a way through which something may go out **2** a chance to use one's powers or express one's feelings

¹**outline** *n* **1** the shape, or a line or flat figure showing the shape, of something **2** the main ideas

²**outline** *v* **-lined, -lining** to make an outline of

outlook *n* **1** a view on which one looks out **2** future probabilities

output *n* production

outrageous *adj* **1** very offensive **2** unexpected and probably offensive: *her outrageous jokes* —~**ly** *adv*

¹**outright** *adv* **1** solely; completely: *She won outright. / owning the car outright* **2** without delay: *be killed outright* **3** openly: *Tell him outright just what you think*

²**outright** *adj* **1** sole; complete: *the outright owner/winner* **2** open

¹**outside** *n* **1** the outer part; the part furthest from the centre **2 at the (very) outside** at the most

²**outside** *adj* **1** facing the outside **2** in the open air **3** coming from or happening elsewhere: *outside help* **4** (of a possibility) unlikely **5** greatest acceptable (amount): *an outside figure of £100*

³**outside** *adv* to or on the outside

⁴**outside** *prep* **1** on or to the outside of **2** more than: *anything outside £100*

outsider *n* **1** a person not accepted as a member of a particular group **2** a person or animal thought unlikely to win

outskirts *n* the outer areas

outspoken *adj* expressing openly what is thought or felt —~**ly** *adv* —~**ness** *n*

outstanding *adj* **1** better than others **2** important **3** not yet settled: *outstanding work/debts* —~**ly** *adv*

outward *adj* **1** outbound: *the outward voyage* **2** towards the outside **3** on the outside: *her outward calm* **4** **outward bound** outbound

outwardly *adv* according to appearances

outwards –also **outward** *adv* **1** sideways (from the centre): *The branch is growing outwards* **2** away (from oneself): *Look outwards*

oval *n, adj* (anything which is) egg-shaped

oven *n* any of several types of heated boxlike spaces used for cooking, baking clay, etc.

¹**over** *adv* **1** downwards from an upright position **2** up, out, and downwards across an edge: *The milk's boiling over!* **3** so that another side is shown: *Turn the page over* **4** right through: *think it over* **5** across a distance: *We must ask our friends over* **6** (showing that something is repeated): *several times over* **7** remaining: *Was there any money over?* **8** so as to be exchanged: *Change these 2 over* **9** from one (person or group) to another: *sign over the money* **10** (*before an adjective or adverb*) too: *over anxious / not over keen* **11** so as to be covered: *Paint it over* **12 and/or over** and/or more: *children of 14 and over*

²**over** *prep* **1** directly above: *The lamp hung over the table* **2** completely or partly covering: *hand over heart* **3** to the other side of, by going up and down: *to jump over the wall* **4** across: *a bridge over/across the river* **5** on the far side of: *over the street* **6** down across the edge of: *to fall over the cliff* **7** in, on, or through

many or all parts of: *They travelled (all) over Europe* **8** (showing command or control): *rule over* **9** higher in rank than: *I don't want anyone over me* **10** more than: *over 30 books* **11** during: *over the years* **12** till the end of: *Are you staying over Christmas?* **13** by means of: *over the telephone* **14** on the subject of: *taking a long time over* **15 over and above** as well as

³**over** *adj* finished: *get it over (with)*

⁴**over** *n* (in cricket) a particular number of balls (usu. 6) thrown by the same bowler

¹**overall** *adj, adv* **1** including everything: *overall measurements* **2** generally: *Overall, prices are still rising*

²**overall** *n* a coatlike garment worn over other clothes

overalls *n* loose trousers worn over other clothes

overboard *adv* **1** over the side of a ship or boat into the water **2 go overboard for/about** to become very attracted to **3 throw overboard** to get rid of

overcoat *n* a warm coat

overcome *v* **-came, -come, -coming 1** to defeat **2** to take control of **3** to make (someone) weak or ill

overdo *v* **-did, -done, -doing 1** to do, ornament, perform, etc., too much **2** to use too much: *Don't overdo the salt in your cooking* **3 overdo it** to work, practise a sport, etc., too much

overdose *n* too much of a drug

overdraft *n* a sum lent to a person by a bank

¹**overflow** *v* 1 to be so full that the contents flow over the edges: *The bath/river overflowed* 2 to be very full (of): *overflowing with kindness*

²**overflow** *n* 1 an act of overflowing, or that which overflows 2 a pipe or channel for carrying away extra water

¹**overhaul** *v* 1 to examine thoroughly and perhaps repair: *overhaul a car* 2 to come up to from behind and pass (something moving)

²**overhaul** *n* a thorough examination

overhead *adj, adv* 1 above one's head 2 of overheads: *overhead costs*

overhear *v* -**heard**, -**hearing** to hear without the speakers' knowledge

¹**overlap** *v* -**pp**- to cover (something) partly and go beyond it

²**overlap** *n* the amount by which 2 or more things overlap each other

overlook *v* 1 to have or give a view of from above 2 to look at but not see; not notice 3 to pretend not to see

overnight *adv, adj* 1 for or during the night 2 suddenly: *Byron became famous overnight*

overreach —also **overleap** *v* to defeat (oneself) by trying to do too much

overriding *adj* more important than anything else

overseas *adv, adj* to, at, or in somewhere across the sea: *overseas news*

overshadow *v* 1 to throw a shadow over 2 to make appear less important

oversight *n* (an) unintended failure to notice or do something

oversleep *v* -**slept**, -**sleeping** to sleep too long

overtake *v* -**took**, -**taken**, -**taking** 1 to come up level with from behind and usu. pass 2 (of something unpleasant) to catch unawares: *overtaken by events*

¹**overthrow** *v* -**threw**, -**thrown**, -**throwing** to remove from power

²**overthrow** *n* 1 removal from power 2 (in cricket) a run made after a fielder has thrown the ball accidentally past the wicket

overtime *n, adv* 1 (time) beyond the usual working time 2 payment for working beyond the usual time

overturn *v* 1 to turn or cause to turn over 2 to remove from power

overweight *n, adj* (of) too great weight, or weighing too much: *an overweight person*

overwhelm *v* 1 (of water) to cover, or (of feelings) to overcome, completely and usu. suddenly 2 to defeat or make powerless by much greater force of numbers —~**ing** *adj* —~**ingly** *adv*

owe *v* **owed**, **owing** 1 to have to pay (a debt) (to) 2 to have an obligation or a moral debt (to): *We owe our parents a lot* —**owing** *adj*

owing to *prep* because of

owl *n* any of several types of flesh-eating night bird with large eyes —~**ish** *adj* —~**ishly** *adv*

¹**own** *adj, pron* 1 that belongs to oneself and to nobody else: *I only bor-*

rowed it; it's not my own **2 come into one's own** to begin to be properly respected for one's qualities **3 for one's very own** to have for oneself **4 hold one's own (against)** to avoid defeat (by) **5 on one's own** alone or without help

²**own** *v* **1** to possess, esp. by lawful right: *Who owns this house?* **2** to admit: *He owns he was wrong* –~**er** *n* –~**ership** *n*

ox *n* **oxen 1** a castrated bull, used for pulling vehicles and for heavy work on farms **2** any of several kinds of large animal of the cattle type, wild or used by man

oxygen *n* a colourless tasteless gas that is an element and is necessary for all life forms on earth

¹**pace** *n* **1** rate or speed in activity or of development **2** a single step in running or walking, or the distance moved in one such step

²**pace** *v* **paced, pacing 1** to walk with slow, regular steps: *They paced up and down* **2** to set the pace for: *Jones paced the runners at a moderate speed*

pacifism *n* the belief that all wars are wrong

pacifist *n* an active believer in pacifism; person who refuses to fight in a war because of such a belief

¹**pack** *n* **1** a number of things together, esp. for carrying on the back **2 a** a group of wild animals (esp. wolves) that hunt together, or a group of hunting dogs **b** (in rugby football) the forwards **3** a collection, group,

etc.: *pack of thieves/lies* **4** a complete set of usu. 52 cards used in playing a game **5** *US* a packet: *a pack of cigarettes* **6** a compress, sometimes containing ice or medicine

²**pack** *v* **1** to put (things) into containers: *a packed meal / We leave tomorrow but I haven't begun to pack yet!* **2** to fit or crush into a space: *Pack those things down to make more room* **3** to cover, fill, or surround closely with a protective material **4** to choose members of (a committee or a jury) favourable to one's own purpose or ideas **5 send somebody packing** *esp. spoken* to cause somebody undesirable to leave quickly

¹**package** *n* **1** an amount or a number of things packed together: *a large package of books* **2** the container of these things

²**package** *v* **-aged, -aging 1** to make into or tie up as a package **2** to place (food) in a special package before selling

packed *adj* full of people; crowded

packet *n* **1** a small package **2** also **packet boat** – a boat that carries mail, and usu. people also, at regular times **3** *sl* a large amount of money

pack up *v adv esp. spoken* **1** to finish work **2** (of a machine) to stop working

¹**pad** *n* **1** a soft material used to protect something or make it more comfortable, or to fill out a shape **2**

also **inkpad, inking pad**– a piece of material which is made thoroughly wet with ink, and used to ink a stamp for printing **3** a number of sheets of paper fastened together along one edge **4** the usu. thick-skinned fleshy underpart of the foot of some 4-footed animals **5** LAUNCHING PAD **6** *sl* the room, house, etc., where one lives

²**pad** *v* **-dd- 1** to protect, shape, or make more comfortable with a pad **2** to make (a speech, story, etc.) longer by adding unnecessary words

³**pad** *v* **-dd-** to walk softly, with the feet flat on the ground

¹**paddle** *n* **1** a short pole with a wide flat blade at one end or (if a **double paddle**) at both ends, used for pushing and guiding a small boat (esp. a canoe) **2** anything shaped like this, such as the foot of a duck

²**paddle** *v* **-dled, -dling 1** to move (usu. a canoe) through water, using one or more paddles; row gently **2** to swim about in water as a dog or duck does

³**paddle** *v* to walk about in water only a few inches deep

¹**padlock** *n* a lock that can be put on and taken away

²**padlock** *v* to fasten or lock by means of a padlock

¹**page** *n* **1** also **page boy** – **a** a boy servant, usu. uniformed **b** (at a wedding) a boy attendant on the bride **2** *old use* a boy of noble birth who was in training to be a knight

²**page** *v* **paged, paging** (in a hotel, club, etc.) to call aloud for (someone who is wanted)

³**page** *n* **1** one side of a sheet of paper in a book, newspaper, etc. **2** the whole sheet (both sides)

pageant *n* **1 a** a splendid public show **b** a steady continuous movement of things developing or passing by: *the pageant of history* **2** a kind of play or show, usu. out of doors, in which scenes from the history of a town are acted

paid *past tense and past part. of* PAY

pail *n* a bucket

¹**pain** *n* **1** suffering; great discomfort of the body or mind **2** a feeling of suffering or discomfort in a particular part of the body **3** also **pain in the neck** – *sl* a feeling of annoyance or displeasure, or a person, thing, or happening that causes this: *She's / it's a real pain/pain in the neck*

²**pain** *v* **1** (of a part of the body) to cause pain; hurt **2** to cause to feel pain in the mind: *It pains me to disobey you, but I must*

painful *adj* causing pain –~**ly** *adv* –~**ness** *n*

¹**paint** *v* **1** to put paint on **2** to make (a picture or pictures of) using paint: *I would very much like to paint him* **3** (of a woman) to cover (the lips, face, or cheeks) with make-up **4** to describe in clear well-chosen words, with lifelike effect

²**paint** *n* **1** liquid colouring matter for

putting or spreading on a surface **2** make-up

¹painter *n* **1** a person whose job is painting buildings, fences, etc. **2** a person who paints pictures; artist

²painter *n technical* a rope fastened to the front end of a small boat for tying it to a ship, a post on land, etc.

painting *n* **1** the act or action of painting **2** the art or practice of painting pictures, or a picture made in this way

¹pair *n* **pairs** *or* **pair 1** something made up of 2 parts that are alike and which are joined and used together: *a pair of trousers* **2 a** 2 things that are alike or of the same kind, and are usu. used together: *a pair of shoes* **b** 2 playing cards of the same value but of different suits: *a pair of kings* **3** 2 people closely connected **4** 2 animals (male and female) that stay together for a certain length of time or for life

²pair *v* to form or cause to form into one or more pairs

palace *n* a very large grand house

¹pale *adj* rather white; not bright: *a pale face / pale blue* –~**ly** *adv* –~**ness** *n*

²pale *v* **paled, paling 1** to make or become pale **2** to seem less important, beautiful, etc., when compared with

¹palm *n* **1** any of a large family of trees which grow mainly in the tropics, and which are usu. very tall with branchless stems and a mass of large leaves at the top **2** the leaf of this tree

²palm *n* **1** the inner surface of the hand between the base of the fingers and the wrist **2 grease/oil somebody's palm (with)** to bribe somebody (with)

³palm *v* to hide in one's palm, esp. when performing a trick

pamper *v* to show too much attention to ; treat too kindly

pamphlet *n* a small book with paper covers

¹pan *n* **1** any of various kinds of metal container used esp. in cooking: *Usually cooking pots have 2 small handles but pans have one long handle* **2** the bowl of a water closet **3** either of the 2 dishes on a small weighing machine **4** a container with holes or mesh in the bottom used for separating precious metals, such as gold, from other materials by washing them in water **5** a part of an old gun that held the explosive

²pan *v* **-nn- 1** to wash (soil or gravel) in a pan looking for a precious metal, or to get (a precious metal) in this way **2** *esp. spoken* criticize very severely

³pan *v* **-nn-** to move (a camera taking moving pictures) from side to side, following action

pander to *v prep* to provide something that satisfies, often for one's own purposes: *The newspapers pander to people's liking for crime stories*

pane *n* a single sheet of glass for use in a frame, esp. of a window

347

¹**panel** *n* **1** a separate usu. 4-sided division of the surface of a door, wall, etc., which is different in some way to the surface round it **2** a piece of cloth of a different colour or material, set in a dress **3** a board on which controls or instruments of various kinds are fastened **4** a group of speakers who answer questions to inform or amuse the public, usu. on a radio or television show: *a panel game* **5** a list of names of people chosen to form a jury, or the group of people on this list: *serve on a panel*

²**panel** *v* **-ll-** to divide into or ornament with panels

¹**panic** *n* (a state of) sudden uncontrollable fear: *panic when the fire started* –~**ky** *adj*

²**panic** *v* **-ck-** to feel or cause to feel panic: *The crowd panicked*

panorama *n* **1** a wide or continuously changing view or scene **2** a thorough representation in words or pictures – **-mic** *adj* – **-mically** *adv*

pansy *n* **-sies 1** a small plant with wide flat flowers **2** *esp. spoken* a girlish young man, or a male homosexual

¹**pant** *v* **1** to breathe quickly, taking short breaths, esp. after great effort or in great heat **2** to desire strongly and eagerly –~**ingly** *adv*

²**pant** *n* a short quick breath

panther *n* **-thers** or **-ther** a leopard, esp. a black one

panties *n* also **pants**– an undergarment worn below the waist and which does not cover the upper part of the leg, worn by women and girls

pantomime *n* a family entertainment usu. produced at Christmas based on a fairy story

pantry *n* **-tries 1** a small room where food is kept or prepared **2** a room in a big house, hotel, ship, where eating utensils are kept

pants *n* underpants, panties, or trousers

¹**paper** *n* **1** material made in the form of sheets from very thin threads of wood or cloth, used for writing or printing on, covering parcels or walls, etc. **2** this material used for making things which are to be thrown away after use: *a paper plate* **3** a newspaper **4** a set of questions used as an examination, or the written answers to these **5** a piece of writing for specialists, or from an official group **6 on paper** as written down or printed, but not yet tested: *These plans seem good on paper*

²**paper** *v* **1** to cover with wallpaper **2** to cover with paper in order to protect or hide

paper clip *n* a small piece of curved wire used for holding sheets of paper together

papers *n* documents

par *n* **1** (in the game of golf) the number of strokes the average player should take to hit the ball into one or all of the holes **2** a level which is equal or almost the same: *These 2 things are on a par (with each other)* **3 below par** also **under par**– not in the usual or average condition **4 (not) up to par** (not) in the usual or average condition

¹**parachute** *n* an apparatus which looks like a large umbrella, fastened to people or objects dropped from aircraft in order to make them fall slowly: *a parachute jump*

²**parachute** *v* **-chuted, -chuting** to drop or jump from an aircraft by means of a parachute – **-chutist** *n*

¹**parade** *n* **1** (esp. of soldiers) a gathering together in ceremonial order, for the purpose of being officially looked at, or for a march: *on parade* **2** a number of people standing or walking together, for the purpose of being looked at or heard **3** an act of showing oneself with the intention of making others look and admire: *made a parade of* **4** also **parade ground**– a large flat area where soldiers parade **5** a wide public path or street, usu. beside the seashore

²**parade** *v* **paraded, parading 1** (esp. of soldiers) to gather together in a parade **2** to walk showily about in order to gain admiration: *parading in her new dress* **3** to show in order to gain admiration: *parading his wealth*

paradise *n* **1** Heaven **2** (in the Bible) the Garden of Eden, home of Adam and Eve **3** a place of perfect happiness **4** a place with everything

needed for a certain activity: *a hunter's paradise* **5** a state of perfect happiness

paraffin *n* **1** also **paraffin oil**– an oil made from petroleum, coal, etc., burnt for heat and in lamps for light **2** also **paraffin wax**– a waxy substance got from petroleum, coal, etc., used esp. in making candles

paragraph *n* **1** a division of a written or printed piece made up of 1 or more sentences, of which the first word begins a new line and is often set inwards a little from the margin **2** a short item in a newspaper

¹**parallel** *adj* **1** (of 2 or more lines or planes) running side by side but staying the same distance apart **2** comparable (to): *My feelings are parallel to yours*

²**parallel** *n* **1** a parallel line, or line of things or surfaces: *on a parallel with* **2** a comparable person or thing: *without (a) parallel* **3** a comparison that shows likeness **4** an electrical arrangement in which a number of electrical apparatuses are connected in such a way that each may receive full electrical power whether or not the others are being used **5** also **parallel of latitude**– a line on a map drawn parallel to the equator

³**parallel** *v* **-l-** *or* **-ll- 1** to equal: *No one has paralleled his success* **2** to compare

paralyse *v* **-lysed, -lysing 1** to cause (some or all of the body muscles) to become uncontrollable or stiff **2**

to make ineffective: *The electricity failure paralysed the train service* – **-lysis** *n*

parasite *n* **1** a plant or animal that lives on or in another and gets food from it **2** a useless person who is supported by the wealth or efforts of others – **-sitic, -sitical** *adj* – **-sitically** *adv*

paratroops *n* a number of soldiers trained to parachute from aircraft, esp. as a fighting group – **-trooper** *n*

parcel *n* also **package**– a thing or things wrapped in paper and tied or fastened in some other way for easy carrying, posting, etc.

¹pardon *n* **1** forgiveness: *I beg your pardon* **2** *law* an action of a court or ruler forgiving a person for an unlawful act, forgiving the act itself, or giving freedom from punishment for such an act

²pardon *v* **1** to forgive **2** to give an official pardon to or for

parent *n* **1** the father or mother of a person **2** any living thing that produces another: *the parent tree* **3** that which starts something else: *Our club is the parent association, and there are now 4 others* – **~al** *adj* – **~ally** *adv* – **~hood** *n*

parish *n* **1** an area in the care of a single priest and served by one main church **2** a small area, esp. a village, having its own local government: *parish council* **3** a usu. small area which someone works in and knows very well

¹park *n* **1** a large usu. grassy enclosed place in a town, used by the public for pleasure **2** also **parkland**– a large enclosed stretch of land round a large country house

²park *v* **1** to stop or leave (a vehicle) for a time: *Don't park here* **2** to leave (something) in a place for a time: *Don't park your books on my papers!* **3** to settle (oneself) with the intention of staying for some time

Parliament *n* **1** a body of people (**Members of Parliament**) wholly or partly elected by the people of a country to make laws **2** (in the United Kingdom) the main lawmaking body, made up of the King or Queen, the Lords, and the elected representatives of the people – **~ary** *adj*

¹parody *n* **-dies 1** (a piece of) writing or music intended to amuse, which recognizably copies a known writer or musician **2** a weak and unsuccessful copy of somebody or something

²parody *v* **-died, -dying** to make a parody of – **-dist** *n*

¹parrot *n* **1** any of a large group of birds, usu. from tropical countries, having a curved beak and usu. brightly coloured feathers. Some can be taught to copy human speech **2** a person who repeats, often without understanding, the words or actions of another

²parrot *v* to repeat like a parrot

parsnip *n* a plant with a thick white

or yellowish root that is used as a vegetable

¹part *n* **1** any of the pieces that make up a whole **2** any of the divisions into which something is or may be considered as being divided: *Parts of this town are beautiful* **3** any of several equal divisions which make up a whole: *3 parts wine and 2 parts water* **4** a necessary or important piece of a machine or other apparatus **5** a share or duty in some activity: *take part in* **6** a side or position: *Tom took my part in the disagreement* **7 a** a character acted by an actor in a play **b** the words and actions of an actor in a play, or a written copy of these words **8** (in music) one of the tunes, esp. for a particular voice or instrument, which make up a piece of music, or a written copy of this **9 in part** in some degree **10 take in good part** not be offended by

²part *v* **1** to separate or no longer be together: *The war parted many men from their families* **2** to separate into parts or spread apart: *The clouds parted and the sun shone* **3** to separate or move apart: *He tried to part the 2 angry dogs* **4** to separate (hair on the head) along a line with a comb

³part *adv* partly: *A centaur is part man, part horse*

⁴part *adj* partial: *part payment*

partial *adj* **1** not complete: *a partial success* **2** favouring one side more than another, esp. in an unfair way **3** having a liking for: *I'm partial to sweets*

partially *adv* **1** partly **2** in a partial way

participate *v* **-pated, -pating** to take part or have a share in an activity or event − **-pant** *n* − **-pation** *n*

participle *n* (in grammar) a form of a verb which may be used as part of a verb (e.g. in compound tenses) or as an adjective

particle *n* **1 a** a single very small piece: *dust/sand particles* **b** *technical* a piece of matter smaller than, and part of, an atom **c** a very small quantity: *particles of food* **2** (in grammar) any of several usu. short words that are not as important in a sentence as the subject, verb, etc.: *Prepositions and conjunctions are particles*

¹particular *adj* **1** worthy of notice; special: *of particular importance* **2** single and different from others; of a certain sort: *I don't like this particular hat* **3** hard to please **4 in particular** especially − **~ity** *n* − **~ly** *adv*

²particular *n* a detail: *correct in every particular/in all particulars / I want all the particulars*

¹partition *n* **1** division into 2 or more parts (esp. of a country) **2** a part formed by dividing **3** something that divides, esp. a thin inside wall

²partition *v* to divide into 2 or more parts

partly *adv* **1** not completely: *partly*

finished **2** in some degree: *partly true*

¹partner *n* **1** a person who shares (in the same activity): *dancing partner* **2** any of the owners of a business, who share the profits and losses **3be partners with** to be a partner of, esp. in a game – ~**ship** *n*

²partner *v* to act as partner to

part-time *adj, adv* (working or giving work) during only a part of the regular working time

party *n* **-ties 1** a group of people doing something together: *a party of schoolchildren* **2** a gathering of people, usu. by invitation, for food and amusement **3** an association of people having the same political aims **4** *esp. law* one of the people or sides in an agreement or argument: *the guilty party* **5 be** (a) **party to** to be concerned in (some action or activity) **6 the party line** the official opinion of a political party

¹pass *v* **1** to go forward: *Because of the crowd the carriage was unable to pass* **2** to reach and move beyond: *That car passed ours at 90mph* **3** to move through, across, over, or between: *No one may pass the gates* **4** to place or be placed (in or for a short space of time): *We can pass a rope round this dead tree* **5** to give or be given: *Please pass the bread* **6** (in various sports) to kick, throw, hit, etc. (esp. a ball) to a member of one's own side **7** to send out from the bowels or kidneys **8 a** (of time) to go by **b** to cause (time) to go by: *She passed the time by picking flowers* **9** happen: *It came to pass that......* **10** to cause (money) to be accepted as lawful , esp. by dishonest means: *Somebody passed me a lead shilling!* **11** to say; speak: *pass a comment/a remark* **12** to give or be given official acceptance: *pass a law* **13** to succeed in (an examination) **14** to accept or be accepted as reaching a required standard: *I can't pass this bad piece of work!* **15** (of feelings, thoughts, etc.) to come to an end **16** (of actions, ideas, etc.) to go beyond the limits of: *It passes my understanding* **17** to give (a judgment, opinion, etc.) **18** to go unnoticed, unchanged, unpunished, etc.: *let something pass* **19** to go from the control or possession of one to that of another **20** (in some games) to let one's turn go by without taking any action

²pass *n* a way by which one may pass, esp. over a range of mountains

³pass *n* **1** an act of moving something (made esp. by the human hand or by an aircraft) over or in front of something else **2** (in various sports) an act of passing a ball **3** (in games) an act of passing **4** a printed piece of paper, which shows that one is permitted to do a certain thing **5** a successful result in an examination **6** a difficult state or condition **7 make a pass at** *sl* to try to make (a member of the opposite sex) sexually interested in one

passage *n* **1** the action of going across,

by, over, through, etc.: *the passage of heavy vehicles* **2** (of time) onward flow **3** a long journey by ship or aircraft or the cost of such a journey **4** a usu. narrow way through: *He forced a passage through the crowd* **5** the right or permission to go through or across something **6** also **passageway** a usu. long narrow connecting way, esp. inside a building **7** a usu. short part of a speech or a piece of writing or music, considered by itself **8 bird of passage a** a bird that regularly migrates **b** a person who often moves from one place to another **9 rough passage a** a stormy sea or air journey **b** a difficult time

passenger *n* a traveller in a vehicle

passerby *n* **passersby** a person who happens to pass by

passion *n* **1** strong feeling, esp. of sexual love **2** a sudden show of anger **3** *esp. spoken* a strong liking –~**less** *adj* –~**lessly** *adv*

passionate *adj* **1** able to feel strongly **2** showing passion : *a passionate speech* **3** very eager: *a passionate interest* –~**ly** *adv*

¹**passive** *adj* **1** not active **2** (esp. of animals) quiet; not dangerous **3** suffering but not opposing **4** *technical* expressing an action done to the subject of a sentence: *'Was thrown' is a passive verb phrase in 'The boy was thrown from his horse'* –~**ly** *adv*

²**passive** *n (in grammar)* the passive forms of a verb

passport *n* **1** a citizen's official document of identification **2** something that permits a person easily to do or get something

¹**past** *adj* **1** (of time) earlier than the present: *past years* **2** ended: *Winter is past* **3** former: *my past successes* **4** (of a verb form) expressing something that happened before now: *the past tense*

²**past** *prep* **1** after: *10 past 7* **2** up to and beyond: *The boys rushed past us* **3 put it past somebody** *esp. spoken* to consider somebody very unlikely: *I wouldn't put it past her to turn up without an invitation!*

³**past** *n* **1** the time before the present:*If only one could change the past* **2 a** (of a country) history **b** (of a person) past life, actions, etc., esp. when these contain scandal: *a woman with a past* **3** the past tense

⁴**past** *adv* to and beyond a point in time or space: *The children hurried past. | The days flew past*

pasta *n* food made from flour paste

¹**paste** *n* **1** a thin mixture used for sticking paper **2** any soft wet mixture easily shaped or spread **3** a mixture of flour, fat, and liquid for pastry **4** a spread for bread made by crushing solid foods: *fish paste* **5** a shining material made of lead and glass, used for imitation jewellery

²**paste** *v* **pasted**, **pasting** to stick with paste

pastime *n* something done to pass one's time pleasantly

pastry *n* **-tries 1** baked paste made of

flour, fat, and milk or water **2** an article of food (esp. a cake) made of this

¹pasture *n* **1** grass as food for cattle **2** land where this is grown

²pasture *v* **-tured, -turing** to put (animals) in a pasture to feed

¹pasty *n* **-ties** a small folded meat pie

²pasty *adj* **-ier, -iest** (of the face) white and unhealthy-looking

¹pat *n* **1** a light friendly stroke **2** a small shaped mass esp. of butter

²pat *v* **-tt-** to touch or strike gently and repeatedly with a flat object, esp. the palm

³pat *adv* **1** at once: *The answer came pat* **2** **have/know something (off) pat** to know something thoroughly

¹patch *n* **1** a piece of material used to cover a hole or a damaged place **2** a part of a surface that is different from the space round it: *wet patches on the wall* **3** a protective piece of material worn over an eye that has been hurt **4** also **beauty patch, beauty spot–** (in the 17th and 18th century) a small round usu. black piece of material worn by woman on the face

²patch *v* to cover (a hole) with a patch

patchwork *n* sewn work made by joining many pieces of cloth of different colours, patterns, and shapes

¹patent *adj* **1** easy to see; obvious **2** protected, by a patent, from being copied **3** concerned with patents

²patent *n* **1** a document from a government office (**Patent Office**) giving someone the right to make or sell an invention **2** the right given in such a document

³patent *v* to obtain a patent for

path *n* **1** a way made by people walking **2** a footpath **3** an open space made to allow forward movement **4** a line along which something moves: *the path of an arrow* **5** a way: *Hard work is the path to success* – ~**less** *adj*

pathetic *adj* **1** causing pity or sorrow **2** hopelessly unsuccessful – **-ically** *adv*

patience *n* **1** the ability **a** to wait calmly **b** to control oneself when angered **c** to suffer without complaining **d** to attend closely to difficult work **2** any of a number of card games, usu. for one player

¹patient *adj* having patience – ~**ly** *adv*

²patient *n* a person receiving medical treatment

patriot *n* a person who loves and will defend his country – ~**ism** *n* – ~**ic** *adj* – ~**ically** *adv*

¹patrol *n* **1** the act or time of patrolling **2** a small group of people, vehicles, etc., sent out to search for the enemy

²patrol *v* **-ll-** to go at regular times round (an area, building, etc.) to see that there is no trouble

patron *n* **1** a person or group that gives money to a person, a group , or some worthy purpose **2** a person who allows his or her name to be used in connection with some group **3** a person who uses a particular shop, hotel, etc.

patronize, -ise *v* **-ized, -izing 1** to be a patron of **2** to act towards as if one is better or more important

¹**patter** *v* to say quickly and without thought

²**patter** *n* very fast continuous amusing talk

³**patter** *v* **1** to make light quickly repeated noises **2** to run with short quick-sounding steps

⁴**patter** *n* the sound of something striking a hard surface lightly, quickly, and repeatedly

¹**pattern** *n* **1** a regularly repeated arrangement with ornamental effect **2** the way in which something develops **3** a sample of cloth **4** a shape used as a guide for making something **5** an excellent example to copy

²**pattern** *v* **1** to copy exactly **2** to make an ornamental pattern on

¹**pause** *n* **1** a short but noticeable break (in activity, or speech) **2** (in music) a mark ( ) over a note, showing that the note is to be played or sung longer than usual

²**pause** *v* **paused, pausing** to make a pause

pavement *n* a hard path at the side of a street

pavilion *n* **1** a building beside a sports field, for the players and spectators **2** a large ornamental esp. temporary building for public amusements or exhibitions **3** a large tent, esp. for shows of flowers, farm goods, etc.

¹**paw** *n* an animal's foot with nails or claws

²**paw** *v* **1** to touch or make a strike at with a paw **2** to strike at (the ground) with the hoof in anger, fear, etc. **3** *esp. spoken* to feel or touch with the hands

¹**pawn** *n* the state of being pawned (esp. in the phrase **in pawn**)

²**pawn** *v* to leave (something of value) with a pawnbroker as a promise that one will repay the money lent

³**pawn** *n* **1** (in chess) one of the 8 least valuable pieces **2** an unimportant person used by somebody else for his own advantage

pawnbroker *n* a person to whom people bring valuables so that he will lend them money

¹**pay** *v* **paid, paying 1** to give (money) for goods bought, work done, etc. **2** to settle (a bill, debt, etc.) **3** to be profitable: *We must make this farm pay* **4** to make or say (esp. in the phrases **pay a visit, pay a call, pay a compliment, pay one's respects**) **5** to give willingly (esp. in the phrases **pay attention/heed**) **6** to suffer for some bad action **−~er** *n*

²**pay** *n* **1** money received for work **2** **in the pay of** employed by: *This man is in the pay of the enemy*

payment *n* **1** paying **2** an amount of money paid **3** something done, said, or given in return

pea *n* **1** a green edible seed **2** any of various climbing plants whose pods contain these seeds

peace *n* **1** a condition or period in

which there is no war **2** freedom from disorder within a country (esp. in the phrases **keep the peace, a breach of the peace**) **3** a state of agreement among people living together **4** calmness; quietness **5** freedom from anxiety: *peace of mind*

peaceful *adj* **1** quiet; untroubled **2** loving peace **–~ly** *adv* **–~ness** *n*

¹peach *n* **1** a small tree or its round fruit with soft yellowish-red skin, sweet juicy flesh, and a large rough seed **2** the colour of this fruit **3** *esp. spoken* a person (esp. a pretty young girl) or thing greatly admired

²peach *v sl* to give information about somebody who has done wrong

peacock *n* **1** (*fem.* **peahen**) –the male of a large ornamental bird (**peafowl**) whose long tail feathers can be spread out showing beautiful colours and patterns **2** a butterfly with large patterned wings

peak *n* **1** a sharply pointed mountain **2** a part that curves to a point: *The wind blew the waves into great peaks* **3** the part of a cap which sticks out above the eyes **4** the highest point of a varying amount: *Sales have reached a new peak*

¹peal *n* **1** the loud ringing of bells **2** *technical* a musical pattern made by ringing several bells one after another **3** *technical* a set of bells on which these patterns can be played **4** a loud long sound: *peals of laughter*

²peal *v* to ring out or sound loudly

pear *n* (a tree bearing) a sweet juicy fruit, tapering towards the stem

pearl *n* **1** a hard silvery-white ball formed inside shell fish, esp. oysters, very valuable as a jewel **2** something which has the shape or colour of this **3** something or somebody very precious

peasant *n* **1** (now used esp. of developing countries or former times) a farm worker , esp. one who owns and lives on a small piece of land **2** a person without education or manners

pebble *n* a small stone found esp. on the seashore

¹peck *v* **1** to strike or eat with the beak **2** to make by striking with the beak: *The bird pecked a hole in the tree* **3** *esp. spoken* to kiss hurriedly

²peck *n* **1** a stroke or wound made by pecking **2** *esp. spoken* a hurried kiss

peculiar *adj* **1** strange; unusual: *This food has a peculiar taste* **2** *esp. spoken* rather ill **3** special; particular

peculiarity *n* **-ties 1** being peculiar **2** something peculiar, strange, or unusual

peculiarly *adv* **1** especially **2** strangely

¹pedal *n* a barlike part of a machine which can be pressed with the foot to control or drive the machine

²pedal *adj technical* of the foot

³pedal *v* **-ll- 1** to work the pedals of a machine **2** to work or move (a machine) by using pedals

pedant *n* a person whose attention to detail is too great **–~ic** *adj* **–~ically** *adv*

pedestal *n* the base on which a pillar or statue stands

¹**pedestrian** *adj* **1** connected with walking **2** lacking in imagination ; uninteresting

²**pedestrian** *n* a person walking

¹**peel** *v* **1** to remove the outer covering from (a fruit, vegetable, etc.) **2** to lose an outer covering: *The walls were peeling* **3** (of an outer covering) to come off: *My skin always peels in the sun*

²**peel** *n* the outer covering, esp. of fruits and vegetables which one peels before eating

¹**peep** *n* a short weak high sound as made by a young bird

²**peep** *v* **1** to look (at something) quickly and secretly **2** to begin slowly to appear

³**peep** *n* a short hurried look

¹**peer** *n* **1** an equal in rank **2** a member of any of 5 noble ranks in Britain (a baron, viscount, earl, marquis, or duke) **3** a person who has the right to sit in the House of Lords

²**peer** *v* to look very carefully or hard, esp. as if not able to see well

¹**peg** *n* **1** a short piece of wood, metal, etc. , esp. **a** for holding esp. wooden surfaces together **b** fixed to a wall for hanging coats and hats on **c** hammered into the ground to hold the ropes supporting a tent **3** a wooden screw to tighten or loosen the strings of certain musical instruments **4** a base for a talk or argument: *a peg to hang an argument on* **5 off the peg** (of clothes) not specially made to fit a particular person's measurements

²**peg** *v* **-gg-** to fasten with a peg

pellet *n* **1** a small ball of soft material made by or as if by rolling **2** a small ball to be fired from a gun **3** *technical* a small mass of feathers, bones, etc., thrown up from the stomach by certain meat-eating birds (e.g. owls)

¹**pelt** *n* **1** the skin of a dead animal with or without the fur or hair **2** the fur or hair of a living animal

²**pelt** *v* **1** to attack by throwing things at **2** (of rain) to fall heavily **3** to run very fast

pelvis *n* **-vises** *or* **-ves** the bowl-shaped frame of bones at the base of the backbone **—pelvic** *adj*

¹**pen** *n* a small piece of land enclosed by a fence, for keeping animals in

²**pen** *v* **-nn-** to shut in a pen or small place

³**pen** *n* **1** an instrument for writing or drawing with ink **2** the profession of writing: *He lives by his pen* **3** *literature* a writer: *a poem by an unknown pen*

⁴**pen** *v* **-nn-** *pompous* to write

penalize, -ise *v* **-ized, -izing 1** to put in a very unfavourable position **2** (in sports) to punish (a team, player, or action) by giving an advantage to the other team **3** to make punishable by law — **-ization** *n*

penalty *n* **-ties 1** punishment for breaking a law, rule, or agreement **2** suffering or loss that is the result of one's action or state **3** (in sports)

a a disadvantage given for breaking a rule **b** an advantage given because the other team have broken a rule (esp. a **penalty kick** in football) **c** also **penalty goal**– a goal scored by this means **4** (in sports) a handicap placed on a very good player or team to give the opponent a better chance of winning

pence *pl. of* PENNY

¹**pencil** *n* **1** a narrow pointed instrument containing a thin stick of lead or coloured material, for writing or drawing **2** a stick of coloured material in a holder, for darkening the eyebrows **3** a narrow beam (of light) beginning from or ending in a small point

²**pencil** *v* **-ll-** to draw, write, or mark with a pencil

penetrate *v* **-trated, -trating 1** to enter, pass, cut, or force a way into **2** to be easily heard at a distance **3** to see into or through **4** to understand **5** to fill: *The country is penetrated with fear* **6** to come to understand the truth behind (something false) – **-tration** *n* – **-trable, -trative** *adj* – **-trability** *n*

penetrating *adj* **1** (of the eye, sight, questions, etc.) sharp and searching **2** able to understand clearly **3** reaching everywhere: *penetrating cold* –~**ly** *adv*

penguin *n* a large black and white flightless swimming seabird of esp. the Antarctic

penicillin *n* a medicine used to destroy certain bacteria in people and animals

peninsula *n* a piece of land almost completely surrounded by water but joined to a larger mass –~**r** *adj*

penis *n* the outer sex organ of male animals

penknife *n* **-knives** a small knife with usu. 2 folding blades

penniless *adj* having no money

penny *n* **-nies** *or* **pence** *or* (*esp. spoken*) **p 1** also (*esp. spoken*) **copper, p**– (in Britain after 1971) a small bronze coin **2** also **old penny**, (*esp. spoken*) **copper**– (in Britain before 1971) a bronze coin, 12 to a shilling; 1d **3** a small amount of money: *It won't cost a penny* **4** **spend a penny** to urinate

¹**pension** *n* an amount of money paid regularly to someone who can no longer earn, esp. because of old age or illness –~**able** *adj*

²**pension** *n French* (not in English-speaking countries) a private boardinghouse

penultimate *adj* next to the last

¹**people** *n* **1** persons in general **2** the persons belonging to a particular place, trade, etc.: *theatre people* **3** persons without special rank or position: *a man of the people* **4** a race; nation **5** one's relatives: *I'll take you home to meet my people* **6** **go to the people** (of a political leader) to hold an election or referendum

²**people** *v* to fill (a place) with people

¹**pepper** *n* **1** a hot powder made from

crushed peppercorns, used for flavouring **2** the capsicum plant, or its fruit (a **red pepper** or **green pepper**) used as a vegetable

²**pepper** *v* to hit repeatedly (esp. with shots)

pep talk *n esp. spoken* a talk intended to encourage the listener to do well, to win, etc.

per *prep* **1** for each: *one apple per child* **2** during each: *40 words per minute / 20 miles per gallon* **3** (esp. in business letters) according to: *We have sent the parcel as per instructions*

perceive *v* -ceived, -ceiving *esp. written* to have or come to have knowledge of ; see – -ceivable *adj*

¹**per cent** *adv* in each 100; %: *I am 100 per cent in agreement*

²**per cent** *n* **per cent** one part in each 100: *This company can supply 30 per cent (= 30% = 30/100 = 3/10) of what we need*

percentage *n* an amount stated as a part of 100; proportion

perceptive *adj* quick to notice and understand – ∼ly *adv* – ∼ness *n* – -tivity *n*

¹**perch** *n* **1** a branch, rod, etc., where a bird rests **2** a high position in which a person or building is placed **3** *humour* a seat

²**perch** *v* **1** (of a bird) to come to rest from flying to go or put into the stated position (esp. on something narrow or high): *She perched on a tall chair*

¹**perennial** *adj* **1** lasting through the whole year **2** lasting forever **3** (of a plant) that lives for more than 2 years – ∼ly *adv*

²**perennial** *n* a perennial plant

¹**perfect** *adj* **1** of the very best possible kind **2** absolutely correct: *His English is almost perfect* **3** satisfying in every way **4** complete: *a perfect stranger* **5** *technical* (of verb forms, tenses, etc.) referring to a time up to and including the present (**present perfect**), past (**past perfect**), or future (**future perfect**) (as in 'He has gone', 'He *had* gone', 'He *will* have gone'): *the perfect tense*

²**perfect** *v* to make perfect – ∼ible *adj* – ∼ibility *n*

perfectly *adv* **1** in a perfect way **2** completely

perforate *v* -rated, -rating **1** to make a hole or holes through (something) **2** to make a line of small holes in (paper), so that a part may be torn off

perform *v* **1 a** to carry out (a piece of work) **b** to fulfil (a promise, order, etc.) **2** to give, act, or show (a play, a piece of music, etc.) **3** to go through the actions of (a ceremony) **4** to work or carry out an activity properly

performance *n* **1** the action of performing something **2** (of people or machines) the ability to do something **3** *esp. spoken* a (troublesome) set of preparations or activities

performer *n* **1** an actor, musician, etc. **2** a person or thing that performs:

He is a good performer on the cricket field (=plays well)

¹**perfume** –also **scent** *n* **1** a pleasant smell, as of flowers **2** sweet-smelling liquid for use on the body

²**perfume** *v* -fumed, -fuming **1** *esp. written* to fill with perfume **2** to put perfume on: *a perfumed handkerchief*

perhaps *adv* **1** it may be: *Perhaps he'll come by train* **2** (in making polite requests): *Perhaps you'll let me know*

peril *n* **1** danger **2** something that causes danger

perilous *adj* dangerous; risky – ~**ly** *adv* – ~**ness** *n*

¹**period** *n* **1** a stretch of time with a beginning and an end **2** a division of a school day: *a history period* **3** a monthly flow of blood (the menses) from a woman's body **4** *esp. US* FULL STOP

²**period** *adj* (of furniture, dress, etc.) belonging to or copying an earlier period in history

periodic –also **periodical** *adj* happening repeatedly, usu. at regular times – ~**ally** *adv*

periodical *n* a periodical magazine

periscope *n* a long tube containing mirrors so that people lower down (esp. in submarines) can see what is above them

perish *v* **1** (esp. in newspapers) to die, esp. suddenly; be completely destroyed **2** to decay or lose natural qualities: *Continuous washing has perished the rubber*

perjure *v* -jured, -juring **perjure oneself** to tell a lie on purpose after promising to tell the truth – ~**r** *n*

perjury *n* -ries **1** perjuring oneself **2** a lie told on purpose

permanent *adj* lasting for a long time or for ever – **-ence, -ency** *n* – ~**ly** *adv*

permission *n* an act of permitting; consent

¹**permit** *v* -tt- **1** to allow **2** to make possible: *weather permitting* **3** to admit: *The facts permit no other explanation*

²**permit** *n* an official written statement giving permission

¹**perpendicular** *adj* **1** exactly upright **2** (of a line or surface) at an angle of 90° to a line or surface **3** of the style of 14th and 15th century English buildings, esp. churches, ornamented with perpendicular lines – ~**ly** *adv*

²**perpendicular** *n* a perpendicular line or position

perpetual *adj* **1** lasting for ever or for a long time **2 a** uninterrupted **b** happening often – ~**ly** *adv*

perplexed *adj* **1** confused and puzzled **2** difficult to understand – ~**ly** *adv*

persecute *v* -cuted, -cuting **1** to treat cruelly (esp. for religious or political beliefs) **2** to annoy – **-cution** *n* – **-cutor** *n*

persevere *v* -vered, -vering to continue firmly in spite of difficulties – **-verance** *n*

persist *v* **1** to continue firmly in spite of opposition **2** to continue to exist

persistent *adj* **1** continuing in a habit or action **2** continuing to exist, happen, or appear: *a persistent cough* –~**ly** *adv* – **-tence** *n*

person *n* **1** a human being **2** a living human body or its appearance: *She was small and neat of person* **3** (in grammar) any of the 3 forms of verbs or pronouns that show the speaker (**first person**), the one spoken to (**second person**), or the one spoken about (**third person**)

personal *adj* **1** concerning, belonging to, or for a particular person; private **2** done directly by a particular person: *a personal visit* **3** of the body or appearance: *personal cleanliness* **4** (of things said) directed against a particular person; rude

personality *n* **-ties 1** the state of existing as a person **2** a person's character: *He has a weak personality* **3** unusual, strong, exciting character **4** a person well known to the public: *a television personality*

personally *adv* **1** directly: *He is personally in charge* **2** speaking for oneself only **3** as a person

personnel *n* **1** all the people employed somewhere **2** the department in a company that deals with (the complaints and difficulties of) these people

perspective *n* **1** the art of drawing solid objects on a flat surface so that they give an effect of depth, distance, and solidity **2** the way in which a matter is judged, so that consideration is given to each part **3** a view, esp. into the distance

perspiration *n* **1** sweating **2** sweat

perspire *v* **-spired, -spiring** to sweat

persuade *v* **-suaded, -suading 1** to cause to feel certain; convince **2** to cause to do something by reasoning, arguing, etc.

persuasion *n* **1** persuading or being persuaded **2** the ability to influence others **3** a strongly held belief **4** a group holding a belief

perverse *adj* **1** (of people, actions, etc.) annoyingly continuing in what is wrong or unreasonable **2** different from what is required or reasonable –~**ly** *adv* –~**ness** *n* – **-sity** *n*

¹pervert *v* **1** to turn away from what is right and natural **2** to use for a bad purpose

²pervert *n* a person of unnatural sexual behaviour

pessimism *n* **1** the habit of thinking that whatever happens will be bad **2** the belief that evil is more powerful than good – **-mist** *n* – **-mistic** *adj* – **-mistically** *adv*

pest *n* **1** a destructive usu. small animal or insect **2** *esp. spoken* an annoying person or thing

pester *v* to annoy continually, esp. with demands

¹pet *n* **1** an animal kept as a companion **2** a specially favoured person or thing

²pet *v* **-tt- 1** to touch kindly with the hands, showing love **2** to show special care for the comfort of **3**

esp. spoken to kiss and touch in sexual play

³**pet** *n* a condition of sudden childish bad temper

petal *n* any of the (usu. coloured) leaflike divisions of a flower

¹**petition** *n* **1** a request made to a government or other body, usu. signed by many people **2** an official letter to a court of law – ~**er** *n*

²**petition** *v* to make a petition to

petrol *n* a liquid obtained esp. from petroleum, used esp. for producing power in engines

petroleum *n* a mineral oil from below the earth's surface, used to produce various chemical substances

petty *adj* **-tier, -tiest 1** unimportant **2** having a limited ungenerous mind – **-tily** *adv* – **-tiness** *n*

phantom *n* **1** a ghost **2** something imaginary

pharmacist *n* **1** a person skilled in making medicine **2** a person who sells medicine; chemist

¹**phase** *n* **1** a stage of development **2** any of a fixed number of changes in the appearance of the moon or a planet at different times

²**phase** *v* **phased, phasing** to plan in separate phases

phenomenal *adj* **1** very unusual **2** *esp. written* concerned with phenomena

phenomenon *n* **-na 1** a fact or event as it appears to the senses, esp. one that is unusual or of scientific interest **2** a very unusual person, thing, event, etc.

philosopher *n* **1** a person who studies or has formed a philosophy **2 a** a person who is governed by reason and calmness **b** a person who thinks deeply

philosophical –also **philosophic** *adj* **1** accepting difficulty or unhappiness with quiet courage **2** of or concerning philosophy – ~**ly** *adv*

philosophy *n* **-phies 1** the study or a theory of the nature and meaning of existence, reality, goodness, etc. **2** a set of rules for living one's life **3** quiet courage

phobia *n* a strong usu. unreasonable fear and dislike –**phobic** *n, adj*

¹**phone** *n esp. spoken* a telephone

²**phone** *v* **phoned, phoning** *esp. spoken* to telephone

photo *n esp. spoken* a photograph

¹**photocopy** *n* **-ies** a photographic copy

²**photocopy** *v* **-ied, -ying** to make a photocopy of – **-ier** *n*

¹**photograph** –also (*esp. spoken*) **photo, picture** *n* a picture obtained with a camera and film sensitive to light

²**photograph** *v* also (*esp. spoken*) **snap**– to take a photograph of – ~**er** *n* – ~**ic** *adj* – ~**ically** *adv*

photography *n* the producing of photographs

¹**phrase** *n* **1 a** a small group of words **b** (in grammar) a group of words without a verb showing tense and subject: *'Walking along the road' and 'a packet of cigarettes' are*

phrases **2** a short passage of music that is part of a longer piece

²phrase *v* **phrased, phrasing 1** to express in words: *a politely-phrased refusal* **2** to perform (music) so as to give full effect to separate phrases

physical *adj* **1** of or concerning matter or material things (as opposed to mind, spirit, etc.) **2** according to the laws of nature: *Is there a physical explanation for these happenings?* **3** of or concerning the body: *physical exercise* **4** connected with physics: *physical chemistry*

physically *adv* **1** according to the laws of nature **2** with regard to the body: *physically fit*

physician *n* a doctor, esp. one who gives medicines (as opposed to a surgeon, who performs operations)

physics *n* the science of matter and natural forces (such as light, heat, movement, etc.)

pianist *n* a person who plays the piano

¹piano *adv, adj, n* **-nos** (a piece of music) played softly

²piano —also (*esp. written*) **pianoforte** *n* **-os** a large musical instrument, played by pressing keys which cause hammers to hit wires

¹pick *v* **1** to choose **2** to pull or break off (part of a plant) by the stem **3** to remove pieces from **4** to steal or take from: *to have your pocket picked* **5** to unlock (a lock) with any instrument other than a key

²pick *n* **1** choice **2** the best (esp. in the phrase **the pick of**)

³pick *n* **1** a sharp pointed instrument: *an ice pick / a toothpick* **2** *esp. spoken* a pickaxe

pickaxe *n* a large tool with a wooden handle fitted into a curved bar with 2 points, used for breaking up roads, rock, etc.

¹pickle *n* **1** liquid (esp. vinegar or salt water) used to preserve meat or vegetables **2** a vegetable preserved in this **3** *esp. spoken* a child who playfully does slightly harmful things

²pickle *v* **-led, -ling** to preserve in pickle

¹picnic *n* **1** a pleasure trip in which food is taken to be eaten in the country **2** such a meal

²picnic *v* **-ck-** to have a picnic —**picnicker** *n*

¹picture *n* **1** a representation made by painting, drawing, photography, or television **2** a cinema film **3** an image in the mind produced by description: *This book gives a good picture of life 200 years ago*

²picture *v* **-tured, -turing** to imagine

pictures *n* the cinema

pie *n* a pastry case filled with meat or fruit, baked usu. in a deep dish

piece *n* **1** a bit, such as: **a** a part which is separated or marked off from a whole: *a small piece of paper* **b** a single object that is an example of a kind: *a piece of furniture* **2 a** any of many parts to be fitted together **b** an object or person forming part of a set: *an 80-piece band* **3** one of a set of small objects or figures used in certain board games, esp. chess

4 a small amount **5** something made by an artist: *a piece of music* **6** a short written statement in a newspaper, magazine, etc. **7** a coin: *a 50-penny piece*

pier *n* **1** a bridgelike framework of wood, metal, etc., built out into the sea, often with small buildings on it, at which boats can take in or land their passengers or goods **2** a pillar to support a bridge or roof

pierce *v* **pierced**, **piercing 1** to make a hole in or through (something) with a point **2** (of light, sound, pain, etc.) to be suddenly seen, heard, or felt

piercing *adj* **1** (of wind) very strong and cold **2** (of sound) very sharp and clear **3** searching: *a piercing look* −~**ly** *adv*

pig *n* **1** any of various fat short-legged animals with a usu. curly tail and thick skin with short stiff hairs, kept on farms for food **2** a person who eats too much, is dirty, or refuses to consider others −~**gish** *adj* −~**gishy** *adv* −~**gishness** *n*

pigeon *n* **pigeons** *or* **pigeon** any of various quite large grey short-legged birds

pigsty *n* **-sties** an enclosure with a small building where pigs are kept

pigtail *n* a length of plaited hair that hangs from the back of the head −~**ed** *adj*

¹**pile** *n* a heavy post hammered upright into the ground to support a building, a bridge, etc.

²**pile** *n* **1** a tidy heap **2** *esp. spoken* a lot: *piles of work* **3** *esp. spoken* a very large amount of money

³**pile** *v* **piled**, **piling 1** to make a pile of **2** to load; fill: *The cart was piled high with vegetables*

⁴**pile** *n*- the soft surface of short threads on some cloths and carpets

pilgrim *n* a person who travels to a holy place as a religious act

pilgrimage *n* **1** (a) journey by a pilgrim **2** a journey to a place in which one has a respectful interest

pill *n* **1** a small ball of solid medicine to be swallowed **2** a pill taken by women as a means of contraception

pillar *n* **1** a tall upright usu. round stone post **2** an active supporter: *She was a pillar of the church*

pillar-box −also **postbox** *n* a round pillar-shaped iron box in the street, with a hole to post letters in

¹**pillow** *n* **1** an oblong cloth bag filled with soft material, for supporting the head in bed **2** an object for supporting the head: *He used his boots for a pillow*

²**pillow** *v* to rest (esp. one's head) on a pillow

¹**pilot** *n* **1** a person who flies an aircraft **2** a person who goes on board and guides ships that use a harbour **3** a person who guides through difficulties

²**pilot** *v* **1** to act as pilot of **2** to guide: *He piloted the old lady to her seat*

³**pilot** *adj* serving as a trial: *a pilot study to see if this product will sell*

pimple *n* a small raised diseased spot on the skin − **-ply** *adj* −~**d** *adj*

¹**pin** *n* 1 a short thin stiff piece of metal like a small nail, for fastening cloth, paper, etc. 2 an ornamented one of these used as jewellery 3 (in golf) a stick with a flag that is put into the hole

²**pin** *v* **-nn-** 1 to fasten with a pin 2 to keep in one position: *In the accident he was pinned under the car*

¹**pinch** *v* 1 to press (esp. a person's flesh) tightly between 2 hard surfaces, or between the thumb and a finger 2 to cause pain or distress to: *pinched with cold and hunger* 3 *esp. spoken* to steal – ~**ed** *adj*

²**pinch** *n* 1 an act of pinching 2 an amount that can be picked up between the thumb and a finger: *a pinch of salt* 3 suffering caused by poverty (esp. in the phrase **feel the pinch**) 4 **at a pinch** if necessary

¹**pine** *v* **pined, pining** 1 to become thin and weak slowly, through disease or esp. grief 2 to have a strong but esp. unfulfillable desire

²**pine** *n* 1 also **pinetree**– any of several types of tall cone-bearing tree with thin sharp leaves (**pine needles**) 2 the white or yellowish soft wood of this tree

pineapple *n* 1 a large dark yellow tropical fruit with thin stiff leaves on top 2 its sweet juicy yellow flesh

¹**pink** *n* a plant with sweet-smelling pink, white, or red flowers

²**pink** *n, adj* pale red

pinnacle *n* 1 a pointed stone ornament like a small tower, on a church or castle roof 2 a tall pointed rock 3 the highest point

pint *n* 1 (a measure equal to) about 0·57 of a litre; half a quart 2 *esp. spoken* this amount of beer

¹**pioneer** *n* 1 one of the first settlers in a new land 2 a person who does something first: *a pioneer of operations on the heart* 3 a member of a group of soldiers who prepare the way for an army's advance

²**pioneer** *v* to begin the development of

pious *adj* respecting God and religion – ~**ly** *adv* – ~**ness** *n*

¹**pip** *n esp. spoken* a star on the shoulder of an army officer's uniform

²**pip** *n* a small fruit seed

³**pip** *n* a short high-sounding note, as given on the radio to show the time

⁴**pip** *v* **-pp-** *esp. spoken* to defeat

¹**pipe** *n* 1 a tube carrying liquids and gas: *a gas pipe* 2 a small tube with a bowl-like container at one end, for smoking tobacco 3 **a** a tubelike musical instrument, played by blowing **b** any of the tubelike parts through which air is forced in an organ

²**pipe** *v* **piped, piping** 1 to carry (esp. liquid or gas) through pipes 2 to play on a pipe or bagpipes 3 **a** (of a bird) to sing **b** (of a person) to speak or sing in a high childish voice

¹**pirate** *n* 1 (esp. formerly) a person who sails the seas robbing ships 2 a person who uses the work of other

people without permission, such as one who prints a book when the copyright is held by someone else, or who works a private radio station and plays records without paying – **-racy** *n* – **-ratical** *adj* – **-ratically** *adv*

²**pirate** *v* **pirated**, **pirating** to make and sell (a book, newly invented article, etc.) without permission or payment

pistol *n* a small gun held and fired in one hand

¹**pit** *n* **1** a hole in the ground **2** a coal mine **3** (in motor racing) a place beside a track where cars can come during a race for repair **4** a hole in the floor of a garage from which the underside of cars can be examined **5** an enclosed hole where fierce animals are kept in a zoo **6** a natural hollow in the surface of a living thing (esp. in the phrase **pit of the stomach**) **7** a small hollow as left on the face after certain diseases, esp. smallpox **8** also **orchestra pit**– the space below and in front of a theatre stage where musicians sit

²**pit** *v* **-tt-** to mark with pits

¹**pitch** *n* any of various black sticky substances used for making protective coverings or for putting between cracks to stop water coming through

²**pitch** *v* **1** to set up (a tent, camp, etc.) **2** (of a cricketer) to make (a ball) hit the ground when bowling **3** (of a ball in cricket or golf) to hit the ground **4** to throw with dislike or annoyance: *We pitched those noisy people out of our club* **5** to set the pitch of (a sound) **6** to fall or cause to fall heavily or suddenly **7** (of a ship or aircraft) to move backwards and forwards with the movement of the waves or air; move along with the back and front going up and down **8** to slope downwards

³**pitch** *n* **1** a place in some public area where somebody regularly tries to gain money from people who are passing, by performing, selling, etc. **2** a marked-out area of ground on which football, rugby, etc., are played **3** the place where the ball hits the ground after being bowled **4** a wicket **5** the degree of highness or lowness of a musical note or speaking voice **6** (esp. in building) the amount of slope **7** (of a ship or aircraft) a backward and forward movement; the action of pitching

piteous –also **pitiful** *adj* **1** causing pity: *The dog gave a piteous cry* **2** feeling or showing pity – **~ly** *adv* – **~ness** *n*

pitfall *n* an unexpected danger or difficulty

pitiful *adj* **1** deserving pity **2** not deserving respect – **~ly** *adv* – **~ness** *n*

¹**pity** *n* **-ies** **1** sensitiveness to and sorrow for the suffering of others **2** a sad or inconvenient state of affairs

²**pity** *v* **-ied**, **-ying** to feel pity for

¹**pivot** *n* **1** a central point or pin on which something turns **2** a person

on whom or thing on which something depends: *The mother is often the pivot of family life* −∼**al** *adj*

²**pivot** *v* **1** to turn on or as if on a pivot **2** to provide with or fix by a pivot

¹**placard** *n* a large notice or advertisement, put up in a public place or carried about

²**placard** *v* **1** to stick placards on **2** to give public notice of, by placards

¹**place** *n* **1** a particular part of space or position in space: *the place where the accident happened* **2** a position of importance: *Sports never had a place in his life* **3** a particular area on a surface: *a sore place on her hand* **4** a (numbered) position in the result of a competition, race, etc.: *John took first place in the examination* **5** any of the first 3 positions in the result of a horse race **6** social rank: *one's place in society*

²**place** *v* **placed, placing** **1** to put in a certain position **2** to pass (an order) to a person, firm, etc. **3** to remember all the details of **4** to state the position of (a runner) at the end of a race **5** *US* to finish second in a race

¹**plague** *n* **1** any disease causing death and spreading quickly **2** a widespread harmful mass or number: *a plague of rats*

²**plague** *v* **plagued, plaguing** to cause continual discomfort or trouble to

plaice *n* **plaice** a European edible flat bony sea fish

¹**plain** *n* a large stretch of flat land

²**plain** *adj* **1** easy to see, hear, or understand **2** simple; without ornament **3** (of paper) without lines **4** (esp. of a woman) rather ugly **5** showing honestly what is thought or felt, often in an impolite way **6** complete; undoubted: *plain foolishness*

plainly *adv* **1** in a plain manner **2** it is clear that: *The door's locked, so plainly they must be out*

¹**plait** −also *(esp. US)* **braid** *n* a length of something, esp. hair, made by plaiting

²**plait** −also *(esp. US)* **braid** *v* to twist 3 or more lengths of (hair, grass, etc.) over and under each other to form one ropelike length

¹**plan** *n* **1** a considered arrangement for some future activity **2** a line drawing of a building or room as seen from above, showing the shape, measurements, etc. **3** a set of drawings showing the parts of a machine

²**plan** *v* **-nn-** to make a plan for: *planning this visit* −∼**ner** *n*

¹**plane** *v* **planed, planing** **1** to use a plane on (something) **2** to cut or make with a plane: *Plane the table smooth*

²**plane** *n* a tool that takes very thin pieces off wooden surfaces to make them smooth

³**plane** *n* **1 a** a completely flat surface **b** (in geometry) a surface such that a straight line joining any 2 points lies only on that surface **2** a level;

standard: *Let's keep the conversation on a friendly plane* **3** *esp. spoken* an aeroplane

planet *n* a large body in space that moves round a star, esp. round the sun −~**ary** *adj*

plank *n* **1** a long piece of board, esp. 2 to 6 inches thick and at least 8 inches wide **2** a main principle of a political party's stated aims

¹plant *v* **1** to put (plants or seeds) in the ground to grow **2** to supply (a place) with plants **3** to fix firmly **4** *esp. spoken* to hide (esp. stolen goods) on a person so that he will seem guilty **5** to put (a person) secretly in a group: *His supporters had been planted in the crowd, and began shouting*

²plant *n* **1** a living thing that has leaves and roots, and grows usu. in earth, esp. the kind smaller than trees **2 a** a machine; machinery: *our power plant for electricity* **b** a factory: *a new chemical plant* **3** *esp. spoken* **a** a person placed in a group of criminals to discover facts about them **b** stolen goods hidden on a person so that he will seem guilty

plantation *n* **1** a large piece of land on which tea, cotton, sugar, or rubber are grown **2** a large group of planted trees

plaque *n* **1** a metal or stone plate, usu. with writing, fixed to a wall as a memorial or ornament **2** *medical* a substance that forms on teeth, in which bacteria can breed

¹plaster *n* **1** a pastelike mixture of lime, water, etc., which hardens when dry- and is used, esp. on walls, to give a smooth surface **2** a medically treated cloth put on the body to produce heat, protect a wound, etc.

²plaster *v* **1** to put plaster on **2** to spread (something) perhaps too thickly on: *They plastered the wall with signs* **3** to cover with a medical plaster

¹plastic *adj* **1** easily formed into shapes by pressing, and able to keep the new shape **2** connected with modelling and sculpture (esp. in the phrase **the plastic arts**) −~**ally** *adv* −~**ity** *n*

²plastic *n* any of various man-made materials produced chemically , which can be made into different shapes when soft and keep their shape when hard

plasticine *n trademark* a soft claylike substance in many colours, for making small models, shapes, etc.

¹plate *n* **1** a flat, usu. round dish with a raised edge from which food is eaten or served **2** metal articles, usu. made of gold or silver, used at meals or in services at church **3** common metal with a covering of gold or silver **4** a flat thin piece of metal, glass, etc., for use in building, in machinery, etc. **5** a thin sheet of glass used in photography, coated with chemicals sensitive to light **6** a set of false teeth **7** a sheet of metal treated so that words or a picture can be printed from it **8** a picture in a book, printed on special paper and often coloured **9** a sheet of metal fixed to the entrance of an office and bearing the name of a person or firm **10** any of the very large movable parts into which the earth's crust is divided

²**plate** *v* **plated, plating 1** to cover (a metal article) with another metal **2** to cover (esp. a ship) with metal plates –**plating** *n*

plateau *n* **-eaus** *or* **-eaux** a large plain much higher than the land around it

platform *n* **1** a raised floor for speakers, performers, etc. **2** a raised flat surface along the side of the track at a railway station **3** the open part at the end of a bus **4** the main aims of a political party **5** an unusually high shoe or sole

platinum *n* a greyish-white metallic element that does not become dirty or impure and is used esp. in jewellery and in chemical industries

plausible *adj* (of a statement, argument, etc.) seeming true or reasonable – **-bly** *adv* – **-bility** *n*

¹**play** *n* **plays 1** activity for amusement only **2** the action in a game: *an interesting day's play in the match* **3 a** a piece of writing to be performed in a theatre **b** a performance of this **4** freedom of movement given by looseness: *Give the rope some play–don't keep it so tight* **5** (somebody's) turn in a game, as in cards **6** risking money on games of chance **7 in play a** (of the ball in cricket, football, etc.) in a position where it may be played **b** without serious intention **8 out of play** (of the ball in ball games) in a position where it may not be played

²**play** *v* **played, playing 1** to pass the time pleasantly ; have fun **2** (of children) to pretend to be: *Let's play doctors and nurses* **3** to allow (a fish caught on a line) to become tired by pulling **4** (of an actor or theatre group) to perform: *Othello was played by Olivier* **5** (of a play or film) to be shown **6** (of a musical instrument or apparatus) to produce sounds **7** to perform on (a musical instrument) **8 a** to perform (a piece of music) **b** to perform the music of (a composer) **9** to reproduce (sounds) on an apparatus **10** to take part in (a sport or game) **11** to be set against in a match **12** to strike and send (a ball) **13** to place (a playing card) face upwards on the table **14** to risk (money) in a game of skill or chance

player *n* **1** a person taking part in a game or sport **2** *esp. old use* an actor **3 a** a person playing a musical instrument **b** an apparatus for reproducing sounds: *a record player*

playful *adj* **1** gaily active **2** not intended seriously: *a playful kiss* –~**fully** *adv* –~**ness** *n*

plea *n* **1** *esp. written* an eager request **2** an excuse **3** *law* a statement made by a person in court, saying whether he is guilty

plead *v* **pleaded** *or* **plead, pleading 1**

to make continual requests **2** to give as an excuse **3** to argue in support of: *pleading the rights of the unemployed* **4** *law* to answer a charge in court **5** *law* to declare that one is: *She pleaded guilty/not guilty* –~**ing** *n*

pleasant *adj* **1** pleasing; enjoyable **2** (esp. of people) likeable; friendly **3** (of weather) fine –~**ly** *adv*

¹**please** *v* **pleased, pleasing 1** to make (someone) happy **2** to choose: *Come when you please*

²**please** *interj* (used to make a request or attract attention) **a** (more politely): *Please pass the sugar* **b** (with more force): *Please, John, do as I say | Please, Miss Jones, Andrew's kicking my chair!*

pleased *adj* satisfied; happy

pleasure *n* happiness or satisfaction resulting from an experience that one likes – **-rable** *adj* – **-rably** *adv*

¹**pledge** *n* **1** a solemn promise **2** something given as a sign of faithful love or friendship **3 a** something valuable left with someone else as proof that one will fulfil an agreement **b** an object of value left, in return for money, with a pawnbroker until the money is repaid **4** the state of being kept for this purpose (esp. in the phrase **in pledge**) **5 sign/take the pledge** *now humour* to promise no longer to drink alcohol

²**pledge** *v* **pledged, pledging 1** to bind with a promise **2** to leave as a pledge

3 *esp. written* to drink to the health, success, etc., of

¹**plenty** *n* the state of having a large supply: *years of plenty, when everyone has enough to eat* – **-tiful** *adj*

²**plenty** *pron* a large quantity or number; enough: *plenty of money / plenty to eat*

pliable *adj* **1** easily bent without breaking **2** willing to accept new ideas **3** easily influenced – **-bility** *n*

pliers *n* a tool made of 2 crossed pieces of metal with long often flat jaws, used to hold small things or to cut wire

plod *v* **-dd- 1** to walk slowly, esp. with effort **2** to work steadily, esp. at something uninteresting

¹**plot** *n* **1** a small piece of ground for building or growing things **2** the connected events on which a story, film, etc., is based **3** a secret plan by several people to do harm

²**plot** *v* **-tt- 1** to mark (the position of a moving aircraft or ship) on a map **2** to represent by pictures or a map **3** to make (a line or curve) on a graph **4** to plan together secretly **5** to make a plot for a story –~**ter** *n*

¹**plough** *n* **1** a farming tool with a heavy cutting blade drawn by a motor vehicle or animal(s). It breaks up and turns over the earth **2** any tool or machine that works like this **3 under the plough** (of farmland) used for growing grain rather than feeding animals

²**plough** *v* **1** to break up or turn over

370

(land) with a plough **2** to force a way: *The ship ploughed across the ocean*

¹**pluck** *v* **1** to pull the feathers off (a bird being prepared for cooking) **2** to pull sharply; pick **3** to play a stringed musical instrument by pulling

²**pluck** *n* courage and will

plucky *adj* **-ier, -iest** brave and determined – **-kily** *adv* – **-kiness** *n*

¹**plug** *n* **1** something used for blocking a hole **2** an electrical connector with projecting metal pins to push into a power socket **3** *esp. spoken* a publicly stated favourable opinion about a record, a book, etc.

²**plug** *v* **-gg- 1** to block with a plug **2** *esp. spoken* to advertise by repeatedly mentioning: *plugging a new book on the radio*

plum *n* **1** (the tree which bears) a roundish sweet smooth-skinned fleshy fruit, usu. dark red, with a single stone **2** a dark reddish-blue colour

plumber *n* a man who fits and repairs water pipes, bathroom articles, etc.

plumbing *n* all the pipes, water tanks, etc., in a building

¹**plume** *n* **1** a feather, esp. a large showy one **2** something that rises in a shape like a feather: *a plume of smoke* –~**d** *adj*

²**plume** *v* **plumed, pluming** (of a bird) to clean or smooth its feathers

plump *adj* **1** (or people) rather fat or nicely rounded **2** (of animals as food) well covered with flesh: *a nice plump chicken* –~**ness** *n*

¹**plunder** *v* to seize (goods) unlawfully or by force from (people or a place) –**plunderer** *n*

²**plunder** *n* **1** goods seized by plundering or stolen **2** the act of plundering

¹**plunge** *v* **plunged, plunging 1** to move or be thrown suddenly forwards and/or downwards **2** (of the neck of a woman's garment) to show a quite large area of the chest: *a plunging neckline*

²**plunge** *n* an act of plunging, esp. a dive

plural *adj, n* (a form or word) that expresses more than one: *'Dogs' is a plural noun* –~**ly** *adv*

¹**plus** *prep* with the addition of: *3 plus 6 is 9 (3+6=9)*

²**plus** –also **plus sign** *n* a sign (+) showing that 2 or more numbers are to be added together, or that a number is greater than zero

³**plus** *adj* **1** *esp. spoken* additional and welcome (often in the phrase **a plus factor**) **2 a** (esp. of age) and above: *All the children are 12 plus* **b** (of a mark given for work) and slightly more: *B plus (B+) is better than B*

p.m. *adv* post meridiem; after midday: *Today the sun sets at 5.49 p.m*

pneumatic *adj* **1** worked by air pressure: *a pneumatic drill* **2** containing air: *a pneumatic tyre* –~**ally** *adv*

¹**poach** *v* to cook (esp. eggs or fish) in gently boiling liquid

²**poach** v to catch or shoot (animals, birds, or fish) without permission

¹**pocket** n 1 a small flat cloth bag sewn into or onto a garment: *my coat pocket* 2 any of the 6 small bags round a billiard table, into which a ball may go 3 a region in the ground containing metal, oil, etc. 4 a small separate area or group: *pockets of mist down by the river* 5 **out of pocket** having paid a certain amount

²**pocket** v 1 to put into one's pocket 2 to take for one's own use, esp. dishonestly

¹**pod** n 1 a long narrow seed vessel of various plants, esp. beans and peas 2 a part of an aircraft or spacecraft that can be separated from the main part

²**pod** v -dd- to take (beans, peas, etc.) from the pod

poem n a piece of writing in patterns of lines and sounds, expressing something in imaginative language

poet n a person who writes poems –~**ical** adj –~**ic** adj –~**ically** adv

poetry n poems: *a book of poetry*

¹**point** n 1 a sharp end 2 a piece of land with a sharp end that stretches into the sea 3 **a** also **decimal point**– a sign (·) separating a whole number from decimals: *When we read out 4·23 we say '4 point 2 3'* **b** a full stop 4 (in geometry) an imaginary place that has position but no size 5 a place: *The bus stops at 4 or 5 points along this road* 6 an exact moment: *It was at that point that I left* 7 also **point of the compass**– **a** any of the 32 marks on a compass, showing direction **b** any of the equal divisions (each of 11⁰ 15¹) between any 2 of these 8 a degree of temperature: *the melting point of gold* 9 a measure of increase or decrease in cost, value, etc. 10 a single quantity used in deciding the winner in games: *We won by 12 points to 3* 11 the meaning of something said or done: *I didn't see the point of his remark* 12 a noticeable quality or ability: *Work isn't her strong point* 13 purpose; use: *There's no point in wasting time* 14 also **power point**– a fixed socket into which a plug can be fitted to connect an apparatus to the supply of electricity 15 (in cricket) (the fielder in) a position directly facing the batsman and about half way to the edge of the playing area

²**point** v 1 to hold out a finger, a stick, etc., in a direction 2 to aim, direct, or turn 3 to fill the spaces between the bricks of (a wall) with cement or a similar substance 4 (of a dog) to show where (a hunted animal or bird) is 5 to bring (the toes) to a point by bending the ankles forward

pointed adj 1 shaped to a point: *pointed fingernails* 2 directed in a noticeable unfriendly way: *a pointed remark* 3 sharply expressed or shown (esp. in the phrase **pointed wit**) –~**ly** adv

pointless *adj* 1 meaningless 2 useless; unnecessary −~**ly** *adv* −~**ness** *n*

point of view −also **viewpoint** *n* **points of view** a way of considering or judging a thing, person, etc.: *From my point of view it would be better to come tomorrow*

¹**poison** *n* 1 a substance that harms or kills if an animal or plant takes it in 2 an evil or unwanted influence

²**poison** *v* 1 to give poison to; harm or kill with poison 2 to put poison into or onto (something) 3 to infect: *a poisoned foot* 4 to make dangerously impure: *Chemicals are poisoning our rivers* 5 to influence in a harmful or evil way: *She poisoned her husband's mind against his sister* −~**er** *n*

poisonous *adj* 1 containing poison: *poisonous snakes* 2 having the effects of poison: *This substance is poisonous* 3 harmful to the mind; evil: *poisonous ideas* 4 very unpleasant: *a poisonous green colour* −~**ly** *adv*

¹**poke** *v* **poked, poking** 1 to push sharply out of or through an opening: *His elbow was poking through his sleeve* 2 to push (a pointed thing) into (someone or something) 3 to move the wood or coal about in (a fire) with a poker or other such object 4 to make (a hole) by pushing, forcing, etc. 5 *esp. spoken* to hit with the hand closed 6 **poke fun at** to make jokes against 7 **poke one's nose into something** *esp. spoken* to enquire into

something that does not concern one

²**poke** *n* 1 an act of poking with something pointed 2 *esp. spoken* a blow with the closed hand: *He took a poke at his opponent*

¹**poker** *n* a thin metal bar used to poke a fire to make it burn better

²**poker** *n* a card game usu. played for money

polar *adj* 1 of, near, like, or coming from lands near the North or South Poles 2 *esp. written* exactly opposite in kind, quality, etc.: *The two brothers were polar opposites*

¹**pole** *n* 1 a long, usu. thin rounded stick or post, used as a support, to guide a flat-bottomed boat, to join 2 animals to a cart, etc.: *a flagpole* 2 **up the pole** *esp. spoken* **a** slightly mad **b** in difficulty

²**pole** *v* **poled, poling** 1 to move (a boat) along by pushing a pole against the bed of the river, lake, etc. 2 to use ski poles or sticks to give oneself more speed

³**pole** *n* 1 either end of an imaginary straight line (axis) round which a solid round mass turns, esp. **a** (the lands around) the most northern and southern points of the earth or another planet **b** the 2 points in the sky to the north and south round which stars seem to turn 2 either of the points at the ends of a magnet where its power is greatest 3 either of the points where wires may be gixed onto a battery to use its electricity: *negative/positive pole* 4

either of 2 completely different qualities, opinions, etc.: *Our opinions are at opposite poles* **5 poles apart** widely separated; having no shared quality, idea, etc.

¹**police** *n* an official body of men and women whose duty is to protect people and property, to make everyone obey the law, to catch criminals, etc.

²**police** *v* **policed, policing** 1 to control (a place) by or as if using police 2 to keep a watch on: *a new body set up to police pay agreements*

policeman –*fem.* **policewoman** *n* -**men** a member of a police force

¹**policy** *n* -**cies** 1 a plan or course of action in directing affairs, chosen by a political party, government, company, etc. 2 sensible behaviour that is to one's own advantage: *It's bad policy to smoke too much*

²**policy** *n* a written statement of an agreement with an insurance company

¹**polish** *v* 1 to make or become smooth and shiny by continual rubbing 2 to make (a person, his behaviour, speech, etc.) less rough 3 to make (a speech, piece of writing, artistic performance, etc.) as perfect as possible: *The musicians gave a very polished performance* –~**er** *n*

²**polish** *n* 1 a liquid, paste, etc., used in polishing a surface 2 a smooth shiny surface produced by rubbing 3 an act of polishing 4 fine quality or perfection (of manners, education, writing, etc.)

polite *adj* 1 having or showing good manners and consideration for others 2 having or showing (or pretending to have or show) fineness of feeling, high development in the arts, manners, etc.; refined: *polite society* –~**ly** *adv* –~**ness** *n*

political *adj* 1 of or concerning public affairs and/or the government of a country: *the loss of political freedoms* 2 of or concerned with (party) politics: *a political party* –~**ly** *adv*

politician *n* 1 a person whose business is politics, esp. a member of a parliament 2 *offensive* a person concerned with party politics for his own selfish purpose or gain

politics *n* 1 the art or science of government: *Tom is studying politics at university* 2 political affairs, esp. considered as a profession and/or as a means of winning and keeping governmental control: *local politics* 3 the political ideas or party that one favours: *What are your politics?* 4 **play politics** *offensive* to speak or act in such a way as to make people argue amongst themselves, distrust each other, etc., in order to gain an advantage for oneself

¹**poll** *n* 1 the giving of votes in writing at an election: *The result of the poll won't be known until midnight* 2 the number of votes recorded at an election: *They expected a large poll* 3 an official list of electors

²**poll** *v* 1 to receive (a stated number of votes) at an election 2 to vote at

an election **3** to question (people) in making a poll **4** to cut off or cut short the horns of (cattle)

pollute *v* **-luted, -luting 1** to make (water, soil, etc.) dangerously impure **2** to destroy the purity of (the mind)

pollution *n* **1** the action of polluting **2** the state of being polluted **3** (an area or mass of) something that pollutes

polythene *n* a type of plastic not easily damaged by water or chemicals, used esp. as a protective covering, for making household articles, etc.

pompous *adj* foolishly solemn and self-important – ∼**ly** *adv* – **-posity,** ∼**ness** *n*

pond *n* an area of still water smaller than a lake

ponder *v* to spend time in considering (a fact, difficulty, etc.)

pony *n* **ponies 1** a small horse **2** *esp. humour* a horse used for racing

¹pool *n* **1** a small area of still water in a hollow, usu. naturally formed: *The rain formed pools of water* **2** a small amount of any liquid poured or dropped on a surface: *The wounded man was lying in a pool of blood* **3** a large water-filled container built into the ground, used for swimming, keeping fish in, etc. **4** a deeper part of a stream where the water hardly moves

²pool *n* **1** a common supply of money, goods, workers, etc., which may be used by a number of people: *Our firm has a car pool* **2** any of various

American billiard games played usu. with 15 numbered balls on a table with 6 pockets

³pool *v* to combine; share

pools –also **football pools** an arrangement by which people bet small amounts of money on the results of certain football matches, and those who guess the results correctly (or nearly correctly) win large shares of the combined money

poor *adj* **1** having very little money and therefore a low standard of living **2** less than is needed or expected; small: *a poor crop of beans* **3** much below the usual standard; low in quality: *The weather has been very poor this summer* **4** (of the bodily system) weak; not good: *in poor health* **5** offensive (of a person or his behaviour) not noble or respected: *He gets angry when he loses a game. He's a poor loser* **6** deserving pity; unlucky: *The poor old man had lost both his sons in the war* **7** *usu. polite or humour* of little worth; humble: *In my poor opinion you're wrong*

¹poorly *adv* **1** in a poor manner or condition; not well **2 think poorly of** to have a low opinion of

²poorly *adj* **-lier, -liest** ill

¹pop *v* **-pp- 1** to make or cause to make a short sharp explosive sound: *The cork popped when he pulled it out* **2** *esp. spoken* to spring: *The child's eyes almost popped out of her head with excitement* **3** *esp. spoken* to move, go, come, enter, etc., suddenly, lightly, or unexpec-tedly: *I've just popped in to see you* **4** *esp. spoken* to put quickly and lightly: *He popped his coat on* **5** *esp. spoken* to ask (a question) suddenly and directly **6 pop the question** *esp. spoken* to make an offer of marriage; propose

²pop *n* **1** a sound like that of a slight explosion: *The lemonade bottle went pop* **2** a sweet fizzy drink

³pop *n* **1** simple modern popular music with a strong beat and not usu. of lasting interest **2 top of the pops** (being) the pop record selling the most copies at a particular time

pope *n* the head of the Roman Cath-olic church

poppy *n* **-pies** any of several types of plant that have a milky juice in the stems and bright, usu. red flowers

popular *adj* **1** favoured by many people: *a popular song* **2** well liked **3** *sometimes offensive* suited to the understanding, liking, or needs of the general public: *popular news-papers* **4** (of prices) cheap

popularity *n* the quality or state of being well liked, favoured, or admi-red

populate *v* **-lated, -lating 1** to live in (a particular area): *a thickly-populated area* **2** to settle in and fill up (an area), esp. with people: *The new land was quickly populated*

population *n* **1** the number of people or animals living in an area **2** the people or animals living in an area: *The population in these villages still uses well water*

porch *n* a built-out roofed entrance to a house or church

porcupine *n* a type of small short-legged animal that has long stiff prickles on its back and sides, and is larger than a hedgehog

pore *n* a very small opening (esp. in the skin) through which liquids (esp. sweat) may pass

pork *n* meat from pigs

pornography *n* the treatment of sexual subjects in books, films, etc., in a way meant to cause sexual excitement – **-pher** *n* – **-phic** *adj* – **-phically** *adv*

porridge *n* a type of soft breakfast food made by boiling oatmeal in milk or water

¹port *n* **1** (a town with a) harbour **2 Any port in a storm** Any means of escape from trouble must be accepted

²port *n* **1** an opening in the side of a ship for loading and unloading goods **2** a porthole

³port *n* the left side of a ship or aircraft as one faces forward: *The damaged ship was leaning over to port*

⁴port *n* strong sweet often dark red Portuguese wine usu. drunk after a meal

portable *adj* that can be carried or moved easily: *a portable television* – **-bility** *n*

¹porter *n* a man in charge of the entrance to a hotel, school, hospital, etc.

²porter *n* 1 a person employed to carry luggage at railway stations, airports, etc. 2 a person employed to carry loads at markets

porthole *n* 1 also **port–** a small usu. circular window or opening in a ship for light or air 2 any of the row of fixed windows along the side of an aircraft

portion *n* 1 a part separated or cut off: *the front portion of the train* 2 a share of something divided among 2 or more people: *A portion of the blame for the accident must be borne by the driver* 3 a quantity of food for one person as served in a restaurant 4 *esp. written & literature* a person's fate; lot

portrait *n* 1 a painting, drawing, or photograph of a real person or animal 2 a lifelike description in words: *He called his book about modern Europe 'A Portrait of Europe'*

portray *v* **-trayed, -traying** 1 to be or make a representation of (someone or something) in painting, drawing, etc. 2 to describe in words 3 to act the part of (a particular character) in a play –~al *n*

¹pose *v* **posed, posing** 1 to sit or cause to sit or stand in a particular effective position, esp. for a photograph, painting, etc. 2 to state; offer for consideration: *You've posed us an awkward question* 3 to set; bring into being: *This rain poses a problem for the farmers* 4 *offensive* to behave or speak unnaturally in an effort to make people notice or admire one

²pose *n* 1 a position of the body, esp. as taken up to produce an effect in art 2 *offensive* a way of behaving which is pretended in order to produce an effect

posh *adj esp. spoken* 1 very fine; splendid 2 *sometimes offensive* fashionable; for people of high social rank: *a posh address*

¹position *n* 1 the place where someone or something is or stands, esp. in relation to other objects, places, etc.: *Can you find our position on this map?* 2 the place where someone or something belongs; the proper place: *One of the chairs is out of position* 3 the place of advantage in a struggle: *The racing drivers manoeuvred for position* 4 the way or manner in which someone or something is placed or moves, stands, sits, etc.: *sitting in a most uncomfortable position* 5 a condition or state, esp. in relation to that of someone or something else: *I'd like to help, but I'm not in a position to do so* 6 a particular place or rank in a group 7 a job; employment 8 an opinion or judgment on a matter: *He takes the position that what his sister does is no concern of his*

²position *v* to put in a position or in the proper position

¹positive *adj* 1 (of a statement) direct: *a positive refusal* 2 certain; beyond any doubt 3 (of people) sure; having no doubt about something 4

thorough; real: *It was a positive delight to hear her sing* **5** (of people or their behaviour) boldly certain of oneself and one's opinions **6** actively noticeable: *In the night, the patient took a positive turn for the worse* **7** (of medical tests) showing signs of disease **8** effective; actually helpful: *positive thinking* **9** (in grammar) of the simple form of an adjective or adverb, which expresses no comparison: *'Good' is the positive form of the adjective; 'better' and 'best' are not* **10** (in mathematics) **a** (of a number or quantity) greater than zero **b** concerning such a quantity: *The positive sign is* + **11** (of or in electricity) of the type that is based on protons and is produced by rubbing glass with silk **12** (of a photograph) having light and shadow as they are in nature, not the other way around; developed

²**positive** *n* **1** (in grammar) the positive degree or form of an adjective or adverb: *The positive of 'prettiest' is 'pretty'* **2** a positive photograph **3** (in mathematics) a quantity greater than zero *esp. written* something that is clearly true or offers proof that something is true

positively *adv* **1** in a positive way, esp. with or as if with certainty **2** really; indeed: *This food is positively uneatable*

possess *v* **1** to own; have as belonging to one, or as a quality **2** (of a feeling or idea) to influence (someone) so completely as to control one's actions: *Fear possessed him and prevented him from moving* **3** (of an evil spirit or the devil) to enter into and become master of (someone)

possession *n* **1** ownership **2** a piece of personal property **3** a country controlled or governed by another **4** the condition of being under or as if under the control of an evil spirit **5 in possession a** having or controlling a place or thing, esp. so that someone else is prevented from doing so: *Wales can't get any points while the England players are in possession* (=have the ball) **b** *often written* having, controlling, keeping, or living in: *He was found in possession of dangerous drugs* **6 Possession is nine tenths/nine points of the law** A person who possesses a thing is in a better position to keep it than someone else who may have a more just claim to it

possibility *n* **-ties 1** the state or fact of being possible **2** a likelihood; chance: *Is there any possibility that you'll be able to come tomorrow?* **3** something that is possible: *The general would not accept that defeat was a possibility* **4** power of developing, or being used or useful in the future: *Although the house is old, it has possibilities if it's properly repaired* **5** *esp. spoken* a suitable person or thing: *Is Jane a possibility as a member of the team?*

¹**possible** *adj* **1** that can exist, happen,

or be done: *I'll do everything possible to help you* **2** that may or may not be, happen, or be expected: *It is possible that I shall go there next week* **3** acceptable; suitable: *one of many possible answers*

²**possible** *n* **1** that which can be or can be done: *Politics has been called the art of the possible* **2** a person or thing that might be suitable

possibly *adv* **1** in accordance with what is possible: *I'll do all I possibly can* **2** perhaps

¹**post** *n* **1** a strong thick upright pole or bar made of wood, metal, etc., fixed into the ground or some other base esp. as a support: *a gatepost* **2** the starting or finishing place in a race, esp. a horse race: *My horse got beaten at the finishing post*

²**post** *v* **1** to make public or show by fixing to a wall, board, post, etc.: *The notice will be posted up today* **2** to make known by putting up a notice: *The ship was posted missing*

³**post** *n* **1** the official system for carrying letters, parcels, etc., from the sender to the receiver **2** the official collection or delivery of letters, parcels, etc. **3** (in former times) any of a number of stopping places on a road where travellers or messengers could rest, change horses, etc., and where letters could be passed to a fresh rider **4 by return of post** by the next post back

⁴**post** *v* **1** to send by post, by taking to a post office or putting into a collection box for sending **2 keep someone posted** to continue to give someone all the latest news about something

⁵**post** *n* **1** a small fort, camp, etc., esp. on a border or in a desert, at which a body of soldiers is kept **2** a special place of duty, esp. on guard or on watch: *All workers must be at their posts by half past 8* **3** a job **4** either of 2 sets of notes played at sunset on a bugle, esp. to call soldiers to their camp: *The soldier played the first post/last post*

⁶**post** *v* **1** to place (soldiers or other men) on duty in a special place, esp. as a guard **2** to send or appoint (someone) to a particular army group, a place or duty with a firm, etc.

postage *n* the charge for carrying a letter, parcel, etc., by post

postage stamp *n* a stamp for sticking on things to be posted

postcard *n* **1** a usu. small card on which a message may be written and sent by post **2** also **picture postcard**– a card like this with a picture or photograph on one side

poster *n* a large printed notice or drawing put up in a public place

postman *n* **-men** a man employed to collect and deliver letters, parcels, etc.

postmortem *n Latin* **1** an examination of a dead body to discover the cause of death **2** an examination of a plan or event that failed in order to discover the cause of failure

post office *n* an office, shop, etc.,

which deals with the post and certain other government business for a particular area, such as telephone bills

postpone *v* **-poned, -poning** to delay; move to some later time –~**ment** *n*

¹**posture** *n* **1** the way of holding the body, esp. the back, shoulders, and head **2** a manner of behaving or thinking on some occasion; attitude

²**posture** *v* **-tured, -turing 1** *often offensive* to place oneself in a bodily position or positions, esp. in order to be admired **2** *offensive* to pretend to be something that one is not: *posturing as a music lover*

¹**pot** *n* **1** any of several kinds of round vessel of baked clay, metal, etc., made to contain liquids or solids: *a pot of paint / a teapot* **2** *esp. spoken* an ornamental clay vessel made by hand **3** *esp. spoken* a large amount (of money): *They've got pots of money* **4** all the money risked on one card game and taken by the winner **5** a stroke which sends the correct ball into a pocket in the game of billiards or snooker

²**pot** *v* **-tt- 1** to shoot (esp. an animal or bird) **2** to set (a plant) in a pot filled with earth **3** (in billiards) to hit (a ball) into one of the 6 bags at the edge of the table

potato *n* **-toes 1** a type of roundish root vegetable with a thin, usu. brown skin, that is cooked and served in many ways **2** a plant which has these growing on its roots

¹**potential** *adj* existing in possibility but not at present active or developed: *Every seed is a potential plant* –~**ly** *adv*

²**potential** *n* **1** possibility for developing or being developed: *The boy has acting potential, but he needs training* **2** the degree of electricity or electrical force (usu. measured in volts)

¹**potter** *n* a person who makes pots, dishes, etc., out of baked clay

²**potter** *v* *esp. spoken* to move slowly or work at small unimportant jobs: *Grandmother just potters about the house* –**potter** *n*

pottery *n* **-ries 1** the work of a potter **2** pots and other objects made out of baked clay **3** baked clay (earthenware), considered as the material of which pots are made: *a pottery dish* **4** a potter's workroom or factory

pouch *n* **1** a small soft, often leather bag for tobacco, carried in the pocket **2** a baglike fold of skin inside each cheek, in which certain animals (such as hamsters) store food **3** a pocket of skin in the lower half of the body, in which certain mammals carry their young **4** a baglike fold of skin that hangs down, esp. under the eye as a result of illness, old age, etc.

poultry *n* **1** farmyard birds, such as hens, ducks, etc., kept for supplying eggs and meat **2** chicken, duck, etc., considered as meat

¹pounce *v* **pounced, pouncing 1** to fly down or spring suddenly in order to seize something, esp. for food: *The bird pounced on the worm* **2** to make a sudden attack, usu. from a hidden place: *Policemen pounced on the criminals*

²pounce *n* an attack made by pouncing

¹pound *n* **1** a standard measure of weight equal to about 0.454 kilograms **2** a measure of weight for gold and silver, equal to about 0·373 kilograms **3 a** the standard of money in several countries: *the Egyptian pound* **b** also (*esp. written or technical*) **pound sterling–** the British standard of money, now divided into 100 pence **4** the British money system; value at any particular time of British money at international exchange rates: *The Bank of England had to support the pound*

²pound *v* **1** to crush into a soft mass or powder by striking repeatedly with a heavy object **2** to strike repeatedly, heavily, and noisily **3** to move with heavy quick steps that make a dull sound

³pound *n* **1** a place where lost dogs and cats, and cars that have been unlawfully parked, are kept by the police until claimed **2** (in former times) an enclosure in which wandering animals were officially kept until claimed and paid for by the owner

pour *v* **1** to flow steadily and rapidly: *Blood poured from the wound* **2** (of people) to rush together in large numbers: *At 5 o'clock workers poured out of the factories* **3** to cause to flow: *Pour away the dirty water* **4** to give or send as if in a flow: *She poured out her sorrows to me* **5 a** to rain hard and steadily: *It's pouring this morning* **b** (of rain) to fall hard and steadily: *The rain is really pouring down* **6** *esp. spoken* to fill cups of tea, coffee, etc., and serve them **7** to supply (someone) with a drink from a vessel: *Please pour me a cup of tea*

poverty *n* **1** the state of being very poor **2** *esp. written & offensive* low quality: *The book is boring because of the poverty of its ideas*

¹powder *n* **1** a substance in the form of very fine dry grains: *He crushed the chalk to powder* **2** a pleasant-smelling, often flesh-coloured substance in this form, for use on the skin: *face powder* **3** explosive material in this form, esp. gunpowder

²powder *v* **1** to put powder on **2** to break into powder

¹power *n* **1** a sense or ability that forms part of the nature of body or mind: *Some animals have the power to see in the dark* **2** force; strength **3** control over others: *Power should be used wisely* **4** right to govern: *Which political party is in power now?* **5** right to act, given by law, rule, or official position: *The army has been given special powers to deal* *with this state of affairs* **6** a person, group, nation, etc., that has influence or control: *There is to be a meeting of the Great Powers* **7** an unearthly force or spirit believed to be able to influence men's fate: *the powers of evil* **8** force that may be used for doing work, driving a machine, or producing electricity: *Mills used to depend on wind or water power* **9** the degree of this force produced by something: *What is the power of this engine?* **10** (in mathematics) **a** the number of times that an amount is to be multiplied by itself: *The amount 2 to the power of 3 is written 2³, and means 2×2×2* **b** the result of this multiplying: *The 3rd power of 2 is 8* **11** (of instruments containing a lens) a measure of the strength of the ability to make objects appear larger **12** *esp. spoken* a large amount: *Your visit did me a power of good* **13 More power to your elbow!** *esp. spoken* May your efforts succeed! **14 power behind the throne** a person who, though he has no official position, has great influence in private over a ruler or leader

²**power** *adj* (of an apparatus or vehicle usu. worked by hand) provided with or worked by a motor: *power steering*

³**power** *v* to supply power to (esp. a moving machine)

powerful *adj* **1** very strong; full of force: *a powerful swimmer* **2** of great ability; easily producing ideas: *a powerful imagination* **3** strong or great in effect: *Onions have a powerful smell* **4** having much control and influence **5** having or using great mechanical power −~**ly** *adv*: *He's very powerfully built*

¹**practical** *adj* **1** concerned with action, practice, or actual conditions and results, rather than with ideas: *At scout camp he made practical use of his cookery lessons* **2** effective or convenient in actual use: *a very practical little table that folds up when not needed* **3 a** sensible; clever at doing things and concerned with facts rather than feelings: *We've got to be practical and buy only what we can afford* **b** *offensive* insensitive and lacking imagination **4** taught by actual experience or practice, not by studying books: *She's never been to cooking classes, but she's a good practical cook* **5 for all practical purposes** actually; in reality: *He does so little work in the office that for all practical purposes it would make no difference if he didn't come* −~**ity** *n*

²**practical** *n esp. spoken* a practical lesson, test, or examination, as in science

practically *adv* **1** usefully; suitably **2** very nearly: *She's practically always late*

practice *n* **1** actual use or performance as compared with the idea, rules, etc., on which the action is based: *We must put our plans into practice*

2 experience; knowledge of a skill as gained by this: *Have you had any practice in nursing?* **3** a repeated performance or exercise in order to gain skill in some art, game, etc.: *We have 3 choir practices a week* **4** a standard course of action that is accepted as correct: *It is the practice in English law to consider a person innocent until he has been proved guilty* **5** *often written* a fixed custom or regular habit: *It's not the usual practice for shops to stay open after 6 o'clock* **6** *often offensive* an act that is often repeated, esp. secretly, in a fixed manner or with ceremony: *The Christian church had to stop magical practices among its people* **7 a** the business of a doctor or lawyer: *Is Doctor Jones still in practice?* **b** his place of business: *Doctor Smith's practice is in the High Street* **c** the kind or number of people using his services: *He has a small practice* **8 sharp practice** *offensive* behaviour or a trick in business or work that is dishonest but not quite unlawful

practise *v* **-tised, -tising 1** to act in accordance with (the ideas of one's religion or other firm belief): *a practising Jew* **2** *esp. written* to show or use (some necessary quality in behaviour): *In dealing with sick old people nurses must practise great patience* **3** *esp. written* to make a habit or practice of: *Our income has decreased and now we have to practise economy* **4** to do (an action) repeatedly or do exercises regularly (esp. on a musical instrument) in order to gain skill: *She's been practising the same tune on the piano for nearly an hour* **5** to do (something needing special knowledge) according to rule: *Some people practise magic* **6** to do (the work of a doctor, lawyer, etc.): *One practises medicine, the other practises law* **7** *esp. written* to make unfair use of (a trick) for one's own advantage **8 practise what one preach**es to do oneself what one is always telling others to do

prairie *n* (esp. in North America) a treeless grassy plain

¹**praise** *v* **praised, praising** to speak favourably and with admiration of

²**praise** *n* **1** expression of admiration: *a book in praise of country life* **2** *esp. written or literature* glory; worship: *Let us give praise to God* **3 praise be** thank God: *At last I've found you, praise be!*

pram —also (*esp. written*) **perambulator** *n* a 4-wheeled carriage for a baby, which is pushed by hand

prance *v* **pranced, prancing 1** (of a horse) to jump high or move quickly by raising the front legs and springing forwards on the back legs **2** to move quickly, gaily, or proudly, with a springing step —**prance** *n*

¹**pray** *v* **prayed, praying 1** to speak, often silently, to God (or the gods), privately or with others, showing love, giving thanks, or asking for something **2** *esp. spoken* to wish or hope very strongly: *We're praying*

for a fine day **3 past praying for** in a hopeless condition (of illness, wickedness, etc.)

²**pray** *adv* please: *Pray be quiet!*

¹**prayer** *n* **1** the act or regular habit of praying to God or the gods **2** a fixed form of church service mainly concerned with praying: *Evening Prayer* **3** a quite informal daily religious service among a group of people: *school prayers* **4** a fixed form of words used in praying: *He said his prayers every night* **5** a solemn request made to God or the gods, or to someone in a position of power: *Her prayer was answered and her husband came home safely*

²**prayer** *n* a person who prays

preach *v* **1** to make known (a particular religion or its teachings) by speaking in public: *Christ preached to large crowds* **2** to give a sermon as part of a church service **3** to advise or urge others to accept (a thing or course of behaviour): *She's always preaching the value of healthy eating* **4** to offer (unwanted advice on matters of right and wrong) in an irritating way: *Mum keeps preaching at me about my untidiness* –~**er** *n*

precarious *adj* **1** unsafe; unsteady **2** doubtful; not based firmly on facts: *precarious reasoning* –~**ly** *adv* –~**ness** *n*

precaution *n* an action done or care taken in order to avoid danger, discomfort, etc.: *We have taken*

every precaution against disease –~**ary** *adj*

precede *v* **-ceded, -ceding 1** to come or go in front of **2** to be higher in rank or importance than: *The king precedes all men* **3** to be earlier than: *The minister's statement preceded that of the president* **4** to introduce (an activity) in the stated way: *He preceded his speech with a warning against inattention*

preceding *adj* that came just before in time or place: *preceding page*

¹**precious** *adj* **1** of great value and beauty: *a precious crystal vase* **2** that must not be wasted: *My time is precious; I can only give you a few minutes* **3** greatly loved or very dear **4** (of an art, use of words, manners, etc.) unnaturally fine; too concerned with unimportant details –~**ly** *adv* –~**ness** *n*

²**precious** *adv esp. spoken* very: *We have precious little time*

³**precious** *n esp. spoken* dear one; a much loved person or animal

precipice *n* **1** a steep or almost upright side of a high rock, mountain, etc. **2 on the edge of a precipice** in very great danger

precise *adj* **1** exact in form, detail, measurements, time, etc. **2** particular; very: *At the precise moment that I put my foot on the step, the bus started* **3** sharply clear: *A lawyer needs a precise mind* **4** careful and correct in regard to the smallest details: *precise manners* –~**ness** *n*

precisely *adv* **1** in a precise way **2**

exactly: *at 10 o'clock precisely* **3** yes, you are right: *'So you think we ought to wait?' 'Precisely'*

predecessor *n* **1** a person who held a position before someone else: *Our new doctor is much younger than his predecessor* **2** something formerly used, which has now been changed: *This new plan is no better than its predecessors*

predicament *n* a difficult or unpleasant state of affairs in which one does not know what to do

predict *v* to see or describe (a future happening) in advance as a result of knowledge, experience, reason, etc.: *The weather scientists predicted a fine summer*

predictable *adj* **1** that can be predicted **2** *offensive* not doing anything unexpected or showing imagination: *I hate predictable men* – **-bility** *n* – **-bly** *adv*

prediction *n* **1** something that is predicted; prophecy **2** the act of predicting – **-tive** *adj* – **-tively** *adv*

¹**preface** *n* **1** an introduction to a book or speech **2** an action that is intended to introduce something else more important

²**preface** *v* **-aced, -acing** **1** to serve as a preface to: *An introduction prefaces the novel* **2** to provide with a preface: *He prefaced his speech with an amusing story* – **-atory** *adj*: *few prefatory remarks*

prefect *n* **1** (in some schools) an older pupil given certain powers and duties with regard to keeping order over other pupils **2** (in ancient Rome and certain countries today) any of various public officers or judges with duties in government, the police, or the army: *the Prefect of Police of Paris*

prefer *v* **-rr-** **1** to choose (one thing or action) rather than another; like better **2** *law* to put forward for official consideration or action according to law: *The police preferred charges on the drunken driver*

preferable *adj* better; to be preferred –**-bly** *adv*

preference *n* **1** desire or liking for one thing rather than another: *I'd choose the small car in preference to the larger one* **2** special favour or consideration shown to a person, group, etc. **3** an example of this: *special trade preferences*

pregnant *adj* **1** (of a woman or female animal) having an unborn child or unborn young in the body **2** full of important but unexpressed or hidden meaning: *His words were followed by a pregnant pause* **3** *literature* clever; inventive: *the artist's pregnant imagination* –~**ly** *adv*

¹**prejudice** *n* **1** unfair and often unfavourable feeling or opinion not based on reason or knowledge, and sometimes resulting from distrust of ideas different from one's own: *A judge must be free from prejudice* **2** damage; harm: *He had to leave the university, to the prejudice of his own future as a scientist*

²**prejudice** *v* **-diced, -dicing** **1** to cause

(someone or someone's mind) to have a prejudice; influence: *His pleasant voice prejudices me in his favour* **2** to weaken; harm (someone's case, expectations, etc.)

¹**preliminary** *n* **-ries** a preparation; preliminary act or arrangement

²**preliminary** *adj* **1** coming before and introducing or preparing for something more important: *The chairman made a preliminary statement before beginning the main business* **2** (of a part of a sports competition) being the first part, in which the weaker people lose and the winners are left to compete in the main competition

prelude *n* **1** something that comes before and acts as an introduction to something more important: *I fear that the riots are a prelude to more serious trouble* **2 a** a short piece of music that introduces a large musical work **b** a short separate piece of piano or organ music: *Chopin's Preludes*

premature *adj* **1** developing, happening, or ripening before the natural or proper time: *his premature death at the age of 32* **2** (of a human or animal baby, or a birth) born, or happening, after less than the usual time inside the mother's body –~**ly** *adv*

premeditate *v* **-tated, -tating** to plan (something) carefully in advance – **-tation** *n* –~**d** *adj*

premises *n* a house or other building with any surrounding land, consi-dered as a piece of property: *Food bought in this shop may not be eaten on the premises*

premium *n* **1** a sum of money paid regularly to an insurance company to protect oneself against some risk of loss or damage **2** an additional payment, esp. to a worker, made as a reward for special effort **3 at a premium a** (of a business share) at a rate above the usual value **b** difficult to obtain, and therefore worth more than usual: *During July and August hotel rooms are at a premium* **4 put a premium on** to cause (a quality or action) to be an advantage: *Work paid according to the amount done puts a premium on speed and not quality*

preoccupy *v* **-pied, -pying** to fill the thoughts or hold the interest of (someone or someone's mind) almost completely, esp. so that not enough attention is given to other matters – **-pied** *adj*

preparation *n* **1** the act of preparing for a future event: *He did too little preparation for his examination* **2** the state of being prepared: *Plans for selling the product are in preparation* **3** something that is made ready for use by mixing a number of substances: *a new preparation for cleaning metal*

prepare *v* **-pared, -paring 1** to put (something) in a condition ready for a purpose: *Please prepare the table for dinner* **2** to put together or make by treating in some special way (such as by mixing or heating substances): *Mother is preparing us a meal* **3** to get or make ready by collecting supplies, making arrangements, planning, studying, etc.: *They are busy preparing to go on holiday* **4** to accustom (someone or someone's mind) to some new idea, event, or condition: *Prepare yourself for a shock*

prepared *adj* **1** got ready in advance: *The chairman read out a prepared statement* **2** willing: *I'm not prepared to listen to your excuses*

preposition *n* a word used with a noun, pronoun, or *-ing* form to show its connection with another word: *In 'a house made of wood' and 'a man like my brother', 'of' and 'like' are prepositions, and so is 'by' in 'she succeeded by working hard'* –~al *adj* –~ally *adv*

prescribe *v* -scribed, -scribing **1** to order (something) as a medicine or treatment for a sick person: *The doctor prescribed a cough medicine* **2** (of a person or body that has the right to do so) to fix (what must happen or be done): *What punishment does the law prescribe for this crime?*

prescription *n* **1** the act of prescribing **2 a** a particular medicine or treatment ordered by a doctor **b** a written order for this: *Take this prescription to the chemist's*

presence *n* **1** the fact or state of being present: *She was so quiet that her presence was hardly noticed* **2** attendance: *Your presence is requested at the meeting* **3** personal appearance and manner, as having a strong effect on others **4** a spirit or an influence that cannot be seen but is felt to be near **5 in the presence of someone** also **in someone's presence**– close enough to be seen or heard by someone

¹present *n* a gift

²present *v* **1** to give (something) away, esp. at a ceremonial occasion: *He presented her with a bunch of flowers* **2** to offer or bring (something) to someone's notice: *Can you present your report this afternoon?* **3** *polite* to offer: *He presented his apologies* **4** to introduce (someone) esp. to someone of higher rank **5** to give the public a chance to see and hear (a play or performer): *The theatre company is presenting Eric Williamson as Hamlet* **6** to show: *Although worried, he always presents a smiling face* **7** (of non-material things) to be the cause of: *He's clever at scientific studies; they present no difficulty to him* **8 present arms** to hold a weapon upright in front of the body as a ceremonial greeting **9 present itself a** (of a thought) to arrive in the mind **b** (of something possible) to happen: *If the chance to buy this farm presents itself, buy it* **10 present oneself** to attend; arrive

³present *adj* **1** (of a person) being in the place talked of or understood: *Who was present at the meeting?* **2**

existing or happening now: *I'm not going to buy a house at the present high prices* **3** *esp. written or literature* felt or remembered as if actually there: *The terrible events of 5 years ago are still present to our minds* **4** *technical* (of a tense or a form of a verb) expressing state or action which is going on now: *'He wants' and 'they are coming' are examples of verbs in present tenses* **5** **'present company excepted'** *polite* 'but the people here are not included in the unfavourable remarks I am making'

⁴**present** *n* **1** the present time **2** *technical* the present tense **3 at present** now; at this time **4 for the present** for now; for the time being **5 live in the present** to experience life as it comes, not thinking about the past or the future **6 (there is) no time like the present** if you must do something, it is best to do it now

presentation *n* **1** the act or action of presenting something: *There are 2 presentations of the show each night* **2** the way in which something is said, offered, shown, explained, etc., to others: *The teacher praised the neat presentation of the homework*

presently *adv* **1** soon: *The doctor will be here presently* **2** *esp. US and Scots* at present; now: *The doctor is presently writing a book*

preservation *n* **1** the act or action of preserving **2** the state of remaining in (a stated) condition after a long time: *The old building is in good preservation*

¹**preserve** *v* **-served, -serving 1** *esp. written or literature* to keep (someone) safe or alive; protect **2** to keep (an article) carefully from destruction for a long time **3** to cause (a condition) to last: *In times of danger he always preserves his calmness* **4** to keep (a substance) in good condition or from decay by some means: *Ancient Egyptians knew how to preserve dead bodies* **5** to keep (a rare animal or plant) in existence – **-servable** *adj*

²**preserve** *n* **1** a substance made from fruit boiled in sugar, used esp. for spreading on bread; jam **2** a stretch of land or water kept for private hunting or fishing **3** something considered to belong to or be for the use of only a certain person or people: *She considers the arranging of flowers in the church to be her own preserve*

preside *v* **-sided, -siding** to be in charge; lead: *the presiding officer*

president *n* **1** the head of government in many modern states that do not have a king or queen: *the President of France* **2** the head of some councils or government departments **3** the head of various societies concerned with art, science, sport, etc.: *the president of the Yorkshire Cricket Club* **4** the head of some British university colleges, and of some American universities **5** the head of a business company, bank, etc. –~**ial** *adj*

¹**press** *n* 1 an act of pushing steadily against something 2 any of various apparatuses or machines used for pressing: *a trouser press* 3 *esp. spoken* an act of ironing a garment 4 newspapers and magazines in general (often including the news-gathering services of radio and tele-vision): *the power of the press* 5 newspaper writers in general: *The minister invited the press to a meeting* 6 treatment given by news-papers in general when reporting a person or event: *The play had a good press* 7 a business for printing (and sometimes also for selling) books, magazines, etc.: *the Univer-sity Press* 8 PRINTING PRESS 9 *esp. written* a crowd or close mass of moving people 10 continual hurry and effort 11 **freedom of the press** the freedom or right to print news or fair opinion on matters of public interest without fear of being stopped or harmed by a govern-ment or other official group 12 **go to press** (of a newspaper for any particular day) to start being printed

²**press** *v* 1 to push firmly and steadily 2 to iron 3 to direct force in order to crush, flatten, shape, pack tightly, or get liquid out 4 to push one's way, esp. in a mass: *People pressed round the famous actress* 5 to force an attack, a demand, etc. on: *She pressed her guest to stay* 6 **time presses** there is not much time

³**press** *v* 1 (in former times) to seize and force (a man) into the navy or army 2 **press into service** to use for some purpose in a time of need

pressure *n* 1 the action of pressing 2 the strength of this force: *a pressure of 10 pounds to the square inch* 3 discomfort caused by a sensation of pressing: *a feeling of pressure in his chest* 4 also **atmospheric pressure**– the force of the weight of the air 5 anxiety and difficulty 6 forcible influence: *We must bring pressure on him* 7 **under pressure** a not of one's own free will b being forced or hurried: *He works best under pressure*

prestige *n* respect or admiration felt by reason of rank, proved quality, etc.: *the prestige of having such a famous brother*

presumable *adj* probable – **-bly** *adv*: *Presumably there's a good reaso*

presume *v* **-sumed, -suming** 1 to take as a fact without proof: *I presume he'll be back* 2 to accept as true until proved untrue: *If a person is missing for 7 years, he is presumed dead* 3 to dare: *He presumed to tell his employer how the work ought to be done*

pretence *n* 1 a false appearance, reason, or show: *She isn't really ill; it's only pretence* 2 a claim to possess (some desirable quality): *He has no pretence to education* 3 **false pre-tences** *law* acts intended to deceive

pretend *v* 1 to give a deceiving appearance of: *He pretended to be* *reading* **2** (usu. of a child) to imagine as a game: *Let's pretend we're cats* **3** to attempt; dare: *I won't pretend to tell you how this machine works*

pretentious *adj* claiming importance that one does not possess – ~**ness** *n* – ~**ly** *adv*

pretext *n* an excuse: *He came under the pretext of seeing Mr Smith, but really to see Smith's daughter*

¹**pretty** *adj* **-tier, -tiest 1** pleasing but not beautiful or grand **2** (of a boy) charming and graceful but rather girlish **3** not nice; displeasing: *a pretty state of affairs* **4 sitting pretty** (of a person) in a favourable situation – **-tily** *adv* – **-tiness** *n*

²**pretty** *adv esp. spoken* rather; quite though not completely: *pretty sure / pretty good*

prevent *v* **1** to keep from happening: *to prevent accidents* **2** to hold (someone) back: *You can't prevent me from going* – ~**able** *adj* – ~**ion** *n*

previous *adj* **1** earlier: *Have you had any previous experience?* **2** *esp. spoken* acting too soon: *You're a little previous in thanking me for something I haven't given you yet* – ~**ly** *adv*

prey *n* **1** an animal that is hunted and eaten by another **2** a way of life based on killing and eating other animals (in the phrases **beast/bird of prey**) **3 be/become/fall a prey to a** (of an animal) to be caught and eaten by (another animal) **b** (of a

person) to be greatly troubled by: *Some people become a prey to fears of being murdered*

¹**price** *n* **1** an amount of money for which a thing is offered or bought **2** that which one must suffer to get something one wants: *Loss of health is the price you pay for taking dangerous drugs* **3** (in betting) the difference between the money asked and the money one will get if one wins **4 a price on one's head** a reward for one's capture **5 have one's price** to be willing to accept bribes

²**price** *v* **priced, pricing 1** to fix the price of (goods for sale) **2** to ask the price of

priceless *adj* **1** of worth too great to be calculated **2** very funny: *You look priceless in those trousers!*

¹**prick** *n* **1** a small hole made by pricking **2** an act of pricking **3** a small sharp pain **4** a prickle **5 kick against the pricks** *esp. literature* to complain uselessly

²**prick** *v* **1** to make a very small hole in the skin or surface of ,with a sharp-pointed object **2** to make (a small hole) in a surface with a pointed tool **3** to give a sensation of light sharp pain

¹**prickle** *n* **1** any of a number of small sharp-pointed growths on the skin of some plants or animals **2** a pricking sensation

²**prickle** *v* **-led, -ling** to give a pricking sensation

prickly *adj* **-lier, -liest 1** covered with

prickles **2** that gives a pricking sensation: *prickly woollen underclothes* **3** *esp. spoken* (of a person) easily made angry – **-liness** *n*

pride *n* **1** too high an opinion of oneself **2** reasonable self-respect: *She wanted to beg him to stay but her pride wouldn't let her* **3** satisfaction in someone or something connected with oneself: *Why can't you take more pride in your appearance?* **4** one's most valuable person or thing **5** a group (of lions) **6 swallow one's pride** to make an effort to forget one's pride

priest *n* **1** (in the Christian church) a person, esp. a man, trained for various religious duties **2** (*fem.* **priestess**)– a person with related duties in certain non-Christian religions –~**hood** *n* –~**ly** *adj* –~**liness** *n*

primary *adj* **1** earliest in time **2** main: *A primary cause of Tom's failure is his laziness* **3** (of education or a school) for children between 5 and 11 **4** *technical* which produces or passes on electricity: *a primary coil*

¹prime *n* **1** the time of greatest perfection, strength, or activity: *in the prime of life* **2** *technical* PRIME NUMBER

²prime *adj* **1** first in importance: *a prime reason* **2** of the very best quality: *a prime joint of beef*

³prime *v* **primed, priming 1** to prepare (a machine) for working **2** to instruct (someone) in advance **3** to cover (a surface) with a base of paint, oil, etc.

prime minister –also (*esp. spoken*) **P M** *n* the chief government minister in Britain and many other countries –~**ship** *n*

prime number *n technical* a number that can be divided exactly only by itself and the number one: *23 is a prime number*

¹primitive *adj* **1** of or belonging to the earliest stage of development: *primitive tools made from stones and bones* **2** old-fashioned and inconvenient: *Life in this village is too primitive for me* –~**ly** *adv* –~**ness** *n*

²primitive *n* **1** an artist who paints simple flat-looking pictures **2** a member of a primitive race or tribe

prince *n* **1** a son or near male relation of a king or queen **2** a ruler of a small country or protected state **3** *esp. in literature* a very great, successful, or powerful man: *Shakespeare, the prince of poets*

princess *n* **1** a daughter or near female relation of a king or queen **2** the wife of a prince

¹principal *adj* chief; most important: *the principal rivers of Africa* –~**ly** *adv*

²principal *n* **1** the head of some universities, colleges, and schools **2** a sum of money on which interest is paid **3** a leading performer in a play, concert, etc.

principle *n* **1** a general truth or belief used as a base for reasoning or action: *the principle of freedom of speech* **2 a** *technical* a scientific law of nature: *the principle of Arch-imedes* **b** such a law as governing the making or working of a machine, apparatus, etc. **3** a rule used as a guide for action **4** honourable behaviour: *a man of principle* **5 in principle a** in regard to the main idea: *They agreed to the plan in principle* **b** according to what is supposed to be true: *There's no reason in principle why man shouldn't travel to* **6 on principle** because of settled fixed beliefs

¹**print** *n* **1** a mark on a surface showing the shape, pattern, etc., of the thing pressed into it: *footprints in the snow* **2** printed letters **3** a picture printed from metal: *a set of Chinese prints* **4** cloth on which a pattern has been printed: *print dresses* **5** a photograph printed from film **6 in print** printed in a book, newspaper, etc.

²**print** *v* **1** to press (a mark) onto a surface **2 a** to press using shapes covered with ink **b** to make (a book, magazine, etc.) in this way **3** to cause to appear in or as a book, newspaper, etc. **4** to ornament with a pattern pressed or rubbed on the surface: *printed wallpaper* **5** to make or copy (a photograph) on paper from film **6** to write without joining the letters

printer *n* **1** a person employed in printing **2** a machine for making copies, esp. photographs

printing press also press, printing machine– *n* a machine that prints books, newspapers, etc.

priority *n* **-ties 1** the state or right of being first: *The badly wounded take priority for medical attention* **2** something that needs attention before others: *The arranging of this agreement is a top priority*

prior to *prep esp. written* before

prison *n* **1** a large building where criminals are kept locked up **2** a place or condition in which one feels a loss of freedom

prisoner *n* **1** a person kept in a prison **2** a person or animal without freedom

¹**private** *adj* **1** personal; not shared: *private letters* **2** not intended for everyone: *a private performance* **3** not connected with government: *a private hospital* **4** not connected with one's public life **5** without official position: *private citizens* **6** quiet; sheltered: *a private corner* **7 in private** secretly **– ~ly** *adv*

²**private** –also **private soldier** *n* a soldier of the lowest rank

privilege *n* **1** a right or favour limited to one person or a few people **2** a right to do or say things without risk of punishment, esp. in parliament **– ~d** *adj*

¹**prize** *n* **1** something of value given to someone who is successful **2** a reward given to a student for good work **3** something of value gained after a struggle: *To some men wealth is the greatest prize in life*

²**prize** *adj* **1** that has gained a prize: *a*

prize rose **2** *esp. spoken* worthy of a prize: *That hen has produced a prize egg* **3** given as a prize: *prize money*

³**prize** *v* **prized, prizing** to value highly

⁴**prize, prise** *v* to pry: *We prized the top off the box*

probable *adj* likely: *a probable result*

probably *adv* almost but not quite certainly

¹**probe** *n* **1** an apparatus (**space probe**) sent into the sky to examine conditions in outer space an act of probing

²**probe** *v* **probed, probing** **1** to poke about in **2** to examine thoroughly: *She tried to probe my mind* –**probing** *adj* –**probingly** *adv*

¹**problem** *n* **1** a difficulty that needs attention **2** a question for which an answer is needed: *simple problems in subtraction*

²**problem** *adj* dealing with, or suffering from, social or moral difficulties: *problem plays / problem children*

procedure *n* **1** the way or order of directing business in an official meeting, a law case, etc. **2** a set of actions necessary for doing something: *Writing a cheque is a simple procedure*

proceed *v* **1** to begin and continue: *Tell us your name and then proceed with your story* **2** to continue after stopping **3** *esp. written* to advance; move forward

proceedings *n* **1** happenings: *the evening's wild proceedings* **2** an action taken in law (esp. in the phrases **start/take proceedings**) **3** the records of the business, activities, etc., of a club

proceeds *n* money gained from sale or from some activity

¹**process** *n* **1** any continued set of natural actions connected with the continuation, development, and change of life or matter: *Coal was formed by chemical processes* **2** a continued set of actions performed intentionally: *the process of learning to read* **3** course; time during which something is done: *in the process of moving to a new factory* **4** a system used in producing goods

²**process** *v* **1** to treat and preserve by a process: *processed cheese* **2** to develop or print (a film) **3** to put (facts, numbers, etc.) into a computer **4** to prepare and examine in detail: *The plans are now being processed*

procession *n* a line of people, vehicles, etc., moving forward in an orderly, often ceremonial, way

proclaim *v* **1** *esp. written* to make known publicly: *The boy was proclaimed king* **2** *literature* to show clearly: *His pronunciation proclaimed that he was an American*

proclamation *n* **1** an official public statement **2** proclaiming

procure *v* **-cured, -curing** **1** *esp. written* to obtain, esp. by effort **2** to provide (a woman) for sexual satisfaction – **-curable** *adj* –~**ment** *n* –~**r** *n*

prod *v* **-dd- 1** to push or press with a finger or pointed object **2** to urge sharply into action or thought —**prod** *n*

prodigy *n* **-gies 1** a wonder in nature **2** an unusually clever child (often in the phrases **child prodigy, infant prodigy**)

¹**produce -duced, -ducing** *v* **1** to show or offer for examination: *The magician produced a rabbit from a hat* **2** to bear (crops) or supply (substances): *Canada produces wheat and furs* **3** to give birth to **4** to lay (an egg) **5** to make from materials **6** to cause: *Gordon's jokes produced a great deal of laughter* **7** (in geometry) to lengthen (a line) to a point

²**produce** *n* something produced, esp. by growing or farming: *The wine bottle was marked 'Produce of Spain'*

product *n* **1** something produced: *Important products of South Africa are fruit and gold* **2** something produced as a result of planning, conditions, etc.: *Criminals are sometimes the product of bad homes* **3** (in mathematics) the number obtained by multiplying 2 or more numbers

production *n* **1** producing or making products: *the production of cloth* **2** the amount produced: *Production has increased* **3** a play, film, or broadcast that is produced

productive *adj* that produces well or much —~**ly** *adv* —~**ness** *n*

profession *n* **1** a form of employment, obtained after education and training (such as law, medicine, and the Church): *He is a lawyer by profession* **2** *esp. written* a declaration of one's belief, opinion, or feeling

¹**professional** *adj* **1** working in one of the professions **2** using the training of a member of a profession: *The magician performed with professional skill* **3** doing for money what others do for enjoyment: *a professional gardener* **4** done by people who are paid: *professional football* —~**ly** *adv*

²**professional** *n* **1** a person who lives on the money he earns by a skill or sport **2** a person employed by a club to play for it and to teach his sporting skills to its members **3** a person who has great experience and high professional standards

profile *n* **1** a side view or edge of something against a background: *He drew her profile* **2** a short description, esp. of a person's life and character, on television or in a newspaper

¹**profit** *n* **1** money gain **2** *esp. written* advantage gained from some action: *Everyone gains profit from exercise* —~**able** *adj* —~**ably** *adv* —~**less** *adj* —~**lessly** *adv*

²**profit** *v* **1** *esp. written* to be of service, use, or advantage to: *It will profit you nothing to do that* **2** to gain advantage: *You can profit by making mistakes*

profound *adj* **1** deep; strongly felt: *profound silence* **2** *esp. written* far below the surface: *the profound depths of the ocean* **3** having or needing deep knowledge: *a profound thinker/subject* **−∼ly** *adv:profoundly grateful*

¹**program** *n* a plan of the operations to be performed by a computer

²**program** *v* **-mm-** to supply (a computer) with a plan of operations

¹**programme** *n* **1** a list of performers or things to be performed at a concert, a sports competition, etc. **2** a complete show or performance, esp. one made up of several acts **3** a fixed plan of a course of action: *The hospital building programme has been delayed*

²**programme** *v* **-grammed, -gramming** to plan or arrange: *The central heating is programmed to start working at 6*

¹**progress** *n* **1** forward movement in space **2** continual improvement: *Jane is still in hospital, but she's making progress* **3** the state of continuing or being done (often in the phrase **in progress**)

²**progress** *v* **1** to advance **2** to improve

progressive *adj* **1** moving forward continuously or by stages **2** (of a tax) higher on larger amounts of money **3** improving in accordance with new ideas: *a progressive firm* **4** modern (esp. in the phrase **progressive jazz**) **−∼ly** *adv* **−∼ness** *n*

prohibit *v* *esp. written* **1** to forbid by law or rule **2** to prevent: *His small size prohibits his becoming a policeman*

¹**project** *n* a plan for work or activity: *The government has begun a project to increase the size of the harbour*

²**project** *v* **1** to stick out: *His ears project noticeably* **2** to aim and throw **3** to direct (heat, sound, light, or shadow): *A singer must project his voice so as to be heard* **4 a** to make a picture of (a solid object) on a flat surface **b** to make (a map) by this means **5** to represent (oneself) favourably: *A politician must project himself if he wants to win an election* **6** to plan: *our projected visit to Australia*

projector *n* an apparatus for projecting films or pictures onto a surface

prolific *adj* producing crops, babies, etc. in large numbers **−∼ally** *adv*

prolong *v* to make longer **−∼ation** *n*

prolonged *adj* continuing for a long time: *a prolonged absence*

prominent *adj* **1** sticking out: *prominent teeth* **2** noticeable **3** of great ability, fame, importance, etc. **−∼ly** *adv*

¹**promise** *n* **1** a statement, which someone else has a right to believe, that one will or will not do something **2** expectation of something good: *The news brings little promise of peace* **3** reasons for such expectation: *The boy shows promise as a cricketer*

²**promise** *v* **-mised, -mising 1** to make a promise **2** to cause one to hope for: *The clear sky promises fine weather*

promising *adj* showing signs of advance towards success −∼**ly** *adv*

promote *v* -**moted, -moting 1** to advance (someone) in rank **2** to help in forming or arranging (a business, concert, etc.): *Who is promoting this boxing match?* **3** to bring (goods) to public notice in order to increase sales **4** to help in the growth of: *Milk promotes health* **5** to bring forward (a bill) in parliament −∼**r** *n*

promotion *n* **1** advancement in rank **2** action to help something develop or succeed: *sales promotions* **3** a product being promoted −∼**al** *adj*

¹**prompt** *v* **1** to cause: *Hunger prompted him to steal* **2** to help (a speaker who pauses) by suggesting how to continue: *The actor forgot his words and had to be prompted*

²**prompt** *adj* acting or done at once: *prompt payment of bills* −∼**ly** *adv* −∼**ness** *n*

prone *adj* **1** (of a person or position) stretched out face downwards **2** having the probability of (usu. something bad): *He is prone to colds* −∼**ness** *n*

pronoun *n* (in grammar) a word used in place of a noun or a noun phrase: *Instead of saying 'the man came' you can use a pronoun and say 'he came'*

pronounce *v* -**nounced, -nouncing 1** to make the sound of (a letter, a word, etc.): *In the word 'knew', the 'k' is not pronounced* **2** to declare officially: *The doctor pronounced the man dead* **3** *esp. law* to give judgement

pronunciation *n* **1** the way in which a word or language is pronounced **2** a particular person's way of pronouncing

¹**proof** *n* **1** a way of showing that something is true: *Have you any proof that you weren't there?* **2** a test to find out whether someone or something has a quality, standard, etc. **3** (in mathematics) the reasoning that shows a statement to be true **4** a test copy made of a piece of printed matter so that mistakes can be put right before the proper printing is done **5** the standard of strength of some kinds of alcoholic drink

²**proof** *adj* **1 a** giving protection: *This tent is proof against water* **b** unyielding; uninfluenced: *His courage is proof against the greatest pain* **2** (of spirits) of standard strength

³**proof** *v* to treat in order to give protection, esp. against water

¹**prop** *n* **1** a support to hold up something heavy **2** a person on whom someone or something depends

²**prop** *v* -**pp- 1** to support by placing something under or against **2** to put in a leaning position: *He propped his bicycle against the fence*

³**prop** *n esp. spoken* an aircraft's propeller

⁴**prop** *n* any small article (such as a weapon, telephone, etc.) used on the stage in a play

propaganda *n often offensive* action

taken, esp. by a government, to influence public opinion by spreading ideas, news, etc.: *propaganda against smoking*

propel *v* **-ll-** to push forward

propeller *n* 2 or more blades fixed to a central bar turned at high speed by an engine, to drive a ship or aircraft

proper *adj* 1 suitable; correct: *proper medical attention* 2 paying great attention to what is considered correct in society 3 complete: *a proper fool* 4 *esp. spoken* real: *a proper dog, not a toy dog* 5 itself; not including additional things: *areas that aren't part of the city proper*

properly *adv* 1 suitably; correctly; sensibly 2 really; actually; exactly

property *n* **-ties** 1 that which is owned: *That car is my property* 2 land, buildings, or both together 3 ownership, with its rights and duties according to the law 4 a quality: *Many plants have medicinal properties* 5 *esp. written* a stage prop 6 **common property** something shared by all

prophecy *n* **-cies** 1 the power of foretelling future events 2 a statement telling something that is to happen in the future

prophesy *v* **-sied, -sying** 1 to give (a warning, statement about the future, etc.) as a result of a religious experience 2 to say in advance: *to prophesy who will win the election*

prophet –(*fem.* **prophetess**) *n* 1 (in the Christian, Jewish, and Muslim religions) a man directed by God to make known God's will or to teach a religion 2 a thinker, poet, etc., who teaches some new idea 3 a person who tells the future: *Farmers are usually good weather prophets* –~ic *adj* –~ically *adv*

proportion *n* 1 the correct relationship between the size, position, and shape of parts 2 compared relationship between the size, amount, etc. of 2 things: *the proportion of men to women in the population* 3 a part; share: *What proportion of your wages do you spend on rent?* 4 (in mathematics) a relation between quantities such that 2 ratios are equal: *2 sets are in proportion if their numbers are in the same ratio, such as {6,4} and {24,16}* 5 **in proportion to a** according to **b** as compared with 6 **in/out of proportion** (not) according to real importance: *When one is angry one often does not see things in proportion* 7 **in the proportion of** in the measure of: *The paint should be mixed in the proportion of one part of paint to 2 of water* 8 **sense of proportion** ability to judge what matters and what does not

proposal *n* 1 a suggestion 2 an offer of marriage

propose *v* **-posed, -posing** 1 to suggest 2 to intend: *I propose to go on Tuesday* 3 *esp. written* to put forward to be voted on (often in the phrase **propose a motion**) 4 to make an offer of (marriage) to someone 5 to ask a social gathering to offer (a wish for success, happiness, etc.) to someone, while drinking (usu. in the phrases **propose a toast/ propose someone's health**) $-\sim$**r** *n*

proposition *n* **1** an unproved statement **2** a suggestion **3** *esp. spoken* a person or thing that must be dealt with: *Be careful with Murray; he's a nasty proposition* **4** a suggested offer of sex (esp. in the phrase **make someone a proposition**) **5** (in geometry) a truth that must be proved, or a question to which the answer must be found $-\sim$**al** *adj*

proprietor $-(fem.$ **-tress**) *n esp. written* an owner

¹**prospect** *n* **1** reasonable hope (of something happening) **2** something considered probable: *the prospect of having to live alone* **3** a view: *a beautiful prospect over the valley* **4** a person who might be offered or might accept a position, office, etc.

²**prospect** *v* to explore an area for gold, oil, etc. $-\sim$**or** *n*

prospective *adj* **1** not yet in effect **2** expected; intended: *her prospective husband*

prosper *v* **1** to become successful and rich **2** to develop favourably

prosperous *adj* successful; wealthy $-\sim$**ly** *adv* $-$ **-rity** *n*

prostitute $-(masc.$ **male prostitute**) *n* a woman who earns money by having sex with anyone who will pay

protect *v* **1** to keep safe, esp. by covering: *He raised his arm to pro-tect his face. / electric wires protected by a rubber covering* **2** to help (local industry or the sale of goods) by taxing foreign goods **3** to guard by means of insurance

protection *n* **1** protecting or being protected **2** a person or thing that protects **3** the condition of being protected by an insurance company

protective *adj* **1** that gives protection: *protective clothing* **2** wishing to protect: *She's too protective towards her daughter* $-\sim$**ly** *adv* $-\sim$**ness** *n*

protein *n* any of many substances that are essential parts of all living things and are necessary in food for building up the body and keeping it healthy. They are found esp. in meat, eggs, and cheese

¹**protest** *n* **1** a complaint or expression of dissatisfaction **2** opposition, dissatisfaction, etc.: *went to bed without protest* **3 under protest** unwillingly

²**protest** *v* **1** to express annoyance or disagreement **2** to declare against disbelief: *We urged her to come but she protested that she was too tired* $-\sim$**er** *n*

Protestant *n, adj* (a member) of the part of the Christian church that separated from the Roman Catholic church in the 16th century $-\sim$**ism** *n*

protocol *n* **1** the ceremonial system of rules and behaviour between rulers or representatives of governments, between people on official occasions, etc. **2** *technical* a first written signed form of an agreement being considered between nations

proton *n* a very small piece of matter that helps to form the central part of an atom and carries a standard amount of positive electricity

prototype *n* the first form of anything, from which later forms develop

¹**proud** *adj* 1 having self-respect: *too proud to beg* 2 having too high an opinion of oneself 3 pleased with something connected with oneself: *proud of his new car* 4 noble; grand: *this proud and great university* – ~**ly** *adv*

²**proud** *adv* **do someone proud** to treat someone splendidly

prove *v* **proved, proved** *or* **proven, proving** 1 to show to be true: *He has proved his courage* 2 to test the quality of 3 to be found to be: *My advice proved to be wrong* 4 technical (of a loaf or cake being baked) to rise properly – **-vable** *adj* – **-vably** *adv*

proverb *n* a short well-known saying: *'A cat has 9 lives' is a proverb*

provide *v* **-vided, -viding** 1 to supply: *That hotel provides meals* 2 (of a law, agreement, etc.) to state a special arrangement: *The law provides that ancient buildings must be preserved* 3 to supply needs: *He has 5 children to provide for*

province *n* 1 one of the main divisions of some countries for purposes of government control 2 an area under an archbishop 3 a division of land in connection with its special plants and animals: *Australia is the province of the kangaroo* 4 a branch of knowledge or activity considered as having fixed limits: *Persian art is quite outside my province*

¹**provision** *n* 1 providing 2 preparation for future needs: *to make provision for the future* 3 a supply 4 a condition in an agreement or law

²**provision** *v* to provide with food and supplies

provisional *adj* for the present time only – ~**ly** *adv*

provisions *n* food supplies

provocation *n* 1 provoking or being provoked 2 a reason for being provoked

provoke *v* **-voked, -voking** 1 to make angry or bad-tempered 2 to cause or force

prowl *v* (esp. of an animal or thief) to move quietly about, trying not to be seen or heard – **prowl** *n* – ~**er** *n*

prudent *adj* sensible and wise, esp. by avoiding risks: *It's prudent to wear a thick coat when it's cold* – **-dence** *n* – ~**ly** *adv*

¹**pry** *v* **pried, prying** to look secretly at or find out about someone else's private affairs

²**pry** –also **prize** *v* to raise, move, lift, or break with a tool: *to pry the cover off a box*

psychiatry *n* the study and treatment of diseases of the mind – **-tric** *adj* – **-trically** *adv*

psychological *adj* 1 of the mind 2

using psychology: *psychological tests* –~**ly** *adv*

psychology *n* **-gies 1** the study of the mind and the way it works, and of behaviour as an expression of the mind **2** a branch of this study that deals with a particular division of human activity – **-logist** *n*

pub –also **public house** *n* a building (not a club or hotel) where alcohol may be bought and drunk

¹**public** *adj* **1** of, to, by, for, or concerning people in general: *a matter of public importance* **2** for the use of everyone: *public gardens* **3** not secret or private: *a public statement* **4** connected with government: *How long has he held public office?* –~**ly** *adv*

²**public** *n* **1** people in general: *The gardens are open to the public* **2** a group in society: *This singer has an admiring public* **3 in public** in the presence of many people

publication *n* **1** the making of something known to the public **2** the offering for sale of something printed **3** something published

publicity *n* **1** public notice **2** the business of bringing someone or something to public notice, esp. for gain

publish *v* **1** to have printed for sale to the public (written work) **2** to make known generally

publisher *n* a person or firm whose business is to publish books, newspapers, etc., or (sometimes) to make and sell records

pudding *n* **1** a dessert **2** a usu. solid sweet dish based on pastry, rice, bread, etc., baked, boiled, or steamed, and served hot **3** a meat dish boiled with a pastry cover: *a steak and kidney pudding* **4** a sausage: *black pudding*

puddle *n* a small amount of rainwater in a hollow

¹**puff** *v* **1** to breathe rapidly and with effort **2** to breathe in and out while smoking (a cigarette, pipe, etc.) **3 a** (of smoke or steam) to blow or come out repeatedly **b** to cause (esp. smoke or steam) to come out repeatedly

²**puff** *n* **1** an act of puffing **2** a sudden short rush of air, smoke, etc. **3** something light that is blown along **4** *esp. spoken humour* breath **5** *esp. spoken becoming rare* written praise of a new book, play, etc. **6** an ornamental part of a garment made by drawing the cloth together so that it swells out **7** a piece of light pastry with a sweet filling: *a cream puff*

¹**pull** *v* **1** to draw (something) along behind one **2** to move (someone or something) by holding and drawing: *to pull the door open* **3** to seize and draw roughly towards one **4** to draw or press (something) towards one to make an apparatus work **5** to stretch and damage: *He's pulled a muscle* **6** to remove by drawing out: *That tooth should be pulled out* **7** to hold back (a horse in a race, or a blow in boxing) so as to avoid victory **8** (esp. in golf) to strike (the ball) to the left of the

intended direction (or right if one is left handed) **9** (in cricket and baseball) to hit (the ball) forward and across the body from right to left (or from left to right) **10** to draw (beer) out of a barrel **11** to draw out (a weapon) ready for use **12** to win, gain, or get (attention, votes, etc.): *The football match pulled in great crowds* **13 pull a fast one** *esp. spoken* to get the advantage by a trick **14 pull to pieces** to point out the faults of

²**pull** *n* **1** an act of pulling **2** a difficult steep climb **3** a natural force that causes movement: *the moon's pull on the sea* **4** *esp. spoken* special influence; (unfair) personal advantage **5** an act of inhaling tobacco smoke from a pipe, cigarette, etc. **6** an act of taking a long drink **7** any article used for pulling something: *a bellpull*

pullover *n* a woollen upper garment pulled on over the head

¹**pulp** *n* **1** soft plant or animal material, such as the inside of many fruits **2** the condition of being soft and liquid **3** vegetable materials softened for making paper **4** a cheap shocking book or magazine $-\sim$**y** *adj*

²**pulp** *v* to make or become pulpy

¹**pulse** *n* **1** the regular beating of blood in the arteries , esp. as felt at the wrist **2** a short sound as sent by radio or a small change in the quantity of electricity going through something

²**pulse** *n* the edible seeds of beans, peas, etc.

³**pulse** *v* **pulsed, pulsing** to beat steadily as the heart does

¹**pump** *n* **1** a machine for forcing liquids or gas into or out of something: *a petrol pump* / *a stomach pump* **2** an act of pumping

²**pump** *v* **1** to move (liquids or gas) by using a pump **2** to empty or fill by means of a pump: *He pumped up his tyres* **3** to work a pump **4** to work like a pump: *His heart was pumping fast* **5** to move up and down like a pump handle **6** *esp. spoken* to ask (someone) questions in the hope of finding out something

³**pump** *n* a light dancing shoe

¹**punch** *v* **1** to strike hard with the fist **2** to make (a hole) using a punch **3** to drive (something) in or out using a punch $-\sim$**er** *n*

²**punch** *n* **1** a quick strong blow with the fist **2** forcefulness: *That statement lacks punch* **3 beat someone to the punch** to take action before someone else can do so

³**punch** *n* **1** a steel tool for cutting holes or pressing a pattern: *a ticket punch* **2** a tool for hammering the heads of nails below a surface

⁴**punch** *n* a usu. alcoholic drink made with fruit juice, sugar, water and spices

punctual *adj* not late; prompt $-\sim$**ity** *n* $-\sim$**ly** *adv*

punctuate *v* **-ated, -ating 1** to divide (written matter) into sentences, phrases, etc., by punctuation marks **2** to break repeatedly into: *The game was punctuated by cheers*

punctuation *n* **1** the punctuating of writing **2** the marks used in doing this

¹**puncture** *n* a small hole made with a sharp point through a soft surface, esp. in a tyre

²**puncture** *v* **-tured, -turing 1** to burst as a result of a puncture **2** to make a small hole in: *a punctured lung*

punish *v* **1** to cause (someone) to suffer for a fault or crime **2** to deal roughly with (an opponent)

punishment *n* **1** punishing or being punished **2** a way in which a person is punished **3** *esp. spoken* rough treatment; damage

¹**pupil** *n* a person, esp. a child, who is being taught

²**pupil** *n* the small transparent round opening in the middle of the coloured part of the eye (iris), that appears black, through which light passes, and which can grow larger or smaller

puppet *n* **1** a jointed figure moved by pulling wires or strings **2** also **glove puppet**– a hollow cloth figure into which the hand is put to move the figure **3** a person or group controlled by the will of someone else: *a puppet government*

puppy –also **pup** *n* **-pies** a young dog

¹**purchase** *v* **-chased, -chasing 1** to buy **2** *esp. written* to gain at the cost of loss –**-chasable** *adj* –~**r** *n*

²**purchase** *n* **1** buying **2** an article just

bought **3** a firm hold for pulling, raising, etc.: *The climber tried to gain a purchase on a ledge*

pure *adj* **1** unmixed: *pure silver* **2** clean **3** of unmixed race: *a pure Arab horse* **4** free from sexual thoughts **5** (of colour or sound) clear **6** complete; thorough: *by pure chance* **7** (of an art or branch of study) considered only as a skill or exercise of the mind, separate from any use: *pure science* **8** *esp. written* clean according to religious rules

purely *adv* completely; only: *purely out of friendship*

¹**purge** *v* **purged, purging 1** to make clean **2** to clear (the bowels) by medicine **3** to get rid of (an unwanted person) by removal from office, exile, killing, etc. – **-gation** *n*

²**purge** *n* **1** a medicine that purges the bowels **2** an act of getting rid of unwanted members of a group, suddenly, and often by force

¹**purple** *adj* of a dark colour between red and blue –**purplish** *adj*

²**purple** *n* **1** (a) purple colour **2** (in former times) dark red or purple garments worn by people of very high rank

¹**purpose** *n* **1** a reason for an action **2** use; effect: *Put your money to some good purpose* **3** willpower **4 on purpose** intentionally

²**purpose** *v* **-posed, -posing** *esp. written* to intend: *He purposes to visit America*

purposely *adv* intentionally

¹purr *n* **1** a low continuous sound produced by a pleased cat **2** a sound like this, made by a powerful machine working smoothly

²purr *v* **1** to make a purr **2** to express contentment in a pleasant low voice

¹purse *n* **1** a small bag for carrying money **2** an amount of money collected for some good purpose or offered as a gift or prize

²purse *v* **pursed, pursing** to draw (esp. the lips) together in little folds

pursue *v* **-sued, -suing 1** to chase **2** to follow closely **3** to follow and cause suffering to: *Bad luck pursued us* **4** to make continual efforts to gain: *to pursue fame* **5** to be busy with: *pursuing his studies* **6** *esp. written* to follow (a way, path, etc.) –~**r** *n*

pursuit *n* **1** the act of pursuing **2** an activity to which one gives one's time: *His favourite pursuit is stamp collecting*

¹push *v* **1** to press (someone or something) forward, away, or to a different position **2** to urge: *My mother is pushing me to learn shorthand* **3** to force on the notice of others: *They aren't pushing their business enough* **4** to hurry or trouble (someone) by continual urging **5** *esp. spoken* to sell (unlawful drugs)

²push *n* **1** an act of pushing **2** a planned advance by an army **3** active will to succeed **4** influence **5 at a push** if really necessary **6 get the push** *sl* to be dismissed from one's job

¹put *v* **put, putting 1** to move, place, or fix (someone or something) in, on, or to a stated place **2** *technical* to guide (a boat or horse) in a stated direction **3** to send: *He put a bullet through the animal's head* **4** to make, set, or fix (something or someone) as an act of the mind: *to put an end to the meeting* **5** to cause to be (in the stated condition): *He put his books in order* **6** to ask (a question) **7** to express in words: *I want to know how to put this in French* **8** to make (a written mark): *Put a cross opposite each mistake* **9** to cause to be busy: *Put the boys to work* **10** to throw (a heavy metal ball) as a sport: *putting the shot* **11 put paid to** to ruin

²put *n* an act of putting a heavy metal ball

³put *adj* **stay put** to remain where placed

put forward *v adv* **1** to offer for consideration **2** to move (some event) to an earlier time **3** *also* **put on–** to cause to show a later time **4** to make (someone) noticed

put off *v adv* **1** to move to a later date **2** to make excuses to: *Don't be put off with a promise* **3** to discourage **4** turn off

put on *v adv* **1** to pretend to have (an opinion, quality, etc.) **2** to increase: *put on speed* **3** to perform (a play, show, etc.) **4** to cover (part of) the body with: *She put her coat on* **5** to put (a clock) forward

put out *v adv* **1** to make (something)

stop burning **2** to trouble or annoy **3** to produce, broadcast, or print **4** **put oneself out** to take trouble

putty *n* a soft oily cement, used esp. in fixing glass to window frames

put up *v adv* **1** to raise: *put up a tent* **2** to put in a public place: *put up a notice* **3** to provide food and lodging for **4** to supply (money) **5** to offer in a struggle: *He didn't put up much of a fight!* **6** to offer for sale **7** to suggest

¹**puzzle** *v* **-zled, -zling 1** to cause difficulty of thought to (someone) in the effort to understand **2** to think hard in order to understand something difficult **–puzzled** *adj* **–puzzler** *n*

²**puzzle** *n* **1** something that one cannot understand or explain **2** a game, toy, or apparatus in which parts must be fitted together correctly: *a crossword puzzle / a jigsaw puzzle* **–~ment** *n*

pygmy, pigmy *n* **-mies 1** a member of a race of very small people **2** any very small person or animal **3** a person of no importance

pyjamas *n* soft loose-fitting trousers and a short coat to be worn in bed

pylon *n* a tall steel framework for supporting electricity wires

pyramid *n* **1** (in geometry) a solid figure with a base and straight flat triangular sides that slope upwards to meet at a point **2** a pile of objects in this shape **3** a very large ancient stone building in this shape, used formerly, esp. in Egypt, as the burial place of a king **4** any ancient stone building like this in shape, found esp. in Latin America

¹**quack** *v, n* (to make) the sound that ducks make

²**quack** a person dishonestly claiming to have special, esp. medical, knowledge **–~ery** *n*

quadruped *n* a mammal with 4 legs

quaint *adj* unusual and attractive, esp. because old **–~ly** *adv* **–~ness** *n*

quake *v* **quaked, quaking** to shake; tremble

qualification *n* **1** qualifying **2** something which limits something said: *I agree, with qualifications* **3** a proof that one has passed examinations: *a medical qualification*

qualifications *n* the necessary ability or knowledge: *the right qualifications for the job*

qualified *adj* **1** limited: *qualified agreement* **2** having qualifications: *a highly qualified man*

qualify *v* **1 -fied, -fying** to gain or give qualifications **2** to limit (meaning): *Qualify that statement– it's too strong*

quality *n* **-ties 1** a (high) degree of goodness **2** something typical of a person or material: *moral qualities*

quandary *n* **-ries** a state of difficulty and inability to decide

quantity *n* **-ties 1** a measurable property of something: *These goods are greater in quantity than in quality* **2** an amount or number

¹**quarantine** *n* a period when someone or something that may be carrying

404

disease is kept separate from others so that the disease cannot spread

²**quarantine** *v* **-tined, -tining** to put in quarantine

¹**quarrel** *n* **1** an argument **2** a point of disagreement: *I have no quarrel with his opinion*

²**quarrel** *v* **-ll-** to have an argument

¹**quarry** *n* **-ries** a creature being hunted

²**quarry** *n* a place from which stone, sand, etc., are dug out

³**quarry** *v* **-ried, -rying** to dig out (stone, sand, etc.)

quart *n* 1/4 of a gallon; 2 pints

¹**quarter** *n* **1** a 4th part of a whole; 1/4 **2** 15 minutes before or after the hour: *a quarter past 10* (=10.15) **3** 3 months of the year: *pay rent by the quarter* **4** 1/4 of an animal including a leg: *hindquarters* **5** a place or person(s) supplying something: *Workers are arriving from all quarters* **6** a part of a town: *the student quarter* **7** the time twice a month when the moon shows 1/4 of its surface: *At the end of the first week the moon is in its first quarter, at the end of the third it is in its last quarter* **8** mercy: *to give no quarter* **9** 1/4 of a pound; 4 ounces **10 at close quarters** near together

²**quarter** *v* **1** to divide into 4 **2** to provide lodgings for (esp. soldiers)

quarters *n* lodgings

quash *v* **1** to make nothing of or officially refuse to accept (esp. something which has been decided) **2** to suppress

quay *n* **-quays** a man-made place where boats can load and unload

queen *n* **1** (the title of) a female ruler of a country or the wife of a king **2** the leading female in a competition **3** the leading female insect of a group which lays eggs: *the queen ant* **4** any of the 4 playing cards with a picture of a queen and usu. a rank between the jack and the king: *the queen of hearts* **5** the most powerful piece in chess

queer *adj* **1** strange: *a queer story* **2** *esp. spoken* not well: *I'm feeling queer* **3** *esp. spoken* mad (esp. in the phrase **queer in the head**) **4 in queer street** *sl* in debt or money trouble −~**ly** *adv* −~**ness** *n*

quench *v* to take away the heat of (flames, steel, desire, etc.) with water or by other methods: *to quench one's thirst*

¹**query** *n* **-ries** a question or doubt

²**query** *v* **-ried, -rying 1** to raise a doubt about: *to query a point* **2** to ask

¹**quest** *n* *literature* a search; attempt to find

²**quest** *v* *literature* to search

¹**question** *n* **1** a sentence or phrase which asks for information **2** a problem: *It's a question of finding time* **3** a doubt: *His honesty is beyond question* **4 in question** being talked about **5 out of the question** impossible **6 there's no question of** there's no possibility of

²**question** *v* **1** to ask a question **2**

to raise doubts about −~**ing** *adj* −~**ingly** *adv* −~**er** *n*

questionable *adj* **1** not certain: *a questionable idea* **2** of doubtful honesty: *questionable friends* − **-bly** *adv*

¹**queue** *n* **1** a line of waiting people, cars, etc. **2** **jump the queue** to go ahead of people who have waited longer than you

²**queue** *v* **queued, queuing** to form or join a line while waiting

¹**quick** *adj* **1** swift; soon finished **2** easily showing anger (in the phrases **a quick temper, quick tempered**) −~**ly** *adv* −~**ness** *n*

²**quick** *n* **1** living matter, usu. the flesh to which the fingernails and toenails are joined **2** **cut (a person) to the quick** to hurt a person's feelings deeply

³**quick** *adv* quickly

¹**quiet** *n* **1** quietness **2** **on the quiet** secretly

²**quiet** *adj* **1** with little noise **2** calm: *a quiet life* **3** (of colours) not bright −~**ly** *adv* −~**ness** *n*

quilt *n* a padded cover for a bed

¹**quit** *adj* finished with; free of

²**quit** *v* **quitted** or **quit, quitting 1** *esp. spoken* to stop (doing something): *I've quit my job* **2** *old use* to leave

quite *adv* **1** completely; perfectly: *quite ready* **2** rather: *quite a good story*

¹**quiver** *n* a container for arrows

²**quiver** *v* to tremble a little

³**quiver** *n* a trembling movement

¹**quiz** *n* **quizzes** a competition or game where questions are put

²**quiz** *v* **-zz-** to ask questions of

quota *n* a stated number or amount, or a limit on numbers: *The quota of foreigners allowed into the country has been reduced*

quotation *n* **1** quoting **2** a sentence or piece taken from a work of art **3** the price of something as at present known: *He gave me a quotation for a new house*

quotation mark *n* either of a pair of marks (" ") or (' ') showing the beginning and end of words said or written by someone else

¹**quote** *v* **quoted, quoting 1** to repeat in speech or writing (the words of another person): *He quotes the Bible* **2** to mention (someone's actions) to add power to one's own point of view **3** to give a price

²**quote** *n esp. spoken* **1** a quotation **2** **in quotes** in quotation marks

¹**rabbit** *n* **1** a small long-eared burrowing animal of the hare family **2 a** its fur **b** its meat

²**rabbit** *v* **-tt- 1** to hunt rabbits **2** *esp. spoken* to talk in a dull complaining way: *He keeps rabbitting on about his health*

¹**race** *n* **1** a competition in speed **2** a strong flow of water: *A mill-race is the stream driving the wheel of a water-mill*

²**race** *v* **raced, racing 1** to compete in a race (against) **2** to go or take very fast: *racing across the road* **3** to cause to run a race: *I can't race my horse* −~**r** *n*

³**race** *n* **1** one of a number of divisions

of human beings, each of a different physical type: *the black/white/brown races* **2** a breed or type of animal or plant **3** a group of people with the same history, customs, etc.: *the German race* **4** a type of creature: *the human race* —**race, racial** *adj* —**racially** *adv*

racialism —also **racism** *n* political and social practices based largely on supposed differences between races of people, and on the belief that one's own race is best —**racialist, racist** *adj, n*

¹**rack** *n* **1** a framework with bars, hooks, etc., for holding things: *a plate rack* **2** a shelf for luggage in a plane, railway carriage, etc. **3** (in former times) an instrument of torture on which people were stretched by turning wheels **4** a bar with teeth on one edge, moved by or moving a toothed wheel

²**rack** *v* **1** to cause great pain **2 rack one's brains** to think very deeply

¹**racket, racquet** *n* a network usu. of nylon stretched in a frame with a handle, for hitting the ball in games such as tennis

²**racket** *n* **1** a loud noise **2** great social activity and hurry **3** *esp. spoken* a dishonest way of getting money **4** *humour* business or trade: *What racket are you in?*

radar —also **radiolocation** *n* a method of finding the position of a solid object by sending out a pulse of high frequency radio waves, and measuring the time taken for that

pulse to bounce off the object and return to the transmitter

radiant *adj* **1** sending out light or heat in all directions: *the radiant sun* **2** *technical* sent out by radiation: *radiant heat* **3** (of a person or his appearance) showing love and happiness: *radiant with joy* – **-ance** *n* –**~ly** *adv*

radiate *v* **-ated, -ating** to send out (light or heat)

radiation *n* **1** radiating **2** something radiated: *harmful radiations* **3** radioactivity

radiator *n* **1** an apparatus consisting of pipes with steam or hot water passing through them, for heating buildings **2** an electric heater for the same purpose **3** an apparatus for cooling a motor-engine

¹**radical** *adj* **1** (of changes) thorough and complete: *radical improvements* **2** in favour of thorough and complete political change: *a radical politician* –**~ly** *adv*

²**radical** *n* **1** a politically radical person **2** *technical* a group of atoms that is found unchanged in a number of compounds and acts like a single atom

¹**radio** *n* **1** the sending or receiving of sounds through the air by electrical waves **2** also **radio set**– an apparatus to receive sounds broadcast in this way **3** the broadcasting industry

²**radio** *v* **-oed, -oing** **1** to send through the air by electrical waves: *The ship radioed for help* **2** to send a message to (a place or person) in this way

radioactivity *n* the quality that some elements have of giving out energy which can harm living things – **-tive** *adj*

radish *n* a small vegetable or its red or white hot-tasting root, eaten raw

radium *n* a rare shining white metal that is an element, radioactive, and used in the treatment of certain diseases, esp. cancer

radius *n* **-dii** **1** (the line marking) the distance from the centre of a circle or sphere to its edge or surface **2** a circular area measured from its centre point **3** *medical* the long bone from the elbow to the thumb joint

¹**raffle** *n* a sale of many low-priced numbered tickets of which one is chosen by chance to win an article of some value

²**raffle** *v* **-fled, -fling** to sell in a raffle

¹**raft** *n* **1** a flat wooden or rubber boat which may be used for lifesaving or as a landing place for swimmers **2** a number of logs fastened together to be sent floating down the river

²**raft** *v* to carry or travel on a raft

rafter *n* one of the sloping beams that hold up a roof

¹**rag** *n* **1** (a small piece of) old cloth **2** an old worn-out garment: *dressed in rags* **3** *esp. spoken* a badly-written newspaper

²**rag** *v* **-gg-** **1** to play about noisily and foolishly **2** to tease: *They ragged him about his big ears*

³**rag** *n* **1** a rough noisy but harmless trick **2** an amusing procession of college students through the streets , collecting money for charity

¹**rage** *n* **1** wild uncontrollable anger **2** a fashion: *Long hair is all the rage now*

²**rage** *v* **raged, raging** **1** to be very angry **2** to be very violent: *a raging headache*

ragged *adj* **1** old and torn **2** dressed in rags **3** uneven: *a ragged beard* **4** unfinished and imperfect: *a ragged performance* – ~**ly** *adv* – ~**ness** *n*

¹**raid** *n* **1** a quick attack on an enemy position **2** a rapid visit to a place, to carry something away **3** an unexpected visit by the police, in search of criminals or forbidden goods

²**raid** *v* to visit or attack on a raid: *raid a bank*

¹**rail** *n* **1** a fixed bar, to hang things on or for protection **2** one of the pair of metal bars along which a train runs **3 by rail** in a train

²**rail** *v* to enclose or separate with rails

³**rail** *v* to curse or complain noisily

railing *n* one rail in a fence

railway *n* **-ways** **1** a track for trains **2** a system of these tracks, with its engines, stations, etc.

¹**rain** *n* **1** water falling in drops from the clouds **2** a thick fall of anything: *a rain of arrows* **3 as right as rain** *esp. spoken* in perfect health – ~**less** *adj*

²**rain** *v* **1** (of rain) to fall **2** to drop or fall like rain: *The bombs came raining down. / Tears rained down her cheeks*

rainbow *n* an arch of different colours that sometimes appears in the sky esp. after rain

raincoat *n* a waterproof coat

rainy *adj* **-ier, -iest** having a lot of rain

raise *v* **raised, raising 1** to lift, push, or move upward **2** to make higher in amount, degree, etc.: *raise the rent* **3** to collect together: *raise an army* **4** *esp. US* to produce and look after (living things); bring up (children): *raise a family* **5** to bring up and talk about (a subject) **6** *esp. written* to build: *raise a monument* **7** to make or cause (a noise): *to raise a laugh* **8** to cause (feelings): *His absence raised fears about his safety* **9** to cause to end (an official rule forbidding something): *raise an embargo* **10** to bring back to life (a dead person) **11** to make a higher bid than (a card player)

¹**rake** *n* **1** a gardening tool consisting of a row of teeth at the end of a long handle, for levelling soil, gathering up leaves, etc. **2** the same kind of tool on wheels, pulled by a horse or tractor

²**rake** *v* **raked, raking 1** to make level with a rake **2** to collect (as if) with a rake: *to rake in money / to rake out some facts* **3** to search by turning over and mixing up a pile **4** to examine or shoot in a sweeping movement along the whole length of: *He raked the hillside with powerful glasses*

¹**rally** *v* **-lied, -lying 1** to come or bring together for a purpose **2** to come or bring back into order, ready to make another effort: *The soldiers rallied and drove the enemy back* **3** to recover, as from illness or unhappiness

²**rally** *n* **-lies 1** an act of rallying **2** a large public meeting **3** a motor race over public roads **4** (in tennis) a long struggle to gain a point

¹**ram** *n* **1** a fully-grown male sheep that can father young **2** any machine that repeatedly drops or pushes a weight

²**ram** *v* **-mm- 1** to run into (something) very hard **2** to force into place with heavy pressure

¹**ramble** *v* **-bled, -bling 1** to go on a ramble **2** to talk or write in a disordered wandering way **3** (of a plant) to grow loosely in all directions

²**ramble** *n* a walk for enjoyment –~r *n: a keen rambler*

rampant *adj* **1** (of crime, disease, etc.) widespread and impossible to control **2** (of an animal drawn on a shield or flag) standing on the back legs with the front legs raised as if to strike –~ly *adv*

ran *past tense of* RUN

¹**random** *adj* made or done aimlessly: *a random shot* –~ly *adv* –~ness *n*

²**random** *n* **at random** aimlessly

rang *past tense of* RING

¹**range** *n* **1** a connected line (of mountains, hills, etc.) **2** an area where shooting is practised, or where missiles are tested **3** (in North

America) a wide stretch of grassy land where cattle feed **4** the distance that a gun can fire or a plane, missile, etc., travel **5** the distance at which one can see or hear **6** the limits between which something varies: *a wide range of temperature* **7** a set of different objects of the same kind: *a range of tools* **8** a cooking fireplace built in a kitchen **9** *technical* **a** (in statistics) the difference between the largest and smallest numbers of a set **b** (in set theory) a set of items to each of which a member of another set is linked

²**range** *v* **ranged, ranging 1** (of a gun) to have a range of **2** to stretch or reach between limits: *ranging between 5 and 15* **3** to wander freely over: *The children ranged the hills* **4** to arrange: *range the goods neatly in the shop window*

¹**rank** *adj* **1** (of a plant) too thick and widespread **2** (of land) thickly covered (with useless plants) **3** (of smell or taste) very strong and unpleasant: *rank tobacco* **4** complete; utter: *a rank beginner* −~**ly** *adv* −~**ness** *n*

²**rank** *n* **1** a degree of value, importance, etc., in a group: *the rank of general* **2** social position: *people of all ranks* **3** a line (of policemen, soldiers, etc.) standing side by side **4** a line (of people or things): *a taxi rank*

³**rank** *v* **1** to be or put (in a certain class): *This town ranks high among*

beauty spots **2** to arrange in regular order: *cups ranked neatly on the shelf*

ransack *v* **1** to search (a place) roughly **2** to search through and rob (a place)

¹**ransom** *n* **1** a sum of money paid to free a prisoner **2 hold someone to ransom** to keep someone prisoner so as to demand payment **3 a king's ransom** *pompous* a great deal of money

²**ransom** *v* to set free by paying a ransom −~**er** *n*

¹**rap** *n* **1** a quick light blow: *a rap on the door* **2 take the rap** *esp. spoken* to receive the punishment (for someone else's crime)

²**rap** *v* **-pp- 1** to strike quickly and lightly **2** to speak severely to: *The judge rapped the police*

¹**rape** *n* a type of European plant grown as food for sheep and pigs and for oil from its seeds

²**rape** *v* **raped, raping** to have sex with, against the other's will −**rapist** *n*

³**rape** *n* **1** the act and crime of raping **2** spoiling: *the rape of our forests*

¹**rapid** *adj* **1** fast **2** (of a slope) descending steeply −~**ity** *n* −~**ly** *adv*

²**rapid** *n* a part of a river where the water moves very fast over rocks

¹**rare** *adj* (of meat, esp. steak) lightly cooked

²**rare** *adj* unusual; uncommon −~**ness** *n*

rarely *adv* not often

¹**rash** *adj* (of a person or his behaviour) not thinking enough of the results: *a rash decision* –~**ly** *adv* –~**ness** *n*

²**rash** *n* **1** a set of red spots on the skin, caused by illness **2** a sudden unpleasant appearance in large numbers: *a rash of complaints* **3 come out in a rash** to become covered with small red spots

raspberry *n* **-ries 1** a type of bush or its a soft sweet usu. red berry **2** *sl* a rude sound made by putting one's tongue out and blowing

¹**rat** *n* **1** any of several types of long-tailed animal with strong sharp teeth related to but larger than the mouse **2** a low disloyal man **3 smell a rat** *esp. spoken* to guess that something wrong is happening

²**rat** *v* **-tt-** *esp. spoken* to break a promise: *They've ratted on us*

¹**rate** *n* **1** a value, speed, etc., measured by its relation to some other amount: *The birth rate is the number of births compared to the number of the people* **2** a (stated) speed: *a steady rate* **3** a payment fixed according to a standard scale: *What rate are you getting?* **4** a local tax paid by owners and tenants of buildings **5** of the (numbered) quality: *first-rate* **6 at any rate** in any case **7 at this/that rate** if events continue in the same way as now/then **8 rate of exchange** the relationship between the money of 2 countries

²**rate** *v* to fix a value on: *I rate him high*

¹**rather** *adv* **1** a little; quite; slightly: *rather cold weather* **2** more willingly: *I'd rather play tennis than swim* **3** more; more exactly: *These shoes are comfortable rather than pretty*

²**rather** *interj* Yes, certainly!: *'Would you like a swim?' 'Rather!'*

ratio *n* **-os** the relation between 2 quantities as shown when one is divided by the other: *£0.14 and £1.00 are in the ratio 14:100 or 7:50*

¹**ration** *n* a share (of food, petrol, etc.) allowed to one person for a period

²**ration** *v* **1** to limit (someone) to a fixed ration **2** to limit and control (supplies)

rat race *n* *esp. spoken* the endless competition for success

¹**rattle** *v* **-tled, -tling 1** to make or cause to make a lot of quick little noises as of objects hitting each other repeatedly **2** *esp. spoken* to make nervous or anxious **3** to say or talk quickly and easily: *He rattled off the poem*

²**rattle** *n* **1** a toy or instrument that rattles **2** a rattling noise

¹**rave** *v* **raved, raving 1** to talk wildly as if mad **2** to speak with excited admiration: *They raved about the new singer*

²**rave** *n* **1** *esp. spoken* very eager praise (esp. of a work of art): *The play got rave reviews* **2** *sl* a wild exciting party

¹**raw** *adj* **1** (of food) not cooked **2** in

the natural state: *raw silk* **3** (of a person) not yet experienced: *a raw recruit* **4** (of a part of the body) without skin; painful: *hands raw with cold* **5** (of weather) cold and wet: *a raw winter day* −~**ness** *n*

²**raw** *n* **1 in the raw a** without civilization: *life in the raw* **b** nude **2 touch (someone) on the raw** to hurt (someone's) feelings by mentioning a sensitive subject

¹**ray** *n* **rays** any of various types of large flat sea fish , related to the shark

²**ray** *n* **1** a narrow beam (of light): *the sun's rays* **2** a very small bit: *a ray of hope*

razor *n* an instrument for shaving

¹**reach** *v* **1** to stretch out a hand or arm for some purpose **2** (of things or places) to be big enough to touch; stretch out as far as: *The ladder won't reach the window* **3** to get to: *They reached London* **4** to get a message to; get in touch with

²**reach** *n* **1** the distance that one can reach: *within reach of the shops* **2** a straight stretch of water between 2 bends in a river

react *v* **1** to act in reply **2** *technical* (of a substance) to change when mixed with another: *An acid can react with a base to form a salt*

reaction *n* **1** a case of reacting: *What was your reaction to the news?* **2** (in science) **a** a force exercised by a body in reply to another force **b** a change caused in a chemical substance by the action of another

¹**read** *v* **read, reading 1** to understand (language in print or writing) **2** to understand (something printed or written): *Can you read French?* **3** to say (printed or written words): *read aloud* **4** to get information from print or writing: *read about the murder* **5** to study (a subject) at university level: *John's reading history at Oxford* **6** (of measuring instruments) to show **7 read between the lines** to find a meaning that is not expressed

²**read** *n* *esp. spoken* **1** an act or period of reading: *a read of the paper* **2** something to be read: *a good read*

reader *n* **1** a person who reads **2** (the job of) a university teacher above the rank of lecturer **3** a type of schoolbook for beginners

readily *adv* **1** willingly **2** with no difficulty

reading *n* **1** the act or practice of reading **2** knowledge obtained through books: *a man of little reading* **3** a figure shown by a measuring instrument **4** matter to be read **5** (in Parliament) one of the 3 official occasions on which a suggested new bill is read aloud and considered

¹**ready** *adj* **-ier, -iest 1** prepared and fit: *The letters are ready* **2** (of a person) willing and eager: *ready to help* **3** (of thoughts or their expression) quick: *ready wit* −**ready** *adv:buy the meat ready cut*

²**ready** *n* the state of being ready: *at the ready*

real *adj* 1 actually existing; true 2 *technical* (of a number) having a square greater than or equal to O

realism *n* 1 determination to face facts and deal with them practically, without being influenced by feelings or false ideas 2 (in art and literature) the showing of things as they really are 3 (in philosophy) the belief that matter really exists outside our own minds – **-list** *n*

realistic *adj* 1 showing realism 2 (of art or literature) life-like – ~**ally** *adv*

reality *n* -ties 1 the quality of being real 2 something real: *Her dream of marrying Frederick became a reality* 3 everything that is real: *to escape from reality by going to the cinema*

realize, -lise *v* -lized, -lizing 1 to understand and believe (a fact): *I didn't realize how late it was* 2 to make real (a hope): *She realized her intention of becoming an actress* – **-lization** *n*

really *adv* 1 in actual fact; truly 2 thoroughly: *I really hate him* 3 (used for showing interest or suprise): *'I collect rare coins.' 'Really?'*

realm *n* 1 *literature & law* a kingdom 2 a world; area: *the realm of science*

reap *v* to cut and gather (a crop of grain) – ~**er** *n*

reappear *v* to appear again after absence – ~**ance** *n*

¹rear *v* 1 to care for until fully grown 2 to lift up (a part of oneself): *reared his head* 3 (of a 4-legged animal) to rise upright on the back legs

²rear *n* 1 the back: *the rear wheel* 2 *polite* the buttocks 3 **bring up the rear** to come last

¹reason *n* 1 the cause of an event; the explanation or excuse for an action 2 what makes one decide on an action: *What is your reason for leaving?* 3 the power to think, understand, and form opinions 4 good sense: *There's a great deal of reason in his advice* 5 **it stands to reason** it is clear to all sensible people 6 **listen to reason** to allow oneself to be persuaded by good advice 7 **with reason** (of something said or believed) rightly: *He thinks, with reason, that I don't like him*

²reason *v* 1 to think: *to reason clearly* 2 to persuade (someone) by arguing: *Try to reason with him* – ~**er** *n*

reasonable *adj* 1 (of a person or his behaviour) sensible: *a reasonable thing to do* 2 (esp. of prices) fair; not too much – **-bleness** *n*

reasonably *adv* 1 sensibly 2 fairly; rather: *reasonably good*

reassure *v* -sured, -suring to comfort and make free from fear (someone anxious) – **-surance** *n* – **-suringly** *adv*

¹rebel *n* a person who rebels

²rebel *v* -ll- to fight, often with violence (against anyone in power, esp. the government)

rebellion *n* an act or the state of rebelling

¹rebound *v* to fly back after hitting

something: *The ball rebounded from the wall*

²**rebound** *n* **on the rebound a** while rebounding **b** as a quick action in reply to failure or unpleasantness: *marry a different girl on the rebound*

rebuild *v* **rebuilt, rebuilding** to build again or build new parts to

¹**rebuke** *v* **rebuked, rebuking** to give a rebuke to

²**rebuke** *n* a short scolding esp. given officially

¹**recall** *v* **1** to remember **2** to call or take back: *The makers have recalled a lot of unsafe cars* −~**able** *adj*

²**recall** *n* **1** a call to return: *the recall of the general from abroad* **2** the power to remember something: *total recall* **3** a signal to soldiers to come back

recede *v* **receded, receding** (of things) to move or incline back or away

receipt *n* **1** a written statement that one has received money **2** the event of receiving: *the receipt of the cheque* **3 be in receipt of** *pompous* to have received

receive *v* **received, receiving 1** to get (something given or sent to one) **2** to suffer; be the subject of: *receive a blow on the head*

receiver *n* **1** a person who deals in stolen property **2** the part of a telephone that is held to one's ear **3** an instrument for receiving radio, television, etc., signals **4** (in British law) the person officially appointed to take charge of affairs of a bankrupt **5** (in tennis, squash, and such games) a player who receives service from his opponent

recent *adj* having happened only a short time ago −~**ly** *adv*

reception *n* **1** an act of receiving: *a friendly reception* **2** a large formal party: *a wedding reception* **3** the office that receives visitors, guests, etc.: *Leave your key at reception* **4** the receiving of radio or television signals: *good reception*

¹**recess** *n* **1** a pause for rest during work **2** a space set back in a wall **3** *literature* a secret inner part of a place, that is hard to reach: *the recesses of his heart*

²**recess** *v* to make or put into a recess: *a recessed bookshelf*

recession *n* a period of reduced activity of trade

recipe *n* a set of instructions for cooking a dish

recital *n* **1** a performance of poetry or music, given by one performer or a small group **2** a telling of a set of facts: *a recital of his experiences*

recite *v* **recited, reciting 1** to say (something learned) aloud from memory: *recite a poem* **2** to give a list of: *recite his complaints* −**recitation** *n* −**reciter** *n*

reckless *adj* (of a person or his behaviour) too hasty; not caring about danger: *reckless driving* −~**ly** *adv* −~**ness** *n*

reckon *v* **1** to regard: *I reckon him as a friend* **2** *esp. spoken* to suppose: *I reckon so* **3** to add up −~**er** *n*

recognition *n* **1** the power to recognize or state of being recognized **2** a reward given in order to recognize someone's behaviour **3 change beyond/out of all recognition** to change so as to be impossible to recognize

recognize, -ise *v* **-nized, -nizing 1** to know again (someone or something one has met before) **2** to admit (someone or something) as really being (something): *They refused to recognize him as king* **3** to show official gratefulness for: *The government recognized his services by making him a lord* – **-nizable** *adj* – **-nizably** *adv*

recollect *v* to remember

recollection *n* **1** the power or action of remembering **2** something in one's memory: *That evening is one of my happiest recollections*

recommend *v* **1** to praise as being good for a purpose: *Can you recommend a good dictionary?* **2** to advise: *I recommend you to wait* **3** (of a quality) to make attractive: *This hotel has nothing to recommend it*

recommendation *n* **1** advice; the act of recommending: *buy the car on Paul's recommendation* **2** a letter or statement that recommends (esp. someone for a job)

reconcile *v* **-ciled, -ciling 1** to make peace between; make friendly again: *They quarrelled but now they're reconciled* **2** to find agreement between (2 conflicting actions or ideas): *I can't reconcile those 2 ideas* – **-cilable** *adj*

reconciliation –also **reconcilement** *n* a peace-making

reconsider *v* to think again and change one's mind about (a subject) –~**ation** *n*

reconstruct *v* **1** to rebuild **2** to build up a description or picture of (something only partly known): *reconstruct a crime* –~**ion** *n*

¹**record** *v* **1** to write down so that it will be known: *record past events* **2** to preserve (sound or vision) so that it can be heard or seen again: *a recorded broadcast* **3** (of an instrument) to show by measuring

²**record** *n* **1** a written statement of facts, events, etc. **2** the known facts about someone's past **3** (often in sport) the best yet done **4** also **gramophone record, disc**– a circular piece of plastic on which sound is recorded **5 for the record** to be reported as official **6 off the record** unofficial(ly) **7 on record** (of facts or events) ever recorded: *the coldest winter on record*

³**record** *adj* more, better, etc., than ever before: *a record crop*

record player –also **gramophone** *n* an instrument which can reproduce the information stored in a record

recover *v* **1** to get back (something lost or taken away) **2** to get well again: *to recover from a cold* **3** to get (oneself) back into a proper state: *She soon recovered herself and stopped crying* –~**able** *adj*

recovery *n* **-ies 1** getting back or being got back **2** getting well

recreation *n* a form of amusement, or way of spending free time

¹recruit *n* **1** someone who has just joined one of the armed forces **2** a new member of any organization

²recruit *v* **1** to find recruits **2** to get (someone) as a recruit: *recruit some new members* –~**ment** *n*

rectangle *n technical* a 4-sided figure with opposite sides equal and parallel, and whose angles are right angles – **-gular** *adj*

recur *v* **-rr-** **1** to happen again or often **2** (of a decimal) to be repeated for ever in the same order: *In 5·1515 ... (also written 5·15) the figures 15 recur, and the number can be read '5·15 recurring'*

¹red *adj* **-dd-** **1** of the colour of blood or of fire **2** (of hair) of a bright brownish orange colour **3** (of wine) of a dark purple colour –~**ness** *n* –~**dish** *adj*

²red *n* **1** (a) red colour: *mix red and yellow to make orange* **2** the state of owing money to the bank: *be in the red* **3 paint the town red** *esp. spoken* to go out and be noisily merry **4 see red** to become angry suddenly

red-handed *adj* in the act of doing something wrong: *They caught the thief red-handed*

reduce *v* **reduced, reducing 1** to make smaller, cheaper, etc. **2** (of a person) to lose weight on purpose –**reducible** *adj*

reduce to *v prep* **1** to bring down to: *The fire reduced the forest to a few trees. / reduced to the ranks* **2** to change (something) to (its parts): *reduce the rocks to dust* **3** to force (someone) into: *She was reduced to begging*

reduction *n* **1** making or becoming smaller; the amount taken off in making something smaller **2** a smaller copy (of a picture, map, or photograph)

redundant *adj* **1** not needed; more than is necessary **2** (of a worker or group of workers) not needed because there is not enough work –~**ly** *adv*

reed *n* **1** (the tall strong hollow stem of) any of various grasslike plants that grow in wet places **2** (in a musical instrument) a thin piece of wood or metal that produces sound by vibrating in an air stream **3 broken reed** *esp. spoken* a weak helper

¹reel *n* **1** a round object on which a length of wire, fishing line, recording tape, etc., can be wound **2** a usu. small wooden or plastic one of these on which sewing thread is sold

²reel *v* to wind on a reel: *reel up the fish*

³reel *v* **1** to walk unsteadily as if drunk **2** to step away suddenly and unsteadily, as after a blow or shock **3** to be confused in the mind: *Numbers make my head reel* **4** to seem to go round and round: *The room reeled*

⁴reel *n* (the music for) a high-spirited Scottish or Irish dance

¹referee *n* **1** a judge in charge of a

team game such as football **2** a person who is asked to settle a disagreement **3** a person who is asked to supply a reference

²**referee** *v* **-eed, -eeing** to act as referee for

reference *n* **1** a case of mentioning: *a reference to Janet* **2** a case of looking at for information: *Keep this dictionary for reference* **3** a statement about someone's character, ability, etc., esp. when he is looking for employment **4 in/with reference to** in connection with

refer to *v prep* **-rr- 1** to mention; speak about **2** to look at for information **3** to concern: *The new law does not refer to farm land* **4** to send back for decision or action: *The shop referred the complaint to the manufacturers* –~**able to** *adj*

refine *v* **refined, refining** to make pure

refined *adj* (of a person, his behaviour, etc.) having or showing education and manners

reflect *v* **1** to throw back (heat, light, sound, or an image) **2** to give an idea of: *Does this letter reflect your opinion?* **3** to consider carefully

reflection *n* **1** the reflecting of heat, light, sound, or an image **2** an image reflected in a mirror or polished surface **3** (a) deep and careful thought

reflex –also **reflex action** *n* a movement that is made by instinct in reply to some outside influence, without power to prevent it

reflexive *n adj* (in grammar) (a word) showing that the action in the sentence has its effect on the person or thing that does the action: *In 'I hurt myself'* **myself** *is a* **reflexive pronoun**

¹**reform** *v* **1** to improve; make or become right: *We should try to reform criminals* **2** to cause reforms in: *try to reform society* –~**er** *n*

²**reform** *n* social action to improve conditions, remove unfairness, etc.

¹**refrain** *v* to hold oneself back (from); avoid: *to refrain from smoking*

²**refrain** *n* a part of a song that is repeated, esp. at the end of each verse

refresh *v* **1** to get rid of the tiredness of; make fresh again **2 refresh one's memory** to cause oneself to remember again

refreshing *adj* producing a feeling of comfort and new strength –~**ly** *adv*

refreshment *n* **1** the experience of being refreshed **2** food and drink

refrigerator –also (*esp. spoken*) **fridge** *n* a machine in which food or drink can be kept for a time at a low temperature

refuge *n* **1** a place that provides protection **2** also **traffic island**– *technical* a place in the middle of a street where people can wait until it is safe to cross the rest of the way

refugee *n* a person who has left his country for political reasons or during a war

refusal *n* **1** a case of refusing **2 first**

refusal the right to decide whether to buy something before it is offered to other people

¹**refuse** *v* **refused, refusing** not to accept, do, or give: *She refused his offer*

²**refuse** *n* waste material: *kitchen refuse*

regain *v* **1** to get or win back **2** to reach again: *to regain the shore* **3 regain one's balance** to get back on one's feet after slipping

¹**regard** *n* **1** respect: *I hold her in high regard* **2 in this regard** on this subject **3 with regard to** regarding

²**regard** *v* **1** to look at **2** to consider: *I have always regarded him highly. / She regarded him as stupid*

regarding –also **as regards** *prep esp. written* on the subject of; in connection with

regardless *adv* whatever may happen: *Get the money, regardless!*

regards *n* **1** good wishes **2 With kind regards** (a friendly but formal way of ending a letter)

¹**regiment** *n* **1** a large military group, commanded by a colonel **2** a very large number (of living creatures): *a regiment of ants* –~**al** *adj*

²**regiment** *v* to control (people) too firmly: *Modern children don't like being regimented* –~**ation** *n*

region *n* **1** a general area: *a tropical region / the region of the heart* **2** *technical* a flat space bounded by curved lines (arcs) **3 in the region of** about: *in the region of £500* **4**

the lower regions hell –~**al** *adj* –~**ally** *adv*

¹**register** *n* **1** a record or list: *a register of births and deaths* **2** a book containing such a record **3** the range of a human voice or musical instrument

²**register** *v* **1** to put into an official list or record **2** (of machines or instruments) to show; record **3** (of a person or his face) to express: *Her face registered anxiety*

¹**regret** *v* **-tt-** to be sorry about

²**regret** *n* sadness –~**ful** *adj* –~**fully** *adv* –~**fulness** *n*

regrettable *adj* that one should regret; worthy of blame: *Your choice of friends is regrettable* – **-bly** *adv*

¹**regular** *adj* **1** happening often with the same length of time between the occasions **2** frequent: *a regular customer* **3** happening every time: *regular attendance* **4** not varying: *a regular speed* **5** proper; according to rule or custom: *He knows a lot about the law but he's not a regular lawyer* **6** evenly shaped: *regular features* **7** *technical* (of a straight-sided flat figure) having all sides and angles equal: *A square is a regular quadrilateral* **8** professional: *the regular army* **9** living under a particular religious rule of life: *Ordinary Roman Catholic priests are not members of the regular clergy, but monks are* **10** (in grammar) following a common pattern: *The verb 'dance' is regular, but the verb 'be' is* **irregular 11 keep regular hours**

to follow the same quiet sensible way of life all the time −~**ity** *n*

²**regular** *n* **1** a soldier who is a member of a regular army **2** a regular visitor, customer, etc.

regularly *adv* **1** at regular times **2** in a regular way: *regularly shaped*

regulate *v* **-lated, -lating 1** to fix or control **2** to make (a machine, esp. a clock or watch) work correctly

regulation *n* **1** control **2** an official rule or order

rehearsal *n* the act or an occasion of rehearsing

rehearse *v* **rehearsed, rehearsing** to learn and practise for later performance: *to rehearse a play*

¹**reign** *n* a period of reigning: *the reign of George VI*

²**reign** *v* **1** to be the king or queen: *Our Queen reigns but does not rule* **2** to exist noticeably: *After the storm, quietness reigned*

¹**rein** *n* **1** a long narrow band usu. of leather, by which a horse (or sometimes a small child) is controlled **2 give rein to** to give freedom to (feelings or desires) **3 take the reins** to become the leader and make the decisions

²**rein** *v* to stop or slow up (a horse) by pulling the reins

reindeer *n* **-deer** a type of deer with long branching horns, native to the coldest parts of Europe

reinforce *v* **-forced, -forcing** to strengthen by adding **a** materials: *to reinforce a coat* **b** men, ships, etc.: *to reinforce an army*

reinforcement *n* the act of reinforcing: *This roof needs some reinforcement*

reinforcements *n* men sent to reinforce an army

¹**reject** *v* **1** to refuse to accept **2** to throw away as useless or imperfect −~**ion** *n*

²**reject** *n* something rejected

rejoice *v* **rejoiced, rejoicing** to feel or show great joy

relate *v* **related, relating 1** to tell (a story) **2** to see a connection between: *to relate 2 ideas*

related *adj* connected; of the same family or kind: *She is related to me by marriage* −~**ness** *n*

relation *n* **1** a member of one's family **2** connection: *the relation between wages and prices*

relationship *n* **1** family connection **2** connection between things or ideas

¹**relative** *n* a relation

²**relative** *adj* **1** compared to each other or to something else: *After his troubles, he's now in relative comfort* **2** esp. written connected (with): *the facts that are relative to this question*

relatively *adv* quite; when compared to other people or things: *She walks relatively fast for a child of 3*

relativity *n* the relationship between time, size, and mass, which are said to change with increased speed: *Einstein's Theory of Relativity*

relax *v* **1** to make or become less active; stop worrying **2** to make or become less stiff or tight: *His muscles relaxed* **3** to make (effort or control) less severe: *Don't relax your efforts*

¹**relay** *n* **relays 1** one part of a team that takes its turn in keeping an activity going continuously: *groups of men working in relays* **2** an electrical apparatus that receives messages by telephone, radio, etc., and passes them on over a further distance **3** *esp. spoken* also **relay race**— a race in which each member of 2 or more teams runs part of the distance

²**relay** *v* **relayed, relaying** to send out by relay: *to relay a broadcast*

¹**release** *v* **released, releasing 1** to set free; allow to come out **2** to allow **a** (a new film or record) to be shown or bought publicly **b** (a news story) to be printed **3** to press (a handle) so as to let something go: *to release the handbrake*

²**release** *n* **1** a setting free **2** a new film or record that has been released **3 on general release** (of a film) able to be seen at all cinemas

relegate *v* **-gated, -gating** to put (someone or something) into a lower or worse position: *relegated to the second division* – **-gation** *n*

relevant *adj* connected with the subject – ~**ly** *adv* – **-vance, -vancy** *n*

reliable *adj* fit to be trusted; dependable – **-bly** *adv*

relic *n* **1** a part of the body or belongings of a holy person, which is kept and respected after his death **2** something old that reminds us of the past: *a relic of ancient times*

relief *n* **1** a feeling of comfort at the ending of anxiety or pain **2** a person or group taking over a duty for another: *a relief driver* **3** help for people in trouble: *send relief to flood victims* **4** the act of driving away an enemy: *the relief of the city* **5** (in art) a shape cut in wood or stone, or shaped in metal, so that it stands out above the surface **6** money that one is allowed not to pay in taxes, for some special reason **7 in bold/ sharp relief** (in art) painted so that it seems to stand out clearly from the rest of the picture **8 in (high/ low) relief** (in art) cut so that it stands out (a long way/a little) above the rest of the surface it is on **9 light relief** pleasant and amusing change

relieve *v* **relieved, relieving 1** to lessen (pain or trouble): *a drug that relieves headaches* **2** to take over a duty from (someone) as a relief **3** to drive away the enemy from (a town, fort, etc.) **4** to give variety to; make more interesting: *to relieve a dull evening* **5 relieve oneself** *polite* to pass urine or empty the bowels **6 relieve someone's mind** to free someone from anxiety

religion *n* **1** belief in one or more gods **2** a particular system of belief and the worship, behaviour, etc., connected with it **3** something that one takes very seriously: *Cricket is a religion with John*

religious *adj* **1** of or concerning religion: *a religious service* **2** obeying the rules of a religion carefully **3** performing the stated duties very carefully: *She washes the floor with religious care* –~**ly** *adv*

relinquish *v* to give up: *He relinquished his claim*

reluctant *adj* unwilling –~**ly** *adv*

rely on –also **rely upon** *v prep* **relied, relying on 1** to depend on (something, or something happening): *You can't rely on the weather* **2** to trust (someone, or someone to do something): *You may rely on me to help you*

remain *v* **1** to stay or be left behind after others have gone **2** to continue to be (in an unchanged state): *Peter became a judge but John remained a fisherman* **3** it **remains to be seen** we shall know later on

remainder *n* what is left over; the rest

remains *n* **1** parts which are left **2** a dead body, usu. of a human being

¹**remark** *v* to say; give an opinion: *He remarked that it was getting late*

²**remark** *n* a spoken or written opinion: *rude remarks*

remarkable *adj* worth speaking of; unusual: *a remarkable man* – **-bly** *adv*: *remarkably well*

¹**remedy** *n* **-dies 1** a way of curing pain or disease: *Warmth is the best remedy for colds* **2** a way of setting right (anything bad): *evils that are past remedy*

²**remedy** *v* to put or make right: *to remedy a fault*

remember *v* **1** to keep in the memory; not forget **2** to give money or a

present to: *Grandfather remembered me in his will*

remind *v* to cause (someone) to remember: *Remind me to write to Mother. / This reminds me of last year* –~**er** *n*

remnant *n* **1** a part that remains: *the remnants of the feast* **2** a small piece of cloth left over from a larger piece

remote *adj* **1** distant: *remote stars / the remote future* **2** quiet and lonely: *a remote village* **3** not close: *a remote connection* **4** (of behaviour) not showing interest in others **5** slight: *Your chances are remote* –~**ly** *adv* –~**ness** *n*

removal *n* an act of removing

¹**remove** *v* **removed, removing 1** to take away; take off: *Remove your hat. / to remove a child from a class* **2 once/twice/etc., removed** (of cousins) different by 1, 2, etc., generations: *a second cousin once removed* –**removable** *adj*

²**remove** *n* **1** a stage or degree: *Great cleverness is only one remove from madness* **2** (in some schools) a class

render *v esp. written* **1** to cause to be: *His fatness renders him lazy* **2** to perform **3** to give: *to render thanks/an account*

¹**rendezvous** *n* **-vous 1** an arrangement to meet **2** the place chosen for meeting **3** a meeting place: *This club is a rendezvous for writers*

²**rendezvous** *v* to meet by arrangement

renew *v* **1** to make as good as new **2** to replace: *to renew one's library* *ticket* **3** to repeat or take up again: *The enemy renewed their attack* –~**able** *adj* –~**al** *n*

renown *n* fame –~**ed** *adj*

¹**rent** *n* money paid regularly for the use of a property or object

²**rent** *v* **1** to pay rent for the use of **2** to allow to be used in return for rent: *to rent a room to Mrs. Smith* –~**able** *adj*

reorganize, -ise *v* **-ized, -izing** to organize again, often in a new way – **-ization** *n*

¹**repair** *v* **1** to mend: *to repair a broken watch/a road* **2** *esp. written* to put right (a wrong, mistake, etc.) –~**able** *adj* –~**er** *n*

²**repair** *n* **1** an act or result of mending: *the repairs to my car* **2** **in good/bad repair** in good/bad condition

repay *v* **repaid, repaying** **1** to pay (money) back **2** to pay (someone) back **3** to reward (an action): *He repaid her kindness with blows* –~**able** *adj* –~**ment** *n*

repeal *v* to do away with (a law) –**repeal** *n*

¹**repeat** *v* **1** to say or do again: *to repeat a word/a mistake* **2** to say (something heard or learnt): *to repeat a poem* **3** (of numbers, esp. decimals) to recur **4** (of a gun) to fire several times without reloading **5** **repeat oneself** to say or do the same thing again and again –~**ed** *adj* –~**edly** *adv*

²**repeat** *n* **1** a performance that is repeated **2** (in music) (a sign (:‖)

showing) a passage to be played again

repel *v* **-ll-** **1** to drive back by force: *to repel an attack* **2** to cause dislike in: *That ugly man repels me* –~**lent** *adj*

repent *v* *esp. written* to be sorry for (wrongdoing) –~**ance** *n* –~**ant** *adj*

repercussion *n* **1** a far-reaching unexpected effect **2** something springing or thrown back: *heard the repercussions of the shot*

repetition *n* **1** the act of repeating **2** the exercise of repeating words learned

repetitious –also **repetitive** *adj* containing parts said or done too many times: *a repetitious speech* –~**ness** *n*

replace *v* **replaced, replacing** **1** to put back in the right place **2** to take the place of: *George replaced Edward as captain* –~**able** *adj*

replacement *n* **1** the act of replacing: *Your tyres need replacement* **2** someone or something that replaces: *We need a replacement for the dead officer*

replica *n* a close copy, esp. of a work of art, often made by the same artist

reply *v* **replied, replying** to answer: *'Of course not,' she replied* –**reply** *n*

¹**report** *n* **1** an account of events, experiences, etc. **2** the noise of an explosion **3** a rumour

²**report** *v* **1** to give an account of: *They reported the disappearance of the ship* **2** to arrive for work or duty:

to report to the police **3** to complain about to someone else: *He reported me to the head* **4** (of a reporter) to write an account of

reporter *n* a person who collects and writes news for a newspaper, radio, etc.

represent *v* **1** to be a picture, sign, etc., of: *This painting represents a storm. / These stones represent armies* **2** to act officially for: *As a member of parliament, he represents Worcester* **3** to be present as an example of (a group):*a soup in which 20 kinds of vegetables were represented* **4** to declare or describe, perhaps falsely: *He represented himself as a friend*

representation *n* **1** representing or being represented **2** something that represents: *This painting is a representation of a storm*

¹**representative** *adj* **1** typical; being an example: *a representative collection of ancient Greek art* **2** (of government) in which the people and their opinions are represented

²**representative** *n* a person acting in place of others

repress *v* **1** to keep under strict and unnatural control **2** to put down by force: *to repress a rising of the people with the army* –~**ive** *adj* –~**ively** *adv*

reprimand *v, n* (to give) a severe official scolding

¹**reproach** *n* **1** blame **2** words of blame: *loud reproaches* **3** something that brings shame: *This dirt is a*

reproach to the city **4** **above/beyond reproach** perfect –~**ful** *adj* –~**fully** *adv*

²**reproach** *v* to blame, not angrily but sadly

reproduce *v* **-duced, -ducing** **1** to produce young: *Birds reproduce by laying eggs* **2** to produce a copy of: *to reproduce a picture* – **-ducible** *adj*

reproduction *n* **1** the producing of young: *human reproduction* **2** copying: *This recording has poor reproduction* **3** a copy, esp. of a work of art, less exact than a replica – **-tive** *adj*

reptile *n* a scaly creature whose blood temperature depends on the temperature around it, such as a snake, turtle, or lizard – **-tilian** *adj, n*

republic *n* **1** a state governed by elected representatives **2** a nation whose chief of state is not a king but a president –~**an** *adj*

repulsion *n* **1** strong dislike and fear: *repulsion at the sight of a diseased animal* **2** (in science) the force by which bodies drive each other away – **-sive** *adj* –~**sively** *adv* –~**siveness** *n*

reputation *n* opinion held by others about someone or something: *to have a high reputation as a farmer*

reputed *adj* **1** generally supposed, but with some doubt: *his reputed father* **2** reported; considered: *She is reputed to be Europe's best singer* –~**ly** *adv*

¹**request** *n* **1** a polite demand: *a request for help* **2** something asked for: *Do*

they play requests on this radio show? **3 in request** very popular **4 on request** when asked for: *The band will play on request*

²**request** *v* to demand politely: *I requested them to stop*

require *v* **required, requiring 1** to need: *The floor requires washing* **2** *esp. written* to demand, expecting obedience: *All passengers are required to show their tickets*

requirement *n* something needed or demanded

¹**rescue** *v* **-cued, -cuing** to save (from harm or danger); set free – **-cuer** *n*

²**rescue** *n* **1** an act of rescuing **2 come/go to someone's rescue** to come/go and help someone

¹**research** *n* **1** advanced study of a subject, so as to learn new facts: *to do research on blood diseases* **2** a piece of work of this kind

²**research** *v* to do research – ~**er** *n*

resemblance *n* likeness: *a strong resemblance between the 2 brothers*

resemble *v* **-bled, -bling** to be like

resent *v* to feel angry or bitter at – ~**ful** *adj* – ~**fully** *adv* – ~**fulness** *n*

resentment *n* the feeling of resenting bad treatment

reservation *n* **1** a limiting condition: *I accept without reservations!* **2** a private doubt: *I have some reservations about his story* **3** (in the US) land set apart for American Indians to live on **4** a booking for a holiday, hotel, etc.

¹**reserve** *v* **reserved, reserving 1** to keep (for a special purpose) **2** to book (a holiday, hotel, etc.)

²**reserve** *n* **1** a quantity kept for future use: *a reserve of food* **2** the military force kept to support the regular army if needed **3** a price limit below which something is not to be sold **4** a piece of land reserved for a stated purpose: *a nature reserve* **5** the quality of being reserved in character: *the well-known reserve of the Scots* **6** a player whose job is to play in a team game instead of any member who cannot play **7 in reserve** ready for use if needed **8 without reserve** *esp. written* **a** freely and openly **b** without conditions: *I believe your story without reserve*

reserved *adj* **1** not liking to talk about oneself or to show one's feelings **2** booked: *reserved seats*

reservoir *n* **1** a place where liquid is stored, esp. water for a city **2** a large supply, often of facts or knowledge

reside *v* **resided, residing** *esp. written* to have one's home (in a stated place)

residence *n* **1** *esp. written* the place where one lives; a house **2** the state of residing: *took up residence in Jamaica*

¹**resident** *adj* living in a place: *a resident doctor* (=living in the hospital)

²**resident** *n* a person who lives in a place and is not just a visitor

resign *v* to give up (a job or position) **2 resign oneself** to become resigned

resignation *n* **1** being resigned: *to accept one's fate with resignation* **2**

an act of resigning **3** a written statement that one resigns

resigned *adj* patiently prepared for, or suffering, something unpleasant –~**ly** *adv*

resist *v* **1** to oppose; fight against **2** to remain unharmed by: *a roof that resists the weather* **3** to refuse to yield to: *She could hardly resist laughing* **4** to force oneself to refuse: *I can't resist baked apples* –~**ant** *adj* –~**er** *n* –~**ible** *adj*

resistance *n* **1** resisting **2** force opposed to anything; opposition: *wind resistance to an aircraft / resistance to the law* **3** the ability to resist disease **4** (a measure of) the ability of a substance to resist the passing through of an electric current **5** an organization that fights secretly against enemy armies that control its country

resolute *adj* firm; determined in purpose –~**ly** *adv* –~**ness** *n*

resolution *n* **1** also (*esp. written*) **resolve–** being resolute **2** the action of resolving: *the resolution of our difficulties* **3** a formal decision by vote: *a resolution against building a new library* **4** also (*esp. written)* **resolve–** a decision to do or stop doing something: *She's always making good resolutions*

resolve *v* **resolved, resolving 1** to decide: *He resolved on going out* **2** to settle or clear up (a difficulty)

resort *n* **1** a holiday place: *a health/ mountain resort* **2** a place that one visits regularly: *This restaurant is*

my favourite resort **3** resorting to: *to pass without resort to cheating* **4** someone or something resorted to: *Her only resort is television* **5 in the last resort** if everything else fails

resort to *v prep* to turn to (often something bad) for help: *When his wife left him he resorted to drink*

resource *n* **1** a part of one's resources: *Oil is an important natural resource* **2** a means of comfort or help: *Religion is her only resource* **3** cleverness in finding a way round difficulties: *a man of great resource*

resourceful *adj* able to get round difficulties –~**ly** *adv* –~**ness** *n*

resources *n* **1** wealth, goods, and other possessions that help one to do things **2 leave someone to his own resources** to leave someone to pass the time as he wishes

¹respect *n* **1** admiration; feeling of honour: *to show respect for one's parents* **2** attention; care: *to have respect for the law* **3** a detail (in such phrases as **in one/no respect, in several/many/all respects**) **4 in respect of** *esp. written* concerning; with regard to **5 without respect to** without considering; without regard to **6 with respect to** *esp. written* (introducing a new subject) with regard to: *With respect to the recent flood...*

²respect *v* to feel or show respect for: *I respect his courage. / I'll respect your wishes*

respectable *adj* **1** having character and standards acceptable to society

2 enough in amount or quality: *a respectable income* – **-bly** *adv* –~**ness** *n* – **-ability** *n*

respectful *adj* feeling or showing respect: *respectful silence* –~**ly** *adv* –~**ness** *n*

respectively *adv* each separately in the order mentioned: *She gave beer to the man and a toy to the baby, respectively*

respond *v* **1** to speak or act in answer: *I offered him a drink but he didn't respond. / The horse responded to his kick by jumping* **2** (of people at a religious service) to make responses

response *n* an answer **2** an action done in answer: *no response to our call for help* **3** one of the parts of a religious service said or sung by the people, in answer to the parts sung by the priest

responsibility *n* **-ties 1** being responsible **2** something for which one is responsible: *A father has many responsibilities*

responsible *adj* **1** having the duty of looking after someone or something, so that one can be blamed if things go wrong: *You are responsible to your mother for keeping the house tidy* **2** trustworthy: *a responsible person* –opposite **irresponsible 3** (of a job) needing a trustworthy person: *a responsible position* **4 be responsible for** to be the cause of – **-ibly** *adv*

¹rest *n* **1** freedom from anything tiring; sleep: *to take a day's rest* **2** a support: *This wall will do as a rest for your camera* **3** (in music) a period of silence of fixed length **4 at rest** not moving **5 come to rest** to stop moving

²rest *v* **1** to take a rest **2** to allow to rest: *rest your feet* **3** to lean or support **4** to lie buried **5** to stop: *Let the argument rest there* **6** (of farming land) to have nothing planted in it **7 rest assured** to be certain: *You can rest assured that we will find him*

³rest *n* what is left: *We'll eat some and keep the rest for breakfast*

restaurant *n* French a place where food is sold and eaten

restless *adj* **1** never quiet or still: *the restless sea* **2** not giving rest: *a restless night* –~**ly** *adv* –~**ness** *n*

restore *v* **restored, restoring 1** to give or put back: *to restore stolen property* **2** to introduce again: *to restore law and order* **3** to bring back to a proper state, esp. of health: *restored after one's holiday* **4** to put (old buildings, furniture, or works of art) back into the original state: *to restore an old painting* –**restoration** *n: the restoration of law and order/This castle is a fine restoration*

restrain *v* to control; hold back: *Restrain your dog from biting the milkman*

restraint *n* **1** being restrained or restraining oneself: *You showed great restraint in not crying. / Dogs don't like restraint in cages* **2** something that restrains: *the restraints of a small town* **3 without**

restraint freely: *She talked to me without restraint*

restrict *v* to keep within limits, often by control or law: *to restrict oneself to 2 sweets a day* –~**ed** *adj*: *a restricted demand for expensive cars* –~**ion** *n*

¹**result** *v* to happen as an effect: *If the police leave, disorder will result*

²**result** *n* **1** what happens because of an action or event; effect: *His illness is the result of bad food* **2** a person's or team's success or failure in an examination, match, etc.: *the football results* **3 with the result that** *esp. written* so that

resume *v* **resumed, resuming** *esp. written* **1** to begin again: *We resumed our journey after a rest* **2** to take again: *to resume one's seat* –**resumption** *n*

retain *v* **1** to avoid losing: *to retain one's balance* **2** to hold in place: *a wall to retain the lake* –**retention** *n* –**retentive** *adj*: *a retentive memory* –**retentively** *adv*

retaliate *v* **-ated, -ating** to pay back evil with evil: *Mary kicked Susan, and Susan retaliated by biting* –**-ation** *n* – **-atory, -ative** *adj*

retire *v* **retired, retiring** **1** to go away to a quiet place: *to retire to one's room* **2** (esp. of an army) to go back, but without being forced to **3** *esp. written* to go to bed **4** to stop working at one's job, usu. because of age

retired *adj* (of a person) having stopped working, usu. because of age: *a retired general* – **-rement** *n He was given a gold watch on his retirement*

retract *v* **1** to draw back or in: *A cat can retract its claws* **2** to take back (a statement or offer made): *to retract his remarks* –~**ion** *n* –~**able** *adj*: *a retractable offer / retractable wheels*

¹**retreat** *n* **1** an act of retreating: *Napoleon's retreat from Moscow* **2** a signal for retreating (often in the phrase **sound the retreat**) **3** a place of peace and safety **4 beat a retreat** to retreat, esp. quickly to avoid something unpleasant

²**retreat** *v* **1** (esp. of an army) to move back, esp. when forced to **2** to escape from something unpleasant

retrieve *v* **retrieved, retrieving** **1** to find and bring back: *to retrieve the lost bag* **2** to put right (a mistake, loss, defeat, etc.) –**retrievable** *adj* –**retrieval** *n*

retrospect *n* the act of looking back towards the past (in the phrase **in retrospect**): *One's school life seems happier in retrospect than in reality*

¹**return** *v* **1** to come or go back: *to return to London / Spring will return* **2** to give or send back: *Please return my keys!* **3** to answer: *'Yes!' she returned* **4** to elect to a political position: *We returned a Liberal as our Member of Parliament* **5** to bring in as profit: *These shares return interest* **6** to state officially: *He returned his earnings on the tax declaration. / The jury returned a*

verdict of 'Guilty' **7 return a favour** to do a kind action in return for another

²return *n* **1** an act of returning: *your return from China* **2** a giving back: *the return of the stolen books* **3** a profit **4** an official statement: *a tax return* **5** a return ticket **6 by return (of post)** by the next post **7 in return** in exchange

³return *adj* (esp. of a ticket) for a trip from one place to another and back again

reunite *v* **-nited, -niting** to come, bring, or join together again

reveal *v* **1** to allow to be seen: *a dress that reveals all* **2** to make known: *to reveal a secret* **–~ing** *adj*

revelation *n* **1** the making known of something secret **2** a surprising fact made known: *revelations about her past*

¹revenge *v* **revenged, revenging 1** to do something in revenge for: *to revenge a defeat* **2** to punish someone for harm done to: *Hamlet revenged his dead father*

²revenge *n* **1** a punishment given in return for harm done: *Hamlet wanted revenge for his father's murder* **2 give someone his revenge** (in sport) to play another game against a defeated opponent **–~ful** *adj* **–~fully** *adv* **–~fulness** *n*

revenue *n* income, esp. that of the government

reverence *n* great respect and admiration mixed with love: *They hold him in great reverence* **– -rent,**

-rential *adj: reverent behaviour* **– -rently, -rentially** *adv*

¹reverse *adj* **1** opposite in position; back: *the reverse side of the cloth* **2 in reverse order** from the end to the beginning

²reverse *v* **reversed, reversing 1** to go or drive backwards or in the opposite direction: *He reversed the car. / The car reversed through the gate* **2** to turn (something) over, showing the back: *She reversed the paper* **3** to change (something) to the opposite: *He reversed the judgment and set the prisoner free after all* **4 reverse arms** (of a soldier) to point one's gun downwards **5 reverse the charges** to make a telephone call to be paid for by the person receiving it **–reversal** *n: By a reversal of fortune he lost his money* **–reversible** *adj* **–reversibility** *n*

³reverse *n* **1** the opposite in position; the back: *the reverse of the cloth* **2** the opposite; the other way round: *Edwin is afraid of Angela, but the reverse is also true* **3** a defeat or change for the worse: *The failure of his business was a serious reverse* **4** the side (of a coin) that does not show the ruler's head **5** the position of controls that causes backward movement: *Put the car into reverse*

¹review *n* **1** an act of reviewing: *a careful review of political events* **2** a grand show of the armed forces **3 a** a magazine containing articles giving judgments on new books, plays, and public events **b** an article of this kind **4 under review** being considered and judged

²**review** *v* **1** to consider and judge; go over again in the mind: *to review the situation* **2** to hold a review of (armed forces) **3** to write a review of (a play, book, etc.)

revise *v* **revised, revising** **1** to read (a piece of writing) carefully, making improvements **2** to change (opinions, intentions, etc.) because of more information or thought: *I'll have to revise my ideas about Tom* **3** to study again (lessons already learnt) **–reviser** *n* **–revision** *n*

revival *n* **1** a rebirth or renewal: *a revival of interest in ancient music* **2** a performance of an old play after many years

revive *v* **revived, reviving** **1** to make or become conscious or healthy again: *The fresh air soon revived him* **2** to bring or come back into use or existence: *to revive an old custom* **3** to perform (an old play) again after many years

¹**revolt** *v* **1** to act violently against those in power so as to win power: *The people revolted against their king* **2** to cause (someone) to feel violent dislike and sickness: *Such cruelty revolted him*

²**revolt** *n* the act of revolting: *The nation is in revolt*

revolting *adj* very nasty: *a revolting smell of bad eggs* **–~ly** *adv*

revolution *n* **1** a great social change, esp. the changing of a political system by force **2** a complete change: *Air travel has caused a revolution in our way of living* **3** (one complete) circular movement round a fixed point: *the revolution of the moon round the earth* **4** (in a machine) one complete circular movement on a central point, as of a wheel: *a speed of 100 revolutions per minute*

¹**revolutionary** *adj* **1** connected with political revolution **2** completely new and different: *a revolutionary machine*

²**revolutionary** *n* **-ries** a person who favours or fights in a revolution

revolve *v* **revolved, revolving** **1** to spin round; make revolutions: *The wheels revolved slowly* **2** *esp. written* to consider carefully: *He revolved the main points in his mind*

¹**reward** *v* **1** to give a reward to **2** to give a reward for: *How can I reward your kindness?*

²**reward** *n* something gained or given for work, service, finding something, etc.: *a reward of £900 for catching the criminal*

rhinoceros –also (*esp. spoken*) **rhino** *n* **-ros** *or* **-roses** one of several kinds of large heavy thick-skinned animal of Africa or Asia, with 1 or 2 horns on its nose

rhubarb *n* **1** a broad-leaved garden plant with thick juicy edible stems **2** *esp. spoken* the sound of many people talking

¹**rhyme** *n* **1** a word that rhymes with another: *'Bold' and 'cold' are rhymes*

2 words that rhyme at the ends of lines in poetry: *Rhyme was not used in ancient poetry* **3** a short and not serious piece of writing, using words that rhyme **4 rhyme or reason** sense; meaning

²**rhyme** *v* **rhymed, rhyming 1** (of words) to end with the same sound: *'House' rhymes with 'mouse'* **2** to put together (2 words that end with the same sound): *You can rhyme 'duty' with 'beauty' but not 'box' and 'backs'*

rhythm *n* **1** (in music or poetry) a regular pattern of beats: *the exciting rhythms of drum music* **2** the quality of happening at regular periods of time: *the rhythm of the seasons* −~**ic,** ~**ical** *adj* −~**ically** *adv*

¹**rib** *n* **1** one of the many pairs of bones (12 in man) running from the backbone round to the front of the chest **2** a piece of meat that includes one of these bones **3** anything like a rib in shape or function: *the ribs of a boat/leaf* −~**bed** *adj: ribbed socks*

²**rib** *v* **-bb-** *esp. spoken* to make fun of in a friendly way

ribbon *n* **1** a long narrow band of cloth used for tying things, for ornament, etc. **2** such a band in a special colour or pattern, worn to show a title or honour: *the ribbon of the Victoria Cross* **3** a long irregular narrow band: *a ribbon of mist*

rice *n* **1** any of several kinds of food grain grown in hot wet places **2** the seed of this, which is cooked and eaten

rich *adj* **1** possessing a lot of money or property **2** containing a lot (of the stated thing): *fish rich in oil* **3** valuable and beautiful: *rich silk/furniture* **4** (of food) containing a lot of cream, sugar, eggs, etc. **5** (of land or soil) good for growing plants in **6** (of a sound or colour) deep, strong, and beautiful −~**ly** *adv* −~**ness** *n*

riches *n* wealth

¹**ricochet** *n* **1** the skipping away in a new direction of a a bullet, stone, etc., when it hits a surface at an angle **2** a blow from an object to which this has happened: *wounded by a ricochet*

²**ricochet** *v* **-cheted** *or* **-chetted, -cheting** *or* **-chetting** to change direction in a ricochet: *The bullet ricocheted off the bridge*

¹**riddle** *n* **1** a difficult and amusing question to which one must guess the answer **2** something one cannot understand: *Robert's character is a complete riddle*

²**riddle** *n* a large sieve

³**riddle** *v* **-dled, -dling 1** to pass (earth, corn, ashes, etc.) through a riddle **2** to shake (a grate) to make the ashes fall through

¹**ride** *v* **rode, ridden, riding 1** to travel along, controlling and sitting on (a horse, bicycle, etc.) **2** to travel on a horse: *teach the children to ride* **3** to go along, across, or over (a place) on a horse: *He rides the borders*

²**ride** *n* **1** a journey (on an animal, in a vehicle, etc.) **2** a path made for horse riding **3 take someone for a ride** *esp. spoken* to deceive someone

rider *n* **1** a person who rides esp. a horse **2** *law* a statement or opinion added to an official judgment

¹**ridge** *n* a long narrow raised part of any surface, such as the top of a mountain range or of a sloping roof

²**ridge** *v* **ridged, ridging** to make ridges in

ridiculous *adj offensive* silly; deserving ridicule **–~ly** *adv* **–~ness** *n*

rid of *v prep* **rid** *or* **ridded, rid, ridding of 1** to make free of: *to rid the town of rats* **2 get rid of** to free oneself from; drive or give away

¹**rifle** *v* **rifled, rifling** to search and steal everything valuable out of: *The thieves rifled his pockets*

²**rifle** *v* to make grooves inside (a gun barrel) so as to make the bullets spin

³**rifle** *n* a gun fired from the shoulder, with a long rifled barrel

¹**right** *adj* **1** on the side of the body that does not contain the heart **2** in the direction of this side: *a right turn* **3** connected with the right in politics

²**right** *n* **1** the right side or direction: *Keep to the right!* **2** political groups that favour fewer political changes and generally support the employers or those in official positions rather than the workers

³**right** *adj* **1** just; morally good **2** correct; true: *the right time* **–~ness** *n*

⁴**right** *n* **1** what is just or good **2** a morally just or lawful claim: *She has a right to half your money* **3 in one's own right** because of one's own just claim: *famous in one's own right* **4 in the right** not deserving blame

⁵**right** *adv* **1** towards the right: *He turned right* **2** directly; straight: *The marmalade's right in front of you* **3** properly; correctly: *to guess right* **4** all the way: *right back to the beginning* **5** all right: *Right! I'll do it*

⁶**right** *v* to put right or upright: *The cat righted itself during the fall, and landed on its feet*

right angle *n* an angle of 90 degrees, as at any corner in a square **–right-angled** *adj*

rights *n* **1** the advantages to which someone has a moral or lawful claim: *women's rights* **2 by rights** if things were done fairly **3 set/put to rights** to make just, healthy, correct, etc.: *This medicine will soon put you to rights* **4 the rights and wrongs of** the true facts of

rigid *adj* **1** stiff; not easy to bend **2** not easy to change: *rigid ideas* **–~ly** *adv* **–~ity** *n*

¹**rim** *n* the outside edge or border of esp. a circular object: *the rim of a wheel* **–~less** *adj*

²**rim** *v* **-mm-** to surround (something circular)

rind *n* **1** the thick outer covering of certain fruits: *lemon rind* **2** the thick outer skin, which cannot be eaten, of certain foods: *cheese rind*

¹ring *n* **1** a circular line or arrangement: *to dance in a ring* **2** a circular band: *the rings of Saturn / a key ring* **3** a metal band worn on the finger: *a wedding ring* **4** any closed-in space where things are shown or performed, as in a circus or for boxing **5** any group of people who work together, often dishonestly, to control some business: *a drug ring*

²ring *v* **1** to make a ring round: *Police ringed the building* **2** to put a ring in the nose of (an animal) or round the leg of (a bird)

³ring *v* **rang, rung, ringing** **1** to cause (a bell) to sound **2** (of a bell, telephone, etc.) to sound: *The telephone's ringing* **3** (of the ears) to be filled with a continuous sound **4** to telephone **5** **ring a bell** *esp. spoken* to remind one of something **6** **ring true/false** to sound true/untrue

⁴ring *n* **1** an act of sounding a bell **2** a loud clear sound like a bell: *the ring of laughter* **3** a quality: *Her story had a ring of truth* **4** **give someone a ring** to telephone someone

ringleader *n* a person who leads others to do wrong

¹rinse *v* **rinsed, rinsing** **1** to wash (esp. clothes) in clean water to take away soap, dirt, etc. **2** to wash (soap, dirt, etc.) out with clean water

²rinse *n* **1** an act of rinsing **2** liquid for colouring the hair

¹riot *n* **1** a lot of violence, noise, etc., by many people together, esp. in a public place **2** *esp. spoken* a very funny and successful occasion or person: *The new show is a riot!* **3** **a riot of colour** a mass of disordered colours **4** **run riot** to become violent and uncontrollable

²riot *v* to take part in a riot **−~er** *n*

riotous *adj* **1** wild and disorderly: *a riotous crowd* **2** noisy and exciting **−~ly** *adv* **−~ness** *n*

¹rip *v* **-pp-** **1** to tear quickly and violently: *The wind ripped the sail* **2** **let rip** *esp. spoken* to let go at top speed or develop without control

²rip *n* a long tear

ripe *adj* **1** (of plants) fully grown and ready to be eaten **2** fully developed: *ripe judgment* **3** ready; fit: *land ripe for development* **4** *esp. spoken* concerned with sex, the lavatory, etc., in a shocking or amusing way: *a rather ripe joke* **−~ly** *adv* **−~ness** *n*

ripen *v* to make or become ripe

¹ripple *v* **-pled, -pling** **1** to move in or form ripples **2** to make a sound like gently running water: *a rippling stream*

²ripple *n* **1** a very small wave or wave-like mark: *ripples on a pool / on the sand* **2** a sound like gently running water

¹rise *v* **rose, risen, rising** **1** (of the sun, moon, or stars) to appear above the horizon **2** to go up; get higher; increase: *The river is rising after the rain. / The price of tea has risen* **−opposite fall** **3** *esp. written* to get out of bed: *She rises before it is light* **4** also (*esp. written*) **arise**– to stand up from lying, kneeling, or sitting **5** (of a river) to begin: *The river Rhine rises in Switzerland* **6** to move up in rank **7** (of uncooked bread) to swell as the yeast works **8** (of wind or storms) to get stronger **9** to show weakness or annoyance in reply to nasty words or behaviour: *He won't rise to your nasty jokes* **10** to come back to life after being dead **11 rise to the occasion** to show that one can deal with a difficult matter

²**rise** *n* **1** the act of growing greater or more powerful: *the rise of the Roman Empire* **2** an increase: *a rise in the cost of living* **3** a small hill **4** an increase in wages **5 get/take a rise out of someone** intentionally to make someone show weakness or annoyance **6 give rise to** to be the cause of

¹**risk** *n* **1** a danger; chance of loss: *a risk of fire* **2** a person who is a possible danger to a project: *a bad risk* **3 at one's own risk** agreeing to bear any loss or danger oneself **4 at risk** *esp. written* in danger: *children at risk* **5 run/take risks/a risk** to take chances –~**y** *adj: a risky business* –~**iness** *n*

²**risk 1** to place in danger: *to risk one's health* **2** to take the chance of: *to risk failure*

¹**rival** *n* a person with whom one competes –**rival** *adj: a rival team* –~**ry** *n: rivalry between our teams*

²**rival** *v* **-ll-** to be as good as: *Ships can't rival planes for speed*

river *n* a wide natural stream of water

road *n* **1** a smooth broad prepared track for wheeled vehicles: *It's not really a road, only a path* **2** also **roadstead**– an open stretch of deep water, as at the mouth of a river, where ships can float at anchor **3 on the road a** on a journey **b** (of esp. a theatrical company) giving performances at different places –~**less** *adj*

roadside *n, adj* (at or near) the edge of the road

roadway *n* **-ways** the part of a road where vehicles drive

roam *v* to wander with no very clear aim –~**er** *n*

¹**roar** *v* **1** to give a roar: *The lion/ engine roared* **2** to go along making a roar **3** to say or express with a roar: *The crowd roared their approval* **4** *esp. spoken* to laugh long and loudly **5** (of a child) to weep or cry noisily **6 do a roaring trade** to sell one's goods very fast

²**roar** *n* a deep loud continuing sound: *the roar of an angry lion*

¹**roast** *v* **1** to cook (esp. meat) by dry heat **2 fit to roast an ox** (of a fire) very hot **3 give someone a roasting** to scold someone severely

²**roast** *n* a large piece of roasted meat

³**roast** *adj* roasted

rob *v* **-bb-** to take the property of (a person or organization) unlawfully –~**ber** *n*

robbery *n* **-ies** the crime of robbing

¹**robe** *n* a long flowing garment **a** for informal occasions: *a bath robe* **b** for official occasions: *a judge's robes*

²**robe** *v* **robed, robing** to dress in robes: *robed in red*

robin –also **robin redbreast** *n* a common type of fat little European bird, with a brown back and a red breast

robot *n* **1** a machine that can do some human work, esp. an imaginary machine figure that acts as if alive **2** a person who acts without thought or feeling

¹**rock** *v* **1** to move backwards and forwards or from side to side **2** to cause great shock and surprise to: *The President's murder rocked the nation* **3** **rock the boat** (of a member of a group) to do something that makes it hard for the group to work together

²**rock** *n* a kind of popular modern music played on electric instruments and with a strong beat

³**rock** *n* **1** stone forming part of the earth's surface **2** a large separate piece of stone **3** a hard sticky sweet made in long round bars **4** **as firm/steady/solid as a rock a** perfectly firm and hard **b** (of people) trustworthy

¹**rocket** *n* **1** a kind of firework that shoots high into the air and lets out coloured flames **2** a machine of this kind driven by burning gases, used in powering aircraft and spacecraft **3** a bomb or missile driven in this way **4** **give someone/get a rocket** *sl* to scold someone/be scolded severely

²**rocket** *v* **1** to rise quickly and suddenly: *rocketing prices* **2** to move very fast: *The train rocketed downhill*

rod *n* **1** a long thin stiff stick of wood, metal, etc. **2** a stick used for beating as a punishment **3** such as punishment **4** a type of cell in the light-sensitive area (retina) of the eye that is sensitive esp. to different amounts of light and allows one to see well in dim light **5** **Spare the rod and spoil the child** A child who is never punished will grow up with bad habits

rode *past tense of* RIDE

¹**rogue** *n* a very dishonest person

²**rogue** *adj* (of a wild animal) living alone and having a bad temper: *a rogue elephant*

role *n* **1** the behaviour or duties expected from one holding a particular position in a social group **2** the part taken by someone in a play or film

¹**roll** *n* **1** a flat piece of some material rolled into a tube shape: *a roll of film/cloth* **2** a small loaf of bread for one person **3** an official list of names: *the College Roll* **4** **call the roll** to read aloud an official list of names to see who is there

²**roll** *v* **1** to move by or as if by turning over and over: *Tears rolled down her cheeks* **2** to turn over and over, round and round, or from side to side **3** to move steadily and

smoothly along on or as if on wheels: *The years rolled by* **4** to form into a circular shape by curling round and round: *He rolled up the map* **5** to make (a tubelike object) by curling round and round **6** (of a ship) to swing from side to side with the movement of the waves **7 a** to make (a surface) flat by pressing with a roller: *roll the grass* **b** to be made flat in this way **8** to make a long deep sound: *The thunder/The drums rolled* **9** to cause (esp. film cameras) to begin working **10** to throw (dice) **11 keep the ball rolling** to keep things active **12 roll one's r's** to pronounce the sound with the tongue beating rapidly against the roof of the mouth, as is common in Scotland **13 set the ball rolling** to be the first to do something, hoping that others will follow

³**roll** *n* **1** a long deep sound: *a roll of thunder/of drums* **2 a** a rolling movement **b** an action which includes this movement: *a roll of the dice*

¹**Roman Catholic** *adj* connected with the branch of the Christian religion (the **Roman Catholic Church**) whose leader (the pope) rules from Rome

²**Roman Catholic** *n* a member of the Roman Catholic Church

¹**romance** *n* **1** a story of love, adventure, strange happenings, etc., more exciting than real life **2** the quality that such stories have: *the romance of life in the Wild West* **3** a love affair

²**romance** *v* **romanced, romancing 1** to tell improbable stories: *Is he romancing about this?* **2** to carry on a love affair

¹**romantic** *adj* **1** belonging to or suggesting romance: *a romantic adventure* **2** fanciful; not practical; dreamy **3** having the quality of romanticism: *romantic poetry* –~**ally** *adv*

²**romantic** *n* **1** a romantic dreamy impractical person **2** a writer, painter, etc., whose work shows romanticism

romanticism *n* (in art, literature, and music) the quality of admiring feeling rather than thought, and wild beauty rather things, and of valuing individual expression – **-cist** *n*

¹**roof** *n* **1** the outside covering on top of a building **2** the top covering of a tent, closed vehicle, etc. **3 a/no roof over one's head** somewhere/nowhere to live **4 raise the roof** to make a loud angry noise **5 the roof of the/one's mouth** the bony upper part of the inside of the mouth

²**roof** *v* to put a roof on; be a roof for

room *n* **1** a division of a building, with its own walls, floor, and ceiling **2** space, esp. which could be filled or is enough for any purpose: *room for 3 more books* **3** the chance to do something: *room to develop as a painter* **4 a** need for: *room for impro-*

vement **b** reason for: *no room for doubt* −∼**ful** *n*

¹root *n* **1** the part of a plant that grows down into the soil **2** the part of a tooth, hair, or organ that holds it to the body **3** origin; central part **4** *technical* (in mathematics) a number that when multiplied by itself a stated number of times gives another stated number: *2 is the 4th root of 16* **5** *technical* (in grammar) the base part of a word to which other parts can be added: *'Music' is the root of 'musician' and of 'unmusical'* **6 root and branch** in all parts: *destroy this system root and branch* **7 take/strike root** (of plants or ideas) to become established

²root *v* to form or cause to form roots

³root −also **rootle** *v* **1** (esp. of pigs) to search for food by digging with the nose **2** to search for something by turning things over

¹rope *n* **1** strong thick cord made by twisting, or a piece of this **2** a fat twisted string (esp. of the stated objects): *a rope of pearls/onions* **3** hanging as a punishment **4 give someone enough rope to hang himself** to allow freedom to a fool or evil person so he can show his true nature **5 give someone rope** to allow someone freedom to act

²rope *v* **roped, roping 1** to tie up with a rope **2** *esp. US* to catch (an animal) with a rope

¹rose *n* **1** any of various bushes with strong prickly stems, divided leaves, and often sweet-smelling flowers **2** the flower of this bush **3** a circular piece of metal or plastic with holes in it fitted to the end of a pipe or watering can **4 a bed of roses** a very pleasant state to be in **5 be not all roses** (of a situation) to include some unpleasant things

²rose *adj* **1** (of a colour) from pink to a deep purplish red **2 see (something) through rose-coloured spectacles** to think (something) is pleasanter than it really is

³rose *past tense of* RISE

¹rot *v* **-tt-** to decay or cause to decay

²rot *n* **1** decay or disease: *a tree full of rot* **2** *sl* foolish remarks or ideas: *Don't talk rot!* **3 the rot sets in** things begin to go wrong

rotate *v* **rotated, rotating 1** to turn round a fixed point: *The earth rotates once a day* **2** to take turns or cause to take turns: *rotate the crops*

rotation *n* **1** the action of rotating **2** one complete turn round a fixed point **3 in rotation** (of events) coming round one after the other in regular order **4 rotation of crops** planting different crops in a field each year

rotten *adj* **1** gone bad: *rotten eggs* **2** wicked; evil **3** *sl* bad: *What rotten weather!* **4 rotten to the core** completely bad morally −∼**ly** *adv* −∼**ness** *n*

¹rough *adj* **1** uneven; not smooth: *a rough road* **2** violent: *rough winds* **3** (of food and living conditions) simple: *a rough dinner* **4** (of plans, calculations, etc.) not yet in detail;

not in finished form: *a rough drawing* **5** (of paper) for making the first attempts at drawing or writing something **6** (of sounds) not gentle or tuneful: *a rough voice* **7** *sl* unfortunate and hard to bear **8 rough and ready** simple and without comfort **9 rough on** (someone) *esp. spoken* unfortunate for (someone)

²**rough** *n* **1** a violent noisy man **2** the uneven ground with long grass on a golf course **3 in rough** unpolished: *Write it out in rough*

³**rough** *v* **rough it** to live in a simple and not very comfortable way

⁴**rough** *adv* **1** in rough conditions, esp. out of doors **2** using too much force **3 cut up rough** *esp. spoken* to become angry **4 sleep rough** (esp. of a homeless wanderer in a city) to sleep out of doors

roughly *adv* **1** in a rough manner **2** about: *roughly 200 people*

¹**round** *adj* **1** circular **2** shaped like a ball **3** curved **4** (of numbers) full; complete: *a round dozen* **5 in round figures** (of numbers) not exactly; about: *The car cost £9,878 – that's £10,000 in round figures* –~**ness** *n*

²**round** *adv* **1** with a circular movement or movements; spinning if in or as if in a circle **2** in a circular position; surrounding a central point **3** all over the place; in or into all parts: *Let's go into the palace and have a look round* **4** so as to face the other way: *Turn the picture round* **5 all the year round** during the whole year **6 round about** in the neighbourhood

³**round** *prep* with a circular movement about (a central point): *The earth goes round the sun* **2** in a circular position on all or some sides of (a central point): *to sit round the fire* **3** into all parts of; all over (a place): *to look round the shop* **4** to or at the other side of: *round the corner* **5** (with times, places, etc.) also **round about** – about: *They arrived round about 5 o'clock* **6 round the clock** all the time

⁴**round** *n* **1** something round like a plate or ball **2** a complete slice, esp. of bread **3** a regular journey to many houses, offices, etc.: *a paper round* **4** a number or set: *a round of wage claims* **5** a share given out to everyone present: *round of drinks* **6** (in sport) one stage, period, or game: *the first round of the FA Cup* **7** one single shot: *I've only 2 rounds left* **8** a song for 3 or 4 voices, in which each sings the same tune, one starting a line after another has just finished it **9 in the round a** (of theatre) with people sitting on most or all 4 sides of the stage **b** (of a figure cut out of stone) not part of a wall but solid and separate **10 one's daily round** one's duties to be done every day

⁵**round** *v* **1** to make or become round: *The child's eyes rounded with excitement* **2** to travel round: *She rounded the corner*

rouse *v* **roused, rousing 1** to waken **2**

to make (someone) more active, angry, or excited: *The speaker tried to rouse the masses*

¹**rout** *n* **1** a complete defeat and disorderly flight **2 put someone to rout** to defeat completely and drive away someone

²**rout** *v* **routed, routing** to put to rout

¹**route** *n* a way planned or followed from one place to another

²**route** *v* **routed, routing** to send by a particular route

¹**routine** *n* **1** the regular ordinary way of doing things **2** a set of steps practised by a dancer

²**routine** *adj* **1** regular: *a routine medical examination* **2** not exciting: *a routine job* –~**ly** *adv*

¹**row** *v* **1** to move through the water with oars **2** to have (a race of this kind): *row against Cambridge* –~**er** *n* –~**ing** *adj: a rowing club*

²**row** *n* a trip in a rowing boat

³**row** *n* a neat line of people or things side by side: *a row of houses*

⁴**row** *n esp. spoken* **1** a noisy quarrel, sometimes with violence **2** a noise: *Stop making such a row!* **3** a scolding **4 kick up/make a row** *sl* to cause trouble

⁵**row** *v esp. spoken* to quarrel, often noisily or violently

¹**royal** *adj* **1** for, belonging to, supported by, or connected with a king or queen **2** splendid: *a right royal feast* –~**ly** *adv*

²**royal** *n sl* a member of the royal family

royalty *n* **-ties 1** royal power and rank **2** members of the royal family **3 a** a percentage of a book's price, paid to the writer on each copy sold. It is also paid to the writer of a play or piece of music, when it is performed **b** a share of the profits, as of a mine or new machine, paid in this way to an owner or inventor

¹**rub** *v* **-bb- 1** to slide one surface with pressure, to and fro or round and round against (another) **2** to slide (2 surfaces against each other) in this way: *He rubbed his hands* **3** (of a surface) to slide in this way against/on another: *My shoe's rubbing* **4** to put (paste, liquid, etc.) on a surface in this way **5** to make (a hole) in this way **6** to bring (something) to a stated condition in this way: *Rub your hair dry*

²**rub** *n* **1** an act of rubbing: *Give the table a good rub* **2** the cause of trouble: *There's the rub*

¹**rubber** *n* **1** a substance, made chemically or from the juice of a tropical tree, which keeps out water and springs back into position after being stretched **2** a piece of this substance used for removing pencil marks; eraser

²**rubber** *n* **1** (when playing cards) a set of 3 games of whist or bridge **2** (in cricket) a set of international matches

¹**rubbish** *n* **1** waste material to be thrown away **2** silly remarks; nonsense –~**y** *adj esp. spoken : a rubbishy story*

²**rubbish** *interj* How silly!

rudder *n* **1** a blade at the back of a ship that controls its direction **2** an apparatus like this on an aircraft −∼**less** *adj*

rude *adj* **1** (of a person or his behaviour) not polite **2** simple and roughly made: *a rude hut* **3** (of people) wild and untaught: *a rude tribe* **4** in the natural state: *rude cotton* **5** sudden and violent (in the phrases **a rude shock, a rude awakening**) **6** connected with sexual jokes **7 in rude health** very healthy −∼**ly** *adv* −∼**ness** *n*

¹**ruffle** *v* **-fled, -fling 1** to make uneven: *He ruffled the child's hair* **2** to make or become rather angry

²**ruffle** *n* a band of fine cloth sewn in folds round an edge, esp. at the neck or wrists of a garment

rug *n* **1** a thick usu. woollen floor mat **2** a large warm woollen covering to wrap round oneself when travelling or camping

rugby also (*esp. written*) **rugby football**, (*esp. spoken)* **rugger** *n* a type of football played with an oval ball, by 2 teams of 13 (**rugby league**) or 15 (**rugby union**) men

rugged *adj* **1** large, rough, uneven, harsh, etc.: *a rugged face / a rugged shore* **2** (of a person or character) rough but strong and good −∼**ly** *adv* −∼**ness** *n*

¹**ruin** *n* **1** the cause, state, or event of destruction and decay **2** a ruined building

²**ruin** *v* **1** to destroy and spoil completely **2** to cause total loss of money to: *I was ruined by that law case*

¹**rule** *n* **1** an order, law, etc., that guides action, describes events, etc.: *the rules of tennis* **2** power to rule: *under foreign rule* **3** a ruler: *a 2 foot rule* **4 as a rule** usually; generally **5 bend/stretch the rules** to allow oneself to be influenced more by special conditions than by strict rules **6 rule of thumb** a quick and not exact way of doing something, based on experience

²**rule** *v* **ruled, ruling 1** to have and use the highest power over (a country, people, etc.), esp. as a government **2** (esp. in law) to decide officially: *The judge ruled that he must leave* **3 a** to draw (a line) as with the help of a ruler **b** to draw parallel lines on (paper) **4 be ruled by** to be guided or influenced by **5 rule (esp. a group) with a rod of iron** to govern (esp. a group) in a very severe way

ruler *n* **1** a person who rules **2** a long narrow piece of hard material with straight edges

¹**ruling** *n* an official decision

²**ruling** *adj* most powerful: *the ruling class*

¹**rumble** *v* **-bled, -bling 1** to make a deep continuous rolling sound **2** to go along making this sound: *The lorry rumbled down the street* **3** to say in a voice of this kind −**rumble** *n*

²**rumble** *v esp. spoken* to understand

the secret or nature of: *I soon rumbled her disguise*

rumour *n* **1** common talk, perhaps untrue **2** a story spread this way: *all kinds of strange rumours* – ~**ed** *adj*

¹**run** *v* **ran, run, running 1** to move on one's legs faster than walking **2** to travel (a distance) in this way **3 a** to take part in or hold (a race) **b** to cause (an animal) to race **4** to move quickly: *I'll run the car into town. / He ran his eyes down the list. / The car ran down the hill* **5 a** (of a machine) to work, often in a stated way: *The engine runs well* **b** to cause (a machine) to work, often in a stated way: *to run the trains on oil* **6 a** (of a public vehicle) to travel as arranged: *This bus runs between Manchester and Liverpool* **b** to cause (a public vehicle) to travel in this way: *They're running a special train* **7** (of liquids, sand, etc.) to flow, often in a stated way: *The water ran cold* **8** (of a container) to pour out liquid, often reaching a stated condition: *Your nose is running. / The well has run dry* **9 a** to cause (liquids, sand, etc.) to flow, esp. from a tap **b** to fill (a bath) for someone **10** to melt and spread by the action of heat or water: *The butter will run if you put it near the fire* **11** to stretch; continue: *The road runs beside the river* **12** to own and drive (a car) **13** to take (somebody or something, to somewhere) in a vehicle **14** to bring (something) into a country, unlawfully and secretly: *to run drugs/guns/arms* **15** to be in charge of and cause to work (an organization or system) **16** to continue in force, playing, being, etc.: *The insurance runs for another month* **17** (of a hole in a stocking) to become a ladder **18** (of words in fixed order, as in a poem or law) to be; consist of: *The line runs 'Time and the bell have buried the day'* **19 be run off one's feet** *esp. spoken* to be very busy, esp. working **20 run (a competitor) close/hard** to be nearly equal to (a competitor) **21 run for it** to escape by running **22 run foul of** to meet difficulty in **23 run (someone) off (someone's) feet** *esp. spoken* to keep someone very busy **24 run (oneself or another) into the ground** to tire (oneself or another) out with hard work **25 run the chance/danger of** to take the risk of

²**run** *n* **1** the action of running, often for a stated time or distance **2** a journey, often of a stated time or distance or to a stated place **3** a usu. enclosed area where animals are kept: *a hen run* **4 a** an eager demand: *a run on beer in hot weather* **b** (in the money market) a general desire to sell **5** (in cricket) a point won by players running from one wicket to the other **6** (in card games) a set of cards with consecutive numbers **7** a continuous set or succession of performances, events, objects, etc.: *a run*

of 3 months **8** a sloping course for a downhill sport: *a ski-run* **9 a good run for one's money** satisfaction for money spent or effort made **10 a run on the bank** a sudden demand by many people to have money back from the bank **11 at a run** running **12 on the run a** trying to escape, or to hide, esp. from the police **b** busy **13 in the long run** after enough time: *It'll be cheaper in the long run to use real leather* **14 in the short run** for the near future **15 the common/ordinary run of** the usual sort of **16 the run of** the freedom to visit or use: *He gave them the run of his garden*

run down *v adv* **1** to knock down and hurt with one's vehicle **2 a** to chase and catch: *to run down a criminal* **b** to find by searching **3** to speak of as being less valuable, important, etc., than appears **4** (esp. of a clock or battery) to lose power and stop working **5** to stop working gradually: *The coal industry is being run down*

¹rung *n* **1** one of the cross-bars that form the steps of a ladder **2 the highest/top/ lowest/bottom rung of the ladder** the highest/ lowest level in an organization or profession

²rung *past part. of* RING

runner *n* **1** a person who runs, esp. in a race **2** one of the thin blades on which a sledge or skate slides over snow or ice **3** one of the stems with which a plant like the strawberry spreads itself along the ground **4** a long narrow piece of cloth

runner-up *n* **runners-up** *or* **runner-ups** the person or team that comes second in a competition

¹running *n* **1** the act or sport of running **2 in/out of the running** with some/no hope of winning **3 make the running** to set the speed at which a race is run, a relationship develops, etc.

²running *adj* **1** (of water) flowing, often from taps **2** done while running along **3** continuous: *a running battle / A* **running commentary** *is an account of an event given while it is actually happening* **4** (of money) spent or needed to keep something working: *the running costs of a car/factory* **5** giving out liquid: *a running nose/sore* **6 take a running jump** *sl, imperative* Go away! You annoy me

³running *adv* one after the other without a break: *3 times running*

runway *n* **-ways** an area with a specially prepared hard surface, on which aircraft land and take off

rural *adj* of or like the countryside or country life −~**ly** *adv*

¹rush *n* any of several types of grass-like water plant whose long thin hollow stems are often dried and made into mats, baskets, and chair seats −**rushy** *adj*

²rush *v* **1** to hurry; act quickly **2** to move suddenly and hastily in the stated direction: *They rushed up the stairs* **3** to do (a job) hastily and usu.

poorly **4** to force (someone) to act hastily: *Don't rush me* **5** to attack suddenly and all together **6 rush someone off his feet** to make someone hurry too much or work too hard

³rush *n* **1** a sudden rapid movement **2** too much haste **3** great activity and excitement: *the Christmas rush* **4** a sudden great demand: *a rush to see the new film*

¹rust *n* **1** the reddish brown surface that forms on iron and some other metals when attacked by water and air **2** the colour of this **3** any of various fungal plant diseases causing reddish-brown spots

²rust *v* to cover or become covered with rust

¹rustle *v* **-tled, -tling 1 a** (of paper, dry leaves, silk, etc.) to make slight sounds when moved or rubbed together **b** to cause (paper, dry leaves, silk, etc.) to make these sounds: *The wind rustled the dead leaves* **2** to move along making these sounds: *The tiger rustled through the bushes* **3** *esp. US* to steal (cattle or horses left loose in open country)

²rustle *n* a sound of rustling

rusty *adj* **-ier, -iest 1** covered with rust **2 a** (of a person) having forgotten much of a subject: *a bit rusty on history* **b** (of one's knowledge of a subject) mostly forgotten **-rustiness** *n*

¹sabotage *n* **1** intentional damage to machines, buildings, etc., esp. to weaken a business or a country at war **2** indirect or secret action to prevent or ruin a plan

²sabotage *v* **-taged, -taging** to practise sabotage on **- -teur** *n*

¹sack *n* **1 a** large bag used for storing or moving goods **b** also **sackful-** the amount in one of these **2** *esp. spoken* the taking away of someone's job by an employer **3 hit the sack** *esp. spoken* to go to bed

²sack *v* to dismiss

sacred *adj* **1** religious, esp. in nature or use **2** holy by connection with God **3** serious, solemn, and important: *a sacred promise* **4** for the honour of a stated person or god **-~ly** *adv* **-~ness** *n*

¹sacrifice *n* **1** an offering to God or a god, esp. of an animal by killing **2** the loss of something of value, esp. for a particular purpose **3** something lost in this way: *His parents made many sacrifices for him* **- -ficial** *adj*

²sacrifice *v* **-ficed, -ficing 1** to offer (something) as a sacrifice **2** to give up or lose, esp. for some good purpose

sacrilege *n* the act of treating a holy place or thing without respect **- -legious** *adj* **- -legiously** *adv*

sad *adj* **-dd- 1** feeling, showing, or causing grief or sorrow; unhappy **2 sadder but wiser** *esp. spoken* having learned from unpleasant experience **3 sad to say** (usu. at the beginning of a sentence) unfortunately **-~ly** *adv* **-~ness** *n*

sadden *v* to make or become sad

¹saddle *n* **1** a usu. leather seat that fits on the back of an animal for a rider to sit on **2** the part of an animal's back where this is placed **3** a piece of meat from the back of a deer or sheep just in front of the back legs **4** a seat on a bicycle, motorcycle, etc. **5 in the saddle a** sitting on a saddle on an animal **b** *esp. spoken* in control

²saddle *v* **-dled, -dling 1** to put a saddle on (an animal) **2** to give (someone) an unpleasant duty, responsibility, etc.: *He's saddled with a large house which he can't sell*

sadism *n* **1** unnatural fondness for causing pain **2** *technical* the unnatural idea or action of getting sexual pleasure from causing pain **–sadist** *n* **–sadistic** *adj* **–sadistically** *adv*

safari *n* a trip through wild country, esp. in Africa

¹safe *adj* **1** out of danger; not able to be hurt; protected **2** not hurt; unharmed: *came through the storm* **safe and sound 3** not allowing danger or harm: *a safe place to swim* **4** not likely to cause risk or disagreement: *It's safe to say that the Queen is popular* **5** (of a seat in Parliament) certain to be won in an election by a particular party **6 as safe as houses** *esp. spoken* very safe from risk **7 on the safe side** taking no risks at all **8 play it safe** *esp.*

spoken to take no risks **–~ly** *adv* **–~ness** *n*

²safe *n* a box or cupboard with thick metal sides and a lock, used to protect valuables

safety *n* **-ties 1** freedom from danger, harm, or risk **2** also **safety catch–** a lock on a weapon to keep it from firing accidentally

sag *v* **-gg-** to sink, settle, or bend downwards, esp. from the usual or correct position: *The branch sagged under his weight. / My spirits sagged when I heard the score* **–sag** *n*

said *past tense and past part. of* SAY

¹sail *n* **1** a piece of cloth fixed on a ship to move it through the water by the force of the wind: *a ship* **in full sail** (=with all its sails spread) **2** a short trip in such a ship **3** any of the broad blades of a windmill **4 set sail** to begin a trip or a new course at sea **5 take the wind out of someone's sails** *esp. spoken* to take away someone's pride or advantage by actions of one's own

²sail *v* **1 a** (of any ship) to travel on water **b** to direct (any ship) on water **2** to travel by water (across) **3** to make short trips as a sport in a sailing boat: *to* **go sailing 4** to move proudly, smoothly, or easily: *sailed easily through the exam*

sailor *n* a person with a job on a ship

saint *n* **1** a person recognized after death by the Christian church as specially holy **2** a person with a holy or completely unselfish way of life −~**ly** *adj*: *a saintly life* −~**liness** *n*

sake *n* **1 for the sake of a** for the good or advantage of: *If you won't do it for your own sake* (=to help yourself), *then do it for my sake* (=to please me) **b** for the purpose of: *Art for art's sake* **2 for God's/ Christ's/goodness/pity's** sake *esp.spoken* (used for giving force to a request, or to express annoyance)

salad *n* **1** a mixture of foods, usu. mainly vegetables, served cold **2** a plant used for such a dish

salary *n* **-ries** fixed regular pay, usu. by the month or year, esp. as for workers of higher rank

sale *n* **1** an act of selling; agreement exchanging something for money **2** a special offering of goods at lower prices than usual **3** the total amount sold of something offered to be bought: *a large sale* **4 for sale** offered to be bought **5 on sale** available to be bought

salesman −*fem.* **saleswoman** *n* **-men 1** also (*esp. written*) **sales representative** − a man who sells a company's goods to businesses, homes, etc. **2** a usu. skilled shop assistant

saliva *n* the natural watery liquid in the mouth − **-vary** *adj*: *salivary glands*

salmon *n* **−on** *or* **−ons 1** a type of large fish of the northern seas with silvery skin and yellowish-pink flesh, which swims up rivers to lay its eggs **2** the flesh of this fish **3** a yellowish-pink colour like that of this flesh

saloon *n* **1** a room for the social use of a ship's passengers **2** also **saloon car**− a car with a roof, closed sides, with windows, and a separate boot **3** (typically in a town in the American wild west) a large public drinking place

¹**salt** *n* **1** a very common colourless or white solid substance (sodium chloride) used to preserve food, improve its taste, etc. **2** any of a class of chemical substances which may be formed by combining an acid and a base **3** pleasant excitement or interest: *Sports give salt to life* **4** *esp. spoken* experienced sailor: *He's* **an old salt 5 rub salt in someone's wounds** to make someone's sorrow, pain, etc., even worse **6 take with a grain/pinch of salt** *esp. spoken* to be cautious in believing (what is said) **7 the salt of the earth** *pompous* a person or people regarded as admirable **8 worth one's salt** *esp. spoken* worthy of respect, or of one's pay

²**salt** *v* **1** to add salt to; put salt on **2** to preserve with salt **3** to add interest or excitement to: *a lecture salted with jokes*

³**salt** *adj* of, containing, or tasting of salt −~**ness** *n*

salty *adj* **-ier, -iest 1** of or containing salt **2** (of talk, stories, etc.) slightly improper in an amusing or exciting way −**saltiness** *n*

¹**salute** *v* **saluted, saluting 1** to make

a salute (to) **2** *esp. written* to greet, esp. with polite words or with a sign **3** *esp. written* to honour formally: *a dinner to salute the president on his birthday*

²**salute** *n* **1** any of several military signs of recognition, such as **a** a raising of the right hand to the forehead **b** a ceremonial firing of guns or lowering of flags **2** a sign or ceremony expressing good feelings or respect **3 take the salute** (of a person of high rank) to stand while being saluted by soldiers marching past

¹**salvage** *n* **1** the act of saving from destruction **2** property saved from being destroyed

²**salvage** *v* **-vaged, -vaging** to save from loss or damage by wrecking, fire, etc.

salvation *n* **1** (esp. in the Christian religion) the saving or state of being saved from the power of evil **2** saving or preservation from loss, ruin, or failure **3** something that saves; a cause or means of saving

¹**same** *adj* **1** being (always) only one single thing, person, etc.: *Father sits in the same chair every evening* **2 a** being the particular one, or one already mentioned: *You've made the same mistakes as last time* **b** like something else in every way; alike in almost every way; not different or changed: **3 amount/come to the same thing** to have the same result or meaning **4 one and the same** exactly the same

²**same** *pron* the same thing, person, etc.: *He ordered apple pie and I had the same*

³**same** *adv* **the same** in the same way

¹**sample** *n* **1** a small part representing the whole; typical small quantity, thing, event, etc. **2** a small trial amount of a product, often given away free

²**sample** *v* **-pled, -pling 1** to examine a sample of: *sampled the wine* **2** to calculate by taking a sample from

¹**sanction** *n* **1** permission, approval, or acceptance **2** an action, such as the stopping of trade, taken by one or more countries against another country **3** a formal action or punishment which is ordered when a law or rule is broken **4** something that forces the keeping of a rule or standard: *societies where shame is the only sanction against wrongdoing*

²**sanction** *v* to accept, approve, or permit

sanctuary *n* **-ries 1** the part of a religious building considered most holy, as in a Christian church the area in front of the altar **2 a** protection from harm **b** a place of safety **3** an area where birds or animals are protected from hunters and animal enemies

¹**sand** *n* loose material of very small fine grains, found along seacoasts and in deserts

²**sand** *v* **1** to make smoother by rubbing with a rough surface, esp. a paper with a covering of sand on

one side (sandpaper) **2** to put sand on, esp. to prevent slipping

sandal *n* a light shoe made of a usu. flat bottom and bands to hold it on the foot

¹sandwich *n* **1** 2 slices of bread with some other food between them **2** also **sandwich cake–** a cake of 2 flat parts with jam and cream between them

²sandwich *v* to put tightly in between 2 things of a different kind

sandy *adj* **-ier, -iest 1** containing or full of sand **2** (esp. of hair) yellowish-brown in colour, like sand **–sandiness** *n*

sane *adj* **1** not mad **2** produced by good reasonable thinking **–~ly** *adv* **– -nity** *n*

sang *past tense of* SING

sank *past tense of* SINK

¹sap *n* the watery juice carrying food, chemical products, etc., through a plant

²sap *v* **-pp-** to weaken or destroy, esp. during a long time

sarcasm *n* speaking or writing which tries to hurt someone's feelings, esp. by expressions which clearly mean the opposite to what is felt **– -castic** *adj* **– -castically** *adv*

¹sash *n* a beltlike length of cloth worn around the waist, or (in ceremonial dress and usu. as a mark of some honour) over one shoulder

²sash *n* a frame holding the glass of a window, door, etc.

sat *past tense and past part. of* SIT

satellite *n* **1** a heavenly body moving around a planet **2** a man-made object intended to move around the earth, moon, etc. **3** something, esp. a country, that is in, and depends on, the power or influence of another

satin *n, adj* (made of) a kind of fine smooth cloth mainly of silk, shiny on one side

satire *n* (a work of) literature, theatre, speaking, etc., intended to show the foolishness or evil of some establishment or practice in an amusing way

satirical –also **satiric** *adj* fond of, being, using, etc., satire **– ~ly** *adv*

satisfaction *n* **1** contentment **2** something that pleases **3** *esp. written* fulfilment of a need, desire, etc. **4** *esp. written* condition of being fully persuaded; certainty

satisfactory *adj* good enough to be pleasing, or for a purpose, rule, standard, etc. **– -rily** *adv*

satisfy *v* **-fied, -fying 1** to make happy; please **2** to be or give enough for; fulfil **3** to persuade fully: *Are you satisfied that I am telling the truth?* **– ~ing** *adj: a satisfying meal*

saturate *v* **-rated, -rating 1** to put as much liquid as possible into **2** to fill completely so that no more can be held **3** *technical* to put into (a chemical solution) as much of the solid substance as possible

Saturday *n* **-days** the 7th day of the week

sauce *n* **1** any of various kinds of usu.

cooked liquids put on or eaten with food **2** cheeky disrespectful talk

saucepan *n* a deep usu. round metal cooking pot with a handle and usu. a lid

saucer *n* a small plate made for setting a cup on

sausage *n* **1** a thin eatable tube of animal skin filled with a mixture of meat, cereal, spices, etc. **2** this meat mixture

¹**savage** *adj* **1** forcefully cruel or violent; uncontrollable; fierce **2** (typical) of an uncivilized place or people **3** *esp. spoken* very angry –~**ly** *adv* –~**ness,** ~**ry** *n*

²**savage** *n* **1** a member of an uncivilized tribe or group **2** a cruel, violent, or wild person

³**savage** *v* **-aged, -aging** (esp. of an animal) to attack and bite fiercely

¹**save** *v* **saved, saving 1** to make safe from danger **2** to keep and add to an amount of money for later use **3** to keep and not spend or use **4** to make unnecessary **5** (in Christianity and some other religions) to free (a person) from the power and effect of evil –~**r** *n*

²**save** *n* (in football) an action by the goalkeeper which prevents a goal

³**save** –also **saving** *prep literature* except: *answered all the questions save one*

savings *n* money saved

saviour *n* a person or thing that saves from danger or loss

¹**saw** *n* a tool for cutting materials, having a thin flat blade with a row of V-shaped teeth on the edge

²**saw** *v* **sawed, sawn** *or* **sawed, sawing 1** to cut with or as if with a saw **2** (of a material) to be able to be cut by a saw

³**saw** *past tense of* SEE

¹**say** *v* **said, saying 1** to pronounce (a sound, word, etc.) **2** to express (a thought, intention, opinion, question, etc.) in words **3** to show: *What time does your watch say?* **4** to suppose: *Let's say your plan fails: then what?* **5** to direct or instruct someone: *She says to meet her at 10* **6 it goes without saying** of course; clearly **7 say for oneself/something** to offer as an excuse or as something in favour or defence: *You're late again! What have you got to say for yourself?* **8 that is to say** also (*abbrev.*) **i.e.–** in other words: *working as hard as before, that is to say not very hard* **9 they say** people say **10 what do you say?** you'll agree, won't you?

²**say** *n* **1** a power or right of acting or deciding: *I've got no say in where we go* **2 have/say one's say** to have/ use the chance to express one's opinion

³**say** *interj US* (used for expressing surprise or a sudden idea): *Say, haven't I seen you before?*

saying *n* a well-known wise statement

scab *n* a hard mass of dried blood which forms over a wound while it is healing –~**by** *adj*

scaffold *n* **1** a framework built up from

poles and boards, as for workmen to stand on **2** a board for a workman to stand on when working high up **3** a raised stage for the execution of criminals

scaffolding *n* poles and boards used for building scaffolds

¹**scald** *v* **1** to burn with hot liquid **2** to clean or treat with boiling water or steam

²**scald** *n* a skin burn from hot liquid or steam

¹**scale** *n* **1** a pair of pans for weighing an object by comparing it with a known weight **2** any weighing machine **3** **turn/tip the scales** to be the fact, action, etc., that decides a result in favour of one thing or the other **4** **tip the scales at** to weigh

²**scale** *n* **1** one of the small nearly flat stiff pieces forming the outer body covering (or part of it) of some animals, esp. fish and reptiles **2** material like this covering a surface, as greyish material forming around the inside of a kettle, water pipes, etc. **3** (a small piece of) dry skin which comes away from the healthy skin below, as in some diseases **4** **the scales fell from my eyes** *esp. literature* I was suddenly able to see what had always been clear

³**scale** *v* **scaled, scaling 1** to remove from or come off a surface in thin small pieces **2** to cover with scale

⁴**scale** *n* **1** a set of numbers or standards for measuring or comparing: *wind forces measured on a standard scale of 0–12* **2 a** a set of marks,

esp. numbers, on an instrument at exactly fixed distances apart **b** a piece of wood, plastic, etc., with such marks on the edge **3** a rule or set of numbers comparing measurements on a map or model with actual measurements **4** size, esp. in relation to other things or to what is usual: *on a large/grand scale* **5** a set of musical notes in upward and downward order and at fixed separations **6** **to scale** according to a fixed rule for reducing the size of something in a drawing, model, etc.

⁵**scale** *v* **1** to climb up **2** to increase or reduce, esp. by a fixed rate: **scale up/down taxes**

¹**scalp** *n* the skin on the top of the human head

²**scalp** *v* to cut off the scalp of (a dead enemy) as a mark of victory as done in former times by American Indians

scamper *v* to run quickly

scan *v* **-nn- 1** to examine closely **2** to look at quickly without careful reading **3 a** to examine (a poem) to show the pattern of music-like beats in each line **b** (of a poem) to have a regular pattern of this kind **4** (of a beam of electrons) to be directed to (a surface) so as to cover with lines which are close together (as in the making of a television picture) **−scan** *n*

scandal *n* **1** a state or action which offends people's ideas of what is right and proper **2** a public feeling or action caused by such behaviour **3** true or false talk which brings harm, shame, or disrespect to another

scandalous *adj* offensive to feelings of what is right or proper − ~**ly** *adv*

scanty *adj* **-ier, -iest** hardly enough; almost too small, few, etc. − **-tily** *adv* − **-tiness** *n*

scapegoat *n* a person or thing taking the blame for others

¹**scar** *n* **1** a mark remaining on the skin or an organ from a wound, cut, etc. **2** a mark of damage like this on objects

²**scar** *v* **-rr-** to mark or be marked with a scar

scarce *adj* **1** not much or many compared with what is wanted; hard to find **2** **make oneself scarce** *esp. spoken* to go away

scarcely *adv* **1** hardly; almost not; barely **2** (almost) certainly not: *You could scarcely have found a better person*

¹**scare** *v* **scared, scaring 1 a** to cause sudden fear to **b** to become fearful **2** to drive, cause to go or become, etc., by fear: *His gun scared off the thief* − ~**d** *adj*

²**scare** *n* a sudden feeling of fear

scarf *n* **scarfs** *or* **scarves** a piece of cloth for wearing around the neck, head, or shoulders

scarlet *adj, n* (of) a very bright red colour

scatter *v* **1 a** to cause (a group) to separate widely **b** (of a group) to do this **2** to spread widely in all directions by or as if by throwing: *scatter seed*

scene *n* **1 a** (in a play) any of the divisions during which there is no change of place **b** (in a film, broadcast, etc.) a single piece of action in one place **2** the background for the action of a play **3** a view of a place: *a beautiful scene* **4** a place where an event happens: *the scene of the crime* **5** an event or course of action regarded as like something in a play or film: *angry scenes in Parliament* **6** a show of anger or feelings, esp. between 2 people in public **7** *esp. spoken* an area of activity: *What's new on the film scene?* **8 behind the scenes** out of sight; secretly **9 on the scene** present; appearing: *came on the scene just when we needed him* **10 set the scene** to prepare; make ready **11 steal the scene** to take attention away from who or what ought to be most important

scenery *n* **1** the set of painted backgrounds and other articles used on a theatre stage **2** natural surroundings, esp. in the country

¹**scent** *v* **1** (esp. of animals) to smell, esp. to tell the presence of by smelling **2** to get a feeling or belief of the presence or fact of: *She scented that all was not well* **3** to fill with a scent

²**scent** *n* **1** a smell, esp. **a** as left by an animal and followed by hunting dogs **b** a particular usu. pleasant smell: *the scent of roses* **2** a way to

the discovering: *a scientist* **on the scent** *of a discovery* **3** (of animals) a power of smelling **4** a feeling of the presence (of something): *a scent of danger* **5** a perfume −~**less** *adj*

sceptical *adj* unwilling to believe a claim or promise −~**ly** *adv*

¹**schedule** *n* **1** a timetable of things to be done **2** a formal list: *a schedule of postal charges* **3 ahead of/on/behind schedule** before/at/after the planned or expected time

²**schedule** *v* **-uled, -uling** **1** to plan for a certain future time **2** to put (a flight, train, etc.) into a timetable; make a regular service

¹**scheme** *n* **1** a clever dishonest plan **2** an official or business plan **3** a general arrangement

²**scheme** *v* **schemed, scheming** to make clever dishonest plans −**schemer** *n*

scholar *n* **1** a person with great knowledge of a subject **2** *old use* a child at school

¹**school** *n* **1** a place of education for children **2 a** attendance or study at such a place **b** one session at such a place: *School begins at 8:30* **3** a university department concerned with a particular subject **4** a group of people with the same methods, opinions, (of artists) style, etc.: *Rembrandt and his school*

²**school** *v* to train

³**school** *n* a large group of one kind of fish, whale, etc.

science *n* **1** (the study of) knowledge which can be made into a system and which usu. depends on seeing and testing facts and stating general natural laws **2** a branch of such knowledge, esp. **a** anything which may be studied exactly: *the science of cooking / military science* engineering (**the sciences**) −**scientist** *n*

scientific *adj* **1** of, being, or concerning science or its principles or rules **2** needing or showing exact knowledge, skill, or use of a system −~**ally** *adv*

scissors *n* **2** sharp blades having handles at one end with holes for the fingers, fastened at the centre so that they open in the shape of the letter X and cut when they close: *a pair of scissors*

¹**scoff** *v* to speak or act disrespectfully; laugh at −~**er** *n*

²**scoff** *v esp. spoken* to eat eagerly and fast

¹**scold** *n* a person, typically a woman, who scolds

²**scold** *v* to speak angrily, esp. to blame −~**ing** *n*

¹**scoop** *n* **1 a** a small deep shovel-shaped or spoonlike tool held in the hand for digging out corn, flour, soft food, etc. **b** a container for loose things weighed on scales **c** the bucket on an earth-moving machine **d** also **scoopful** − the amount held by any of these **2** an action of taking with or as if with one of these **3** a usu. exciting news report made by a newspaper before any other newspapers

²**scoop** *v* to take up or out, with or as

if with a scoop: *scoop up a handful of sand*

scope *n* **1** the area within the limits of a question, subject, action, etc. **2** space or chance for action or thought

¹**scorch** *v* **1 a** to burn a surface or part of it so as to change its colour, taste, or feeling but not completely destroy it **b** (of such a surface) to burn in this way **2** to dry up (plants): *fields scorched by the sun*

²**scorch** *n* a scorched place; mark made by burning on a surface

¹**score** *n* **1** the number of points, runs, goals, etc., made by opponents in a game, sport, etc. **2** one of these points **3** a total of points won esp. in an examination **4** also **score mark –** a line made or cut on a surface with a sharp instrument **5** a reason; account (esp. in the phrases **on this/that score, on the score of**): *It's not the colour I wanted but it's no less pretty on that score* **6** an old disagreement or hurt kept in mind: *a score to settle* **7 a** written copy of a piece of music, esp. for a large group of performers **b** music for a film or play **8 know the score** *esp. spoken* to understand the true and usu. unfavourable facts of a matter

²**score** *v* **scored, scoring 1** to gain (one or more points, goals, etc.) in a sport, game, or competition **2** to give (a certain number of points) to in a sport, game, or competition **3** to keep an official record of the score of a sports match as it is played **4** to win (a total of points) in an examination **5** to gain or win (a success, victory, prize, etc.) **6** to make (a clever and successful point), esp. in an argument against someone **7** to mark or cut 1 or more lines with something sharp

³**score** *adj, n* **score** *or* **scores 1** 20 **2 scores (of)** large numbers (of)

¹**scorn** *n* **1** strong, usu. angry feeling of disrespect; contempt **2** an object of such a feeling **3 laugh someone/ something to scorn** also **pour scorn on–** to express scorn for; treat with scorn –~**ful** *adj* –~**fully** *adv*

²**scorn** *v usu. literature* **1** to refuse because of pride **2** to feel scorn for

scorpion *n* any of several types of tropical insect having a long body and curving tail which stings poisonously

¹**scourge** *n* a cause of great punishment, harm, or suffering: *the scourge of war*

²**scourge** *v* **scourged, scourging 1** to beat with a whip **2** to cause great harm or suffering to

¹**scout** *v* **1** to go looking for something: *Scout around for a meal* **2** to go through or look carefully at (a place) to get information about it

²**scout** *n* **1** a soldier sent out to search the land ahead of an army, esp. for information about the enemy **2** a person who gets information for a sports team about players who should be hired **3** also **boy scout–** a member of an association (the

451

(boy) **scouts**) for training boys in character and initiative **4** a servant at Oxford University who looks after students living in college rooms **5** an act of scouting: *took a scout round*

scowl *v* to make an angry threatening frown –

¹**scramble** *v* **-bled, -bling 1** to move or climb quickly, esp. over a rough or steep surface **2** to struggle or compete with others or against difficulty: *scrambling out of the way* **3** to mix together without order **4** to mix the white and yellow parts of (1 or more eggs) together while cooking them **5** to change the signals in (a radio or telephone message) with a machine (a **scrambler**) so that it can be understood only on a special receiver

²**scramble** *n* **1** an act of moving or climbing, esp. over a rough surface **2** an eager and disorderly struggle **3** a motorcycle race over rough ground

¹**scrap** *n* **1** a small piece: *a scrap of paper* **2** material which cannot be used for its original purpose but which may have some value

²**scrap** *v* **-pp- 1** to get rid of as no longer useful or wanted **2** to make into scrap

³**scrap** *v* **-pp-** *esp. spoken* to quarrel or fight **–scrap** *n*

¹**scrape** *v* **scraped, scraping 1-** to remove (material) from a surface by moving an edge firmly across it repeatedly **2** to clean or make

smooth in this way **3** to rub roughly **4** to hurt or damage in this way: *He scraped his knee when he fell* **5** to make in this way: *She scraped a hollow in the ground* **6 a** to live with no more than the necessary money **b** to succeed by doing work of the lowest acceptable quality **7 scrape the bottom of the barrel** *esp. spoken* to take, use, suggest, etc., something of the lowest quality

²**scrape** *n* **1** an act or sound of scraping **2** a hurt made by scraping **3** *esp. spoken* an unpleasant position or affair, esp. caused by one's breaking a rule

¹**scratch** *v* **1** to rub and tear or mark with something pointed or rough **2** to make a sound or movement as if doing this **3** to remove in this way: *scratched the paint off the wall* **4** to hurt in this way: *scratched her elbow on a nail* **5** to write or make in this way: *scratched his name on the tree with a knife* **6** to rub lightly, as to stop itching **7** to remove (oneself, a horse, etc.) from a race or competition before it starts **8 scratch the surface** to deal with only the beginning of a matter or only a few of many cases

²**scratch** *n* **1** a mark or injury made by scratching **2** a sound made by or as if made by scratching **3** an act of scratching **4** a golf handicap of 0 **5** something put together in a hurry: *a scratch cricket team* **6 from scratch** *esp. spoken* starting from zero or with nothing **7 up**

to **scratch** *esp. spoken* up to an acceptable standard **8 without a scratch** *esp. spoken* completely unhurt

scrawl *v* to write in a careless, irregular, or unskilful way −**scrawl** *n*

¹**scream** *v* **1** to cry out loudly on a high note **2** to say or express in this way: *He screamed out a warning*

²**scream** *n* **1** a sudden loud cry on a high note **2** *sl* a very funny person, thing, joke, etc.: *It was a scream!*

screech *v* **1** to cry out on a very high sharp note **2** (of machines, esp. of tyres and brakes) to make a noise like this −**screech** *n*

¹**screen** *n* **1** any of various kinds of upright covered frames, used for protecting people from cold or heat, or for hiding something from view **2** something that protects, shelters, or hides **3** a large flat surface on which films or slides are shown **4** *esp. pompous* the cinema industry **5** the front surface of an electrical instrument showing information, esp. the surface of a television set on which the picture appears **6** a frame holding a thin wire net, put in a window to keep out insects **7** a frame holding a net or surface with holes, used for separating large things from smaller ones

²**screen** *v* **1** to shelter or protect, as from light, wind, etc. or from view **2** to protect or try to protect from harm or punishment **3** to examine or prove the ability or suitability of (people for a job, requests to be allowed to do something, etc.) **4** to show (a film)

¹**screw** *n* **1** a device like a nail having a thread winding round it which helps to hold it in place **2** an act of turning one of these **3** a propeller **4** *sl* (used by prisoners) a prison guard **5 a** a small twisted piece (of paper) **b** the amount contained by one of these **6 a screw loose** *humour* something wrong or not working properly (esp. in one's mind) **7 put the screws on/to someone** *sl* to force someone to do as one wishes, esp. by threatening

²**screw** *v* **1** to fasten with 1 or more screws **2 a** to turn or tighten (a screw or something that moves in the same way) **b** (of such a thing) to turn or tighten: *The 2 pieces screw together* **3** to twist **a** (a part of the face) **b** (paper or cloth) carelessly or to make a ball **4** to get by forcing or twisting or by great effort or threats **5** *sl* to cheat **6 have one's head screwed on (right)** to be sensible

screwdriver *n* a tool with a narrow blade to fit into the heads of screws for turning them

scribble *v* **-bled, -bling 1** to write (meaningless marks) **2** to write carelessly or in a hurry −**scribble** *n*

script *n* **1** writing done by hand, esp. with the letters of words joined **2** the set of letters used in writing a language: *Arabic script* **3** a written form of a speech, play, or broadcast to be spoken **4** a piece of writing done by a student in an examination, to be read and given a mark by a teacher

¹**scrub** *n* low-growing plants including bushes and short trees growing in poor soil

²**scrub** *v* **-bb- 1** to clean by hard rubbing, as with a stiff brush **2** to remove in this way: *scrubbed the spot out* **3** to remove from consideration or from a list

³**scrub** *n* an act of scrubbing

scrupulous *adj* **1** carefully doing only what is right **2** carefully correct in the smallest detail: *scrupulous care* –~**ly** *adv* –~**ness** *n*

scrutinize, -nise *v* **-nized, -nizing** to examine closely

scrutiny *n* **-nies** a close study; careful and thorough examination

sculptor –(*fem.* **sculptress**) *n* an artist who makes works of sculpture

¹**sculpture** *n* **1** the art of shaping solid figures (as people or things) out of stone, wood, clay, metal, etc. **2** (a piece of) work produced by this art – **-ral** *adj*

²**sculpture** –also **sculpt** *v* **-tured, -turing 1** to make by shaping **2** to make a figure of (a person or thing) in sculpture

scum *n* **1** a filmy covering that typically forms over a pool of still water **2** impure material in a liquid which rises and floats on the surface **3** *offensive* worthless evil people –~**my** *adj*

sea *n* **1** the great body of salty water that covers much of the earth's surface **2** a large body of water smaller than an ocean, as **a** part of the ocean: *the North Sea* **b** a body of water almost or wholly enclosed by land: *the Dead Sea* **3** a large mass or quantity regarded as being like one of these: *a sea of faces* **4** the seaside (often in names of towns in the phrase **-on-sea**) **5** movement of waves: *heavy seas* **6** any of a number of broad plains on the moon: *the Sea of Tranquillity* **7** **at sea a** during a ship's voyage on the sea **b** *esp. spoken* bewildered: *I'm all at sea when people talk about the government* **8** **by sea** on a ship or using ships

seafood *n* fish and fishlike animals (esp. shellfish) as food

¹**seal** *n* **seals** *or* **seal** any of several types of large fish-eating animals having broad flat limbs (flippers) for swimming

²**seal** *n* **1 a** an official often round pattern as of a government, university, company, or (esp. in former times) a powerful person **b** a piece of wax or soft metal into which such a pattern is pressed and which is fixed to some official writings **c** such a pattern pressed into a piece of writing on paper **2** a metal tool with such a pattern for pressing it into paper or hot metal or wax **3** a small piece of paper, wax, etc. which is fixed across an opening, and which must be broken in order

to open it **4 a** a part of a machine for keeping a gas or liquid in or out **b** a tight connection allowing no liquid or gas to escape **5** a mark or sign **6 set the seal on** *literature* to bring to an end in a suitable way

³**seal** *v* **1** to make or fix a seal onto **2** to fasten or close with or as if with a seal or a tight cover or band **3** to settle; make certain, formal, or solemn: *sealed their agreement*

¹**seam** *n* **1** a line of stitches joining 2 pieces of cloth, leather, etc., at or near their edges **2** the crack, line, or raised mark where 2 edges meet **3** a narrow band of one kind of mineral, esp. coal, between masses of other rocks – **~less** *adj*

²**seam** *v* **1** to mark with lines like seams **2** to sew 1 or more seams in

seaman *n* **-men 1** a member of the navy with any of the lowest group of ranks (below Petty Officer) **2** a man skilled in handling ships at sea

¹**search** *v* **1** to look at, through, into, etc., or examine carefully and thoroughly to try to find something **2 search me!** *esp. spoken* I don't know! – **~er** *n*

²**search** *n* an act of searching

searching *adj* sharp and thorough: *a searching look* – **~ly** *adv*

seashore *n* land along the edge of the sea

seaside *n* the edge of the sea, esp. as a holiday place

¹**season** *n* **1** a period of time each year, as **a** spring, summer, autumn, or winter **b** marked by weather: *the cold season* **c** for a particular activity: *the planting season* **2 for a season** *literature* for a short time **3 in season a** (of fresh foods) at the time of usual fitness for eating **b** (esp. of holiday business) at the busiest time of year: **c** (of certain female animals) on heat **d** (of animals) permitted to be hunted at the time

²**season** *v* **1** to give special taste to (a food) by adding salt, pepper, a spice, etc. **2 a** to make (wood) fit for use by gradual drying **b** (of wood) to become fit for use **3** to give long experience to: *a seasoned traveller*

¹**seat** *n* **1** a place for sitting **2** the part on which one sits **3** a place of a particular power or activity; centre **4** a place as a member of an official body: *a seat in Parliament* **5** *technical* a way of sitting on a horse **6 take/have a seat** please sit down **7 in the driver's seat** *esp. spoken* in charge **8 take a back seat** *esp. spoken* to allow someone else to take control or have the more important job

²**seat** *v* **1** to cause or help to sit **2** (of a room, table, etc.) to have room for seats for (a certain number of people)

seaweed *n* any of various plants growing in the sea

secluded *adj* very quiet and private: *a secluded house* – **-usion** *n*

¹**second** *adj, adv, n, pron* **1** 2nd **2**

a person who helps another, esp. someone who is fighting in a match **3** an article of imperfect quality for sale at a lower price **4** a formal act of seconding a motion **5** a British university examination result of middle quality **6 second to none** *esp. spoken* the best

²**second** *n* **1** a length of time equal to 1/60 of a minute **2** a measure of an angle equal to 1/3600 of a degree **3** a moment

³**second** *v* **1** to make a second person's statement in favour of (a motion at a meeting) **2** to support in an argument, decision, or effort – ~**er** *n*

⁴**second** *v* to move (someone) from usual duties to a special duty – ~**ment** *n*

secondary *adj* **1** of 2nd, or less than 1st, rank, value, importance, etc. **2** later than, developing from, taken from, etc., something earlier or original **3** (of education or a school) for children over 11 years old **4** *technical* carrying or being an electric current caused by another electric current – -**arily** *adv*

second-hand *adj, adv* **1** used or worn by an earlier owner; not new **2** from somewhere other than the original place or person

secrecy *n* **1** the practice of keeping secrets **2** the state of being secret

¹**secret** *adj* **1** kept from the knowledge of others, or of all except a few **2** (of a person) undeclared; unad-mitted: *a secret admirer* **3** secretive – ~**ly** *adv*

²**secret** *n* **1** something known to only a few **2** something (so far) unexplained: *the secret of life* **3** a single or most important means of gaining a good result: *the secret of success*

secretary *n* **-ries** **1** a person with the job of preparing letters, keeping records, arranging meetings, etc., for another **2** any of various government officers, as a minister, or the highest nonelected officer in a department **3** an officer of an organization who keeps records, writes official letters, etc. – -**rial** *adj*

secretive *adj* hiding one's intentions or plans – ~**ly adv** – ~**ness** *n*

¹**section** *n* **1** a part of a larger object, place, etc., that is, or is regarded as, more or less separate **2** any of the equal parts of some fruits, such as an orange **3** a representation of something as if it were cut from top to bottom and looked at from the side **4** (in mathematics) the figure formed by the points where a solid body is cut by a plane **5** a very thin flat piece cut from skin, plant growth, etc., to be looked at under a microscope

²**section** *v* **1** to cut or divide into sections **2** to cut or show a section from

¹**secure** *adj* **1** safe; protected against danger or risk **2** sure; certain: *a secure job* – ~**ly** *adv*

²**secure** *v* **secured, securing** **1** *esp. written* to get, esp. as the result of

effort: *to secure a place in the team* **2** to make safe **3** to hold or close tightly: *They secured the windows when the storm began*

security *n* **-ties 1** the state of being secure **2** something which protects or makes secure **3** property of value promised to a lender in case repayment is not made or other conditions are not met **4** protection against lawbreaking, violence, enemy acts, etc. **5** a writing giving the owner the right to some property: *government securities*

seduce *v* **seduced, seducing 1** to persuade (esp. someone inexperienced) to have sex **2** to cause or persuade (someone) to do something more or less wrong by making it seem attractive **−seducer** *n*

seductive *adj* having qualities likely to seduce; attractive: *a seductive voice* **−~ly** *adv* **−~ness** *n*

¹**see** *v* **saw, seen, seeing 1** to use the eyes; have or use the power of sight **2** to look at; get sight of; notice, examine, or recognize by looking: *Can you see that? / Let me see your ticket* **3** to understand or recognize: *Do you see what I mean?* **4** to find out or try to find out or determine: *I'll see what I can do* **5** to make sure; take care: *See that you're ready* **6** to form a picture in the mind of: *I can't see myself lending her money* **7** *literature* to be an occasion of (an event or course in history): *The 19th century saw many changes* **8** to have experience of: *This old house has* **seen better days 9** to visit, call upon, or meet: *The doctor can't see you yet* **10** to go with: *to see her home* **11** (in the game of poker) to answer (an opponent) by risking an equal amount of money **12 see the back/last of** *esp. spoken* to be through with; have no more to do with **13 see things** to think that one sees something that is not there

²**see** *n* the office of, area governed by, or centre of government of a bishop

see about *v prep* **1** to attend to; make arrangements for: *to see about dinner* **2 We'll see about that!** *esp. spoken* I will put a stop to that!

¹**seed** *n* **1** the part of a plant from which a new plant can grow **2** something that starts growth or development:*seeds of trouble* **3** a seeded player **4** kept for planting or producing seeds **5 go/run to seed a** (of a plant) to produce seed **b** (of a person) to lose one's power of freshness **6** *in seed* (of a plant) in the condition of bearing seeds **−~less** *adj*

²**seed** *v* **1** to grow and produce seed **2** to plant seeds in (a piece of ground) **3** to place (a sports, esp. tennis, player at the start of a competition) in order of likelihood to win

seek *v* **sought, seeking 1** *usu. written or literature* to make a search for; look for; try to find or get **2** to ask for: *to seek advice* **3** *esp. literature* to try: *They sought to punish him* **4**

to move naturally to: *Water seeks its own level* **5 not far to seek** easily seen or understood – ~**er** *n*

seem *v* **1** to give the idea or effect of being; be in appearance; appear **2** to appear to be true

seemingly *adv* **1** as far as one can tell: *Seemingly there is nothing we can do* **2** according to what appears, usu. opposed to what actually is so

seen *past part. of* SEE

see over *v adv* **1** to examine: *to see over a report* **2** also **see round**– to visit and examine: *to see over the house*

¹seesaw *n* (play on) a board for children to sit on at opposite ends, balanced so that when one end goes up the other goes down

²seesaw *v* **1** to move backwards and forwards, up and down, or between opponents or opposite sides **2** to play on a seesaw

see through *v prep* **1** to recognize the truth about (an excuse, false statement, etc.) **2** to provide for or support throughout (a time or difficulty)

see to *v prep* to attend to

segment *n* **1** any of the parts into which something may be cut or divided **2** the region inside a circle between its edge and a straight line across it; a region bounded by part of a circle and a chord

seize *v* **seized, seizing 1** to take possession of **a** by official order **b** by force: *The army seized the fort* **2** to take hold of eagerly, quickly, or forcefully; grab **3** to attack or take control of (someone's body or mind): *He was seized with pain*

seldom *adv* not often; rarely

¹select *adj* **1** chosen, or choosing, from a larger group **2** carefully chosen by quality; limited and exclusive: *a select group*

²select *v* to choose as best, most suitable, etc., from a group – ~**or** *n*

selection *n* **1** the act of selecting **2** one that is selected **3** a collection of things of a kind: *a selection of cheeses*

selective *adj* **1** acting with, or concerning, only certain articles; not general: *selective controls on goods* **2** careful in choosing – ~**ly** *adv* – ~**ness** *n* – -**tivity** *n*

self *n* **selves 1** a person with his whole nature, character, etc.: *He put his whole self into the job* **2** a particular part of one's nature **3** one's own advantage or profit **4** (written; esp. in business matters) the person concerned; the signer

self-confidence *n* a feeling of power to do things successfully – -**dent** *adj*

self-control *n* control over one's feelings – -**trolled** *adj*

self-defence *n* the act or skill of defending oneself

self-employed *adj* running one's own business; not working for another

self-government –also **self-rule** *n* government free from outside control; independence –**self-governing** *adj*

selfish *adj* concerned with or directed towards one's own advantage without care for others −∼**ly** *adv* −∼**ness** *n*

selfless *adj* caring only for others; completely unselfish −∼**ly** *adv* −∼**ness** *n*

self-respect *n* proper respect for, or pride in, oneself

self-service *adj, n* (working by) the system in many restaurants, shops, petrol stations, etc., in which buyers collect what they want and then pay at special desks

sell *v* **sold, selling 1** to give to another for money or other value **2** to cause to be bought: *Bad news sells newspapers* **3** to offer (goods) for sale **4** to be bought; get a buyer or buyers **5** *sl* to persuade (someone) to like, believe, or agree to something **6** *sl* trick; cheat: *The things we bought are no good: we've been sold!* **7 sell oneself a** to make oneself or one's ideas attractive to others **b** to give up one's principles for gain **8 sell short** to sell something, esp. shares in a company, not yet owned but expected to be bought later at a lower price **9 sell something/ someone short** to value something or someone too low

seller *n* **1** a person who sells **2** a product that sells well

¹sellotape *n trademark* sticky thin clear plastic material in long narrow lengths sold in rolls, for sticking paper, mending light objects, etc.

²sellotape *v* **-taped, -taping** *trademark* to put together or mend with sellotape

semicircle *n* **1** half a circle **2** a group arranged in this shape: *to sit in a semicircle* − **-cular** *adj*

semidetached −also (*esp. spoken*) **semi** *n* a house joined to another house by one shared wall −**semidetached** *adj*

semifinal *n* either of a pair of matches whose winners will compete in the final

semitone *n* a difference in pitch equal to that between 2 neighboring notes on a piano

send *v* **sent, sending 1** to cause or order to go or be taken to a place, in a direction, etc. **2** to put or bring into a particular state: *The news sent us into great excitement* **3** to cause a message, request, or order to go out **4** (of a natural object) to produce from itself: *branches sending forth their fruit* **5** literature (esp. of God) to give or provide: *Heaven send us a safe journey!* **6** (of a radio or radio operator) to transmit −∼**er** *n*

senior *adj* **1** older **2** of higher rank or position −**senior** *n* −∼**ity** *n*

sensation *n* **1** a direct feeling, as of heat or pain, from the senses **2** a general feeling in the mind or body **3** a state of excited interest or the cause of it: *The new discovery caused a great sensation*

sensational *adj* **1** *often offensive* causing excited interest or attention

2 (esp. of writing or news reports) intended to cause quick excitement or shock 3 *sl* wonderful; very good – ~**ly** *adv*

¹**sense** *n* 1 a meaning 2 any of the 5 senses 3 power to understand and make judgments about something: *a good business sense* 4 a feeling, esp. one hard to describe exactly 5 good and esp. practical understanding and judgment 6 **in a sense** in one way; partly 7 **make sense a** to have a clear meaning **b** to be a wise course of action 8 **make sense of** to understand 9 **no sense in** *esp. spoken* no good reason for 10 **talk sense** *esp. spoken* to speak reasonably

²**sense** *v* **sensed, sensing** to feel; perceive; detect: *The horse sensed danger and stopped*

senseless *adj* 1 in a sleeplike state, as after a blow on the head; unconscious 2 marked by a lack of meaning or thinking; foolish; purposeless – ~**ly** *adv* – ~**ness** *n*

senses *n* 1 the 5 natural powers (sight, hearing, feeling, tasting, and smelling) which give a living thing information about the outside world 2 one's powers of thinking: *Have you taken leave of/lost your senses?*

sensible *adj* 1 reasonable; having good sense 2 *esp. written* recognizing; aware: *sensible of the trouble he caused* 3 noticeable; that can be sensed 4 sensitive – -**bly** *adv*

sensitive *adj* 1 quick to show or feel the effect of a force 2 (of an apparatus) measuring accurately 3 showing delicate feelings or judgment 4 *sometimes offensive* easily hurt in the feelings, esp. of self-respect; easily offended – ~**ly** *adv* – -**tivity** *n*

sent *past tense and past part. of* SEND

¹**sentence** *n* 1 a punishment for a criminal found guilty: *a heavy/light* (=long/short) *sentence* 2 a group of words that forms a statement, command, exclamation, or question, contains a verb and usu. a subject, and (in writing) begins with a capital letter and ends with one of the marks '.!?' 3 **a life sentence** an order to spend an unlimited amount of time in prison

²**sentence** *v* -**tenced, -tencing** (of a judge or court) to give a punishment to

sentiment *n* 1 a feeling, usu. of a stated kind 2 a tender or fine feeling, as of pity, love, etc: *There's no place for sentiment in business* 3 an expression of a wish or feeling

sentimental *adj* marked by, arising from, or appealing to tender feelings, esp. rather than reasonable or practical ones – ~**ly** *adv* – ~**ism**, ~**ity**, ~**ist** *n*

¹**separate** *v* -**rated, -rating** 1 to set or move apart; make or become disconnected 2 to keep apart; mark a division between: *a wall separating the rooms* 3 to divide up into parts forming the whole 4 **a** to cause (a part of a mixture) to leave a

mixture and form a mass by itself **b** (of a part of a mixture) to do this **5 a** (of a husband and wife) to live apart, esp. by formal? agreement **b** to cause (a husband and wife) to do this

²**separate** *adj* **1** not the same; different **2** not shared with another; individual: *everyone thinking of his own separate interests* **3** apart; not joined – ~**ness** *n* – ~**ly** *adv*

separation *n* **1** a breaking or coming apart **2** a distance apart **3** esp. a person's being or living apart: *his separation from his mother* **4** *law* a formal agreement by a husband and wife to live apart

sepsis *n* **-ses** *medical* a poisoning of part of the body by bacteria, often producing infection there

September *n* the 9th month of the year

septic *adj* **1** infected; marked by sepsis **2** causing, or related to decomposition caused by bacteria

sequel *n* **1** a book, film, etc., which continues the story, or has the same characters, as an earlier one **2** something that follows on, esp. as a result

sequence *n* **1** a group of things arranged in an order, esp. following one another in time **2** the order in which things or esp. events follow one another **3** a part of a story, esp. in a film, about a single subject or action; scene **4** (in mathematics) a set of terms derived according to a rule: *A common number pattern is*

the fibonacci sequence: 1, 1, 2, 3, 5, 8, 13, -----, where each number is the sum of the two before it – -**ntial** *adj* – -**ntially** *adv*

sergeant *n* **1** a noncommissioned officer of upper rank in the army, airforce, or marines, usu. having 3 v-shaped marks on the upper arm of the uniform **2** a police officer with next to the lowest rank, usu. also with such uniform marks

¹**serial** *adj* **1** of, happening, or arranged in, or concerning a series **2** of, being, or concerning a serial – ~**ly** *adv*

²**serial** *n* **1** a story appearing in parts at fixed times **2** *technical* (a book, magazine, etc. printed as one of) a continuing set with a single name and numbered 1, 2, 3, etc.

series *n* **series** **1** a group of related objects, events, etc., coming one after another or in order **2** (in mathematics) the sum of the members of a sequence: *The series* $1+x+x^2+x^3+$ ... **3** an electrical arrangement connected without branches, so that the same current passes through each part: *lamps in series*

serious *adj* **1** solemn; not gay or cheerful; grave **2** not joking or funny; to be considered as sincere **3** not easily or lightly dealt with: *serious damage* **4** of an important kind; needing or having great skill or thought: *a serious artist* – ~**ly** *adv* – ~**ness** *n*

sermon *n* **1** a talk usu. based on a

sentence from the Bible, given in a church service **2** *esp. spoken* a long and solemn warning or piece of advice

servant *n* **1** a person who works for another, esp. in the other's house, as a cook, gardener, maid, etc. **2** a person or thing willing to be used for the service of another:*Politicians are the servants of the people*

¹**serve** *v* **served**, **serving 1** to work or do a useful job for: *Serve your country* **2** to have an office or job, often for a stated period: *served in the army* **3** to provide with something: *a pipeline serving the houses with water* **4** to be good enough for (a purpose or need): *This stone should serve my purpose* **5** to give food to or be food for (people) **6** to attend to (someone buying something) **7** to spend (time) in prison: *served 10 years* **8** (in tennis, volleyball, etc.) to begin play by striking (the ball) to the opponent **9** *law* to deliver (an order to appear in court) to (someone) **10** *technical* (of a male animal) to mate with (a female) **11 serve someone right** *esp. spoken* to be a fair punishment for someone

²**serve** *n* an act or manner of serving, as in tennis

¹**service** *n* **1** work or duty done for someone **2** *esp. written* an act or job done for someone: *the services of a lawyer* **3** *now rare* employment as a servant in someone 's home **4** any of the armed services **5** duty in the army, navy, etc.: *He saw active service in the war* **6** any of several government departments **7** attention to buyers in a shop or esp. to guests in a hotel, restaurant, etc. **8** the dishes, tools, etc., needed to serve a stated food, meal, or number of people **9** a fixed form of public worship; a religious ceremony **10** a useful business or job that usu. does not produce goods: *a good postal service* **11** a/the repair of a machine: *Take your car for regular services* **12** an act or manner of serving, as in tennis: *a fast service* **13** *technical* the act of serving a female animal **14 at your service** *polite* yours to command or use **15 do someone a service** to do something which helps someone **16 of service** of use; helpful

²**service** *v* **-viced**, **-vicing** to repair or put in good condition

session *n* **1 a** a formal meeting of an organization, esp. an official body **b** a time during which such meetings take place: *Parliament will be in session for 3 months* **2** *US & Scots* one of the parts of the year when teaching is given at a university **3** a meeting or period used esp. by a group for a particular purpose: *a dancing session*

¹**set** *v* **set**, **setting 1** to put in a place **2** to put in a stated condition: *Set the bird free* **3** to fix or determine (a rule, time, standard, etc.) **4** to give (a piece of work) for (someone) to do: *He set them to write reports* **5** to put into a position, arrange:

set the clock / He set his jaw and refused **6 a** to put (a broken bone) into position for proper joining **b** (of a broken bone) to become joined in a fixed position **7** to put into action: *He set the machine going* **8 a** to cause (a liquid, paste, etc.) to become solid **b** (of such materials) to become solid **9 a** to fix (a colour) against being changed as by water **b** (of a colour) to become fixed **10** *technical* to put (a bird) onto eggs to hatch them **11** (of a heavenly body) to pass downwards out of sight: *The sun is setting* **12** to arrange type for printing **13 a** to arrange (hair) when wet to give the desired style when dry **b** (of hair) to dry after being arranged in this way **14** (of a plant) to form and develop seed or fruit **15** to give a particular setting to (a story, play, etc.)

²**set** *adj* **1** placed; located **2** determined: *He's set on going* **3** fixed; prescribed **4** given or fixed for study: *set books* **5** (of part of the body, manner, etc.) fixed in position; unmoving: *a set smile* **6** ready; prepared: *Are you set?* **7** (of a restaurant meal) complete and at a fixed price

³**set** *n* **1** a group of naturally connected things: *a set of tools* **2** (in mathematics) a formal object which is a collection of members clearly defined either by a rule or by listing the members: *the set of all numbers greater than 3* **3** a group of people of a similar social type or age group **4 a** position of part of the body, a garment, etc.: *the set of a collar* **5 a** direction, as of movement, opinion, etc.: *The wind had a western set* **6** an electrical apparatus, esp. a radio or television **9** a place, usu. built and provided with furniture, scenery, etc., where a play or film is acted **10** a part of a tennis match including at least 6 games **11** a young plant to be set out **12** an act or result of setting hair **13 make a dead set at a** to combine to attack (someone) **b** to try to gain the favour of (someone of the opposite sex)

setback *n* **1** a going or return to a less good position than before: *She seemed better until her setback* **2** a defeat; reverse

set off *v adv* **1** also **set out**, (*esp. literature*) **set forth**– to begin a journey **2** to cause to explode **3** to cause (sudden activity): *The news set off a rush of activity* **4** to make (something) more noticeable or beautiful by putting it near something different: *Black sets off the jewels*

settee *n* a long seat with a back and usu. arms for more than 1 person

setting *n* **1** the action of a person or thing that sets: *the setting of the sun* **2** the way or position in which something is set **3 a** a set of surroundings **b** the time and place where the action of a book, film, etc., happens **4** a set of articles (dishes, knives, forks, spoons, etc.) arranged on a table or at one place on a table

settle *v* **-tled, -tling 1** to live or cause to live in a place **2** to provide people to live in (a place): *We settled the desert* **3** to bring or place down, often in a comfortable position: *settled himself in his chair* **4** to sink or come down, usu. to a position of rest **5** to make or become quiet, calm, still, etc.: *to settle one's nerves* **6 a** to separate (solid material or a liquid containing it) each from the other, usu. by causing the solid to fall slowly to the bottom: *to settle the wine/dregs* **b** (of the solid or liquid) to separate like this **7** (of a building, the ground etc.) to sink slowly to a lower level; subside **8** to decide on; fix; arrange **9** to end (an argument, esp. in law); bring (a matter) to an agreement **10** to pay (a bill or money claimed) **11 settle one's affairs** to put all one's business into order, esp. for the last time

settled *adj* **1** unlikely to change: *settled habits* **2** not moving about: *a desert with no settled population* **3** (of a place) having people living in homes **4** established; fixed: *settled principles*

settle down *v adv* **1** to sit or cause to sit comfortably **2** to establish a home and live quietly **3** to become used to a way of life, job, etc. **4** to give one's attention to a job, working, etc.

settlement *n* **1** the movement of new people into a place to live there **2** a usu. recently-built small village in an area with few people **3** an agreement or decision ending an argument, question, etc. **4** a payment of money claimed **5** a formal gift of money or property: *made a settlement on his daughter*

set up *v adv* **1** to establish (an organization, business, etc.) **2** to provide (someone) with what is necessary or useful

seven *adj n, pron* the number 7 *– ~*th *adj, n, pron, adv*

seventeen *adj n, pron* the number 17 *– ~*th *adj, n, pron, adv*

seventy *adj, n, pron* **-ties** the number 70 *–* **-tieth** *adj, n, pron, adv*

¹**several** *adj esp. written (with pl. nouns)* **1** of the stated people or things; separate: *busy with their several jobs* **2** various; different

²**several** *adj, pron* more than 2 but fewer than many; some but not many

severe *adj* **1** not kind or gentle; not allowing failure or change in rules, standards, etc.; strict: *a severe look* **2** very harmful or painful; serious or uncomfortable: *a severe winter* **3** needing effort; difficult: *a severe test of ability* **4** plain; without ornament: *the severe beauty of the building* *– ~*ly *adv –* **-rity** *n*

sew *v* **sewed, sewn, sewing 1** to join or fasten (cloth, leather, paper, etc.) by stitching with thread; make or mend with needle and thread **2** to enclose in this way: *sewed a £5 note into his pocket* −~**er** *n*

sewage *n* the waste material and water carried in sewers

sewer *n* a man-made passage or large pipe under the ground for carrying away water and waste material, esp. in a city, to a body of water or for chemical treatment (**sewage disposal**)

¹sex *n* **1** the condition of being either male or female **2** the set of all male or female people: *a member of the opposite sex* **3** the act of sexual intercourse between people, or related activity −**sex** *adj*

²sex *v esp. technical* to find out the sex of (esp. an animal)

sexual *adj* of, related to, or concerning sex −~**ly** *adv*

sexy *adj* **-ier, -iest** exciting in a sexual way −**sexily** *adv* −**sexiness** *n*

shabby *adj* **-bier, -biest 1** appearing poor because of wear **2** (of a person) wearing such clothes **3** ungenerous or not worthy; unfair; mean: *a shabby trick* − **-bily** *adv* − **-biness** *n*

¹shade *n* **1** slight darkness, shelter from direct light, or somthing that provides this **2** something that keeps out light or its full brightness: *a lampshade* **3** representation of shadow or darkness in a picture, painting, etc. **4** a slightly different colour: *light blue and a deeper shade* **5** a slight difference or varying: *a word with several shades of meaning* **6** *esp. literature* a ghost **7** (*often* before adjectives or adverbs) a little bit: *a shade too loud* **8 put someone/ something in the shade** *esp. spoken* to make someone/something seem less important by comparison

²shade *v* **shaded, shading 1** to shelter from direct light or heat **2** to represent the effect of shade or shadow on (an object in a picture) **3** to change slowly or by slight degrees: *blue shading off into grey*

¹shadow *n* **1** greater darkness where direct light is blocked **2** a dark shape made on a surface by something between it and direct light: *The tree cast its shadow on the wall* **3** a dark place like this: *shadows under the eyes* **4** a form without real substance: *He is but a shadow of his former self* **5** a person or thing who follows another closely: *The dog is your shadow* **6** a slightest bit: *no shadow of an excuse* **7** the very strong power or influence of someone or something: *He lived in the shadow of his famous father* **8** an unhappy or threatened feeling **9 be afraid of one's own shadow** to be fearful or nervous

²shadow *v* **1** to darken as with a shadow **2** to follow and watch closely, esp. secretly

³shadow *adj* **1** belonging to a group of politicians (the **shadow cabinet**) in the opposition party in Parliament who each study the work of a particular minister and are themselves ready to form a government **2** able to be active or become the stated thing when the proper or expected occasion comes

shadowy *adj* **-ier, -iest 1** hard to see or know about clearly: *a shadowy figure* **2** full of shade

shaft *n* **1** a long or thin pole, such as the body of a spear or arrow **2** the long handle of a hammer, axe, golf club, etc. **3** one of the pair of poles that an animal is fastened between to pull a vehicle **4** a bar which turns, or around which a belt or wheel turns, to pass power through a machine **5** a beam of light **6** *literature* something shot like an arrow: *well-aimed shafts of wit* **7** a long passage, usu. in an up and down or sloping direction: *a mine shaft*

shaggy *adj* **-gier, -giest** being or covered with long, uneven, and untidy hair – **-gily** *adv* – **-giness** *n*

¹shake *v* **shook , shaken, shaking 1** to move quickly up and down and to and fro: *The explosion shook the house* **2** to put or remove by such action: *He shook salt on his food* **3** to take (someone's right hand) in one's own for a moment, moving it up and down, as a sign of greeting, goodbye, agreement, etc. (esp. in the phrase **shake hands (with someone))** **4** to trouble the feelings of; upset **5** to make less certain **6** *sl* to escape from; get rid of: *Try to shake him off* **7 shake one's head** to move one's head from side to side to show 'no' or disapproval

²shake *n* **1** an action of shaking **2** *sl* a moment: *I'll be ready in 2 shakes*

shaky *adj* **-ier, -iest 1** shaking or unsteady **2** not firm; easily shaken; undependable **–shakily** *adv* **–shakiness** *n*

shall *v* **should,** *negative short form* **shan't 1** (used with *I* and *we* to express) **a** (the simple future tense): *I shall have finished my work by next Friday* **b** (a question or offer): *Shall I get you a chair?* **2** (used to express a promise, command, or strong intention): *The enemy shall not enter*

¹shallow *adj* **1** not deep; not far from top to bottom **2** lacking deep or serious thinking: *shallow arguments* **3** (of breathing) not taking in much air **–~ly** *adv* **–~ness** *n*

²shallow *v* to become shallow

¹sham *n* **1** something false pretending to be the real thing: *The agreement is just a sham* **2** falseness; pretence

²sham *adj* not real; imitation

³sham *v* **-mm-** to pretend to be or have (some disease, condition, etc.)

shambles *n* a place or scene of great disorder; wreck: *After the party the house was a shambles*

¹shame *n* **1** painful feeling of guilt, wrongness, inability, or failure **2** the condition in which this should be felt; disgrace: *behaviour which brings shame on us all* **3** something that deserves blame; something that ought not to be: *What a shame that it rained today* **4 put someone/ something to shame a** to cause shame to someone/something **b** to show someone/something to be lacking in ability, quality, etc., by comparison **5 Shame!** (called out against a speaker) You ought to be ashamed to say that!

²**shame** *v* **shamed, shaming 1** to bring dishonour to **2** to appear very much better than: *a record which shames other companies* **3** to cause to feel shame **4** to force or urge by causing shame: *I shamed her into voting in the election*

shameful *adj* deserving blame; causing shame –~**ly** *adv* –~**ness** *n*

¹**shampoo** *v* **-pooed, -pooing 1** to wash (the head and hair) **2** to clean (heavy woven material) with shampoo

²**shampoo** *n* **-poos 1** an act of shampooing **2** a usu. liquid soaplike product used for shampooing

¹**shape** *v* **shaped, shaping 1** to make in a particular usu. finished form **2** to influence and determine: *a powerful person who can shape events* **3** to develop well or in the stated way: *Our plans are shaping up well*

²**shape** *n* **1** the appearance or form of something seen: *Houses come in all shapes and sizes* **2** the organization or form in which something is expressed, arranged, etc. **3** condition: *Our garden is in good shape* **4** a way of appearing; form **5 get/put something into shape** to arrange or plan something properly **6 in/out of shape** in/out of good condition of the body **7 take shape** to begin to have a shape, esp. like the finished form –~**less** *adj* –~**lessly** *adv* –~**lessness** *n*

¹**share** *n* **1** the part belonging to or done by a person: *Do your fair share of the work* **2** any of the equal parts into which the ownership of a company may be divided **3 go shares** to divide the cost, profit, etc., among 2 or more people

²**share** *adj* of or concerning company shares

³**share** *v* **shared, sharing 1** to use, pay, have, take part in, etc., with others or among a group: *Everyone shares the bathroom* **2** to divide and give out in shares **3** to tell others about: *He shared the story with us* **4** to join with others esp. in (an opinion or idea) **5 share and share alike** *esp. spoken* to have an equal share in everything –**sharer** *n*

¹**shark** *n* any of several kinds of large fierce flesh-eating fish which have several rows of sharp teeth, and can be dangerous to people

²**shark** *n sl* a person who cleverly and mercilessly gets money from others as by lending money at high rates

¹**sharp** *adj* **1 a** having or being a thin cutting edge **b** having or being a fine point **2** quick and sensitive in thinking, seeing, hearing, etc.: *a sharp mind* **3** causing a sensation like that of cutting, biting, stinging: *a sharp wind* **4** not rounded; marked by angles: *a sharp nose* **5**

sudden and steep; strong, etc.: *a sharp rise/fall in prices* **6** clear in shape or detail; distinct: *a sharp image* **7** (of a pain) severe and sudden **8** (as of words) intended to hurt; harsh **9** clever and usu. dishonest: *This sale sounds like* **sharp practice 10** (of a note in music) raised by 1/2 tone (in the phrases **F sharp**, **C sharp**, etc.) −∼**ly** *adv* −∼**ness** *n*

²**sharp** *adv* **1** exactly at the stated time **2** sharply (esp. in such phrases as **turn sharp left/right**) **3** higher than the correct note: *She sang sharp* **4** **look sharp** *sl* **a** to watch out; be careful **b** to hurry up

³**sharp** *n* (in music) **1** a note higher by 1/2 tone than a named note **2** a sign, (♯), used before a note to raise it by this amount

sharpen *v* to make or become sharp or sharper −∼**er** *n*

shatter *v* **1** to break suddenly into small pieces **2** to damage badly; wreck: *Illness shattered his health* **3** to shock the feelings of: *a shattered look* **4** *esp. spoken* to cause to be very tired and weak

¹**shave** *v* **shaved, shaving 1** to cut off (hair) close to the skin with a razor **2** to cut off in very thin pieces **3** *esp. spoken* to come close to or touch in passing: *The car just shaved the wall*

²**shave** *n* **1** an act or result of shaving **2 a close/narrow shave** *esp. spoken* an almost unsuccessful avoiding of something bad; narrow escape

shawl *n* a piece of usu. soft heavy cloth for wearing over a woman's head or shoulders or wrapping round a baby

¹**she** *pron* **1** that female person or animal: *She's a pretty girl* **2** (used esp. of vehicles and countries) that thing regarded as female: *What's wrong with the car? She won't start*

²**she** *n esp. spoken* a female: *Is the cat a he or a she?*

sheaf *n* **sheaves 1** a bunch of grain plants tied together, esp. to stand in a field to dry after gathering **2** a handful of long or thin things laid together: *a sheaf of notes*

shears *n* large scissors or any similar but heavier cutting tool

sheath *n* **1** a closefitting case for a knife, blade, etc. **2** a usu. rubber covering worn over a man's sex organ when having sex to keep the woman from having a child and to prevent infection

¹**shed** *v* **shed, shedding 1** *literature* to cause to flow out: *She shed tears. / to shed new light on a question* **2** (of a surface) to keep (a liquid) from entering: *A duck's back sheds water* **3** (as of a plant or animal) to throw off or get rid of naturally (outer skin, leaves, hair, etc.) **4** (of a vehicle) to drop (a load of goods) by acccident **5 shed blood** to cause wounding or esp. killing

²**shed** *n* a lightly built, often partly enclosed, building, usu. for storing things

sheep *n* **sheep 1** a type of grass-eating

animal farmed for its wool and meat (mutton, lamb) **2 a black sheep** an unsatisfactory or shameful member of a group **3 make/cast sheep's eyes at someone** *sl* to behave fondly towards someone, esp. in a foolish way

¹sheer *adj* **1** very thin, fine, light, and almost transparent: *sheer stockings* **2** pure; unmixed with anything else: *sheer luck* **3** very steep; straight up and down: *a sheer cliff*

²sheer *adv* straight up or down

³sheer *v* to turn as if to avoid hitting something; change direction quickly: *The boat sheered away*

¹sheet *n* **1** a large 4-sided piece of cloth used usu. in a pair on a bed **2** a piece of paper **3** a broad stretch, piece, mass of something thin: *a sheet of ice* **4 white as a sheet** *esp. spoken* very pale in the face, as because of fear or a shock

²sheet *n technical* a rope or chain controlling the angle between a sail and the wind

shelf *n* **shelves 1** a flat usu. long and narrow board fixed against a wall or in a frame, for placing things on **2** a group of things filling one of these: *a shelf of books* **3** something shaped like this, such as a narrow surface of rock **4 on the shelf** *sl* (esp. of a person) not active, esp. put aside by others as of no use

¹shell *n* **1** a hard covering, as of an animal, egg, nut, etc. **2** the outer surface of something, not the contents or substance **3** the outside frame of a building **4** an explosive for firing from a large gun **5 come out of one's shell** *sl* to begin to be friendly or interested in others

²shell *v* **1** to remove a natural covering from: *to shell peas/oysters* **2** to fire shells at

¹shelter *n* **1** anything that protects, esp. a building **2** protection or the state of being protected: *the shelter of a tree*

²shelter *v* **1** to protect from harm; give shelter to **2** to take shelter; find protection: *We sheltered in the doorway*

¹shepherd *n fem.* ~**ess**– a man or boy who takes care of sheep in the field

²shepherd *v* to lead, guide, or take care of like sheep: *The teacher shepherded the children into the bus*

sherry *n* **-ries** a pale or dark brown strong wine, often drunk before a meal

¹shield *n* **1** a broad piece of metal, wood, or leather once carried by soldiers to protect them from arrows, blows, etc. **2** a representation of this used for a coat of arms, badge, etc.

²shield *v* to protect or hide from harm or danger

¹shift *v* **1** to change in position or direction: *The wind shifted and blew the mist away* **2** to take care of oneself; manage (esp. in the phrase **shift for oneself**)

²shift *n* **1** a change in position or direction **2 a** a group of workers which takes turns with other groups: *the day/night shift* **b** the period worked by such a group **3** a loosefitting straight simple woman's dress **4** a means or trick used in a difficulty **5 make shift** to use what can be found; make do

shilling *n* an amount of money in use in Britain until 1971, equal to 12 old pence and 1/20 of £1 **2** a coin worth this amount, now 5 new pence

¹**shin** *n* the bony front part of the leg below the knee

²**shin** *v* **-nn-** to climb (a tree, pole, etc.), esp. quickly and easily, using the hands and legs

¹**shine** *v* **shone, shining 1** to give off light; look bright **2** to direct (a lamp, beam of light, etc.) **3** to appear clearly as excellent: *He really shines at sports* – **-ning** *adj*

²**shine** *v* **shined, shining** to polish; make bright by rubbing

³**shine** *n* **1** brightness; shining quality **2** an act of polishing, esp. of shoes **3 rain or shine** in good or bad weather; whatever happens

shiny *adj* **-ier, -iest** (esp. of a smooth surface) looking polished; bright **–shininess** *n*

¹**ship** *n* **1** a large boat **2** *esp. spoken* a large aircraft or spacecraft **3 when one's ship comes in/home** *esp. spoken* when one becomes rich

²**ship** *v* **-pp- 1** to send by ship **2** to send (esp. a large article) over some distance by post or other means: *We ship our products everywhere in*

Britain **3** (of a boat) to take (water) over the side **4** to take a job on a ship **5** to hold one's oars to the side of the boat without rowing

shipment *n* **1** the action of sending, carrying, and delivering goods **2** a load of goods sent together

¹**shipwreck** *n* a/the destruction of a ship, as by hitting rocks or sinking

²**shipwreck** *v* **1** to cause to suffer shipwreck **2** to wreck; ruin

shirk *v* to avoid (unpleasant work) **–~er** *n*

shirt *n* **1** a piece of clothing for the upper body, usu. of light cloth with a collar and sleeves **2 lose one's shirt** *sl* to lose all one has; lose a lot of money **3 stuffed shirt** *sl* a person who acts grand and important; pompous person

¹**shiver** *v* to shake, esp. from cold or fear

²**shiver** *n* a feeling of fear or cold: *a shiver up my spine*

¹**shock** *n* **1** violent force, as from a hard blow, crash, explosion, etc. **2** the strong feeling caused by something unexpected and usu. very unpleasant **3** something causing this; an unpleasant piece of news: *His death was a shock* **4** the sudden violent effect of electricity passing through the body **5** *medical* the weakened state of the body with less activity of the heart, lungs, etc., usu. following damage to the body

²**shock** *v* **1** to cause usu. unpleasant or angry surprise to (someone) **2** to give an electric shock to

³**shock** *n* a thick bushy mass of hair

shocking *adj* **1** causing shock; very improper, or sad **2** very bad (though not evil): *What a shocking waste of time!* **–~ly** *adv*

¹**shoddy** *n* **1** cloth made using wool from old used cloth **2** poor cheap material

²**shoddy** *adj* **-dier, -diest 1** made or done cheaply and badly: *shoddy workmanship* **2** ungenerous or not worthy; dishonourable: *a shoddy trick* **– -dily** *adv* **– -diness** *n*

¹**shoe** *n* **1** an outer covering for the human foot, usu. of leather and having a hard base (sole) and a support (heel) under the heel of the foot **2** either of a pair of curved plates around a vehicle wheel which may press against it to stop it or slow it down: *Your car has worn brake shoes* **3** a horseshoe **4 to fill someone's shoes** to take the place or job of someone **5 in someone's shoes** in someone's position

²**shoe** *v* **shod** *or* **shoed, shoeing** to fix a shoe on (an animal)

shoelace *n* a thin cord passed through holes on both sides of the front opening of a shoe and tied to fasten the shoe on

shone *past tense. and past part. of* SHINE

shook *past tense of* SHAKE

¹**shoot** *v* **shot, shooting 1** to let fly with force (a bullet, arrow, etc.) **2** to fire (a weapon) **3** to hit or kill with something as from a gun: *He was shot in the arm* **4** to make (one's way) by firing a gun at anyone in the way: *He shot his way out of prison* **5** to cause to go or become by hitting with something from a gun: *His foot was shot away* **6** to send out as from a gun: *Everyone shot questions at the chairman* **7** to go fast or suddenly: *Pain shot through his arm* **8** to kick, throw, etc., a ball in order to score in a game **9** to make a photograph or film (of): *This story was shot quickly* **10** *US* to play (a game of billiards, pool, marbles, etc.) **11** to pass quickly by or along: *a boat shooting the rapids* **12** (esp. in cricket) (of a ball) to keep very low after bouncing **13 a** to move (a bolt) across **b** (of a bolt) to move across **14** *drug-users' sl* to take (a drug) directly with a needle

²**shoot** *n* **1** a new growth from a plant, esp. a young stem and leaves **2** an occasion for shooting guns

¹**shop** *n* **1** (*US* **store**)– a room or building where goods are regularly kept and sold **2** such a place, esp. small or selling special kinds of goods **3** a place where things are made or repaired; workshop **4** business; activity (esp. in the phrases **set up shop, close/shut up shop**) **5 (talk) shop** (to talk about) one's work

²**shop** *v* **-pp- 1** to visit 1 or more shops in order to buy; buy goods (often in the phrase **go shopping**) **2** *sl* to

tell the police about (a criminal) −~**per** *n*

shop floor *n* the place where ordinary workers do their work: *What's the feeling on the shop floor?*

shopkeeper *n* a person, usu. the owner, in charge of a small shop

shoplift *v* to steal from a shop −~**er** *n*

¹**shore** *n* **1** the land along the edge of a large stretch of water **2 on shore** on land; away from one's ship

²**shore** *v* **shored, shoring 1** to support, esp. with timbers: *shored up the wall* **2** to strengthen or give support to (something weak); keep from failing or falling: *to shore up farm prices*

¹**short** *adj* **1** not far from one end to the other; little in distance of length (opposite **long**) or height (opposite **tall**) **2** lasting only a little time; brief: *a short visit* −opposite **long 3** lacking enough; insufficient or scarce: *short weights/measures* **4** rudely impatient; curt: *I'm sorry I was short with you* **5** (of pastry) falling easily into pieces; crumbly **6** (of a drink) of a kind (such as spirits) usu. served in a small glass **7** (in cricket) **a** (of a fielder) in a position close to the batsman **b** (of a bowled ball) hitting the ground quite far from the batsman **8 for short** as a shorter way of saying something **9 in short** to put it into a few words; all I mean is **10 little/ nothing short of** *pompous* little/ nothing less than; almost/

completely **11 short and sweet** not wasting time; short and direct **12 short for** a shorter way of saying −~**ness** *n*

²**short** *adv* **1** suddenly; abruptly: *The driver stopped short* **2 be taken/ caught short** *esp. spoken* to have a sudden need to empty the bowels or esp. pass water from the body **3 cut short** to stop suddenly before the end: *They cut their holiday short* **4 fall short (of)** to be less than good enough (for) **5 go short** to be without enough **6 run short a** to use almost all one has and not have enough left **b** to become less than enough

shortage *n* a condition of having less than needed; an amount lacking: *a food shortage*

shortcoming *n* a failing to reach what is expected or right: *his shortcomings as a sailor*

short cut *n* a quicker more direct way

shorten *v* to make or become short or shorter

shorthand *n* rapid writing in a system using signs for letters, words, phrases, etc.

short-lived *adj* lasting only a short time

shortly *adv* **1** soon **2** at a short distance **3** in a few words **4** impatiently; not politely: *He answered shortly*

shorts *n* trousers ending above the knees

shortsighted *adj* **1** unable to see things clearly if they are not close to the eyes **2** not considering the likely future effects of present action −~**ly** *adv* −~**ness** *n*

¹**shot** *n* **1** an action of shooting a weapon **2** a person who shoots with the stated degree of skill **3** a kick, throw, etc., of a ball intended to score a point: *His shot went wide* **4** a sending up of a space vehicle or rocket **5** a chance or effort to do something; try: *I'd like a shot at cooking* **6** nonexplosive metal balls for shooting from some kinds of guns, such as shotguns **7** the heavy metal ball used in the shot put **8** a photograph **9** a single part of a cinema film made by one camera without interruption: *an action shot* **10** a taking of a drug through a needle; injection **11** *esp. spoken* a bill for drinks (esp. in the phrase **pay one's shot**) **12** a chance at the stated degree of risk: *The horse is an 8 to 5 shot* **13** a small drink, esp. of whisky, for swallowing at once **14 a shot in the arm** something to bring back a happy active condition **15 a shot in the dark** a wild guess **16 big shot** *offensive* an important person **17 like a shot** quickly or without delay

²**shot** *adj* **1** woven in 2 different colours, one along and one across the material **2** *esp. spoken* rid of; finished with

³**shot** *past tense and past part. of* SHOOT

should *v negative short form* **shouldn't** **1** (used in indirect speech) shall: *We said we shouldn't arrive till 6* **2** (used usu. with *that*, after certain verbs and adjectives esp. expressing an intention or wish): *He was keen that she should go to college* **3** (used with *I* and *we* in conditional sentences): *I should have been very lonely without my dog* **4** (expressing duty or what is necessary) ought to: *The lid should go on like this* **5** (expressing what is likely): *It should be fine tomorrow* **6** (expressing what is possible but not likely): *If I should see him, I'll tell him*

¹**shoulder** *n* **1 a** the part of the body at each side of the neck where the arms are connected **b** the part of a garment that covers this part **2** the upper part of the back including these, esp. considered as where loads are carried **3** something like these in shape, such as an outward curve on a bottle or a slope on a mountain near the top **4** either edge of a road outside the travelled part **5** the upper part of the front leg of an animal as meat **6 head and shoulders above** very much better than **7 rub shoulders with** to meet socially **8 shoulder to shoulder a** side by side **b** together; with the same intentions **9 straight from the shoulder** expressed plainly and directly

²**shoulder** *v* **1** to place (as a load) on the shoulder(s) **2** to push with the shoulders: *He shouldered his way to the front*

¹**shout** *v* to speak or say very loudly

²shout *n* **1** a loud cry or call **2** *sl* a particular person's turn to buy alcoholic drinks for others

¹shove *v* **shoved**, **shoving 1** to push, esp. in a rough or careless way: *Shove this furniture aside* **2** *esp. spoken* to move oneself: *Shove over, friend, and make room for me*

²shove *n* a strong push

¹shovel *n* **1** a long-handled tool with a broad blade for lifting and moving loose material **2** also **shovelful** – the amount of material carried in any of these

²shovel *v* **-ll- 1** to take up, move, make, or work with a shovel **2** to move roughly as if with a shovel: *He shovelled the papers into his desk*

¹show *v* **showed**, **shown**, **showing 1** to offer for seeing; allow or cause to be seen: *He showed his ticket* **2** to appear; be in or come into view; be visible: *His happiness showed in his smile* **3** to point to as a mark or number; indicate: *The clock showed 20 past 2* **4** to go with and guide or direct: *May I show you to your seat?* **5** to state or prove: *His speech showed no understanding of the subject* **6** to explain; make clear to by words or esp. actions; demonstrate **7 a** to offer as a performance **b** (esp. of a cinema film) to be offered at present **8** to allow to be easily seen: *A white dress will show dirt* **9** to prove (oneself) to be: *He showed himself a brave soldier* **10** *literature* to make to be felt in one's actions: *They showed their enemies kindness*

11 *sl* to arrive; show up: *My friend never showed* **12 show one's face** to be present in a company

²show *n* **1** a showing of some quality; display: *a show of strength* **2** an outward appearance, esp. as opposed to what is really true, happening, etc.: *a show of interest* **3** grandness; splendid appearance or ceremony **4** a public showing; collection of things for looking at; exhibition **5** a performance, esp. in a theatre or nightclub or on radio or television **6** *esp. spoken* an organization or activity: *He's in charge of the whole show* **7** *esp. spoken* an effort; act of trying (often in such phrases as **put up a good show**) **8 get this show on the road** *esp. spoken* to start to work; get going **9 Good show!** *esp. spoken* Very good! Well done! **10 steal the show** to get all the attention and praise expected by someone else

¹shower *n* **1** a short-lasting fall of rain or snow **2** a fall of many small things or drops of liquid: *A shower of paint fell on the men below* **3** a quantity or rush of things coming at the same time: *a shower of cards* **4 a** a washing of the body by standing under an opening from which water comes out in many small streams **b** an apparatus for this, with controls for water and usu. built as an enclosure in a bathroom **5** *esp. spoken offensive* a group of unpleasant, lazy, etc., people

²shower *v* **1** to rain or pour down in

showers **2 a** to pour (on), scatter heavily (on) **b** to give in large quantity: *They showered her with gifts* **3** to take a shower

showing *n* **1** an act of putting on view **2** a record of success or quality; performance: *a good showing by the local team*

shown *past part. of* SHOW

show off *v adv* **1** to behave so as to try to get admiration for oneself, one's abilities, etc. **2** to show, esp. as something fine, beautiful, etc. **−show-off** *n*

shrank *past tense of* SHRINK

¹**shred** *n* **1** a small narrow piece torn or roughly cut off **2** a smallest piece; bit: *a shred of truth*

²**shred** *v* **-dd-** to cut or tear into shreds **−~der** *n*

shrewd *adj* **1** clever in judgment, esp. of what is to one's own advantage: *a shrewd lawyer* **2** well-reasoned and likely to be right **−~ly** *adv* **−~ness** *n*

shriek *v* to cry out with a high sound; screech **−shriek** *n*

shrill *adj* **1** high and sounding sharp or even painful to the ear; piercing **2** marked by continuous complaining **−~y** *adv* **−~ness** *n*

shrimp *n* **shrimp** *or* **shrimps 1** any of many types of small sea creature with long legs and a fanlike tail **2** *usu. offensive* a small person

shrink *v* **shrank, shrunk** *or* **shrunken, shrinking 1** to make or become smaller, as from the effect of heat or water **2** to move back and away; retire: *The dog shrank into a corner*

shrub *n* a low bush with several woody stems

shrug *v* **-gg-** to raise (one's shoulders), esp. as an expression of doubt or lack of interest **−shrug** *n*

shudder *v* to shake uncontrollably for a moment, as from fear, cold, or strong dislike; tremble **−shudder** *n*

¹**shuffle** *v* **-fled, -fling 1** to mix up the order of (playing cards) so as to produce a chance order ready for a game to begin **2** to move or push to and fro or to different positions: *to shuffle papers around* **3** to walk by dragging (one's feet) slowly along **−~r** *n*

²**shuffle** *n* **1** a slow dragging walk **2** an act of shuffling cards

shun *v* **-nn-** to avoid with determination; keep away from

shut *v* **shut, shutting 1** to move into a covered, blocked, or folded-together position; close **2** to keep or hold by closing: *He shut himself in his room* **3** to stop in operation; close

¹**shutter** *n* **1** a wood or metal cover that can be placed, usu. by unfolding in pairs, in front of a window to block the view or keep out the light **2** a part of a camera which opens for an exact usu. very short time in taking a picture to let light fall on the film

²**shutter** *v* to close as with shutters

¹**shy** *adj* **shyer** *or* **shier, shyest** *or* **shiest 1** nervous in the company of

others; not putting oneself forward **2** having doubts or distrust: *I'm shy of acting in this case* **3** (of animals) unwilling to come near people **4** **fight shy of** to try to avoid −∼**ly** *adv* −∼**ness** *n*

²**shy** *v* **shied, shying 1** (esp. of a horse) to make a sudden movement, as from fear **2** to avoid something unpleasant, as by moving aside

³**shy** *v* **shied, shying** *esp. spoken* to throw with a quick movement −**shy** *n*

sick *adj* **1** ill; having a disease **2** upset in the stomach so as to want to throw up what is in it **3** causing or typical of this feeling **4** feeling something so unpleasant as (almost) to cause this feeling **5** having a dislike from too much of something: *I'm sick of winter* **6** unhealthy; unnaturally cruel in likings, humour, etc.; morbid: *a sick joke* **7** for or related to illness: *sick pay* **8** **go/report sick** to excuse oneself from work because of illness

sicken *v* **1** to cause strong (almost) sick feelings of dislike in **2** to become ill; show signs of a disease

sickly *adj* **-lier, -liest 1** habitually ill; weak and unhealthy **2** unpleasantly weak, pale, or silly: *a sickly yellow* **3** causing a sick feeling

sickness *n* **1** a/the condition of being ill; illness or disease **2** the condition of feeling sick

¹**side** *n* **1** a more or less upright surface of something, not the top, bottom, front, or back **2** any of the flat surfaces of something: *Which side of the box is up?* **3** a part, place, or division according to a real or imaginary central line: *the other side of town* **4** the right or left part of the body, esp. from the shoulder to the top of the leg **5** the place next to someone, often regarded as the place of a helper, friend, tool, etc. **6** an edge or border: *A square has 4 equal sides* **7** either of the 2 surfaces of a thin flat object **8** a part to be considered, usu. in opposition to another: *Try to look at all sides of the question* **9** (a group which holds) a position in a quarrel, disagreement, war, etc. **10** a sports team: *cricket side* **11** the part of a line of a family that is related to a particular person: *He's Welsh on his mother's side* **12** either half of an animal body cut along the backbone **13** **hold/split one's sides** to be weak with uncontrollable laughter **14** **on the side** as a usu. cheating or dishonest additional activity **15** **put on/to one side** to take out of consideration, for the present; keep for possible use later **16** **this side of** *esp. spoken* without going as far as

²**side** *adj* **1** at, from, towards, etc., the side **2** beside or in addition to the main or regular thing: *the drug had serious side effects*

³**side** *v* **sided, siding** to be a party in a quarrel, disagreement, etc.; take a side

sidelight *n* **1** (a piece of) interesting

though not very important information **2** either of a pair of lamps at the sides of a vehicle

sideshow *n* **1** a separate small show at a fair or circus usu. with strange people (a sword swallower, bearded lady, etc.) on view **2** a usu. amusing activity beside a more serious main one

sidestep *v* **-pp- 1** to take a step to the side, (as) to avoid (a blow) **2** to avoid (an unwelcome question, duty, etc.) as if by moving aside

sideways *adv, adj* **1** with one side (and not the front or back) forward or up: *The fat lady could only get through the door sideways* **2** to or towards one side

siege *n* an operation by an army surrounding a defended place to force it to yield, by repeated attacks, blocking of its supplies, etc.: *to lay siege to a fort*

¹**sieve** *n* **1** a tool of wire or plastic net on a frame, or of a solid sheet with holes, used for separating large and small solid bits, or solid things from liquid **2 a head/memory like a sieve** *esp. spoken* a mind that forgets quickly

²**sieve** *v* **sieved, sieving** to put through or separate by means of a sieve

sift *v* **1** to put through a sieve or net **2** to make a close examination of (things in a mass or group): *He sifted through his papers* **3** to separate or get rid of in either of these ways **4** (of a fine-grained material)

to pass (as) through a sieve: *Snow sifted through the crack*

¹**sigh** *v* **1** to let out a deep breath slowly and with a sound, usu. expressing tiredness, sadness, or satisfaction **2** (as of the wind) to make a sound like this **3** *literature* to feel fondly sorry, esp. about something past, far away, etc.

²**sigh** *n* an act or sound of sighing

¹**sight** *n* **1** something that is seen **2** the seeing of something **3** the sense of seeing; the power of the eye; eyesight; vision **4** presence in one's view; the range of what can be seen: *within sight of land* **5** something worth seeing, esp. a place visited by tourists: *the sights of London* **6** something which looks very bad or laughable: *What a sight you are!* **7** a part of an instrument or weapon which guides the eye in aiming **8** a lot; a great deal: *It cost me a sight more than expected* **9 in sight a** in view; visible **b** within a little of being reached; near: *Peace was in sight* **10 lose sight of a** to cease to see **b** to cease to have news about; lose touch with **c** to forget; fail to consider **11 out of sight a** out of the range of being seen **b** *esp. spoken* very high, great, etc.: *Costs have gone out of sight*

²**sight** *v* **1** to get a view of, esp. after a time of looking; see for the first time: *to sight land* **2** to aim or look in a certain direction −~**ing** *n*

sightseeing *n* the activity of visiting

places of interest, esp. while on holiday – **-seer** *n*

¹sign *n* **1** a standard mark; something which is seen and represents a known meaning; symbol **2** a movement of the body intended to express a meaning; signal **3** a board or other notice giving information, warning, directions, etc. **4** something that shows a quality, or the presence or coming of something else: *Swollen ankles can be a sign of heart disease* **5** also **sign of the zodiac–** any of the 12 divisions of the year represented by groups of stars **6 a sign of the times** something that is typical of the way things are just now

²sign *v* **1** to write (one's name) on (a written paper), esp. for official purposes, to show one's agreement, show that one is the writer, etc. **2** to make a movement as a sign to (someone); signal: *The policeman signed me to stop*

¹signal *n* **1** a sound or action intended to warn, command, or give a message **2** an action which causes something else to happen **3** a railway apparatus (usu. with coloured lights) near the track to direct train drivers **4** TRAFFIC LIGHT **5** a sound, image, or message sent by waves, as in radio or television

²signal *v* **-ll-** **1** to give a signal **2** to express, warn, or tell by a signal or signals **3** to be a sign of; mark: *The defeat of 1066 signalled the end of Saxon rule in England*

³signal *adj* *literature* noticeable, important, and usu. excellent; outstanding: *signal courage*

signature *n* **1** a person's name written by his own hand, as at the end of a written statement, letter, cheque, etc. **2** the act of signing one's name: *to witness a signature*

significance *n* importance; meaning; value

significant *adj* **1** of noticeable importance or effect **2** having a special meaning: *a significant smile* **–~ly** *adv*

signify *v* **-fied, -fying** **1** *esp. written* to be a sign of; represent; mean; denote **2** *esp. written* to make known (esp. an opinion) by an action: *to signify (agreement) by raising hands* **3** *esp. spoken* to matter; have importance (for)

signpost *n* a sign showing directions and distances, as at a meeting of roads **–~ed** *adj*

¹silence *n* **1** absence of sound; stillness **2** the state of not speaking or making a noise **3** failure to write a letter or letters **4** failure to mention or say a particular thing: *Why silence on this matter?* **5** a moment or period of any of these conditions

²silence *v* **silenced, silencing** **1** to cause or force to stop making a noise **2** to force to stop expressing opinions, making opposing statements,- etc.: *They were silenced by imprisonment*

silent *adj* **1** not speaking; not using spoken expression **2** free from noise; quiet **3** making no statement; expressing no opinion, decision, etc.: *The law is silent on this point* **4** (of a letter in a word) not pronounced: *silent 'w' in 'wreck'* **5** being or concerning films with no sound −∼**ly** *adv*

silk *n* **1 a** fine thread which is produced by a type of caterpillar (silkworm) and made into thread for sewing and into cloth **b** smooth soft cloth made from this **2 silk and satins** *literature* fine rich clothes

¹**silly** *adj* **-lier, -liest 1** having or showing little judgment; foolish; stupid; not serious ; ridiculous **2** *esp. spoken* senseless; stunned: *That speaker bores me silly* **3** (of a player or his position in cricket) very close to the batsman (in the phrases **silly point, silly mid-on, silly mid-off**)

²**silly** *n* **-lies** a silly person

¹**silver** *n* **1** a soft whitish precious metal that is an element, carries electricity very well, can be brightly polished, and is used esp. in ornaments and coins **2** silver money; coins made of this, or of some white metal like it, and not of copper **3** spoons, forks, dishes, etc., for the table, made of this or a metal like it

²**silver** *adj* **1** made of silver **2** like silver in colour **3** *literature* pleasantly musical

³**silver** *v* **1** to cover with a thin shiny silver-coloured surface: *to silver the back of a mirror* **2** *literature* to make or become silver-coloured

similar *adj* **1** like or alike; of the same kind; partly or almost the same **2** *technical* exactly the same in shape but not size: *similar triangles* −∼**ly** *adv*

similarity **-ties 1** the quality of being alike or like something else; resemblance **2** a point of likeness

simile *n* an expression making a comparison in the imagination between 2 things, using the words *like* or *as*: *'As white as snow' is a simile*

simmer *v* **1** to cook gently in liquid at or just below boiling heat **2** to be filled (with hardly controlled excitement, anger, etc.) −**simmer** *n*

simple *adj* **1** not ornamented; plain **2** easy to understand or do; not difficult **3** of the ordinary kind, without special qualities, rules, difficulties, etc.; not complicated; basic **4** not (able to be) divided; of only one thing or part: *A simple sentence has only 1 verb* **5** not mixed with anything else; with nothing added; pure: *a simple statement* **6** sincere; natural and honest: *a woman of simple goodness* **7** easily tricked; foolish **8** *literature* of low rank or unimportant position: *a simple farm worker* **9** *old use* weak-minded **10 the simple life** *esp. spoken* life considered as better without the difficulties of having many possessions, using machines, etc.

simplicity *n* **1** the state of being simple **2 simplicity itself** *esp. spoken* very easy

simplify *v* **-fied, -fying** to make

plainer, easier, or less full of detail: *to simplify an explanation* – **-fica-tion** *n*

simply *adv* **1** in a simple way; easily, plainly, clearly, or naturally **2** just; only: *I drive simply to get to work each day* **3** really; very (much): *It's simply wonderful to see you!*

simultaneous *adj* happening or done at the same moment: *they made a simultaneous appearance* –~**ly** *adv* – **-neity,** ~**ness** *n*

¹**sin** *n* **1** disobedience to God; the breaking of law regarded as holy **2** an example of this **3** *esp. humour* something that should not be done; a serious offence **4 live in sin** *usu. polite or humour* (of 2 unmarried people) to live together as if married

²**sin** *v* **-nn-** to break God's laws; do wrong according to·some standard –~**ner** *n*

¹**since** *adv* **1** at a time between then and now; subsequently; from then until now: *He came to England 3 years ago and has lived here ever since* **2** ago: *I've long since forgotten our quarrel*

²**since** *prep* from (a point in past time) until now; during the period after: *I haven't seen her since her illness*

³**since** *conj* **1 a** after the past time when **b** continuously from the time when: *We've been friends since we met* **2** as; as it is a fact that: *Since you can't answer, I'll ask someone else*

sincere *adj* free from deceit or false-ness; real, true, or honest; genuine –~**ly** *adv* – **-rity** *n*

sing *v* **sang, sung, singing 1** to produce (music, musical sounds, songs, etc.) with the voice **2** to make or be filled with a ringing sound: *My ears sang after the crash* **3** *literature* to speak, tell about, or praise in poetry –~**able** *adj* –~**er** *n*

¹**single** *adj* **1** being (the) only one **2** having only one part, quality, etc.; not double or multiple **3** separate; considered by itself: *Food is our most important single need* **4** unmarried **5** for the use of only one person **6** (of a ticket or its cost) for a trip from one place to another but not back again

²**single** *n* **1** a single ticket **2** (in cricket) a single run **3** a record with only one short song on each side **4** *esp. spoken* a single room

single file –also **Indian file** *n, adv* (moving or standing in) a line of people, vehicles, etc., one behind another

single-handed *adj, adv* done by one person; working alone, without help

single-minded *adj* having or showing one clear purpose and effort to serve it –~**ly** *adv* –~**ness** *n*

singular *adj* **1** of or being a word or form representing exactly one: *'Mouse' is the singular form of 'mice'* **2** of unusual quality; extraordinary **3** *becoming rare* very unusual or strange; peculiar –~**ity** *n*

sinister *adj* threatening, intending, or leading to evil: *a sinister look*

¹**sink** *v* **sank, sunk, sinking 1** to go or cause to go down below a surface, out of sight, or to the bottom (of water) **2** to fall to a lower level or position: *The flames sank* **3** to get smaller; go down in number, value, strength, etc.: *His voice sank to a whisper* **4** to fall (as) from lack of strength: *She sank to the ground* **5** to become weaker; fail: *He's sinking fast* **6** to dig out or force into the earth: *to sink fence posts/a well* **7** to stop considering; forget: *to sink a disagreement* **8** to put (money, labour, etc.) into; invest **9** (in games like golf and billiards) to cause (a ball) to go into a hole **10 sink or swim** to fail or succeed without help from others – ~**able** *adj*

²**sink** *n* a large basin in a kitchen, for washing pots, vegetables, etc., fixed to a wall and usu. with pipes to supply and carry away water

sip *v* **-pp-** to drink, taking only a little at a time into the front of the mouth –**sip** *n*

sir *n* **1** (a respectful address to an older man or one of higher rank; to an officer by a soldier; to a male teacher by a British school child; to a male customer in a shop; etc.) **2** *pompous* (an angry scolding form of address): *Come here at once, sir!*

siren *n* **1** an apparatus for making a loud long warning sound, as used on ships, police cars, fire engines, and for air-attack warnings **2** (in ancient Greek literature) any of a group of woman-like creatures whose sweet singing charmed sailors and caused the wreck of their ships **3** a dangerous beautiful woman

¹**sister** *n* **1** a female relative with the same parents **2** a woman in close association with the speaker **3** (a title for) a nurse in charge of a ward of a hospital **4** (a title for) a woman member of a religious group, esp. a nun – ~**hood** *n*

²**sister** *adj* (of women or things considered female) with the same purpose; in the same group; fellow: *a sister ship*

sister-in-law *n* **-s-in-law 1** the sister of one's husband or wife **2** the wife of one's brother **3** the wife of the brother of one's husband or wife

sit *v* **sat, sitting 1** to rest in a position with the upper body upright and supported at the bottom of the back, as on a chair or other seat **2** to go or cause to go into this position; take or cause to take a seat: *She sat the baby on the grass* **3** (of an animal or bird) to be in or go into a position with the tail end of the body resting on a surface **4** to have a position in an official body **5** (of an official body) to have 1 or more meetings: *The court sat longer than expected* **6** to lie; rest; have a place (and not move): *books sitting unread on the shelf* **7** to have one's picture painted or photographed; pose **8** to take (a written examination) **9** (of a hen) to cover eggs to bring young birds to life **10 sit on one's hands** *esp. spoken* to take no action **11 sit pretty** to be in a very good position

¹**site** *n* **1** a place where something was or happened **2** a piece of ground for building on

²**site** *v* **sited**, **siting** to provide with a site; locate

situated *adj* **1** in a particular place; located **2** *esp. spoken* placed among possibilities; in a condition

situation *n* **1** a position or condition at the moment; state of affairs **2** *esp. written* a job; position in work **3** a position with regard to surroundings: *an island situation*

¹**six** *adj, n, pron* **1** the number 6 **2** a cricket hit worth 6 runs **3 at sixes and sevens** in disorder, esp. of mind; confused or undecided −∼**th** *adj, n, pron, adv*

sixteen *adj, n, pron* the number 16 −∼**th** *adj, n, pron, adv*

sixty *adj, n, pron* **-ties** the number 60 − **-tieth** *adj, n, pron, adv*

¹**size** *n* **1** (a degree of) bigness or smallness **2** bigness: *not of any size* **3** any of a set of measures in which objects are made (such as clothes, for fitting people) **4 cut someone down to size** to show someone to be really less good, important, etc. **5 That's about the size of it** *esp. spoken* That's a fair statement of the matter

²**size** −also **sizing** *n* pastelike material used for giving stiffness and a hard shiny surface to paper, cloth, etc.

³**size** *v* **sized**, **sizing** to cover or treat with size

skate *n* either of a pair of metal blades fitted to the sole of boots to enable the wearer to move swiftly on ice −**skate** *v* −∼**r** *n*

¹**skeleton** *n* **1** the framework of all the bones in a human or animal body **2** a set of these bones (or models of them) held in their positions, as for use by medical students **3** an unnaturally very thin person **4** something forming a framework **5** *esp. spoken* a secret of which a person or family is ashamed

²**skeleton** *adj* enough to keep an operation or organization going, and no more: *a skeleton rail service*

¹**sketch** *n* **1** a rough not detailed drawing **2** a short description in words **3** a short informal piece of literature or stage acting

²**sketch** *v* **1** to draw sketches **2** to make a sketch of **3** to describe roughly with few details: *to sketch in/out the main points* −∼**er** *n*

¹**ski** *n* **skis** either of a pair of long thin narrow pieces of wood, plastic, or metal curving up in front, for fastening to a boot for travelling (often in sports) on snow

²**ski** *v* **skied**, **skiing** to go on skis for travel or sport −∼**er** *n*

¹**skid** *n* **1** a piece of usu. wood placed under a heavy object to raise it off the floor or move it **2** an act or path of skidding: *The car went into a skid* **3 put the skids on/under** *esp.*

spoken **a** to stop or defeat; frustrate **b** to force to hurry

²**skid** *v* **-dd-** (of a vehicle or a wheel) to fail to stay in control on a road; slip sideways out of control

skilful *adj* having or showing skill −~**ly** *adv*

skill *n* (a use of) practical knowledge and power; ability to do something (well): *a writer of great skill* −~**ed** *adj*

skim *v* **-mm-** **1** to remove (floating fat or solids) from the surface of a liquid: *skim cream from milk* **2** to remove unwanted floating material from (liquid) **3** to read quickly to get the main ideas; scan **4** to move swiftly in a path near or touching (a surface): *to skim stones over a lake*

¹**skin** *n* **1** the natural outer covering of an animal or human body, from which hair may grow **2** this part of an animal body for use as leather, fur, etc. **3** a natural outer covering of some fruits and vegetables; peel **4** an outer surface built over a framework or solid inside **5** the more solid surface that forms over a liquid, as when it gets cool **6** a case for a sausage **7 by the skin of one's teeth** *esp. spoken* narrowly; only just **8 get under someone's skin** *esp. spoken* to annoy or excite someone deeply **9 save one's skin** *esp. spoken* to save oneself, esp. in a cowardly way, from death, ruin, punishment, etc. −~**less** *adj*

²**skin** *v* **-nn-** **1** to remove the skin from

2 to hurt by rubbing off some skin: *He skinned his knee*

¹**skip** *v* **-pp-** **1** to move in a light dancing way, as with quick steps and jumps **2** to move in no fixed order: *to skip from one subject to another* **3** to pass over or leave out (something in order); not do or deal with (the next thing) **4** to fail to attend or to take part in (an activity); miss: *to skip school* **5** to jump over a rope passed repeatedly beneath one's feet **6** *esp. spoken* to leave hastily and secretly, esp. to avoid being punished or paying money: *She skipped off without paying*

²**skip** *n* a light quick stepping and jumping movement

³**skip** *n* a builder's large metal container for carrying away heavy materials, esp. old bricks, wood, etc.

skipper *v, n esp. spoken* **1** (to be) a ship's captain **2** (to be) a captain of a sports team

¹**skirmish** *n* **1** a fight between small groups of soldiers, ships, etc., at a distance from the main forces and not part of a large battle **2** a slight or unplanned exchange of arguments between opponents

²**skirmish** *v* to fight in a skirmish −~**er** *n*

¹**skirt** *n* **1** a woman's outer garment that fits around the waist and hangs down with one lower edge all round **2** a part of a coat or dress that hangs below the waist **3** *sl* girls or women considered as sexual objects: *a nice bit of skirt*

²**skirt** *v* **1** to be or go around the outside of; go around: *a road skirting the town* **2** to avoid (a question, subject, difficulty, etc.)

skulk *v* to move about secretly or hide, through fear or for some evil purpose −~**er** *n*

skull *n* **1** the bone of the head which encloses the brain **2** *esp. spoken* this regarded as the mind or its covering

¹**sky** *n* **skies 1** the upper air; the space above the earth where clouds and the sun, moon, and stars appear **2** **The sky's the limit** *esp. spoken* There is no upper limit (esp. to the amount of money that may be spent)

²**sky** *v* **skied, skying** to knock (a ball) high into the air in a game, esp. by mistake

skyline *n* a shape or picture made by scenery (esp. tall city buildings) against the background of the sky

skyscraper *n* a very tall city building

slab *n* a thick flat usu. 4-sided piece of metal, stone, wood, food, etc.

¹**slack** *adj* **1** (of a rope, wire, etc.) not pulled tight **2** not firm; weak; loose **3** not busy or active: *Business is slack* **4** not properly careful or quick −~**ly** *adv* −~**ness** *n*

²**slack** *v* **1** to be lazy; not work well or quickly enough: *scolded for slacking* **2** to reduce (in) speed, effort, or tightness: *to slack off towards the end of the day*

³**slack** *n* the part of a rope, wire, etc., that hangs loose

slain *past part. of* SLAY

¹**slam** *n* the act or loud noise of a door closing violently

²**slam** *v* **-mm- 1** to shut loudly and with force **2** to push, move, etc., hurriedly and with great force: *He slammed the papers down* **3** to attack with words

¹**slander** *n* **1** an intentional false spoken report, story, etc., that unfairly damages a person's good reputation **2** the making of such a statement, esp. as an offence in law

²**slander** *v* to speak slander against; harm by making a false statement −~**er** *n* −~**ous** *adj* −~**ously** *adv*

¹**slang** *n* language that is not usu. acceptable in serious speech or writing, including words, expressions, etc., regarded as very informal or not polite, and those used among particular groups of people. These are marked *sl* in this dictionary −~**y** *adj* −~**iness** *n*

²**slang** *v* *esp. spoken* to attack with rude angry words

¹**slant** *v* **1** to be or cause to be at an angle from straight up and down across; slope **2** to express (facts, a report, etc.) in a way favourable to a particular opinion −~**ingly** *adv*

²**slant** *n* **1** a slanting direction or position: *a steep upward slant* **2** a particular way of looking at or expressing: *an interesting new slant on the news*

¹**slap** *n* a quick blow with the flat part of the hand

²**slap** *v* **-pp- 1** to strike quickly with the flat part of the hand **2** to place

quickly, roughly, or carelessly: *to slap paint on a wall*

³**slap** *adv esp. spoken* directly; right; smack: *to run slap up against a wall*

¹**slash** *v* **1** to cut with long sweeping forceful strokes, as with a knife or sword **2** to move or force with this kind of cutting movement: *He slashed his way through the bush* **3** to attack fiercely in words **4** to reduce (an amount, price, etc.) steeply

²**slash** *n* a long sweeping cut or blow

¹**slate** *n* **1** fine smooth rock formed from mud by heat or pressure, easily splitting into thin flat pieces **2** a small piece of this or other material used for laying in rows to cover a roof **3** a small board made of this or of wood, used for writing on with chalk **4** an imaginary record of the past, esp. of mistakes, faults, disagreements, etc.: *Let's wipe the slate clean and forget our past quarrels*

²**slate** *v* **slated, slating** to blame severely or attack in words; scold

¹**slaughter** *n* **1** (a) killing of many people or animals, esp. cruelly, wrongly, or as in a battle; massacre **2** the killing of animals for meat

²**slaughter** *v* **1** to kill (animals) for food; butcher **2** to kill (esp. many people) cruelly or wrongly; massacre

¹**slave** *n* **1** a person owned in law by another; servant without personal freedom **2** a person completely in the control of another person or thing; one who must obey: *a slave*

to duty **3** *usu. humour* a person who works hard at uninteresting work for another

²**slave** *v* **slaved, slaving** to work like a slave; work hard with little rest

slavery *n* **1** the system of having slaves **2** the condition of being a slave

slay *v* **slew** , **slain, slaying** *literature* to kill, esp. violently; put to death –~**er** *n*

¹**sledge** –also (*esp. US*) **sled** *n* **1** a vehicle made for sliding along snow or ice on 2 metal blades. Small light kinds are used in play and sport for going fast down slopes **2** one of these made for carrying heavy loads across snow

²**sledge** *v* **sledged, sledging** to go or race down slopes on a sledge

sledgehammer *n* a large heavy hammer for swinging with both hands to drive in posts, break stones, etc.

¹**sleep** *n* **1** the natural resting state of unconsciousness of the body **2** a period of time of this **3** the substance that sometimes gathers in the corners of the eyes when one is tired or asleep **4 go to sleep a** to begin to sleep; fall asleep **b** (of an arm, leg, etc.) to become unable to feel, or to feel slight pricking pains **5 put to sleep a** to kill (a suffering animal) mercifully **b** to make (a person) unconscious, as for an operation

²**sleep** *v* **slept, sleeping 1** to rest in sleep; be naturally unconscious, as

at night **2** to provide beds or places for sleep for (a number of people)

sleepless *adj* **1** not providing sleep: *a sleepless night* **2** *literature* unable to sleep − ~**ly** *adv* − ~**ness** *n*

sleepy *adj* **-ier, -iest 1** tired and ready for sleep **2** quiet; inactive or slow-moving: *a sleepy country town* −**sleepily** *adv* −**sleepiness** *n*

¹**sleet** *n* partly frozen rain; ice falling in fine bits mixed with water −**sleety** *adj*

²**sleet** *v* (of sleet) to fall

sleeve *n* **1** a part of a garment for covering (part of) an arm **2** a stiff envelope for keeping a gramophone record in usu. with information about the contents **3** a tube with 2 open ends for enclosing something, esp. a machine part **4 have/keep something up one's sleeve** to keep a secret for use in the future **5 roll up one's sleeves** to get to work − ~**less** *adj*

slender *n* **1** delicately or gracefully thin in the body; not fat; slim **2** pleasingly thin compared to length or height; not wide or thick **3** slight; small and hardly enough: *a slender chance of success* − ~**ly** *adv* − ~**ness** *n*

slept *past tense and part. of* SLEEP

¹**slew** *v* to turn or swing violently: *The car slewed out of control*

²**slew** *past tense of* SLAY

¹**slice** *n* **1** a thin flat piece cut from something **2** a kitchen tool with a broad blade for lifting and serving pieces of food **3** (in sports like golf

and tennis) a flight of a ball away from a course straight ahead and towards the side of the player's stronger hand

²**slice** *v* **sliced, slicing 1** to cut into slices **2** to cut off as a slice **3** to cut with a knife: *He sliced his fingers* **4** to hit (a ball) in a slice

¹**slide** *v* **slid, sliding 1** to go or cause to go smoothly over a surface **2** to pass smoothly or continuously; go slowly and unnoticed; slip **3 let something slide** *esp. spoken* to pay no attention; do nothing

²**slide** *n* **1** a slipping movement over a surface: *The car went into a slide on the ice* **2** a sliding machine part, such as the U-shaped tube on a trombone **3** a track or apparatus for sliding down: *a children's slide* **4** a usu. square piece of framed film for passing strong light through to show a picture on a surface **5** a small piece of thin glass to put an object on for seeing under a microscope

¹**slight** *adj* **1** not strong-looking; thin; frail **2** not great; not considerable; small or weak − ~**ly** *adv* − ~**ness** *n*

²**slight** *v* to treat rudely, without respect, or as if unimportant −**slight** *n* − ~**ingly** *adv*

¹**slim** *adj* **-mm- 1** (esp. of people) attractively thin; not fat **2** (of hope, probability, etc.) poor; slight; not considerable − ~**ly** *adv* − ~**ness** *n*

²**slim** *v* **-mm-** to make or try to make

oneself slim; lose weight $-\sim$**mer** *n* $-\sim$**ming** *n*

slime *n* **1** partly liquid mud, esp. regarded as ugly, bad-smelling, etc. **2** thick sticky liquid produced by the skin of various fish and snails

slimy *adj* **-ier, -iest 1** like, being, or covered with slime; unpleasantly slippery **2** very unpleasant and offensive; disgusting **–sliminess** *n*

¹**sling** *v* **slung, slinging 1** to throw, esp. roughly or with effort: *He slung his coat over his shoulder* **2** to throw (a stone) in a sling $-\sim$**er** *n*

²**sling** *n* **1** a piece of material for hanging from the neck to support a damaged arm or hand **2** an apparatus of ropes, bands, etc., for lifting or carrying heavy objects **3** a length of cord with a piece of leather in the middle, held at the ends and swung, for throwing stones with force

¹**slip** *v* **-pp- 1** to slide out of place or fall by sliding **2** to move slidingly, smoothly, secretly, or unnoticed: *She slipped into/out of the room* **3** to put on or take off (a garment) **4** to fall from a standard; get worse or lower: *He has slipped in my opinion* **5** to make a slight mistake **6** to give secretly **7** to get free from (a fastening): *The dog slipped his collar* **8** to escape from (one's attention, memory, etc.); be forgotten or unnoticed by **9 let slip a** to fail to follow (a chance, offer, etc.) **b** to say without intending **10 slip a disc** to get a slipped disc

²**slip** *n* **1** an act of slipping or sliding **2** a usu. slight mistake **3** a woman's dresslike undergarment not covering the arms or neck **4** a long surface sloping down into water, for moving ships into or out of water, or for ships to land at **5** (the position of) a cricket fielder who stands close behind and to the right of a (right handed) batsman, to catch balls that come off the edge of the bat **6 give someone the slip** *esp. spoken* to escape from someone

³**slip** *n* **1** a usu. small or narrow piece of paper **2** a small branch cut for planting; cutting **3** *becoming rare* a small thin one: *a slip of a boy*

slipper –also (*esp. written*) **carpet slipper** *n* a light indoor shoe with the top made from soft material

slippery *adj* **-ier, -iest 1** difficult to hold or to stand, drive, etc., on without slipping **2** difficult to understand exactly **3** *esp. spoken* not to be trusted; shifty **– -iness** *n*

slit *v* **slit, slitting** to make a narrow cut or opening in **–slit** *n*

slogan *n* a short phrase expressing a usu. political or advertising message

¹**slope** *v* **sloped, sloping** to lie or move in a sloping direction; be or go at an angle

²**slope** *n* **1** a surface that slopes; a piece of ground going up or down **2** a degree of sloping; a measure of an angle from a level direction

sloppy *adj* **-pier, -piest 1** (as of clothes) loose, informal, and careless-

or dirty-looking **2** not careful or thorough enough **3** wet and dirty **4** silly in showing feelings – **-pily** *adv* – **-piness** *n*

¹**slot** *n* **1** a long straight narrow opening or hollow place, esp. in a machine or tool **2** *esp. spoken* a place or position in a list, system, organization, etc.

²**slot** *v* **-tt- 1** to cut a slot in **2** to put into a slot **3** to find a place for

¹**slow** *adj* **1** not moving or going on quickly; having less than a usual or standard speed **2** taking a long time or too long: *slow to act* **3** not good or quick in understanding **4** not very active; dull; not brisk **5** (of a clock) showing a time that is earlier than the true time **6** (of a surface) not allowing quick movement: *a slow wicket* **7 slow off the mark** slow to understand (esp. the point of a joke) – ~**ly** *adj* – ~**ness** *n*

²**slow** *adv* slowly

³**slow** *v* to make or become slower

¹**slug** *n* any of several types of small limbless plant-eating creature, related to the snail but with no shell, that often do damage to gardens

²**slug** *n* a lump or piece of metal, esp. a bullet

³**slug** *v* **-gg-** *US esp. spoken* to strike with a heavy blow, esp. with the closed hand and so as to make unconscious

¹**slum** *n* **1** a city area of poor living conditions and dirty unrepaired buildings **2** *esp. spoken* a very untidy place – ~**my** *adj*

²**slum** *v* **-mm-** *esp. spoken* **1** to amuse oneself by visiting a place on a much lower social level **2 slum it** to live very cheaply, not having things that others find necessary

¹**slump** *v* **1** to sink down; fall heavily or in a heap; collapse **2** to go down in number or strength; fall off; decline

²**slump** *n* a time of seriously bad business conditions and unemployment; depression

slung *past tense and past part. of* SLING

sly *adj* **slyer** *or* **slier**, **slyest** *or* **sliest 1** clever in deceiving; dishonestly tricky; crafty **2** playfully unkind **3 on the sly** secretly (as of something done dishonestly or unlawfully) – ~**ly** *adv* – ~**ness** *n*

¹**smack** *n* a particular taste; flavour

²**smack** *v* **1** to open and close (one's lips) noisily **2** to strike loudly, as with the flat part of the hand **3** to put so as to make a short loud sound

³**smack** *n* **1** a quick loud noise; sound of smacking **2** a loud kiss **3** a quick loud forceful blow

⁴**smack** *adv* *esp. spoken* with force: *run smack into a wall*

⁵**smack** *n* a small sailing boat used for fishing

¹**small** *adj* **1** little in size, weight, force, importance, etc. **2** doing only a limited amount of a business or activity: *a small farmer* **3** very little; slight – ~**ness** *n*

²**small** *adv* in a small manner: *to write small*

³**small** *n* the small narrow part of something, esp. the middle part of the back where it curves in

¹**smart** *v* **1** to cause or feel a painful stinging sensation, usu. in one part of the body and not lasting long **2** to be hurt in one's feelings

²**smart** *adj* **1** quick or forceful; lively; vigorous: *a smart blow* **2** good or quick in thinking **3** neat and stylish in appearance **4** used by, concerning, etc., very fashionable people –~**ly** *adv* –~**ness** *n*

³**smart** *n* **1** a smarting pain **2** something that hurts the feelings or pride

¹**smash** *v* **1** to break into pieces violently **2** to go, drive, throw, or hit forcefully, as against something solid; crash **3** to be or cause to be destroyed or ruined **4** (in games like tennis) to hit (the ball) with a smash

²**smash** *n* **1** a powerful blow **2** a breaking into pieces **3** also **smash hit**– a great success, as of a new play, book, film, etc. **4** a hard downward attacking shot, as in tennis

smashing *adj esp. spoken* very fine; wonderful

¹**smear** *n* **1** a spot made by an oily or sticky material; mark made by smearing **2** *esp. medical* a small bit of some material prepared for examining under a microscope **3** an unproved charge made intentionally to try to turn public feelings against someone

²**smear** *v* **1 a** to cause (a sticky or oily material) to spread on or go across (a surface) **b** (of such material) to do this **2** to lose or cause to lose clearness in this way or by rubbing **3** to charge unfairly

¹**smell** *v* **smelled** *or* **smelt, smelling 1** to use the nose; have or use the sense of the nose **2** to notice, examine, discover, or recognize by this sense **3** to notice, come to know of, recognize, etc., by some natural unexplained ability: *I smelt trouble* **4** to have an effect on the nose; have a particular smell, often unpleasant

²**smell** *n* **1** the power of using the nose; the sense that can discover the presence of gases in the air **2** a quality that has an effect on the nose; something that excites this sense **3** an act of smelling something

¹**smile** *v* **smiled, smiling 1** to have or make (a smile) **2** to act or look favourably: *The weather smiled on us* –**smilingly** *adv*

²**smile** *n* an expression of the face with the mouth turned up at the ends and the eyes bright, that usu. expresses amusement, happiness, approval, or sometimes bitter feelings

¹**smoke** *n* **1** gas mixed with very small bits of solid material (esp. carbon) that can be seen in the air and is usu. given off by burning **2 a** *esp. spoken* something (esp. a cigarette)

for smoking **b** an act of smoking
–~**less** *adj*

²**smoke** *v* **smoked, smoking 1** to suck
or breathe in smoke from (esp.
tobacco, as in cigarettes, a pipe,
etc.) **2** to give off smoke **3** to darken
(a surface with smoke) **4** to preserve
and give a special taste to (meat,
fish, cheese, etc.) by hanging in
smoke

¹**smoking** *n* the practice or habit of
sucking in tobacco smoke from
cigarettes, a pipe, etc.

²**smoking** *adj* where one may smoke

smoky *adj* **-ier, -iest 1** filled with or
producing (too much) smoke **2** with
the taste or appearance of smoke
–**smokiness** *n*

¹**smooth** *adj* **1** having an even surface
without sharply raised or lowered
places, points, lumps, etc.; not
rough **2** even in movement without
sudden changes or breaks: *bring to
a smooth stop* **3** (of a liquid mixture)
without lumps; evenly thick **4** not
bitter or sour **5** very or too pleasant,
polite, or untroubled in manner;
avoiding or not showing difficulties
–~**ly** *adv* –~**ness** *n*

²**smooth** *v* to make smooth

smother *v* **1** to cover thickly or
heavily: *cake smothered with cream*
2 to die or kill from lack of air;
suffocate **3** to put out or keep down
(a fire) by keeping out air

smoulder *v* **1** to burn slowly without
a flame **2** to have, be, or show
violent feelings that are kept from
being expressed

smuggle *v* **-gled, -gling** to take from
one country to another unlawfully
(esp. goods without paying the
necessary duty) – **-gler** *n* – **-gling** *n*

snack *n* an amount of food smaller
than a meal; something eaten informally between meals

¹**snag** *n* **1** a dangerous, rough, sharp
part of something that may catch
and hold or cut things passing
against it **2** a pulled thread in a
cloth, esp. a stocking **3** a hidden or
unexpected difficulty

²**snag** *v* **-gg-** to catch on a snag

snail *n* any of several kinds of small
animal with a soft body, no limbs,
and usu. a hard spiral-shaped shell
on its back

¹**snake** *n* **1** any of many kinds of reptile
with a long limbless body, large
mouth, and fork-shaped tongue,
usu. feeding on other animals and
often with a poisonous bite **2** a
system in which the values of certain countries' money are allowed
to vary against each other within
narrow limits **3 a snake in the grass**
usu. humour a false friend

²**snake** *v* **snaked, snaking** to move in
a twisting way; wind (one's way or
body) in moving –**snaky** *adj*

¹**snap** *v* **-pp- 1** to close the jaws
quickly (on) **2** to break suddenly off
or in 2: *The branch snapped under
all that snow* **3** to make or cause to
make a sound as of either of these
actions **4** to move so as to cause
such a short sound: *The lid snapped
shut* **5** to say quickly, usu. in an

annoyed or angry way **6** *esp. spoken* to photograph; take a snapshot of **7** **snap out of it** *esp. spoken* to make oneself quickly get free from a bad state of mind

²**snap** *n* **1** an act or sound of snapping **2** a type of card game in which players lay down cards one after the other and try to be the first to notice and call out 'Snap!' when 2 like cards are laid down together **3** *esp. spoken* a snapshot

³**snap** *adj* done, made, arrived at, etc., in haste or without (long) warning

snapshot *n* an informal picture taken with a hand-held camera

¹**snare** *n* **1** a trap for catching an animal, esp. one with a rope which catches the animal's foot **2** something in which one may be caught; a course which leads to being trapped

²**snare** *v* **snared, snaring 1** to catch (as if) in a snare **2** to get by skilful action: *snare a good job*

¹**snarl** *n* a knotty twisted confused mass or state; tangle

²**snarl** *v* to put into a snarl; make confused or difficult; tangle: *Traffic was snarled (up) near the accident*

³**snarl** *v* **1** (of an animal) to make a low angry sound while showing the teeth **2** (of a person) to speak or say in an angry bad-tempered way —**snarl** *n*

¹**snatch** *v* to get hold of (something) hastily: make every effort to get: *snatch at a chance* −~**er** *n*

²**snatch** *n* **1** an act of snatching (at) something **2** a short period of time or activity: *to sleep in snatches* **3** a short and incomplete part of something that is seen or heard

¹**sneak** *v* **1** to go or cause to go, quietly and secretly; go or take so as not to be seen: *sneak past a guard* **2** *sl* to steal secretly **3** *school sl* to give information, esp. to a teacher, about the wrongdoings (of another pupil) −~**y** *adj*

²**sneak** *n* **1** a sneaky person; one who acts secretly and should not be trusted **2** unexpected; secret until the last moment; surprise **3** *school sl* a person who sneaks

sneaking *adj* **1** secret; not expressed, as if shameful **2** (of a feeling or suspicion) not proved but probably right

¹**sneer** *v* to express proud dislike; treat something as if not worthy of serious notice −~**er** *n* −~**ingly** *adv*

²**sneer** *n* a sneering expression of the face, way of speaking, or remark

¹**sneeze** *v* **sneezed, sneezing 1** to have a sudden uncontrolled burst of air out of the nose and mouth, usu. caused by discomfort in the nose **2** **not to be sneezed at** *esp. spoken, often humour* worthy of consideration

²**sneeze** *n* an act, sound, etc., of sneezing

¹**sniff** *v* **1** to draw air into the nose with a sound, esp. in short repeated actions **2** to do this to discover a

smell in or on **3** to say in a proud complaining way −∼**er** *n*

²**sniff** *n* an act or sound of sniffing

snob *n* **1** a person who dislikes or keeps away from those he feels to be of lower social class **2** a person who is too proud of having special knowledge or judgment in a subject −∼**bish** *adj* −∼**bishly** *adv* −∼**bishness** *n*

¹**snore** *v* **snored, snoring** to breathe heavily and noisily through the nose and mouth while asleep −**snorer** *n*

²**snore** *n* a noisy way of breathing when asleep; a noise of snoring

¹**snort** *v* **1** to make a rough noise by blowing air down the nose **2** to express (esp. impatience or anger, or sometimes amusement) (as) by this sound

²**snort** *n* an act or sound of snorting

¹**snow** *n* **1** water frozen into small flat 6-sided flakes that fall like rain in cold weather and may cover the ground thickly **2** a fall of this

²**snow** *v* (of snow) to fall

¹**snowball** *n* a ball pressed or rolled together from snow, as thrown at each other by children

²**snowball** *v* to increase in size faster and faster or uncontrolledly: *Prices are snowballing*

snug *adj* **-gg-** giving or enjoying warmth, comfort, peace, protection, etc.; cosy −∼**ly** *adv* −∼**ness** *n*

¹**so** *adv* **1** in the way I show: *Push the needle so* **2** in that way; in the way

stated **3 a** to such a degree: *You mustn't worry so* **b** in such a way: *The book is so written in order to offend* **4** (used in place of an idea, expression, etc., stated already): *He hopes he'll win and I hope so too* **5** in the same way; also: *You have pride and so have I* **6** indeed; certainly: *'Father, you promised!' 'So I did.'* **7** up to a limit; to a certain degree: *I can hold so much and no more* **8** in that same way/time: *As the wind blew harder, so the sea grew rougher*

²**so** *conj* **1** with the result that: *I broke my glasses, so I couldn't see* **2** with the purpose (that) **3** therefore: *I had a headache, so I went to bed*

³**so** *adj* **1** in agreement with the facts; true: *It just isn't so* **2** (used in place of an adjective already stated): *He's clever−probably too much so for his own good*

¹**soak** *v* **1** to remain or leave in a liquid, esp. to become soft or completely wet **2** (of a liquid) to enter (a solid) through the material of a surface −∼**ed** *adj* −∼**ing** *adj, adv*

²**soak** *n* **1** an act or state of soaking **2** *sl* a person who is often or usually drunk

so-and-so *n* **so-and-sos 1** someone or something; a certain one (not to be named) **2** (used instead of a stronger word) a rude, wicked, etc., person

¹**soap** *n* a product made from fat and alkali, for use with water to clean the body or other things −**soapy** *adj*

²**soap** *v* to rub soap on or over

soar *v esp. in literature* **1** to fly; go fast or high (as) on wings; sail in the air **2** to go upwards, esp. far or fast: *The temperature soared to 80°* **3** to go beyond what is ordinary or limiting: *a soaring imagination* **4** (of a glider or people in it) to go through the air

sob *v* **-bb-** to breathe while weeping, in sudden short bursts making a sound in the throat —**sob** *n* —**sobbingly** *adv*

¹**sober** *adj* **1** in control of oneself; not drunk **2** thoughtful, serious, or solemn; not silly; grave **3** not ornamental or brightly-coloured; restrained —~**ly** *adv*

²**sober** *v* to make or become serious or thoughtful

so-called *adj* **1** called or named the stated thing **2** improperly or falsely named so

soccer —also **football, Association Football** *n* a football game between 2 teams of 11 players who kick or head a round ball without using the arms or hands

sociable *adj* fond of being with others; enjoying social life; friendly — -**bility** *n* – -**bly** *adv*

¹**social** *adj* **1** of or concerning human society, its organization, or quality of life **2** of, concerning, or spent in time or activities with friends **3** forming groups or living together by nature: *social insects like ants* —~**ly** *adv*

²**social** *n* a planned informal friendly gathering of members of a group or esp. church

socialism *n* any of various beliefs or systems (sometimes considered to include communism) aiming at public ownership of the means of production and the establishment of a society in which every person is equal

socialist *n, adj* (a follower) of socialism, or of any of various esp. W European parties who support more equality of wealth and government ownership of business

society *n* **-ties** **1** a large group of people with a particular organization and shared customs, laws, etc. **2** people living and working together considered as a whole **3** an organization of people with like aims, interests, etc. **4** the companionship or presence of others **5** the fashionable group of people of a high class in a place: *a society occasion*

sociology *n* the scientific study of societies and human behaviour in groups – -**gical** *adj* – -**gically** *adv* – -**gist** *n*

¹**sock** *n* a covering of soft material for the foot and usu. part of the lower leg, usu. worn inside a shoe

²**sock** *v esp. spoken* to strike hard —**sock** *n*

socket *n* an opening, hollow place, or machine part that forms a holder or into which something fits: *an electric light socket*

sofa *n* a comfortable seat with raised

arms and a back and wide enough for usu. 2 or 3 people

soft *adj* **1** not firm against pressure; giving in to the touch; changeable in shape; not hard or stiff **2** less hard than average: *Lead is one of the softer metals* **3** smooth and delicate to the touch **4** restful and pleasant to the senses, esp. the eyes: *soft lights* **5** quiet; not making much noise; not loud **6** not violent; gentle **7** easily persuaded; easy to make agree or do what one wishes; weak **8** (of a drink) containing no alcohol and usu. sweet **9 a** (of *c*) having the sound of c in 'acid' **b** (of *g*) having the sound of g in 'age' **10** (of water) free from certain minerals; allowing soap to act easily **11** not of the worst, most harmful, etc., kind: *soft drugs* **12** *esp. spoken* foolish or mad –~**ly** *adv* –~**ness** *n*

soften *v* to make or become soft, gentle, less stiff, or less severe

softhearted *adj* having tender feelings; easily moved to pity; merciful –~**ness** *n*

software *n technical* the set of systems (in the form of programs rather than machine parts) which control the operation of a computer

soggy *adj* **-gier**, **-giest** completely wet; heavy and usu. unpleasant with wetness – **-gily** *adv* – **-giness** *n*

¹**soil** *v* to make or become dirty, esp. slightly or on the surface

²**soil** *n* material that soils; dirt

³**soil** *n* the top covering of the earth in which plants grow; ground

solar *adj* **1** of, from, or concerning the sun **2** using the power of the sun's light and heat

solar system *n* the sun together with all the bodies going around it

sold *past tense and past part. of* SELL

soldier *n* a member of an army, esp. a man and esp. one of low rank (not an officer) –~**ly** *adj*

¹**sole** *n* **1** the bottom surface of the foot, esp. the part on which one walks or stands **2** the part of a piece of footwear covering this, esp. the flat bottom part of a shoe not including the heel

²**sole** *v* **soled**, **soling** to put a sole on (a shoe)

³**sole** *n* sole *or* soles any of various kinds of flat fishes with small mouths, eyes, and fins, of which large types make fine food

⁴**sole** *adj* **1** having no sharer; being the only one **2** belonging or allowed to one and no other; unshared –~**ly** *adv*

solemn *adj* **1** done, made, etc., seriously, having a sense of religious-like importance **2** too serious for humour; grave –~**ly** *adv* –~**ness** *n*

solicitor *n* (esp. in England) a kind of lawyer who gives advice, appears in lower courts, and prepares cases to be argued in a high court

¹**solid** *adj* **1** not needing a container to hold its shape; not liquid or gas **2** having an inside filled up; not

hollow **3** made of material tight together; dense; compact: *They hit solid rock* **4** that may be depended on; reputable: *solid citizens* **5** completely of the stated material without mixture of others **6** in or showing complete agreement **7** being or concerning space with length, width, and height; 3-dimensional: **Solid geometry** *is the study of lines, figures, angles, measurements, etc., in space* –~**ly** *adv* –~**ness** *n*

²**solid** *n* **1** a solid object; something that does not flow **2** any of the solid material in a liquid **3** (esp. in geometry) an object that takes up space; object with length, width, and height **4** an article of non-liquid food: *He's still too ill to take solids*

solitary *adj* **1** alone without companions **2** fond of, or habitually, being alone **3** in a lonely place **4** single; sole – **-tarily** *adv*

solitude *n* the quality or state of being alone away from companionship

¹**solo** *n* **solos** a piece of music played or sung by one person

²**solo** *adj, adv* **1** without a companion **2** of, for, or played or heard as, a musical solo

soluble *adj* **1** that can be dissolved **2** solvable – **-bility** *n*

solution *n* **1** an answer to a difficulty or problem **2** (a) liquid containing a solid or gas mixed into it, usu. without chemical change **3** the

state or action of being mixed into liquid like this

solve *v* **solved, solving** to find a solution to; come to an answer, explanation, or way of dealing with (something) –**solvable** *adj* –**solver** *n*

¹**some** *adj, pron* **1** a little, few, or certain or small number or amount (of): *I saw some people I knew* **2** an unknown one; a certain: *Come back some other time*

²**some** *adv* (used usu. before a number) about: *There were some 40 or 50 people there*

somebody –also **someone** *pron* a person; some but no particular or known person

somehow *adv* by some means; in some way not yet known or stated: *We must reach an agreement somehow*

somersault *n, v* (to make) a jump or rolling backward or forward movement in which the feet go over the head before the body returns upright

something *pron* some unstated or unknown thing: *Something must be done!*

¹**sometime** *adv* at some uncertain or unstated time: *We'll take our holiday sometime in August*

²**sometime** *adj* former: *sometime chairman of the company*

sometimes *adv* at times; now and then; occasionally: *Sometimes he comes by train, and sometimes by car*

somewhat *adv* by some degree or amount; a little; rather: *a price somewhat higher than expected*

somewhere *adv* (in/at/to) some place

son *n* **1** someone's male child **2** (used by an older man in speaking to a much younger man or boy)

song *n* **1** a usu. short piece of music with words for singing **2** the act or art of singing **3** the music-like sound of a bird or birds **4 for a song** *esp. spoken* for a very small price; very cheaply

soon *adv* **1** within a short time **2** (making comparisons) readily; willingly: *He'd just as soon have water as coffee* **3 no sooner...than** when...at once: *No sooner had we sat down, than we found it was time to go*

soot *n* black powder produced by burning, and carried into the air and left on surfaces by smoke – ~**y** *adj*

soothe *v* **soothed, soothing 1** to make less angry, excited, or anxious; comfort or calm **2** to make less painful –**soothingly** *adv*

sophisticated *adj* **1** having or showing a knowledge of social life and behaviour **2** having many parts; complicated; complex – **-cation** *n*

¹**sore** *adj* **1** painful or aching from a wound, infection, or (of muscles) hard use **2** likely to cause pain of mind or offence: *It's a sore subject with him* – ~**ness** *n*

²**sore** *n* a painful usu. infected place on the body

¹**sorrow** *n* (a cause of) unhappiness over loss or wrongdoing; sadness; grief – ~**ful** *adj* – ~**fully** *adv* – ~**fulness** *n*

²**sorrow** *v esp. in literature* to feel or express sorrow; grieve

¹**sorry** *adj* **-rier, -riest 1** grieved; sad **2** having a sincere feeling of shame or unhappiness at one's past actions, and expressing a wish that one had not done them **3** (used for expressing polite refusal, disagreement, excusing of oneself, etc.) (esp. in the phrase **I'm sorry**) **4** causing pity mixed with disapproval: *a sorry sight*

²**sorry** *interj* **1** (used for expressing polite refusal, disagreement, excusing of oneself, etc.) **2** (used for asking someone to repeat something one has not heard properly)

¹**sort** *n* **1** a group of people, things, etc., all having certain qualities; type; kind **2 a sort of** a weak, unexplained, or unusual kind of **3 out of sorts** in a bad temper; feeling unwell or annoyed

²**sort** *v* to put (things) in order; place according to kind, rank, etc.; arrange – ~**er** *n*

sort of *adv esp. spoken* in some way or degree; rather; kind of

sought *past tense and past part. of* SEEK

¹**soul** *n* **1** the part of a person that is not the body and is thought not to die **2** a person: *She's a dear old soul* **3** a fine example; embodiment

²**soul** *adj US esp. spoken* of or concerning black people

¹**sound** *adj* 1 in good condition; without disease or damage 2 solid; firm; strong: *a sound basis for study* 3 based on truth or good judgment; not wrong 4 (of sleep) deep and untroubled 5 severe; hard: *a sound slap* –~**ly** *adv* –~**ness** *n*

²**sound** *n* 1 what is or may be heard; (something that causes) a sensation in the ear 2 a quality of something read or heard –~**less** *adj* –~**lessly** *adv*

³**sound** *v* 1 to have the effect of being; seem when heard: *Your idea sounds a good one* 2 to make or cause to make a sound; produce an effect that can be heard 3 to express as a sound; pronounce

⁴**sound** *n* 1 a fairly broad stretch of sea water mostly surrounded by coast 2 a water passage connecting 2 larger bodies of water

⁵**sound** *v* to measure the depth of (esp. the bottom of a body of water), as by using a weighted line

soup *n* 1 liquid cooked food often containing small pieces of meat, fish, or vegetables 2 **in the soup** *esp. spoken* in trouble

¹**sour** *adj* 1 having the taste that is not bitter, salty, or sweet, and is produced esp. by acids 2 having or expressing a bad temper; unsmiling –~**ly** *adv* –~**ness** *n*

²**sour** *v* to make or become sour

source *n* 1 a place from which something comes; producing place or force 2 the place where a stream of water starts 3 a person or thing that supplies information

¹**south** *adv* towards the south

²**south** *n* 1 (the direction of) one of the 4 main points of the compass, on the right of a person facing the rising sun 2 (of a wind) (coming from) this direction

¹**southeast** *adv* towards the southeast

²**southeast** *n* 1 (the direction of) the point of the compass that is halfway between south and east 2 (of a wind) (coming from) this direction

southerly *adj* 1 towards or in the south 2 (of a wind) coming from the south

southern *adj* of or belonging to the south part, esp. of the world or a country

southwards *adv* towards the south

¹**southwest** *adv* towards the southwest

²**southwest** *n* 1 (the direction of) the point of the compass which is halfway between south and west 2 (of a wind) (coming from) this direction

souvenir *n* an object (to be) kept as a reminder of an event, trip, place, etc.

¹**sovereign** *n* 1 the person with the highest political power in a country; a ruler such as a king or queen; monarch 2 a former British gold coin worth £1

²**sovereign** *adj* 1 in control of a country; ruling: *Sovereign power must lie with the people* 2 (of a country) independent and self-governing

Soviet *adj* of or concerning the USSR (the **Soviet Union**) or its people

¹sow *n* a fully grown female pig

²sow *v* **sowed, sown** *or* **sowed, sowing** to plant or scatter (seeds) on (a piece of ground) −∼**er** *n*

¹space *n* **1** something limited and measurable in length, width, or depth and regarded as not filled up; distance, area, or volume; room **2** a quantity or bit of this for a particular purpose **3** that which surrounds all objects and continues outward in all directions **4** what is outside the earth's air; where other heavenly bodies move **5** (an area of) land not built on (esp. in the phrase **open space**) **6** a period of time **7** an area or distance left between written or printed words, lines, etc.

²space *v* **spaced, spacing** to place apart; arrange with spaces between

spacecraft *n* **spacecraft** a vehicle able to travel in space

spaceship *n* (esp. in stories) a space vehicle for carrying people

spacesuit *n* a suit for wearing in space, covering the whole body and provided with an air supply

spacious *adj* having a lot of room; not narrow −∼**ly** *adv* −∼**ness** *n*

¹spade *n* a tool like a shovel for digging earth, with a broad metal blade for pushing with the foot into the ground

²spade *n* a playing card with 1 or more figures shaped like a pointed leaf printed on it in black

spaghetti *n* an Italian food made of pasta in long strings, usu. sold in dry form for making soft again in boiling water

¹span *n* **1** a stretch between 2 limits, esp. in time **2** a length of time over which something continues or works well **3** (the length of) a bridge, arch, etc., between supports **4** the distance from the end of the thumb to the end of the little finger in a spread hand; about 9 inches or 0..23 metres

²span *v* **-nn-** **1** to form an arch or bridge over **2** to enclose in space or time; reach over: *His interest spans many subjects*

spaniel *n* any of various breeds of small short-legged dogs with long ears and long wavy hair

¹spank *v* to strike with quick force (as if) with the open hand, esp. on the buttocks −**spank** *n* −∼**ing** *n*

²spank *v* to go or esp. sail quickly

spanner *n* a metal hand tool with jaws (**open-ended spanner**) or a hollow end (**ring spanner**), for fitting over and twisting nuts

¹spare *v* **spared, sparing** **1** to keep from punishing, harming, or attacking: *Spare my life!* **2** to save (someone) (need or trouble) **3** to give up as not completely needed; afford to give: *Can you spare me 5 minutes?* **4 to spare** left over; extra

²spare *adj* **1** not in use but kept for use **2** not needed for use; free: *spare time* **3 go spare** *sl* to become very anxious and/or angry

³**spare** *n* a second object of the same kind that is kept for possible use

¹**spark** *n* 1 a small bit of burning material thrown out by a fire or by the striking together of 2 hard objects 2 a light-producing passage of electricity across a space 3 a very small but important bit, esp. of a quality 4 **bright spark** *esp. spoken* a clever or cheerful person

²**spark** *v* 1 to throw out sparks 2 to produce a spark

¹**sparkle** *v* **-kled, -kling** 1 to shine in small flashes 2 (of a drink) to give off gas in small bubbles 3 to show spirit and excitement; be bright

²**sparkle** *n* an act, or the quality, of sparkling

sparrow *n* any of various kinds of small brownish birds very common in many parts of the world

sparse *adj* scattered; with few members; thin; scanty −∼**ly** *adv* −∼**ness, sparsity** *n*

spasm *n* 1 a sudden uncontrolled tightening of muscles 2 a sudden violent effort, feeling, or act; fit: *spasms of laughter*

spastic *n, adj* (a person) suffering from a disease (**spastic paralysis**) in which some parts of the body will not move because the muscles stay tightened

spate *n* 1 a large number or amount, esp. coming together in time 2 **in spate** flooding; full of rushing water

speak *v* **spoke, spoken, speaking** 1 to say things; express thoughts aloud; use the voice; talk 2 to express

thoughts, ideas, etc., in some other way than this: *Actions speak louder than words* 3 to be able to talk in (a language) 4 to express or say

speaker *n* 1 a person making a speech, or who makes speeches in a stated way 2 a person who speaks a language 3 the person who controls the course of business in a law-making body (note the phrase **Mr Speaker**) 4 a loudspeaker

speak out *v adv* to speak boldly, freely, and plainly

speak up *v adv* 1 to speak more loudly 2 SPEAK OUT

¹**spear** *n* a pole with a sharp point at one end used esp. formerly for throwing as a weapon

²**spear** *v* to make a hole in or catch (as) with the point of a spear

¹**special** *adj* of a particular kind; not ordinary or usual

²**special** *n* 1 something not ordinary or usual 2 *esp. spoken* an advertised reduced price in a shop

specialist *n* 1 a person who has special interests or skills in a limited field of work or study; expert 2 a doctor who gives treatment in a particular way or to certain kinds of people or diseases

speciality *n* **-ties** 1 a special field of work or study 2 a particularly fine or best product: *Fish is a speciality of this restaurant*

specially *adv* 1 for one particular purpose 2 in a special way 3 especially

species *n* **-cies** 1 a group of plants or animals that are of the same kind, which are alike in all important ways, and which can breed together to produce young of the same kind **2** a type; sort

specific *adj* **1** detailed and exact; clear in meaning; careful in explanation; not vague **2** particular; certain; fixed, determined, or named – ∼**ity** *n*

specifically *adv* **1** exactly and clearly **2** of the stated kind and no other; particularly

specify *v* **-fied, -fying** to mention exactly; describe fully so as to choose or name

specimen *n* **1** a single typical thing or example **2** one or a piece or amount of something for being shown, tested, etc.

speck *n* a small spot, coloured mark, or dot

spectacle *n* **1** a grand public show or scene **2** a silly sight; object of laughing or disrespect: *to make a spectacle of oneself*

spectacles –also (*esp. spoken*) **specs** *n* glasses, esp. of the usual kind with side parts fitting on top of the ears

¹spectacular *adj* grandly out of the ordinary; attracting excited notice – ∼**ly** *adv*

²spectacular *n* a spectacular entertainment

spectator *n* a person who watches (esp. an event or sport) without taking part

spectrum *n* **-tra 1** a set of bands of coloured light in the order of their wavelengths, into which a beam of light may be separated (as by a prism) **2** a range of any of various kinds of waves

speculate *v* **-lated, -lating 1** to think (about a matter) in a light way or without facts that would lead to a firm result **2** to buy or deal in goods, shares etc., whose future price is still very uncertain, in the hope of a large profit – **-lation** *n* – **-lator** *n*

speech *n* **1** the act or power of speaking; spoken language **2 a** an act of speaking formally to a group of listeners **b** the words so spoken **3** a usu. long set of lines for an actor to say in a play

¹speed *n* **1** rate of movement; distance divided by time of travel: *a speed of 55 miles per hour* **2** the action, ability, or state of moving swiftly

²speed *v* **speeded** *or* **sped, speeding 1** to go or send quickly **2** to go or drive too fast; break the speed limit

¹spell *n* **1 a** a condition caused by magical power: enchantment **b** the magic words producing this condition **2** a strong attractive power

²spell *v* **spelt** *or* **spelled, spelling 1** to name in order the letters of (a word) **2** (of letters in order) to form (a word) **3** to form words correctly from letters – ∼**er** *n*

³spell *v* **spelled, spelling** to take the turn of; allow (another) to rest by taking over work; relieve

⁴spell *n* an unbroken period of time of usu. unstated length: *a spell of work abroad*

spelling *n* **1** the action or proper way

of forming words from letters **2** an ordered set of letters forming a word

spend *v* **spent, spending 1** to give out (esp. money) in payment **2** to pass or use (time) **3** *esp. written or literature* to wear out or use completely: *The storm soon spent itself*

sphagnum *n* any of a large group of mosses growing in wet areas which can go to make peat and which are used by gardeners for packing plants

sphere *n* **1** a round figure in space; ball-shaped mass; solid figure all points of which are equally distant from a centre **2** an area or range of existence, force, meaning, action, etc.: *famous in many spheres* **3** (in ancient science) any of the transparent shells which were thought to turn around the earth with the heavenly bodies fixed in them

¹**spice** *n* **1** any of various vegetable products used esp. in powder form for flavouring foods **2** interest or excitement, esp. as added to something else

²**spice** *v* **spiced, spicing** to add spice to

spicy *adj* **-ier, -iest 1** containing or tasting like spice **2** exciting, esp. from being slightly improper or rude **-spicily** *adv* **-spiciness** *n*

spider *n* any of many kinds of small 8-legged creatures which make silk threads, sometimes into nets for catching insects to eat

spike *n* **1** a long pointed piece of esp. metal with an outward or upward point **2** any of several pieces of metal fixed in the bottom of shoes for holding the ground, esp. in sports **-spiky** *adj*

¹**spill** *v* **spilt** *or* **spilled, spilling 1** to pour out accidentally, as over the edge of a container **2** to spread or rush beyond limits **3** *esp. literature* to cause (blood) to flow by wounding

²**spill** *n* **1** an act or amount of spilling **2** a fall from a horse, bicycle, etc.

³**spill** *n* a thin piece of wood or twisted paper for lighting lamps, pipes, etc.

¹**spin** *v* **spun, spinning 1** to make (thread) by twisting (cotton, wool, etc.) **2** (of a spider or silkworm) to produce (thread, esp. in a mass or net) **3** to turn round and round fast; whirl **4** to move fast on wheels **5** to produce in a threadlike form

²**spin** *n* **1** an act of spinning **2** fast turning movement **3** a short trip for pleasure

spinach *n* a type of widely-grown vegetable whose broad green leaves are eaten cooked

spindly *adj* **-dlier, -dliest** long, thin, and weak-looking

spine *n* **1** also **spinal column-** the row of bones in the centre of the back of higher animals that supports the body and protects the thick cord of nerves (spinal cord) by which nervous messages are carried to the body **2** the end of a book where the pages are fastened and the title is usu. printed **3** any of various stiff sharp-pointed plant or animal parts; prickle

spinster *n* 1 an unmarried woman 2 *sometimes offensive* old maid –~**hood** *n*

¹**spiral** *n* 1 a curve on a plane formed by a point winding round a centre and getting always closer to or further from it 2 a curve in space winding round a central line 3 a continuous upward or downward change: *the inflationary spiral*

²**spiral** *v* -ll- 1 to move in a spiral; rise or fall esp. in a winding way 2 to fall or esp. rise continuously

spire *n* a roof rising steeply to a point on top of a tower, as on a church; (the top of a) steeple

¹**spirit** *n* 1 *literature* a person apart from the body; one's mind or soul 2 a being without a body, such as a ghost 3 a power regarded as able to take control of a person 4 life or thought regarded as independently existing 5 a person of the stated kind or temper 6 an intention or feeling in the mind; attitude: *to take a remark in the right spirit* 7 excitement, force, or effort shown; energy; liveliness 8 the central quality or force of something 9 an alcoholic drink (such as whisky or brandy) produced by distillation from a weaker alcohol-containing drink or mixture 10 any of various liquids such as alcohol used esp. for breaking down solids or as fuels

²**spirit** *v* to carry away; take, esp. in a secret or mysterious way; make off with

spirited *adj* full of spirit; forceful

¹**spiritual** *adj* 1 nonmaterial; of the nature of spirit 2 religious; sacred –~**ly** *adv*

²**spiritual** *n* a religious song of the type sung originally by the black peoples of the US

¹**spit** *n* 1 a thin pointed rod for sticking meat onto and turning, for cooking over a fire 2 a small usu. sandy point of land running out into a stretch of water

²**spit** *v* **spat** *or* **spit, spitting** 1 to force (liquid) from the mouth 2 **spit it out** *esp. spoken* Go ahead and say what is on your mind

³**spit** *n* 1 the liquid in the mouth; saliva 2 *esp. spoken* the exact likeness (esp in the phrases **the spit and image of, the dead spit of**)

¹**spite** *n* 1 unreasonable dislike for and desire to annoy another person, esp. in some small way 2 **in spite of** in opposition to the presence or efforts of; despite –~**ful** *adj* –~**fully** *adv* –~**fulness** *n*

²**spite** *v* **spited, spiting** to treat with spite; annoy intentionally

¹**splash** *v* 1 to move or hit usu. noisily in a liquid 2 **a** (of a liquid) to fall, strike, or move noisily, in drops, waves, etc. **b** to cause (a liquid) to do this 3 *esp. spoken* to give a lot of space to (esp. a news story); report as if very important 4 to spend (money) on unnecessary but fine things

²**splash** *n* 1 a splashing act, movement, or noise 2 a mark made by splashing

³**splash** *adv* with a splash

splendid *adj* 1 grand in appearance; glorious 2 very fine; excellent —~**ly** *adv*

splendour *n* excellent or grand beauty; magnificence

splint *n* a flat piece of wood, metal, etc., used for protecting and keeping a damaged part of the body, esp. a broken bone, in position

¹**splinter** *n* a small needle-like piece broken off something

²**splinter** *v* 1 to break into small needle-like pieces 2 to separate from a larger organization

³**splinter** *adj* (of a group) that has separated from a larger body

¹**split** *v* **split, splitting** 1 to divide along a length, esp. with force or by a blow or tear 2 to divide into separate parts 3 to end a friendship, marriage, etc. 4 *sl* to tell secret information (about someone) 5 *sl* to leave quickly 6 **split an infinitive** to put a word such as an adverb between

²**split** *n* 1 a cut or break made by splitting 2 a division or separation 3 a dish made from fruit (esp. a banana) cut into 2 pieces with ice cream on top

split second *n* a small part of a second; flash; instant —**split-second** *adj*

¹**spoil** *n* things taken without payment, as **a** by an army from a defeated enemy or place **b** by thieves

²**spoil** *v* **spoiled** *or* **spoilt, spoiling** 1 to make or become of no use or value; ruin 2 to make (esp. a child) selfish from having too much attention or praise —~**er** *n*

¹**spoke** *n*- any of the bars which connect the outer ring of a wheel to the centre, as on a bicycle

²**spoke** *past tense of* SPEAK

spoken *past part. of* SPEAK

spokesman —(*fem.* **spokeswoman**) *n* **-men** a person who speaks as a representative of others

¹**sponge** *n* 1 any of a group of sea creatures which grow a spreading rubber-like skeleton full of small holes 2 a piece of this animal's frame or of rubber or plastic like it, which is used in washing surfaces 3 *esp. spoken* a person who sponges on other people 4 *also* **sponge cake**- a soft light sweet cake

²**sponge** *v* **sponged, sponging** 1 to clean (as if) with a wet cloth or sponge 2 to remove (liquid) with a cloth, sponge, etc. 3 to get (money, meals, etc.) free by taking advantage of another's good nature —**sponger** *n*

¹**sponsor** *n* 1 a person who takes responsibility for a person or thing 2 a business which pays for a show, broadcast, sports event, etc., usu. in return for advertising —~**ship** *n*

²**sponsor** *v* to act as sponsor for

spontaneous *adj* produced from natural feelings or causes without outside force; unplanned: *a spontaneous cheer* −~**ly** *adv* −~**ness, -neity** *n*

¹spoon *n* **1** a tool for mixing, serving, and eating food, consisting of a small bowl with a handle **2** a spoonful

²spoon *v* to take up or move with a spoon

spoonful *n* **-s** *or* **spoonsful** the amount that a spoon will hold

¹sport *v* to wear or show publicly; show off

²sport *n* **1** an outdoor or indoor game, competition, or activity carried on by rules and needing bodily effort **2** active amusement; play: *It's great sport, swimming in the sea* **3** a generous-minded person of a kind who accepts defeat or a joke good-temperedly **4** *technical* a plant or animal that is different in some way from its usual type

sporting *adj* **1** offering the kind of fair risk that is usual in a game: *a sporting chance* **2** of or fond of field sports like hunting or horse racing −~**ly** *adv*

¹spot *n* **1** a part or area different from the main surface, as in colour, usu. of a round shape **2** a particular place: *the spot where it happened* **3** a small part of something: *a bright spot in the news* **4** a dirty mark **5** a pimple **6** an area of mind or feelings: *I have a soft spot for my old school* **7** a usu. difficult state of affairs; fix: *We're really in a spot!* **8** a little bit; small amount **9** a place

in a broadcast **10 on the spot a** at once **b** at the place of the action **c** in a position of having to make the right action or answer: *The question put me on the spot*

²spot *v* **-tt- 1** to pick out, esp. with the eye; see; recognize **2** to mark with coloured or dirty spots **3** to place in position: *Guards were spotted around the building*

³spot *adv esp. spoken* exactly (in the phrase **spot on**): *spot on time*

⁴spot *adj* limited to a few times or places as representing all: *to make spot checks*

spotless *adj* completely clean −~**ly** *adv* −~**ness** *n*

¹spotlight *n* **1** (a bright round area of light made by) a lamp with a directable narrow beam **2** public attention

²spotlight *v* **-lighted, -lighting** to direct attention to, with, or as if with a spotlight

spotted *adj* marked with coloured or dirty spots

¹spout *v* **1** to throw or come out in a forceful stream **2** to pour out in a stream of words: *to spout Shakespeare* −~**er** *n*

²spout *n* **1** an opening from which liquid comes out from a container **2** a forceful esp. rising stream of liquid **3 up the spout** *esp. spoken* ruined; in a hopeless condition

¹sprain *n* an act or result of spraining a joint

²sprain *v* to damage (a joint in the body) by sudden twisting

sprang *past tense of* SPRING

¹sprawl *v* **1** to stretch out (oneself or one's limbs) awkwardly: *sprawled out in a chair* **2** to spread ungracefully: *The city sprawls for miles*

²sprawl *n* **1** a sprawling position **2** an irregular spreading mass or group

¹spray *n* **sprays** (an arrangement of flowers, jewels, etc. in the shape of) a small branch with leaves and flowers

²spray *n* **1** water in very small drops blown from the sea, a waterfall, etc. **2** (a can or other container holding) liquid to be sprayed out under pressure

³spray *v* **sprayed, spraying 1 a** to scatter (liquid) in small drops under pressure **b** (of liquid) to be scattered in this way **2** to throw or force out liquid in small drops upon (a surface, field of crops etc.) −~**er** *n*

¹spread *v* **spread, spreading 1** to open, reach, or stretch out; be or make longer, broader, wider, etc.: *a ship with sails spread* **2** to put (a covering) on: *spread butter on bread* **3** to share or divide over an area, period of time, etc.: *spread the cost over 3 years* **4** to make or become (more) widely known **5** to have or give a wider effect: *The fire soon spread* **6** to prepare (a table or meal) for eating −~**able** *adj*

²spread *n* **1** the act or action of spreading **2** a distance, area, or time of spreading: *a tree with a spread of 100 feet* **3** a newspaper or magazine article or advertisement running across one or more pages **4** a large or grand meal **5** a soft food for spreading on bread

¹spring *v* **sprang, sprung, springing 1** to move quickly as if by jumping; bound **2** to come into being or action quickly; arise: *A wind suddenly sprang up* **3** to come out (as if) in a spring of water; issue **4** to crack or split: *The weight sprang the beam* **5** to open or close (as if) by the force of a spring: *The box sprang open* **6** *sl* to cause to leave prison, lawfully or by escaping **7** to produce as a surprise **8** **spring a leak** to begin to let liquid through a crack, hole, etc.

²spring *n* **1** a place where water comes up naturally from the ground **2** the season between winter and summer **3** a metal spiral, which tends to push, pull, or twist and return to its original shape **4** the quality of this object; elasticity **5** an act of springing −~**less** *adj*

sprinkle *v* **-kled, -kling 1** to scatter in drops or small grains **2** to scatter liquid, small bits, etc., on or among: *a book sprinkled with humour* −**sprinkle** *n*

¹sprint *v* to run at one's fastest speed −~**er** *n*

²sprint *n* **1** an act of sprinting **2** a short race; dash

¹sprung *past part. of* SPRING

²sprung *adj* supported by springs

spun *past tense and past part. of* SPIN

¹spur *n* **1** a U-shaped object worn on a rider's boot to direct a horse **2** a force leading to action; incentive **3** a railway track that goes away from a main line **4** a length of high ground coming out from a range of mountains **5 on the spur of the moment** without preparation

²**spur** *v* **-rr- 1** to prick (a horse) with spurs **2** to urge to (faster) action or effort

¹**spurt** *n* a short sudden increase of activity; burst

²**spurt** *v* to make a spurt

³**spurt, spirt** *v* to flow or send out suddenly or violently; gush; spout

⁴**spurt, spirt** *n* a sudden usu. short coming out, as of liquid; surge: *a spurt of steam from the teapot*

¹**spy** *v* **spied, spying 1** to watch secretly: *spy on one's neighbours* **2** to try to get information secretly **3** to catch sight of

²**spy** *n* **spies 1** a person employed to find out secret information, usu. from an enemy **2** a person who keeps watch secretly

¹**squabble** *n* a petty quarrel

²**squabble** *v* **-bled, -bling** to quarrel, esp. noisily

squad *n* **1** a small group of soldiers **2** a group of people working as a team

squadron *n* **1** a body of usu. 500–1,000 soldiers with tanks or (formerly) horses **2** a large group of warships; any of the largest parts of a fleet **3** the main size of a fighting organization in an airforce; any of the parts of a wing

squalid *adj* **1** very dirty and uncared-for; filthy **2** having, expressing, or about low moral standards −~**ly** *adv*

¹**squall** *v* to cry noisily −**squall,** ~**er** *n*

²**squall** *n* a sudden violent gust of wind −**squally** *adj*

squalor *n* the condition of being squalid

squander *v* to spend foolishly; waste −~**er** *n*

¹**square** *n* **1** a figure with 4 straight equal sides forming 4 right angles **2** a piece of material in this shape **3** a straight-edged often L-shaped tool for testing right angles **4** an open space surrounded by buildings **5** a number equal to another number multiplied by itself: *16 is the square of 4* **6** *esp. spoken* a person who does not know or follow the latest ideas, styles, etc. **7 square one** the very beginning

²**square** *adj* **1** having 4 equal sides and 4 right angles **2** forming a (nearly) right angle: *a square jaw* **3** being a measurement of area equal to that of a square with sides of the stated length **4** being the stated length from a corner in both directions: *The room is 10 feet square* **5** fair; honest: *a square deal* **6** paid and settled: *Our account is all square* **7** *esp. spoken* old fashioned **8** (in cricket) in a position at (about) right angles to the batsman **9 a square meal** a good satisfying meal −~**ly** *adv* −~**ness** *n*

³**square** *v* **squared, squaring 1** to put into a shape with straight lines and right angles: *square up a wall* **2** to mark squares on; divide into squares **3** to multiply (a number) by itself once **4** to fit to a particular explanation or standard **5** to pay or pay for; settle: *square an account* **6** to cause (totals of points or games won) to be equal

⁴**square** —also **squarely** *adv esp. spoken* **1** fairly; honestly **2** directly: *He looked her square in the eye*

¹**squash** *v* **1** to force or be forced into a flat shape; crush **2** to push or fit into a small space; squeeze: *May I squash in next to you?* **3** to force into silence; put down

²**squash** *n* **1** an act or sound of squashing **2** a crowd of people in a small space **3** a game played in a 4-walled court by 2 or 4 people with rackets and a small rubber ball **4** a sweet fruit drink without alcohol

¹**squat** *v* **-tt- 1** to sit on a surface with legs drawn fully up or under the body **2** to live in a place without owning it or paying rent

²**squat** *n* **1** a squatting position **2** *sl* an empty building for squatting

³**squat** *adj* ungracefully short or low and thick

¹**squeak** *v* **1** to make a high but not loud sound **2** *sl* to tell a secret to avoid punishment; squeal —~**er** *n*

²**squeak** *n* **1** a short high soft noise: *the squeak of a mouse* **2** a **narrow squeak** a narrow escape; near thing

¹**squeal** *v* **1** to make a long very high sound or cry **2** *sl* to tell criminal secrets; squeak; inform —~**er** *n*

²**squeal** *n* a high cry or noise: *squeals of delight*

¹**squeeze** *v* **squeezed, squeezing 1** to press together, esp. from opposite sides: *squeeze out a wet cloth* **2** to fit by forcing, crowding, or pressing **3** to get or force out (as if) by pressure: *squeeze the juice from an orange* **4** to cause money difficulties to

²**squeeze** *n* **1** an act of pressing in from opposite sides or around **2** a small amount squeezed out **3** a condition of crowding or pressing; squash: *There's room for one more, but it'll be a squeeze* **4** a difficult state of affairs caused by short supplies or high costs: *a credit squeeze*

¹**squint** *v* **1** to look with almost closed eyes, as at a bright light **2** to have a squint

²**squint** *n* **1** a disorder of the eye muscles causing the eyes to look in 2 different directions **2** an act of looking hard, usu. through nearly closed eyes

squirrel *n* a small 4-legged animal with a long furry tail that climbs trees and eat nuts

¹**squirt** *v* **1** to force or be forced out in a thin stream **2** to hit or cover with such a stream of liquid: *I was squirted with water*

²**squirt** *n* **1** a quick thin stream; jet **2** *esp. spoken* a silly person, who makes big claims

¹**stab** *n* **1** a wound made by a pointed weapon **2** an act of stabbing **3** a sudden painful feeling; pang: *a stab of guilt* **4** an act of trying; go: *have a stab at the job* **5 a stab in the back** an attack from someone supposed to be a friend; betrayal

²**stab** *v* **-bb-** to strike forcefully into with something pointed, esp. with a weapon – ~**ber** *n*

¹**stable** *n* **1** a building for keeping and feeding animals, esp. horses, in **2** a group of racing horses with one owner or trainer

²**stable** *v* **-bled, -bling** to put or keep (animals) in a stable

³**stable** *adj* **1** not easily moved or changed; steady **2** purposeful in mind; dependable **3** (of a substance) tending to keep the same chemical or atomic state; not breaking down naturally – **-bly** *adv*

¹**stack** *n* **1** a usu. orderly pile or heap of things one above another: *a stack of papers* **2** a large pile of grain, grass, etc., for storing outdoors **3** *esp. spoken* a large amount or number **4** a pipe, or group of pipes in a chimney, for carrying away smoke

²**stack** *v* **1** to form a neat pile or put piles of things on or in: *stack (up) books* **2** *esp. US spoken* to arrange unfairly and dishonestly **3 a** (of an aircraft) to fly in a pattern with others waiting for a turn to land **b** to make (an aircraft) wait like this

stadium *n* **-diums** *or* **-dia** a large usu. unroofed building with rows of seats surrounding a sports field

¹**staff** *n* **staves** *or* **staffs** a thick stick of the kind carried in the hand when walking, or used as a mark of office **2** a pole for flying a flag on **3** also **stave**– a set of one or more groups of the 5 lines on which music is written **4 the staff of life** *pompous* bread

²**staff** *n* **1** the group of workers who do the work of an organization **2** members of such a group

³**staff** *v* to supply with staff: provide the workers for

¹**stage** *n* **1** a period in a course of events; state reached at a particular time: *a plan in its early stages* **2** the raised floor on which plays are performed in a theatre **3** *usu. literature* the art or life of an actor; work in the theatre **4** a part of a trip: *We travelled by easy stages* **5** a self-contained driving part of a rocket **6 set the stage for** to prepare for; make possible

²**stage** *v* **staged, staging** **1** to perform or arrange for public show; put on **2** to cause to happen, esp. for show or public effect

¹**stagger** *v* **1** to have trouble standing or walking; move unsteadily on one's feet **2** to seem almost unbelievable to; shock **3** to arrange not to come at the same place or time: *Working hours are staggered*

²**stagger** *n* an unsteady movement of a person having trouble walking or standing

stagnant *adj* 1 (as of water) not flowing or moving 2 not developing or growing; inactive −~**ly** *adv*

¹**stain** *v* to discolour or darken in a way that is lasting

²**stain** *n* 1 a stained place or spot 2 a chemical for darkening or colouring (esp. wood) 3 *literature* a mark of guilt or shame

stair *n* any of the steps in a set of stairs

staircase −also **stairway** *n* a length of stairs

stairs *n* a fixed length of steps connecting floors in a building (often in the phrase **a flight of stairs**)

¹**stake** *n* 1 a pointed piece of wood, metal, etc., for driving into the ground 2 (in former times) a post to which a person was bound for being killed, esp. by burning 3 something that may be gained or lost; interest 4 **at stake** at risk; dependent on what happens

²**stake** *v* **staked, staking** 1 to risk (money, one's life, etc.) on a result; bet: *I've staked all my hopes on you* 2 to fasten or strengthen with stakes 3 to mark (an area of ground) with stakes 4 **stake (out) a claim** to make a claim

stale *adj* 1 no longer fresh 2 no longer interesting: *stale jokes* 3 (of a person) worn out; without new ideas −~**ness** *n*

stalemate *n* 1 (in the game of chess) a position from which a player can only move into check and back again 2 a condition in which neither side in a quarrel, argument, etc., can get an advantage

¹**stalk** *v* 1 to hunt (esp. an animal) by following quietly and staying hidden 2 to walk stiffly, proudly, or with long steps −~**er** *n*

²**stalk** *n* 1 the main upright part of a plant 2 a long narrow part of a plant supporting one or more leaves, fruits, or flowers; stem

¹**stall** *n* 1 an indoor enclosure (as in a barn or stable or inside a room) for one animal or person 2 a table or open-fronted shop in a public place 3 any in a row of seats along the sides in the central part of some churches

²**stall** *v* 1 **a** (of an engine) to stop for lack of power **b** to cause or force (an engine) to do this 2 to go or put into a stall when flying

³**stall** *n* a loss of control in an aircraft caused by trying to climb too steeply too slowly

⁴**stall** *v esp. spoken* to delay; intentionally take little or no action

stamina *n* the strength of body or mind to fight tiredness, discouragement, or illness

¹**stammer** *v* to speak with pauses and repeated sounds, because of excitement, fear, etc. −~**er** *n* −~**ingly** *adv*

²**stammer** *n* the fault of stammering in speech

¹**stamp** *v* 1 to strike (esp. a surface) downwards with (the foot) 2 to mark (a pattern, letters, etc.) on (a surface) by pressing 3 to stick a

stamp onto **4** to put into a class; distinguish: *His manners stamped him a military man* **5** to produce by a forceful blow (as by factory machinery): *stamp out a car body*

²**stamp** *n* **1** also **postage stamp**– a small usu. 4-sided piece of paper sold by post offices for sticking on a piece of mail to be sent **2** a piece of paper like this for sticking to certain official papers to show that tax (**stamp duty**) has been paid **3** an instrument or tool for pressing or printing onto a surface **4** a mark or pattern made by this **5** an act of stamping, as with the foot **6** a lasting result; effect: *The events left their stamp on his mind*

¹**stampede** *n* **1** a sudden rush of frightened animals **2** a sudden mad rush

²**stampede** *v* **-peded, -peding** to go or drive in a stampede

stance *n* **1** a way of standing, esp. in various sports **2** a way of thinking; standpoint; attitude

¹**stand** *v* **stood, standing** **1** to support oneself on the feet upright **2** to rise or raise to a position of doing this **3** to be in or take a stated position (of doing this): *Stand clear of the doors, please* **4** to be in height: *He stands 5 feet 10 inches* **5** to be in a particular state of affairs or condition: *How do things stand ?* **6** to have a position in a range of values **7** to be in a position to gain or lose **8** to rest in a position, esp. upright **9** to remain unmoving: *machinery standing idle* (unused) **10** to accept;

bear; tolerate **11** to be found in a particular form in writing: *Copy it as it stands* **12** to remain true or in force: *My offer still stands* **13** to pay the cost of (something) for (someone else); give as a treat: *Let me stand you a dinner* **14** to make oneself a choice in an election; be a candidate **15 know how/where one stands (with someone)** to know how someone feels about one **16 stand a chance** to have a chance **17 stand on one's own (two) feet** to be able to do without help from others **18 stand something on its head** to change or upset violently –~**er** *n*

²**stand** *n* **1** a strong effort or position of defence: *the army made a stand* **2** a fixed public decision or opinion (often in the phrase **take a stand**) **3** a place or act of standing **4** a raised stage, esp. at a public place **5** a small often outdoor shop or place for showing things; stall **6** a frame, desk, or other piece of furniture for putting something on **7** a place where taxis wait to be hired **8** an open-fronted building at a sports ground with rows of seats or standing space rising behind each other

¹**standard** *n* **1** a level of quality that is considered proper or acceptable: *He sets high standards for his pupils* **2** something fixed as a rule for measuring weight, purity, etc. **3** any of various ceremonial flags **4** a pole with an image or shape at the top

formerly carried by armies **5** the system of using one particular material (esp. gold) for fixing the value of a country's money

²**standard** *adj* **1** ordinary; of the usual kind: *standard sizes* **2** generally recognized as correct or acceptable: *It's one of the standard books on the subject*

standard of living –also **living standard** *n* **standards of living** the degree of wealth and comfort in everyday life enjoyed by a person, group, country, etc.

standpoint *n* a position from which things are seen and opinions formed; point of view

¹**star** *n* **1** a very hot heavenly body of great size, such as the sun **2** *esp. spoken* any heavenly body (such as a planet) that appears as a bright point in the sky **3** a 5- or more pointed figure **4** a piece of metal in this shape for wearing as a mark of office, honour, etc. **5** a heavenly body regarded as determining one's fate **6** a sign used with numbers from usu. 1 to 5 in various systems, to judge quality: *a 3 star hotel* **7** a famous or very skilful performer ~**ry**, ~**less** *adj*

²**star** *v* **-rr- 1** to mark with one or more stars **2** to have or appear as a main performer

¹**stare** *v* **stared, staring 1** to look fixedly with wide-open eyes **2 stare one in the face** to be so near or so obvious as to be very easily seen

²**stare** *n* an act or way of staring; long fixed look: *admiring stares*

¹**start** *v* **1** to begin (a course, journey, etc.); set out (on) **2** to come or bring into being; begin **3** to go or cause to go into (movement or activity); begin: *Give it a push to start it* **4** to begin doing a job or a piece of work **5** to go from a particular point: *Prices start at £5* **6** to begin using: *Start each page on the 2nd line* **7** to make a quick uncontrolled movement, as from sudden surprise; be startled **8 to start with** also **for a start–** (used before the first in a list of facts, reasons, etc.)

²**start** *n* **1** a beginning of activity; condition or place of starting **2** a sudden uncontrolled movement, as of surprise: *to wake with a start* **3** an advantage, esp. in a race

startle *v* **-led, -ling** to cause to jump; give an unexpected slight shock to – **-lingly** *adv*

starvation *n* suffering or death from lack of food

starve *v* **starved, starving 1** to die or kill by lack of food **2** to suffer or cause to suffer from great hunger **3** to suffer or cause to suffer from not having some stated thing: *starved for companionship*

¹**state** *n* **1** a condition in which a person or thing is: *the state of one's health* **2** a very anxious or excited condition (esp. in the phrases **in/into a state**) **3** the government of a country **4** the ceremony connected

with high-level government: *The Queen drove to the palace in state* **5** any of the smaller parts making up certain nations

²**state** *v* **stated, stating 1** to say or put into words, esp. formally **2** to set in advance; specify: *only to be used on the stated date*

statement *n* **1** something that is stated, esp. of a formal kind **2** a list showing amounts of money paid, received, etc., and their total: *a bank statement*

statesman *n* **-men** a political or government leader – ~**ship** *n*

¹**static** *adj* **1** not moving or changing; stationary **2** lacking the effect of action, and usu. uninteresting **3** of or being electricity not flowing in a current: *static electricity* **4** *technical* of or concerning objects at rest

²**static** *n* radio noise caused by electricity in the air

¹**station** *n* **1** a building on a railway (or bus) line where passengers or goods arrive or leave **2** a building that is a centre for the stated kind of service: *a police station* **3** a company or apparatus that broadcasts on television or radio **4** a place or building for some special scientific work: *a research station* **5** a usu. small military establishment **6** *literature* one's position in life; social rank: *She married beneath her station*

²**station** *v* to put into a certain place;

post: *Guards were stationed around the prison*

stationary *adj* standing still; not moving

stationery *n* materials for writing; paper, ink, pencils, etc.

statistic *n* a single number in a collection of statistics

statistics *n* **1** collected numbers which represent facts or measurements **2** a branch of mathematics dealing with the collection, representation, and analysis of numerical data which may be drawn from many sources – **-tical** *adj* – **-tically** *adv* – **-tician** *n*

statue *n* a human or animal figure, made in some solid material (such as stone, metal, or plastic)

stature *n* **1** a person's natural height **2** quality or position gained by development or proved worth: *a man of stature*

status *n* **1** a condition that determines one's formal position: *What's your status in this country? Are you a citizen?* **2** high social position; prestige **3** a state of affairs

¹**stay** *n* **stays** a strong rope used for supporting a mast on a ship

²**stay** *v* **stayed, staying 1** to stop and remain **2** to continue to be; remain **3** to live in a place for a while; be a visitor or guest **4** to last out; continue for the whole length of: *stay the course in a mile race* **5** to stop from going on, moving, or having effect; hold back **6 be here/ come to stay** to become generally

accepted **7 stay put** to remain in one place; not move

³stay *n* **stays 1** a usu. limited time of living in a place **2** a stopping or delay by order of a judge: *The prisoner was given (a) stay of execution*

¹steady *adj* **-ier, -iest 1** firm; not shaking: *a steady hand* **2** moving or developing evenly; regular: *a steady speed* **3** not changing; stable: *a steady job* **4** dependable; serious −**steadily** *adv* −**steadiness** *n*

²steady *v* **-ied, -ying** to make or become steady or settled

³steady −also **steady on** *interj esp. spoken* be careful; watch what you're doing

steak *n* **1** a flat piece of beef, or meat from a stated animal or fish, cut from the fleshy part and in a direction across the animal **2** beef of a less good quality, usu. used in small pieces in pies or stews

steal *v* **stole, stolen, stealing 1** to take (what belongs to another) without any right **2** to take quickly, without permission: *steal a kiss* **3** to move secretly or quietly

stealth *n* the action of going or acting secretly or unseen (esp. in the phrase **by stealth**) −∼**y** *adj* −∼**ily** *adv*

¹steam *n* **1** water in the state of a gas produced by boiling **2** the mist formed by water becoming cool **3** feelings and power considered as trapped by self-control (esp. in the phrases **let off/work off steam**) **4 get up steam** to begin to move with

power and speed **5 under one's/its own steam** by one's/its own power or effort

²steam *v* **1** to give off steam, esp. when very hot **2** to travel by steam power: *The ship steamed into the harbour* **3** to cook by allowing steam to heat **4** to use steam on, esp. for unsticking or softening

³steam *adj* using steam under pressure to produce power or heat

¹steamroller *n* a heavy usu. steam-powered machine for driving over and flattening road surfaces

²steamroller *v esp. spoken* to crush or force using very great power or pressure

¹steel *n* **1** iron in a hard strong form containing some carbon and sometimes other metals **2** great strength

²steel *v* to make hard or determined: *He steeled himself to say he was sorry*

¹steep *adj* **1** rising or falling quickly: *steep rise in prices* **2** *esp. spoken* (of a demand or esp. a price) unreasonable; too much −∼**ly** *adv* −∼**ness** *n*

²steep *v* **1** to stay, or leave, in a liquid, for softening, cleaning, bringing out a taste, etc.; soak **2 steeped in** thoroughly filled or familiar with

steeple *n* a church tower with a top part rising to a usu. high sharp point

¹steer *n* a male animal of the cattle family with its sexual organs removed

²steer *v* **1** to direct the course of (as a ship or vehicle) **2** to go in or hold to (a course); follow (a way) **3** to allow being directed: *Does your car steer well?* **4 steer clear (of)** to keep away from; avoid

¹**stem** *n* **1** the central part of a plant above the ground, or the smaller part which supports leaf or flower **2** any narrow upright part which supports another: *the stem of a wine glass* **3** the narrow part of a tobacco pipe, through which smoke is drawn **4** the part of a word which remains the same, even when combining with different endings **5** a large block of wood set upright in the bow of a ship

²**stem** *v* **-mm- 1** to stop (the flow of): *to stem the blood* **2** to prevent; stand against: *to stem the tide of public opinion*

stem from *v prep* to have as origin

¹**step** *n* **1** the act of putting one foot in front of the other in order to move along **2** the sound this makes **3 a** the distance between the feet when stepping **b** a short distance: *It's just a step from here* **4** a flat edge, esp. in a set of surfaces each higher than the other, on which the foot is placed for climbing up and down; stair, rung of a ladder, etc. **5** an act, esp. in a set of actions, which should produce a certain result **6** a type of movement of the feet in dancing **7 in step a** (esp. of soldiers) stepping with the left and right leg at the same time as one or more others **b** (of a person or behaviour) in accordance or agree-

ment with others **8 keep step** to march together in step **9 take steps (to do something)** to take action **10 watch one's step** to behave or act carefully

²**step** *v* **-pp- 1** to put one foot down usu. in front of the other, in order to move along **2** to walk **3** to bring the foot down (on); tread **4 step on it** *esp. spoken* to go faster **5 step out of line** to act differently from others or from what is expected

stepchild *n* **-children** the child of one's husband/wife by an earlier marriage; a **stepson** or **stepdaughter**

stepladder *n* a short ladder with flat steps, which can be folded together for storing

stepparent *n* the person to whom one's father or mother has been remarried; one's **stepmother** or **stepfather**

stepping-stone *n* **1** one of a row of large stones with a level top, which one walks on to cross a river or stream **2** a way of improvement or getting ahead

stereo —also **stereo set** *n* **-os** a record player or radio which gives out sound by means of 2 loudspeakers —**stereo(phonic)** *adj*

sterile *adj* **1** (of living things) which cannot produce young **2** made free from all germs and bacteria **3** (of land) not producing crops **4** lacking new thought, imagination, etc. — **-ization** *n*

sterilize, -ise *v* **-ized, -izing** to make sterile – **-ization**

¹**stern** *adj* **1** very firm or hard towards others' behaviour **2** difficult or hard to bear: *a stern punishment* **3** showing firmness, esp. with disapproval – ~**ly** *adv* – ~**ness** *n*

²**stern** *n* the back end of a ship

¹**stew** *n* **1** a meal with meat, vegetables, etc., cooked together in liquid **2** *esp. spoken* a confused anxious state of mind (in the phrase **in a stew**)

²**stew** *v* to cook (something) slowly and gently in liquid in a closed vessel

¹**steward** *n* **1** a man who controls supplies of food in a place such as a club or college **2** one of a number of men who serve passengers on a ship or plane **3** one of a number of men who arrange a public amusement, such as a horse race, a meeting, etc. **4** a man who is employed to look after a house and lands, such as a farm

²**steward** *v* to act as a steward

stewardess *n* a woman who serves passengers on a plane

¹**stick** *n* **1** a small thin piece of wood **2** a thin rod of wood used for supporting the body when walking; walking stick **3** a thin rod of any material: *a stick of rock* (=a hard kind of sweet) **4** an uninteresting person (in the phrases **dull/dry old stick**) **5** **get the wrong end of the stick** to misunderstand

²**stick** *v* **stuck, sticking 1** to push (in)

(esp. a pointed object): *to stick pins into the material* **2** to fix or be fixed with a sticky substance **3** to remain or become fixed **4** *esp. spoken* to put: *Stick it on the table* **5** *esp. spoken* to bear (a person or activity) **6** **stick in one's throat a** to be hard to accept **b** to be hard to say

sticky *adj* **-ier, -iest 1** made of or containing material which can stick to or around anything else **2** *esp. spoken* difficult: awkward **3** (**come to/meet**) **a sticky end** *esp. spoken* at last to suffer ruin, dishonour, death, etc. **–stickily** *adv* **–stickiness** *n*

¹**stiff** *adj* **1** not easily bent **2** painful when moving or moved: *stiff muscles* **3** firm: *Beat the eggs until stiff* **4** formal; not friendly **5** (of a drink of strong alcohol) large and without water or other liquid added **6** difficult to do: *a stiff job* **7** *esp. spoken* too much to accept; unusual in degree – ~**ly** *adv* – ~**ness** *n*

²**stiff** *adv* **1** **bore someone stiff** to make someone very tired with dull talk **2** **scare someone stiff** to make someone very afraid

stiffen *v* **1** to make or become hard or firm **2** to make or become stiff and painful **3** to become anxious or less friendly: *He stiffened at her rude remarks*

stifle *v* **-fled, -fling 1** to stop or cause to stop breathing properly **2** to prevent from happening or continuing: *Their ideas were stifled*

¹**still** *adj* **1 a** not moving **b** without

wind **2** quiet or silent **3** (of drinks) not containing gas — ~**ness** n

²**still** v **1** to make quiet or calm: *The food stilled the baby's cries* **2** to prevent from moving

³**still** adv **1** (even) up to and at the present time/the time referred to: *Does this dress still fit you?* **2** even so; nevertheless **3** even; yet: *He gave still another reason*

⁴**still** n **1** quietness or calm: *the still of the evening* **2** a photograph printed from one frame of a cinema film

⁵**still** n an apparatus for making alcohol

stillborn adj born dead

stimulate v **-lated, -lating 1** to increase in activity: *Exercise is stimulating* **2** to encourage or excite – **-lation** n

¹**sting** v **stung, stinging 1** to cause sharp pain to, or to feel such a pain **2** (of an insect) to prick with a sting **3** sl to take too much money from: *They stung him for 1000 dollars*

²**sting** n **1** a sharp organ used as a weapon by some animals, often poisonous **2** a pain-producing substance contained in hairs on a plant's surface **3** a sharp pain, wound, or mark caused by a plant or animal **4** a strong burning pain, usu. on the outer skin **5** an ability to cause pain or hurt feelings: *the sting of her tongue*

stipulate v **-lated, -lating** to demand as a condition – **-ation** n

¹**stir** v **-rr- 1** to move around and mix (esp. something mainly liquid) by means of an object such as a spoon

2 to put in by such a movement **3** to move from a position: *She stirred in her sleep* **4** esp. spoken to cause oneself to move or wake **5** to excite (the feelings) (of): *He was stirred by stories of battle* **6** sl to cause trouble between others, esp. by telling stories

²**stir** n **1** an act of stirring **2** a movement

¹**stitch** n **1** a movement of a needle and thread into cloth at one point and out at another in sewing **2** a turn of the wool round the needle in knitting: *to drop a stitch* **3** the piece of thread or wool seen in place after the completion of such a movement **4** a particular style of sewing or knitting and the effect which it gives **5** technical a piece of thread which sews the edges of a wound together **6** a sharp pain in the side, esp. caused by running **7** esp. spoken clothes (esp. in the phrases **haven't got a stitch, not a stitch on**) **8 in stitches** laughing helplessly

²**stitch** v to sew; put stitches on to fasten together or for ornament

¹**stock** n **1** a supply (of something) for use **2** goods for sale **3** a piece of wood used as a support or handle, as for a gun or tool **4 a** a plant from which cuttings are grown **b** a stem onto which another plant is grafted **5** a group of animals used for breeding **6** farm animals, usu. cattle **7** a family line, esp. of the stated character **8** money lent to a govern-

ment at a fixed rate of interest **9** the money (capital) owned by a company, divided into shares **10** a type of garden flower with a sweet smell **11** a liquid made from the juices of meat, bones, etc., used in cooking **12** (in former times) a stiff cloth worn by men round the neck of a shirt **13 take stock (of)** to consider the state of things so as to take a decision

²**stock** *v* **1** to keep supplies of **2** to supply

³**stock** *adj* **1** commonly used, esp. without much meaning **2** kept in stock, esp. because of a standard or average type: *stock sizes*

Stock Exchange —also **stock market** *n* **1** the place where stocks and shares are bought and sold **2** the business of doing this

stocking *n* a garment for a woman's foot and leg which is shaped to fit closely

stockpile *v, n* **-piled, -piling** (to keep adding to) a store of (materials), esp. in case of future need

stodgy *adj* **-ier, -iest** *esp. spoken* **1** (of food) heavy and uninteresting **2** dull; lacking excitement —**stodginess** *n*

stole *past tense of* STEAL

stolen *past part. of* STEAL

¹**stomach** *n* **1** a baglike organ in the body where food is digested after being eaten **2** *esp. spoken* the front part of the body below the chest; abdomen **3 a** desire to eat **b** liking; acceptance

²**stomach** *v* to accept without displeasure: *I can't stomach his jokes*

¹**stone** *n* **1** a piece of rock, either of natural shape or cut out specially for building **2** solid mineral material; (a type of) rock **3** a single hard seed inside some fruits, such as the cherry, plum, and peach **4** a piece of hard material formed in an organ of the body, esp. the bladder or kidney **5** a gravestone

²**stone** *v* **stoned, stoning 1** to throw stones at **2** to take the seeds or stones out of (usu. dried fruit)

³**stone** *n* **stone** *or* **stones** (a measure of weight equal to) 14 pounds (lbs)

stony *adj* **-ier, -iest 1** containing or covered with stones **2** cruel; hard: *a stony stare* —**stonily** *adv*

stood *past tense and past part. of* STAND

stool *n* **1** a seat without a supporting part for the back or arms **2** *esp. written & technical* a piece of solid waste matter passed from the body

¹**stoop** *v* **1** to bend (the head and shoulders) forwards and down **2** to stand habitually with the head and shoulders bent over **3** to allow oneself (to do something), so falling to a low standard of behaviour

²**stoop** *n* a habitual position with the shoulders bent or rounded

¹**stop** *v* **-pp- 1** to cease or cause to cease moving or continuing an activity **2** to prevent: *You can't stop me* **3** to end **4** to pause **5** to remain: *Stop here a moment* **6** to block **7** to prevent from being given or paid: *to stop a cheque* **8** (in music) to use

the fingers on (holes or strings) in order to change the note played by an instrument −~**pable** *adj*

²**stop** *n* **1** the act of stopping or state of being stopped **2** a place on a road where buses or other public vehicles stop for passengers **3** a dot as a mark of punctuation, esp. a full stop **4** a movable part of a musical instrument used for changing the pitch **5** a set of pipes on an organ **6** the part of a camera which moves to control the amount of light entering **7 pull all the stops out** to do everything possible to complete an action

stoppage *n* **1** a blocked state which stops movement, as in a waste pipe or a pipe in the body **2** the state of being held back **3** the act of stopping work, as in a strike

stopper *n* an object which fits in and closes the opening to esp. a bottle or jar

storage *n* **1** the act of storing **2** a place for storing goods (esp. in the phrase **in storage**)

¹**store** *v* **stored, storing 1** to make up and keep a supply of **2** to keep in a warehouse **3** to put away for future use: *to store one's winter clothes*

²**store** *n* **1** a supply for future use **2** a place for keeping things **3** a warehouse **4** a large shop **5** a large number or amount: *a store of jokes* **6 in store a** kept ready (for future use) **b** about to happen **7 set store by** to feel to be of importance

storey *n* **-reys** a floor or level in a building

¹**storm** *n* **1** a rough weather condition with wind, rain, and often lightning **2** a sudden violent show of feeling: *a storm of tears* **3** a loud noise **4 take by storm a** to conquer by a sudden violent attack **b** to win success from (those who watch a performance)

²**storm** *v* **1** to attack with sudden violence: *to storm the city* **2** to blow violently **3** to show or express violent anger

stormy *adj* **-ier, -iest 1** having one or more storms: *stormy weather* **2** showing noisy expressions of feeling −**stormily** *adv*

story *n* **-ries 1** an account of events, real or imagined **2** *esp. spoken* (*used by and to children*) a lie (esp. in the phrase **to tell stories**) **3** the plot of a book, film, play, etc. **4** (material for) an article in a newspaper, magazine, etc. **5 the same old story** the usual excuse or difficulty

¹**stout** *adj* **1** rather fat and heavy **2** strong; thick; too solid to break **3** brave; determined: *a stout supporter of the team* −~**ly** *adv* −~**ness** *n*

²**stout** *n* a kind of strong dark beer

stove *n* an enclosed apparatus for cooking or heating which works by burning coal, oil, gas, etc., or by electricity

¹**straight** *adj* **1** not bent or curved: *A straight line is the shortest distance between 2 points* **2** level or upright **3** tidy; neat **4** honest; truthful **5**

518

correct (esp. in the phrases **set/put someone/the record straight) 6** (of alcohol) without added water **7** (in the theatre) serious; of the established kind **8** (of the face) not laughing; with a serious expression –~**ness** *n*

²**straight** *adv* **1** in a straight line **2** directly: *go straight home* **3 go straight** to leave a life of crime

³**straight** *n* a straight part or place, esp. on a racetrack

straightaway –also (*esp. spoken*) **straight off** *adv* at once

straighten *v* to make or become straight, level, or tidy

straightforward *adj* **1** honest, without hidden meanings **2** expressed or understood in a direct way, without difficulties –~**ly** *adv*

¹**strain** *n* **1** *esp. in literature* a tune; notes of music **2** a manner or style of using words: *Her letters were written in a happy strain* **3** a breed or type of plant or animal **4** a quality which tends to develop, esp. one passed down a family

²**strain** *v* **1** to stretch or pull tightly **2** to use the whole of: *to strain one's ears* **3** to make great efforts **4** to damage or weaken (a part of the body) **5** to press against or hold closely: *She strained the child to her* **6** to separate (a liquid and solid) by pouring through a narrow space, esp. the fine holes in a sieve or filter

³**strain** *n* **1 a** the condition of being strained **b** the force causing this **2** a state of tension: *She's under a lot of strain* **3** damage to a part of the body caused by too great effort and often stretching of muscles

stranded *adj* in a helpless position; unable to get away

strange *adj* **1** hard to accept or understand; surprising **2** not known or experienced before; unfamiliar **3** *old use* foreign: *a traveller in a strange country* –~**ly** *adv* –~**ness** *n*

stranger *n* **1** a person who is unfamiliar **2** a person in a new or unfamiliar place

strangle *v* **-gled, -gling** to kill by pressing on the throat

¹**strap** *n* **1** a strong narrow band of material, such as leather, used as a fastening **2** the giving of punishment by beating with a thick narrow piece of leather

²**strap** *v* **-pp- 1** to fasten in place with one or more straps **2** to beat with a strap **3** to bind (a part of the body that has been hurt, esp. a limb) with bandages

stratagem *n* a trick or plan to deceive an enemy or to gain an advantage

strategy *n* **-gies 1** the art of planning movements of armies or forces in war **2** a particular plan for winning success in a particular activity, as in war, a game, a competition, or for personal advantage – **-gic** *adj* – **-gically** *adv* – **-gist** *n*

straw *n* **1** dried stems of grain plants, such as wheat, used for animals to sleep on, for making baskets, mats, etc. **2 a** one stem of wheat, rice, etc. **b** a thin tube of paper or plastic for sucking up liquid **3 clutch at straws** to attempt to save oneself from trouble by means which cannot succeed

strawberry *n* **-ries 1** a type of plant which grows near the ground, or its juicy fruit, eaten fresh and in jam **2** the colour of this fruit, dark pink to red

¹stray *v* **strayed, straying 1** to wander away **2** (of thoughts or conversation) to move away from the subject

²stray *n* **strays 1** an animal lost from its home **2** a child without a home (in the phrase **waifs and strays**)

³stray *adj* **1** lost; separated from home or others of the kind **2** met by chance; scattered: *hit by a stray shot*

¹streak *n* **1** a thin line or band, different from what surrounds it **2** a quality which sometimes appears among different qualities of character

²streak *v* **1** to move very fast **2** to cover with streaks

¹stream *n* **1** a natural flow of water, usu. smaller than a river **2** anything flowing or moving on continuously: *a stream of people* **3** (the direction of) a current of water: *float with the stream* **4** (in schools) a level of ability within a group of pupils of the same age, esp. of a class

²stream *v* **1** to flow fast and strong; pour out **2** to move in a continuous flowing mass **3** to float in the air:

The wind caught her hair, and it streamed out **4** to group (pupils) –in streams

streamline *v* **-lined, -lining 1** to form into a smooth shape which moves easily through water or air **2** to make (a business, organization, etc.) more simple but more effective in working –~**d** *adj*

street *n* **1** a road with houses or other town buildings on one or both sides **2 up one's street** in one's area of interest or activity

strength *n* **1** the quality or degree of being strong or something that provides this **2** force, esp. measured in numbers: *They came in strength to see the fight* **3 on the strength of** because of

strengthen *v* **1** to make strong or stronger **2** to gain strength: *The wind strengthened*

strenuous *adj* **1** taking great effort **2** showing great activity: *a strenuous supporter of women's rights* –~**ly** *adv* –~**ness** *n*

¹stress *n* **1** force or pressure caused by difficulties in life **2** force of weight caused by something heavy **3** a sense of special importance: *not enough stress on the need for exactness* **4** the degree of force put on a part of a word, making it seem stronger than other parts: *In 'under', the main stress is on 'un'*

²stress *v* **1** to give a sense of importance to (a certain matter) **2** to give force to (a word or part of a word)

¹stretch *v* **1** to make or become wider

or longer **2** to cause to reach full length or width: *to stretch a rope between 2 poles* **3** to spread out **4** to be elastic **5** to straighten (the limbs or body) to full length **6** to cause to go beyond a limit (of rule, or time) **7** to last —~**able** *adj*

²**stretch** *n* **1** an act of stretching, esp. the body **2** the (degree of) ability to increase in length or width: *There's not much stretch in this collar* **3** a level area (of land or water) **4** *technical* a mathematical transformation in which all lengths are increased by a constant amount **5** a part, esp. one of 2 straight sides, of a race track, considered as a part of a race (esp. in the phrases **the final/finishing/home stretch**) **6** a continuous period of time **7** *sl* a period of time in prison

stretcher *n* **1** a covered framework on which a sick person can be carried lying down **2** an apparatus for stretching something

strict *adj* **1** severe, esp. in rules of behaviour **2 a** exact: *a strict analysis* **b** complete; not to be broken: *strict secrecy* —~**ly** *adv* —~**ness** *n*

stride *v* **strode, stridden, striding** to walk with long steps or cross with one long step —**stride** *n*

strife *n* trouble between people

¹**strike** *v* **struck, striking** **1** to hit **2** to give (a blow) **3** to make suddenly or unexpectedly: *They were struck silent* **4** to light by hitting against a hard surface: *strike a match* **5** (of a person or machine) to make (a

sound), by a finger or moving part which hits an object **6** to have a (strong) effect on: *How does the room strike you?* **7** to come suddenly to the mind of: *An idea struck me* **8** to find (a material or place) **9** *technical* to produce (a coin or like object) **10** to stop working because of disagreement **11** to produce or reach (agreement) (esp. in the phrases **strike a bargain, strike a balance**) **12** to take up and hold (a bodily position) for effect: *to strike a pose* **13 strike camp** to take down tents when leaving a camping place

²**strike** *n* **1** a time when no work is done because of disagreement, as over pay or working conditions **2** an attack, esp. by aircraft whose bombs hit the place attacked **3** success in finding esp. a mineral in the earth: *an oil strike*

striking *adj* which draws the attention, esp. because of being attractive or unusual —~**ly** *adv*

¹**string** *n* **1** thin cord **2** anything like this, esp. used for tying things up **3** a thin piece of material, often one of several, stretched across a musical instrument, to give sound **4** a set (of things) connected together on a thread: *a string of onions* **5** a set (of words, actions, etc.) following each other closely **6 no strings attached** (esp. of an agreement) with no limiting conditions

²**string** *v* **strung, stringing** **1** to put one or more strings on (a musical

instrument) **2** to thread (beads) on a string **3 highly strung** very sensitive and easily excited, hurt in feelings, etc. **4 strung up** very excited, nervous, or worried

¹**strip** *v* **-pp- 1** to remove (the covering or parts of) **2** to undress or be undressed **3** to tear the twisting thread from (a gear or screw)

²**strip** *n* **1** a narrow piece **2** an occasion or performance of taking the clothes off, esp. when performed as a show **3** the clothes of a particular colour worn by a team in football

stripe *n* **1** a band of colour, among one or more other colours **2** a band of colour worn on a uniform as a sign of rank

strive *v* **strove, striven, striving** to struggle hard (to get or conquer) −**striver** *n*

strode *past tense of* STRIDE

¹**stroke** *v* **stroked, stroking** to pass the hand over gently, esp. for pleasure

²**stroke** *n* **1** a blow, esp. with (the edge of) a weapon **2** a sudden illness in part of the brain which damages it and can cause loss of the ability to move some part of the body **3** an unexpected piece (of luck) **4** a single movement, esp. in a sport or game **5** a line made by a single movement of a pen or brush in writing or painting **6** a rower who sets the speed for others rowing with him **7** the sound made by a clock on the hour

stroll *v* to walk, esp. slowly, for pleasure −**stroll** *n* −~**er** *n*

strong *adj* **1** having (a degree of) power **2** powerful against harm; not easily broken, spoilt, moved, or changed: *strong beliefs* **3** of a certain number: *Our club is 50 strong* **4** (esp. of drinks) having a lot of the material which gives taste **5** (of a verb) which does not add a regular ending in the past tense, but may change a vowel: *'Speak'' is a strong verb; its past tense is 'spoke''* **6** technical of worth: *Is the pound stronger today?* −~**ly** *adv*

strove *past tense of* STRIVE

struck *past tense and past part. of* STRIKE

¹**structure** *n* **1** the way in which parts are formed into a whole **2** anything formed of many parts, esp. a building − **-ral** *adj* − **-rallyb** *adv*

²**structure** *v* **-tured, -turing** to form (esp. ideas) into a whole form, in which each part is related to others

¹**struggle** *v* **-gled,-gling** to make violent movements, esp. when fighting against a person or thing

²**struggle** *n* a hard fight or effort

¹**stub** *n* **1** a short end left when something has been used, esp. of a cigarette or pencil **2** the piece of a cheque or ticket left in a book of these as a record after use

²**stub** *v* **-bb-** to hurt (one's toe) by hitting against something

stubborn *adj* determined; with a strong will −~**ly** *adv* −~**ness** *n*

¹**stuck** *adj* **1** fixed in place, not moving **2** unable to go or do anything further, esp. because of difficulties **3**

esp. spoken having to do or have, esp. unwillingly: *We were stuck with unexpected visitors* **4 get stuck in(to)** *esp. spoken* to start work or action (on) forcefully

²stuck *past tense and past part. of* STICK

student *n* **1** a person who is studying at a place of education or training **2** a person with a stated interest: *a student of human nature*

studio *n* **-os 1** a workroom for a painter, photographer, etc. **2** a room from which broadcasts are made **3** a specially equipped room or place where cinema films are made

¹study *n* **-ies 1** the act of studying one or more subjects **2** a subject studied **3** a room used for studying and work **4** a drawing or painting of a detail, esp. for combining later into a larger picture

²study *v* **-ied, -ying 1** to spend time in learning (one or more subjects) **2** to examine carefully

¹stuff *n* **1** *esp. spoken* things in a mass; matter: *I can't carry all my stuff alone* **2** material of any sort, of which something is made

²stuff *v* **1** to fill with a substance **2** to fill the skin of (a dead animal), to make it look real **3** to put stuffing inside: *to stuff a chicken* **4** *esp. spoken* to cause (oneself) to eat as much as possible

stuffing *n* **1** material used as a filling for something **2** finely cut-up food with a special taste placed inside a

bird or piece of meat before cooking

stuffy *adj* **-ier, -iest 1** (having air) which is not fresh **2** (having a way of thought) which is dull, old-fashioned, etc. **-stuffily** *adv* **-stuffiness** *n*

stumble *v* **-bled, -bling 1** to catch the foot on the ground while moving along and start to fall **2** to stop and/or make mistakes in speaking or reading aloud **-~r** *n*

¹stump *n* **1** the base of a tree left after the rest has been cut down **2** the remaining part of a limb which has been cut off **3** the stub of a pencil or the useless end of something long which has been worn down, such as a tooth **4** (in cricket) one of the 3 upright pieces of wood at which the ball is thrown

²stump *v* **1** to move, esp. heavily **2** (in cricket) to end the innings of (a batsman) who has moved outside the hitting area, by touching the stumps with the ball **3** *esp. spoken* to put an unanswerable question or point to

stun *v* **-nn- 1** to make unconscious by hitting the head **2** to cause to lose the senses or sense of balance **3** to shock into helplessness: *He was stunned by their unfairness* **4** to delight

stung *past tense and past part. of* STING

¹stunt *v* to prevent (full growth) (of)

²stunt *n* **1** an act of bodily skill, often dangerous **2** an action which gains attention, as in advertising **3** any trick movement, as of a plane

stupid *adj* silly or foolish, either generally or in a certain action – ~**ity** *n* – ~**ly** *adv*

sturdy *adj* **-dier, -diest 1** strong and firm, esp. in body **2** determined in action: *a sturdy opposition* –**sturdily** *adv* –**sturdiness** *n*

¹sty *n* **sties** a pigsty

²sty, stye *n* **sties, styes** an infected place on the edge of the eyelid, usu. red and swollen

¹style *n* **1** a type of choice of words, esp. which marks out the speaker or writer as different from others **2** a general manner or way of doing anything which is typical or representative of a person or group, time in history, etc.: *the modern style of building* **3** high quality of social behaviour, appearance, or manners **4** fashion, esp. in clothes **5** a type or sort, esp. of goods – ~**less** *adj*

²style *v* **styled, styling 1** to form in a certain (good) pattern, shape, etc. **2** to give (a title) to

¹subconscious *adj* (of thoughts, feelings, etc.) not fully known or understood by the mind in its conscious workings; present at a hidden level of the mind – ~**ly** *adv*

²subconscious –also **unconscious** *n* the hidden level of the mind and the thoughts that go on there, beyond conscious knowledge

subdue *v* **-dued, -duing 1** to conquer or control the actions of **2** to make gentler or less rough in effect

subdued *adj* **1** gentle; reduced in strength of light, sound, movement, etc. **2** quiet in behaviour, not forceful, esp. unnaturally or not habitually so

¹subject *n* **1** a person owing loyalty to a certain state or royal ruler **2** something being considered, as in conversation **3** a branch of knowledge studied, as in a system of education **4** a cause: *His clothes were the subject of amusement* **5** a certain occasion, object, etc., represented in art **6** a person or animal chosen to experience something or to be studied in an experiment **7** (in music) a group of notes forming the tune on which a longer piece is based **8** (in grammar) the noun, pronoun, etc., about which a statement is made or a question asked

²subject *adj* **1** governed by someone else; not independent **2** tending or likely (to have): *subject to ill health*

³subject *v* to cause to be controlled or ruled – ~**ion** *n*

¹submarine *adj technical* growing or used under or in the sea

²submarine –also (*esp. spoken*) **sub** *n* a ship, esp. a warship, which can stay under water

submerge *v* **-merged, -merging** to go or cause to go under the surface of water – ~**nce** *n*

submission *n* **1** submitting or being submitted **2** obedience **3** *esp. written* a suggestion

submit *v* -tt- **1** to cause (oneself) to yield or agree to obey **2** to offer for consideration **3** *law* to suggest or say

¹subordinate *adj* of a lower rank or position − ∼**ly** *adv*

²subordinate *n* a person who is of lower rank in a job, and takes orders from his superior

³subordinate *v* -nated, -nating to put in a position of less importance − -ation *n* − -ative *adj*

subscribe *v* -scribed, -scribing **1** to give (money) **2** to pay regularly in order to receive a magazine, newspaper, etc.

subscription *n* **1** the act of subscribing **2** also (*esp. spoken*) **sub**− an amount of money given, esp. regularly to a society

subsequent *adj* coming after something else, sometimes as a result of it − ∼**ly** *adv*

subside *v* -sided, -siding **1** (of land) to fall away suddenly, because of lack of support **2** (of bad weather or other violent conditions) to go back to the usual level **3** to sink down; settle

subsidiary *adj* connected but of second importance to the main company, plan, work, etc. −**subsidiary** *n*

subsidize, -dise *v* -dized, -dizing (of someone other than the buyer) to pay part of the costs of (something) for (someone) − -dization *n* − -dizer *n*

subsidy *n* -dies money paid, esp. by the government or an organization, to make prices lower, make it cheaper to produce goods, etc.

substance *n* **1** a material; type of matter **2** the important part or quality; strength: *no substance in the speech* **3** the real meaning, without the unimportant details: *Tell me the substance of what he said* **4** solidity **5** *esp. old use* wealth: *a man of substance*

substantial *adj* **1** solid; strongly made **2** big or important enough to be satisfactory **3** concerning the important part or meaning: *in substantial agreement* **4** wealthy

¹substitute *n* a person or thing acting in place of another

²substitute *v* -tuted, -tuting **1** to put (something or someone) in place of another **2** to act as a substitute; be used instead of − -tution *n*

subtle *adj* **1** delicate, hardly noticeable, and esp. pleasant: *a subtle taste* **2** very clever in noticing and understanding **3** clever in arrangement − -tly *adv*

subtract *v* to take (a part or amount) from something larger − ∼**ion** *n*

suburb *n* an outer area of a town or city, where people live

suburban *adj* of or in the suburbs, esp. when considered uninteresting and full of dull ideas, lack of change, etc.

succeed *v* **1** to gain a purpose or reach an aim **2** to do well, esp. in gaining position or popularity in life **3** to follow after **4** to be the next heir after, or the next to take a position or rank

success *n* 1 the act of succeeding in something 2 a good result 3 a person or thing that succeeds or has succeeded –~**ful** *adj* –~**fully** *adv*

succession *n* 1 the act of following one after the other: *His words came out in quick succession* 2 a number (of people or things) following on one after the other 3 the act of succeeding to an office or position

successor *n* 1 a person or thing that comes after another 2 a person who takes an office or position formerly held by another

such *adj, pron* 1 so great: *Don't be such a fool!* 2 of the same kind; like: *flowers such as roses, sunflowers, etc.* **3 and such** and suchlike **4 any/no/some such** any/no/some (person or thing) like that **5 as such** in that form or kind **6 such as** *esp. written* any that **7 such as it is/they are** although it/they may not be of much worth

suck *v* 1 to draw (liquid) into the mouth by using the tongue, lips, and muscles at the side of the mouth, with the lips tightened into a small hole 2 to eat (something) by holding in the mouth and melting by movements of the tongue –**suck** *n*

sudden *adj* happening, done, etc., unexpectedly –~**ly** *adv* –~**ness** *n*

sue *v* **sued, suing** to bring a claim in

law against, esp. for an amount of money

suffer *v* 1 to experience pain or difficulty 2 to experience (something painful): *She suffered the loss of her pupils' respect* 3 to grow worse; lessen in quality 4 *Bible* to allow 5 to accept without dislike (esp. in the phrase **to suffer fools gladly**)

suffering *n* pain and difficulty generally

sufficient *adj* enough

suffocate *v* **-cated, -cating** to kill or die by lack of air – **-cation** *n*

¹**sugar** *n* 1 a sweet usu. white substance used in food 2 *technical* any of several types of sweet substance formed in plants –~**less** *adj*

²**sugar** *v* 1 to put sugar in 2 to make less unpleasant (esp. in the phrase **to sugar the pill**)

suggest *v* 1 to cause to come to the mind 2 to say or write (an idea to be considered) 3 to give signs (of)

suggestion *n* 1 something suggested 2 a slight sign; trace 3 (in psychology) a way of causing an idea to be accepted by the mind by indirect connection with other ideas

suicidal *adj* 1 of or with a tendency to suicide 2 wishing to kill oneself 3 which leads or will lead to death or destruction –~**ly** *adv*

suicide *n* 1 the act of killing oneself 2 an example of this 3 *law* a person who does this 4 an act which destroys the position of the person concerned

¹**suit** *n* 1 **a** a set of outer clothes which

match, usu. including a jacket with trousers or skirt **b** a garment or set of garments for a special purpose **2** one of the 4 sets of cards used in games **3** also **lawsuit**– a civil case in a law court

²**suit** *v* **1** to satisfy or please; be convenient for **2** to match or look right with **3** to be good for (the health of)

suitable *adj* fit (for a purpose); right; convenient – **-bility** *n* –~**ness** *n* – **-bly** *adv*

suitcase *n* a flat bag for carrying clothes and possessions when travelling

suite *n* **1** a set (of furniture) for a room, esp. a settee and 2 chairs (**3-piece suite**) **2** a set (of rooms), esp. in a hotel **3** (in music) a piece of music for instruments that has several loosely connected parts

sulk *v* to show lasting annoyance against others, esp. silently and for slight cause –**sulks, sulkiness** *n* –~**y** *adj* –~**ily** *adv*

sulphur *n* an element that is found in different forms (esp. a light yellow powder) and is used in the chemical and paper industries and in medicines –~**ous** *adj*

sum *n* **1** the total produced when numbers, amounts, etc., are added together **2** an amount: *a large sum of money* **3** a usu. simple calculation, adding, multiplying, dividing, etc. **4** the whole; a complete summary (esp. in the phrase **sum total**)

summarize, -ise *v* **-ized, -izing** to be or make a short general account out of (something longer or more detailed)

¹**summary** *adj esp. written* **1** short; expressed as a summary **2** done at once without attention to formalities or details, esp. (of punishments) without considering mercy – **-rily** *adv*

²**summary** *n* **-ries** a short account giving the main points

¹**summer** *n* the season between spring and autumn when the sun is hot and there are many flowers

²**summer** *v* to cause (animals) to live and feed during the summer

summit *n* **1** the top, esp. the highest part on the top of a mountain **2** the highest point, degree, etc. **3** a meeting between heads of state

summon *v esp. written* to give an official order (to come, do, etc.)

¹**summons** *n* **-monses** an order to appear, esp. in court, often written

²**summons** *v* to give a summons to; order to appear in court

¹**sun** *n* **1** the very hot bright body in the sky, which the earth goes round and from which it receives light and heat **2 a** light and heat from the sun **b** a place with sunlight: *Let's lie over there in the sun* **3** a star round which planets may turn

²**sun** *v* **-nn-** to place (oneself) or stay in sunlight; allow sunlight to fall on (oneself)

sunbathe *v* **-bathed, -bathing** to spend time in strong sunlight, usu. sitting or lying, in order to make the body brown $-\sim$r *n*

sunburn *n* the condition of having sore skin after experiencing the effects of strong sunlight

sunburnt –also **sunburned** *adj* having a brown skin; suntanned

Sunday *n* **-days** the first day of the week; day before Monday, on which Christians worship

sung *past part. of* SING

sunglasses *n* glasses with dark glass in them to protect the eyes from sunlight

sunk *past part. of* SINK

sunlight *n* the light from the sun

sunny *adj* **-nier, -niest 1** having bright sunlight **2** cloudless **3** cheerful – -**nily** *adv* – -**niness** *n*

sunrise –also (*esp. spoken*) **sun-up** *n* the time when the sun is seen to appear after the night

sunset *n* the time when the sun is seen to disappear as night begins

sunshine *n* **1** strong sunlight, as when there are no clouds **2** a place where there is bright light and heat from the sun

super *adj esp. spoken* wonderful

superb *adj* perfect in form, quality, etc.; wonderful $-\sim$**ly** *adv*

superficial *adj* **1** on the surface; not deep **2** not serious, complete, or searching in thought, ideas, etc. $-\sim$**ity** *n* $-\sim$**ly** *adv*

superfluous *adj* more than is necessary; not needed or wanted $-\sim$**ly** *adv* $-\sim$**ness, -fluity** *n*

¹**superior** *adj* **1** *esp. written & tech-*

nical higher in position; upper **2** good or better in quality or value **3** of higher rank or class **4** (as if) thinking oneself better than others $-\sim$**ity** *n*

²**superior** *n* **1** a person of higher rank, esp. in a job **2** (a title for) the head of a religious group: *Mother Superior*

superman *n* **-men 1** (in stories) a man with powers of mind and body much greater than others' **2** *esp. spoken* a man of great ability

supermarket *n* a large shop where one serves oneself with food and goods

supernatural *adj* **1** not explained by natural laws but (esp.) by the powers of spirits, gods, and magic **2** connected with unknown forces and spirits $-\sim$**ly** *adv*

supersonic *adj* faster than the speed of sound

superstition *n* (a) belief which is not based on reason or fact but on association of ideas, as in magic – -**tious** *adj* – -**tiously** *adv*

supervise *v* **-vised, -vising** to keep watch over (work and workers) as the person in charge – -**vision** *n* – -**visor** *n* – -**visory** *adj*

supper *n* the last meal of the day, taken in the evening $-\sim$**less** *n*

¹**supplement** *n* **1** an additional amount of something **2** an additional written part, at the end of a book, or as a separate part of a newspaper, magazine, etc.

²**supplement** *v* to make additions to

supplies *n* food and/or necessary materials for daily life, esp. for a group of people over a period of time

¹**supply** *v* **-plied, -plying** to provide (something) – **-lier** *n*

²**supply -plies** *n* **1** a store which can be used **2** an amount: *a large supply of food* **3** the rate at which an amount is provided **4 in short supply** scarce

¹**support** *v* **1** to bear the weight of, esp. preventing from falling **2 a** to provide money for (a person) to live on **b** to help, with sympathy, or practical advice, money, food, etc. **3** to approve of and encourage **4** to be in favour of – ~**ive** *adj*

²**support** *n* **1** the act or means of supporting **2** a piece of material which bears the weight of something **3** an apparatus which holds a weak or displaced part of the body **4** a person who provides money to live, esp. for his family **5** the amount of attendance or number of people who are loyal attenders: *The theatre gets a lot of support*

supporter *n* a person who gives loyalty and attendance to (an activity), defends (a principle), etc.

¹**suppose** *v* **-posed, -posing** to take as likely; consider as true **2 a** to expect, because of duty, responsibility, law, or other conditions: *Everyone is supposed to wear a seat belt in the car* **b** to allow:*not supposed to smoke*

²**suppose** –also **supposing** *conj* **1** why not?; I suggest **2** if: *Suppose it rains, what shall we do?*

suppress *v* **1** to crush (esp. an action or state) by force **2** to prevent from appearing: *to suppress the truth* **3** to prevent from being printed and made public – ~**ion** *n*

supreme *adj* **1** highest in position, esp. of power **2** highest in degree – ~**ly** *adv*

¹**sure** *adj* **1** having no doubt **2** certain: *It's sure to rain* – ~**ness** *n*

²**sure** *adv esp. spoken esp. US* certainly: *'Are you all right?' 'Sure'*

surely *adv* **1** safely: *slowly but surely* **2** certainly **3** I believe or hope (something must be or become so)

¹**surface** *n* **1** the outer part: *the earth's surface* **2** the top of a body of liquid

²**surface** *v* **-faced, -facing 1** to come to the surface of water **2** to cover (esp. a road) with hard material

³**surface** *adj* (of post) travelling by land and sea

surge *v* **surged, surging 1** to move, esp. forward, in or like powerful waves: *The crowd surged past him* **2** (of a feeling) to arise powerfully – **surge** *n*

surgeon *n* a doctor whose job is to perform medical operations

surgery *n* **-ries 1** a place where one or a group of doctors or dentists receives people to give them advice on their health and medicines to treat illnesses **2** the time during which this takes place **3** the skill and practice of performing medical operations **4** the performing of such an operation, usu. including the cutting open of the skin

surly *adj* **-lier, -liest** angry, bad-mannered, etc., esp. habitually

surname *n* the name one shares with the other members of one's family, often the last name

surpass *v* to go beyond, in amount or degree –~**ing** *adj* –~**ingly** *adv*

surplus *n, adj* (an amount) additional to what is needed or used, as of money

¹**surprise** *n* **1** (the feeling caused by) an unexpected event **2** the act of coming on (someone, often an enemy) unprepared (esp. in the phrase **take by surprise**)

²**surprise** *v* **-prised, -prising 1** to cause surprise to **2** to shock or cause to disbelieve **3** to come on or attack when unprepared

surprising *adj* unusual; causing surprise –~**ly** *adv*

¹**surrender** *v* **1** to yield to the power of esp. an enemy, as a sign of defeat **2** *esp. written* to give up possession of (esp. a paper, in return for money or services)

²**surrender** *n* the act of surrendering

¹**surround** *v* **1** to be all around on every side **2** to go around on every side –~**ing** *adj*

²**surround** *n* an edge, esp. ornamental as part of the furnishing in a house, or an open space around a carpet

surroundings *n* the place and conditions of life

¹**survey** *v* **-veyed, -veying 1** to look at (a person, group, place, or condition) as a whole **2** to examine the condition of and give a value for (a building) **3** to measure, judge, and record on a map the details of (an area of land)

²**survey** *n* **-veys 1** a general view or considering (of a place or condition) **2** (an) examination of a house, esp. for someone who may buy it **3** (an) act of surveying land **4** a map showing the details and nature of such land

survival *n* **1** the fact or likelihood of surviving **2** something which has continued to exist from an earlier time, (esp.) which is not useful now

survive *v* **-vived, -viving 1** to continue to live, esp. after coming close to death **2** to continue to live after: *She survived her sons*

survivor *n* a person who has continued to live, esp. in spite of coming close to death

¹**suspect** *adj* of uncertain truth, rightness, quality, etc.

²**suspect** *n* a person who is suspected of guilt, esp. in a crime

³**suspect** *v* **1** to believe to exist or be true; think likely **2** to believe to be guilty **3** to be doubtful about the truth or value of

suspend *v* **1** to hang from above **2** to hold still in liquid or air: *Dust could be seen suspended in the beam of light* **3** to put off or stop (esp. the fulfilment of a decision) for a period of time **4** to prevent from taking part in a team, belonging to a group, etc., for a time, usu. because of misbehaviour or breaking rules

suspense *n* a state of uncertain expectation

suspension *n* 1 the act of suspending or state of being suspended 2 a liquid mixture with very small pieces of solid material contained but not combined in the liquid 3 the pieces of apparatus fixed to the wheels of a car, motorcycle, etc., to lessen the effects of rough road surfaces

suspicion *n* 1 the act or feeling of suspecting or state of being suspected 2 a slight amount (of something seen, heard, tasted, etc.)

suspicious *adj* 1 likely to suspect (guilt) 2 causing to suspect guilt, wrongness, etc.; suspect −~**ly** *adv*

sustain *v* 1 a to bear (difficulty) b to do this without loss of strength 2 to keep in continuance: *to sustain a note in music* 3 to keep strong; strengthen 4 *esp. written* to hold up (the weight of)

¹swagger *v* 1 to walk with a swinging movement, as if proud 2 to talk in a boasting way −~**er** *n* −~**ingly** *adv*

²swagger *n* a proud manner of walking

¹swallow *n* a type of small insect-eating bird with pointed wings and a tail that comes to 2 points, which comes to the northern countries in summer

²swallow *v* 1 to move (food or drink) down the throat from the mouth 2 to make the same movement of the throat, esp. as a sign of nervousness

3 a to accept patiently **b** *esp. spoken* to believe, in spite of doubt −~**er** *n*

³swallow *n* an act of swallowing

swam *past tense of* SWIM

¹swamp *n* (an area of) soft wet land; (a) bog −~**y** *adj*

²swamp *v* 1 to fill with water, esp. causing to sink 2 to crush with a large amount, as of work or difficulties

swap, swop *v* **-pp-** *esp. spoken* to exchange −

¹swarm *n* 1 a large group (of insects) moving in a mass, esp. bees with a queen 2 a crowd (of people) or moving mass (of animals)

²swarm *v* 1 (of bees) to leave the hive or other living place in a mass to find another 2 to move in a crowd or mass

³swarm *v becoming rare* to climb using the hands and feet

¹sway *v* **swayed, swaying** 1 to swing from side to side or to one side 2 to influence

²sway *n* 1 swaying movement 2 influence 3 *old use & literature* power to rule

swear *v* **swore, sworn, swearing** 1 to promise formally or by an oath 2 *esp. spoken* to state firmly 3 to take or cause to take an oath, as in court: *They swore him to silence* 4 a to take (an oath) b to declare the truth of by oath: *a sworn statement* 5 to curse −~**er** *n*

¹sweat *v* 1 to have sweat coming out on the skin 2 to cause to do this: *to* *sweat a horse* **3** to show liquid on the surface, from inside: *The cheese is sweating* **4** to work or force to work very hard for little money **5** **sweat blood** *esp. spoken* to work unusually hard

²**sweat** *n* **1** also **perspiration**– liquid which comes out from the body through the skin to cool it **2** the action of sweating **3** fever with sweating **4** *esp. spoken* hard work –~**y** *adj*

sweater *n* **1** a heavy woollen garment for the top of the body **2** a knitted top garment; jumper

¹**sweep** *v* **swept, sweeping** **1** to clean by brushing **2** to move or touch with a brushing movement: *The wind swept the leaves away* **3** to move in, or extend in, a curve: *The hills sweep round the valley* **4** to cover quickly: *A storm swept over the country* **5** to spread throughout: *The new fashion swept the country* **6** to move in a grand manner: *She swept from the room* **7** **sweep the board** to win easily and completely **8** **sweep someone off his feet** to cause someone to fall suddenly in love with one

²**sweep** *n* **1** an act of sweeping **2** a swinging movement, or the distance covered by this: *the sweep of his sword* **3** a long curved line or area: *the sweep of the hills* **4** a strong forward movement **5** an act of moving out over a broad area to search, attack, etc. **6** *technical* one

of the large broad arms of a windmill

¹**sweet** *adj* **1** tasting like or containing sugar **2** having a pleasant taste, smell, or sound: *sweet music* **3** gentle or attractive in manner **4** small and charming: *a sweet little kitten* **5** (of wine) not dry **6** pleasant: *the sweet smell of success* **7** **sweet on** *esp. spoken* in love with –~**ly** *adv* –~**ness** *n* –~**ish** *adj*

²**sweet** *n* **1** a small sweet thing, mainly sugar or chocolate, eaten for pleasure **2** a dessert

sweeten *v* **1** to make or become sweet **2** to make pleasanter: *Holidays sweeten life* –~**er** *n*

sweetheart *n* a person whom another loves

¹**swell** *v* **swelled, swollen** *or* **swelled, swelling** **1** to increase in fullness and roundness **2** to increase the amount of **3** to fill with strong feeling: *Her heart swelled*

²**swell** *n* **1** the movement of large stretches of the sea **2** an increase of sound: *the great swell of the organ* **3** roundness and fullness

³**swell** *adj US esp. spoken* very good: *a swell teacher*

swelling *n* **1** swelling or being swollen **2** a swollen place on the body

swept *past tense and past part. of* SWEEP

¹**swerve** *v* **swerved, swerving** **1** to turn suddenly to one side, when moving **2** to change from a course or purpose

²**swerve** *n* a swerving movement

¹**swift** *adj* rapid, fast, short, or sudden −∼**ly** *adv* −∼**ness** *n*

²**swift** *n* a type of small bird with long wings

¹**swim** *v* **swam, swum, swimming 1** to move through water by moving limbs or tail **2** to cross or complete (a distance) by doing this: *to swim a river* **3** to be full of or covered with liquid: *swimming in fat* **4** to feel dizzy: *His head swam* **5 swim with the tide** to follow the behaviour of others −∼**mer** *n*

²**swim** *n* **1** an act of swimming **2 in the swim** knowing about and concerned in what is going on

swimming bath −also **swimming baths** *n* a public swimming pool

swimming pool *n* a special pool for swimming in

¹**swindle** *v* **-dled, -dling** to cheat (someone) −∼**r** *n*

²**swindle** *n* **1** an example of swindling **2** something which is not of the value paid for

swine *n* **swine 1** *old use or technical* a pig **2** *sl* a disliked unpleasant person − **-nish** *adj*

¹**swing** *v* **swung, swinging 1** to move backwards and forwards, round and round, or in a curve from a fixed point **2** to move (oneself) in this way: *swinging on the gate* **3** to wave (something) around in the air: *He swung his sword* **4** *esp. spoken* to be hanged to death, as a punishment **5** to turn quickly: *He swung round* **6** to change by a large degree: *She swung from happiness to tears* **7** to move or start to move smoothly and rapidly: *swing into action* **8 no/not enough room to swing a cat** very little space

²**swing** *n* **1** the/an act or method of swinging: *the swing of his arms* **2** the distance covered by a swinging movement: *a wide swing* **3** a strong regular beat: *walk with a swing* **4** a type of jazz music of the 1930's and 40's with a strong regular beat **5** a seat on which one can swing **6** a large change: *a swing in public opinion* **7 go with a swing** to happen successfully **8 in full swing** fully active

¹**switch** *n* **1** an apparatus for interrupting an electric current **2** a change: *a switch of plan* **3** a small thin stick, esp. taken from a tree

²**switch** *v* **1** to change or exchange: *He switched positions* **2** to change by a switch **3 a** to hit with a switch **b** to move quickly; twitch: *He switched his hand away* −∼**able** *adj*

¹**swollen** *adj* **1** of an increased size, often because of the presence of surplus water or air within **2** too great: *a swollen opinion of oneself* −∼**ness** *n*

²**swollen** *past part. of* SWELL

¹**swoop** *v* to descend sharply or rush on someone, esp. in attack −∼**er** *n*

²**swoop** *n* **1** a swooping action **2 at one fell swoop** all at once

sword *n* a weapon with a long blade and a handle

swore *past tense of* SWEAR

sworn *past part. of* SWEAR

swum *past part. of* SWIM

swung *past tense and past part. of* SWING

syllable *n* a word or part of a word which contains a vowel sound or consonant acting as a vowel: *There are 2 syllables in "button"* – **-abic** *adj*

symbol *n* **1** a sign, shape, or object which represents a person, idea, value, etc. **2** a letter or figure which expresses a sound, number, or chemical substance: *'H$_2$O' is the symbol for water* –~**ic,** ~**ical** *adj* –~**ically** *adv*

sympathetic *adj* **1** of, feeling, or showing sympathy **2** connecting ideas or events as cause and result, because one follows the other: *sympathetic magic* –~**ally** *adv*

sympathize, -ise *v* **-thized, -thizing** to feel or show sympathy or approval – **-thizer** *n* – **-thizingly** *adv*

sympathy *n* **1** the ability to share or understand the feelings of another **2** pity **3** agreement: *sympathy for his opinions* **4 come out in sympathy** to stop work in support of workers who have gone on strike

symphony *n* **-nies** a musical work for an orchestra – **-onic** *adj*

symptom *n* **1** an outward sign of inner change **2** a change in body or mind which shows disease or disorder –~**atic** *adj* –~**atically** *adv*

synchronize, -nise *v* **-nized, -nizing 1** to happen or cause to happen at the same speed: *They synchronized their steps* **2** to set (clocks and watches) to the same time **3** to match (recorded sound) correctly to a piece of film – **-nization** *n*

syndrome *n* **1** a collection of symptoms which represent a disorder of the body or the mind **2** any pattern of qualities, happenings, etc., typical of a general condition

synthesize, -sise *v* **-sized, -sizing 1** to make up or produce by combining parts **2** to make by combining chemicals: *to synthesize a drug* – **-sis** *n*

synthetic *adj* **1** of or concerning synthesis **2** produced by synthesizing; artificial –~**ally** *adv*

syrup *n* **1** sweet liquid, esp. sugar and water **2** treacle or sugarcane juice –~**y** *adj*

system *n* **1** a group of related parts working together **2** an ordered set of ideas, methods, or ways of working **3** a plan

systematic *adj* based on a regular plan or fixed method; thorough: *a systematic search* –~**ally** *adv*

¹table *n* **1** a piece of furniture with a flat top supported by legs **2** such a piece of furniture made for a specific activity: *a card table* **3** the people sitting at a table **4** a collection of information arranged in an orderly way: *a bus timetable* **5** also **multiplication table** – a list which young children repeat to learn what number results when a number from 1 to 12 is multiplied by any of the numbers from 1 to 12 **6 under the table** *esp. spoken* (of money) given in order to influence somebody dishonestly

²table *adj* made to be placed and used on a table: *a table lamp*

³table *v* **tabled, tabling 1** to suggest; bring forward (a matter, report, etc.) for consideration **2** to put (facts, information, etc.) into the form of a table

tablespoon *n* a large spoon used for serving food from a bowl or dish –~**ful** *n*

tablet 1 a hard flat block of some substance, esp. a small round one of medicine **2** a small slab of stone or metal with words cut into it **3** a thin sheet of clay or wax used as a writing surface in ancient times

taboo *n* **taboos 1** a strong social custom forbidding an act or the naming of certain things **2** religious, social, or magical rules forbidding the naming, use, or touching of a person or object considered too holy or evil –**taboo** *adj:a taboo act*

¹tack *n* **1** a small nail with a broad flat head **2** the course of a sailing ship in relation to the position of its sails **3** a course of action: *to try a new tack* **4** a long loose stitch

²tack *v* **1** to fasten with a tack **2** to change tack **3** to sew with long loose straight stitches

¹tackle *n* **1** the apparatus used in a sport, such as the rod, line, hooks, etc., used in fishing **2** a system of ropes and wheels for working a ship's sails, raising heavy weights, etc. **3** (in games such as football) an act of trying to take the ball from an opponent

²tackle *v* **-led, -ling 1** to try to take the ball away from (an opponent) **2** *esp. spoken* **a** to deal with: *The children didn't know how to tackle the question* **b** to deal with by speaking forcefully: *If Bill's late again I'll have to tackle him about it*

tact *n* skill in handling people without causing offence –~**ful** *adj* –~**fully** *adv* –~**less** *adj* –~**lessly** *adv* –~**lessness** *n*

tactic *n* a means of getting a desired result

tactics *n* **1** the art of arranging military forces and moving them during battle **2** the art of using existing means to get a desired result – **-tical** *adj* – **-tically** *adv*

tadpole *n* the young of a frog or toad

¹tag *n* **1** a small narrow length of paper, material, etc., fixed to something to show what it is, details about it, etc. **2** a metal or plastic point at the end of a cord, shoelace, etc. **3** a phrase or sentence spoken (too) often, esp. one in Latin

²tag *v* **-gg- 1** to fasten a tag to (something) **2** to put (someone) into a kind or class **3** to follow closely: *tagging along behind*

¹tail *n* **1** the movable part growing at the back of a creature's body **2** anything like this in appearance, shape, or position **3** the back, last, or lowest part of various things **4**

the side of a coin which does not bear the head of a ruler (esp. in the phrase **heads or tails**) **5** *sl* a person employed to watch and follow someone **6 turn tail** to run away −~**less** *adj*

²**tail** *v esp. spoken* **1** to follow closely behind (someone): *The police have been tailing me* **2** to cut the stems off the bottom of (berries)

¹**tailor** *n* a person who makes outer garments to order, esp. for men

²**tailor** *v* to make an outer garment by cutting and sewing cloth

¹**take** *v* **took, taken, taking 1** to get possession of; gain; seize; win **2** to hold with the hands **3** to borrow or use without asking permission or by mistake **4** to hold: *This bottle takes a litre* **5** to carry from one place to another **6** to carry (to a person): *Take him a cup of tea* **7** to use in getting from one place to another: *take the bus* **8** to gain: *If he wins he will take the title* **9** to buy: *We take 2 newspapers a day* **10** to eat, drink, breathe in, etc.: *Take your medicine* **11** to have: *taking a walk* **12** to test, measure, etc.: *Take your temperature* **13** to subtract: *Take 5 from 12* **14** to follow: *a difficult course to take* **15** to swear (an oath) **16** to understand: *The girl took his smile to mean yes* **17** to attract; delight: *really taken by the little dog* **18** to study as a course: *take history* **19** to last: *How long does the flight take?* **20** to need: *It takes a thief to know a thief* **21** to

cost: *Keeping a horse takes a lot of money* **22** to accept: *This machine only takes 5-pence coins* **23** to make by photography: *I had my picture taken* **24** to have an intended effect: *The colour took and her white dress is now red* **25** to become or cause to become: *John was taken ill* **26** to write down: *He took my name and address* **27** to jump over: *The horse took that fence well* **28** to accept: *I won't take less than £500* **29 take to one's heels/legs** to run away −**taker** *n*

²**take** *n* **1** a scene that has been or is to be photographed for a film: *6 takes before the director was satisfied* **2** the amount of money taken by a business, thief, etc. **3** a share of this

take in *v adv* **1** to provide lodgings for **2** to include: *The British Empire once took in a quarter of the world* **3** to reduce the size of (a garment) **4** to understand: *It took me a long time to take it all in* **5** to deceive; cheat

takeoff *n* **1** the beginning of a flight, when a plane, spacecraft, etc., rises from the ground **2** *esp. spoken* a copy of someone's typical behaviour, usu. done to amuse others: *a takeoff of the headmaster*

take off *v adv* **1** to remove (a garment) **2** *esp. spoken* to copy (someone, esp. his speech or manners) **3** (of a plane, spacecraft, etc.) to rise into the air at the beginning of a flight

take over *v adv* to gain control over and responsibility for

tale *n* 1 a story of real or imaginary events 2 a piece of news, esp. when false or intended to hurt: *to tell tales*

talent *n* (a) special natural or learnt ability or skill, esp. of a high quality 2 people of such ability: *The school has plenty of talent* −~**ed** *adj*

¹**talk** *v* 1 to use words; have the power of speech; speak 2 to make thoughts, ideas, etc., known by means of speech 3 to express thoughts as if by speech: *People who cannot speak or hear can talk by using signs* 4 to speak about: *We talked music all night* 5 **talk big** to boast

²**talk** *n* 1 a particular way of speech or conversation: *baby talk* 2 a conversation 3 an informal speech 4 a subject of conversation: *She's the talk of the street* 5 empty speech: *His threats were just talk*

talkative *adj* liking to talk a lot −~**ness** *n*

tall *adj* 1 having a greater than average height 2 having the stated height: *4 feet tall* −~**ish** *adj* −~**ness** *n*

¹**tame** *adj* 1 gentle and unafraid; not fierce; trained to live with man 2 unexciting; uninteresting −~**ly** *adv* −~**ness** *n*

²**tame** *v* **tamed, taming** 1 to train (a wild or fierce animal) to be gentle and unafraid in man's presence 2 to make (something dangerous) useful and safe −**tamable** *or* **tameable** *adj* −**tamer** *n*

tamper with *v prep* to make changes in (something) without permission

¹**tan** *v* **-nn-** 1 to make (animal skin) into leather by treating with an acid (tannin) made from the bark of certain trees 2 to make or become brown, esp. by sunlight 3 *esp. spoken* to beat (someone) severely: *I'll tan your hide!*

²**tan** *n* 1 a yellowish brown colour 2 the brown colour given to the skin by sunlight

tangible *adj* 1 that can be felt by touch 2 real; not imaginary − **-bility** *n* − **-bly** *adv*

¹**tangle** *v* **-gled, -gling** to make or become a confused mass of disordered and twisted threads

²**tangle** *n* 1 a confused mass of hair, thread, string, etc. 2 a confused disordered state

tank *n* 1 a large container for storing liquid or gas 2 an enclosed heavily armed armoured vehicle that moves on 2 metal belts

tanker *n* a ship, plane, or railway or road vehicle built to carry large quantities of gas or liquid

tantalize, -lise *v* to worry or annoy (a person or animal) by keeping something strongly desired just out of reach; cause anger by raising hopes that cannot be satisfied

¹**tap** *n* 1 any apparatus for controlling the flow of liquid or gas from a pipe, barrel, etc. 2 **on tap** *esp. spoken* ready for use when needed

²**tap** *v* **-pp-** 1 to use or draw from: *to tap the nation's natural mineral*

wealth **2** to make a connection to (a telephone) in order to listen to conversations

³**tap** *v* **-pp-** to strike lightly against something

⁴**tap** *n* a short light blow

¹**tape** *n* **1** narrow material in the form of a band **2** a string stretched across the winning line in a race and broken by the winner **3** (a length of) narrow material covered with a magnetic substance on which sound can be recorded **4** also **tape recording–** a length of this on which a recording has been made

²**tape** *v* **taped, taping 1** also **tape-record–** to record on tape **2** to fasten or tie (a parcel, packet, etc.) with tape **3 have someone taped** *sl* to understand a person, esp. their weakness, thoroughly

¹**taper** *n* **1** a gradual decrease in the width of a long object **2** a length of string covered in wax, used for lighting candles, pipes, etc. **3** a very thin candle

²**taper** *v* to make or become gradually narrower towards one end

tape recorder *n* an instrument which can record and play back sound using tape

tapestry *n* **-tries 1** a heavy cloth into which a picture or pattern is woven **2** a wall-hanging made of this – **-tried** *adj*

¹**tar** *n* a black substance used for making roads, preserving wood, etc.

²**tar** *v* **-rr- 1** to cover with tar **2 tar and feather** to put tar on (someone) and then cover with feathers as a punishment

target *n* **1** anything at which shots, missiles, etc. are aimed **2** a person or thing that is made the object of unfavourable remarks, jokes, etc. **3** a total or object which one desires to reach

¹**tarnish** *v* to make or become dull or discoloured

²**tarnish** *n* dullness; loss of polish

tarpaulin *n* (a sheet or cover of) heavy waterproof cloth

¹**tart** *adj* **1** sharp to the taste **2** spoken sharply and unkindly –~**ly** *adv* –~**ness** *n*

²**tart** *n* **1** fruit or jam cooked on a pastry base **2** *sl* a girl or woman who is regarded as having a sexually immoral character

tartan *n* **1** woollen cloth with checks of various colours **2** a special pattern on this cloth worn by a group of Scottish families (clan)

task *n* **1** a piece of work (that must be) done, esp. if hard or unpleasant **2 take someone to task** to scold someone

¹**taste** *v* **tasted, tasting 1** to test the taste of (food or drink) by taking a little into the mouth **2** to experience the taste of **3** to eat or drink: *He had not tasted food in 3 days* **4** to have a particular taste: *This soup tastes of chicken* **5** to experience: *to taste freedom*

²**taste** *n* **1** the sense by which one knows one food from another by

its sweetness, bitterness, etc. **2** the quality special to any food or drink which makes one able to recognize it by taste **3** a small quantity of food or drink: *a taste of soup* **4** the judgement of beauty, art, music, etc.; choice and use of manners, fashions, etc.: *good/bad/poor taste* **5** a personal liking for something: *a taste for adventure* **6** an experience: *a taste of success*

tasteful *adj* having or showing good taste −∼**ly** *adv* −∼**ness** *n*

tasteless *adj* **1** having no taste **2** having or showing poor taste −∼**ly** *adv* −∼**ness** *n*

tasty *adj* **-ier, -iest** pleasing to the taste −**tastily** *adv*

tattered *adj* torn; ragged

¹tattoo *n* **-toos 1** a rapid beating of drums played late at night to signal that soldiers should go to their rooms **2** a rapid continuous beating of drums **3** an outdoor military show with music, usu. at night

²tattoo *n* **-toos** a pattern, picture, or message put on the skin by tattooing

³tattoo *v* **-tooed, -tooing** to mark (a pattern, message, etc.) on the skin by pricking it and putting in coloured dyes −∼**ist** *n*

taught *past tense & past part. of* TEACH

taut *adj* **1** stretched tight **2** showing signs of anxiety: *a taut expression* −∼**ly** *adv* −∼**ness** *n*

¹tax *v* **1** to charge a tax on **2** to make heavy demands (on); tire −∼**ability** *n* −∼**able** *adj*

²tax *n* **1** (a sum of) money paid to the government according to income, property, goods bought, etc. **2** a heavy demand: *a tax on your strength*

taxation *n* **1** the act of taxing **2** money raised from taxes

taxi −also *esp. written* **taxicab** *n* a car which may be hired by the public with its driver

tea *n* **1** a type of bush mainly grown in South and East Asia for its leaves **2** (a drink made by pouring boiling water onto) the dried and cut leaves of this bush **3** a cup of this: *3 teas please!* **4** a small meal, served in the afternoon **5** a medicinal drink made by putting roots or leaves in hot water: *herb tea* **6 one's cup of tea** the sort of thing one likes

teabag *n* a small bag with tea leaves inside, put into boiling water to make tea

teach *v* **taught, teaching** to give knowledge or skill of, or training or lessons to

teacher *n* a person who teaches, esp. as a profession

teacup *n* **1** a cup in which tea is served **2 storm in a teacup** a lot of worry over something unimportant

tealeaf *n* **-leaves** one of the pieces of leaf used for making tea

team *n* **1** 2 or more animals pulling the same vehicle: *a team of horses* **2** a group of people who work, play, or act together

teapot *n* a vessel in which tea is made and served

¹**tear** *n* **1** a drop of liquid from the eye **2 in tears** crying

²**tear** *v* **tore, torn, tearing 1** to pull apart or into pieces by force **2** to make by doing this: *tear a hole* **3** to remove by force: *Our roof was torn off* **4** to become torn: *This material tears easily* **5** to divide by the pull of opposing forces: *torn apart by war* **6** to move excitedly with great speed: *They tore down the street*

³**tear** *n* a torn place in cloth, paper, etc.

tease *v* **teased, teasing 1** to make fun of playfully or unkindly **2** to separate and straighten threads

teaspoon *n* a small spoon used for stirring tea −∼**ful** *n*

tea towel *n* a cloth for drying cups, plates, etc.

technical *adj* **1** having special knowledge, esp. of an industrial or scientific subject **2** of or related to a particular and esp. a practical or scientific subject **3** belonging to a particular art, science, profession, etc. −∼**ly** *adv*

technicality *n* **-ties** a technical point, detail, or expression

technique *n* **1** the method or manner in which a skilled activity is carried out **2** skill in art or some specialist activity

technology *n* **-gies** the branch of knowledge dealing with scientific and industrial methods and their practical use in industry; practical science − **-gical** *adj* − **-gically** *adv* − **-gist** *n*

tedious *adj* long and boring −∼**ly** *adv* −∼**ness** *n*

teenage −also **teenaged** *adj* of, for, or being a teenager

teenager *n* a person aged between 13 and 19

¹**teeth** *n* **1** *esp. spoken* effective force or power: *When will the police be given the necessary teeth to deal with young criminals?* **2 armed to the teeth** very heavily armed **3 escape by the skin of one's teeth** to have a narrow escape **4 get one's teeth into** to do (a job) very actively and purposefully **5 in the teeth of** against the strength of **6 set someone's teeth on edge** to give someone the unpleasant sensation caused by certain acid tastes or high sounds **7 show one's teeth** to act threateningly

²**teeth** *pl. of* TOOTH

teetotal *adj* never drinking, or opposed to the drinking of, alcohol −∼**ler** *n*

telecommunications *n* the various methods of receiving or sending messages by telephone or telegraph

telegram *n* **1** a message sent by telegraph **2** a piece of paper on which this message is delivered

¹**telegraph** *n* **1** a method of sending messages along wire by electric signals **2** the apparatus that receives or sends messages in this way

²**telegraph** *v* to send by telegraph

¹**telephone** −also *(esp. spoken)* **phone** *n* **1** a method of talking over distances by electrical means: *radio*

telephone 2 the apparatus that receives or sends sounds in this way

²**telephone** –also *(esp. spoken)* **phone** *v* **-phoned, -phoning** 1 to speak (a message) to (someone) by telephone: *I telephoned your aunt the news* 2 to send (something) to (someone) by telephone: *We telephoned Jean a greetings telegram* 3 to reach or try to reach by telephone

teleprinter *n* a machine used for sending and receiving written messages by telegraphic methods

¹**telescope** *n* an instrument used for seeing distant objects

²**telescope** *v* **-scoped, -scoping** to make or become shorter by crushing, as in a violent accident

televise *v* **-vised, -vising** to broadcast or be broadcast by television

television –also *(esp. spoken)* **telly** *n* 1 the method of transmitting pictures and usu. sound by means of electrical waves 2 the news, plays, etc., broadcast in this way: *the television news* 3 also **television set**– a boxlike apparatus for receiving television pictures and sound 4 the industry of making and broadcasting plays, films, etc., on television 5 **on (the) television a** broadcast by television: *What's on television?* **b** broadcasting by television: *The President spoke on television*

¹**telex** *n* 1 an international service provided by post offices whereby written messages are passed by teleprinter 2 a message sent in this way

²**telex** *v* to send (a message, news, etc.) to (a person, place, etc.) by telex

tell *v* **told, telling** 1 to make (something) known in words to (someone) 2 to warn; advise: *I told you so* 3 to show; make known: *This light tells you if the machine is on* 4 to find out; know: *It's impossible to tell who'll win* 5 to order; direct: *I told you to get here early* 6 to recognize; know: *I can't tell if it's him or not* 7 to be noticeable; have an effect: *Her nervousness began to tell* 8 to speak someone's secret to someone else 9 **all told** altogether 10 **tell me another** *esp. spoken* I don't believe you 11 **tell the time** to read the time from a clock or watch 12 **there is/was/will be no telling** it is/was/will be impossible to know: *There's no telling what will happen* 13 **you're telling me** *esp. spoken* (a strong way of saying) I know this already

¹**temper** *n* 1 a particular state of mind with regard to anger: *in a good temper* 2 an angry or impatient state of mind: *John's in a temper today* 3 **fly/get into a temper** to become angry suddenly 4 **keep one's temper** to stay calm 5 **lose one's temper** to become angry 6 **out of temper** *esp. written* angry

²**temper** *v* 1 to bring (metal, clay, etc.) to the desired degree of toughness or firmness by treatment 2 to make less severe: *justice tempered with mercy*

temperament *n* a person's nature, esp. as it influences his thinking or behaviour

temperamental *adj* **1** caused by one's nature **2** having frequent changes of temper — ~**ly** *adv*

temperate *adj* **1** practising self-control **2** (of places, climate, etc.) free from very high or very low temperatures

temperature *n* **1** the degree of heat of a place, object, etc. **2 have/run a temperature** to have a bodily temperature higher than normal **3 take someone's temperature** to measure the temperature of someone's body

tempest *n literature* a violent storm

tempestuous *adj* stormy; violent — ~**ly** *adv*

¹**temple** *n* a place for worship in various religions

²**temple** *n* one of the flattish places on each side of the forehead

tempo *n* **-pos** *or* **-pi 1** the rate of movement, work, or activity **2** the speed at which music is played

temporary *n* lasting for a limited time — **-rarily** *adv* — **-rariness** *n*

tempt *v* **1** to persuade or try to persuade (someone) to do something unwise or wrong **2 tempt Providence** to take an unnecessary risk — ~**er** (*fem.* ~**ress**) *n* — ~**ingly** *adv*

temptation *n* **1** the act of tempting or the state of being tempted **2** something very attractive: *the temptations of a city*

ten *adj, n, pron* **1** the number 10 **2 ten a penny** *esp. spoken* very

common **3 ten to one** very likely: *Ten to one he will be late* —**tenth** *adj, n, pron, adv*

¹**tenant** *n* a person who pays rent for a building, land, etc.

²**tenant** *v* to pay rent for the use of (a building, land, etc.)

¹**tend** *v* to take care of; look after

²**tend** *v* **1** to move in a certain direction: *Interest rates are tending upwards* **2** to have a tendency: *Janet tends to get angry if you annoy her*

tendency *n* **-cies 1** a likelihood of developing or acting in a particular way **2** a natural skill

¹**tender** *adj* **1** not hard; soft **2** delicate: *tender flowers* **3** painful; sore **4** gentle; kind: *a tender heart* — ~**ly** *adv* — ~**ness** *n*

²**tender** *n* **1** a wagon carrying coal and/or water behind a railway engine **2** a small boat for travelling between the shore and a larger boat

tendon *n* a strong cord connecting a muscle to a bone

tenement *n* a large building divided into flats, esp. in a poor town area

tennis *n* a game for 2 (**singles**) or 2 pairs (**doubles**) who use rackets to hit a ball across a net dividing a court

tenor *n* **1** (a man with) the highest male singing voice in general use **2** an instrument with the same range of notes **3** *esp. written* (esp. of a person's life) the general direction or style **4** *esp. written* (of speech or writing) the general meaning: *the tenor of his speech*

¹tense *n* any of the forms of a verb that show the time of the action or state expressed by the verb

²tense *adj* 1 stretched tight 2 nervous or anxious – ~**ly** *adv* – ~**ness** *n*

³tense *v* **tensed, tensing** to make or become tense

tension *n* 1 the degree of tightness of a wire, rope, etc. 2 the amount of a force stretching something 3 nervous anxiety, worry, or pressure 4 an anxious, untrusting relationship between people, countries, etc. 5 electric power: *high tension*

tent *n* a movable shelter made of cloth supported by a framework of poles and ropes

tentative *adj* made or done only as a suggestion – ~**ly** *adv* – ~**ness** *n*

tenth *n, pron, adv, adj* 10th

tepid *adj* only slightly warm – ~**ity** *n* – ~**ly** *adv* – ~**ness** *n*

¹term *n* 1 one of the periods of time into which the school, university, legal, etc., year is divided 2 a fixed period of time: *a 4-year term* 3 a period of time after which something is to end: *Our agreement is getting near its term* 4 a word or expression with a special meaning or used in a technical sense: *a medical term* 5 each of the quantities in a ratio, a sum, or an algebraic expression: *The expression $X^2 + 3XY$ contains the terms X^2 and $3XY$* 6 **in the long/short term** over a long/short period of time

²term *v* to call: *You wouldn't term this house beautiful*

¹terminal *adj* 1 *technical* of or happening at the end of a term 2 related to an illness that will cause death 3 of or at the end or limit – ~**ly** *adv*

²terminal *n* 1 a place in the centre of a town for passengers travelling to or from an airport 2 a point at which connections can be made to an electric circuit 3 an apparatus by which a user can give instructions to and get information from a computer

terminate *v* **-nated, -nating** to come to or bring to an end – **-ation** *n*

terminus *n* **-ni** *or* **-nuses** the last stop on a railway or bus route

terms *n* 1 the conditions of an agreement, contract, etc. 2 conditions with regard to payment, prices, etc. 3 **come to terms with** to accept (something one does not want to accept) 4 **in no uncertain terms** clearly and usu. angrily 5 **in terms of** with regard to: *In terms of money we're quite rich, but not in terms of happiness* 6 **on equal terms** as equals 7 **on good/bad/ speaking/ friendly terms** having a stated relationship

¹terrace *n* 1 a flat level area cut from a slope 2 a flat outdoor living area next to a house or on its roof 3 a row of houses joined to each other

²terrace *v* **-raced, -racing** to form into terraces

terrestrial *adj* 1 of or related to the earth rather than to the moon, space, etc. 2 of, being, related to, or living on land rather than in water −~**ly** *adv*

terrible *adj* very bad indeed

terribly *adv* 1 very badly, severely, etc. 2 *esp. spoken* very: *terribly lucky*

terrier any of several types of small active dogs

terrific *adj esp. spoken* 1 very good: *a terrific party* 2 very great: *terrific speed*

terrify *v* **-fied, -fying** to fill with terror or fear

territory *n* **-ries** 1 an area of land, esp. ruled by one government 2 an area regarded by a person, animal, group, etc., as belonging to it alone 3 an area for which one person or branch of an organization is responsible

terror *n* 1 very great fear 2 someone or something that causes such fear 3 *esp. spoken* an annoying person

terrorism *n* the use of violence to obtain political demands − **-ist** *adj, n*

terrorize, -ise *v* **-ized, -izing** to fill with terror by violence

¹**test** *n* 1 a number of questions, tasks, etc., set to measure someone's ability or knowledge 2 a short medical examination 3 a practical examination or trial: *a test drive* 4 something used as a standard: *a test case*

²**test** *v* 1 to study or examine by means of a test 2 to be a severe or difficult test of or for: *These roads test a car's*

tyres 3 to search by means of tests: *testing for oil* −~**er** *n*

testify *v* **-fied, -fying** 1 to bear witness 2 to serve as proof: *Her red face testified to her guilt*

testimonial *n* 1 a formal written statement of a person's character 2 something given or done as an expression of respect, thanks, etc.

testimony *n* **-nies** 1 a formal statement that something is true 2 any information in support of a fact or statement

test tube *n* a small glass tube, closed at one end, used in scientific tests

¹**tether** *n* 1 a rope or chain to which an animal is tied so as to limit movement 2 **at the end of one's tether** unable to suffer any more

²**tether** *v* to fasten (an animal) with a tether

text *n* 1 the main body of writing in a book 2 the original words of a speech, article, etc. 3 any of the various forms in which a book, article, etc., exists: *the original text* 4 a textbook

textbook *n* a book for the study of a particular subject

textile *n* material made by weaving

texture *n* the degree of roughness or smoothness, coarseness or fineness, of a substance

than *conj, prep* (used for introducing the second part of a comparison of inequality): *I know him better than you*

thank *v* 1 to express gratefulness to 2 **have (oneself) to thank** to be responsible **3 thank God/goodness/heaven** (an expression of great thankfulness)

thankful *adj* showing, feeling, or expressing thanks –~**ly** *adv* –~**ness** *n*

thankless *adj* **1** ungrateful **2** not likely to be rewarded with thanks –~**ly** *adv* –~**ness** *n*

thanks *n* **1** words expressing gratefulness **2 thanks to** on account of; because of

thank you –also (*esp. spoken*) **thanks** *interj* I am grateful to you

¹**that** *adj, pron* **those 1** (being) the one or amount stated, shown, or understood: *Those sweets tasted very nice. / Who told you that?* **2** (being) the one of 2 or more people or things that is further away:- *This is my glass and that is yours*

²**that** *adv esp. spoken* so; to such a degree: *I like him but not all that much!*

³**that** *conj* **1** (*used for introducing various kinds of clause*): *It's true that he's French. / He was so rude that she refused to speak to him* **2** who, whom, or which: *It's Jean that makes the decisions here. / Did you see the letter that I sent him?* **3** in, on, for, or at which: *the day that he arrived*

¹**thatch** *v* to cover with thatch

²**thatch** *n* **1** roof covering of straw, reeds, etc. **2** *humour* a mass of thick or untidy hair on the head

¹**thaw** *v* **1** to warm to above freezing point and so make or become liquid, soft, or bendable **2** (of the weather) to become warm enough for snow and ice to melt **3** (of a person) to become friendlier, less formal, etc.

²**thaw** *n* a period of warm weather during which snow and ice melt

¹**the** *definite article* **1** (*used when it is clearly understood who or what is meant*): *We have a cat and a dog. The cat is black and the dog white. / This is the book you wanted* **2 a** (*used with a person, thing, or group that is the only one of its kind*): *the sun / the year 2,000 / sitting on the ground* **b** (*used to suggest that a person, thing, or group is the only or best or most important one of its kind*): *Her wedding was the event of the year. / You didn't meet the Charlie Chaplin!* **3** (*used with or as part of a title or proper name*): *Peter the Great / the Rhine* **4** (*used with an adjective or participle to make it into a noun*): *the impossible / the dead / the English* **5** (*used with a singular noun to make it general*): *The lion is a wild animal*

²**the** *adv* **1** (*used before each of a pair of comparative adjectives or adverbs, to show that 2 things increase or decrease together*): *The more he has the more he wants* **2** (*used before a comparative adjective or adverb, to mean*) in or by that; on that account; in or by so much; in some degree: *He's had a holiday and looks the better for it* **3** above all others; very much: *He likes you*

the best. / He has the greatest difficulty

theatre *n* **1** a special building or place for the performance of plays **2** the work or activity of people who write or act in plays: *the modern theatre*

theft *n* the crime of stealing

their *adj* (*possessive form of* THEY) belonging to them: *They cooked their own breakfast*

theirs *pron* (*possessive form of* THEY) that/those belonging to them: *They used our phone while theirs was out of order*

them *pron* (*object form of* THEY): *He bought them drinks. / Where are my shoes? I can't find them*

theme *n* **1** the subject of a talk or piece of writing **2** a short simple tune on which a piece of music is based

themselves *pron* **1** (*reflexive form of* THEY): *The children seem to be enjoying themselves* **2** (*strong form of* THEY): *They built the house themselves* **3** *esp. spoken* (in) their usual state of mind or body: *When they came to themselves they found their money had been stolen* **4 in themselves** without considering the rest: *These little things aren't important in themselves*

then *adv* **1** at that time: *We lived in the country then. / When you see her, then you'll understand* **2** next in time, space, or order: *The elephants were followed by the camels and then came the horses* **3** in that case: *If you want to go home, then go* **4** as a

result: *Go into the cave, then they won't see you* **5 but then** (**again**) however: *I like watching television but then (again) I wouldn't miss it if I didn't have one*

thence *adv* **1** from that place on: *We can drive to London and thence to Paris by air* **2** for that reason: *He was recently in Africa; thence we may argue that it was there he caught this tropical disease*

theology *n* **-gies 1** the study of religion and religious ideas and beliefs **2** a particular body of opinion about religion: *Muslim theology* – **-ogical** *adj* – **-ogically** *adv* – **-ogian** *n*

theoretical –also **theoretic** *adj* **1** based on theory, not on experience **2** existing only in theory – ~**ly** *adv*

theory *n* **-ries 1** an explanation of a particular fact or event for which certain proof is still needed but which appears to be reasonable **2** the part of a science or art that deals with general principles, rules and methods **3** an opinion based on limited information or knowledge

therapy *n* **-pies** the treatment of illnesses or disorders of the mind or body, esp. without drugs or operations

¹**there** *adv* **1** to, at, or in that place: *Paul's hiding there, under the trees. / There goes John!* **2** at that point of time: *I washed the car and decided to stop there* **3 all there** *esp. spoken* healthy in the mind

²**there** *adv* (*used as the first word in a sentence or clause or as the second*

word in a question, as the subject of the verb when the real subject follows later): *There's a man at the door. / Is there something wrong?*

³**there** *interj* (used for comforting someone or for expressing various feelings, the meaning changing according to the setting and the way it is expressed): *There! Do you feel better now? / There, there. Stop crying. / There. I told you I was right!*

thereabouts *adv* near that place, time, number, degree, etc.: *at 9 o'clock or thereabouts / The people who lived thereabouts were very worried*

thereby *adv* **1** *esp. written* by that means; by doing or saying that: *He treated everyone fairly, and thereby gained the trust of the school* **2** (**and**) **thereby hangs a tale** There is an interesting story connected with what I have just said

therefore *adv* **1** as a result; for that reason; so: *I've never been to China and therefore I don't know much about it* **2** (used in reasoning) as this proves; it follows that: *I think. Therefore, I exist*

thermometer *n* an instrument for measuring and showing temperature

thermos —also **thermos flask** *n trademark* a vacuum flask

thermostat *n* an apparatus that can control temperature

these *pl. of* THIS

they *pron* **1** those people, animals, or things: *They arrive on Monday* **2** people in general: *They say prices are going to increase again*

¹**thick** *adj* **1 a** having a large distance between opposite surfaces; not thin **b** (of a round solid object) wide: *thick wire* **2** measuring in depth, width, or from side to side: *ice 5 centimetres thick* **3** (of liquid) not watery: *thick soup* **4** difficult to see through: *thick mist* **5** (esp. of an accent) very noticeable **6** full of; covered with: *thick with smoke/dust* **7** (of a voice) not clear in sound **8** made of many objects set close together: *a thick forest* **9** *sl* (of a person) stupid: *as thick as two short planks* **10** *sl* beyond what is reasonable or satisfactory: *It's a bit thick* **11** *esp. spoken* very friendly: *Jean and John seem very thick* **12 lay it on thick** *esp. spoken* to praise, thank, etc., someone too much –~**ly** *adv*

²**thick** *adv* so as to be thick; thickly: *The flowers grew thickest near the wall*

³**thick** *n* **1** the most packed part; place or time of greatest activity **2** the thick part of anything **3 through thick and thin** through both good and bad times

thicken *v* **1** to make or become thick **2** to make or become more involved or confused: *The plot thickened*

thickness *n* **1** the state, degree, or quality of being thick **2** a layer: *3 thicknesses of newspaper*

thief *n* **thieves** a person who steals

thieve *v* **thieved, thieving** to act as a

thief – **-ving** *n, adj* – **-vish** *adj* – **-vishly** *adv* – **-vishness** *n*

thigh *n* **1** the top part of the leg between the knee and the hip **2** a part like this on the back legs of certain animals

thimble *n* a protective cap put over the finger that pushes the needle during sewing

¹**thin** *adj* **-nn- 1 a** having a small distance between opposite surfaces; not thick **b** (of a round solid object) narrow: *thin string* **2** having little fat on the body; not fat **3** (of a liquid) watery: *This soup's too thin* **4** not closely packed: *Your hair's getting thin* **5** easy to see through: *thin mist* **6** (esp. of a sound) lacking in strength: *thin high notes* **7** lacking force: *a thin excuse* **8 a thin time** an unpleasant, uncomfortable, or esp. unsuccessful time **9 thin on the ground** scarce – ~**ly** *adv*: *Spread the butter thinly* – ~**ness** *n*

²**thin** *adv* so as to be thin; thinly: *Don't cut the bread so thin*

³**thin** *v* **-nn- 1** to make or become thin **2** to pull up the weaker of (a mass of young plants) so that the stronger ones have room to grow

thing *n* **1** any material object; an object that need not or cannot be named **2** that which is not material; subject; matter: *What a nasty thing to say!* **3** a creature **4** an act: *the next thing to do* **5** an event: *The murder was a terrible thing wasn't it?* **6** *sl* an activity satisfying to one personally: *to do one's thing* **7 first**

thing early; before anything else **8 for one thing** (used for introducing a reason): *For one thing I think you're stupid, for another I don't like you* **9 have a thing about** to have a strong like or dislike for

things *n* **1** personal belongings **2** the general state of affairs **3 be seeing things** to see things which do not exist

¹**think** *v* **thought, thinking 1** to use one's reason; make judgments; use the mind to form opinions; have (a thought) **2** to imagine; understand; believe; consider carefully **3** to remember: *I can't think what his name is* **4** to expect: *We didn't think we'd be this late* **5 to think aloud** to speak one's thoughts as they come **6 think twice** to think very carefully – ~**er** *n*

²**think** *n esp. spoken* an act of thinking

¹**thinking** *n* **1** the act of using one's mind to produce thoughts and ideas **2** opinion; judgment; thought **3 put on one's thinking cap** *esp. spoken* to think seriously about something

²**thinking** *adj* thoughtful; reasoning; that can think clearly and seriously

think of *v prep* **1** also **think about**– to consider before making a decision: *We're thinking of going to France* **2 not think much of** to have a low opinion of **3 think better of someone** to have a higher opinion of someone **4 think better of something** to change one's opinion about something **5 think highly/**

well/little/poorly/etc. of to have a good/bad/etc. opinion of **6 think nothing of** to regard as usual or easy

third *adj, adv, n, pron* **1** 3rd **2** the lowest passing degree standard at many British universities

thirst *n* **1** a sensation of dryness in the mouth caused by the need to drink; desire for drink **2** a strong desire: *the thirst for excitement*

thirsty *adj* **-ier, -iest 1** feeling thirst **2** causing thirst **–thirstily** *adv*

thirteen *adj, n, pron* the number 13 **–~th** *adj, pron, adv*

thirty *adj, n, pron* **-ties** the number 30 **– -tieth** *adj, n, pron, adv*

¹this *adj, pron* **these 1** (being) the one or amount stated, going to be stated, shown, or understood: *I saw Mrs Jones this morning. / Wait until you've heard this story! / Who's this? / Would you like this?* **2** (being) the one of 2 or more people or things that is nearer: *You look in this box here. / This is my sister*

²this *adv esp. spoken* so; this degree: *I've never been out this late before*

thistle *n* any of several types of wild plant with prickly leaves and yellow, white, or purple flowers. The thistle is the national sign of Scotland

thorn *n* **1** a prickle growing on a plant **2** any of various types of bush, plant, or tree having such prickles **3 a thorn in one's flesh/side** a continual cause of annoyance

thorny *adj* **-ier, -iest 1** prickly; having thorns **2** troublesome: *a thorny matter* **–thorniness** *n*

thorough *adj* **1** complete in every way **2** careful with regard to detail **–~ly** *adv* **–~ness** *n*

thoroughfare *n* **1** a road for public traffic **2 No thoroughfare** (as written on signs) not open to the public; no way through

those *pl. of* THAT

¹though *adv* in spite of the fact; nevertheless: *It's hard work. I enjoy it though*

²though *conj* **1** in spite of the fact that; even if: *Even though it's hard work, I enjoy it. / He spoke firmly though pleasantly* **2 as though** as if

¹thought *n* **1** the act of thinking **2** serious consideration **3** (a) product of thinking; idea, opinion, etc. **4** the particular way of thinking of a period, country, etc: *Ancient Greek thought* **5** regard: *with no thought for her own safety*

²thought *past tense and past part. of* THINK

thoughtful *adj* **1** given to or expressing thought **2** paying attention to the feelings of other people **–~ly** *adv* **–~ness** *n*

thoughtless *adj* not thinking; selfish **–~ly** *adv* **–~ness** *n*

thousand *adj, n, pron* **-sand** *or* **-sands 1** the number 1,000 **2 one in a thousand** very good indeed **–~th** *adj, n, pron, adv*

thrash *v* **1** to beat with a whip or stick **2** to defeat thoroughly **3** to move wildly: *The fish thrashed about in the net*

thrashing *n* **1** a severe beating **2** a severe defeat

¹**thread** *n* **1** (a length of) very fine cord **2** a logical connection: *to lose the thread* **3** a raised line that winds around the outside of a screw; a bolt, or the inside of a nut

²**thread** *v* **1** to pass one end of a thread through the eye of (a needle) **2** to put a film in place on a projector **3** **thread one's way through** to make one's way carefully through

threadbare *adj* **1** (of cloth, clothes, etc.) worn thin **2** having been so much used as to be no longer interesting

threat *n* **1** an expression of an intention to hurt, punish, cause pain, etc. **2** a person, thing, or idea regarded as a possible danger

threaten *v* **1** to express a threat against (someone) **2** to give warning of (something bad) –~**ingly** *adv*

three *adj, n, pron* the number 3

three-dimensional *adj* having or seeming to have length, depth, and height

threshold *n* **1** a piece of wood or stone forming the bottom of a doorway **2** the point of beginning **3** *technical* (in psychology) the lowest level at which an influence can be perceived: *on the threshold of pain*

threw *past tense of* THROW

thrice *adj, adv* 3 times

thrifty *adj* **-ier, -iest** avoiding waste in the use of money –**thriftily** *adv* –**thriftiness** *n*

¹**thrill** *v* to feel or cause to feel a thrill –~**ingly** *adv*

²**thrill** *n* a wave of joy, fear, etc.

thrive *v* **thrived** *or* **throve**, **thrived** *or* **thriven**, **thriving** to develop well and be healthy; be successful

throat *n* **1** the passage inside the neck, that divides into 2, one taking air to the lungs, the other food to the stomach **2** the front of the neck: *The murderer cut the old man's throat*

¹**throb** *v* **-bb-** to beat strongly and rapidly

²**throb** *n* a strong low continuous beat

throne *n* **1** the ceremonial chair of a king, bishop, etc. **2** the rank or office of a king or queen

throng *v* to move (as if) in a crowd in –**throng** *n*

¹**throttle** *v* **-tled, -tling** **1** to seize (someone) tightly by the throat **2** to reduce the flow of fuel (e.g. petrol) to (an engine) so lessening speed

²**throttle** *n* a valve that opens and closes to control the flow of fuel into an engine

¹**through** *prep* **1** in at one side, end, or surface of (something) and out at the other **2** by means of: *I got this book through the library* **3** as a result of: *The war was lost through bad organization* **4** from the beginning to the end of **5** over the surface of or within the limits of: *through France and Belgium* **6** among or between the parts or single members of: *through the trees* **7** having

finished, or so as to finish, successfully: *Did you get through your examinations?*

²**through** *adv* **1** in at one side, end, or surface, and out at the other **2** all the way; along the whole distance: *right through to London* **3** from the beginning to the end: *Have you read the letter through?* **4** to a favourable or successful state: *I got through with good marks* **5** (when telephoning) in a state of being connected to a person or place: *Can you put me through to Mr Jones?* **6** in every part; thoroughly: *I got wet through in the rain*

throughout *adv, prep* in, to, through, or during every part (of)

¹**throw** *v* **threw, thrown, throwing 1** to send (something) through the air by a sudden movement of the arm **2** to move (oneself or part of one's body) suddenly and with force **3** to cause to go or come into some place, condition, etc., as if by throwing **4** to put on or take off (a garment) hastily **5** *technical* (of an animal) to give birth to (a young one) **6** to move (a switch, handle, etc.) in order to connect or disconnect parts of a machine, apparatus, etc. **7** to shape (an object) on a potter's wheel **8** to cause to fall to the ground **9** to roll (a dice) **10** to get (a particular number) by rolling a dice **11** *esp. spoken* to give (a party) **12 throw a fit** to have a sudden attack of uncontrolled

temper **13 throw oneself into** to work very busily at −~**er** *n*

²**throw** *n* **1** an act of throwing **2** the distance to which something is thrown: *a throw of 100 metres*

¹**thrust** *v* **thrust, thrusting 1** to push forcefully and suddenly as with a sword, knife, etc. **2** to make a sudden forward stroke with a sword, knife, etc. **3 thrust oneself forward** to draw attention to oneself

²**thrust** *n* **1** an act of thrusting; forceful forward push **2** a swift forward stroke with a knife, sword, etc.

thud *v, n* -**dd**- (to make) a dull sound as caused by a heavy object striking something soft

thug *n* a violent criminal −**thuggery** *n*

¹**thumb** *n* **1** a short movable part of the human hand set apart from the fingers **2** the part of a glove that fits over this **3 stick out like a sore thumb** *esp. spoken* to seem very out of place **4 under somebody's thumb** *esp. spoken* under the control of someone

²**thumb** *v esp. spoken* to ask for or get a lift by holding out one's hand with the thumb raised

¹**thump** *v* to strike with a heavy blow; produce a knocking sound

²**thump** *n* **1** a heavy blow **2** the dull sound produced by this

¹**thunder** *n* **1** the noise that follows a flash of lightning **2** any loud noise like this

²**thunder** *v* **1** to produce thunder **2** to

produce loud sounds like this −~**er** *n*

thunderbolt *n* **1** a flash of lightning from which thunder is heard **2** a sudden event which causes great shock, anxiety, etc.

thunderous *adj* producing thunder or a loud noise like thunder −~**ly** *adv*

Thursday *n* **-days** the 5th day of the week

thus *adv* **1** in this manner; in the way or by the means stated **2** with this result; hence **3 thus far** until now; to this point

¹**tick** *n* any of various types of small blood-sucking animals

²**tick** *n* **1** a short sudden regularly repeated sound made by a clock or watch **2** a mark (usu. √) put against something to show that it is correct

³**tick** *v* **1** (of a clock, watch, etc.) to make a regularly repeated tick **2** to show that (an item) is correct by marking with a tick **3 make someone or something tick** to make a person or thing act, behave, etc., in a particular way

⁴**tick** *n esp. spoken* credit

¹**ticket** *n* **1** a printed piece of paper or card entitling a person to a service such as a journey on a bus, entrance into a cinema, etc. **2** a piece of card or paper fastened to an object giving its price, size, quality, etc. **3** a printed notice of an offence against the driving laws

²**ticket** *v* to put a ticket, tag, or label on (something)

¹**tickle** *v* **-led, -ling** **1** to touch lightly to produce laughter, nervous excitement, etc. **2** to (cause (someone) to) feel nervous excitement **3** to delight or amuse **4 tickled pink** *sl* very pleased or amused

²**tickle** *n* the act or sensation of tickling

tide *n* **1** the regular rise and fall of the seas **2** a current of water caused by this **3 swim/go with/against the tide** to act in accordance with/ opposition to what most other people are doing or thinking

¹**tidy** *adj* **tidier, tidiest** **1** neatly arranged or liking things to be so **2** *esp. spoken* fairly large: *a tidy income* − **-dily** *adv* − **-diness** *n*

²**tidy** *v* **tidied, tidying** to make (something or someone) neat

¹**tie** *n* **1** a band of cloth worn round the neck and tied in a knot **2** a cord, string, etc., used for fastening something **3** something that unites; bond **4** something that limits one's freedom: *Young children can be a tie* **5** an equality of results, score, etc. **6** a length of wood, metal, etc., that joins parts of a framework and gives support **7** a curved line connecting 2 printed musical notes of the same level showing that they are to be played or sung as one unbroken note

²**tie** *v* **tied, tying** **1** to fasten with a cord, rope, etc. **2** to fasten or be fastened by drawing together and knotting string, laces, etc.: *tie your shoes* **3** to be fastened by string, laces, etc., that are drawn together

and knotted **4** to make (a knot or bow) **5** to finish (a match, competition) with equal points **6** to connect (musical notes of the same level) so that there is no interruption in playing or singing

tiger –(*fem.* **tigress**) *n* **tigers** *or* **tiger** a large fierce Asian cat that is yellowish with black stripes

¹**tight** *adj* **1** closely fastened, held, knotted, etc.; fitting too closely **2** drawn out as far as possible; fully stretched **3** leaving no free room or time; fully packed **4** closely or firmly put together **5** *esp. spoken* (of money) in short supply **6** *sl* drunk –~**ly** *adv* –~**ness** *n*

²**tight** *adv* closely; firmly; tightly

tighten *v* to make or become tight or tighter

tights a very close fitting garment covering the legs and lower part of the body

¹**tile** *n* a thin shaped piece of baked clay, plastic, etc., used for covering roofs, floors, etc.

²**tile** *v* **tiled, tiling** to cover (a roof, floor, etc.) with tiles –**tiler** *n*

¹**till** *v* to cultivate (the ground) –~**er** *n*

²**till** *n* **1** a drawer in a shop where money is kept **2 have one's fingers in the till** *esp. spoken* to steal money from the shop where one works

³**till** *prep, conj* until

¹**tilt** *v* to slope or cause to slope as by raising one end

²**tilt** *n* **1** a slope **2** an act of tilting; tilting movement **3 (at) full tilt** at full speed; with full force

¹**timber** *n* **1** wood for building **2** trees suitable for building **3** a wooden beam

²**timber** *interj* (a warning shouted when a cut tree is about to fall down)

¹**time** *n* **1** a continuous measurable quantity from the past, through the present, and into the future **2** the passing of the days, months, and years, taken as a whole **3** a system of measuring this **4** a limited period **5** a period in history: *in ancient times* **6** a period or occasion and the particular experience connected with it: *a good time* **7** the rate of pay received for an hour's work: *double time for Sundays* **8** *sl* a period of imprisonment: *to do/ serve time* **9** free or unfilled time: *no time to watch television* **10** a particular point in the day stated in hours, minutes, seconds, etc.: *What's the time?* **11** a particular point in the year, day, etc.; moment for a particular activity or event: *summertime / bedtime* **12** an unlimited period in the future: *In time you'll forget him* **13** *technical* the rate of speed of a piece of music **14 ahead of one's time** having ideas too modern or original for the period in which one is living **15 all the time** continuously **16 at one time** formerly **17 bide one's time** to wait for a suitable chance **18 from time to time** sometimes **19**

have no time for *esp. spoken* to dislike **20 in no time (at all)** very quickly **21 keep time** (of a clock, watch, etc.) to work correctly **22 kill time** to make time pass by doing something **23 many a time** frequently **24 on time** at the right time **25 once upon a time** (often used at the beginning of children's stories, to mean) at a time in the past **26 pass the time of day** to have a short conversation

²**time** *v* **timed, timing 1** to arrange or set the time at which (something) happens or is to happen **2** to record the time taken by/for (something or someone) **3** to choose the right moment to hit (a ball) or make (a shot)

time limit *n* a period of time within which something must be done

timely *adj* **-lier, -liest** happening at just the right time – **-liness** *n*

¹**times** *prep* multiplied by: *3 times* (usu. written x) *3=9*

²**times** *n* **1** the present: *a sign of the times* **2** occasions **3 behind the times** old-fashioned **4 for old times' sake** because of or as a reminder of happy times in the past

¹**timetable** *n* **1** a table of the times at which buses, planes, etc., arrive and leave **2** a table of the times of classes in a school, college, etc.

²**timetable** *v* **-bled, -bling 1** to plan for a future time **2** to arrange according to a timetable

timid *adj* fearful; lacking courage – ~**ity** *n* – ~**ly** *adv* – ~**ness** *n*

¹**tin** *n* **1** a soft metal that is an element, used to plate metal objects with a protective surface **2** a small metal box or container

²**tin** *v* **-nn-** to preserve (esp. food) by packing in tins

³**tin** *adj* made of tin

¹**tinge** *v* **tinged, tingeing** *or* **tinging 1** to give a slight degree of a colour to (an object or colour) **2** to show signs of

²**tinge** *n* a slight degree (of colour or some quality)

tingle *v* **-gled, -gling** to feel a slight prickly sensation – **tingle** *n*

tinkle *v* **-kled, -kling** to make or cause to make light metallic sounds – **tinkle** *n*

tinsel *n* **1** thin lengths of shiny material used for ornaments **2** anything showy that is really worthless – ~**ly** *adj*

¹**tint** *n* **1** a pale or delicate shade of a colour **2** any of various dyes for the hair **3** an act of tinting the hair

²**tint** *v* to give a slight colour to (e.g. the hair) – ~**er** *n*

tiny *adj* **tinier, tiniest** very small

¹**tip** *n* **1** the end of something **2** a small piece or part serving as an end, cap, or point **3 have (something) on the tip of one's tongue** to be about to remember (a name, word, etc.)

²**tip** *v* **-pp- 1** to lean or cause to lean at an angle **2** to upset or cause to upset; fall or cause to fall over **3** to throw or leave (unwanted articles) somewhere **4** to pour (a substance)

from one container into another, onto a surface, etc.

³tip *n* a place where unwanted waste is left

⁴tip *v* **-pp-** to give (a tip) to (a waiter, waitress, etc.) –~**per** *n*

⁵tip *n* a small amount of money given for a small service

⁶tip *n* a helpful piece of advice

tiptoe *v* **-toed, -toeing** to walk on one's toes

tire *v* *tired, tiring* to make or become tired

tired *adj* **1** having or showing a lack of power in the mind or body, esp. after activity; having or showing a need for rest or sleep **2** no longer interested: *I'm tired of your conversation* –~**ly** *adv* –~**ness** *n*

tiresome *adj* **1** annoying **2** tiring or uninteresting, esp. because of dullness –~**ly** *adv*

tissue *n* **1** animal or plant cells of the same type that make up a particular organ **2** also **tissue paper**– light thin paper used for wrapping, packing, etc. **3** a piece of soft paper

titbit *n* **1** a small piece of particularly nice food **2** an interesting piece of news

title *n* **1** a name given to a book, painting, play, etc. **2** a word or name, such as 'Mr', 'Lord', 'Doctor', etc., given to a person to be used before his name as a sign of rank, profession, etc. **3** *technical* the lawful right to ownership or possession **4** the position of

unbeaten winner in certain competitions

¹to *prep* **1** in a direction towards **2** in the direction of; so as to have reached: *sent to prison* **3** as far as **4** reaching the state of: *She sang the baby to sleep* **5** as far as the state of: *until the lights change to green* **6** in a touching position with: *cheek to cheek* **7** facing or in front of: *face to face* **8** until and including: *Count (from 10) to 20* **9** for the attention or possession of: *to Mildred from George* **10** for; of: *the key to the lock* **11** in relation with; in comparison with: *5 goals to 3* **12** forming; making up: *100 pence to every pound* **13** in honour of: *a temple to Mars* **14** (of time) before: *5 (minutes) to 4* **15** in the position of: *to the north of England* **16** in connection with: *What's your answer to that? / kind to animals* **17** **(a number) to (a number) a** between (a number) and (a number): *in 10 to 12 feet of water* **b** compared with: *100 to 1 he'll lose* (=100 times as likely)

²to *adv* **1** into consciousness: *John didn't come to for half an hour after he'd hit his head* **2** into a shut position: *The wind blew the door to*

³to (*used before a verb to show it is the infinitive*)

toad *n* an animal like a large frog, that usu. lives on land, but goes into water for breeding

toadstool *n* any of several types of fleshy fungus, often poisonous

¹toast *v* **1** to make (bread, cheese,

etc.) brown by holding close to heat **2** to warm thoroughly

²**toast** *n* bread made brown by being held in front of heat

³**toast** *v* to drink or suggest a drink to the success, happiness, etc., of (someone) —**toast** *n*

tobacco *n* **-cos** a type of leafy plant, specially prepared for use in cigarettes, pipes, etc.

tobacconist *n* a person who sells tobacco, cigarettes, etc.

today *adv, n* **1** (during or on) this present day **2** (during or at) this present time: *young people of today*

toddle *v* **-dled, -dling** to walk with short unsteady steps, as a small child does

toddler *n* a child who has just learnt to walk

¹**toe** *n* **1** one of the 5 movable parts on each foot **2** the part of a sock, shoe, etc., that fits over these **3 on one's toes** ready for action

²**toe** *v* **toed, toeing toe the line** to obey orders

toffee, toffy *n* (a piece of) a hard sticky sweet brown substance made by boiling sugar and butter with water

together *adv* **1** in or into one group, body, or place; in or into a relationship **2** in or into union **3** at the same time **4** without interruption: *for 4 days together*

¹**toil** *n esp. written* hard or continuous work

²**toil** *v esp. written* **1** to work hard and untiringly **2** to move with difficulty or pain

toilet *n* a lavatory

token *n* **1** an outward sign; small part representing something greater **2** a souvenir **3** a piece of metal used instead of coins for a particular purpose **4** a receipt, usu. fixed to a greetings card, which one can exchange for the stated thing in a shop

tolerable *adj* fairly good; that can be tolerated

tolerance *n* **1** the quality of being able to suffer pain, hardship, etc., without being damaged **2** the quality of allowing people to behave in a way that may not please one, without becoming annoyed **3** *technical* (in engineering) the amount by which a value can vary from the amount intended without causing difficulties **4** *technical* the degree to which a cell, animal, plant, etc., can successfully oppose the effect of a poison, drug, etc.

tolerant *adj* showing or practising tolerance —**~ly** *adv*

tolerate *v* **-rated, -rating 1** to allow (something one does not agree with) to be practised or done freely without opposition **2** to suffer (someone or something) without complaining

¹**toll** *n* **1** a tax paid for the right to use a road, harbour, etc. **2** the cost in health, life, etc., from illness, an accident, etc.

²**toll** *v* (of a bell) to ring or cause to ring slowly and repeatedly

³**toll** *n* the sound of a tolling bell

tomato *n* **-toes** a type of yellow-flowered plant, or its red fruit used as a vegetable

tomb *n* a grave

tomorrow *adv* **1** (during or on) the day following today **2** (in) the future: *tomorrow's world*

ton *n* **tons** *or* **ton 1** a measurement of weight equal in Britain to 2,240 pounds (**long ton**) and in the United States to 2,000 pounds (**short ton**) **2** also **tonne**, **metric ton–** a measurement of weight equal to 1,000 kilos **3** a measurement of **a** the size of a ship equal to 100 cubic feet **b** the amount of goods a ship can carry equal to 40 cubic feet **4** *sl* a very large quantity or weight: *tons of fruit* **5** *sl* 100 miles per hour **6** *sl (*in cricket) a century

tone *n* **1** any sound considered with regard to its quality, highness or lowness, strength, etc. **2** the quality or character of a particular instrument or singing voice as regards the sound it produces **3** *technical* a difference in the pitch of a musical note equal to 2 semitones **4** a manner of expression **5** a particular (change of) pitch of a speech sound **6** a variety of a colour, different from the ordinary colour because of more light or darkness **7** *technical* the effect in painting of light and shade together with colour **8** the general quality or nature: *the tone of the neighbourhood*

tongs *n* an instrument consisting of 2 movable arms joined at one end, used for holding or lifting various objects

tongue *n* **1** the large movable fleshy organ in the mouth **2** this organ taken from an animal, cooked as food **3** any of various objects like this in shape or purpose **4** a language **5 get one's tongue around** to pronounce (a difficult word, name, etc.) correctly

¹**tonic** *adj* **1** *esp. written* strengthening: *the tonic quality of sea air* **2** (in music) of or based on the tonic

²**tonic** *n* **1** anything which increases health or strength **2** a medicine intended to give the body more strength, esp. when tired **3** the first note of a musical scale of 8 notes

tonight *adv*, *n* (on or during) the night of today

tonsil *n* either of 2 small roundish organs at the sides of the throat near the top

too *adv* **1** (*before adjectives and adverbs*) more than enough; to a higher degree than is necessary or good; excessively **2** also; in addition; as well **3 only too** very: *only too pleased*

took *past tense of* TAKE

¹**tool** *n* **1** any instrument or apparatus for doing special jobs **2** anything necessary for doing one's job: *Words are his tools* **3** a person unfairly or

dishonestly used by another for his own purposes **4 down tools** to stop working

²**tool** *v* to shape or make (something) with a tool

tooth *n* **teeth 1** one of the small hard bony objects growing in the upper and lower mouth of most animals **2** any of the narrow pointed parts that stand out from a comb, saw, cog, etc. **3 long in the tooth** *esp. spoken* old **4 tooth and nail** very violently: *They fought tooth and nail* –~**less** *adj*

toothbrush *n* a brush used for cleaning the teeth

toothpaste *n* a substance used for cleaning the teeth

¹**top** *n* **1** the highest part or point **2** the upper surface **3** the most important part of anything **4** the highest leaves of a plant: *turnip tops* **5** the lid **6** a garment worn on the upper part of the body **7 in top (gear)** in the highest gear

²**top** *v* -**pp**- **1** to reach the top of **2** to provide or form a top for: *topped with cream* **3** to be higher, better, or more than: *Our profits have topped £1,000* **4** to remove the top from (a vegetable, fruit, etc.) **5** (esp. in golf) to hit (a ball) above the centre **6 top the bill** to be the chief performer in an entertainment

³**top** *adj* of, related to, or being at the top

⁴**top** *n* **1** a toy that is made to balance on its point by spinning **2 sleep like a top** to sleep deeply

top-heavy *adj* too heavy at the top in relation to the bottom; not properly balanced for this reason

topic *n* a subject for conversation, talk, writing, etc.

topical *adj* of, related to, dealing with, or being a subject of present interest –~**ly** *adv* –~**ity** *n*

topple *v* -**pled, -pling** to fall down

torch *n* **1** a small electric light carried in the hand **2** a mass of burning material used for giving light

¹**torment** *n* **1** (a) very great pain or suffering in mind or body **2** something or someone that causes this

²**torment** *v* **1** to cause to suffer great pain in mind or body **2** to annoy –~**or** *n*

tornado *n* -**does** *or* -**dos** a violent storm in the form of a very tall wide pipe of air that spins at speeds of over 300 miles per hour

¹**torpedo** *n* -**does** a self-propelled explosive shell that travels underwater

²**torpedo** *v* -**doed, -doing** to attack or destroy (a ship) with a torpedo

torrent *n* a violently rushing stream, esp. of water –~**ial** *adj*

tortoise *n* a slow-moving land reptile that has a body covered by a hard shell into which the legs, tail, and head can be pulled for protection

¹**torture** *n* **1** the act of causing someone severe pain, done out of cruelty, as a punishment, etc. **2** severe pain or suffering caused in the mind or body **3** a method of causing such pain or suffering

²**torture** *v* **-tured, -turing** to cause great pain or suffering to (a person or animal) out of cruelty, as a punishment, etc. –~**r** *n*

Tory *n, adj* **Tories** (a member or supporter) of the British Conservative party –~**ism** *n*

¹**toss** *v* **1** to throw **2** to move about rapidly and pointlessly: *tossed about in the sea* **3** to mix lightly: *Toss the vegetables in butter* **4** to throw (a coin) to decide something according to which side lands face upwards

²**toss** *n* **1** an act of tossing: *a toss of the head* **2** a tossing movement

¹**total** *adj* complete; whole –~**ly** *adv*: *I totally agree*

²**total** *n* the sum obtained as the result of addition; complete amount

³**total** *v* **-ll- 1** to equal a total of; add up to **2** to find the total of

totter *v* to move in an unsteady way as if about to fall –~**y** *adj*

tot up *v adv* **-tt-** to add up

¹**touch** *v* **1** to be separated from (something) by no space **2** to feel with a part of the body, esp. the hands or fingers **3** to eat or drink a little of **4** to compare with; be equal to: *Your work will never touch the standard set by Robert* **5** to deal with; concern: *a serious matter that touches your future* **6** to cause (someone) to feel pity, sympathy, etc. **7** to mark with light strokes; put in with a pencil or brush –~**able** *adj* –~**er** *n*

²**touch** *n* that sense by which a material object is felt and by which it is known to be hard, smooth, rough, etc. **2** the effect caused by touching something; way something feels **3** an act of touching **4** a slight amount: *a touch of fever* **5** an addition or detail that improves or completes something: *the finishing touches* **6** a special ability to do, or a particular way of doing, something needing skill: *I hope you're not losing your touch* **7** field of play **8 in/out of touch a** regularly/not regularly exchanging news and information **b** having/not having information about something

¹**tough** *adj* **1** strong; able to suffer uncomfortable conditions **2** not easily cut, worn, or broken: *as tough as leather* **3** difficult **4** unyielding; hard: *The government will get tough with tax evaders* **5** rough; violent **6** *esp. spoken* too bad; unfortunate –~**ly** *adv* –~**ness** *n*

²**tough** –also **toughie** *n esp. spoken* a rough violent person

¹**tour** *n* **1** a journey during which several places of interest are visited **2** a short trip to or through a place in order to see it **3** a period of duty at a single place or job, esp. abroad **4** a journey from place to place as made by a company of actors in order to perform, by an important person to make official visits, by a sports team, etc.

²**tour** *v* to visit as a tourist

tourism *n* **1** the practice of travelling for pleasure, esp. on holiday **2** the business of providing holidays, tours, hotels, etc., for tourists

tourist *n* **1** a person travelling for pleasure **2** a sportsman on tour

tournament *n* **1** a series of competitions of skill between players, the winner of one match playing the winner of another, until the most skilful is found **2** also **tourney–** (in former times) a competition of courage and skill between knights

¹**tow** *v* to pull (a vehicle) along by a rope or chain

²**tow** *n* **1** an act of towing **2** the state of being towed **3 in tow** *esp. spoken* following closely behind

towards –also **toward** *prep* **1** in the direction of, without necessarily reaching **2** in a position facing: *with his back towards me*

¹**towel** *n* a piece of cloth or paper used for rubbing or drying wet skin, dishes, etc. **2 throw in the towel/ sponge** *esp. spoken* to admit defeat

²**towel** *v* **-ll-** to rub or dry with a towel

¹**tower** *n* **1** a tall building standing alone or forming part of a castle, church, etc. **2** a tall metal framework

²**tower** *v* to be very tall in relation to the height of the surroundings

town *n* **1** a large group of houses and other buildings where people live and work **2** the business or shopping centre of such a place: *We went to town* **3** the people who live in a town: *The whole town is angry* **4** towns and cities in general, as opposed to the country

town hall *n* a building used for a town's local government offices and public meetings

toxic *adj* **1** of, related to, or caused by poisonous substances **2** poisonous: *a toxic drug* –∼**ity** *n*

toy *n* **toys 1** an object for children to play with **2** a small breed of dog

¹**trace** *v* **traced, tracing 1** to follow the course or line of (something or someone) **2** to find the origins of **3** to find or discover: *I can't trace the letter you sent* **4** to copy by drawing on transparent paper (a drawing, map, etc.) placed underneath **5** to draw the course or shape of –∼**able** *adj*

²**trace** *n* **1** a mark or sign showing the former presence or passing of some person, vehicle, or event **2** a very small amount of something

³**trace** *n* either of the ropes, chains, or lengths of leather by which a cart, carriage, etc., is fastened to an animal that is pulling it

¹**track** *n* **1** a line or number of marks left by a person, animal, vehicle, etc., that has passed before **2** a rough path or road **3** the metal lines of a railway **4** the course taken by something **5** an endless belt used over the wheels of some very heavy farm, building, or military vehicles **6** a course prepared for racing **7** one of the pieces of music on a long-playing record or tape **8** one of the bands on which material can be recorded on a tape **9 on the**

right/wrong track thinking or working correctly/incorrectly

²**track** *v* **1** to follow the track of **2** (of a television or film camera or the person working it) to move round while taking a picture –~**er** *n*

tracksuit *n* a loose-fitting suit of warm material worn by sportsmen when training but not when playing, racing, etc. –~**ed** *adj*

tractor *n* a powerful motor vehicle used for pulling farm machinery or other heavy objects

¹**trade** *n* **1** the business of buying, selling, or exchanging goods **2** a particular business or industry **3** the people who work in a particular business or industry **4** a job, esp. one needing special skill with the hands: *a printer by trade* **5** amount of business: *a good trade in flowers*

²**trade** *v* **traded, trading 1** to carry on trade **2** to buy, sell, or exchange (a product, goods, etc.) –~**r** *n*

trademark *n* **1** a particular producer's own mark on a product **2** a distinctive habit or characteristic by which a person may be recognized

tradesman *n* -**men** a person who buys and sells goods, esp. a shopkeeper

trade union –also **trades union** *n* an organization of workers to represent their interests and deal as a group with employers –~**ism** *n* –~**ist** *n*

tradition *n* **1** the passing down of beliefs, customs, etc., from the past to the present **2** belief, custom, etc., passed down in this way **3** the body of beliefs, practices, etc., passed down –~**al** *adj* –~**ally** *adv*

traffic *n* **1** the movement of people or vehicles along roads or streets, of ships in the seas, planes in the sky, etc. **2** the people, vehicles, etc., in this movement **3** trade; buying and selling **4** business done by a railway, ship or air travel company, etc., in carrying goods or passengers

traffic lights –also **traffic signals** *n* a set of coloured lights used for controlling and directing traffic

tragedy *n* -**dies 1** a serious play that ends sadly, esp. with the main character's death **2** this type of play, film, etc. **3** a terrible, unhappy, or unfortunate event

tragic *adj* of or related to tragedy –~**ally** *adv*

¹**trail** *v* **1** to drag or allow to drag behind **2** to be dragged along behind **3** to follow the tracks of **4** to walk tiredly **5** (of a plant) to grow over or along the ground

²**trail** *n* **1** the track or smell of a person or animal **2** a path across rough country made by the passing of people or animals **3** a stream of dust, smoke, people, vehicles, etc., behind something moving **4 blaze a/the trail** to be the very first in doing something

¹**train** *n* **1** a line of connected railway carriages drawn by an engine **2** a series or line of people, things, events, etc. **3** a part of a long dress that spreads behind the wearer **4** a

group of servants or officers attending a person of high rank

²**train** *v* **1** to direct the growth of (a plant) by bending, cutting, tying, etc. **2** to give teaching or practice, esp. in an act, profession, or skill **3** to be taught or given practice, esp. in an art, profession, or skill: *I trained to be a doctor* **4** to make ready for a test of skill: *training for the race* **5** to aim (a gun) at something or someone –~**able** *adj* –~**er** *n*

training *n* **1** the act of training or being trained **2** a course of special exercises, practice, food, etc., to keep sportsmen or animals healthy and fit

traitor *n* a person who is disloyal, esp. to his country

¹**tramp** *v* **1** to walk with firm heavy steps **2** to walk steadily through or over

²**tramp** *n* **1** the sound of heavy walking **2** a long walk **3** also **tramp steamer**– a ship that takes goods to any port **4** a person with no home or job, who wanders from place to place

trample *v* **-pled, -pling** to step heavily with the feet; crush under the feet

trance *n* a sleeplike condition of the mind in which one does not notice the things around one

transact *v*– to carry (a piece of business, matter, etc.) through to an agreement –~**ion** *n*

transatlantic *adj* **1** on the other side of the Atlantic ocean **2** crossing the Atlantic ocean **3** concerning countries on both sides of the Atlantic ocean

¹**transfer** *v* **-rr- 1** to move officially from one place, job, etc., to another **2** to move or change from one vehicle to another **3** to move (a pattern, set of marks, etc.) from one surface to another **4** to give the ownership of (property) to another person –~**ability** *n* –~**able** *adj* –~**ence** *n*

²**transfer** *n* **1** the act of transferring **2** someone or something that has transferred **3** a drawing, pattern, etc., for sticking or printing onto a surface

transform *v* to change completely in appearance or nature –~**able** *adj*

transformation *n* (an example of) the act of transforming; complete change

transfuse *v* **-fused, -fusing** to put (the blood of one person) into the body of another – **-fusion** *n*

transistor *n* **1** a small solid electrical apparatus for controlling the flow of an electrical current **2** also **transistor radio**– a radio that uses these instead of valves

transition *n* the act of changing or passing from one form, state, subject, or place to another –~**al** *adj* –~**ally** *adv*

translate *v* **-lated, -lating** to express in another language – **-latable** *adj* – **-lator** *n*

translation *n* **1** the act of translating or being translated **2** something that has been translated **3** *technical* (in mathematics) the process of moving from one position to another so that each point of the object moves the same distance in the same direction as every other point; movement without turning

transmission *n* **1** transmitting or being transmitted **2** something broadcast **3** the parts in a vehicle which carry power from an engine to the road wheels

transmit *v* **-tt- 1** to send or pass from one person, place, or thing to another **2** to broadcast **3** to allow to travel through or along itself **4** to carry (force, power, etc.) from one part of a machine to another

transmitter *n* **1** someone or something that transmits **2** an instrument in a telegraphic system that sends out messages **3** an apparatus that sends out radio or television signals

transparent *adj* **1** allowing light to pass through so that objects behind can be clearly seen **2** clear; easily seen or understood −~**ly** *adv*

¹**transplant** *v* **1** to move (a plant) from one place and plant in another **2** to move (an organ, piece of skin, hair, etc.) from one part of the body to another or from one person or animal to another −~**ation** *n*

²**transplant** *n* **1** something transplanted **2** an act of transplanting

¹**transport** *v* **1** to carry (goods, people, etc.) from one place to another **2** (in former times) to send (a criminal) to a distant land as a punishment −~**able** *adj*

²**transport** *n* **1** transporting or of being transported **2** a means or system of transporting **3** a ship or aircraft for carrying soldiers or supplies

¹**trap** *n* **1** an apparatus for catching and holding animals **2** a position in which one is caught ; plan for catching a person **3** a U or S shaped part of a pipe, which holds water and so prevents gas from waste escaping **4** a light 2-wheeled vehicle pulled by a horse **5** *sl* a mouth: *Keep your trap shut* **6** an apparatus from which a dog is set free at the beginning of a race

²**trap** *v* **-pp- 1** to catch by a trick or deception **2** to block: *to trap water* **3** to catch (an animal) in a trap

¹**travel** *v* **-ll- 1** to go from place to place; make a journey **2** *sl* to go very quickly: *We were really travelling when the police caught us*

²**travel** *n* the act of travelling

traveller *n* **1** a person on a journey **2** also **travelling salesman**− a person who goes from place to place trying to sell goods

travesty *n* **-ties** a copy, account, or example of something that misrepresents the real thing

tray *n* **trays** a flat piece of material with raised edges, used for carrying small articles or holding papers

treacherous *adj* **1** disloyal; deceitful **2** dangerous −~**ly** *adv*

treachery *n* **-ries 1** disloyalty; deceit;

unfaithfulness; falseness **2** a treacherous action

treacle *n* a thick dark sticky liquid produced when sugar is being refined

¹tread *v* **trod, trodden, treading 1** to walk on, over, or along **2** to press or crush with the feet **3 tread on air** *sl* to be very happy **4 tread on somebody's toes** to offend somebody **5 tread water** keep oneself upright in deep water

²tread *n* **1** the act, manner, or sound of walking **2** the part of a step or stair on which the foot is placed **3** the raised lines on a tyre

treason *n* disloyalty to one's country – ~**able** *adj:a treasonable crime* – ~**ably** *adv*

¹treasure *n* **1** wealth in the form of gold, silver, etc. **2** a very valuable object **3** *esp. spoken* a person considered precious

²treasure *v* **-sured, -suring** to keep as precious; regard as valuable

treasurer *n* a person in charge of the money belonging to a club, organization, etc.

Treasury *n* the government department that controls and spends public money

¹treat *v* **1** to act or behave towards **2** to deal with; handle **3** to regard; consider: *My employer treated our request as a joke* **4** to try to cure by medical means **5** to buy or give (someone) something special **6** to put (a substance) through a chemical or industrial action in order to

change it in some way – ~**able** *adj* – ~**er** *n*

²treat *n* **1** something that gives pleasure **2 one's treat** one's act of treating

treatment *n* **1** the act or manner of treating someone or something **2** a substance or method used in treating someone medically

treaty *n* **-ies** an agreement made between countries and formally signed by their representatives, or between people

¹treble *n* **1** (a person with or a musical part for) a high singing voice **2** (of a family of instruments) the instrument with this range of notes **3** the upper half of the whole range of musical notes

²treble *adv, adj* high in sound

³treble *adj* 3 times as big, as much, or as many as

⁴treble *v* **-led, -ling** to make or become 3 times as great

tree *n* **1** a type of tall plant with a wooden trunk and branches **2** a bush or other plant with a treelike form **3** a wooden object with a special purpose, such as a shoe tree, clothes tree, etc. **4** a diagram with a branching form, esp. as used for showing family relationships – ~**less** *adj*

¹tremble *v* **-bled, -bling** to shake uncontrollably – **-blingly** *adv*

²tremble *n* an act of trembling; shudder

tremendous *adj* **1** very great in size,

amount, or degree **2** wonderful: *a tremendous party* –~**ly** *adv*

¹**trench** *n* a deep ditch dug in the ground (e.g. as a protection for soldiers)

²**trench** *v* to dig trenches in

¹**trend** *v* to have a certain tendency, course, or direction of development

²**trend** *n* a general direction or course of development; tendency

¹**trendy** *adj* -ier, -iest *esp. spoken* very fashionable –**trendiness** *n*

²**trendy** *n* -ies *esp. spoken* a trendy person

trespass *v* **1** to go onto private land without permission **2** *old use &* *Bible* to sin –**trespass** *n* –~**er** *n*

trial *n* **1** the act of hearing and judging a person, case, or point of law in a court **2** the act of testing: *horse trials* **3** an attempt; effort; try: *trial and error* **4** an annoying thing or person: *That child is a trial* **5** **on trial a** for the purpose of testing: *He took the car on trial* **b** being tried in a court of law

triangle *n* **1** a flat figure with 3 straight sides and 3 angles **2** an object or piece of that shape **3** a 3-sided musical instrument made of a bent steel rod played by being struck with another steel rod **4** a group of 3

triangular *adj* **1** of or shaped like a triangle **2** having 3 people or groups

tribe *n* **1** a social group made up of people of the same race, language,

etc. **2** a group of related plants or animals –**tribal** *adj*

tribunal *n* a court of people appointed officially, with powers to deal with special matters

tributary *n* -ries a stream or river that flows into a larger one

tribute *n* **1** (a) payment made by one ruler, government, or country to another as the price of peace, protection, etc. **2** something done, said, or given to show respect or admiration

¹**trick** *n* **1** an act needing special skill, esp. done to confuse or amuse **2** a special skill: *the trick of adding up quickly* **3** something done to deceive or cheat someone **4** something done to someone to make him look stupid **5** a strange or typical habit **6** the cards (one from each player) played or won in one round of some card games **7 not/ never miss a trick** *esp. spoken* to know everything that is going on –~**ery** *n*

²**trick** *adj* **1** made for playing tricks: *a trick spoon* **2** full of hidden and unexpected difficulties **3** of, concerned with, or related to a special skill

³**trick** *v* to cheat (someone)

¹**trickle** *v* -led, -ling to flow or cause to flow in drops or in a thin stream

²**trickle** *n* a small thin flow

tricky *adj* -ier, -iest **1** difficult to handle or deal with **2** deceitful; sly –**trickiness** *n*

tricycle *n* a bicycle with 3 wheels

¹tried *adj* found to be good by experience: *a tried method*

²tried *past tense and past part. of* TRY

trifle *n* **1** an article or thing of little importance **2** a dish of plain cakes set in fruit and jelly and covered with cream or custard **3 a trifle** rather

¹trigger *n* the tongue of metal pressed by the finger to fire a gun

²trigger *v* to start; set off

¹trim *v* **-mm- 1** to make neat, even, or tidy by cutting **2** to ornament: *trimmed with fur* **3** to move or be moved into the desired position: *Trim the sail* **4** to adjust the load of (a ship or aircraft) for balance **5** to reduce: *trim one's costs*

²trim *adj* **-mm-** tidy **– ~ly** *adv*

³trim *n* **1** an act of cutting **2** proper shape, order, or condition

trinket *n* a small ornament or piece of jewellery of low value

trio *n* **-os 1** any group of 3 people or things **2** a group of, or a piece of music written for, 3 singers or musicians

¹trip *v* **-pp- 1** to catch or cause to catch one's foot and lose one's balance **2** to make or cause to make a mistake: *The teacher tripped me with that question* **3** to move with quick light steps **4** to start or set free (a switch, spring, etc.)

²trip *n* **1** a journey from one place to another **2** a journey with a particular purpose or happening regularly **3** a mistake: *a trip of the tongue* **4** an act of tripping **5** a

switch, wire, etc., for starting some apparatus or movement **6** *drug users' sl* a period under the influence of a mind-changing drug

tripe *n* **1** the rubbery wall of the stomach of the cow or ox, eaten as food **2** *esp. spoken* worthless or stupid talk, ideas, etc.

¹triple *v* **-led, -ling** to multiply by 3

²triple *adj* **1** having 3 parts or members **2** 3 times repeated

tripod *n* a 3-legged support

trite *adj* (of remarks, ideas, etc.) too often repeated to be effective **– ~ly** *adv* **– ~ness** *n*

¹triumph *n* **1** a complete victory or success **2** the joy or satisfaction caused by this **3** (in Ancient Rome) a procession in honour of a victorious general **– ~al** *adj*

²triumph *v* **1** to be victorious (over) **2** to show joy and satisfaction because of success or victory

triumphant *adj* **1** victorious; successful **2** rejoicing in one's success or victory **– ~ly** *adv*

trivial *adj* of little worth or importance **– ~ly** *adv* **– ~ity** *n*

trod *past tense of* TREAD

trodden *past part. of* TREAD

trolley *n* **-leys 1** any of various low carts, esp. one pushed by hand **2** a small table on small wheels from which food and drinks are served

¹troop *n* **1** a band of people or wild animals **2** a body of soldiers, esp. a group of cavalry **3** a group of about 32 boy scouts

²troop *v* **1** to move together in a

band **2** to carry (the regimental flag (**colour**)) in a ceremonial way

trophy *n* **-phies 1** a prize given for winning at sport **2** something taken after much effort, esp. in war or hunting

tropic *n* one of the 2 lines of latitude drawn around the world at about 23 1/2° north (the **tropic of Cancer**) and south (the **tropic of Capricorn**) of the equator

tropical *adj* **1** of, related to, concerning, or living in the tropics **2** very hot: *tropical weather* –~**ly** *adv*

tropics *n* the area between the tropics

¹**trot** *n* **1** (of a horse) a way of moving at a speed between a walk and a gallop **2** a ride on a horse moving at this speed **3** a human speed between a walk and a run **4** a journey at this speed

²**trot** *v* **-tt-** to move or cause to move at a trot; to hurry

¹**trouble** *v* **-bled, -bling 1** to cause worry, anxiety, etc. to (someone) **2** to cause inconvenience to (someone or oneself) **3** to cause (someone) pain as a disease does: *troubled with a bad back* **4 fish in troubled waters** to try to win some advantage from a confused state of affairs

²**trouble** *n* **1** (a) difficulty, worry, annoyance, dangerous state of affairs, etc.; an inconvenience **2** the position where one is blamed for doing wrong or thought to have done wrong: *in trouble* **3** a fault **4** a medical condition; illness **5**

ask/look for trouble to behave so as to cause difficulty or danger for oneself **6 get (a girl) into trouble** *esp. spoken* to make (a girl) pregnant

troublesome *adj* causing trouble, anxiety, or difficulty

trough *n* **1** a long narrow boxlike object, esp. for holding water or food for animals **2** a long narrow hollow area; depression **3** *technical* (in meteorology) a long area (of fairly low pressure) between 2 areas of high pressure

trousers *n* an outer garment divided into 2 parts each fitting a leg, worn from the waist down **–trouser** *adj: a trouser factory*

trout *n* **trout** any of various types of esp. river fish, highly regarded for sport and food

trowel *n* **1** a tool for spreading cement, plaster, etc. **2** a garden tool for digging small holes, lifting up plants, etc.

truant *n* **1** a pupil who purposely stays away from school without permission **2 play truant–** to stay away from school in this way – **-ancy** *n*

truce *n* (an agreement between 2 enemies for) the stopping of fighting for a period

¹**truck** *n* **have no truck with** to have nothing to do with

²**truck** *n* **1** an open railway goods vehicle **2** a simple goods vehicle, pulled or pushed by hand **3** a fairly large motor vehicle for carrying goods **4** *esp. US* a lorry

¹**trudge** *v* **trudged, trudging** to walk

with heavy steps, slowly and with effort

²**trudge** *n* a long tiring walk

¹**true** *adj* **1** in accordance with fact or reality; actual; not false **2** faithful; loyal; sincere **3** exact; proper; correct; sure **4** correctly fitted, placed, or formed: *The door's not exactly true* **5 true to type** behaving or acting just as one would expect from a person or thing of that type

²**true** *n* **1** that which is true: *the good, the beautiful, the true* **2 out of true** not having the exact position or correct shape or balance

³**true** *adv* in a true manner

truly *adv* **1** exactly; in accordance with the truth; sincerely; certainly; really **2 yours truly** (used at the end of a formal letter before the signature)

¹**trump** *n* **1** any card of a suit chosen to be of higher rank than the other 3 suits **2 turn/come up trumps** to behave in a helpful way, esp. unexpectedly

²**trump** *v* to beat (a card that is not a trump) or win (a trick) by playing a trump

¹**trumpet** *n* **1** a brass wind instrument consisting of a long metal tube curved round once or twice, controlled by 3 valves on top **2** something shaped like the bell-shaped end of this **3** the loud cry of an elephant **4 blow one's own trumpet** to praise oneself

²**trumpet** *v* **1** to play a trumpet **2** (of an elephant) to make a loud sound

3 to declare or shout loudly – ~**er** *n*

trunk *n* **1** the main stem of a tree **2** the human body without the head and limbs **3** a large case or box **4** the long muscular nose of an elephant

¹**trust** *n* **1** firm belief in the honesty, worth, power, etc., of someone or something **2** solemn responsibility **3** care; keeping **4** the act of holding and controlling property or money for the advantage of someone else: *in trust / a trust fund* **5** a group of people doing this **6** a property or sum of money so held and controlled **7** belief in the intention of a person to pay in the future for goods received now: *supplied on trust* **8** a group of firms that have combined to reduce competition and control prices to their own advantage **9 take on trust** to accept without proof or close examination

²**trust** *v* **1** to believe in the honesty and worth of (someone or something); have faith in; depend on **2** to hope: *I trust you enjoyed yourself*

trustworthy *adj* worthy of trust; dependable – **-thiness** *n*

truth *n* the true facts; the state or quality of being true

truthful *adj* telling the truth – ~**ly** *adv* – ~**ness** *n*

¹**try** *v* **tried, trying 1** to test by use and experience, in order to find the quality, worth, effect, etc. **2** to attempt **3** to attempt to open (a door, window, etc.): *Try the door* **4**

to examine (a person thought guilty or a case) in a court of law **5** to cause to suffer; annoy

²**try** *n* **tries 1** an attempt **2** (in rugby) points won by placing the ball on the ground behind the opposing team's try line

T-shirt, tee shirt *n* a close-fitting collarless shirt

tub *n* **1** a large round vessel for packing, storing, washing, etc. **2** a bath

tube *n* **1** a hollow round pipe of metal, glass, rubber, etc. **2** a small soft container of this shape for holding toothpaste, paint, etc. **3** any hollow pipe or organ in the body **4** an underground railway: *travel by tube* – **-bular** *adj*

tuberculosis *n* a serious infectious disease that attacks esp. the lungs – **-lar** *adj*

¹**tuck** *v* to put into a convenient narrow space for protection, safety, etc.

²**tuck** *n* **1** a flat fold of material sewn into a garment **2** cakes, sweets, etc., esp. as eaten by people at school

Tuesday *n* **-days** the third day of the week

tuft *n* a bunch (of hair, grass, etc.) growing or held closely together at a base – **~ed** *adj*

¹**tug** *v* **-gg-** to pull hard with force or much effort

²**tug** *n* a sudden strong pull

tugboat –also **tug** *n* a small powerful boat used for guiding large vessels

tulip *n* a type of garden plant that grows from a bulb, or its flowers

¹**tumble** *v* **-bled, -bling 1** to fall suddenly or helplessly; roll over or down quickly or violently **2** to fall to pieces; fall down; collapse

²**tumble** *n* **1** a fall **2** a state of disorder and confusion

tumbler *n* **1** a flat-bottomed drinking glass with no handle or stem **2** the part in a lock that must be turned by a key before the lock will open **3** an acrobat; gymnast

tumour *n* a mass of diseased cells, often a cancer, in the body

tumult *n* the confused noise and excitement of a big crowd; state of confusion and excitement

¹**tune** *n* **1** a number of musical notes, one after the other, that produce a pleasing pattern of sound **2 call the tune** to be in a position to give orders, command, etc. **3 change one's tune** to change one's opinion, decision, behaviour, etc. **4 in/out of tune a** at/not at the correct pitch **b** in/not in agreement or sympathy

²**tune** *v* **tuned, tuning 1** to set (a musical instrument) at the proper pitch **2** to put an engine in good working order

tunic *n* **1** a loose-fitting short-armed or armless knee length outer garment **2** a specially-shaped short coat worn by policemen, soldiers, etc., as part of a uniform

¹**tunnel** *n* an underground or underwater passage; passage for a road,

railway, etc., through or under a hill, river, etc.

²tunnel *v* **-ll-** to make or make like a tunnel –~**ler** *n*

turban *n* a head-covering worn by men in parts of North Africa and southern Asia –~**ed** *adj*

turbine *n* an engine or motor in which the pressure of a liquid or gas drives a wheel and thus changes into circular movement

¹turf *n* **-s** *or* **turves** (a piece of) soil with grass and roots growing in it

²turf *v* to cover land with turf

turkey *n* **-keys** a type of large bird bred for its meat

turmoil *n* a state of confusion, excitement, and trouble

¹turn *v* **1** to move round a fixed point **2** to change direction **3** to aim in a particular direction **4** to make or become: *to turn brown* **5** to make or become sour: *The heat's turned the milk* **6** to shape wood or metal: *to turn wood* **7** to feel or cause to feel uncomfortable, sick, etc.: *Fat turns my stomach* **8** to change the form or nature of: *She turned her old dress into a skirt* **9** to cause to go; send; drive: *My father would turn me out if he knew I played truant* **10** to throw into disorder or confusion: *The robbers had turned the room upside down* **11** to change position so that the bottom becomes the top, the hidden side uncovered, etc.

²turn *n* **1** a single movement completely round a fixed point **2** a

change of direction **3** a point of change in time: *the turn of the century* **4** a movement or development: *a turn for the worse* **5** a place or appointed time in a particular order: *You've missed your turn* **6** a deed or action with the stated effect: *a good turn* **7** *esp. spoken* a shock: *You gave me quite a turn* **8** *esp. spoken* an attack of illness: *She's had one of her turns* **9** **at every turn** at every moment

turn down *v adv* **1** to lessen the force, strength, loudness, etc., of (something) by using controls: *Turn that radio down* **2** to refuse

turning *n* a place where one road branches off from another

turnip *n* a type of plant grown for its large round edible root

turn out *v adv* **1** to stop (a gas, oil, or electric light, heating apparatus, etc.) **2** to come out or gather as for a meeting, public event, etc. **3** to produce **4** to clear or empty a cupboard, drawer, etc. **5** to be in the end: *His statement turned out to be false*

turntable *n* **1** a flat round apparatus, sunk into the ground to be level with the surface, on which railway engines can be turned round or matched to different tracks **2** the round spinning part or the whole machine on which a record is placed to be played

turret *n* **1** a small tower, usu. at an angle of a larger building **2** (on a tank, plane, warship, etc.) a heavily-armoured dome that spins round to allow its guns to be aimed

turtle *n* **-tles** *or* **-tle 1** a cold-blooded animal living esp. in water and having a hard shell into which the soft head, legs, and tail can be pulled **2 turn turtle** (of a ship) to turn over

tusk *n* a long pointed tooth that comes out beyond the mouth in certain animals such as the elephant

¹**tutor** *n* **1** a teacher who gives private instruction to a single pupil or a very small class **2** (in British universities and colleges) a teacher who directs the studies of students whom he also meets separately –~**ial** *adj*

²**tutor** *v* to act as a tutor to

tweed *n* a coarse woollen cloth woven from threads of several different colours

tweezers *n* a v-shaped tool used for picking up, pulling out, and handling small objects

twelfth *adj, adv, n, pron* 12th

twelve *adj, n, pron* the number 12

twenty *adj, n, pron* **-ties** the number 20 – **-tieth**

twice *adj, adv* 2 times

¹**twig** *n* a thin stem going off from a branch –**twiggy** *adj*

²**twig** *v* **-gg-** *sl* to understand

twilight *n* **1** the time when night is about to become day or (more usually) day night **2** a period or condition of decay, failure, etc., before or following one of growth, glory, success, etc.

¹**twin** *n* **1** either of 2 children born of the same mother at the same time **2** either of 2 people or things closely related or connected

²**twin** *v* **-nn-** to join (a town) closely with another town in another country

¹**twine** *n* strong cord or string made by twisting together 2 or more threads or strings

²**twine** *v* **twined, twining 1** to twist **2** to make by twisting

¹**twinkle** *v* **-kled, -kling 1** to shine with an unsteady light that rapidly changes from bright to faint **2** (of the eyes) to be bright with cheerfulness, amusement, etc. **3** (of the eyelids, feet in dancing, etc.) to move rapidly up and down

²**twinkle** *n* **1** a repeated momentary bright shining of light **2** a brightness in the eyes as from cheerfulness, amusement, etc. **3** a twinkling

¹**twist** *v* **1** to wind strands together or round something else **2** to make (something) by doing this **3** to move in a winding course **4** to turn: *Twist the handle* **5** to hurt (a joint or limb) by pulling and turning sharply **6** to pull or break off by turning and bending forcefully **7** to change the true or intended meaning of (a statement, words, etc.)

²**twist** *n* **1** something made by twisting 2 or more lengths together **2** a particular tendency of mind or character **3** a bend **4** an unexpected change or development: *a twist of fate* –**twisty** *adj*

¹twitch *v* to move suddenly and quickly, usu. without control –~**er** *n*

²twitch *n* **1** a repeated short sudden movement of a muscle, done without control **2** a sudden quick pull

¹twitter *v* **1** (of a bird) to make a number of short rapid sounds **2** (of a person) to talk rapidly, as from nervous excitement –~**er** *n*

²twitter *n* **1** short high rapid sounds made by birds **2** a state of nervous excitement –~**y** *adj*

two *adj, n, pron* **twos 1** the number 2 **2 put two and two together** to calculate the meaning of what one sees or hears

tycoon *n* a businessman or industrialist with great wealth and power

¹type *n* **1** a particular kind, class, or group **2** a person or thing considered an example of such a group or class **3** one or many small block(s) of metal or wood with the shape of a letter on the upper end, dipped in ink and pressed on paper to print the letter(s) **4** printed words

²type *v* **typed, typing** to write (something) with a typewriter

typewriter *n* a machine that prints letters by means of keys which press onto paper through an inked ribbon

typhoon *n* a violent tropical storm in the western Pacific

typical *adj* combining and showing the main signs of a particular kind, group, or class –~**ly** *adv*

typist *n* a secretary employed mainly for typing letters

tyranny *n* **-nies** the use of cruel or unjust power to rule a person or country – **-nical** *adj* – **-nically** *adv*

tyrant *n* a person with complete power who rules cruelly and unjustly

tyre *n* **1** a thick rubber band, solid or filled with air, that fits round the outside edge of a wheel **2** a protective metal band fitted round a wooden wheel

ugly *adj* **uglier, ugliest 1** unpleasant to see **2** threatening; bad-tempered – **-liness** *n*

ultimate *adj* **1** (the) last or farthest distant; being at the end or happening in the end **2** considered as an origin or base: *The ultimate responsibility lies with the president*

ultimately *adv* in the end; after all else or all others

ultimatum *n* **-tums** *or* **-ta** a statement of conditions to be met

umbrella *n* **1** an arrangement of cloth over a frame , used for keeping rain off the head **2** a protecting power or influence

¹umpire *n* a judge in charge of a game such as cricket or of a swimming competition

²umpire *v* **umpired, umpiring** to act as umpire for (a game or competition)

unaccustomed *adj* unusual; not accustomed

unanimous *adj* **1** (of people) all agreeing **2** (of agreements, statements, etc.) supported by everyone in the same way −~**ly** *adv* − -**mity** *n*

unarmed *adj* **1** not carrying a weapon **2** using no weapons

unawares *adv* **1** unintentionally or without noticing **2 take someone unawares** to surprise someone by one's presence

uncanny *adj* -**nier**, -**niest** mysterious; not natural or usual − -**nily** *adv*

uncertain *adj* **1** not certain; doubtful **2** changeable: *uncertain weather* −~**ly** *adv* −~**ness** *n* −~**ty** *n*

uncle *n* **1** the brother of one's father or mother, the husband of one's aunt, or a man whose brother or sister has a child **2** a man who is a friend of a small child or its parents

unconcerned *adj* **1** not worried, anxious, or interested **2** not about: *unconcerned with details* −~**ly** *adv*

unconditional *adj* not limited by any conditions −~**ly** *adv*

¹**unconscious** *adj* **1** having lost consciousness **2** not intentional −~**ly** *adv* −~**ness** *n*

²**unconscious** *n* subconscious

uncouth *adj* not having good manners −~**ly** *adv* −~**ness** *n*

uncover *v* **1** to remove a covering from **2** to find out (something unknown or kept secret)

¹**under** *adv* in or to a lower place

²**under** *prep* **1** in or to a lower place than; directly below **2** less than: *under £5* **3** lower in rank than; serving or obeying: *They work under a kind leader* **4** beneath the surface, covering, or concealment

of **5** during; in the state or act of: *under discussion* **6** in; during: *under difficulties* **7** *technical* (of land) bearing (a crop) **8 under age** legally too young

undercarriage *n* the wheels and lower part of an aircraft, which support it on the ground

undercover *adj* acting or done secretly

undergo *v* -**went**, -**gone**, -**going** to experience (esp. suffering or difficulty)

¹**underground** *adv* **1** under the earth's surface **2** secretly

²**underground** *adj* **1** below the surface of the earth **2** representing a political view which is not publicly accepted

³**underground** −also **tube** *n* a railway system in which the trains run under the earth

underline −also **underscore** *v* -**lined**, -**lining** **1** to emphasise (one or more words) by drawing a line underneath **2** to give force to (an idea, feeling, etc., which has been expressed or shown)

undermine *v* -**mined**, -**mining** to wear away or destroy gradually

underneath *prep*, *adv* (so as to go) under (something)

underpants *n* short underclothes for men, covering the lower part of the body

understand *v* -**stood**, -**standing** **1** to know or get the meaning of (something) **2** to know or feel closely the nature of (a person, feelings, etc.)

3 *often written or polite* to have been informed **4** to take or judge (as the meaning): *'Children' is understood to mean those under 14* **5** to add (esp. a word) in the mind for completion: *When I say 'Come and help', the object 'me' is understood* –~**able** *adj* –~**ably** *adv*

understanding *n* **1** the act of understanding; power to judge sympathetically **2** power of the brain; intelligence **3** a private agreement

understatement *n* (a) statement which is not strong enough to express facts or feelings with full force (such as *not bad* meaning *rather good*)

undertake *v* **-took**, **-taken**, **-taking 1** to take up (a position); start on (work) **2** to promise or agree

undertaker *n* a person whose job it is to arrange funerals

underwater *adj, adv* (used, done, etc.) below the surface of a stretch of water

underwear –also **underclothes, underclothing** *n* the clothes worn next to the body under other clothes

underwent *past tense of* UNDERGO

underworld *n* **1** (in ancient Greek stories) the place where the spirits of the dead live **2** the criminal world

¹**undesirable** *adj* unpleasant; not wanted – **-bility** *n* – **-bly** *adv*

²**undesirable** *n* a person not thought good or useful

undo *v* **undid, undone, undoing 1** to unfasten or untie **2** to remove the effects of: *In 10 minutes he undid my whole day's work*

undoing *n* the cause of ruin, shame, failure, etc.

undoubted *adj* known for certain to be so –~**ly** *adv:That is undoubtedly true*

¹**undress** *v* **1** to take one's clothes off **2** to take the clothes off (someone)

²**undress** *n* lack of clothes

undue *adj* too much: *undue haste*

uneasy *adj* **-ier, -iest 1** not comfortable or at rest **2** worried; anxious – **-sily** *adv* – **-siness** *n*

unemployed *adj* not having a job

unemployment *n* the condition of lacking a job or jobs

unfold *v* **1** to open from a folded position **2** to make or become clear, more fully known, etc. **3** (of a bud) to open into a flower

unfortunate *adj* **1** unlucky **2** deserving of pity **3** unsuitable: *an unfortunate remark* **4** unsuccessful: *an unfortunate business venture*

unfortunately *adv* **1** by bad luck **2** it is/was a bad thing that . . .: *Unfortunately, we crashed*

unheard-of *adj* very strange and unusual

¹**uniform** *adj* the same; even; regular –~**ity** *n* –~**ly** *adv*

²**uniform** *n* clothing which all members of a group wear –~**ed** *adj: uniformed soldiers*

unilateral *adj* done by or having an effect on only one of the groups in an agreement –~**ly** *adv*

union *n* **1** the act of joining or state

of being joined into one **2** a group of countries or states joined together **3** a state of agreement and unity, esp. in marriage **4** a club, society, or trade union **5** *technical* a connecting part for pipes **6** *technical* (in mathematics) the set of members that occur in either or both of two sets

unique *adj* **1** being the only one of its type **2** *often considered bad usage* unusual: *a rather unique position* –~**ly** *adv* –~**ness** *n*

unit *n* **1** one complete thing **2** a group of things or people forming a complete whole but usu. part of a larger group: *an army unit* **3 a** the number 1 **b** any whole number less than 10 **4** an amount or quantity taken as a standard of measurement: *The pound is the standard unit of money in Britain* **5** an article, esp. of furniture, which can be fitted with others of the same type: *a kitchen unit*

unite *v* **united, uniting 1** to join together into one **2** to act together for a purpose **3** to join in marriage

united *adj* **1** in agreement **2** with everyone concerned having the same aim: *a united effort* –~**ly** *adv*

unity *n* **-ties 1** the state of being united: *church unity* **2** agreement of aims and interests **3** *technical* the number one: *greater than unity*

universal *adj* **1** concerning all members of a group **2** for all people or every purpose; widespread **3** in all parts of the world: *universal travel* –~**ity** *n* –~**ly** *adv*

universe *n* all space and the matter which exists in it

university *n* **-ties** a place of education at the highest level, or the members of this place

unknown *n, adj* (something or someone) whose name, value, or origin is not known

unless *conj* if ... not; except in the case that: *I will leave at 9, unless you want to go earlier*

unlike *adj, prep* not like; different (from)

unlikely *adj* **-lier, -liest 1** not expected; improbable **2** not likely to happen or be true – **-liness, -lihood** *n*

unload *v* **1** to remove (a load) from; get rid of (a load) **2** to get rid of (something unwanted) **3** to remove the charge from (a gun) or film from (a camera) –~**er** *n*

unlock *v* to unfasten the lock of

unmistakable *adj* clearly recognizable – **-bly** *adv*

unpleasant *adj* causing dislike; not enjoyable; displeasing or unkind –~**ly** *adv* –~**ness** *n*

unreasonable *adj* **1** unfair in demands; not sensible **2** (of prices, costs, etc.) too great – **-bly** *adv* –~**ness** *n*

untie *v* **untied, untying** to undo

until –also **till** *prep, conj* up to (the time that)

unusual *adj* **1** rare **2** interesting

because different from others –~**ly** *adv*

unwell *adj* ill, esp. for a short time

¹**up** *adv* **1** towards or into a higher position; from below to a higher place **2** above; at or in a higher position **3** to, into, or in a sitting or standing position **4** from or off a surface: *The dog jumped up* **5** to the surface from below it: *to come up for air* **6** so as to be completely finished: *The money's all used up* **7** so as to be all in small pieces: *to tear up the newspaper* **8** out of the stomach through the mouth, when vomiting **9** in or towards (the north) **10** to or in a city or place of importance: *up to London* **11** to or towards a point away from the speaker: *up to the shop* **12** towards and as far as the speaker: *up to me* **13** firmly; tightly; so as to be closed, covered, or joined: *to tie up* **14** (showing or making an increase or higher level of price, quantity, or quality): *The price is going up* **15** to a state of greater activity, force, strength, power, etc.: *Please turn the radio up* **16** so as to be together: *Add up the figures* **17** to or in a higher or better condition: *come up in the world* **18** (so as to be) in a raised position or on top: *He turned up his collar* **19** Up (**with**) We want or approve of: *Up the workers!*

²**up** *adj* **1** in a raised position; so as to be in place or be seen: *high up in the mountains* **2** out of bed: *to get up* **3** directed or going up: *the up*

train **4** at a higher level: *The temperature is up today* **5** finished; ended: *Time's up!* **6** (of a road) being repaired; with a broken surface **7** charged with an offence: *had up for stealing* **8** **be up** to be happening; be the matter **9** **be well up in/on** to know a lot about **10** **not up** (in tennis and like games) (of a ball) having bounced more than once before being hit **11** **up for** intended or being considered for: *The house is up for sale*

³**up** *v* **-pp-** *esp. spoken* **1** to raise; increase: *to up the price of petrol* **2** to get or jump up (and): *He upped and left*

⁴**up** *prep* **1** to or in a higher or rising position; along; to the far end of: *He climbed up the hill* **2** against the direction of the current: *to go up river* **3** **up and down** away and back along: *His eyes moved up and down the rows* **4** **up yours** *vulgar sl* (used for expressing great dislike for or annoyance at a person)

upheaval *n* a great change and movement

uphill *adj* **1** on an upward slope **2** difficult (esp. in the phrase **an uphill task**) –**uphill** *adv*

uphold *v* **upheld, upholding 1** to support: *to uphold a right* **2** to declare to be right: *The judge upheld the court's decision* –~**er** *n*

upon *prep esp. written* on

¹**upper** *adj* **1** in a higher position **2** farther from the sea: *the upper*

reaches of the Nile **3** of greater importance or higher rank

²upper *n* the top part of a shoe or boot above the heel and sole

¹upright *adj* **1** standing straight up; vertical **2** honest, fair, responsible, etc. –~**ly** *adv* –~**ness** *n*

²upright *adv* straight up; not bent

³upright *n* a supporting beam which stands straight up

uprising *n* a rising; rebellion

uproar *n* confused noisy activity

upset *v* **upset, upsetting 1 a** to turn over, causing confusion **b** to overflow or cause to overflow or scatter by a knock **2** to cause to worry, not be calm, etc. **3** to make ill, usu. in the stomach –**upset** *n, adj*

upside down *adv* **1** in a position with the top turned to the bottom **2** in disorder

upstairs *adv, adj* at, on, or to the upper floor or floors of a building –**upstairs** *n*

up to *prep* **1 a** as far as; to and including a number: *up to 10 men* **b** a higher degree or position in a set: *Everyone works, from the lift boy up to the President* **2** also **up till**– until **3** equal to; good, well, clever enough for: *Michael's not really up to that job* **4** the duty or responsibility of: *It's up to you* **5 be/get up to** to do (something bad): *The children are always getting up to mischief*

up to date *adj* **1** modern **2** having the latest information

upward –also **upwards** *adj* incre-

asing, getting higher, etc.; going up: *an upward movement*

upwards –also **upward** *adv* towards a higher level, position, or price: *A tree grows upwards*

urban *adj* of a town or city

¹urge *v* **urged, urging 1** to drive or force (forward) **2** to beg or persuade with force **3** to tell of with force: *She urged its importance*

²urge *n* a strong wish or need

urgent *adj* **1** very important, esp. which must be dealt with quickly **2** showing that something must be done quickly: *He was urgent in his demands* –~**ly** *adv* – **-gency** *n*

urine *n* waste liquid passed out of the body

us *pron* **1** (*object form of* WE): *They helped us.* | *The waiter brought us the drinks we had ordered* **2** *bad usage* me: *'Lend us your pen a minute'*

¹use *n* **1** the act of using or state of being used **2** the ability or right to use something **3** the purpose or reason for using something: *What use does this tool have?* **4** the usefulness or advantage given by something: *Is this book any use?* **5** custom; habit; practice **6 make use of** to use well; take advantage of **7 of use** useful **8 out of use** no longer used

²use *v* **used, using 1** to employ; put to use **2** *esp. written* to treat in the stated manner: *to use someone ill* (= badly) **3** to finish: *All the paper has been used* **4** to treat (someone) with consideration only for one's own advantage −**user** *n* −**usable** *adj*

³**use** *v* **used**, *negative short form* **usedn't, usen't** to have done regularly or habitually: *We used to go there every year. | Usen't you to keep a dog? | This used to be a shabby house*

used *adj* **1** (usu. of goods) which has already had an owner; second-hand **2** accustomed: *to get used to Indian food*

useful *adj* **1** effective in use **2** helpful −∼**ly** *adv* −∼**ness** *n*

useless *adj* **1** not of any use **2** not giving hope of success **3** *esp. spoken* not able to do anything properly −∼**ly** *adv* −∼**ness** *n*

usual *adj* **1** customary **2** **as usual** as is common −∼**ly** *adv*

utensil *n* a tool

¹**utmost** *adj* of the greatest degree

²**utmost** *n* the most that can be done (esp. in the phrase **to do one's utmost**)

¹**utter** *adj* complete −∼**ly** *adv*

²**utter** *v* to pronounce; express −∼**ance** *n*

vacancy *n* **-cies** **1** the state of being vacant **2** an unfilled place or job **3** emptiness of mind

vacant *adj* **1** empty; not filled with anything **2** (of a house, room, or seat) not being used or lived in **3** (of a job) not at present filled **4** (of the mind) not thinking; foolishly empty; senseless −∼**ly** *adv*

vacate *v* **vacated, vacating** to cease to occupy or live in

vacation *n* **1 a** one of the periods of holiday when universities, law courts, etc., are closed **b** *US* a holiday **2** an act or the action of vacating

vaccinate *v* **-ated, -ating** to introduce vaccine into the body of (someone) − **-ation** *n*

vaccine *n* a substance used for protecting people against diseases, esp. smallpox

¹**vacuum** *n* **-uums** or (*technical*) **-ua** **1** a space that is completely, or almost completely, empty of all gas **2** emptiness: *Her death left a vacuum in his life*

²**vacuum** *v esp. spoken* to clean (a room, floor, etc.) using a vacuum cleaner

vacuum cleaner −also (*esp. spoken, trademark)* **hoover** *n* an apparatus which cleans floors and floor coverings by sucking up the dirt

vague *adj* not clear −∼**ly** *adv* −∼**ness** *adv*

vain *adj* **1** too admiring of one's appearance, abilities, etc. **2** without result; useless: *vain attempt* **3** **in vain** uselessly; without a successful result −∼**ly** *adv*

valiant −also **valorous** *adj esp. written or literature* (of a person or act) very brave −∼**ly** *adv*

valid *adj* **1** (of a reason, argument, etc.) having a strong firm base; that can be defended **2** *law* written or done in a proper manner so that a court of law would agree with it **3** having value; that can be used lawfully for a stated period or in certain conditions – ~**ity** *n: the validity of a statement* – ~**ly** *adv*

valley *n* **-leys 1** the land lying between 2 lines of hills or mountains **2** the land through which a stated river or great river system flows: *the Thames Valley*

¹**valuable** *adj* **1** worth a lot of money **2** having great usefulness or value

²**valuable** *n* something (esp. something small) that is worth a lot of money

¹**value** *n* **1** the (degree of) usefulness or desirability of something, esp. in comparison with other things **2** the worth of something in money or as compared with other goods for which it might be changed **3** qualities: *One way of judging a society is to consider its values* **4** (in the science of numbers) the quantity expressed by a letter of the alphabet or other sign: *Let 'x' have the value 25* – ~**less** *adj*

²**value** *v* **-ued, -uing 1** to calculate the value, price, or worth of (something) **2** to consider (someone or something) to be of great worth – **-uation** *n*

valve *n* **1** a doorlike part of a pipe (or of a pipelike part inside the body), which opens and shuts so as to control the flow of liquid, air, gas, etc., through the pipe **2** a closed glass tube with no air in it, used for controlling a flow of electricity, esp. in radios and televisions **3** a hard shell protecting the soft body of certain sea creatures, esp. one of 2 enclosing the animal

¹**van** *n esp. written or literature* a vanguard

²**van** *n* a covered vehicle for carrying goods and sometimes people

vandal *n* a person who intentionally damages or destroys beautiful or useful things

vandalism *n* intentional needless damage

vanguard *n* **1** the soldiers sent on ahead of an army to protect it against surprise attack **2** the leading part of any marching body of people, or of ships in battle **3** the leading part of any kind of advancement in human affairs

vanish *v* **1** to disappear; go out of sight **2** to cease to exist; come to an end

vanity *n* **-ties** the quality or state of being too proud of oneself or one's appearance, abilities, etc.

vapour *n* **1** a gaslike form of a liquid (such as mist or steam) **2** *technical* the gas to which the stated liquid or solid can be changed by the action of heat: *water vapour* – **vaporous** *adj*

¹**variable** *adj* **1** changeable; not staying the same; not steady **2** that can be intentionally varied – **-bly** *adv* – ~**ness** *n*

²**variable** *n usu. technical* **1** something which represents something (such as temperature) which can vary in quantity or size **2** a letter representing this

variation *n* 1 the action of varying 2 an example or degree of this 3 one of a set of repeated parts of a piece of music each with certain different developments made to it 4 (an example of) change from what is usual in the form of a group or kind of living things, such as animals

varied *adj* 1 of different kinds 2 not staying the same

variety *n* -ties 1 the state of varying; difference of condition or quality 2 a group or collection containing different sorts of the same thing or people 3 a type which is different from others in a group to which it belongs: *new varieties of wheat* 4 a show in which a number of short performances are given (such as singing, dancing, acts of skill, etc.)

various *adj* 1 different from each other; of (many) different kinds 2 several; a number of: *various people*

¹varnish *n* 1 (any of several types of) liquid based on oil, which, when brushed onto articles and allowed to dry, gives a clear hard bright surface 2 the shiny appearance produced by using this substance

²varnish *v* 1 to cover with varnish or with nail varnish 2 to cover (something unpleasant) over with a smooth appearance

vary *v* -ied, -ying to be or cause to be different

vase *n* a container used either for flowers or as an ornament

vast *adj* great in size or amount

vastly *adv* very greatly

¹vault *n* 1 a number of arches that form a roof or ceiling 2 a burial room beneath the floor of a church or in a churchyard 3 an underground room in which things are stored 4 a room at a bank used to store money, important papers, etc. 5 *poetic* a covering like a large curved roof

²vault *v* to jump over (something) in one movement using the hands or a pole to gain more height —~**er** *n*

³vault *n* a jump made by vaulting

vaulting horse —also **horse** *n* a wooden apparatus over which people can vault for exercise

veal *n* meat from a calf

¹vegetable *n* 1 a (part of a) plant that is grown for food 2 plant life 3 a human being who exists but has little or no power of thought (or sometimes also movement)

²vegetable *adj* of, related to, growing like, or made or obtained from plants

vegetation *n* plant life

vehicle *n* 1 something in or on which people or goods can be carried from one place to another 2 a means by which something can be passed on or a person's abilities shown off

¹veil *n* 1 a covering of fine cloth or net for all or part of the head or face 2 something which covers or hides something else —~**ed** *adj*

²veil *v* to cover (as if) with a veil

vein *n* 1 a tube that carries blood from any part of the body to the heart 2 one of a system of thin lines which run in a forked pattern through leaves and wings **3** a thin coloured line found in some kinds of stone and certain other substances **4** a crack in rock, filled with useful material: *a vein of silver* **5** a small but noticeable amount (of some quality): *a vein of cruelty* – ~**ed** *adj*

velvet *n* a fine closely-woven cloth made of silk, nylon, cotton, etc.,having a short soft thick raised surface of cut threads on one side only – ~**y** *adj*

vendor, -er *n* **1** a seller of small articles **2** *law* a seller of anything

¹veneer *n* **1** a thin covering of good quality wood on some cheaper material **2** an outer appearance which hides the unpleasant reality

²veneer *v* **1** to cover with a veneer **2** to hide (an unpleasant quality) under a pleasing appearance

venereal disease –also **VD** *n* a disease passed from one person to another during sexual activity

vengeance *n* **1** a punishment for harm done to oneself, one's family, etc. **2 with a vengeance** *esp. spoken* to a high degree; with greater force than is usual

venom *n* **1** liquid poison **2** great hatred

venomous *adj* **1** (of a creature) having an organ that produces poison **2** (of speech, behaviour, etc.) showing a strong desire to hurt – ~**ly** *adv*

ventilate *v* **-lated, -lating 1** to allow or cause fresh air to enter and move around inside (a room, building, etc.) **2** to permit or cause full public examination of (a subject or question) – **-lation** *n*

ventriloquism *n* the art of speaking or singing with little or no movement of the lips or jaws, in such a way that the sound seems to come from someone else or from some distance away – **-ist** *n*

¹venture *v* **-tured, -turing 1** to risk going somewhere or doing something (dangerous) **2** to take the risk of saying (something that may be opposed or considered foolish)

²venture *n* a course of action of which the result is uncertain – ~**r** *n*

veranda, -dah *n* an outside part of a house with its own floor and roof

verb *n* a word or phrase that tells what someone or something is, does, or experiences: *In 'She is tired' and 'He wrote a letter', 'is' and 'wrote' are verbs*

verbal *adj* **1** spoken, not written: *a verbal description* **2** connected with words and their use **3** of, coming from, or connected with a verb – ~**ly** *adv*

verdict *n* the official decision in a court of law at the end of a trial **2** *esp. spoken* a judgment or decision given on any matter

verge *n* an edge or border

verify *v* **-fied, -fying** to make sure that (a fact, statement, etc.) is correct or true – **-fiable** *adj* – **-fication** *n*

vermin *n* **1** any kind of insect that lives on the body of man or animals

2 any kind of animal or bird that destroys crops, spoils food, or does other damage, and is difficult to control – ~**ous** *adj*

versatile *adj* **1** having many different kinds of skill or ability; easily able to change from one kind of activity to another **2** having many different uses: *Nylon is a versatile material* – **-tility** *n*

verse *n* **1** writing arranged in regular lines, with a pattern of repeated beats as in music **2** a set of lines that forms one part of a poem or song, and usu. has a pattern that is repeated in the other parts **3** one of the numbered parts of a chapter in the Bible

version *n* **1** one person's account of an event, as compared with that of another person **2** a translation **3** a form of a written or musical work that exists in more than one form **4** a slightly different form, copy, or style of something

versus *prep esp. written* against

vertical *adj* **1** upright; forming an angle of 90 degrees with the level ground, or with a straight line in a figure **2** pointing or moving directly upwards or downwards – ~**ly** *adv*

¹**very** *adj* **verier, veriest** (used for giving force to an expression): *He wrote his novels with this very pen. / the very top of her profession*

²**very** *adv* **1** especially; in a high degree: *a very good cake / very quickly / How very annoying!* **2** in the greatest possible degree: *the very best butter / the very same house*

vessel *n esp. written* **1** a container used esp. for holding liquids **2** a ship or large boat **3** a tube (such as a vein) that carries blood or other liquid through the body, or sap through a plant

vest *n* **1** a short undergarment worn on the upper part of the body **2** *US* a waistcoat

vestige *n* **1** a sign, track, or other proof that someone or something formerly existed or was present **2** the very small slight remains (of something) **3** the smallest possible amount: *not a vestige of truth* **4** the remains or imperfectly developed form of some limb or organ that was formerly important but is not now used – **-gial** *adj*

¹**vet** –also (*esp. written*) **veterinary surgeon** *n* an animal doctor

²**vet** *v* **-tt-** *esp. spoken* to examine (something or someone) carefully for correctness, past record, etc.

veteran *n, adj* **1** a person who in the past has had experience in the stated form of activity **2** old: *Every year a race is held in England for veteran cars* (=those made before 1916)

vex *v* to displease (someone) – ~**ation** *n* – ~**atious** *adj* – ~**atiously** *adv*

via *prep* **1** travelling or sent through (a place) on the way **2** by means of: *I sent a message to Mary via her sister*

viable *adj* able to succeed in operation – **-bility** *n* – **-bly** *adv*

vibrate *v* **vibrated, vibrating** to shake continuously and very rapidly with a fine slight movement

vibration *n* **1** a slight continuous shaky movement **2** a regular to and fro movement of a stretched or touched wire **3** *esp. spoken* an influence, favourable or unfavourable, felt by a sensitive person as coming from someone or something else

vicar *n* **1** (in the Church of England) a priest in charge of a church and its parish who receives a yearly payment for his duties **2** (in the Roman Catholic Church) a representative: *The Pope is known as the vicar of Christ*

¹**vice** *n* **1** evil living **2** a serious fault of character ﹐

²**vice** *n* a tool with jaws that can be tightened, used for holding material so that it can be worked on

vice versa *adv Latin* in the opposite way from that just stated

vicinity *n* **-ties 1** the neighbourhood **2** *esp. written* nearness

vicious *adj* **1** having or showing hate and the desire to hurt **2** able or likely to cause severe hurt – ~**ly** *adv* – ~**ness** *n*

victim *n* a person, animal, or thing that suffers pain, death, etc., as a result of other people's actions, or bad luck, etc.

victor *n esp. written, literature, or pompous* **1** a conqueror in battle **2** a winner in a race, competition, or other struggle

victorious *adj* **1** having won or conquered **2** of, related to, or showing victory – ~**ly** *adv*

victory *n* **-ries** the act of winning or state of having won

video *adj* **1** *technical* connected with or used in the showing of pictures by television **2** using videotape: *a video recording*

¹**videotape** *n* a long band of magnetic tape on which television pictures and sound are recorded

²**videotape** *v* **-taped, -taping** to make a recording of (a television show) on videotape

¹**view** *n* **1** ability to see or be seen from a particular place **2** something seen, esp. a stretch of pleasant country **3** a picture or photograph of a piece of scenery, a building, etc. **4** a general consideration of a matter in all its details **5** a personal opinion, belief, idea, etc., about something

²**view** *v* **1** *esp. technical* to examine; look at thoroughly: *to view the house* **2** to consider; regard; think about: *He viewed his son's lawless behaviour as an attack on himself*

viewpoint *n* POINT OF VIEW

vigilant *adj* continually watchful or on guard – ~**ly** *adv* – **-ance** *n*

vigorous *adj* **1** forceful; strong; healthy **2** (of a plant) healthy; growing strongly – ~**ly** *adv*

vigour *n* forcefulness; strength

vile *adj* **1** hateful; shameful; low **2**

esp. spoken very bad: nasty: *a vile temper* −~**ly** *adv* −~**ness** *n*

village *n* 1 a small collection of houses and other buildings, smaller than a town 2 the people in this place as forming a society

villain *n* 1 (in a story or a play) the bad man 2 *esp. spoken* a criminal −~**ous** *adj*

vine *n* −also **grapevine** a type of climbing plant that produces grapes 2 **a** any creeping or climbing plant **b** the main stem of this: *a hop vine*

vinegar *n* an acid liquid made usu. from malt or sour wine −~**y** *adj*

¹**vintage** *n* (a fine wine made in) a particular year, and named by the date of the year

²**vintage** *adj* 1 *esp. spoken* (of wines) of a type that is of a high enough quality to be given a named vintage 2 high quality, esp. from the past 3 (of a car) made between 1916 and 1930

violate *v* -lated, -lating 1 to disregard or act against something solemnly promised 2 *esp. written* to break, spoil, or destroy what should be respected or left untouched 3 to rape (a person) − -**lation** *n*

violence *n* 1 very great force in action or feeling 2 rough treatment; use of bodily force on others, esp. to hurt or harm

violent *adj* 1 fierce and dangerous in action 2 forceful beyond what is usual or necessary 3 produced by

or being the effect of damaging force −~**ly** *adv*

violet *n, adj* 1 a small plant with purplish-blue flowers 2 (having) a purplish-blue colour 3 *humour* a modest person (esp. in the phrase **shrinking violet**)

violin *n* 1 a type of 4-stringed wooden musical instrument, supported between the left shoulder and the chin and played by drawing a bow across the strings 2 *esp. spoken* a person who plays this instrument in a band −~**ist** *n*

VIP *n esp. spoken* a very important person

¹**virgin** *n* a person (esp. a woman or girl) who has not had sexual relations with a member of the opposite sex −~**ity** *n*

²**virgin** *adj* 1 without sexual experience 2 fresh; unspoiled; unchanged by human activity

virtual *adj* almost what is stated; in fact though not in name: *the virtual ruler of the country*

virtually *adv* almost; very nearly: *My book's virtually finished; I've only a few changes to make*

virtue *n* 1 goodness; nobleness 2 any good quality of character or behaviour 3 an advantage: *Plastic has many virtues* 4 **by virtue of** also (*esp. written*) **in virtue of**− as a result of; by means of 5 **woman of easy virtue** a woman who has sex with many men

virus *n* a living thing smaller than

bacteria which causes infectious disease in the body, in plants, etc.

visibility *n* **-ties 1** ability to give a clear view **2** the degree of clearness with which objects can be seen according to the condition of the air and the weather: *poor visibility*

visible *adj* **1** that can be seen **2** noticeable to the mind: *This object serves no visible purpose*

vision *n* **1** the ability to see **2** wisdom and power of imagination esp. with regard to the future **3** something seen in or as if in a dream **4** a picture seen in the mind, as a fulfilment of a desire **5** a rare or beautiful sight: *a brief vision of the mountain top*

¹**visit** *v* **1** to go and spend some time in (a place or someone's house) **2** to go to (a place) in order to make an official examination

²**visit** *n* **1** an act or time of visiting **2 pay a visit** to visit someone or something usu. for a short time

visitor *n* **1** a person who visits or is visiting **2** a bird which spends only part of the year in a country

visual *adj* **1** gained by seeing: *visual knowledge of a place* **2** having an effect on the sense of sight: *The visual arts are painting, dancing, etc., as opposed to music and literature* **3** *technical* concerned with the power of sight

vital *adj* **1** very necessary; of the greatest importance **2** full of life and force: *a vital and cheerful manner* **3** necessary in order to stay alive: *a vital organ* (=any organ without which life cannot continue, such as the heart, brain, etc.)

vitality *n* **1** liveliness of character or manner **2** ability to stay alive or working in an effective way

vitamin *n* **1** any one of several chemical substances which are found in small quantities in certain foods, and lack of which causes weaknesses and diseases **2** any particular type of this, named by a letter of the alphabet (A, B, C, etc.): *Oranges contain vitamin C*

vivid *adj* **1** (of light or colour) bright and strong **2** that produces sharp clear pictures in the mind **3** (of a person's power of expression) full of life and force – ~**ly** *adv* – ~**ness** *n*

vocabulary *n* **-ries 1** all the words known to a particular person **2** the special set of words used in a particular kind of work: *the vocabulary of the lawcourts* **3** also (*esp. spoken*) **vocab** – a list of words much shorter than a dictionary

¹**vocal** *adj* **1** connected with the voice; used in speaking **2** produced by or for the voice; spoken or sung: *vocal music* – ~**ly** *adv*

²**vocal** *n* a performance of a popular song by a singer

vocation *n* **1** a job which one does because one believes one has a special ability to give service to other people **2** a special call from God for the religious life **3** a person's work or employment

¹voice *n* **1** the sound or sounds produced by man in speaking and singing or his ability to produce them **2** the quality of such sound as particular to a certain person: *The boy's voice is breaking* (= becoming lower like a man's) **3** the expressing of an opinion; the right to influence other opinions, decisions, etc. **4** ability as a singer: *a good voice* **5** an expression of ideas: *the voice of reason* **6** the form of the verb which shows whether the subject of a sentence acts (**active voice**) or is acted on (**passive voice**) **7 at the top of one's voice** very loudly **8 raise one's voice a** to speak louder **b** to speak loudly and angrily (to someone) **c** to express one's displeasure, disagreement, etc. **9 with one voice** with everyone expressing the same opinion

²voice *v* **voiced, voicing 1** to express in words, esp. forcefully **2** to produce (a sound, esp. a consonant) with vibration of the vocal cords: *'D' and 'g' are voiced consonants, but 't' and 'k' aren't*

volcano *n* **-noes** *or* **-nos** a mountain with a large opening (crater) at the top through which melted rock (lava), steam, etc., escape from time to time: *An* **active volcano** *may explode at any time. / A* **dormant volcano** *is quiet at present. / An* **extinct volcano** *has ceased to be able to explode*

¹volley *n* **-leys 1** a number of shots fired at the same time by soldiers, police, etc. **2 a** an attack with stones, arrows, etc. **b** a number of blows given, words spoken, etc., with speed and force **3** (of a ball) the condition of not having hit the ground after being thrown, kicked, or hit **4** a kicking or hitting of a ball in this condition, esp., in tennis, a stroke by which the player returns the ball to his opponent without allowing it to touch the ground first

²volley *v* **-leyed, -leying 1** (of shots fired or objects thrown) to come flying together through the air **2** to hit or kick (a ball) on the volley **3** (in tennis) to make a volley against (one's opponent)

volt *n* the amount of electrical force needed to produce one standard measure (ampere) of electrical current where the resistance of the conductor is another standard measure (ohm)

voltage *n* electrical force measured in volts

volume *n* **1** one of a set of books of the same kind **2** a book, esp. a large one **3** size or quantity thought of as measurement of the space inside or filled by something: *The volume of this container is 100,000 cubic metres* **4** *esp. technical* amount produced by some kind of (industrial) activity: *the volume of passenger travel* **5** loudness of sound

volumes *n* **1** a large quantity or mass (esp. of something that pours or flows) **2 speak volumes (for some-**

thing) to show or express (something) very clearly or fully

voluntary *adj* **1** (of a person or an action) acting or done willingly, without payment **2** supported by people who give their money, services, etc., of their own free will **3** *technical* under the control of the will: *voluntary movements* – **-tarily** *adv:He made the promise quite voluntarily*

¹**volunteer** *n* a person who volunteers

²**volunteer** *v* **1** to offer one's services or help without payment **2** to offer to join the army, navy, or airforce of one' own free will **3** to tell (something) without being asked

¹**vomit** *n* **1** food or other matter that has been vomited **2** an act of vomiting

²**vomit** *v* **1** to throw up (the contents of the stomach) through the mouth; be sick **2** to pour out suddenly with force and in great quantity (usu. something unpleasant or unwanted)

¹**vote** *n* **1** an act of making a choice or decision on a matter by means of voting **2** a (person's) choice or decision, as expressed by voting **3** the piece of paper on which a choice is expressed **4** the whole number of such choices made either for or against someone or something **5** **put something to the vote** to try to obtain a decision about something by asking everyone to vote on it

²**vote** *v* **voted, voting 1** to express

one's choice officially (usu. done by marking a piece of paper secretly, or by calling out or raising one's hand at a meeting) **2** to elect **3** to agree, as the result of a vote, to provide (something)

voucher *n* **1** a kind of ticket that may be used instead of money for a particular purpose: *a travel voucher* **2** a kind of ticket that gives the right to receive certain goods free or at a lower price

¹**vow** *n* **1** a solemn promise or declaration of intention **2** **take vows** to begin to live in a religious house (as a monk or nun)

²**vow** *v* **1** to declare or swear solemnly **2** to promise (something) by swearing solemnly, esp. to God: *Priests vow their lives to the service of the church*

vowel *n* **1** any one of the more open sounds uttered when speaking **2** a letter used for representing any of these: *The vowels in the English alphabet are a, e, i, o, u, and, sometimes, y*

¹**voyage** *n* a journey, usu. long, made by boat or ship

²**voyage** *v* **-aged, -aging** *literature or esp. written* to make a long journey by sea –~r *n*

vulgar *adj* **1** (of a person or behaviour) very rude, low, or having bad manners **2** showing a lack of feeling or judgment in the choice of what is suitable or beautiful, esp. in matters of art: *vulgar furniture* –~ly *adv*

vulnerable *adj* **1** (of a place, thing, or

person) not well protected **2** (of a person or his feelings) easily harmed or wounded – **-bility** *n* – **-bly** *adv*

vulture *n* **1** a large bird with almost featherless head and neck, which feeds on dead animals **2** a person who has no mercy and who uses people for his own advantage

¹**wad** *n* **1** a thick mass of material pressed into a hole used for filling space, etc. **2** a thick piece of cloth, or pieces of paper folded or fastened together: *a wad of letters* **3** a large amount of paper money rolled up

²**wad** *v* **-dd- 1** to make a wad of: *Wad the newspaper and hit the flies with it* **2** to fill with a wad

¹**waddle** *v* **-dled, -dling** to walk with short steps, bending from one side to the other, as if having short legs and a heavy body: *Ducks waddle*

²**waddle** *n* a way of walking like that of a duck

wade *v* **waded, wading** to walk through water

wafer *n* a thin crisp biscuit

¹**wag** *v* **-gg- 1** to shake to and fro: *The dog wagged its tail* **2 a case of the tail wagging the dog** *esp. spoken* a state of affairs in which the followers control the leader **3 Their tongues wagged** *esp. spoken* They talked a lot

²**wag** *n* an act of wagging; shake

³**wag** *n* a clever and amusing talker

¹**wage** *v* **waged, waging** to begin and continue (a struggle) (esp. in the phrase **wage war**)

²**wage** *n* **1** wages: *a high wage level* **2 a living wage** an amount of pay large enough to buy food, clothing, etc.

¹**wager** *n* a bet

²**wager** *v* to bet

wages *n* a payment for labour or services usu. received daily or weekly

waggon, wagon *n* **1** a 4-wheeled vehicle, mainly for heavy loads, drawn by horses, oxen, railway engines, or road vehicles **2 on the waggon** *sl* unwilling to drink alcohol

wail *v* **1** to make a long cry suggesting grief or pain **2** to cry out in grief or pain: *"You've taken my apple,"* he *wailed* **3** to complain **–wail** *n*

waist *n* **1** the narrow part of the human body just above the hips **2** the part of a garment that goes round this: *the waist of a dress* **3** the narrow middle part of any apparatus, such as a musical instrument

waistcoat *n* a close-fitting armless garment that reaches to the waist

¹**wait** *v* **1** to stay somewhere without doing anything until somebody comes or something happens: *Don't keep her waiting* **2** to be ready: *Your tea is waiting for you* **3** to remain not dealt with: *This news can't wait* **4** to hold back until (the stated occasion): *just waiting his chance to strike* **5 wait at table** to serve meals

²**wait** *n* **1** an act or period of waiting: *a long wait* **2 lie in wait** to hide,

waiting to attack: *robbers lying in wait for the traveller*

waiter –(*fem.* **waitress**) *n* a person who serves food at the tables in a restaurant

¹**wake** *v* **woke** *or* **waked, woken, waking 1** to cease to sleep or stop someone sleeping: *She usually wakes early* **2** to make or become active: *The lonely child woke our pity* **3** *literature* to begin moving: *A light wind woke among the trees*

²**wake** *n* a gathering to watch and grieve over a dead person on the night before the burial

³**wake** *n* **1** a track or path, esp. that left by a moving body in water: *the broad white wake of the great ship* **2** **in the wake of** following as a result of: *hunger and disease in the wake of the war*

¹**walk** *v* **1** to move at a walk: *to walk to town* **2** to pass over, through, or along on foot: *to walk a tightrope* **3** to take for a walk: *walking the dog / I walked her home* **4** to cause to move in a manner suggesting a walk: *Let's walk the heavy ladder to the other end of the room* **5** (of a spirit) to move about visibly: *Spirits walk at night* **6 walk (someone) off (their) feet/legs** *esp. spoken* to tire (someone) by making (them) move about on foot too much **–~er** *n*

²**walk** *n* **1** (of people and creatures with legs) a natural and unhurried way of moving on foot **2** a journey on foot: *Let's go for a short walk* **3** a place for walking: *a beautiful walk along the river* **4** a distance to be walked: *a 10-minute walk from here* **5** the style of walking: *His walk is like his father's*

walkover *n sl* an easy or unopposed victory

¹**wall** *n* **1** an upright dividing surface (esp. of stone or brick) enclosing something: *fields surrounded by stone walls / the city wall* **2** the side of a room: *Hang that picture on the wall* **3** an upright mass: *a wall of water* **4** something that separates; barrier: *a wall of silence* **5** the covering of something hollow: *the walls of a blood vessel* **6 bang one's head against a wall** *esp. spoken* to try to do the impossible **7 to the wall** into a hopeless position **8 up the wall** into a state of or near madness

²**wall** *v* **1** to provide with a wall: *an old walled town* **2** to close or enclose with a wall: *to wall up a door / a prisoner* **3** to separate with walls

wallet *n* a small flat leather case for papers and paper money

wallflower *n* **1** a sweet-smelling European yellow or red flower that grows best near walls **2** a person who sits by the wall at a dance because no one has asked them to dance

¹**wallpaper** *n* ornamental paper to cover the walls of a room

²**wallpaper** *v* to cover with wallpaper

walnut *n* a brain-shaped eatable nut which grows on a **walnut tree**, and has a rough shell easily divided into 2 parts

¹waltz *n* (music for) a social dance for a couple, made up of 6 steps in 3/4 time

²waltz *v* **1** to dance a waltz **2** *esp. spoken* to move easily or showily: *We can't just waltz up to a complete stranger*

wand *n* a thin stick carried in the hand, esp. by a person who does magic tricks

wander *v* **1** to move about aimlessly **2** to follow a winding course: *The river wanders through beautiful country* **3** (of people or thoughts) to become confused: *His mind is wandering*

wanderer *n* a person who wanders

wandering *adj* **1** aimless, slow, and irregular: *the wandering course of a stream* **2** moving from place to place: *wandering tribes*

wane *v* **waned, waning** to grow gradually smaller or less powerful

¹want *v* **1** to have a desire for **2** to need: *The house wants painting* **3** ought: *You don't want to work so hard* **4** to lack; be without: *His answer wants politeness* **5** to look for in order to catch: *He is wanted for murder*

²want *n* **1** lack, absence, or need: *The plants died from want of water* **2** severe lack of the things necessary to life: *How terrible to live in want!*

¹war *n* **1** armed fighting between nations **2** a period of this **3** a struggle: *a war against disease* **4**

(having) been in the wars *esp. spoken* (having) been hurt or damaged

²war *v* **-rr- 1** *literature* to take part in a war **2** to struggle: *warring beliefs*

ward *n* **1** a separate room or division of a hospital: *the heart ward* **2** a political division of a city **3** a person who is under the protection of another , or of a law court

warden *n* a person who looks after a place and people: *the warden of an old people's home*

wardrobe *n* **1** a room or cupboard in which one hangs up clothes **2** a collection of clothes: *a new summer wardrobe* **3** a collection of theatre costumes and ornaments

warehouse *n* a building for storing things

wares *n* articles for sale

warfare *n* **1** war **2** struggle

warlike *adj* **1** threatening war: *a warlike appearance* **2** liking war: *a warlike nation*

¹warm *adj* **1** having or producing enough heat: *a warm fire* **2** able to keep in heat: *warm clothes* **3** feeling hot: *We were warm from exercise* **4** showing good feeling: *a warm welcome* **5** marked by excitement or anger: *a warm argument* **6** recently made; fresh (esp. in the phrases **warm scent/smell/trail**) **7** (esp. in children's games) near a hidden object, the right answer to a question, etc. **8** giving a cheerful feeling: *warm colours* —~**ish** *adj* —~**ly** *adv* —~**ness** *n*

²**warm** *v* to make or become warm

³**warm** *n* 1 a warm place: *Come into the warm* 2 the act of making oneself warm

warmth *n* the quality of being warm

warn *v* 1 to tell of something bad that may happen, or of how to prevent something bad 2 to tell of some future need or action: *You should warn the police when you go away on holiday*

warning *n* 1 warning or being warned 2 something that warns: *Let that be a warning to you* 3 an example of what *not* to do: *He is a warning to us all of what happens to people who drink too much*

¹**warp** *n* 1 the downward threads running along the length of cloth 2 a twist out of a straight line: *a warp in a board* 3 a rope or wire for pulling a net along behind a fishing boat

²**warp** *v* to turn or twist out of shape

¹**warrant** *n* 1 proper reason for action 2 a written order signed by an official of the law

²**warrant** *v* 1 to cause to appear reasonable 2 to guarantee 3 *esp. spoken* to declare as if certain: *I'll warrant he's there*

warrior *n* 1 *literature* a soldier 2 a man who fights for his tribe: *The Indian warriors charged bravely*

wart *n* a small hard ugly swelling on the skin – ~y *adj*

wary *adj* **-ier, -iest** careful; looking out for danger **–warily** *adv* **–wariness** *n*

was 1st and 3rd person sing. past tense of BE: *I/He was happy*

¹**wash** *v* 1 to clean or clean oneself with liquid: *to wash clothes / to wash before dinner* 2 *esp. spoken* to be easy to believe: *His story just won't wash* 3 to flow over or against continually: *The waves washed against the shore* 4 to cause to be carried with liquid: *I washed the dirt off. / The waves washed the swimmer away* 5 **wash one's hands of** *esp. spoken* to refuse to accept any more responsibility for

²**wash** *n* 1 washing or being washed: *to have a wash* 2 things to be washed; laundry 3 the flow, sound, or action of a mass of water: *the wash of the waves* 4 water thrown back by a boat 5 a movement of air caused by an aircraft passing through it 6 the liquid with which something is washed or coloured: *mouthwash / a copper-coloured hairwash* 7 **come out in the wash** *esp. spoken* to turn out all right in the end

washbasin *n* a fixed basin for washing hands and face

washing *n* clothes washed or to be washed

washing-up *n* the washing of dishes, plates, etc. after a meal

wasp *n* any of many types of flying stinging insect related to the bee, usu. yellow and black

wastage *n* wasting or that which is wasted: *a wastage of 25% of all the goods produced*

¹waste *n* **1** *often literature* a wide empty lonely stretch of water or land: *stony wastes* **2** loss, wrong use, or lack of full use: *Waste of food is wicked while people are hungry* **3** used, damaged, or unwanted matter: *poisonous waste from the chemical works* **4 go/run to waste** to be wasted

²waste *v* **wasted, wasting 1** to use wrongly, not use, or use too much of **2** (esp. of a disease) to cause to lose flesh, muscle, strength, etc., slowly **3** to make useless by damage: *Long dry periods wasted the land* **4 waste one's breath** *esp. spoken* to speak without persuading anyone

³waste *adj* **1** (esp. of land) not productive; ruined or destroyed **2** got rid of as worthless: *waste material* **3** used for holding or carrying away what is worthless: *waste pipes*

wasteful *adj* tending to waste: *wasteful habits* −∼**ly** *adv* −∼**ness** *n*

wastepaper basket *n* a container for unnecessary material, esp. waste paper

¹watch *v* **1** to look at (some activity or event): *Do you often watch television? / Watch how to do this* **2** to look for; expect and wait: *She watched to see what I would do* **3** to take care of: *I'll watch the baby while you are away* **4** *literature* to stay awake at night: *She watched beside her sick mother's bed* **5 watch it!** *esp. spoken* Be careful! **6 watch one's step** *esp. spoken* to act with

great care **7 watch the clock** *esp. spoken* to be waiting for one's working day to end instead of thinking about one's work −∼**er** *n*

²watch *n* **1** a small clock to be worn or carried **2** one or more people ordered to watch: *In spite of the watch set on the house, the thief escaped* **3** any of the periods into which the night was once divided for policing duty: *the watches of the night* **4** (sailors who have to be on duty during) a period of 2 or 4 hours at sea **5 keep a close/careful watch on** to fix one's attention on, carefully **6 on the watch for** waiting for

watchdog *n* **1** a fierce dog kept to guard property **2** a person or group that tries to guard against undesirable practices: *a watchdog of public morals*

watchful *adj* careful to notice things −∼**ly** *adv* −∼**ness** *n*

watchman *n* **-men** a guard, esp. of a building

¹water *n* **1** the most common liquid, without colour, taste, or smell, which falls from the sky as rain, forms rivers, lakes, and seas, and is drunk by people and animals **2** a liquid like or containing this liquid, produced by some part of the body **3** the tide: *high/low water* **4 above water** *esp. spoken* out of difficulty (esp. in the phrase **keep one's head above water** (=keep out of difficulty)) **5 in/into deep water(s)** *esp. spoken* in/into trouble **6 in/into hot**

water *esp. spoken* in/into trouble related to anger or punishment **7 like water** *esp. spoken* in great quantity and without considering the cost: *The wine flowed like water* **8 make/pass water** *polite* to pass urine from the body **9 hold water** to be true or reasonable: *Your story just doesn't hold water* **10 throw cold water on** *esp. spoken* to speak against; point out difficulties in **11 water on the brain/knee/etc.** liquid on the brain, knee, etc. as the result of disease

²**water** *v* **1** to pour water on **2** to supply with water: *to water the horses* **3** (esp. of the eyes or mouth) to form or let out water **4** (esp. of rivers) to flow through and provide with water: *Colombia is watered by many rivers*

water closet *n esp. written* a WC

water down *v adv* **1** to weaken (a liquid) by adding water **2** to weaken the effect of: *His political statement has been watered down so as not to offend anyone*

waterfall *n* water falling straight down over rocks

watering can *n* a container from which water can be poured through a long spout

waterlogged *adj* full of water, as of wet earth

¹**waterproof** *adj, n* (an outer garment) which does not allow water to go through

²**waterproof** *v* to make waterproof

watertight *adj* **1** through which no

water can go **2** allowing of no mistakes: *a watertight argument*

watt *n* (a standard measure of electrical power equal to) the amount produced when a voltage of one volt causes a current of one ampere to flow: *A kilowatt is 1000 watts*

¹**wave** *v* **waved, waving 1** to move in the air, backwards and forwards, up and down **2** to move one's hand as a signal, esp. in greeting **3** to lie, or cause to lie, in regular curves: *Her hair waves naturally*

²**wave** *n* a raised curving line of water on the surface, esp. of the sea **2** the movement of the hand in waving **3** an evenly curved part of the hair **4** a suddenly rising and increasing feeling, way of behaviour, etc., passed on from person to person: *a wave of fear* **5** a form in which some forms of energy move: *radio waves*

wavelength *n* **1** the distance between one energy wave and another **2** a radio signal sent out on radio waves a particular distance apart

waver *v* to be unsteady or uncertain **−waverer** *n* **−waveringly** *adv*

wavy *adj* **-ier, -iest** in the shape of waves; having regular curves **−waviness** *n*

¹**wax** *n* a solid material made of fats or oils and changing to a thick liquid when melted

²**wax** *v* to put wax on, esp. as a polish

³**wax** *v* (esp. of the moon) to grow

way *n* **ways 1** a road or path: *a cycle way* **2** the right direction to follow: *Is this the way out?* **3** the distance to be travelled to reach a place: *a long way from home* **4** a method: *the right way of addressing the Queen* **5 by way of a** by going through: *by way of London* **b** as a sort of: *by way of help* **6 go out of one's way** to take the trouble **7 have it both ways** to gain advantage from opposing opinions or actions **8 mend one's ways** to improve one's behaviour **9 out of the way** unusual or not commonly known **10 pay one's way** never to owe money **11 set in one's ways** having very fixed habits **12 to my way of thinking** in my opinion

waylay *v* **-laid**, **-laying** to stop (a person moving somewhere) for a purpose

wayside *n* **1** the side of the road **2 fall by the wayside** to fail and give up

WC —also (*esp. written*) **water closet** *n* a lavatory which is emptied by a flow of water from the pipes

we *pron* **1** (*pl. of* I) the people speaking: *We came together* **2** (used by a king or queen) I: *We are grateful to our people for their greetings*

weak *adj* **1** not strong enough to work or last properly: *a weak wall / heart* **2** not strong in character **3** not well: *His legs felt weak* **4** containing mainly water: *weak soup* **5** (of a verb) forming the past in a regular way, with the usual endings: *Stepped is a weak form; swam and swum are strong* **−~ly** *adv*

weaken *v* **1** to make or become weak **2** to become less determined: *She asked so many times that in the end we weakened and let her go*

weakness *n* **1** the state of being weak **2** a weak part or fault: *Drinking is his weakness* **3** a strong liking: *a weakness for chocolate*

wealth *n* **1** a large amount of money and possessions **2** a large number: *a wealth of examples*

wealthy *adj* **-ier**, **-iest** rich **−wealthily** *adv*

weapon *n* a tool for harming or killing **−~less** *adj* **−~ry** *n*

¹wear *v* **wore**, **worn**, **wearing** **1** to have (esp. clothes) on the body **2** to have (a look): *She wore an angry expression* **3** to reduce by continued use: *The noise wore her nerves to shreds* **4** to last: *Considering her age, she has worn well* **5** *esp. spoken* to find acceptable: *Fiji would be lovely for our holiday, but I don't think father will wear it* **−~able** *adj*

²wear *n* **1** clothes of the stated type: *evening wear* **2** use or damage which reduces the material: *This mat has had a lot of wear* **3** the quality of lasting in use: *There's a lot of wear in these shoes* **4 the worse for wear** in bad condition after use

¹weary *adj* **-ier**, **-iest** **1** very tired **2** which makes one tired: *a weary day* **−wearily** *adv* **−weariness** *n*

²weary *v* **-ied**, **-ying** to make or become weary

weasel *n* a small thin furry fierce animal with a pointed face

¹weather *n* **1** the condition of wind,

rain, sunshine, snow, etc., at a certain time **2 keep one's weather eye open** to be ready for trouble **3 make heavy weather of** to make (something) seem difficult **4 under the weather** not very well or happy

²**weather** v **1** to pass safely through (a storm or difficulty) **2** to change by the air and weather: *Rocks weather until they are worn away*

¹**weave** v **wove, woven, weaving 1** to form threads into material by drawing one thread at a time under and over a set of longer threads on a loom **2** to make by doing this: *to weave a mat* **3** to form by twisting or winding: *to weave a nest out of sticks* **4** to make up (a story or plan) **5 get weaving** *esp. spoken* to start working hard

²**weave** n the way in which a material is woven and the pattern formed by this

³**weave** v **weaved, weaving** to move along, changing direction frequently: *weaving in and out between the cars*

web n **1** a net of threads spun by some insects and esp. spiders **2** a length of material still on a loom **3** the skin between the toes of swimming birds and animals

wedding n a marriage ceremony, esp. with a party after a religious service

¹**wedge** n **1** a piece of (esp.) wood with a V-shaped edge, one end thin and the other quite wide, used for making or filling a space **2** something shaped like this: *shoes with wedge heels* **3** a golf club with a heavy metal head for driving the ball high **4 the thin end of the wedge** the part which seems least important but will open the way for more important things

²**wedge** v **wedged, wedging** to fix with a wedge **2** to pack tightly: *The people wedged me into the corner*

Wednesday n **-days** the 4th day of the week

¹**weed** n **1** an unwanted wild plant **2** cigarettes or tobacco **3** *usu. offensive* a tall thin weak-bodied person

²**weed** v to remove weeds from: *to weed the garden*

week n **1** a period of 7 days (and nights), esp. from Sunday to Saturday **2** the period of time during which one works

weekday n **-days 1** a day not at the weekend **2** a day not Sunday

weekend n Saturday and Sunday, esp. when considered a holiday

¹**weekly** adj, adv happening once a week

²**weekly** n **-lies** a magazine or newspaper which appears once a week

weep v **wept, weeping 1** to let fall tears from the eyes; cry **2** to lose liquid from a part of the body, esp. because of illness: *The wound is weeping*

weigh v **1** to find the weight of, esp. by a machine **2** to have a certain weight: *I weigh less than I used to* **3** to consider carefully: *He weighed the ideas in his mind* **4** to be important: *Your suggestion does not weigh with me* **5** to raise (an anchor)

weigh down *v adv* to make heavy: *weighed down with grief*

weigh out *v adv* to measure in amounts by weight

¹**weight** *n* **1** heaviness: *She is losing weight* **2** *technical* the force with which a body is drawn towards the centre of the earth: *The weight of an object is related to the force of gravity, which is fixed, and to its mass* **3** a piece of metal of a standard heaviness: *a one-pound weight* **4** a heavy object for holding something down: *a paperweight* **5** a system of measures of weight: *metric weight* **6** value or importance: *a man of political weight* **7** a worry: *The loss of the money is a weight on my mind* **8 pull one's weight** to join in work equally with others **9 throw one's weight about** to give orders because one thinks oneself important

²**weight** *v* to add something heavy to: *Fishing nets are weighted*

weird *adj* **1** strange; unnatural **2** *esp. spoken* not sensible or acceptable: *weird ideas* −∼**ly** *adv* −∼**ness** *n*

¹**welcome** *v* **-comed, -coming 1** to greet with pleasure (a person) when arriving in a new place **2** to receive (an idea): *They welcomed the idea with little interest*

²**welcome** *adj* **1** acceptable and wanted: *a welcome suggestion* **2** allowed freely: *You're welcome to try, but you won't succeed* **3 You're welcome** (a polite expression when thanked for something) **4 make (someone) welcome** to receive (a guest) with friendliness

³**welcome** *n, interj* a greeting to someone on arrival: *The crowd gave a joyful welcome to the home team.* / *'Welcome home!' said my father*

¹**weld** *v* to join (usu. metals) by pressure or melting together when hot −∼**er** *n*

²**weld** *n* the part joined in welding

¹**welfare** *n* **1** well-being; comfort and happiness **2** government help for those in special need: *on welfare*

²**welfare** *adj* helping with living conditions, social difficulties, etc.: *the welfare officer*

welfare state *n* a country, or system, based on the principle that the economic welfare of every citizen is the shared responsibility of the community

¹**well** *n* **1** a place where water comes from underground **2 a** such a place with walls leading down to the water **b** a hole through which oil is drawn from underground

²**well** *v* (of liquid) to flow: *Blood welled from the cut*

³**well** *adv* **better, best 1** in the right manner; satisfactorily: *well clothed* **2** to a high standard: *She paints very well* **3** thoroughly: *Wash it well* **4** much; quite: *He was well within the time* **5** with kindness or favour: *They speak well of him* **6 as well** in addition; also **7 do well out of** to gain profit from **8 just as well**

There's no harm done; There's no loss **9 may well** could suitably: *You may well ask!* **10 may as well** could with the same result: *You might as well ask for the moon as for a bicycle* **11 pretty well** almost **12 well out of** lucky enough to be free from: *It's lucky you left before the trouble; you were well out of it* **13 well up in** well informed about

⁴**well** *interj* **1** (an expression of surprise, doubt, acceptance, etc.): *She's got a new job. Well, well!* **2** (used when continuing a story): *Well, then she said...*

⁵**well** *adj* **better, best 1** in good health **2** right; acceptable: *All is well* **3** most suitable: *It would be just as well to let them know* **4 It's all very well** (an expression of dissatisfaction): *It's all very well to say that, but what can I do?*

wellbeing *n* personal and bodily comfort, esp. good health

wellington *n* a waterproof, usu. rubber, boot

well-known *adj* known by many people

well-off *adj* **1** rich **2** lucky (esp. in the phrase **you don't know when you're well off**)

went *past tense of* GO

wept *past tense and past part. of* WEEP

were *pl. and 2nd person sing. past tense of* BE: *You/We/They were happy*

¹**west** *adv* **1** towards the west **2 go west** to die or be damaged or broken

²**west** *n, adj* **1** (in the direction of) one of the 4 main points of the compass, which is on the left of a person facing north: *The sun sets in the west* **2** (of a wind) coming from this direction

West *n* **1** the western part of the world, esp. western Europe and the United States **2** the part of a country which is further west than the rest **3** (in the US) the part of the country west of the Mississippi

westerly *adj* **1** towards or in the west: *in a westerly direction* **2** (of a wind) coming from the west

¹**western** *adj* of or belonging to the west: *the Western nations*

²**western** *n* a story, usu. on a film, about life in the US West in the past, esp. about cowboys, gunfights, etc.

westward *adj* going towards the west: *in a westward direction*

westwards *adv* towards the west: *They travelled westwards*

¹**wet** *adj* **-tt- 1** covered in liquid or not dry: *wet ground / wet paint / to get wet* **2** rainy: *wet weather* **3** *esp. spoken* lacking in strength of mind; weak: *Don't be so wet! Of course you can do it* –~**ly** *adv* –~**ness** *n*

²**wet** *n* rainy weather: *to go out in the wet*

³**wet** *v* **wet** *or* **wetted, wetting 1** to make wet **2 wet the bed** to pass water from the body in bed, because of a loss of control while asleep

¹**whack** –also **thwack** *v* to hit with a blow making a loud noise

²**whack** *n* –also **thwack 1** (the noise made by) a hard blow **2** *esp. spoken*

a fair share: *Have you all had your whack?* **3** *esp. spoken* a try; attempt

whale *n* **1** any of several types of very large animals which live in the sea and look like fish, but are mammals, and therefore warm-blooded **2 a whale of a time** *esp. spoken* a very enjoyable experience

¹**what** *adj, pron* **1 a** which (thing or person)?: *What time will you come? / What are you doing?* **b** (used for having words repeated): *'I got up at half past 4.' 'What?'* **2** that which; a/the thing that: *I believed what he told me* **3 and what not** and other things: *sugar, tea, and what not* **4 give someone what for** *esp. spoken* to punish and/or scold someone **5 what have you** *esp. spoken* anything (else) like that: *In his pocket I found a handkerchief, string, and what have you* **6 what's what** the important things (in the phrase **know what's what**) **7 what it takes** *esp. spoken* the qualities necessary for success **8 what though** *literature* even if (used in comparing something bad with something better): *What though the battle be lost? We can fight again!*

²**what** *adj* (an exclamation showing surprise): *What a big house! / What pretty flowers!*

³**what** *adv* **1** in what way?; to what degree?: *What do you care about it?* **2 what with** (used for introducing the causes of something): *What with the bad weather and the bad news, no wonder we're miserable!*

¹**whatever** –also (*literature*) **whatsoever** *adj, pron* **1** anything at all that: *They eat whatever they can find* **2** no matter what: *Whatever I said, he'd disagree*

²**whatever** *pron* **1** anything else like that: *bags, boxes, or whatever* **2** (showing surprise) what?: *Look at that strange animal! Whatever is it?*

³**whatever also whatsoever**– *adj* at all: *Have you any interest whatever?*

wheat *n* **1** a plant from whose grain flour is made **2** the grain from this plant

¹**wheel** *v* **1** to push (a wheeled object or something on one): *He wheeled his bicycle into the street. / The mother wheeled the baby round the park* **2** to turn suddenly: *I called him and he wheeled to face me* **3** to fly round and round in circles: *gulls wheeling over the sea*

²**wheel** *n* **1** a circular object with an outer frame which turns around an inner part (hub) to which it is joined, used for turning machinery, making vehicles move, etc. **2** the steering wheel of a car or ship **3 at the wheel** driving or steering **4 oil the wheels** to make matters go more smoothly **5 on wheels** by car: *meals on wheels* (= delivered to the homes of old people) **6 put one's shoulder to the wheel** to start work **7 wheels within wheels** hidden influences

wheelbarrow –also **barrow** *n* a movable container with one wheel at the front, 2 handles at the back, 2 legs, and a part in which things can be carried

wheelchair *n* a wheeled chair in which a person who cannot walk can move himself or be pushed

¹**when** *adv* **1** at what time?: *When will they come?* **2** (of time) at or on which: *the day when we met*

²**when** *conj* **1** at the time at which: *When I came home she was cooking dinner* **2** if: *No one can make a dress when they haven't learnt how* **3** although: *She stopped trying, when she might have succeeded next time* **4 hardly/scarcely when** only just... when: *Hardly had I opened the door when he hit me*

³**when** *pron* **1** what time?: *Since when has that been so?* **2** which time: *She wrote a month ago, since when we've heard nothing*

whence *adv* **1** *old use* from where?: *Whence come you?* **2** from which: *the bridge over the river Cam, whence came the name of the town of Cambridge*

¹**whenever** *conj* **1** at any time at all that: *Come whenever you like* **2** every time: *Whenever we see him we speak to him*

²**whenever** *adv* **1** at any such time: *tonight, tomorrow, or whenever* **2** (showing surprise) when?: *Whenever did you find time to do it?*

¹**where** *adv* **1** at/to what place?: *Where will you go?* **2** (of place) at or to which: *the office where I work*

²**where** *conj* **1** at, to the place (at) which: *Keep him where you can see*

him **2** whereas **3 where it's at** *sl* very good, esp. as being fashionable: *This party's really where it's at, man!*

¹**whereabouts** *adv* (used when an exact answer is not expected) where?: *Whereabouts did I leave my bag?*

²**whereabouts** *n* the place a person or thing is in: *The escaped prisoner's whereabouts is/are still unknown*

whereas *conj* **1** (*used for introducing an opposite*) but: *They want a house, whereas we would rather live in a flat* **2** *law* (at the beginning of a sentence) since; because of the fact that

whereby *adv* *esp. written* **1** by means of which: *a system whereby a new discovery may arise* **2** according to which: *a law whereby all children are to receive cheap milk*

whereupon *conj* at once after that: *He saw me coming, whereupon he offered me his seat*

¹**wherever** *adv* **1** (showing surprise) where?: *Wherever did you get that idea?* **2** at any such place: *at home, at school, or wherever*

²**wherever** *conj* at/to all places or any place: *Wherever you go, I go too*

whether *conj* **1** if . . . or not: *He asked whether she was coming* **2** no matter if...: *I shall go, whether you come with me or stay at home*

which *adj, pron* **1** (*used when a choice is to be made*) what (thing or person)?: *Which shoes shall I wear?* **2** being the one or ones that: *the* book which I like best **3** (*used esp. in written language, with commas*) and/because it/they, them: *Books, which you can change at the shop, make good presents* **4** (and) this: *He changed his mind, which made me very angry* **5 which is which?** what is the difference between the 2?

whichever *adj, pron* **1** any one that: *I'll give it to whichever of you wants it* **2** no matter which: *It has the same result, whichever way you do it* **3** (showing surprise) which: *Whichever did you choose?*

¹**whiff** *n* **1** a short-lasting smell **2** a breath in: *A few whiffs of this gas and she'll fall asleep*

²**whiff** *v esp. spoken* to smell bad –~y *adj*

¹**while** *n* **1** a space of time: *a long while* **2 once in a while** sometimes, but not often **3 worth one's while** worthwhile to one

²**while** –also **whilst** *conj* **1** during the time that: *While I was out he started to misbehave* **2** although ; whereas: *You like sports, while I'd rather read*

¹**whine** *v* **whined, whining 1** to make a high sad sound: *The dog whined at the door* **2** to complain unnecessarily: *Stop whining, child!*

²**whine** *n* the sound of whining

¹**whip** *n* **1** a long piece of rope or leather fastened to a handle used for hitting animals or people **2** a Member of Parliament responsible for making other members attend **3** an order given to Members of Parliament to attend and vote **4** a

sweet food made of beaten eggs and other foods whipped together

²**whip** *v* **-pp- 1** to beat with a whip **2** to conquer; beat: *Ali really whipped Frazier* **3** to move quickly: *He whipped it into his pocket* **4** to beat until stiff (esp. cream or white of egg): *whipped cream* **5** to sew over (the edge of material) with a close stitch **6** to cover (the end of a stick or rope) closely with thread, string, etc. **7** to spin (a top) by means of a whip

¹**whirl** *v* **1** to move round and round very fast **2** to move away in a hurry: *The car whirled them off to the wedding*

²**whirl** *n* **1** the act or sensation of whirling: *My head's in a whirl* **2** very fast confused movement: *a whirl of activity* **3 give something a whirl** *esp. spoken* to try something

whirlpool *n* a circular current of water in a sea or river, which can draw objects into it

whirlwind *n* a tall pipe-shaped body of air moving rapidly in a circle

¹**whisk** *n* **1** a quick movement, esp. to brush something off: *with a whisk of his hand* **2** a small brush consisting of a bunch of feathers, hair, etc., tied to a handle: *a flywhisk* **3** a small hand-held apparatus for beating eggs, whipping cream, etc.

²**whisk** *v* **1** to move (something) quickly, esp. so as to brush something off: *The horse was whisking its tail* **2** to remove suddenly: *She*

whisked the cups away **3** to beat (esp. eggs), esp. with a whisk

whisker *n* one of the long stiff hairs near the mouth of a cat, rat, etc.

whiskers *n* hair allowed to grow on the sides of a man's face, not meeting at the chin

whisky *n* **-kies** strong alcoholic drink made from grain, produced esp. in Scotland

¹**whisper** *v* **1** to speak with noisy breath, but not much of the voice: *'Listen!' she whispered* **2** to make a soft sound: *the wind whispering in the roof* **3** to tell (a secret) widely: *His adventures have been whispered everywhere* −~**er** *n*

²**whisper** *n* **1** whispered words: *She said it in a whisper* **2** a soft windy sound **3** a rumour

¹**whistle** *n* **1** a simple musical instrument for making a high sound by passing air or steam through **2** the high sound made by passing air or steam through an instrument, a mouth, or a beak: *gave a loud whistle of surprise* **3 wet one's whistle** *humour* to drink (esp. alcohol)

²**whistle** *v* **-tled, -tling 1** to make the sound of a whistle **2** to produce (music) by doing this: *He whistled 'God save the Queen'*

¹**white** *adj* **1 a** of the colour of snow or milk: *white hair* **b** pale: *white wine* **2** (of a person) of a pale-skinned race **3** (of coffee) with milk or cream −~**ness** *n*

²**white** *n* **1** the colour that is white:

dressed in white **2** a person of a pale-skinned race **3** the white part of the eye **4** the part of an egg which is white after cooking

white-collar *adj* of office workers: *a white-collar job*

white elephant *n* a usu. big object not useful to its owner , which he wants to get rid of

whitewash *n, v* **1** (to cover with) a white liquid mixture made from lime, used for covering walls: *whitewashing farm buildings* **2** (to make) an attempt to hide something wrong: *What he said was just to whitewash the politician's actions*

Whitsun −also **Whit** *n* **1** also **Whit Sunday**− the 7th Sunday after Easter **2** also **Whitsuntide**− the public holiday including this Sunday

whiz, whizz *v* **-zz-** *esp. spoken* to move very fast, often with a noisy sound: *Cars were whizzing past*

who *pron* **1** what person or people?: *Who's at the door?* **2** that one person/those ones: *a man who wants to see you* **3** (used esp. in written language, with commas) and/but he, she, etc.: *George, who lives in Scotland, came late*

whoever *pron* **1** anybody that: *I'll take whoever wants to go* **2** no matter who: *The business would be a success, whoever owned it* **3** (showing surprise) who?: *Whoever can that be?*

¹**whole** *adj* **1** not spoilt or divided: *a whole cake* **2** all (the): *the whole*

truth **3 swallow something whole** to accept something without thinking

²**whole** *n* **1** the complete amount, thing, etc.: *the whole of that area* **2** the sum of the parts: *2 halves make a whole* **3 on the whole** generally; mostly

whole-hearted –also **full-hearted** *adj* with all one's ability, interest, sincerity, etc. –~**ly** *adv*

¹**wholesale** *n* the business of selling goods in large quantities, esp. to shopkeepers –~**r** *n*

²**wholesale** *adj, adv* **1** of or concerned in selling in large quantities or at the lower prices fixed for such sales: *They sell machines wholesale* **2** in unlimited numbers: *a wholesale rush from the burning cinema*

wholesome *adj* good for people; with no bad effects: *wholesome food* –~**ness** *n*

wholly *adv* completely

whom *pron* (*object form of* WHO): *the man with whom he talked*

whose *adj, pron* **1** of whom?: *Whose house is this?* **2 a** of whom: *the man whose house was burned down* **b** of which: *a factory whose workers are all women*

¹**why** *adv* for what reason?: *Why did you do it?*

²**why** *conj* the reason for which: *I don't see why it shouldn't work*

wick *n* **1** a piece of twisted thread in a candle, which burns as the wax melts **2** a tubelike piece of material in an oil lamp which draws up oil while burning

wicked *adj* very bad; evil: *wicked cruelty / a wicked man* –~**ly**

wicket *n* **1** (in cricket) **a** either of 2 sets of 3 stumps, with 2 small pieces of wood (bails) on top, at which the ball is bowled **b** also **pitch**– the stretch of grass between these 2 sets **2** (in cricket) one turn of a player to bat: *England have lost 3 wickets* (= 3 of their players are out) **3** also **wicket gate** – a small gate or door which is part of a larger one

¹**wide** *adj* **1** large from side to side: *The skirt's too wide. / 4 inches wide* **2** covering a large range: *wide interests* **3** *sl* clever in cheating: *a wide boy* **4 wide of the mark** not suitable, correct, etc., at all: *What he told me was quite wide of the mark* –~**ly** *adv*

²**wide** *adv* completely (open): *wide-eyed with amazement*

³**wide** *n* (in cricket) a ball bowled too far to the right or left of the wicket

widen *v* to make wider

widespread *adj* found in many places: *a widespread disease*

widow *n* a woman whose husband has died, and who has not married again –~**hood** *n*

widower *n* a man whose wife has died, and who has not married again

width *n* **1** size from side to side **2 a** piece of material of the full width, as it was woven

wield *v* to control the action of: *to*

wield power / (old use) to wield a weapon −~**er** *n*

wife *n* **wives** the woman to whom a man is married

wig *n* an arrangement of false hair to cover the head

wigwam *n* a tent of the type used by some North American Indians

¹**wild** *adj* **1** usu. living in natural conditions and having natural qualities not produced by man, esp. (in animals) violence; not tame or cultivated: *a wild elephant / wild flowers* **2 a** not civilized; savage: *wild tribes* **b** disordered in appearance or behaviour: *a wild party* **3** (of places) natural; without the presence of man **4** (of natural forces) violent; strong: *a wild wind* **5** having strong feelings: *I felt so wild when she hit the baby. / He was wild about racing cars* **6** without (much) thought or control: *a wild idea / a wild guess* −~**ly** *adv* −~**ness** *n*

²**wild** *n* natural areas full of animals and plants, with few people: *lost in the wilds of an unknown country*

³**wild** *adv* **1** wildly **2 run wild** to behave without control **3 go wild** to be filled with anger or joy: *They went wild over his good looks*

wilderness *n* an area of land with little life and no sign of human presence

wild-goose chase *n* a useless search

wildlife *n* animals and plants which live and grow wild

wilful *adj* **1** doing what one likes, in spite of other people: *a wilful child*

2 done on purpose: *wilful misbehaviour* −~**ly** *adv* −~**ness** *n*

¹**will** *v* **would**, *present short form* **-'ll,** *negative short form* **won't 1** (expressing the simple future tense): *They say that it will rain* **2 a** to be willing to: *Will you come now?* **b** (expressing a polite request or question): *Will you have some tea?* **3 a** is/are/proved or expected to: *These things will happen. / Oil will float on water* **b** is/are able to: *This car will hold 6 people* **4** may likely (be): *That's your knife, so this will be mine*

²**will** *n* **1** the power in the mind to choose one's actions: *Free will makes us able to choose our way of life* **2** intention to make things happen: *the will to live* **3** what is wished: *to do God's will* **4** the wishes of a person in regard to sharing his property among other people after his death, esp. in an official written form: *Have you made your will yet?*

³**will** *v* **1** *old use* to wish **2** to try to make happen by power of the mind: *We willed him to stop, but he went past* **3** to leave (possessions) in a will: *Grandfather willed me his watch*

willing *adj* eager; ready: *willing to help* −~**ly** *adv* −~**ness** *n*

willow *n* a tree which often grows near water, or its wood

willpower *n* strength of will

willy-nilly *adv* regardless of whether wanted or not

wilt *v* **1** (of a plant) to become less

fresh and start to die: *The flowers are wilting for lack of water* **2** (of a person) to become tired and weaker: *I'm wilting in this heat*

wily *adj* **-ier**, **-iest** clever in tricks: *a wily fox*

¹win *v* **won**, **winning** **1** to be the best or first in (a struggle, competition, or race) **2** to get as the result of success in a competition, race, or game of chance: *He won a prize* **3** to guess successfully (the result of a race or game of chance): *to win at cards* **4 win the day** to succeed

²win *n* (esp. in sport) a victory or success

¹wind *n* **1** moving air: *heavy winds* **2** breath or breathing: *He couldn't get his wind* **3** air or gas in the stomach **4** woodwind players: *The wind are playing too loud* **5 break wind** *polite* to pass air or gas from the bowel **6 put/get the wind up** *esp. spoken* to make/become afraid or anxious **7 (sail) close to the wind** to be near to dishonesty or improper behaviour **8 second wind** steady breathing regained during hard exercise

²wind *v* **winded**, **winding** to make breathless: *He hit him in the stomach and winded him*

³wind *v* **wound**, **winding** **1** to turn round and round: *to wind the handle* **2** to follow a twisting direction: *The path winds through the woods* **3** to tighten the working parts of by turning: *to wind a clock* **4 wound up** very excited

⁴wind *n* a bend or turn

windfall *n* **1** a fruit fallen from a tree **2** an unexpected lucky gift: *a windfall of £100*

windmill *n* **1** a building containing a machine that crushes corn into flour and is driven by large sails turned round by the wind **2** a toy consisting of a stick with usu. 4 small curved pieces at the end which turn round when blown

window *n* a space in a wall to let in light and air, esp. of glass which can be opened

windowsill *n* the flat shelf below a window, inside or outside

windpipe *n* the air passage from the throat to the top of the lungs

windscreen *n* the front window of a car

wind up *v adv* **wound**, **winding up** **1** to bring to an end: *to wind up a company* **2** *esp. spoken* to put oneself in a certain state or place, accidentally: *He wound up drunk*

windy *adj* **-ier**, **-iest** **1** with a lot of wind: *windy weather* **2** *sl* afraid **—windily** *adv* **—windiness** *n*

wine *n* alcoholic drink made from grapes or other fruit, plants, etc.

¹wing *n* **1** one of the 2 feathered limbs by which a bird flies, or a limb of flight on an insect **2** one of the parts of a plane which support it in flight **3** any part which stands out from the side: *the west wing of the house* **4** a group of 3 squadrons in an airforce **5** (in sport) the position or player on the far right or left of the field **6** an extreme group in a political party: *the right wing of the Labour party* **7 under someone's wing** being protected, helped, etc., by someone – **~less** *adj*

²**wing** *v* **1** to fly **2** to wound in the arm or wing

¹**wink** *v* to close and open (one eye) rapidly, usu. as a signal

²**wink** *n* **1** a winking movement **2** (used of sleep) a short time: *I didn't sleep a wink*

winner *n* a person, animal, or idea that has won or is thought likely to win: *That idea's a real winner*

winnings *n* money which has been won

¹**winter** *n* the cold season between autumn and spring – **-try, ~y** *adj*

²**winter** *v* to spend the winter: *to winter in a warm country*

¹**wipe** *v* **wiped, wiping** to pass something against (something) to remove dirt, liquid, etc.: *Wipe your feet*

²**wipe** *n* a wiping movement: *Give your nose a wipe*

wipe out *v adv* to destroy all of: *The enemy wiped out the whole nation*

¹**wire** *n* **1** a thin metal thread **2** *esp. spoken* a telegram

²**wire** *v* **wired, wiring 1** to connect up wires in (something), esp. in an electrical system: *to wire a house* **2** to fasten with wire **3** to send a telegram to

wireless *n* **1** radio **2** a radio set **3** radio broadcasts

wiring *n* the wired electrical system in a building

wisdom *n* being wise

wise *adj* **1** sensible, clever, and able to understand **2 get wise to** *sl* to learn to understand the tricks of – **~ly** *adv*

¹**wish** *v* **1** to want (what is at present impossible): *I wish we had a cat* **2** to try to cause a particular thing by magic: *Go to the well and wish* **3** to want (something or someone) to be or to have: *We wish you a merry Christmas* **4** *polite* to want: *Do you wish to eat alone?*

²**wish** *n* **1** a feeling of wanting: *a wish to see the world* **2** an attempt to make a particular thing happen by magic **3** what is wished for

¹**wit** *v* **to wit** *esp. law* that is (to say)

²**wit** *n* **1** power of thought; intelligence: *He had the wit to say no* **2** (a person who has) the ability to say clever amusing things – **~ty** *adj* – **~tily** *adv* – **~tiness** *n*

witch *n* a woman who has magic powers, esp. who can cast spells on people – **~ery** *n*

with *prep* **1** in the presence of; beside, near, among, or including: *staying with a friend / with his dog* **2** having: *a book with a green cover* **3** by means of; using: *to eat with a spoon* **4** in the same direction as: *to sail with the wind* **5** against: *Don't fight with your brother* **6** concerning; in the case of: *Be careful with the baby* **7** because of: *wild with excitement*

withdraw *v* **-drew, -drawn, -drawing 1** to take away or out: *to withdraw*

£5 *from a bank account / He withdrew his horse from the race* **2** to move away or back: *The army withdrew* **3** to take back (a remark): *I withdraw that point* –~**al** *n*

wither *v* **1** to become reduced in size, colour, etc.: *The flowers withered in the cold* **2** to crush or humiliate by a look or remark: *One look withered her opponent* –~**ing** *adj* –~**ingly** *adv*

withhold *v* **-held**, **-holding** to keep back on purpose: *to withhold the money*

within *adv, prep* inside; not beyond or more than

without *adv, prep* **1 a** not having; lacking: *to go out without a coat* **b** not: *He left without telling me* **2** *old use* outside: *The King waits without* –opposite **within**

withstand *v* **-stood**, **-standing** to oppose or resist without yielding: *to withstand an attack / Children's furniture must withstand kicks and blows*

¹**witness** *n* **1** also **eyewitness**– a person who is present when something happens: *a witness of the accident* **2** a person who tells in a court of law what he saw or knows **3** a person who is present at the writing of an official paper, and who signs it **4** what is said about an event, person, etc., esp. in court

²**witness** *v* **1** to be present and notice: *We witnessed a strange change in her* **2** to be a witness of (an official

paper) **3** to be a sign of: *His tears witnessed the shame he felt*

wizard *n* **1** (esp. in stories) a man who has magic powers, esp. to cast spells **2** a person with unusual abilities: *He's a wizard at playing the piano* –~**ry** *n*

¹**wobble** *v* **-bled**, **-bling** to move unsteadily from one direction to another

²**wobble** *n* a wobbling movement –**wobbly** *adj*

woeful *adj* **1** very unhappy **2** regrettable: *a woeful lack of understanding* –~**ly** *adv*

woke *past tense of* WAKE

woken *past part. of* WAKE

¹**wolf** *n* **wolves** **1** a wild animal of the dog family which hunts in a pack **2** a man who charms women to seduce them **3 cry wolf** to call for help unnecessarily **4 keep the wolf from the door** to earn enough to eat and live –~**ish** *adj*

²**wolf** *v* to eat quickly, in large amounts: *wolfed his meal*

woman *n* **women** **1** a fully grown human female **2** women in general: *Woman lives longer than man in most countries* **3** a man's wife or lover –~**ly**

womb *n* the female sex organ of a mammal where her young develop

won *past tense and past part. of* WIN

¹**wonder** *n* **1** a feeling of strangeness usu. combined with admiration and curiosity: *filled with wonder at the sight of the great new aircraft* **2** a wonderful act, object, or person **3 It's a wonder** It's surprising: *It's a*

wonder you recognized me **4** (**It's**) **no wonder** naturally; of course

²**wonder** v **1** to be surprised: *I wonder at his rudeness* **2** to wish to know: *wondering how to do it* –~**ingly** *adv*

wonderful *adj* unusually good: *wonderful news* –~**ly** *adv*

¹**wood** n **1** the material of which trunks and branches of trees are made **2** a place where trees grow, smaller than a forest: *We went for a ride in the wood* **3** one of the set of 4 golf clubs with wooden heads used for driving a ball long distances

²**wood** *adj* wooden

wooden *adj* **1** made of wood **2** stiff; unbending: *wooden movements* –~**ly** *adv* –~**ness** n

woodland n wooded country

woodwind n (the players of) the set of instruments in an orchestra, usu. wooden, which are played by blowing

woodwork n **1** the skill of making wooden objects **2** the objects produced **3** the parts of a house that are made of wood

wool n **1** the soft thick hair of sheep and some goats **2** thread or cloth made from this **3** soft material from plants, such as cotton before it is spun: *cotton wool* –~**len** *adj*

¹**woolly** *adj* **-lier, -liest** **1** of or like wool: *woolly socks* **2** not clear in the mind: *woolly ideas* – **-liness** n

²**woolly** n **-lies** *esp. spoken* a garment made of wool, esp. knitted: *winter woollies*

¹**word** n **1** a sound or sounds which form a unit of meaning and can be used to express an idea: *Tell me in your own words* **2** the written representation of this **3** a short speech or conversation: *Can I have a word with you?* **4** news: *Word came of his success* **5** a number of units of information (e.g. 12, 32, or 64 bits) treated as a unit in a computer **6** a promise: *I give you my word I'll go* **7 eat one's words** to admit to having said something wrong –~**less** *adj* –~**lessly** *adv* –~**lessness** n

²**word** v to express in words: *He worded the explanation well*

wording n the words chosen to express something: *The wording of a business agreement should be exact*

wore past tense of WEAR

¹**work** n **1** activity which uses effort, esp. with a special purpose, not for amusement **2** a job or business: *My work is in medicine* **3** what is produced by work: *This mat is my own work* **4** *technical* force multiplied by distance. **5** an object produced by writing, painting, etc.: *Shakespeare's works*

²**work** v **1** to do an activity which uses effort, esp. as employment: *working in a factory* **2** (of a plan, machine, etc.) to be active in the proper way, without failing: *Your idea won't work* **3** to make (a person) work: *They work us too hard* **4** to make (a machine) work **5** to get through by effort: *He worked his way to the*

front **6** to produce (an effect): *to work a change* **7** to shape with the hands: *to work clay* **8** to stitch: *a baby's dress worked by hand* **9 work to rule** to obey the rules of one's work exactly in such a way as to cause inconvenience

worker *n* **1** a person or animal which works **2** a person who works with his hands rather than his mind: *a factory worker*

working class *n, adj* (of) the social class to which people belong who work with their hands

workman *n* **-men** a man who works with his hands

work out *v adv* **1** to calculate the answer to: *to work out a sum* **2** to have a good result: *I wonder how their ideas worked out in practice?* **3** *esp. spoken* to exercise: *to work out in the gymnasium* **4** to complete the use of (esp. a mine)

¹**works** *n* the moving parts (of a machine)

²**works** *n* **works** a factory: *a gas works*

workshop *n* a place where heavy work on machines is done

world *n* **1 a** the earth **b** a particular part of it: *the Third World* **2** a planet or star system: *Is there life on other worlds?* **3** people generally: *The whole world knows about it* **4** a particular group or area of common interest: *the cricket world* **5** *esp. written* material standards (not spiritual): *to give up the world and serve God* **6** a large amount: *The fire makes a world of difference* **7** a

group of living things: *the animal world* **8 world without end** (in prayers) for ever

worldwide *adj, adv* in or over all the world

¹**worm** *n* **1** a small thin tubular fleshy creature with no backbone or limbs, esp. the one which lives in earth **2** a person who is thought worthless, cowardly, etc. **3** the curving line round a screw

²**worm** *v* **1** to remove living worms from the body of, esp. by chemical means: *to worm the dog* **2** to move by twisting or effort: *He wormed himself out of the way*

worn *past part. of* WEAR

worn-out *adj* **1** completely finished by continued use: *worn-out shoes* **2** very tired

¹**worry** *v* **-ried, -rying 1** to make or be anxious: *a worrying state of affairs / worrying about your health* **2** (esp. of a dog) to chase and bite: *The dog was worrying sheep* **3** to keep trying to persuade: *She worried him for a present* –~**ingly** *adv*

²**worry** *n* **-ries 1** a feeling of anxiety **2** a person or thing which makes one worried: *Money is just one of our worries* – **-ried** *adj* – **-riedly** *adv*

¹**worse** *adj* **1** (*comparative of* BAD) more bad or less good: *I'm worse at sums than Jean* **2** (*comparative of* ILL) more ill: *At least, he's no worse*

²**worse** *adv* (*comparative of* BADLY) in

a worse way: *people who behave worse than animals*

¹**worship** *n* **1** great respect to God or a god **2** a religious service

¹**worst** *adj* (*superlative of* BAD) most bad: *the worst accident for years*

²**worst** *n* **1** the most bad thing or part: *The worst of it is I could have prevented the accident* **2** **at** (**the**) **worst** if one thinks of it in the worst way **3** **do one's worst** to do as much harm as one can **4** **if the worst comes to the worst** if the worst happens

³**worst** *adv* (*superlative of* BADLY) most badly: *the worst-dressed woman*

¹**worth** *prep* **1** of the value of: *a piece of land worth £4,500* **2** deserving: *You're not worth helping* **3** **for all one is worth** with all possible effort **4** **for what it's worth** though I'm not sure it's of value **5** **worth it** useful; worth the trouble

²**worth** *n* value: *I know the true worth of his friendship* **–~less** *adj* **–~lessly** *adj* **–~lessness** *adv*

worthwhile *adj* worth doing: *a worth-while job*

¹**worthy** *adj* **-thier, -thiest** deserving: *worthy of help* **– -thily** *adv* **– -thiness** *n*

²**worthy** *n* **-thies** *sometimes humour* a person of importance

would *v* *short form* **'d**, *negative short form* **wouldn't 1** past tense of WILL: *They said it would be fine* **2** (used to show that one is annoyed at something that always happens): *That's exactly like Jocelyn–she*

would lose the key! **3** **would rather** (expressing a choice): *Which would you rather do, go to the cinema or stay at home?*

¹**wound** *n* an injury to the body caused by violent means, or an injury to one's feelings: *a gun wound / a wound to her pride*

²**wound** *v* to cause a wound to

³**wound** *past tense and past part. of* WIND

wove *past tense of* WEAVE

woven *past part. of* WEAVE

¹**wrap** *v* **-pp-** to cover; fold round: *I wrapped the present in paper*

²**wrap** *n* an outer garment or covering, such as a scarf, shawl, or rug

wreath *n* **1** a circle of flowers and/or leaves **2** a curl of smoke, mist, etc.

¹**wreck** *n* **1** a ship lost at sea or destroyed on rocks **2** the state of being ruined: *the wreck of her hopes* **3** a person whose health is destroyed

²**wreck** *v* **1** to destroy (a ship) **2** to destroy: *The weather has wrecked our plans*

wreckage *n* the broken parts of a destroyed thing: *the wreckage of the cars*

¹**wrench** *v* **1** to pull violently with a twisting or turning movement **2** to twist and damage (a joint of the body): *to wrench one's ankle*

²**wrench** *n* **1** an act of twisting and pulling **2** twisting to a joint of the body **3** painful grief at a separation: *the wrench of leaving home* **4** a spanner with adjustable jaws

wrestle *v* **-tled, -tling 1** to fight by holding and throwing one's opponent to the ground **2** to fight (someone) in this way as a sport (**wrestling**) –**wrestler** *n*

wretch *n* a poor unhappy person –~**ed** *adj* –~**edly** *adv* –~**edness** *n*

¹wriggle *v* **-gled, -gling 1** to twist from side to side **2** to move (a part of the body) in this way

²wriggle *n* a wriggling movement

¹wring *v* **wrung, wringing 1 a** to twist (esp. the neck, causing death) **b** to press hard on; squeeze: *He wrung my hand* **2** to remove water from, by twisting and pressing: *Wring those wet things out* **3** to force: *They wrung the truth out of her*

²wring *n* **1** an act of wringing **2** a machine which presses cheese into shape or presses the juice out of apples

¹wrinkle *n* **1** a line in something which is folded or crushed, esp. on the skin **2** *esp. spoken* a clever piece of advice – **-kly** *adj*

²wrinkle *v* **-kled, -kling** to form into wrinkles: *She wrinkled her nose at the bad smell*

wrist *n* the joint between the hand and the lower arm

wristwatch *n* a watch made to be fastened on the wrist

write *v* **wrote , written, writing 1** to make (marks that represent letters or words), esp. with a pen or pencil on paper **2** to express and record in this way, or by means of a type-writer: *to write a letter* **3 writ large** *esp. pompous* made larger or grander

write-off *n* anything which is completely ruined

writer *n* a person who writes

writing *n* **1** the activity of writing, esp. books **2** handwriting: *I can't read the doctor's writing* **3** anything written

written *past part. of* WRITE

¹wrong *n* **1** standards according to which some things are bad: *to know right from wrong* **2** any bad action **3 in the wrong** mistaken or deserving blame

²wrong *adj* **1** not correct: *the wrong answer* **2** evil: *Telling lies is wrong* **3** not suitable: *the wrong time to make a visit* –~**ly** *adv*

³wrong *adv* **1** wrongly **2 get it wrong** to misunderstand **3 go wrong a** to make a mistake **b** to end badly: *The day went wrong* **c** to act badly, immorally, etc.: *His so-called friends helped him go wrong*

⁴wrong *v* to be unfair to or cause difficulty, pain, etc., to

wrote *past tense of* WRITE

wrung *past tense and past part. of* WRING

wry *adj* **wryer, wryest** showing dislike, lack of pleasure, etc.: *a wry face/ smile* –~**ly** *adv*

xerox *v, n* *trademark* (to make) a photographic copy of (printed or written matter) from a special electric copying machine

Xmas *n* Christmas

x-ray *v* **x-rayed, x-raying** to photograph, examine, or treat by X-rays

X-ray *n* **x-rays 1** a powerful unseen beam of light which can pass through substances that are not transparent, and which is used for photographing conditions inside the body, for treating certain diseases, and for various purposes in industry **2** a photograph taken using this

yacht *n* **1** a light sailing boat, esp. one used for racing **2** a large pleasure boat, often large and luxurious –~**ing** *n:They went yachting*

¹**yard** *n* **1** a measure of length that is a little less than a metre; 3 feet **2** a long pole that supports a square sail

²**yard** *n* **1** an enclosed area next to a building **2** an area enclosed for a special purpose: *shipyard / coal-yard*

¹**yarn** *n* **1** spun thread **2** an adventure story

²**yarn** *v* *esp. spoken* to tell yarns

¹**yawn** *v* **1** to open the mouth wide involuntarily as when tired or bored **2** to become wide open: *The hole yawned before him*

²**yawn** *n* an act of yawning

year *n* **1** the time (365 1/4 days) it takes the earth to travel round the sun **2** –also **calendar year** a period of 365 or 366 days beginning on January 1st and ending on December 31st **3** a period of 365 days measured from any point: *2 years ago today* **4** a period of about a year in the life of an organization: *the school year*

yearly *adj, adv* happening once a year

yearn *v* to have a strong, loving, or sad desire: *She yearned for his return* –~**ing** *n*

yeast *n* a form of very small plant life used to produce alcohol and for making bread rise

yell *v* to shout loudly; cry out –**yell** *n*

¹**yellow** *adj* **1** of the colour of butter, gold, or the yolk of an egg **2** having a light brown or yellowish skin

²**yellow** *n* (a) yellow colour –~**ish** *adj*

¹**yes** *adv* (in an answer expressing willingness or agreement): *'Is this a dictionary?' 'Yes.' / 'Michael?' 'Yes, Mum?'*

²**yes** *n* a vote, voter, or reply in favour of an idea, plan, law, etc.

yesterday *adv, n* **-days 1** (on) the day before this one **2** only a short time ago: *the fashions of yesterday* –**yesterday** *adj*

¹**yet** *adv* **1** at this moment; then; so far; still; at a future time; even; in addition; again **2** **as yet** up to this moment

²**yet** *conj* but even so; but: *strange yet true*

¹**yield** *v* **1** to give, produce, bear, etc.: *That tree yields fruit* **2** to give up control (of); surrender **3** to bend, break, etc., because of force: *The shelf is beginning to yield under that heavy weight*

²**yield** *n* the amount produced: *The trees gave a high yield*

yoga *n* an Indian system of exercises to free the self from the body, will, and mind

¹**yoke** *n* **1** a wooden bar used for joining 2 animals together to pull heavy loads **2** a frame fitted across a person's shoulders for carrying 2 equal loads **3** that piece of a garment from which the rest hangs, such as the part of a shirt around the shoulders **4** power, control, etc.: *under the yoke of the king* **5** something that binds people or things together: *the yoke of marriage*

²**yoke** *v* **yoked, yoking** to join with a yoke

yolk *n* the yellow central part of an egg

you *pron* **1** the person or people being spoken to: *You are kind* **2** one; anyone: *You have to be careful with people you don't know*

¹**young** *adj* **1** in an early stage of life **2** fresh and good: *young vegetables* **3** inexperienced – ~**ish** *adj*

²**young** *n* **1** young people or animals as a group **2** **with young** (esp. of animals) pregnant

youngster *n* a child

your *adj* (*possessive form of* YOU) belonging to you: *your book*

yours *pron* **1** (*possessive form of* YOU) that/those belonging to you: *a friend of yours* **2** (written at the end of a letter): *yours faithfully*

yourself *pron* **-selves** **1** (*reflexive form of* YOU): *You'll hurt yourself* **2** (*strong form of* YOU): *You yourself know it* **3** *esp. spoken* (in) your usual state of mind or body: *You don't seem yourself today*

youth *n* **1** the period of being young; early life **2** the appearance, health, etc., of someone young **3** a young male person **4** young people as a group: *the youth of the country* – ~**ful** *adj* – ~**fully** *adv* – ~**fulness** *n*

zeal *n* eagerness; keenness

zebra *n* **zebras** *or* **zebra** an African wild animal, horselike with dark brown and white stripes

zebra crossing *n* a street crossing marked by black and white lines

zero *n* **zeros** *or* **zeroes** **1** the figure 0; a nought; nothing **2** the point between + and − on a scale; on the centigrade scale, the temperature at which water freezes

zigzag *v, n* **-gg-** (to go in) a line shaped like a row of Z's **−zigzag** *adv*

zinc *n* a bluish-white metallic element, used in alloys and for plating metal surfaces

¹**zip** *v* **-pp-** **1** to open or fasten with a zip **2** to make the sound of something moving quickly through the air

²**zip** *n* **1** also **zip fastener**− a fastening device with interlocking teeth, opened and shut with a sliding tag **2** a zipping sound **3** *esp. spoken* energy: *full of zip*

zodiac *n* **1** an imaginary belt in space along which the sun and planets appear to travel, divided into 12 signs each named after a group of stars **2** a circular representation of this used by astrologers – ~**al** *adj*

zombie, -bi *n* **1** (according to certain African and Caribbean religions) a corpse made to move by magic **2** someone who moves very slowly and behaves as if he were not really alive

¹**zone** *n* **1** a division or area marked off from others: *a war/danger zone* **2** one of the 5 divisions of the earth's surface according to temperature, marked by latitude: *the torrid zone, the 2 temperate zones and the 2 frigid zones* – **-nal** *adj*

²**zone** *v* **zoned, zoning** to divide into zones

zoo –also **zoological gardens** *n* **zoos** a park where animals are kept for show

¹**zoom** *v* **1** *esp. spoken* to go or rise quickly **2** (of a cinema camera) to move quickly between a distant and a close-up view

²**zoom** *n* (the deep low sound of) the upward flight of an aircraft